STUDIES IN THE EARLY HISTORY OF BRITAIN

General Editor: Nicholas Brooks

South-western Britain in the Early Middle Ages

South-western Britain in the Early Middle Ages

Susan Pearce

Leicester University Press
London and New York

G

Leicester University Press
A Continuum imprint
The Tower Building, 11 York Road, London SE1 7NX
15 East 26th Street, New York, NY 10010

First published 2004

British Library Cataloguing-in-Publication Data
A catalogue record for this book is available from the British Library.

ISBN 0-7185-0055-5 (hardback)

Library of Congress Cataloging-in-Publication Data

Pearce, Susan M.
    South western Britain in the early Middle Ages / Susan Pearce.
        p.   cm.– (Studies in the early history of Britain)
    Includes bibliographical references and index.
    ISBN 0-7185-0055-5
        1. West Country (England)–Antiquities. 2. Great Britain–Civilization–To 1066.
3. Anglo-Saxons–England–West Country. 4. Britons–England–West Country. 5. West
Country (England)–History. 6. Romans–England–West Country. I. Title. II. Series.

DA670.W49P43   2003
942.3′01–dc21   2003043573

Typeset by RefineCatch Limited, Bungay, Suffolk
Printed and bound in Great Britain by Antony Rowe, Chippenham, Wiltshire

Contents

List of figures and tables

Figures

Tables

Foreword

The aim of the *Studies in the Early History of Britain* is to promote works of the highest scholarship which open up new fields of study or which straddle the barriers of traditional academic disciplines. As scholarship becomes ever more specialized, interdisciplinary studies are needed not only by students and lay people but also by professional scholars. This series has therefore included research monographs, works of synthesis and also collaborative studies of important themes by several scholars, whose training and expertise has lain in different fields. Our knowledge of the early Middle Ages will always be limited and fragmentary, but progress can be made if the work of the historian has secure foundations in philology, archaeology, geography, literature, numismatics, art history and liturgy – to name only the most obvious fields. The need to cross and to remove academic frontiers also explains the extension of the geographical range of this series to include the whole island of Britain, where its predecessor had been limited to 'early English history'. The previous editor, the late Professor H. P. R. Finberg, whose pioneering work helped to inspire, or to provoke, the interest of a new generation of early medievalists in the relations of Britons and Saxons, would have welcomed the change. The approach of this series is therefore deliberately wide-ranging. Early medieval Britain can only be understood in the context of contemporary developments in Ireland and on the Continent.

It is a particular pleasure to welcome to the series a further volume, which seeks to provide a brief, well-illustrated and up-to-date synthesis of the settlement and history of one of the principal regions of early medieval Britain. Professor Susan Pearce's study of *South-western Britain* overlaps with Barbara Yorke's earlier volume on *Wessex*. The decision to encourage them both to include Devon within their remit has proved an effective means of allowing this area to be seen both against its Celtic Dumnonian and its Germanic West Saxon backgrounds. Here Susan Pearce brings to this volume the distinctive advantages of her long association with the material culture of Devon and Cornwall and her experience of presenting that evidence in both the museum and the university worlds. It is a fascinating, rich and well-told history of changes in the social economy, in regime and in ethnic identities. It also provides an instructive example of acculturation under changing circumstances over more than six hundred years.

This volume brings to an end the series which Leicester University Press bravely permitted me to establish some twenty-eight years ago. It has been a privilege to assist a large number of scholars to reach a substantial lay and scholarly market by publishing their interpretations of the early Middle Ages in such an attractively presented format. Under successive owners and through times of rapid changes in publishing, Leicester University Press has maintained the commitment it then made to high-quality production and fine scholarship. I have had an opportunity to work with a succession of able and committed Press secretaries, commissioning editors, managers and copy- and production-editors in a very happy collaboration. It is particularly pleasing that this series should be brought to its end with a volume written by the long-term chairman of the Leicester University Press committee. Under Susan Pearce's wise guidance, the university's interest in the Press has been exercised in an entirely constructive meeting of academe and commerce. I am happy to salute her achievement in bringing this volume to publication amid her own very heavy administrative obligations.

N. P. Brooks
University of Birmingham
November 2002

Preface

This book has been in the making for many years, and it draws upon innumerable conversations, site visits and archaeological meetings from which I have benefited, in the West Country and elsewhere. In terms of the kind of story it tells, and the type of evidence it draws upon, this book has an archaeological, rather than documentary, thrust. In it, I have been more concerned to discuss questions relating to the exploitation and organization of the landscape and the meaning of sites and material culture than those bearing upon political or literary history. Some recent, major publications have made this much easier. Readers are directed towards Sims-Williams'[1] study for religious and literary matters in the seventh and eighth centuries, and Conner's[2] for the cultural history of tenth-century Exeter. In particular, I have tried not to retread too much of the ground covered by Yorke in her volume[3] on Wessex in the *Studies in the Early History of Britain* series.

The volumes of Domesday Book published by Caroline and Frank Thorn for the British counties are very helpful. References to these have been made under the names of manors. References to counties relate to the pre-1974 names and boundaries, now mostly officially restored, to general satisfaction. Unless otherwise stated, maps and morphological outlines of sites are taken from the Ordnance Survey 1:2500 (25.344 inches to the mile) historical series as revised in the early twentieth century and available at *www.ordnancesurvey.co.uk*.

I wish to record my thanks to the British Academy for a grant to investigate the morphology of Devon churchyards, to the University of Leicester for granting me study leave and to Alison Yarrington for her willingness to take over the duties of Dean of the Faculty of Arts a semester early in order to make the study leave possible. I am grateful to Jody Humphrey, who served as my research assistant for the morphology project. I thank Miriam Gill, who worked as my research assistant, and my University for providing funding for her. I am very grateful to Jim Roberts, who produced roughly half of the line drawings, and to Kathy Baddeley, who performed the amazing task of putting a handwritten script onto disc while coping with newly born Rebekah.

Many people in libraries, record offices, museums and sites and monuments registers gave help unstintingly. Singling out individuals is impossible, but I am particularly grateful to Vince Russett, Janet Tall and Chris Webster in Somerset; Peter Garrod and Matthew Jones in Dorset; Nicholas Johnson and Christine North in Cornwall; and John Draisey and John Allan in Devon. Norman Quinnell

---

1.   P. Sims-Williams, *Religion and Literature in Western Europe* (1990).
2.   P. Conner, *Anglo-Saxon Exeter: A Tenth-century Cultural History* (1993).
3.   B. Yorke, *Wessex in the Early Middle Ages* (1995).

provided valuable information about the Ordnance Survey's early mapping programme.

I am very grateful to Sam Turner, who allowed me to quote from his unpublished material, based on his forthcoming doctoral research. David Petts provided me with copies of his published papers and helpful discussion. Thomas Head kindly allowed me to quote unpublished material. Oscar Aldred kindly permitted me to draw upon his unpublished work on Devon minsters, and Henrietta Quinnell allowed me to read a pre-publication draft of the Trethurgy publication.

I wish to give my particular thanks to those to read drafts of this book. Henrietta Quinnell read Chapter 2 and Harold Fox Chapters 2, 5 and 6; I am grateful for their comments and suggestions. Nicholas Brooks read the whole book in draft: his detailed criticisms saved me from many errors, and were invaluable in many ways, and I am very grateful to him. It goes without saying that all remaining mistakes are my own responsibility.

Finally, as always, I thank my husband Mac, for his unfailing support and encouragement.

Susan Pearce
1 November 2003

Abbreviations

Antiq. J.	*Antiquaries Journal*
Arch.	*Archaeologia*
Arch. Camb.	*Archaeologia Cambrensis*
Arch. Rev.	*Archaeological Review*
Arch. J.	*Archaeological Journal*
BAR(S)	British Archaeological Reports (S, International Series)
Cam. Med. Celtic S.	Cambridge Medieval Celtic Studies
CBA	Council for British Archaeology
Corn. Arch.	*Cornish Archaeology*
CRAGS	Committee for Rescue Archaeology in Avon, Gloucester and Somerset
DAS News	*Devon Archaeological Society Newsletter*
DCNQ	*Devon and Cornwall Notes and Queries*
Devon Arch.	*Devon Archaeology*
EHR	*English Historical Review*
Gent's Mag.	*Gentleman's Magazine*
Gover MSS	Gover J. *The Place Names of Cornwall*. MSS Royal Institution of Cornwall, Truro.
J. Brit. Arch. Assoc.	*Journal of the British Architectural Association*
JRIC	*Journal of the Royal Institution of Cornwall*
JRS	*Journal of Roman Studies*
Med. Arch.	*Medieval Archaeology*
PDAS	*Proceedings of the Devon Archaeological Society*
PDNHAS	*Proceedings of the Dorset Natural History and Archaeological Society*
Proc. Soc. Antiq. Scot.	*Proceedings of the Society of Antiquaries of Scotland*
Proc. U. Brist. Spel. Soc.	*Proceedings of the University of Bristol Spelaeological Society*
Proc. Soc. Ant.	*Proceedings of the Society of Antiquaries*
PSANHS	*Proceedings of the Somerset Archaeological and Natural History Society*
RCAHM	Royal Commission on Ancient and Historical Monuments
RCAHMW	Royal Commission on Ancient and Historical Monuments of Wales
RCHMS	Royal Commission on Historical Monuments of Scotland

S (followed by number)	Sawyer P., 1968, *Anglo-Saxon Charters: An Annotated List.* Royal Historical Society London; also available at http://www.trin.cam.ac.uk/sdk13/chartwww/eSawyer.99
SDNQ C	*Somerset and Dorset Notes and Queries*
TASC	Trans-national Atlas of Saintly Cults
TBGAS	*Transactions of the Bristol and Gloucester Archaeological Society*
TDA	*Transactions of the Devonshire Association*
TRAC	*Theoretical Roman Archaeology Conference*
Trans. Hon. Soc. Cymmrodorion	*Transactions of the Honourable Society of Cymmrodorion*
VCH	*Victoria County History*
WAM	*Wiltshire Archaeology Magazine*

1 Contexts of research

Introduction

The purpose of this book is to suggest how society in south-western Britain was transformed from that visible in the late Roman period, roughly the fourth century AD, to that which appears in the tenth century, quite a long period of six hundred years, or some eighteen human generations. The changes are part of a rich broader context which embraces north-western Europe and its Atlantic peninsulas and islands; they are dynamic, but piecemeal and characterized by geographical and chronological complications; and, crucially, they have a great deal to do with those most inscrutable of trajectories, human thoughts and feelings, now collected under the phrase 'cultural history'. Only this kind of study can tell us why and how people started to see themselves as Christians, and to value something they saw as 'holiness'; why they wanted to express prestige differently, how they felt about what we see as the implosion and decay of the late Roman imperial infrastructure, how they conceived identity in a world where 'Romans' and 'barbarians' mixed and why they used material things: these are just a few of the most difficult but most fascinating questions which run through this book.

The south-western peninsula is bounded by the sea on three sides, and only on the east does the question of regional definition arise. In this book, I shall take the Bristol Avon as (broadly) marking the regional border in the north-east, and continue the line roughly southwards to the sea at the Isle of Purbeck, so including the modern counties of Cornwall, Devon, Somerset and most of Dorset, although it should be said immediately that my coverage of Dorset, for which considerable literature exists, is much less full than that of the other three counties. This is roughly the region to the west of the great early medieval forest of Selwood, which covered the area where the counties of Somerset, Dorset and Wiltshire meet, and was regarded as a major boundary by contemporaries. The northern and western parts of the peninsula are united in their large expanses of upland – Mendip, Exmoor, Dartmoor, Bodmin Moor and the other areas of Cornish granite – and by the marshland of the Somerset Levels. Even though most southern British regions possessed large open expanses in the early medieval period, those of the south-west tend to be larger and higher, and are certainly richer in metallic and other mineral deposits. The south-western peninsula occupies a pivotal position in the western seaways between Wales, Ireland and the Irish Sea, the Atlantic coast southwards to the Mediterranean and the Channel route northwards to the Low Countries and the Baltic.

Above all – and this is one of the main themes of this book – the south-west occupied a 'border area', akin to those of the Welsh marches or Cumbria, between what became part of an English kingdom, and what remained a native, post-Roman society long enough for us to see something of what was happening within it. Within this perspective, the later medieval and modern county of Cornwall becomes part of a broader regional story rather than one on its own, and the cultural position of Devon is pivotal. Early medieval Devon has been a relatively neglected topic, but evidence relating to its history is beginning to accumulate, and I hope I have done something to redress the balance. If we are to improve our understanding of post-Roman times, there is an urgent need to see the south-western peninsula as a cultural whole.

The past two decades have seen both a great deal of work devoted to explaining the character of life in south-western Britain between roughly AD 350 and AD 1050 and a substantial development in the ways in which our understanding of the past, both archaeologically and historically, and how these aspects interweave, can be perceived. There is a tension between ideas of structure, in which inevitable trends are seen as determining the course of events, and ideas of agency, in which the aspirations and feelings of people, individually and in the aggregate, are seen as capable of creating changes, even though these feelings are themselves in part bound up with broader trends. There is an essential tension between broad general concepts of why and how societies move through historical time and site-specific studies which show local detail which may or may not be 'typical'.[1] An obvious question here is why and how the people of the south-west became Christians, and what 'being a Christian' meant at different times and places. Embracing the explanatory poles of structure and agency, also, are a number of overarching points of view, the 'histories' which constitute the historiography of the subject. These are the main ways in which the past has been seen, and the purposes to which its study has been put. On a different level, but crucial to our understanding of the time and place, are the three principal groups of evidence: the inscribed stones, the imported pottery and the limited body of particularly relevant documents. All these issues will be briefly examined in the following pages.

Themes of structure

The extreme of a structuralist or determinant view of the past[2] is represented in studies which posit a catastrophic global climatic event in the 530s to 540s, either a comet impact or a volcanic upheaval similar to, but more significant than, the eruption of Krakatoa in 1893, that may have caused cold temperatures, crop failure and (or, at least, contributed to) the sickness of 565 which killed the Emperor Justinian and was known in western Britain and Ireland as the Yellow Plague. Its effects can be seen as the decline of the British kingdoms in the later sixth century which led to the success of the Anglo-Saxon kingdoms, in a style which (leaving aside the correctness or otherwise of the various calculations of date) reduces complex events to simple causes. This kind of environmentalist argument is frequently made distressingly crudely, although the fine-grained sensitivity in which it can be embodied is demonstrated by Alan Everitt and his idea of 'river and wold', of great

---

1.   See, for example, the various discussions in J. Bintliff (ed.), *The Annales School and Archaeology* (1991) and *Structure and Contingency* (1999).

2.   D. Keys, *Catastrophe* (1990); M. Baillie, *Exodus to Arthur* (1999). See also J.Gunn (ed.), *The Years without Summer: Tracing AD 536 and its Aftermath* (2000), which brings a number of studies together.

importance in the patchwork landscape of the south-west, where the detailed mixture of low-lying, sheltered river valleys and harsher, open upland is very obvious.[3]

The south-west has an impressive geomorphology (Fig. 1), which comprises a series of granite upland 'islands' surrounded by lower, more fertile ground, much of it coastal strip; in the eastern part the granite is replaced by the predominantly slates and sandstones of Exmoor, the sandy heathland of east Devon and west Dorset and the chalk and limestone hills of Mendip and north and south Dorset, differences which may be more important to modern geologists and connoisseurs than they were to early settlers. The granite bosses, from Dartmoor westward, were the sources of mineral wealth, particularly tin, copper and especially good potting clays, while Mendip produced lead and some silver. The distinctiveness of this south-western landscape in its social impact is debatable, because much of the island of Britain, and indeed much of Europe in general, is composed of small-scale landscapes in which the character of the countryside changes rapidly, giving local communities relatively easy access to a range of resources. The important question is the extent to which, in the south-west as elsewhere, the nature of the landscape determines the kind of lives which can be lived within it. The character of a region's landscape used to be seen as a major shaper of its history, but more recently stress has been placed on understanding the ways in which landscapes can be seen as actors in the social story, which we shall discuss shortly.

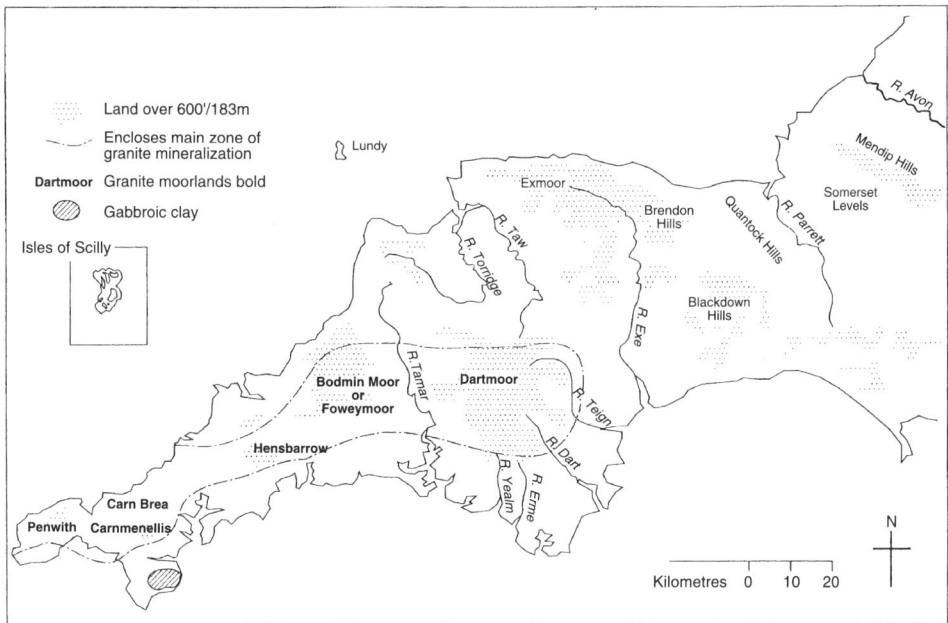

Figure 1 South-western Britain: physical features

3.   A. Everitt, 'River and Wold: reflections on the historical origins of regions and pays', *J. Historical Geography*, 3 (1977): 1–19.

During the 1970s and 1980s, the deterministic view of the landscape fed into, and helped to elaborate, a systems theory view of society in which each of the main elements in social action and interaction could be isolated and explored in ways which generated broadly, or even universally, applicable theories of social change which relied upon mechanisms of feedback, overload and eventual dysfunction to explain what was perceived. In 1982, Philip Rahtz[4] produced an interesting analysis of events in Somerset from 400 to 700 by setting what was known against the general model of systems collapse and consequent 'Dark Ages' which Renfrew had developed for the collapse of Mycenae in Greece and the Maya in Central America (Table 1). The fit, as Rahtz justly says, is very good, particularly in those areas where the Somerset evidence is reasonably abundant,[5] although we might home in, for example, on the 'end of rich burials' (*collapse of elite class*) in the model and question why 'not applicable' was the response for Somerset, given the cultural significance of burial sites; here the outcome of state collapse might be not a 'transition to lower/earlier

Table 1 Model of sytems collapse during the 'Dark Ages'

Dark Age societies (Mycenae, Maya, etc.)	*Parallels in Dark Age western Britain*
Collapse of central administration organization:	
• decline in central places	decline of Roman towns
• fragmentation of military organization	withdrawal or disintegration of Roman military units
• survival of small, independent political units	possible survival of *civitas* nuclei
• abandonment of palaces, storage	not applicable
• eclipse of temples as major centres	destruction or devolution of Roman temples and Roman Christian churches
• survival as local shrines	survival of Roman shrines and building of new ones
• loss of literacy, secular and religious	decline in epigraphy, etc.
• end of public buildings and works	decline of Roman works in 5th century or earlier
Collapse of traditional elite class:	
• end of rich burials	not applicable
• end of rich residencies	decline of Roman villas and wealthy town houses
• their reuse for different purposes	villa 'squatters' and industrial use
• end of luxury goods (except as survival)	end of Roman luxuries (some objects survive into post-Roman period)
Collapse of centralized economy:	
• end of large-scale trade, distribution/exchange	end of Roman external and internal trade
• end of coinage	end of coinage *c.* 400–410

4.   P. Rahtz, 'The Dark Ages 400–700', in M. Aston and I. Burrow, *The Archaeology of Somerset* (1982), pp. 98–107.
5.   *Ibid.*, p. 107.

Dark Age societies (Mycenae, Maya, etc.)	*Parallels in Dark Age western Britain*
• survival of pieces	coins reused in Dark Age and Anglo-Saxon contexts
• end of craft/specialist activity	end of pottery manufacture, building, etc.
• end of specialized/organized agriculture	decline in organized villa economy
• new local homesteads	not yet found
Collapse of settlement and population:	
• settlement abandoned	widespread in 5th century
• shift to dispersed pattern	not yet shown
• choice of defensible locations, the 'flight to the hills'	reoccupied hill-forts
Aftermath development of romantic Dark Age myth:	
• attempt by new power groups to legitimize themselves by genealogies linking to former state or relating to deeds by which invaders achieve power by arms	Dark Age genealogies with Roman names – later also by Anglo-Saxon battle myths
• tendency for early chroniclers to personalize historical explanation; individual deeds, battles, invasions; decline attributed to external hostile powers	Gildas, *Hist. Brit.*, Arthur, etc.; later Bede and Anglo-Saxon Chronicle; ultimately Geoffrey Monmouth
• confusion between old golden age and new heroic age	Dark Age? *Romanitas* and glorification of deeds against English
• paucity of archaeological evidence after collapse	sparse evidence for Dark Ages
• tendency among historians to accept as evidence traditional narratives first set down in writing centuries after collapse	old-style Dark Age 'history'
• slow development of Dark Age archaeology, hampered by above and by focus on larger and more obvious central place sites of the vanished state	old-style 'alien' Roman archaeology
Aftermath transition to 'lower/earlier' socio-political organization:	
• new segmentary societies analogous to those of centuries or millennia before; fission of realm to smaller units	'Celtic re-emergence' ?= Iron Age systems
• boundaries of earlier polities	not yet shown; possible hill-fort territorial survival or re-emergence
• ?peripheral survival of organized communities retaining features of a collapsed state	?Carlisle
• survival of religious elements as folk-cults or beliefs	sub-Roman religion in shrines of 5th–7th centuries
• peasant craft imitating former specialists	hand-made pottery, etc.
• local population movement	not yet demonstrated but likely in view of abandonment of Roman sites
• language change?	Latin/Celtic/English
• regeneration of chiefdom or state, influenced by earlier remains	'British Kings' of Dumnonia, etc. – later by Anglo-Saxons

socio-political organizations' but the shift to a new religious universalism rooted in the older state.

A development of the systems approach takes in the concept of 'core and periphery' which, when applied to pre-modern history, offers a way of analysing the 'growth and nature of long-distance interactions and their capacity for producing social transformations'.[6] So the history of Late Antiquity can be seen as the need by the central imperial organization for taxes in kind to ensure the survival of locally based units of the army and the state bureaucracy, which in turn made it possible for local army commanders to control the tax themselves and set up rival governments to that of the emperor: here the interaction between centre and periphery creates a temporal sequence in which the centre declines, and the old periphery becomes the seat of new centres where, in various ways, history repeats itself through the inevitability of successive crises. In the south-west, this notion can be used to help to explain how powerful local people on the very edge of the Roman Empire were able to take over what had been the functions of imperial agents and use them to create what we eventually see as the kingdoms of Wessex and (dimly) Dumnonia.

A very differently based structural approach is represented by Stark's analysis of the rise of Christianity in which, as his subtitle tells us, 'a sociologist reconsiders history'.[7] This draws from studies of the nature and progress of twentieth-century cults through use of established growth curves, conversion processes, differential mortality and the like. The quantitative approach to the growth of the Church in the Empire is refreshingly new, and does indeed provide an interesting slant on the traditional document-based analysis of events. Unfortunately, the information available from the south-west, as from post-Roman Britain generally, does not make a local analysis of this kind possible.

Notions of agency

If the geophysical landscape has traditionally been seen as a determining factor bearing upon social development, an interesting recent approach has begun to explore the idea of landscape as a form of individual and collective experience which can then contribute largely to the sense and the expression of community and difference and to the creation of social power through the manipulation of access to sites, and to knowledge and experience connected with them.[8] The most cursory glance at the past of the peninsula shows a series of hilltops – Glastonbury Tor, Brent Tor, Maiden Castle hill, St Michael's Mount – which have occupied a significant

---

6.   M. Rowlands, 'Introduction', in M. Rowlands (ed.), *Centre and Periphery* (1987), p.11. See also Rowland's volume in general; and T. Chapman, *Centre and Periphery: Comparative Studies in Archaeology* (1989).

7.   R. Stark, *The Rise of Christianity. A Sociologist Reconsiders History* (1994).

8.   For broad discussions, see R. Bradley, 'Ruined buildings, ruined stones: enclosures, tombs and natural places in the Neolithic of south-west England', *World Archaeology*, 30 (1): 13–22 (1998); G. Nash (ed.), *Semiotics of Landscape: Archaeology of Mind* (1997); C. Holtorf, 'Megaliths, monumentality and memory', *Arch. Review from Cambridge*, 14 (2): 45–65 (1997); C. Tilley, *A Phenomenology of Landscape. Places, Paths and Monuments* (1994). For specific south-west studies see Bradley, 'Ruined buildings'; and B. Bender, S. Hamilton and C. Tilley, 'Leskernick: the biography of an excavation', *Corn. Arch.*, 34 (1995): 58–73.

role in social definition in the long term and continued to do so in the post-Roman period. The same may be true of landmarks – the tors – on the granite moorlands, and of local rock outcrops like those in the St Keverne area of south-west Cornwall.[9] In this sense, there is an archaeology of natural places which helps to explain why hills, rocks, rivers, streams and springs take on a sacred character, and how the sacred content could be continually reworked to accommodate and sustain new definitions of group unity and new hierarchies of power.

This phenomenological view of the landscape applies equally cogently to human-made structures. There is considerable evidence[10] that disused occupation sites were considered appropriate places for later burial grounds, and that sometimes ancient constructions, like barrows or standing stones, were thought to be rightly used as burial places or boundary points. Here there may have been a blurring together in the understanding of a distinction between nature and artificial features. The notion of the landmark, which distinguishes the human from the wild, and defines rights and access, offers an opportunity to claim authority through proclaimed relationships with the ancestors who built the marks and used the land. The same feelings may well have been generated by standing Roman masonry like the city walls of Exeter or Bath, or a temple building like Pagans Hill, Somerset. We can see the same processes focusing upon the local church and its attached burial ground, which through time came to assume all the emotions which we attach to the idea of the ancient parish church.

What applies to landscape applies to material culture.[11] Objects are not simply a reflection of social structure, but play a dynamic role in expressing and creating, that is changing, social patterning. Material goods acquire meanings, which then make them seem able to embody desire, political messages and self-identity, and so to create new associations and meanings. So, objects in Roman Britain (and early medieval Britain) can be seen as part of the dynamic of consumption and cultural creation[12] and as a way of investigating the relationship between exchange and social relations.[13] To put it crudely, if a woman of any background in sixth-century Britain started to wear the jewellery of a group which saw itself as having a particular Germanic identity, then she 'became' a member of that group, and if she took the ornaments to her grave, which is excavated by an archaeologist, she is likely to be

---

9. C. Johns and P. Herring, *St Keverne: Historic Landscape Assessment* (1996), pp. 78–81.
10. See Ch. 3.
11. I. Hodder, *Reading the Past* (1986); see also S. Pearce (ed.), *Researching Material Culture* (2000) and J. Bintliff and H. Hamerow, *Europe between Late Antiquity and the Middle Ages* (1995).
12. I. Ferris, 'Shoppers' paradise: consumers in Roman Britain', in P. Rush (ed.), *Theoretical Roman Archaeology Conference Proceedings* (1995), pp. 132–40; J. Evans, 'Roman finds assemblages, towards an integrated approach', in Rush, *Theoretical Roman Archaeology*, pp. 91–103; M. Fulford, 'Pottery production and trade at the end of Roman Britain: the case against continuity', in P. Casey, *The End of Roman Britain* (1979), pp. 120–32.
13. P. Rush, 'Economy and space in Roman Britain', in Rush, *Theoretical Roman Archaeology*, pp. 141–7; and more generally Rush, *Theoretical Roman Archaeology*. See also M. Whyman, 'Invisible people? Material culture in "Dark Age" Yorkshire', in M. Carver (ed.), *In Search of Cult* (1993), pp. 61–8; C. Scull, 'Approaches to material culture and social dynamics of the migration period in eastern England', in Bintliff and Hamerow, *Europe between Late Antiquity and the Middle Ages* (1995), pp. 17–24; H. Cool, 'The parts left over: material culture into the fifth century', in T. Wilmot and P. Wilson (eds), *The Late Roman Transition in the North* (2000), pp. 47–65.

counted as a group member. Everything which we are coming to know about the fifth and sixth centuries suggests that it would be rash to underestimate the extent to which this kind of manipulation was going on during these generations. It has potentially profound implications for our interpretation of the degree of 'Christianity' particular burial customs suggest,[14] the gender that beads, earrings and bracelets may represent,[15] how gender was viewed or political issues of changing power and hierarchy revealed, for example, by imported African red slipware.[16] In all these areas we are beginning to appreciate the difference an individual or a small group can make, how they could make it and how what they made might appear in the record, but there is a long way to go.

The effort of understanding has its own implicit problems. The proper appreciation of the context of material culture is seen as the way to gain closest understanding of its specific meanings in the given time and place, but of course this is a circular process, because the context itself takes meaning from the material it includes, and we have to conclude that there never is a starting point, a 'founding story' about what the artefact was 'originally' about; we are always telling bits of stories, not beginning new stories in the here and now.

Histories

A pervasive theme in the way in which the past of the south-west has been perceived has been in terms of 'Celticity', a theme with its roots in pan-European early nineteenth-century Romanticism of 'blood and soil' nationalism and the preceding views of antiquarians.[17] This is the result of complex factors,[18] including the interlinked psychology of invaders and natives, of defence strategies and of pseudo-history developed to sustain notions of an idealized past, and it has, of course, become entangled with notions of culture, ethnicity and race, and consequently with the self-image of individuals.

Among many other manifestations this has given us the figures of 'Celt' and 'Saxon' as interpretative tools for the post-Roman period, promoting a range of studies from Kerslake's 1873 paper, 'The Celt and the Teuton in Exeter', which offers the notion of a long-standing 'British Quarter' in the city based chiefly on parish

---

14. A. Schülke, 'On Christianisation and grave-finds', *European Journal of Archaeology*, 2 (1): 76–106 (1999).

15. A. Allason-Jones, ' "Sexing" small finds', in Rush, *Theoretical Roman Archaeology*, pp. 22–30; W. Frazer and A. Tyrrell (eds), *Social Identity in Early Medieval Britain* (2000); R. Gilchrist, *Gender and Archaeology* (1999); N. Wicker and B. Arnold (eds), *From the Ground Up: Beyond Gender Theory* (1999).

16. J. Hawthorne, 'Post processual economics. The role of African red slipware vessel volume in Mediterranean demography', in K. Meadows, C. Lemke and J. Heron (eds), *Proceedings of the Sixth Annual Theoretical Roman Archaeology Conference, Sheffield, 1996* (1997), pp. 29–37.

17. N. Merriman, 'Value and motivation in pre-history: the evidence for the "Celtic spirit" ', in I Hodder (ed.), *The Archaeology of Contextual Meanings* (1987), pp. 111–16 and refs there; S. James, *The Atlantic Celts* (1999). Recent work on human genetics may have an important bearing on all this, see edition of *Nature*, Spring 2000.

18. P. Sims-Williams, 'The visionary Celt: the construction of an ethnic preconception', *Cam. Med. Celtic. St.*, 11 (1986): 71–96.

dedications,[19] to *Celt and Saxon: Studies in the Early British Border* edited by Chadwick in 1963.[20] A very influential element in the complex has been the concept of the 'Celtic Church' seen as geographically and qualitatively different from the Church in eastern Britain, and, indeed, in western Europe.[21] Equally persuasive has been the tendency to see post-Roman society, particularly in western Britain, as 'reverting' to what is seen as the ancestral 'Celtic' culture, located somewhere in the pre-Roman Iron Age and featuring an 'heroic' lifestyle for the upper class, a vision first propounded by W. P. Ker[22] and Hector and Nora Chadwick,[23] and followed by Leslie Alcock.[24]

The historic county of Cornwall is the smallest of the areas which had a substantial Celtic-speaking population through the medieval period, and retained some such speakers into modern times. This is often seen to qualify the native-born Cornish as 'Celts' with a separate cultural history, which should be understood in its own terms, so creating a fundamental rift in the history of the south-western peninsula which runs along the Tamar. Recent work has stressed the cultural diversity and the complex blurring and re-creation of identity which characterized late Roman and post-Roman Britain, as it did western Europe generally, and this presumably included a complex linguistic mix within the broadly British speech of the population of the southern part of the island of Britain. Early kingdoms of both the west and east, including 'Wessex' and 'Cornwall', crystallized out of this multicultural mix, and in their own interests began the long process of defining cultural distinctions upon which, ultimately and in very different circumstances, Celticists of many kinds could draw from the seventeenth century onwards. In the south-west, the early stages of the whole historical process can be explored only by treating the peninsula as a whole, and by not reading back onto its early cultural history events which had not yet happened and might not have happened at all.

In cultural terms, issues of 'Celticity' have much in common with what has come to be called the 'post-colonial perspective',[25] and analysis of the workings of Roman imperialism in these terms is proving interesting, particularly in terms of concepts of knowledge, power and hegemony, and, specifically, of British perceptions of Roman society given that we ourselves are in a post-imperial phase. Some of the analyses which these ideas have generated[26] have an obvious relevance to Christianity as a 'later imperial' phenomenon, to ideas of cultural mix and to the aspirations which shaped the successor states.

Embedded in all these differences of perception are those which see the progression from 'Roman Britain' around AD 400 to 'Anglo-Saxon England' around AD 700 as

---

19. T. Kerslake, 'The Celt and the Teuton in Exeter', *Arch. J.*, 30 (1873): 211–25.
20. N. Chadwick, *Celt and Saxon: Studies in the Early British Border* (1963).
21. See Ch. 4.
22. W. Ker, *Epic and Romance. Essays on Medieval Literature* (1957).
23. H. Chadwick and N. Chadwick, *The Growth of Literature* (1932–40).
24. L. Alcock, *Arthur's Britain* (1973).
25. E. Said, *Orientalism* (1978); C. Spivak, 'Can the subaltern speak?', in P. Williams and L. Chrisman (eds), *Colonial Discourse and Post-colonial Theory* (1993), pp. 66–111.
26. J. Webster and N. Cooper, *Roman Imperialism: Post-colonial Perspectives* (1996); B. Kurchin, 'Romans and Britons on the northern frontier: a theoretical evaluation of the archaeology of resistance', in Rush, *Theoretical Roman Archaeology*, pp. 124–31.

characterized either by a very substantial degree of dysfunction or by a considerable degree of cultural carry-over, often described in the past by matched alternatives, like Finberg's[27] 'continuity or cataclysm', or Wilson's[28] 'continuity or discontinuity'. It is noticeable that those who see little evidence of 'Roman survivals' tend to interpret from a Romanist perspective,[29] and those who do see some such evidence interpret from that of a medievalist.[30] Ideas from cultural studies have opened up this debate along the lines already discussed, where change is now seen to be an immensely complex mosaic of similarities, differences and rewritings. The investigation of how the existing cultural stock was changed and transformed is likely to give a more finely grained appreciation than simplistic notions of endings and beginnings.[31]

Principal groups of evidence

This is not the place to canvass the complex arguments which surround the requirement upon any investigator in the field AD 350–1100 to use both documentary historical information, and artefactual archaeological findings, conceived as both movable (material culture in the circumscribed sense) and immovable (landscape and the structures upon it). The scope of this problem, both methodological and philosophical, has been ably set out by Driscoll, who discusses our own (mistaken) cultural creation of the primacy of language, the meaningful nature of artefacts and the suggestion that the creation of both should be treated as 'discursive practice, which is ultimately grounded on the reality of power' and which should both be used as 'expressions of knowledgeable social actors'.[32] Crucial here are three principal groups of evidence: the inscribed memorial stones which are both written monuments and contemporary objects; the pottery imported from the Continent between roughly AD 480 and 700; and those documents which survive in later manuscripts but which have been claimed to embody historical details with a bearing on the post-Roman history of the south-west. These all range well beyond the south-west, but are highly relevant to it.

The range of evidence provided by the inscribed stones is so important that, one way and another, they will figure in many of the discussions in the course of this book. South-western Britain has some 70[33] certain or possible inscribed

27.   H. Finberg, 'Continuity or cataclysm', in Finberg (ed.), *Lucerna* (1964), pp. 1–20.
28.   P. Wilson 'Romano-British and Welsh Christianity: continuity or discontinuity?', *Welsh Historical Review*, Part 1 (1966), 3: 5–19; Part 2 (1967), 4: 103–20.
29.   M. Todd, *The South-West to AD 1000* (1987), esp. p. 259; S. Cleary, 'Review of *Civitas to Kingdom* by K. R. Dark', *Britannia*, 26 (1995): 32.
30.   P. Sawyer, *From Roman Britain to Norman England* (1978), esp. pp. 132–67. Sawyer saw these possibilities as early as the mid-1970s.
31.   J. Evans, 'From the end of Roman Britain to the "Celtic West" ', *Oxford Journal of Archaeology*, 9 (1): 91–103 (1990).
32.   S. Driscoll, 'The relationship between history and archaeology: artefacts, documents and power', in S. Driscoll and M. Nieke, *Power and Politics in Early Medieval Britain and Ireland* (1988), p. 178.
33.   C. Thomas, *And Shall These Mute Stones Speak?* (1994) and *Christian Celts: Messages and Images* (1998); E. Okasha, *Corpus of Early Christian Inscribed Stones of South-West Britain* (1993); Celtic Inscribed Stones Project (CISP) – see *http://www.ucl.ac.uk/archaeology/cisp*; Okasha *Supplement* (1998–9), pp. 137–52.

pillar stones (Fig. 2), that is pieces of undressed or roughly dressed stone, which Okasha included in her Category I.[34] Of these, over 50 bear simple formulae usually with the name of the person commemorated in the genitive, indicating 'The stone of X', and any further text referring to filiation (or possibly lineage). Some of these carry a second inscription, in the south-west always a version of the Latin text, in Irish ogham script, and a few, with or without ogham script, carry a personal name identified as primitive Irish. Some ten carry texts with longer Latin memorial formulae, usually of the HIC IACET ('here lies') type. Some of these also bear various carved cross forms, including the later, simpler monogram form of the chi-rho

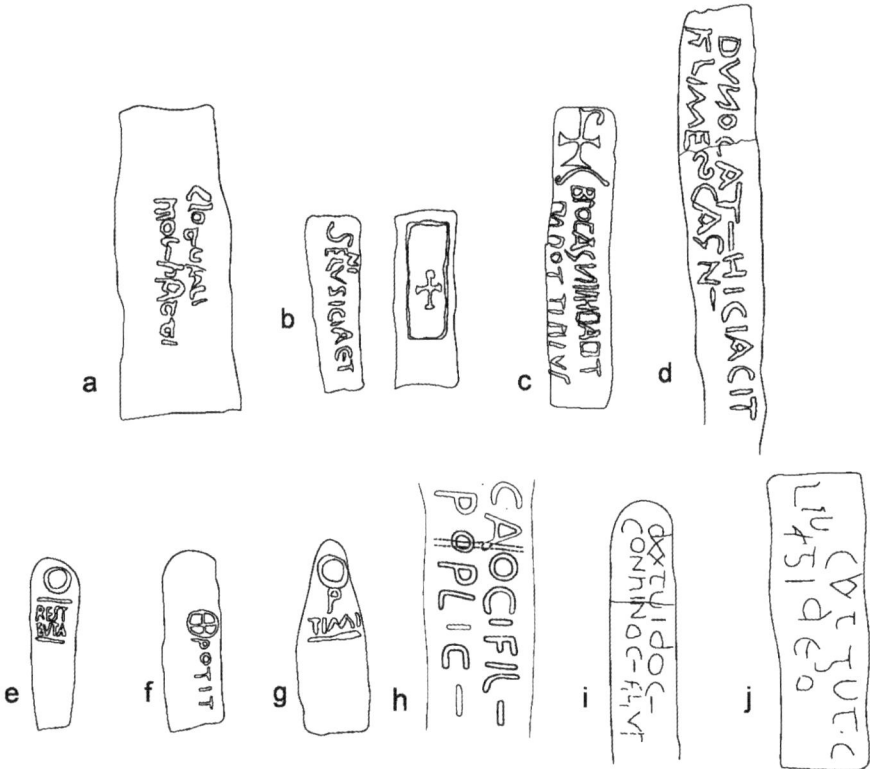

Figure 2 Inscribed stones from south-western Britain: a. Phillack (CLO[TUALI] MO[BRAJTTI]); b. St Just (NI SELUS IC IACET); c. St Endellion (BROCAGNIIHICIACIT?); d. Lancarfe (DNVO ?ATI HIC IACIT FILIMECAGNI); e. Beacon Hill, Lundy (?RESTEUTA); f. Beacon Hill, Lundy (POTITI); g. Beacon Hill (?TIMI); h. East Ogwell (CAOCI FILI POPLICI); i. Lustleigh (DATUIDOCI CONHINOCI FILI V?); j. Lady St Mary, Wareham (CATGUG C[FI] LIUS GEIDO) (not to scale)

a–i Various readings; for variants, see E. Okasha, *Corpus of Early Christian Inscribed Stones of South-West Britain* (1993), pp. 201–4, 243–7, 232–5, 126–8, 154–66, 100–2, 167–70, for a–i; for j see Radford and Jackson 1970, pp. 130–312

---

34. Okasha, *Inscribed Stones*.

symbol,[35] which Hamlin[36] has suggested could be used as late as the eighth century.[37] There are some fourteen carved crosses with inscriptions. There are also several – St Columb, Cornwall, possibly Culbone, Somerset, East Linnacombe, Devon, Belstone, Devon – slabs carved with just crosses, of which two, from Cape Cornwall and Phillack, if they are genuinely ancient, carry the early, Constantinian form of the chi-rho, and are likely to date from the fifth century. The others are difficult to date.[38] There are also two altar slabs (Camborne, Treslothan, Cornwall), three slabs inscribed but undecorated and a few stones which Okasha deemed impossible to classify. Table 2 gives a brief summary of the inscribed pillar stones, from which it will be seen that the simple commemorative filiation style and vertical inscription belong together, but that the other characteristics cut across each other. Reasonably clear evidence of an original relationship to what became a later medieval Christian graveyard also cuts across the characteristics.

All these stones are usually assumed to be Christian, although some of the simple commemorative ones not set up in graveyards need not be. The south-western stones form part of a large corpus of related material which includes (most closely related) the Welsh inscribed and decorated stones, those of northern Britain and Ireland and those of Gaul, the old Western Empire and Brittany.[39] The suggested sources of inspiration for the western British stones include the late and sub-Roman Christian traditions of Gaul, Iberia and Africa; the Irish commemorative tradition, which itself probably has a debt to Roman commemorative styles; and, closer to home, the very similar looking imperial milestones (the St Hilary stone is a reused milestone) and the local prehistoric standing stones.

The conventional chronology of the stones relies upon historical associations (of which there are none directly for the south-west), the epigraphy of the letter forms and dates for the symbols and sculptural features, drawn from analysis of the art

---

35.   The symbol known as the chi-rho derives from the first two letters of the title Christ ('the Anointed One') in Greek, *Christos*, superimposed, where the Greek capital 'chi' is like our X and the Greek capital 'rho' is like our P. This symbol became very popular after 313, when the Emperor Constantine had a vision of the sign before his crucial battle against Maxentius at Ponte Milvio (the Milvian Bridge) outside Rome. The sign appeared with the words *in hoc signe vince* ('in this sign conquer'); Constantine ordered his troops to put it on their shields and was victorious. This, the early or Constantinian form of the sign, began to be used in a simplified form from around the later fourth century, in which the rho has a short horizontal cross-piece below the loop. After *c.* 500 a number of variants appear.

36.   A. Hamlin, 'A chi-rho-carved stone at Drumaqueran, Co. Antrim', *Ulster J. Archaeology*, 35 (1972): 24.

37.   Three – St Clement, Sourton, Whitestyle – were later recut to give them cross heads, and two – Lanteglos, Cardinham II (both Cornwall) – had cross heads attached in the nineteenth century; Okasha, *Inscribed Stones*, p. 12.

38.   For comparable Welsh evidence, see T. Gwyn, 'An early monument in Caernarvonshire', *Arch. Camb.*, 141 (1992): 183; J. Knight *et al.*, 'New finds of early Christian monuments', 126 (1977): 60–73.

39.   For Wales, see V. Nash-Williams, *The Early Christian Monuments of Wales* (1950). New catalogues of the north, British, Irish and Gaulish stones are needed; for Brittany, see W. Davies, J. Graham-Campbell and M. Handley, *The Inscriptions of Early Medieval Brittany* (2000). For a discussion of date, see M. Handley, 'The origins of Christian commemoration in Late Antique Britain', *Early Medieval Europe*, 10 (2): 177–99 (2001), and for function see N. Edwards, 'Early medieval inscribed stones and stone sculpture in Wales: context and function', *Med. Arch.*, 45 (2001): 15–40.

Table 2 Inscribed stones in the south-west

Site	Irish ogham/place-name	Filiation – simple formula	Vertical	Horizontal	Cross	Latin memorial formulae	Associated with churchyard		Mostly capitals	Mostly insular script	Notes[a]
							Yes	No			
Boskena		×	×					×	×		
Boslow		?	×					×		×	
Bosworgey		×	×				?		×		
Bowden	×	×						×	×		
Buckland		×	×					×	×		
Cardinham		×	×				×		?.		
Castledore		×	×					×	×		
Cubert		×	×				×		×		
East Ogwell		×	×				×		×		
Fardel	×	×	×					×			FANONI SAGRAWI QVEBATAVCLLC
Guival	×	×	×					×	×		
Hayle				×		×		×	?.		
Indian Queens		×	×					×	?.		
Kenidjack			×					×	×	?	poss. modern CAR[A]SI[VN]I[A]VS
Kerris		×	×			×		×	×		
Lancarffe		×	×					×	×		
Lanivet		×	×				×		×		
Lanteglos			×	×				×	×		
Lewannick I	×		×	×		×	×				
Lewannick II	×		×	×		×	×				
Lundy I		×	×				×		×		TIGERNI
Lundy II		?	×		×		×		×		POTITI
Lundy III		?		×	×		×		×		OPTIMI
Lundy IV		?		×	?		×		×		RESTEUTA
Lustleigh		×	×				×			×	

Table 2 *Continued*

Site	Irish ogham/place-name	Filiation – simple formula	Vertical	Horizontal	Cross	Latin memorial formulae	Associated with churchyard		Mostly capitals	Mostly insular script	Notes[a]
							Yes	*No*			
Linton		×	×					×	×		
Madron I	?	×	×					×	×		RIALOBRANA
Madron II		×	×					×	×		NR/QON[FIL-]
Mawgan		×	×		×		×		×		
Nanscow	×	×	×					×	×		
Parracombe								×	×		Stone lost
Phillack		×	×				×			×	
Redruth		?	×				×				Stone lost
Rialton			×			?					
St Clement	?	×	×				×		×		
St Endellion	×	×	×	×	×		×		×		
St Hilary		×	×				×		×		
St Just	×	×	×		×		×		×		
St Kew	×	?	×			?	×		×		
Sampford		?	×				?	?	×		[-]IRENR[-]
Sourton		?	×		×	?	?	?	×		
Southill			×		×			?			
Stowford		×	×							×	
Tavistock I		×	×				?		×		NEPRANI (from Tavistock)
Tavistock II	×	×						×	×		SABINI (from Buckland Monochorum)
Tavistock III	×	×	×					×	×		DOBUNN (from BucklandMonochorum)
Tawna	×	×	×					×			Very worn
Tregony		×	×				×		×		

Table 2 *Continued*

Site	Irish ogham/place-name	Filiation – simple formula	Vertical	Horizontal	Cross	Latin memorial formulae	Associated with churchyard		Mostly capitals	Mostly insular script	Notes[a]
							Yes	No			
Tresco		×	×				×		×		
Trevalgan		?	×		×			×	×		DISN
Trevarrack		?	×				×		?		
Treveneagae		?	×		??			×	×		
Welltown	×	×	×					×	×		
Whitestyle		×	×					×	×		
Winsford						×		×	×		CARAACI NEPUS
Worthyvale	×	×	×					×	×		
Yealhampton		×	×					×	×		
Wareham I		×	×				×				VIDCU...
Wareham II		×	×				×				IUDNNE....
Wareham III		×	×				×				CATGUG...
Wareham IV		×	×			×	×			×	DIENIEL
Wareham V		×	×				×			×	GONGORIE
Trencrom											illegible
Tintagel Is		?	?			?		×	×		?not memorial
Tintagel Ch								×			?not inscribed
Porthgwarra			×					×			stone lost
Sancreed		×					?		?		reworked as cross
Combwich	??	?									lost doubtful
Ilsington	?		×					×			possible
Lewannick III	?						?				Ogham only, Thomas 1994: 330
Totnes		×	×					×			lost
St Columb Major		?	?				×				cross-slab, doubtful text

Note: The details given here are not formal readings, but merely indications of which stone is meant

history of Late Antiquity, all of which have been reviewed by Thomas,[40] Okasha,[41] Dark[42] and Knight.[43] Ogham material has been reviewed by McManus,[44] who suggests that the use of ogham on stone monuments seems to belong to the fifth to the seventh centuries, and that it probably derives from ecclesiastical contact between Britain and Ireland. Okasha concludes that in general the inscribed stones can be dated from the fifth or sixth to the eighth century; that those with ogham texts or primitive Irish names have the same date span; that those with a Latin name or a monogram chi-rho, and those with the horizontal I, are likely to belong in the sixth to eighth centuries; and that those with insular script are probably eighth or ninth century onwards.[45] Okasha further believes that neither the horizontal/vertical character of the inscriptions nor the formulae used – broadly filial or HIC IACET – is of chronological significance, but rather represents different traditions, with the Latin memorial formulae being introduced from western Gaul in the mid to late fifth century.[46] The use of capital letters may belong mostly in the fifth/sixth to eighth centuries although they continue to appear until the eleventh century. The inscribed carved standing crosses and the two altar slabs are likely to date from the ninth to the eleventh centuries, and so overlap the range of the pillar stones.

A radical revision of this dating has been put forward by Handley.[47] He suggests that the stones date from the late fourth century and are therefore late Roman rather than post-Roman. They should be seen as the British contribution to the larger pattern of epigraphic practice which appeared across Spain, Italy, Gaul and North Africa during Late Antiquity, rather than as a new departure in western Britain with its origins in any particular set of contacts. The inscription from Hayle, Cornwall, with its lengthy memorial formulae, would therefore be not the result of specific post-Roman contacts with Gaul, but, rather, a late fourth-century local response demonstrating Britain's integral place in the culture of the Late Antique world. Handley suggests that features like the HIC IACET and other formulae, the layout of inscriptions and the use of particular letter-forms, words and abbreviations can all be paralleled with the broad Late Antique world. Handley's interpretation, which puts

---

40.   Thomas, *Mute Stones*, pp. 187–207.

41.   Okasha, *Inscribed Stones*, pp. 55–7.

42.   K. Dark, 'Epigraphic art-historical, and historical approaches to the chronology of Class I inscribed stones', in N. Edwards and A. Lane (eds), *The Early Church in Wales and the West* (1992), pp. 51–61.

43.   J. Knight, 'The early Church in Gwent II: the early medieval Church', *Monmouth Antiquary*, 9 (1992): 45–50; 'Seasoned with salt: insular-Gallic contacts in the early memorial stones and cross slabs', in K. Dark, *External Contacts and the Economy of Late Roman and Post-Roman Britain* (1996), pp. 109–20.

44.   D. McManus, 'Ogham: archaising, orthography and the authenticity of the manuscript key to the alphabet', *Erin*, 37 (1986): 1–31; *A Guide to Ogham* (1991).

45.   Okasha, *Inscribed Stones*, pp. 14–42. The Lanteglos (Cornwall) stone is a complete, roughly trimmed pillar stone of normal type, but carries a relatively lengthy text in early Middle English which is unlikely to date from before the eleventh century. Other English inscriptions are known from Cornwall, dated from the ninth century onwards, but are on more elaborately carved and shaped stone monuments, usually cross-shafts or basses. The Lanteglos stone presumably represents either deliberate archaizing, or some local reason for an inexpert job; Okasha, *Inscribed Stones*, pp. 141–5.

46.   See Dark, 'Epigraphical art-historical', p. 50.

47.   Handley, 'Origins of Christian commemoration', pp. 177–99.

some of the western stones, particularly those with more complex, Latin formulae, into the same broad cultural and chronological framework as the inscriptions from Silchester (with ogham) and Wroxeter, seems to have some merit.[48]

In a major recent study, drawing on the detail of the phonology of the British stones, Sims-Williams suggests that these linguistic criteria provide an independent check on the non-linguistic relative chronologies. He concludes that 'the phonology of the Brittonic inscriptions broadly vindicates the relative chronologies that have been suggested for them'.[49] This broadly endorses the chronologies of Thomas, Dark and Okasha which were based on epigraphic and typological grounds.

All this suggests that the inscribed stones can be seen as belonging within the late fourth to seventh centuries (or even possibly later) with all that this implies for sites and social practices. Difficulty still surrounds the chronological relationship of the stones to the standing crosses and the various carved slabs. It seems safest to assume, at present, that inscribed stones with the simpler filiation formulae continued to be erected and used through the fifth and sixth centuries, at least. It is unlikely that this will be the last word on the chronological issues of the stones, particularly probably in relation to the dating of Latin memorial formulae, but it is for the present a useful working chronology which, with its looser conformation, assists consideration of social developments.

Since Radford's recognition of pottery imported from the Mediterranean in post-Roman levels at Tintagel and Thomas' original paper,[50] the considerable body of subsequent study, of which that by Campbell[51] is particularly significant, has begun to illumine the production of the pottery, suggest the mechanisms of exchange and, most fundamentally, foster a broad consensus relating to the chronology of the imported types, principally Phocean red slipware (PRS), African red slipware (ARS), B ware amphorae, D ware and E ware (Fig. 3). At the time of writing, some 30 south-western sites with these wares are known, and more appear routinely: the pottery is a crucial indicator of date and social practice. Table 3 gives a currently generally acceptable chronological scheme which will be used in this book together with probable sources and previous classificatory names.

The written material with evidential potential divides into two types. There are inscriptions on a wide range of media, like the lead alloy curse tablets from Bath, or the legal document written on a wooden board from Chew, and coins; these require specialized expertise but what they have to say can be directly applied to the better understanding of the period. In contrast, there are the written texts from a wide range of contexts. These very seldom survive in anything like contemporary

---

48. For Silchester, see M. Fulford, M. Handley and A. Clarke, 'The Silchester Ogham Stone rehabilitated', *Med. Arch.*, 44 (2000); M. Fulford and B. Sellwood, 'The Silchester Ogham Stone: a reconsideration', *Antiquity*, 54 (11): 95–9 (1980); for Wroxeter, R. White and P. Barker, *Wroxeter: Life and Death of a Roman City* (1998), p. 106, colour plate 13.

49. Sims-Williams, *Celtic Inscriptions* (2003), p. 351.

50. C. Radford, 'Imported pottery found at Tintagel, Cornwall', in D. Harden (ed.), *Dark Age Britain* (1956), pp. 59–70; C. Thomas, 'Imported pottery in Dark Age western Britain', *Med. Arch.*, 3 (1959): 89–111.

51. E. Campbell, 'Imported goods in the early medieval Celtic west; with special reference to Dinas Powys', Vols 1–3 (1991). See also for useful summary, D. Peacock and D. Williams, *Amphorae and the Roman Economy: An Introductory Guide* (1986), pp. 67–127.

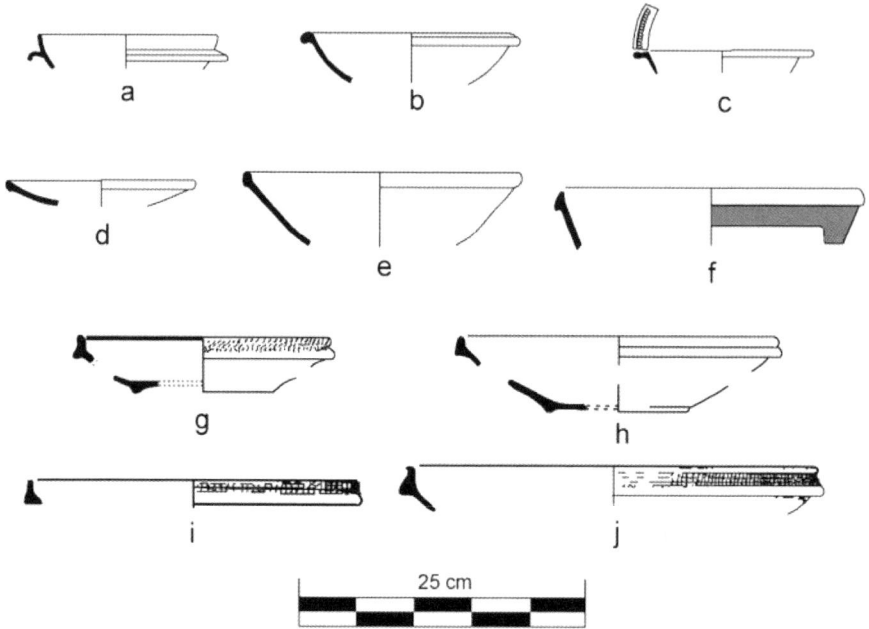

Figure 3 Forms of imported pottery found in Britain
a–f. African red slipware (after Fulford and Peacock 1984, Figs 17, 18, 19, 20)
g–j. Phocean red slipware (after Campbell 1991, Illus. 59)

manuscripts, posing important issues of transmission, and it has been recognized for a century and a half that many of them are composite documents in content and date embodying much special pleading; nevertheless, texts like Gildas' *De Excidio Britannia*,[52] Nennius' *Historia Brittonum*[53] and the *Liber Landavensis*,[54] to name three very different but among the most quoted of the British texts, have often been used as quarries from which solid histories of the fifth and sixth centuries can be built.

In a series of articles published in the 1970s, David Dumville[55] systematically cast doubt on most of the Celtic textual sources, saying that 'most of the available written "evidence" is more apparent than real'[56] and that much then recent work 'has given us

---

52.   In an accessible edition, M. Winterbottom, *Gildas. The Ruin of Britain and Other Works* (1978).

53.   In an accessible edition, J. Morris, *Nennius: British History and the Welsh Annals* (1980).

54.   W. Davies, *The Llandaff Charters* (1979), pp. 258–80. Davies argued that, 'The witness list is therefore a crucial key to the credibility of the records' (p. 81) i.e., the information contained in (some of) the records derived from pre-800.

55.   D. Dumville, 'Some aspects of the chronology of the *Historia Brittonum*', *Bulletin of the Board of Celtic Studies*, 4 (1974): 439–45; ' "Nennius" and the *Historia Brittonum*', *Studia Celtica*, 10–11 (1975–6): 78–95; 'Kingship, genealogies and regnal lists', in P. Sawyer and I. Wood (eds), *Early Medieval Kingship* (1977), pp. 72–104.

56.   D. Dumville, 'Sub-Roman Britain: history and legend', *History*, 62 (1977): 173.

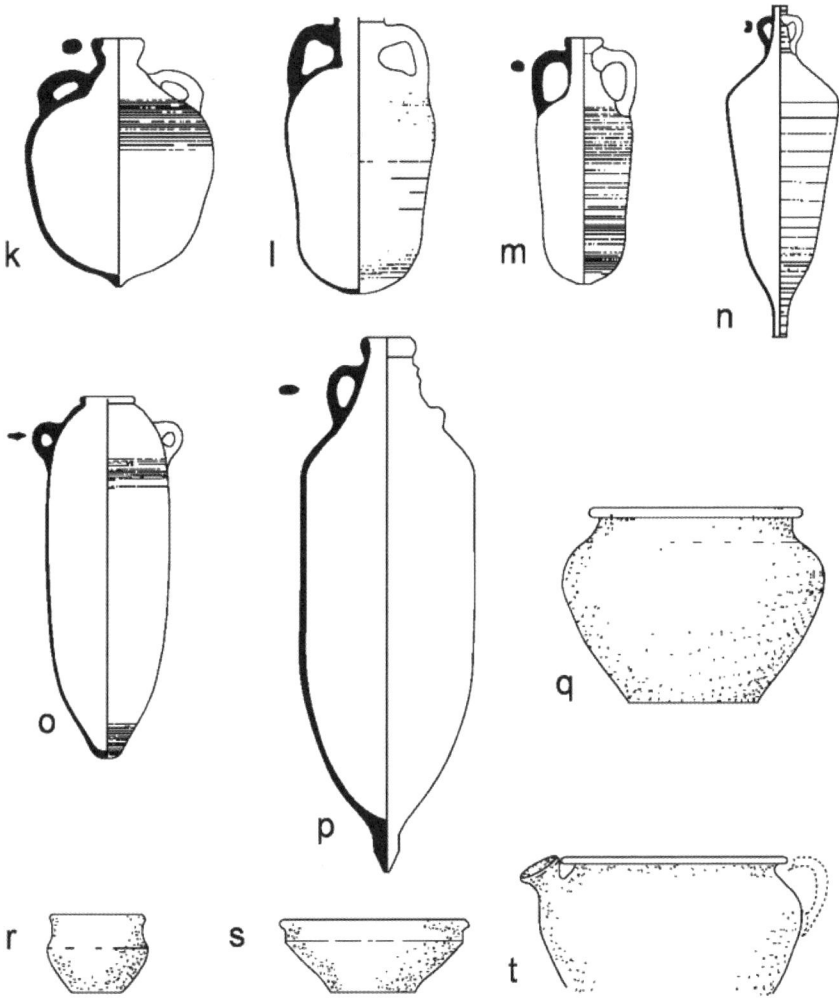

Figure 3 *Cont.* k–p. types of B ware amphorae (after Peacock and Williams 1986, Figs 101, 104, 107, 116, 81)
q–t. types of E ware (after Campbell 1991, Illus. 182) (Various scales)

what is in all essentials a medieval view of the period'.[57] A few years later, Philip Bartholomew[58] published two papers, one on the incapacity of the literary sources to permit a political history of Britain in the fifth century, and the other on the similar position in relation to the Saxon settlement, the *Adventus Saxonum*. A similar work of undermining, in relation to the historical weight which can be placed upon

---

57.   *Ibid.*, p.192.
58.   P. Bartholomew, 'Fifth-century facts', *Britannia*, 15 (1982): 261–70; 'Fourth-century Saxons', *Britannia*, 15 (1984): 169–85.

Table 3 Imported pottery in south-west Britain

Ware	Dating	Source	Previous classifications
PRS	Made fourth to sixth centuries but only Hayes' Forms 3C, D, E, F certainly found in Britain, suggesting date range 480–520	Western Turkey (ancient Phocea)	Radford's A ware; late Roman C
ARS	Insular post-R finds *c.* 550	Carthage region	Radford's A ware
B wares	Amphorae, all long-lived types; insular fragments generally only datable with ref to assoc. PRS and ARS		
Bi	As B	Argolid, Peloponnese, Greece	Radford's B ware
Bii	As B	?south-east Turkey (Cilicia)	
Biv	2-handled forms post *c.* 400		
Bv		'Africana Grande' – N. Africa	
Bvi		Palestine – not known to occur in post-R insula contexts	
Bmisc	Uncertain	unidentified amphorae	Thomas' Bmisc
D	Belongs in Atlantic group of Gaulish R and post-R stamped fine wares. *c.* 500–600, ?into seventh century	various: Bordeaux, Loire Valley, Poitiers, poss others	D ware
E	Undercrafted coarse ware, dating problematic but ?broad currency *c.* 575–700	unresolved: Nantes, Rouen and Charente regions candidates	E ware

the charter material and the Narrations attached to some of them in the *Liber Landavensis*, has been published by Maund,[59] who concluded '*Liber Landavensis* holds an important ... place in the history of the Normanization of the twelfth-century Welsh church: as a witness to the period before this time, the testimony of its Narrations, at least, should be handled with the greatest care.'[60]

This does not, of course, mean that these, and other texts, should not be taken seriously as presenting sixth-, or ninth-, or even twelfth-century views of the past.

---

59.   K. Maund, 'Fact and narrative fiction in the Llandaff Charters' *Studia Celtica*, 31 (1997): 173–93.
60.   *Ibid.*, p. 189.

De Excidio[61] is still generally considered to be a genuine sixth-century work written by a single man, Gildas, although he did not set out to write an historical narrative. The *Historia Brittonum* is probably a north Welsh compilation made in the early ninth century, although uncertainties about the author and his sources remain. What emerges is the general ill-advisability of using the literary sources to create a framework onto which other kinds of evidence can be manoeuvred in order to make sense, and this is quite apart from the standard difficulties posed by bringing historical sources and archaeological evidence together.

Two written sources are of prime significance, although they cannot be wholly separated from the problems surrounding the 'literary' material. The first is the body of charters mostly issued by West Saxon kings.[62] Naturally, the charter texts do not lack their own multitudinous problems, but, these issues notwithstanding, as a group they have much evidence which bears directly on the period in which they were issued. The second are the place-names of the peninsula, which have occasionally been manipulated to further special interests or views, but which generally offer genuine information to be disentangled.[63] It is regrettable that Somerset remains the only county on which the English Place-Name Society has published no work.

Themes and problems

During the last century of Roman rule, life in south-western Britain was lived out in the broad contexts which can be represented upon the map (Fig. 4). These included a basic road system, four 'civic' settlements, a range of 'Romanized' rural houses conventionally called 'villas'[64] and a few small communities like *Abonae* (Sea Mills), Gatcombe, Camerton and Shepton Mallet, clustered in the east, where a number of people seem to have been involved in industrial and commercial activity, usually

61. See M. Lapidge and D. Dumville, *Gildas: New Approaches* (1984); N. Higham, *The English Conquest. Gildas and Britain in the Fifth Century* (1994); M. Herren, 'Gildas and early British monasticisms', in A. Bammesberger and A. Wollmann (eds), *Britain 400–600: Language and History* (1990), pp. 65–78.
62. The essential listing of Anglo-Saxon charters is P. Sawyer, *Anglo-Saxon Charters: An Annotated List and Bibliography* (1968), with an updated version on the Web at *http://www.trin.cam.ac.uk/chart*; for a survey of modern scholarship, see N. Brooks, *Anglo-Saxon Myths: State and Church 400–1066* (2000), esp. pp. 181–202 and 202–15. See also D. Hooke, *The Pre-Conquest Charter-bounds of Devon and Cornwall* (1994).
63. O. Padel, *Cornish Place-name Elements* (1985); *A Popular Dictionary of Cornish Place-names* (1988); J. Gover, A. Mawer and F. Stenton, *The Place-names of Devon*, Parts 1 and 2 (1931, 1932); A. Mills, *The Place-names of Dorset*, Parts 1 and 2 (1977, 1980); A. Fagersten, *The Place-names of Dorset* (1933).
64. J. Smith, 'Villas as a key to social structure', in M. Todd (ed.), *Studies in the Romano-British Villa* (1978); information from Devon County Council Sites and Monuments Register. Villa sites continue to be recognized, especially in Devon, as at Crediton (see F. Griffith, 'A Romano-British villa near Crediton', *PDAS*, 46 (1988): 137–42). There is also Scobchester (Ashbury) in north-west Devon, recorded in 1242 (Gover *et al.*, (1931) *Place-names of Devon*, p. 126). The first element seems to be an English personal name but no explanation has yet appeared for the second.

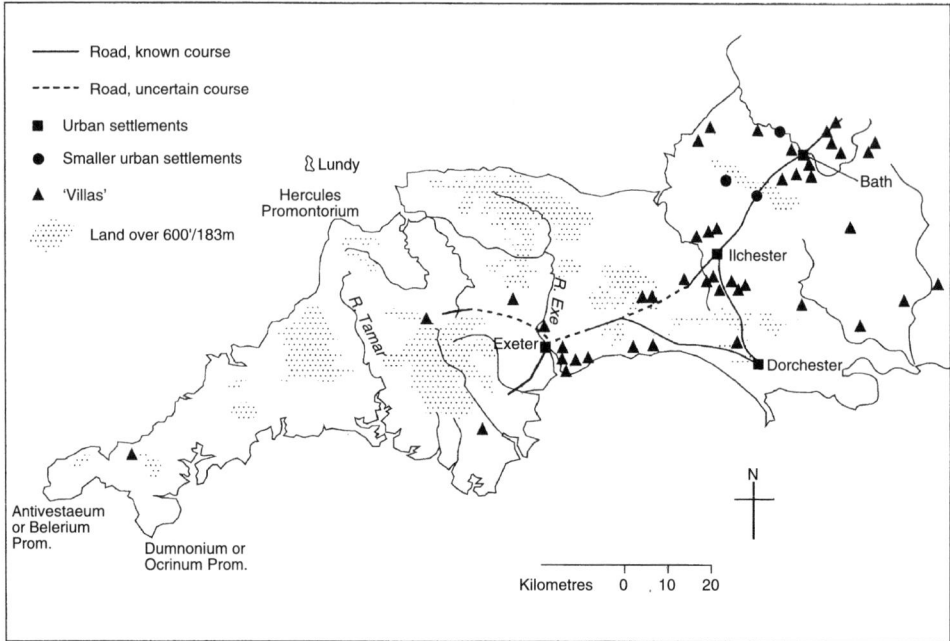

Figure 4 The late Roman south-west

called 'towns'.[65] There are places where coins[66] are known to have been deposited, and places identified as the sites of non-Christian religious activity.[67] There is also relatively considerable evidence in the shape of 'Roman' material culture for widely, and sometimes densely, distributed rural settlement, with its associated structures and landscape use.[68]

By the fourth century the peninsula formed part of one of the four (perhaps eventually five) provinces into which Britain was divided, probably Britannia Prima with its capital at Cirencester, and which embraced the old broadly self-governing tribal groupings of the Dumnonii, the Dubunni and perhaps the Durotiges.[69] Ptolemy's *Geography*[70] tells us that the three great south-western headlands were known as *Antivestaeum* or *Belerium* (Land's End), *Damnonium* (= presumably *Dumnonium*) or *Ocrinum* promontory (The Lizard), and *Hercules* promontory (presumably Hartland Point). Padel suggests that *Ocrinum* 'may not be Celtic at all' and

65.   See for general account, R. Smith, *Roadside Settlements in Lowland Roman Britain* (1987).
66.   See A. Robertson, *An Inventory of Romano-British Coin Hoards* (2000); S. Archer, 'Late Roman gold and silver coin hoards in Britain: a gazetteer', in Casey, *End of Roman Britain*, pp. 29–64.
67.   P. Rahtz and L. Watts, 'The end of the Roman temples in the west of Britain', in Casey, *End of Roman Britain*, pp. 183–210.
68.   Information held in Sites and Monuments Registers, Devon, Cornwall, Somerset and Dorset County Councils.
69.   S. Cleary, *The Ending of Roman Britain* (1989), pp. 28–42; B. Jones and D. Mattingley, *An Atlas of Roman Britain* (1990), Map 5.1.
70.   Jones and Mattingley, *Atlas*, Maps 2.4, 2.5, 2.8, 2.13 and 4.30.

that *Damnonium* is a derivative name (of purely Graeco-Roman invention?), this time taken from the tribe which occupied the south-western peninsula in the Roman period. However, the use of that tribal name is at least significant. It shows 'that a headland, indeed the Lizard itself, could be named from a national territory'.[71] He draws attention to the place-name Predannack or Pradnick in Mullion parish which appears to come from early *Britanakon*, later *Bridanoc*, meaning 'the British one', and was 'the name of the Lizard Point in the late British or Old Cornish period, say from the fifth century on'. Presumably this did not arise locally but as the name of the most significant north-western landfall given by those who made the voyage between western Britain and the opposite Atlantic/Channel coasts.

Ptolemy[72] names three rivers as *Isca* (Exe), *Tamarus* (Tamar) and *Cenio* (doubtful); the only settlement name he knew was *Isca* (Exeter), the old military base and later cantonal capital. The *Antonine Itinerary* names *Moridunum*, unidentified but somewhere in east Devon, and the *Ravenna Cosmography* gives a run of some sixteen further names which include *Nemetostatio* (as generally emended), which must take its name from 'nemeton' ('sacred grove'), still marked by place-names in north-central Devon, and *Statio Deventiasteno*, perhaps somewhere near west Dartmoor: both names have the element *statio*, meaning an 'official post'. *Tamaris* was presumably on the Tamar, and evidently immediately to its west was *Duro-Cornoviorum*, meaning 'fort of the Cornovii', the earliest reference we have to the collective name for the people who inhabited what is now known (in English) as Cornwall. If it is permissible to put all these fragments together, they suggest that the whole peninsula apparently was recognized as the tribal area of the pre-Roman Dumnonii, whose name seems to mean 'worshippers of the god Dumnonos', perhaps 'the Mysterious One', and which of course survives in 'Devon'; and the Cornovii[73] were a recognized subgroup west of the Tamar, whose name from British **corn*, meaning 'horn', refers either to the curving peninsula or, and more probably, to a horned god of the *Cernunnos* (stag-god) type whom they worshipped.

The location of the tripartite interface between the Roman Dumnonii, the Durotiges and the Dubunni has been much debated.[74] It seems likely that the original cantonal boundaries roughly followed those of the Iron Age tribes (with some scope for changes in what is now east Devon), but in the late second-century imperial reorganization a new administrative area was created, centred on Ilchester, giving the divisions which became, broadly, the later shires of Devon, Dorset, and Somerset and Gloucester. Gardner makes the interesting suggestion that the marshlands of central Somerset may have been originally an intertribal zone with a sacred character running back into earlier prehistory, paralleling similar sacred boglands in Denmark and the Fens.

The five British provinces were grouped into the diocese of the Britains which had a governor-general, the *Vicarius*, based in London. He was responsible for civil affairs and for the collection of the *annona militaris*, apparently a poll tax-based

71. O. Padel, 'Predannack or Pradnick, in Mullion', *Cornish Studies*, 15 (1987): 12–13.
72. For what follows, see A. Rivet and C. Smith, *The Place-names of Roman Britain* (1979) under place-names, and esp. pp. 342–3.
73. Rivet and Smith, *Place-names of Roman Britain*, pp. 324–5.
74. K. Gardner, 'The PRIA tribal boundaries', *DAS News*, 74 (1999): 8–9.

requisitioning of supplies for the army. In London were also the officials of the *sacrae largitiones*, the ministry of finance, responsible for tax collecting and disbursements to the civil service, and those of the *resprivata*, the ministry of Crown property, in charge of the large imperial estates. All of these officials were responsible up a bureaucratic ladder which ended ultimately with the emperor in person.[75] The cities of Exeter and Dorchester, and also Ilchester, presumably continued to appoint civic magistrates and a city council as long as they could, through whom the detail of local government within the tribal areas was managed.

Militarily speaking,[76] Britain lay under the western imperial command, and was controlled by the *Dux* ('duke') *Britanniarum* in charge of frontier defence, largely in the north, the *Comes* ('count') *Britanniae* who commanded the strategic reserve, and the *Comes litoris Saxonici*, the Count of the Saxon Shore, in control of coastal defence, particularly in the south-east. No military installations of this date have been found in the south-west; the nearest along the south coast were the Saxon shore forts at Porchester and possibly Carisbrooke. There was, however, a major fort with artillery bastions, state-of-the-art military architecture, at Cardiff, matched by another similar one at Caer Gybi, Holyhead, on Anglesey. Where these fitted into the command structure has been debated, but it seems likely that their operations included naval patrols in the Bristol Channel and the Irish Sea. The social role of the military community has taken on a new significance in recent work, but this cannot have been very influential directly in the peninsula.[77]

What emerges most interestingly from this is the locality and sense of communal identity, which the tribal areas, with their roots in the pre-Roman Iron Age, embodied in the long term. The fourth-century governmental superstructure, both civilian and military, disappeared because it had never entered the mindset of the general population, but Devon, Cornwall, Dorset, Gloucestershire and even perhaps Somerset have maintained very roughly their ancient boundaries to the present day because they have always had meaning for their inhabitants. Similarly, through a number of vicissitudes, so have the administrative centres at Exeter and Dorchester, although Ilchester, less deeply rooted as a centre than the others, was superseded. Cornwall never had a Roman capital, rather oddly but presumably in recognition of its subtribal status, a lack of focus which is reflected in its subsequent administrative history.

A map like Figure 4 produced for around AD 950 would show the same four civic settlements and much the same road system, but most of the small communities have gone, and instead there are a number of 'urban settlements' or 'market towns', many of them fortified. The social texture is now Christian, embodied in a broad range of religious houses, urban churches and rural churches. The material culture has changed completely. In the countryside, some areas look very different, but others appear to have changed less. What mapping cannot show, but what must have been at least as significant to people living at the time, were the impact of new languages (Germanic, perhaps some Irish), the arrival and departure of individuals across north-western Europe, new social structures and some new ways of defining individuals in relation to them. At the centre is the cultural shift in the working of hearts and minds which we call Late Antiquity, which created new feelings about

75.   Jones and Mattingley, *Atlas*, p. 150 and Table 5.2.
76.   Jones and Mattingley, *Atlas*, pp. 97–149 and Map 5.8.
77.   James 1999b, pp. 14–25.

bodies, living and dead, new ideas about how God might intervene in the world and the novel psychological landscape of potential experience which this opened up, and a new stress on locality as the natural scale of life.

The approach to these themes and issues in this book is partly thematic and partly chronological. Chapter 2 is devoted to an analysis of the ways in which the late and post-Roman landscape of the south-west was exploited to produce most of the food, clothing and building materials the way of life required, ways which (as we have seen) have a complex relationship to social culture. The most obvious and spectacular change between *c.* 300 and *c.* 800 is the development of Christian institutions, which by 900 had come to dominate the cultural and physical landscape. Chapters 3 and 4 will assess how this change came about, by concentrating on the roles of the various possible players – villa households, urban populations and clergy, monks, royal patrons and rural communities needing to dispose of their dead – and the institutions which emerged.

Chapter 5 tries to pull the preceding three chapters into an analysis of how social relationships were gradually redrawn to express the imaginative power of the old Roman world, of Christian belief and practice and of new linguistic and cultural combinations. This was made possible through the exploitation of imported goods, of significant sites like hilltops and of legitimating devices like inscribed and decorated standing stones. It worked through the organization of the landscape and the capacity of some individuals to create new forms, or rework old forms, of access to resources, especially land. These themes are pursued in Chapter 6 for the period 800–1050, concentrating here on the western part of the peninsula, chiefly modern Devon and Cornwall. Chapter 7 tries, briefly, to draw the threads together, and set them in a broader cultural and historical context.

Before we can embark on all this, some problems of nomenclature and definition need to be canvassed briefly. In this book, *Cornwall, Devon, Somerset* and *Dorset* will be used to mean the areas of the old counties (i.e., pre-1974, now largely restored); *'the south-west'* means the whole of the peninsula; *western Britain* means the south-west and present-day Wales; and *northern Britain* all of the island roughly north of the Humber. *Britain* means either the island of Britain or the Roman provinces of Britain, depending upon the context, *Ireland* means the island of Ireland and the *British Isles* the whole archipelago. The *Western* and *Eastern* Empires refer to the fluctuating but broadly understood division in the Roman Empire effective during the fourth century AD and its eastern continuation. The term *post-Roman* represents the period *c.* 400–600 and is usually used for Britain. *Primitive Christian* represents AD 1–*c.* 300, and *Early Christian c.* 300–700: these terms should be restricted to religious issues, but this has proved difficult to stick to. *Late Antique/Antiquity* are useful, and now fashionable, phrases which represent the late Roman culture of the Eastern Empire and the Western Empire and its aftermath from *c.* 300 to 600.[78]

I have left the most difficult until last. *Wessex* is a fluctuating area meaning strictly the region under the rule of the West Saxon king at the relevant time, but in practice used more generally as the sense requires; *England* is employed in the same way. Following Gildas, *Dumnonia* is used to mean the area of the south-west governed (whatever this means) by presumed local rulers during the sixth century. *Celtic* means the speakers of a Celtic language, *Germanic* the speakers of a Germanic language (although probably many people in the period grew up bi-, or even trilingual) and

78.   E.g., A. Cameron, *The Mediterranean World in Late Antiquity AD 395–600* (1993).

Irish means coming from, or affiliated with, the island of Ireland. Finally, *Armorica(n)* means the north-western peninsula of Roman Gaul, and *Brittany/ Breton* refers to its status during and following the emigration from Britain.

If this book has an overarching perspective, it is the analysis of what constituted social understanding in a community trying to make collective sense through which life could be lived in the world in which it found itself; it recognizes that this discourse[79] is the site of constant struggle as circumstances and people change and new social practices emerge. It allows some analysis of how the past has been understood and also, perhaps, a useful way of thinking about the past itself.

79.   D. Nunan, *Introducing Discourse Analysis* (1993).

2 Living landscapes

Introduction

The significance of landscape rests not in what it is, but in what we think it is, and therefore how we use it. The standard archaeo/historical presentation of the land as a map or photograph in which time is compressed, the three-dimensional flattened and feeling smoothed away, is a poor apology for the living land, while the observer is removed from the frame, and given what Harraway[1] has called a god-like vantage in which everything is seen from nowhere in particular. We need to see the landscape as lived and experienced, an arena in which particular places have to be identified within surrounding space in order for social life to carry on, and where the inheritance of the past will be an important strand within this process.

The first part of this chapter emphasizes the significance of place in human experience. It then discusses the farming settlements and changes within them, and the importance of woodland. It assesses the enormous importance of the large areas of open grazing and the mineral resources of the uplands. Finally, it considers what life in the early medieval south-west was like for most people.

Places and people

The south-western peninsula is dense with particularly impressive coastlines, river valleys and skylines: an observer standing on Woodbury Common in east Devon can see westwards over the Exe Valley to Haldon Hill and the heights of Dartmoor beyond, with the glimmer of Exmoor to the north, while someone on Branscombe Cliffs looking west can see the whole trend of the coast in a series of overlaid head-lands running from High Peak to Start Point. Within this landscape are weathered rock stacks known as tors on the moorlands, with their impressively statuesque qualities, particular coastal formations like the rock arches at Ladrum Bay, the caves at Boscastle or the jagged ridges at Hartland Point, and isolated hills like Glastonbury Tor or Carn Brea: all these featured at the same time as focuses of poetic significance between people and land, as points of reference in a network of land-marks within which the landscape could be understood and so drawn into a web of social reference and as a means of legitimizing land exploitation and the exercise of authority. Probably no important distinction was made between natural and 'ancient' man-made formations, so that the visual relationship between granite tor formations and Neolithic megalithic tombs would have stood as an experiential fact that helped

---

1. D. Harraway, *Simians, Cyborgs and Women* (1991), p. 31.

to give the landscape its especial qualities. In the same way, the medieval Stannary Parliament used the natural granite foundations at Crockern Tor, Dartmoor, to create a meeting place and judgement seat from which a wide swathe of the tin-bearing country could be seen,[2] eloquent witness to the emotional and emotive creation of socially endorsed special places within the landscape.

At the level of daily life, each individual moved through a densely detailed landscape. Tracks and rights of way linked particular places across the wilder spaces. Prehistoric barrows, natural mounds, rock formations, ancient trees and standing stones were used as reference points from which field systems were drawn out, and as boundary marks in the crucial business of land allotment where they gave physical reality to abstract notions like rights, and the creation of ancestral, legitimating narratives. To an age which perceived the past as an individual whole and did not differentiate between the various categories which we would wish to impose, the interrelation between past and present was immediately significant. In the same way, every act of earth-moving or stone shifting was of significance on the landscape stage, either as an endorsement of the past working on in the present, or as a deliberate shift of scene. The ways in which people worked the landscape to produce food and other necessities such as shelter and clothing, in the damp, and sometimes cold, climate of the south-west, and how this both sustained and affected social organizations, are questions of crucial significance, and this chapter is concerned with the lives of that great majority of the population who were physically working the land, exploiting its resources at the hands-on level, and making goods deemed useful.

Questions about how individuals saw themselves as social beings fitting in to community patterns are notoriously difficult especially when they depend, as post-Roman indications must do, on 'reading back' better perceived material. Charles-Edwards[3] has discussed a Welsh legal text about the position of women which bears such a close resemblance to Hindu legal texts that it may describe early, very widespread arrangements, which possibly also have a bearing on Roman and post-Roman Britain. This shows us several types of recognized marriage (some six to nine, possibly) which suggest a considerable variety of arrangements including union by gift of kin, in which the woman moves to her husband's house accompanied by goods, union in which the woman does not leave her home but is visited there openly by her man, and secret unions, where sex takes place out of doors. If life in the post-Roman south-west was anything like this, it suggests a strong sense of self-possession leading to a range of birth circumstances where what mattered was recognized membership of a broader family group who possessed access to resources. Families themselves are understood not as the long-term monoliths which result from cousin marriage (as in much of the world) but as local and temporal sites

---

2.   V. Smith, *Portrait of Dartmoor* (1972), p. 22.
3.   T. Charles-Edwards, *'Nau Kynywedi Teithiauc'*, in D. Jenkins and M. Owen (eds), *The Welsh Law of Women* (1980), pp. 35–9. See also E. Wrigley, 'Mortality and the European marriage system', in G. Geissler and D. Oddy (eds), *Food, Diet and Economic Change Past and Present* (1993), pp. 35–9, for an interesting discussion relating to Hartland, Devon, though at a much later period, which considers morality and European marriage patterns, and the relatively favourable circumstances in early Modern England which arose, in part, from late marriages. For an interesting general discussion, see J. Goody, *The European Family: An Historical Anthropological Essay* (1983), esp. pp. 39–45.

where the bundle of blood links and widely ramifying affine (in-law) relationships happens to coalesce densely enough to provide sufficient labour to manage the various resources properly. Conceivably, also, the freedom of choice (some?) women enjoyed, for whom marriage was not arranged and consummated when they were pubescent, meant relatively low birth rates, with the favourable relationships to resource and mortality that this can imply.

Population size is an equally thorny issue. Millet, in a careful summary of the available evidence and the bases of previous estimates, concluded that the rural population of Roman Britain, both free and less free, was about 3.3 million, and the urban population less than 250,000.[4] At an extremely crude estimate this suggests that Exeter's population in, say, 300 was scarcely more than a couple of thousand, with Bath and Dorchester much the same, and Ilchester perhaps a little smaller, and that the rural population of the whole peninsula may not have numbered much more than 300,000 to 500,000 people. The human consequences of this, among others, meant that each person could have known individually a relatively large proportion of those alive at the same time, allowing all the connecting threads of mutual obligation which characterize small-scale societies.

Farming settlements

It is important to note that the density of archaeological work across the peninsula has differed very considerably, with the result that we know much more about Dartmoor than the rest of Devon, more about Cornwall in later prehistory than in the early medieval period and more about Romano-British settlement in Dorset and Somerset than we do about settlement pre-1000. Across the whole peninsula, in fact, early medieval settlements have been relatively infrequently excavated. Secondly, the place-name evidence, because it reflects the two main languages spoken in the peninsula at the time, British/Cornish and Anglo-Saxon, together with the generally county-based character of most important studies, tends to create an expectation of difference between the eastern and western areas, which may obscure significant similarities.

Excavation, field survey and aerial reconnaissance have demonstrated the existence of a substantial number of enclosures, and these have been considered in detail by Bastide, who compares the south-western material, including that from Dorset and Somerset, with comparable evidence from Brittany in a broad chronological sweep which extends from later prehistory to the Roman period, and takes known post-Roman occupation into account. For the south-west Bastide draws upon work by Johnson and Rose, Preston-Jones and Rose,[5] and Griffith.[6] In Cornwall, enclosed settlements are becoming known by the hundred (Fig. 5) and, while density differs from place to place, in some areas it is as high as two per square kilometre: when field survey is complete, the number of recorded sites may well reach the 1000

4. M. Millett, *The Romanization of Roman Britain* (1990), pp. 181–6.
5. T. Bastide, *Les Structures de l'habitat rural protohistorique dans le sud-ouest de l'Angleterre et le nord-ouest de la France* (2000); N. Johnson and P. Rose, 'Defended settlement in Cornwall – an illustrated discussion', in D. Miles (ed.), *The Romano-British Countryside* (1982), pp. 151–208; A. Preston-Jones and P. Rose, 'Medieval Cornwall', *Corn. Arch.*, 25 (1986): 135–86.
6. F. Griffith, 'A Romano-British villa near Crediton', *PDAS*, 46 (1988): 137–42; 'Changing perceptions of the context of prehistoric Dartmoor', *PDAS*, 52 (1994): 85–100.

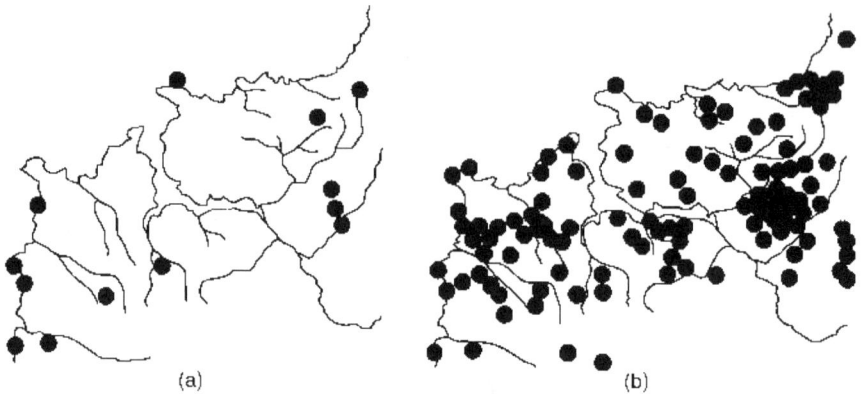

(a)   (b)

Figure 5 The known distribution of Iron Age/Romano-British sites before (a) and after (b) the National Mapping Programme Initiative in northern Cornwall (by 1996). (After Hartgroves 1996 copyright, Cornwall County Council)

level.[7] In Devon[8] they are being recognized in increasing number through air survey, while, in Somerset, Bastide has accumulated evidence for some 179 and in Dorset for some 266.[9] The bulk of the sites are of the type known as 'rounds' in Cornwall, and which sometimes appear in Cornish place-names with the prefix 'car', from the Cornish **ker*, 'fort, round'.[10] Further east, they have no particular name, outside the pages of archaeologists. The enclosed area at these sites is relatively small, ranging from approximately 2 hectares to 0.25 ha, and the enclosure itself normally has a relatively simple entrance, clearly not intended primarily for defence. The enclosures are usually situated on hill slopes and spurs rather than hilltops. Some of the Cornish examples have survived physically as obvious upstanding monuments in the present landscape, with enclosure banks which incorporate substantial lumps of stone, but the majority of all the sites can now only be recognized through careful fieldwork. Together they belong within the general tradition in later prehistoric Britain of roundhouses, often clumped together within a round enclosure. They are probably best imagined as hamlets rather than single-family farmsteads.

In Devon and Cornwall, the enclosed settlements have demonstrated in excavation a date range from later prehistory to the sixth century AD, or later. Of the twenty enclosures outside Dartmoor excavated in Devon (Fig. 6), only one, Hayes Farm II, gave positive evidence of post-Roman date, although Turnspit, Rewe Cross and Overland may have continued in use, and possibly some of the others.[11] Equivalent evidence[12] for Cornwall (Fig. 7) suggests a similar broad date range, showing that we

---

7.   A. Young, *The National Mapping Programme. Cornwall and the Isles of Scilly Mapping Project: Annual Progress Report 2000/2001*; see also H. Quinnell, *Excavations at Trethurgy Round, St Austell: Insights into Roman and Post-Roman Cornwall* (forthcoming), Ch. 12.

8.   Through the work of the Cornish Sites and Monuments Register; S. Hargroves, 'The Sites and Monuments Record', *Archaeology Alive*, 4 (1996): 5; and Devon Sites and Monuments Register through the work of Frances Griffith.

9.   Bastide, *Les Structures*, figs 2.3, 2.4.

10. O. Padel, *Cornish Place-names Elements* (1985), p. 50.

11. Griffith, 'Changing perceptions of prehistoric Dartmoor', pp. 85–100.

12. Johnson and Rose, 'Defended settlement in Cornwall', pp. 151–86.

Site name	Parish	NGR	Plan	Excavation	Dating	Reference
Sourton enclosure	Sourton	SX54917		Full excavation by CEU, 1986	Few finds; C14 date 3590BP Uncal	Weddell & Reed 1997
Gittisham	Gittisham	SY140996		Evaluation trenches by EA, 1994	ceramic: ?lat BA/early IA	Reed & Manning 1994a
Rewe (Uglow site R5)	Rewe	SS941008		Trench, 1982	ceramic: 'mid 1st mill. BC'	Uglow et al.1985
Black Horse	Clyst Honiton	SX978933		Evaluation trenches by EA, 1994	ceramic: ?mid-late IA	Reed & Manning 1994b
Holcombe	Uplyme	SY315928		Partial area excavation, 1967-9	ceramic: R-B and ?IA	Pollard 1974
Milber Little Camp	Coffinswell	SX886697		Trench, 1938	ceramic: AD 50–80	Fox et al. 1949; Vachell 1964; Watts 1993
North Wood	Dartington	SX787634		Trench, 1966, by M. Biddle	'R-B coarse pottery'	anon, DAS Newsletter, June 1966
Hayes Farm I	Clyst Honiton	SX991944		Partial area excavation, 1987	Ceramic and C14: C3–4 AD	Simpson et al. 1989
Rudge	Morchard Bishop	SS746078		Partial area excavation, 1988	ceramic: 'second half C1 AD'	Todd 1988
Butland Farm	Modbury	SX644506		Recording of pipe trench, 1993	1 R-B sherd	Homer 1993
Lower Well Farm	Stoke Gabriel	SX864576		Area excavation, 1958–60	ceramic and coins: C1–4 AD	Masson Phillips 1966
Pond Farm	Exminster	SX922884		Trench, 1975	ceramic: late C2	Jarvis 1976
Turnspit (Uglow R28)	Rewe	SS938011		Trenches, 1988–9	ceramic: C3	Uglow 1993a
Rewe Cross (Uglow R8)	Rewe	SX947998		Trench, 1992	ceramic: C2–3	Uglow 1993b
Overland (Uglow T22)	Thorverton	SS934025		Trench, 1988	ceramic: C2–4	Uglow 2000
Hayes Farm II	Clyst Honiton	SX991944		Partial area excavation by EA, 1987	C14: AD 390–630 cal	Simpson et al.1989
Sourton Down	Sourton	SX542917		Full excavation by EA, 1991	ceramic: C13–15 AD	Weddell & Reed 1997
West Wortha	Germansweek	SX431917		Full excavation by EA, 1989–90	ceramic: medieval	Stead & Weddell 1991
Shop	Broadwoodwidger	SX423912		Sample trenches by EA, 1989–90	ceramic: medieval	Silvester 1980
Castle Field	Dunkeswell	ST141077		Trench, 1977	ceramic: C12–14AD	Ponsford 1992
Hayes Barton	St Thomas, Exeter	SX991943	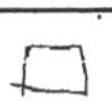	Full excavation by EA, 1989	ceramic: C16 AD	

Notes
1. The enclosure at Bow is omitted.
2. Where enclosures are shown incomplete, this does not necessarily indicate that the site itself is not fully enclosed, merely that its perimeter is not fully recorded.
3. Some sites, such as Clancombe, have too little of their perimeter known to be shown here.

0   200
metres

Figure 6 Devon enclosures outside Dartmoor (after Griffiths 1994, Fig. 2)

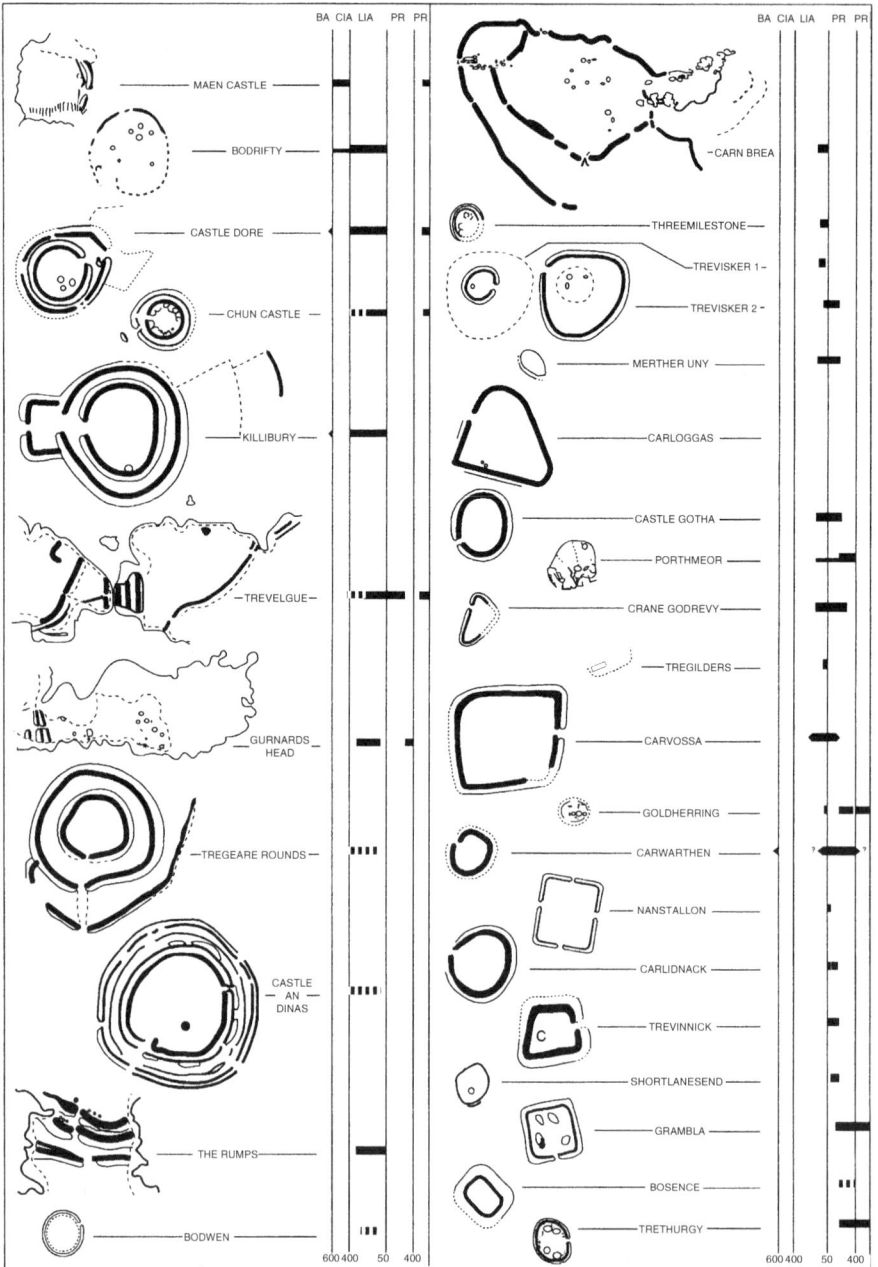

Figure 7 Cornish enclosures (after Johnson and Rose 1982, Fig. 13)

are looking at a complicated palimpsest of settlements which makes it well-nigh impossible to tell how many were being used in the late-Roman/post-Roman period, or generally which ones they were.

In the west of Penwith, and with some related structures in Scilly, are some 60 or so sites called courtyard houses: the majority of the known sites lie on the high ground of Lands End peninsula and on the cliff slope between Zennor and Morvah. These are in attractive areas and often show substantial surviving remains, and have consequently attracted a disproportionate amount of attention. Some sites, like those excavated at Chysauster and Carn Euny,[13] comprise substantial groups of hut sites, but most are small groups or single houses, often with associated buildings and attached field systems. Courtyard houses are roughly oval in plan, extending around 20 m on their long axes, with a massive external wall, through which an entrance gives onto a central space, open and sometimes paved, off which there are a number of rooms, usually three or four, some of which seem to have been for living and others for work and stock management. If several such houses clump together, the result often presents the appearance of a strong enclosure with a number of units, in which the spaces between the sides and backs of the dwellings are filled in with stones, leaving access routes and the courtyards open to the sky.[14]

The origin of the type seems to belong in the Roman period, and some of them, like that at Halangy[15] (St Mary's), seem to have grown out of successive buildings and additions. New courtyard houses were being built into the second and third centuries, as at Chysauster and Porthmeor (Fig. 8), which had post-Roman material.[16] The courtyard houses are probably best regarded as the local variant on the general theme of Iron Age/Romano-British settlement, and, like related sites, could easily in some cases have remained in occupation into the post-Roman period: that at Halangy certainly did.

The shape of the simpler enclosures occupied in the period shows considerable variation. In Devon, Hayes Farm[17] had a sharp-cornered rectangular enclosure, followed by a loosely circular (or conceivably D-shaped) enclosure, while Rewe Cross[18] and Overland,[19] both with Romano-British material, are like early Hayes Farm. At Stoke Gabriel,[20] a subrectangular enclosure with a dependent enclosure had an attached field system with early Roman and fourth-century material, and at Clannacombe[21] the settlement was enclosed by a ditch which was deliberately filled in around AD 200. Rectangular crop marks have appeared near Exminster (Fig. 9). In Cornwall, Grambla,[22] with a date range spanning the Roman/post-Roman period,

13. For broad account of Chysauster, see C. Weatherhill, *The Courtyard Houses of West Penwith* (1982). For Carn Euny, see P. Christie, 'The excavation of an Iron Age souterrain and settlement at Carn Euny, Sancreed, Cornwall', *Proceedings of the Prehistoric Society*, 44 (1978): 309–434.

14. This is the generally accepted view, but see J. Wood, 'A new perspective on West Cornwall courtyard houses', *Corn. Arch.*, 2 (1997): 95–106, for a suggestion that some, at least, of the whole complexes were roofed over.

15. For full account of the Halangy excavations, see P. Ashbee, 'Halangy Down, St Mary's, Isles of Scilly, excavations 1964–1977', *Corn. Arch.*, 35 (1996): 5–201.

16. F. Hurst, 'Excavations of Porthmeor, 1933–5', *JRIC*, 24 (1936), App 2: 1–81.

17. S. Simpson, F. Griffith and N. Holbrook, 'The prehistoric, Roman and early post-Roman site at Hayes Farm, Clyst Honiton', *PDAS*, 47 (1989): 1–28.

18. Devon sites and Monuments Register, Rewe Cross SX947998.

19. Griffith, 'Changing perceptions of prehistoric Dartmoor', p. 95.

20. M. Phillips, 'Excavations at a Romano-British site at Lower Well Farm, Stoke Gabriel', *PDAS*, 23 (1966): 3–29.

21. J. Green and K. Green, 'Excavations at Clannacombe, Thurlstone', *PDAS*, 94 (1970): 130–8.

22. A. Saunders, 'Excavations at Castle Gotha, St Austell: interim report', *Procs. West Cornwall Field Club*, 2 (5): 50–2 (1972).

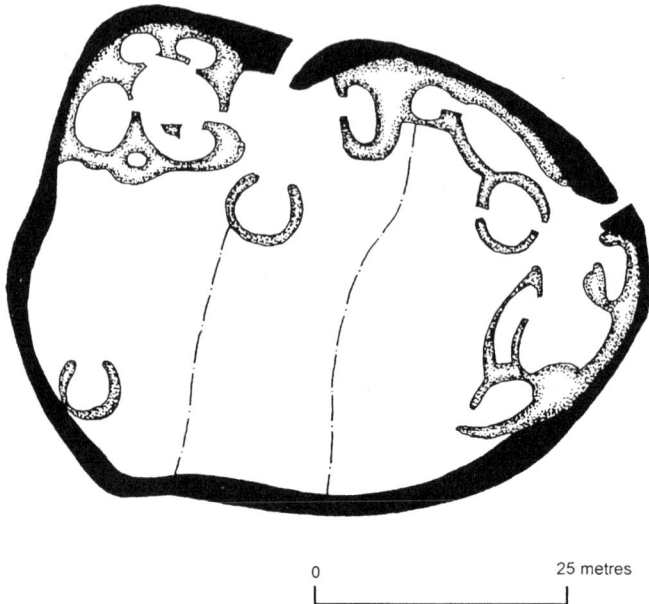

0   25 metres

Figure 8 Plan of Porthmeor showing outer enclosure (solid) and hut plans (after Hurst 1936, Fig. 1)

is rectangular, and early Romano-British Trevinnick[23] is roughly rectangular, while Trethurgy,[24] Roman with some post-Roman use, is roughly circular. Reawla,[25] with a date range of first to fourth century AD, showed during the second century the replacement of the original small round enclosure by a larger stronger one, and Shortlanesend[26] also had a circular enclosure. The substantial enclosures look large in the record, and in the minds of investigators, but it would be a mistake to suppose that unenclosed farming sites, encompassing sometimes just one house and sometimes more, did not feature in the landscape either before or after 400, although if they are unexcavated, or lack diagnostic material, they will be impossible to date. Port Godrevy[27] is one example of such a small site and probably there were many others.

Trethurgy[28] is the only round where the interior has been completely excavated

23.   A. Fox and W. Ravenhill, 'Excavation of a rectilinear earthwork at Trevinnick, St Kew 1968', *Corn. Arch.*, 8 (1969): 89–97.

24.   H. Quinnell, *Excavations at Trethurgy Round, St Austell: Insights into Roman and Post-Roman Cornwall* (forthcoming), Ch. 1.

25.   N. Appleton-Fox, 'Excavations at a Romano-British round: Reawla, Gwinear, Cornwall', *Corn. Arch.*, 31 (1992): 69–123.

26.   D. Harris, 'Excavation of a Romano-British round at Shortlanesend, Kenwyn, Truro', *Corn. Arch.*, 19 (1980): 63–75.

27.   See P. Fowler, 'A native homestead of the Roman period at Porth Godrevy, Gwithian', *Corn. Arch.*, 1 (1962): 61–84. Evidence continues to accumulate: the site at Ruthvoes, Cornwall, with a ditch complex, has produced several radiocarbon dates representing the fifth-sixth centuries AD; see A. Jones, *Brear's Down to Ruthvoes, Cornwall Archaeological Watching Brief*, (2001).

28.   Quinnell, *Excavations at Trethurgy Round.*

Figure 9 Crop mark north-east of Exminster, near Exeter, Devon, showing double rectangular enclosure, possibly of Romano-British farmstead. Other crop marks can also be seen. (Photo: Cambridge University collection of air photographs, copyright reserved)

(Fig. 10). Occupation of the site appears to have started in the late second century, with four large oval houses set around the inside edge of the embankment together with a possible store and space for farm activities. By the early third century, further houses and other buildings were built and used until the early fourth century, when there may have been a short gap in occupation. When the farmers moved in again they had four houses, together with a large byre, or similar building. By the late fourth century, the houses, although smaller, had increased to five, and during the fifth century, the accommodation gradually dropped back to two with three again in the sixth (Fig. 11). We get an impression of considerable flexibility, in which changes in extended family and farming circumstances could easily be reflected in new buildings or changed usage.

The admittedly thin evidence suggests that this sort of pattern was probably fairly typical, regardless, perhaps, of the shape of the enclosure. Stoke Gabriel[29] had (at

---

29.   Phillips, 'Excavations at Lower Well Farm', pp. 3–29.

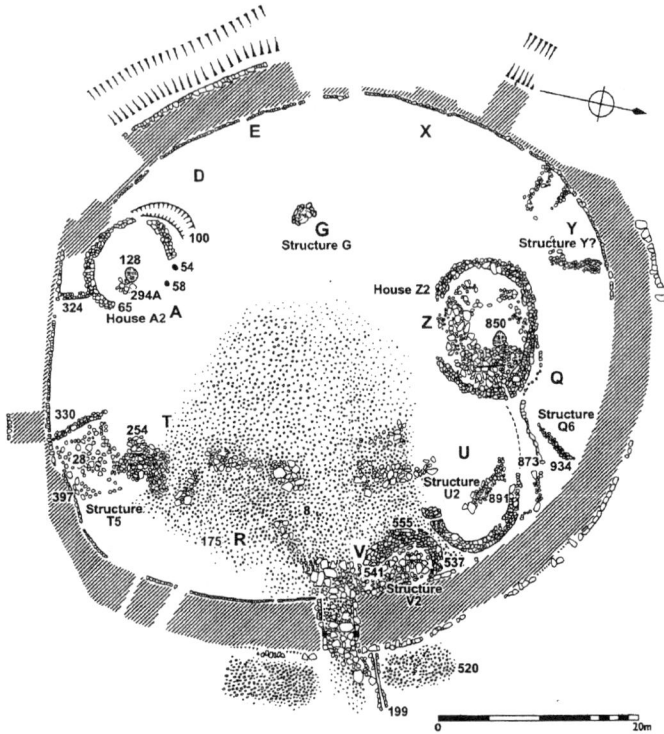

Figure 10 Plan of round settlement at Trethurgy *c.* AD 450–500 showing the entrance area, two roundhouses and a range of structures/outbuildings (after Quinnell forthcoming, Fig. 87, reproduced with kind permission of H. Quinnell and English Heritage).

least) one internal house in the fourth century; at Reawla[30] by then the excavated houses had been used as a rubbish dump, although further houses may have existed. The enclosed sites generally had drainage gullies like those at Shortlanesend[31] and Trethurgy, often some rough cobbling, and space for workshops, storage and stock management. As Quinnell[32] cogently points out, 'it is difficult to find a true round-house of the Cornish Roman period.' At Trethurgy, Castle Gotha,[33] Grambla[34] and perhaps Crane Goddrevy[35] and Shortlanesend,[36] the houses were oval, often con-structed so as to leave the interiors open, without posts holding up the roofs. The houses were up to 13 m in length, giving a floor space of 80–100 m², and the floors were well made of tamped rab (beaten earth) or paving, each with a hearth and a

30.   Appleton-Fox, 'Romano-British round', pp. 69–123.
31.   Harris, 'Romano-British round', pp. 63–75.
32.   H. Quinnell, 'Cornwall during the Iron Age and Roman period', *Corn.Arch.*, 24 (1986): 126.
33.   A. Saunders and D. Harris, 'Excavations at Castle Gotha, St Austell', *Corn. Arch.*, 21 (1982): 109–53.
34.   Saunders, 'Excavations at Castle Gotha', pp. 215–20.
35.   C. Thomas, 'Excavations at Crane Godrevy, Gwithian, 1969: interim report', *Corn. Arch.*, 8 (1968): 84–8.
36.   Harris, 'Romano-British round', pp. 63–75.

Figure 11 The settlement site at Trethurgy, St. Austell, Cornwall, in process of excavation. The entrance is on the left (photo by courtesy of English China Clays)

cooking pit beside it. At Trethurgy, the many small nails found bear witness to wooden fittings, presumably pegs, shelves or even basic cupboards and box-beds. These houses must have had a roof ridge, with roofs made of timber.

The richest sources of finds are the rubbish dumps, which are known from Trethurgy[37] (late fourth century), Kilhallon[38] (third century) and Carvossa[39] (fourth century). All of these had been allowed to accumulate in disused buildings or ditches, and it was clearly normal practice to clear out the middens periodically and spread the contents, including presumably animal and human waste, on the fields (adding, of course, further perplexities to dating issues, since the crucial chronological sequences of the pottery became muddled in the process). Across its periods of occupation Trethurgy produced sherds of over 600 vessels, mostly of gabbroic ware produced in the Lizard,[40] in a range of jars and bowls, some flanged.

---

37. Quinnell, *Excavations at Trethurgy Round* (forthcoming).
38. P. Carlyon, 'A Romano-British site at Kilhallon, Tywardreath: excavation in 1975', *Corn. Arch.*, 21 (1982): pp. 155–70; 'Excavation at Kilhallon', *Corn. Arch.*, 23 (1994): 181–3.
39. P. Carlyon, 'Finds from the earthwork at Carvossa, Probus', *Corn. Arch.*, 26 (1987): 103–41. There are also a few stray finds, some from possible settlements; see Todd, 'Silver Brooch from Capton' (1983).
40. The gabbroic clays of the Lizard produced a particularly fine potting clay – see later this chapter, pp. 68–71; Quinnell, *Excavations at Trethurgy Round* (forthcoming).

Common remains of iron objects suggest a basic tool kit[41] containing knives, sickles, nails and shears. Smooth pebbles, like those at Reawla,[42] were perhaps used for food processing, and leather and cloth finishing and spindle whorls, also found here and at Stoke Gabriel,[43] are common generally, together with loom weights. Presumably a range of woollen clothes could be produced, from something like rough flannel to heavier tweeds, dyed with soft vegetable dyes. Several of the sites have produced evidence of metalworking. Trethurgy[44] produced a tin ingot, a droplet of silver and the mould cover from a flan casting, and Halangy[45] part of a mould; however, the supposed evidence for iron smelting at Reawla[46] and Carvossa[47] now looks more suspect. The fourth- and fifth/sixth-century inhabitants, particularly in Penwith, possessed hard stone mortaria[48] and other objects like weights, which were made in the farming settlements from at least the third century.

Assemblages like these do not readily convert into detailed assessments of life-style. The quality of time-specific data is generally very poor, so that its correlation with a specific lifetime – the unit of experience – is impossible, while 'roughly contemporary' does not mean 'in use at the same time'. Archaeological assessment tends to rely on ideas like 'trend', 'normative', 'highly differentiated' and 'aggregate', while actual life is lived as complex, messy and in the spirit of 'make do and mend' in which individual categories and contexts are paramount. Added to this is the undoubted fact that some things, like children's gear or some cooking equipment, wear out very quickly, while others, like stone bowls, have a much longer lifespan. Unless we postulate a state of affairs where the whole population renounced worldly goods and determined to use only biodegradable materials,[49] there must have been objects in use at the end of the fourth century and well on into the early fifth.

Analysis of fourth-century assemblages outside the south-west suggest a possible distinctive very late fourth-century material set, which also hinted at social changes. This set included black jewellery and Samian fragments reworked into counters and spindle whorls, perhaps valued for their red colour. It was accompanied by a marked decline in hairpins, suggesting a female fashion shift from elaborate coiffures which needed pins to hold them up, to short hair (perhaps the least likely), hair bundled into some sort of bonnet, possibly suggesting influence from the early Christian fathers, or plaits, hinting at 'Germanic' fashion. During the fourth century there also seems to have been a curtailment of the range of pots in use, suggesting that habits of eating, drinking and cooking were changing and simplifying. The nature of the south-western finds do not permit this level of analysis, but the outside evidence may throw light on some specific south-western finds, like the reuse of Samian at Cadbury

---

41.   See W. Manning, *Catalogue of Romano-British Iron Tools, Fittings and Weapons in the British Museum* (1985).

42.   Appleton-Fox, 'Romano-British round', pp. 106–13.

43.   Phillips, 'Excavations at Lower Well farm', p. 26.

44.   Quinnell, *Excavations at Trethurgy Round* (forthcoming).

45.   P. Ashbee, 'Halangy Down', (1996), pp. 102–4.

46.   Appleton-Fox, 'Romano-British round', pp. 102–4.

47.   H. Douch and S. Beard, 'Excavations at Carvossa, Probus, 1968–1970: preliminary report', *Corn. Arch.*, 9 (1970): 93–7; Carlyon, 'Finds from Carvossa', pp. 103–41.

48.   H. Quinnell, 'A sense of identity: distinctive Cornish stone artefacts in the Roman and post-Roman periods', in M. Carver, *In Search of Cult* (1993), pp. 69–78.

49.   H. Cool, 'The parts left over: material culture into the fifth century', in T. Wilmot and P. Wilson (eds), *The Late Roman Transition in the North* (2000), pp. 47–65.

Congresbury, Somerset,[50] and the general premise that life had already begun to change in the later fourth century may be pertinent for the south-west.

The domestic archaeology of the sites cannot produce evidence of planned allotments of space to specific groups (by gender, age or seniority, for example) or to specific activities either within the settlement as a whole or within individual houses, for even hearths can have been used for cooking or metalworking, through differential allocations by time or place, with all the social distinctions this implies. To put it at its simplest, we do not really know what was going on, involving whom and why, in all the various areas of the hamlets during the course of either their lifetimes, or the lifetimes of their inhabitants. The existence of a range of buildings within the enclosures suggests both that a good deal had and was happening, and that there was an urge to create separate sites, but we have little information about what these were, and how they related to social distinctions, beyond obvious need to keep animals away from metalworking, for example. Studies of later prehistoric houses have recently shown interest in the orientation of house doorways, which seem frequently to face east (the sunrise) or south-east (the midwinter sunrise), and in the internal layout of house usage (Fig. 12), which seems to mirror this cosmological scheme.[51] This opens up an interesting line of speculation but the present level of excavated evidence does not allow the argument to be pursued.

The farming landscape was not static and the present state of evidence suggests that a major change was taking place in the west in the early medieval centuries. The distribution of the Cornish rounds is broadly similar to that of the early medieval settlements,[52] with a concentration on reasonable farming land. In the parishes of

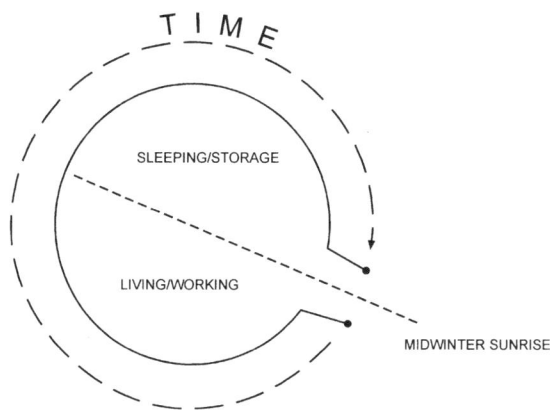

Figure 12 Cosmological house schemes (after Giles and Pearson 1999, Fig. 13.2)

50. I. Burrow, *Hillfort and Hill-top Settlement in Somerset in the First to Eighth Centuries AD* (1981), esp. pp. 270–4.

51. A. Fitzpatrick, 'Everyday life in Iron Age Wessex', in A. Gwilt and C. Haselgrove (eds), *Reconstructing Iron Age Societies: New Approaches to the British Iron Age* (1997), pp. 73–86; M. Giles and M. Pearson, 'Learning to live in the Iron Age: dwelling and praxis', in B. Bevan (ed.), *Northern Exposure: Interpretative Devolution and the Iron Age in Britain* (1999), pp. 217–31.

52. P. Rose and A. Preston-Jones, 'Changes in the Cornish countryside AD 400–1100', in D. Hooke and S. Burnell, *Landscape and Settlement in Britain AD 400–1066* (1995), p. 56.

Padstow and St Merryn, a relatively low-lying area on the north coast, at least twelve enclosures have been identified, and they follow the same broad distribution as the later medieval settlements (Fig. 13). The same pattern appears in the Fal Valley, although there the later settlements seem to shun the high ground, suggesting perhaps some shrinkage of settlement. These later settlements have the Old Cornish habitative place-name prefix *tre* or *tref* meaning 'hamlet, farmstead, estate'.[53] The later settlements are often on new sites which fieldwork shows were not enclosed, or sometimes on the old sites (rounds), the enclosures of which were allowed to decay, a landscape dynamic visible in the St Keverne area. The evidence from Devon is much more patchy but may eventually suggest the same.[54] Here the place-name element equivalent to *tre* seems to be *tun*, Old English meaning 'farmstead, estate'.[55] Fieldwork suggests that these are unenclosed settlements, and apparently replaced the

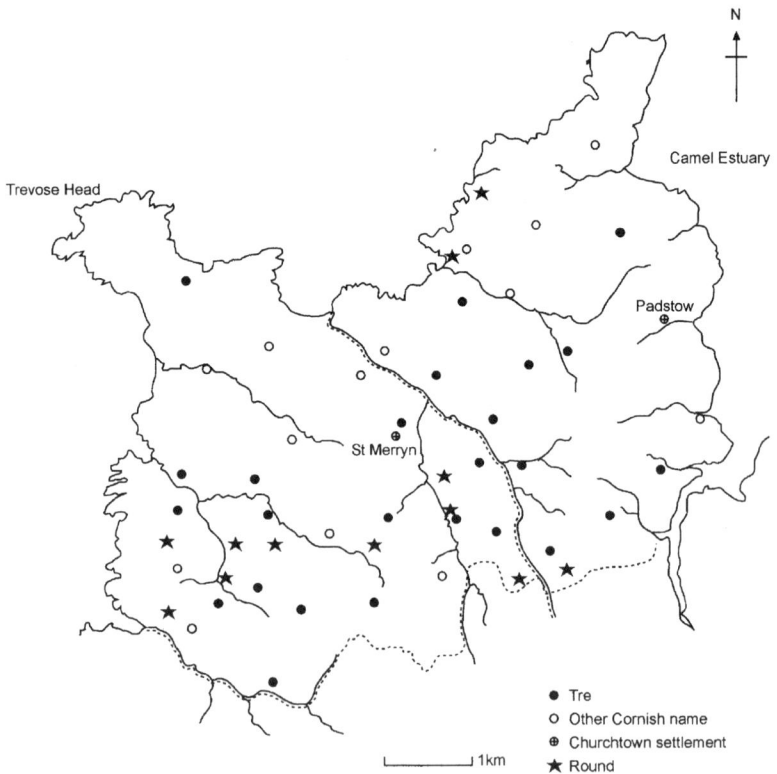

Figure 13 Rounds and later medieval settlements in the parish of Padstow and St Merryn (after Rose and Preston-Jones, 1992, Fig. 3.4)

53.   Padel, *Cornish Place-name Elements*, pp. 223–32.
54.   For a broader discussion of these place-names across Devon and Cornwall, see pp. 303–4.
55.   O. Padel, 'Place-names', in R. Kain and W. Ravenhill (eds), *Historical Atlas of South-West England* (1999), pp. 88–94.

enclosed farmsteads, although they may of course have had a fence or a hedge.

This model is broadly matched by what seems to have been happening in south Wales,[56] where excavations at a group of small defended enclosures at Llawhaden, Dyfed, have shown a succession of short-lived settlements in which, by the later Iron Age, an increased number of enclosed farmsteads had replaced fewer, larger sites, possibly as a result of a population increase balanced against the pressures of limited production. Some of these enclosed farmsteads were abandoned in their turn in the Romano-British period,[57] and, eventually, unenclosed settlements, marked as in Cornwall by names in *tre*, emerged across the region.

The model suggested by the present state of evidence across the peninsula west of the Exe, or even the Axe, presents a picture of dense, in Cornwall especially frequently, enclosed, rural settlement in the Roman period, followed by a certain retraction of settlement in the sixth and seventh centuries and perhaps in the following centuries, in which some settlements were deserted, and in which, too, many settlements moved a little way to a new, unenclosed hamlet, although the inhabitants probably continued to work the same land. Probably, too, older enclosed settlements and newer open ones existed side by side for some time. The pattern of earlier medieval settlement within the landscape, and so much of later medieval and contemporary settlement, probably continues the Roman (and probably later prehistoric) pattern, albeit with considerable modification and development, but exactly which sites are involved in these processes, and how long this took, are open questions.

Questions of settlement status are as important as they are difficult. The settlements marked by the place-name elements *tre* and *tun* seem in later medieval records, like the Welsh laws[58] and some Anglo-Saxon evidence,[59] to be the major units of food production, and their holders to be in a relatively substantial proprietorial position. If – as seems quite possible – the social and economic role of these open settlements succeeded to that of the enclosed settlements, then we are perhaps looking at several generations of non-noble but personally free landholders, who knew how to farm the land with their own hands, but who normally had dependants to do most of the work.

Further east, the few enclosed sites for which we have evidence seem to be prehistoric in date, suggesting that the type had gone out of use by the later (or even possibly the earlier) Roman period. Here the 'natural' development of the pattern of land use was 'interrupted', by the deliberate creation of Roman-style systems. Probably[60] both east and west of the Parrett the region was well populated in the pre-Roman period, but in the first and second centuries AD the area east of the Parrett was reorganized to create large estates in which 'native' settlements were tenuously associated with the newly built villas. The economic collapse of the villa system from

56. See, for broad account, papers in N. Edwards, *Landscape and Settlement in Medieval Wales* (1997).
57. G. Williams and H. Mytum, *Llawhaden, Dyfed: Excavations on a Group of Small Defended Enclosures, 1980–4* (1998), p.144.
58. M. Richards (ed. and trans.), *The Laws of Hywel Dda (The Book of Blegywryd)* (1954), pp. 55–72.
59. See, for example, P. Stafford, 'The "farm of one night" and the organisation of King Edward's estates in Domesday', *Economic History Review*, 33 (1980): 491–502.
60. For the broad account, see R. Leech, 'The Roman interlude in the south-west: the dynamics of economic and social change in Romano-British south Somerset and north Dorset', in D. Miles (ed.), *The Romano-British Countryside* (1982); for Bradley Hill, see R. Leech, 'The excavation of a Romano-British farmstead and cemetery on Bradley Hill, Somerset', *Britannia*, 12 (1981): 117–252.

the later fourth century meant that in this area the medieval settlement pattern was a relic form of that of the Roman period, with a widely varying density of settlements, many abandoned at the end of the Roman period, while, in the west, the changes were relatively few and the Roman settlement pattern underlies the medieval one. To put it differently, east of the Parrett, the settlement pattern had been distorted in the interests of the local and imperial Roman economy during the first to fourth centuries AD, and then reverted to type, while to the west of the river no distortion had happened; in both areas, after AD 400 (perhaps some time after in the east), 'normal' settlement was resumed, which we see as an early medieval pattern. In the east, as well, some new settlements were founded, like that at Bradley Hill north of Ilchester, where the two rectangular houses and a byre were quite quickly turned over to metalworking and infant burials, and lasted in use until at least the middle of the fifth century. The Somerset Roman and post-Roman settlements seem to be generally unenclosed.

A very broadly similar pattern may have evolved in Dorset,[61] where there seem to have been fluctuations in land use; there was perhaps an expansion in the fourth century, which may be linked with the growth of Dorchester, and perhaps also of the local villa economy. Some sites, like those in the Whitcombe area, all near Dorchester, were reoccupied, while the site at Alington Avenue, in the same area, was occupied continuously from the second to the late fifth century.

Generalizations are extremely insecure, but if one is to be hazarded, it is that, in the east of the peninsula, enclosed hamlets belong to prehistory, and were superseded by open farms in the Roman period onwards, while, west of the Tamar, the broadly prehistoric type continued to be thought appropriate until at least the fifth century, when it was gradually replaced by open settlements associated with the place-name element *tref*. Devon, as we would expect, shows a mixed picture, but here, too, enclosed settlements may have been the Roman norm, gradually replaced by open hamlets. There may have been pressing agricultural or tenurial reasons for the change, but it seems also to embody a shift in cultural attachment from domestic space, which was curved inside and out, with many small spaces for individual people, work and animals, to more open homes with possibly fewer, rather larger, spaces defined by straight(ish) lines and angles, suggesting joint activity. Another way of putting this would be to say that, by the later fourth century, many of the eastern settlers were already living in 'medieval'-style homesteads of the kind that are often called longhouses, which humans and beasts shared, while, in the west, traditional separations took longer to die out. This cultural distinction, of course, also more or less matches that of broader *Romanitas*, as indicated by the distribution of 'villas', and just possibly, too, with the area where many ordinary farm workers had some vulgar Latin of the kind spoken in Britain, and that where they did not.

Clearly, so major a change must relate to very important cultural shifts. The enclosing earthwork gave out a message of boundaries which suggests a community which wished to make its distinctiveness, perhaps as a blood kin, clear, and to assert its independence, standing and capacity to defend itself, at least to a degree. The move to unenclosed settlement hints at the communal understanding of a higher degree of vulnerability, and perhaps the recognition that status and the right to deny access have passed elsewhere. It is possible that this shift is linked with the emergence of larger landed units, which had come to occupy a median position between

---

61.   G. Aitken and G. Aitken, 'Excavations at Whitcombe 1965–1967', *PDNHAS*, 112 (1990): 89–94.

hamlets, now grouped together, and the overarching higher authority, a shift which had perhaps happened earlier further east. It would be surprising if these changes were not part of the broader change which was slowly creating a Christian society.

Fields and woods

The issues and possibilities show up most clearly within specific areas. The St Keverne area[62] of south-west Cornwall is based geologically on gabbro, with assorted other volcanic rocks on the northern side (Fig. 14). There are several upstanding rocky tors rising dramatically from the landscape as highly visible landmarks, especially at Carrick Crane Crags, where the weathered tops standing looking out to sea. It comprises a coastal strip of clifftop rough ground, rough upland mostly in the south-east and large areas of anciently enclosed land. There are indications that the region earlier possessed seven enclosed settlements,[63] all but two of which are close to presumed later open settlements, and perhaps there were other open settlements in use at the same time as the rounds, which await discovery.

The open settlements with their names in *tre* show a fairly even distribution across the country: some of them carry names which relate to the landscape, such as Treloyon (*Tre* + *legh*, 'flat stone') and Trenance (*Tre* + *nans*, 'valley'); some perpetuate the name of the first (or an early) farmer, such as Tregellast, Trevalsoe and Tregoning; and others have names descriptive of their character, such as Trevean (*Tre* + *bygan*, 'small') and Trebarveth (*Tre* + *perveth*, 'middle'). The names also testify to a time frame, which shows that the creation of the open farmsteads took some time: Tredinnick embodies *Tre* + *redenn* 'bracken', suggesting that it was cut later than most of the others out of rough ground; and Trenoweth, *Tre* + *noweth*, 'new', speaks for itself.[64] Both these are in less desirable positions on the lip of steep valleys.[65]

Oliver Rackham[66] realized that the area between Main Dale and the sea is taken up with a large ancient coaxial field system, in which a series of parallel boundaries run across country some 30m apart. The boundaries themselves are substantial banks of earth and stone, incorporating large stones, some on edge and some earthfast, reaching about 1 m high and 0.5 m wide. The transverse boundaries are sometimes smaller, but over the generations may have acquired lynchets, the build-up of soil as a result of ploughing and of stone clearance from the fields. This field system seems, like broadly similar ones in Penwith, Bodmin Moor and Dartmoor, to be Bronze Age in date, although it probably has its own history. The fields became the arable attached first (presumably) to the rounds, and then to the open *trefs*. With the fields go the trackways and lanes which connect them and the settlements, and these must be equally ancient. The axial boundaries are laid out by taking a line from the tors of

62. C. Johns and P. Herring, *St Keverne: Historic Landscape Assessment* (1996).
63. Johns and Herring, *St Keverne*, p. 81.
64. Johns and Herring, *St Keverne*, pp. 81–7.
65. Poor quality excavation at Trebarveth in the 1920s and 1930s produced settlement remains and much pottery (see D. Peacock, 'A Romano-British salt working site at Trebarveth, St Keverne', *Corn. Arch.*, 8 (1969): 47–65; Carlyon, 'Romano-British site at Kilhallon' but none of the material appears to be post-Roman (information from Henrietta Quinnell).
66. O. Rackham, *The History of the Countryside* (1987), p. 161.

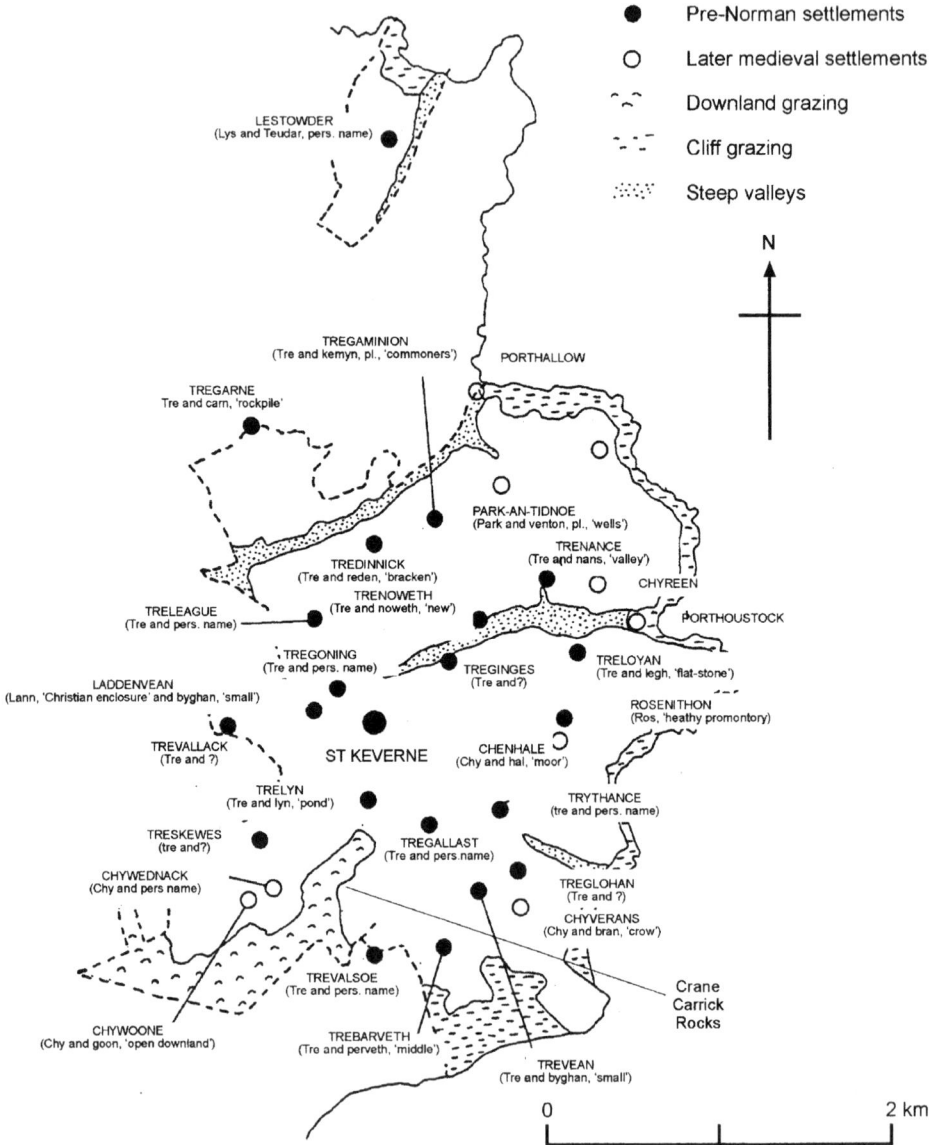

Figure 14 Settlement patterns in the St Keverne area. Solid lines denote principal field pattern elements; dotted lines denote trackways

Carrick Crane Crags, which received offerings in the Neolithic period[67] and may have been accounted rocks of power.

A broadly similar pattern (Fig. 15) appears on the north coast behind Tintagel Island.[68] Here again some ten enclosed settlements were eventually superseded by

---

67.   Johns and Herring, *St Keverne*, pp. 75–6, 126.
68.   Rose and Preston-Jones, 'Changes in the Cornish countryside' (1995), p. 54.

Figure 15 Settlement patterns south and west of Tintagel Island (after Rose and Preston-Jones 1992, Fig. 3.1)

some 30 open settlements, of which the earliest are likely to be post-Roman and the later founded any time up to about 1100. They are embedded in a system of small, often squarish fields and trackways, which may be contemporary with the earlier settlements or may have been already ancient when they were established. In a few places it looks as if older fields were reorganized into strip cultivation, perhaps after *c.* 850, but most of the old system continued to be used. On the seaward side, there seem to be at least three field blocks laid out with reference to major headlands, including that of Tintagel.

Similar settlement landscapes are more elusive in Devon off Dartmoor, but examples have been identified on the limestone plateau in south Devon,[69] including the areas a few kilometres from Denbury Camp and East Ogwell, both potential post-Roman sites of broader social significance (Fig. 16). The dating of these field systems is difficult; they are likely to have been on very marginal land only brought into cultivation in times of pressure on better land, and they have produced a very broad scatter of finds from all periods from Neolithic to medieval. They undoubtedly represent a palimpsest landscape of multi-period use and development, but their association with the late prehistoric site at Dainton shows that some of the fields, at least, date to the pre-Roman period, and these and their immediate successors would have been available for cultivation in the post-Roman period. Tornewton shows a complex of two circular enclosures together with one subdivided squarish enclosure, which may be Roman in origin; Orley Common has a circular enclosure and has produced surface finds of fourth-century pottery; and Kerswell Down produced a hoard of about 2000 late Roman coins found in 1838, presumably (like most of these very large finds) of the late third century, but now lost.

Similar patterns, problems and possibilities show up on the chalklands further east, with the best surviving sites in north Dorset appearing in the Tarrant

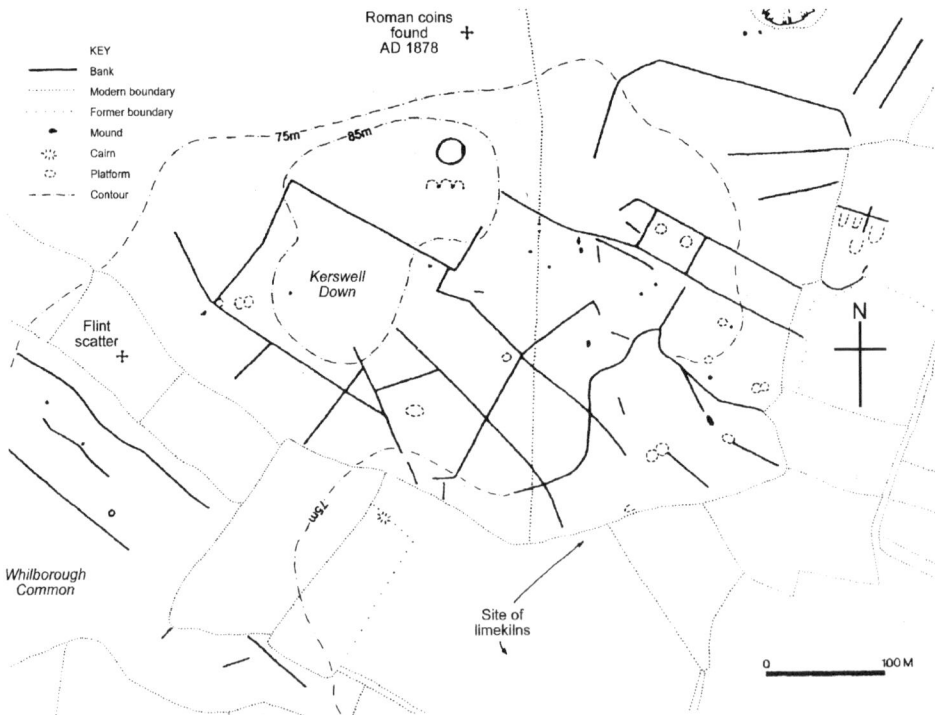

Figure 16 Field systems on Kerswell Down, south Devon (after Quinn 1995, Fig. 2)

69.   L. Gallant, N. Luxton and M. Collman, 'Ancient fields on the south Devon limestone plateau', *PDAS*, 43 (1985): 23–38; G. Quinn, 'A new survey of the prehistoric field system in Kerswell Down and Wilborough Common', *PDAS*, 53 (1995): 131–4.

Valley.[70] Buzbury Rings, a double enclosure of which the inner ring encloses approx 0.5 ha, for example, has produced from this inner area a mixture of occupation debris running from the Iron Age through to the fourth century AD, with ox and sheep bones and fragments of wattle and daub, presumably from houses. South and east of the settlement run areas of characteristic fields (Fig. 17). Comparable field systems have been traced in the Bristol region, where that at Worthy Farm, Pilton, produced Roman–British sherds, that on Brean Down (Fig. 18) may have been associated with the Roman temple complex and that on Bathampton Down presumably bore a relationship to Bath itself (Fig. 19). Two types[71] of system can be distinguished, one of which shows fields in linear blocks.

Figure 17 Occupation systems around Buzbury Rings, north Dorset (after RCHM 1972, endpaper)

70. Royal Commission on Historical Monuments (RCHM), *Dorset, Vol. IV North* (1972), pp. xxvi–xxvii, 99–100.
71. P. Fowler, 'Pre-medieval fields in the Bristol region', in (1978), pp. 29–47.

Figure 18 Brean Down, Somerset, from the north-west. The field system is below the crest, between the track and the cliff. The temple site is on the eastern summit, close to where the Down joins the flat coastland. The burials were on the seaward side of the temple, slightly further east. The hill-fort is on the opposite side, also further east. Prehistoric burials and a find of Bronze Age gold armrings of about 800 BC suggest that the Down had been a significant site for a long time. (Photo: West Air Photography)

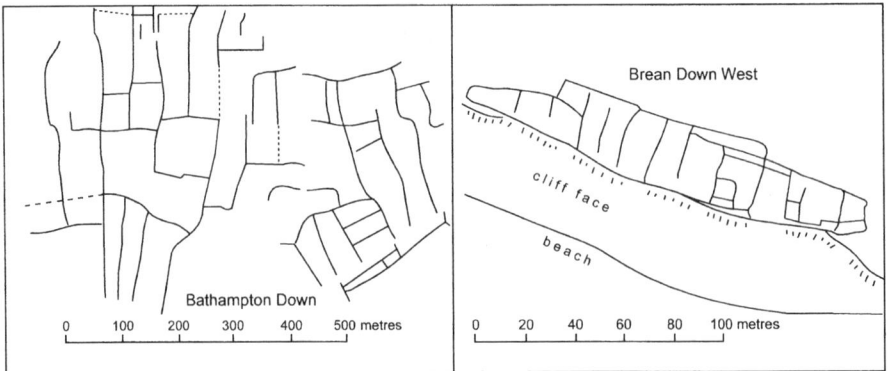

Figure 19 Field systems on Bathampton Down and Brean Down, Somerset (after Fowler 1978, Fig. 5.4)

Our evidence of how the farming landscape as a whole was exploited is exceedingly scanty. The nature of the enclosed field systems suggests that they were cultivated on a rotation basis, which left, say, a third of the total fallow every year, which, coupled with manuring and the feeding of those cattle earmarked for retention on the stubble for as long as possible into the autumn, maintained fertility. The crops, too, are likely to have been rotated through the field system. Plant remains from Britain generally suggest that rye, spelt, wheat, bread wheat, peas and Celtic beans were all grown. The late phase at Hayes Farm produced only a few dubious grains of wheat and barley but its Roman predecessor had spelt, barley, oats and beans. Work on the experimental farm at Butser, Hampshire, suggests that the average yield on the chalklands may have been about 2.4 tonnes per hectare (1 ton per acre) of the bread cereals and will perhaps have been a little less in most of the south-west. This, amazingly, is similar to the British figure for 1951. The fields needed intensive weeding to maintain the yield: as late as the 1930s, charlock could be responsible for total crop failure. Farming could be very efficient, but only with unremitting back-breaking effort.[72]

Plough-oxen were kept on the farm all the year, stall-fed with hay during the winter, and worked until they grew too old. They are likely to have counted almost as members of the family (and to this day, in English, the plural form *oxen* shares, in a complex way, an ancient plural form with *children* and *brethren*, all part of the family circle[73]). Riding horses and cows, kept perhaps primarily for their milk, must also have been stall-fed during the cold months, suggesting that various byres and stores were a necessary part of the farm buildings. The hay must have come from areas set aside as meadow, presumably along the wetter valley bottoms. It, like the cereals, had to be sickle-cut. Cattle were in outside pasture during the summer, and, judging by the bone evidence, bullocks were slaughtered for their meat. Sheep, kept for wool, meat and perhaps milk, are likely to have spent most time outside.

Exploitation of woodland will have been a crucial element in this farming economy. In the eastern part of the peninsula there were considerable stretches of woodland, of oak together with ash, beech and other species. It included Selwood, which ran for some 10 km wide and 30 km long along what finally became the boundaries between Somerset and Wiltshire and the point where the Dorset boundary joined them.[74] The lower flanks of Exmoor, and the hills surrounding the Somerset Levels and south Dartmoor, all supported useful stretches of lighter woodland. The lower river valleys of the Exe, the Taw and Torridge, the Dart, the Tamar, the Fal and the Fowey seem to have carried heavy woodland as they still do today. Judging by the place names,[75] north Devon also carried substantial expanses of heavy woods, as the place-name 'Morchard', a British name meaning 'great wood', testifies. All these woodland areas had considerable open stretches interspersed among the trees, and

72.   P. Reynolds, 'The Pimperne House', *Current Archaeology*, 171 (2000): 94–7.
73.   M. Wakelin, *English Dialects* (1977), p. 109.
74.   J. Jackson, 'Selwood Forest', *WAM*, 23 (1987): 268–94; R. Grant, 'Royal forests: Selwood', in E. Crittall, *Victoria County History: Wiltshire*, Vol. 4 (1959), pp. 414–17; M. McGarvie, *The Bounds of Selwood* (1978).
75.   For Morchard, see J. Gover, A. Mawer and F. Stenton, *The Place-names of Devon* (1932), Part 2, p. 380, Cruwys Morchard, and p. 408 for Morchard Bishop. Gover suggests that because these places are ten miles apart they are unlikely to refer to the same wood, but a 'great wood' could easily have been this large. For *leah* see Gover, p. 679, and refs there.

such open woodland is implied by the common local place-name *leah*. Central and western Cornwall may have had few large woods, but it is important to realize what a mosaic the whole countryside was, and probably most small areas had patches of locally important woodland. Near Bath, for example, the place-name Woolley means 'Wolf Clearing', and *kelli*, 'grove, small wood', is found throughout Cornwall with over 40 known examples.[76]

There is no reason to doubt that the woods were a carefully managed resource, and we should envisage the small local woods as carefully integrated into the detail of small-scale economies, while the large woods operated more like substantial expanses of common land. Clearly, timber trees needed protection, but 'the axe is not a thief'[77] and nor is the man who wields it responsibly. Local stands of trees yielded firing, building timber, hazel, coppiced and cropped to grow rods for hurdles, and materials for a wide range of containers, tool handles and equipment, such as honeysuckle or old-man's-beard ties, as well as blackberries, rose-hips, elderberries, hazelnuts, crab apples and edible fungi. The large woodlands[78] contributed forage for domestic pigs, and pork from the not very different wild pigs, venison, wild cattle and wild goats, together with furs from animals like foxes, beavers and wild cats. The woods also held wolves, evidently a genuinely ever-present menace, and the woodlands had patches dense with impenetrable brambles, nettles, holly, fallen and rotting timber and stinging insects, including malaria-carrying mosquitoes. Not the least significance of the deep woodland was its power to symbolize confusion and terror, together with a particular kind of wild freedom.

We can, then, using a good deal of inference and a little imagination, build up a picture of how the farmers on the land behind Tintagel Island, for example, or the south Devon limestone went about producing food, suggesting that each group would need a considerably larger area of maintenance than the surviving field systems suggest. Moreover, each community would have occupied a farming microclimate of its own, resulting from small differences in geology, wind direction, height above sea level and orientation, requiring a multitude of minor adjustments to the basic pattern which will have emerged as specializations in material goods and foodstuffs. But the peninsula also offered a further significant resource.

Wider pastures

A glance at any map shows that, with the partial exception of Penwith with its courtyard houses, the farmsteads avoid the granite uplands which are so conspicuous a feature of the western part of the peninsula, but this does not mean that the upland was an unused wilderness; rather, it seems to mean that farmland and moorland were knitted together into integrated patterns of landscape exploitation, in which use of the upland was regulated by the observation of customs and practices. Dartmoor, the largest, absorbs the heart of Devon, and, in Cornwall, Bodmin Moor, Hensbarrow, Carnmenellis and Penwith string out like beads along a chain.

76.   Padel, *Cornish Place-name Elements*, p. 47.
77.   As in Ine's Laws, see F. Attenborough, *The Laws of the Earliest English Kings* (1922).
78.   D. Kirby, 'The Old English forest', in T. Rowley (ed.), *Anglo-Saxon Settlement and Landscape* (1974), pp. 120–30.

A twelfth-century reference in John of Cornwall's *Prophetia Merlini* says, 'Brentigie, formerly described, is in Cornwall, and in our language is called "Goen Bren" and in the Saxon tongue "Fawi-mor".'[79] John seems to be saying that 'Brentigie', presumably a local reference to what is now called Bodmin Moor, was not permanently settled, and that the area was called in Cornish *Goen Bren* and in English *Fawi-mor*. *Fawi-mor* may be expressed as 'Foweymoor': it was the normal English medieval name of the area taken from its largest river, and matches 'Dartmoor' and 'Exmoor'. *Goe* is *goon*, 'downland, unenclosed pasture', with a sense since about the sixteenth century of 'unenclosed upland pasture', and *bren* means 'hill'.[80] Sharing the same rough treeless 'upland' character in the post-Roman period, although on a mixture of sedimentary rock bases, are Exmoor and the Quantocks, the Polden Hills, Mendip, the heathlands of west Dorset and east Devon, parts of north-west Devon, St Breock Down and the Lizard. In Somerset, the Levels occupy the same kind of heartland position that Dartmoor does in Devon.

The prehistoric and later medieval exploitation of the upland, especially of Dartmoor and Bodmin Moor, has been much studied, if not well understood, since the nineteenth century, but little attention was paid to the long stretch of time between the end of late Bronze Age/Early Iron Age occupation around 700 BC and the documented work of medieval tinners which begins around 1200, until interest developed in the practice of transhumance.[81] 'Transhumance' means both the movement of stock over very large distances, often called 'the greater, or Mediterranean, transhumance', and smaller journeys characteristic of the Alpine region, for example, which involved the local movement of stock from lower permanent settlements to high pastures for summer grazing. It is this kind of smaller-scale movement that is widely attested in many parts of the medieval British Isles. Studies of contemporary Mediterranean stock movement stress the scanty archaeological evidence its past practices are likely to leave.[82]

As early as 1942, Pounds[83] had drawn attention to a series of Cornish place-names and elements, particularly *hendre* ('the old settlement') and *havos* (correctly 'summer dwelling'); *hendre* has the meaning of 'the home or winter farmstead', and the way in which Cornish and Welsh share this usage suggests that the origins of the practice to which it refers predates the separation of Wales and Cornwall in the seventh century.[84] Pounds linked these names with the practice of transhumance, in which open moorland is used as summer grazing, partly to make use of the resources available on the moors, and partly, perhaps primarily, to free the arable and fallow land, where the stock had been feeding over winter, for ploughing in the late spring. Herring[85] has studied the evidence in depth, and shows that *havos* names are spread across Cornwall, often located on relatively small areas of grazing. Some *hendra* and *havos* sites are known to have been linked in the post-900 period, suggesting that

79. Curley, (1982), p. 239.
80. Padel, *Cornish Place-name Elements*, pp. 31, 108.
81. E.g. E. Davies, 'The patterns of transhumance in Europe', *Geography*, 25 (1940): 155–75.
82. J. Segui, 'Ethnoarchaeology of pastoralism in a Mediterranean mountain area' (2000), for general account.
83. N. Pounds, 'Note on transhumance in Cornwall', *Geography*, 27 (1942): 34.
84. Padel, *Cornish Place-name Elements*, pp. 127, 129.
85. P. Herring, 'Transhumance in medieval Cornwall', in H. Fox, *Seasonal Settlement* (1996), pp. 35–44.

specific farmsteads or communities had rights of pasture over specific areas of moorland, but this system could have developed as a result of post-800 pressures which involved firmer regulation, and we cannot be sure that such a system operated as early as the post-Roman period.

A striking cluster of *hendre* and *havos* names appears on Bodmin Moor. Archaeologically, *havos*-type occupation is represented by the groups of poorly dated but probably post-Roman huts located on Bodmin Moor at, for example, Brown Willy, Roughtor and Brockabarrow Common (Fig. 20). The huts are small, generally about 3.5 m by about 2.0 m internally, giving enough space for a bed (of sorts), an open fire and some storage. Obviously, only one or two people, rather than a whole family, could live in such quarters. At Brockabarrow, the huts were spread out over quite a wide area, and the workers seem to have shared an animal pen.

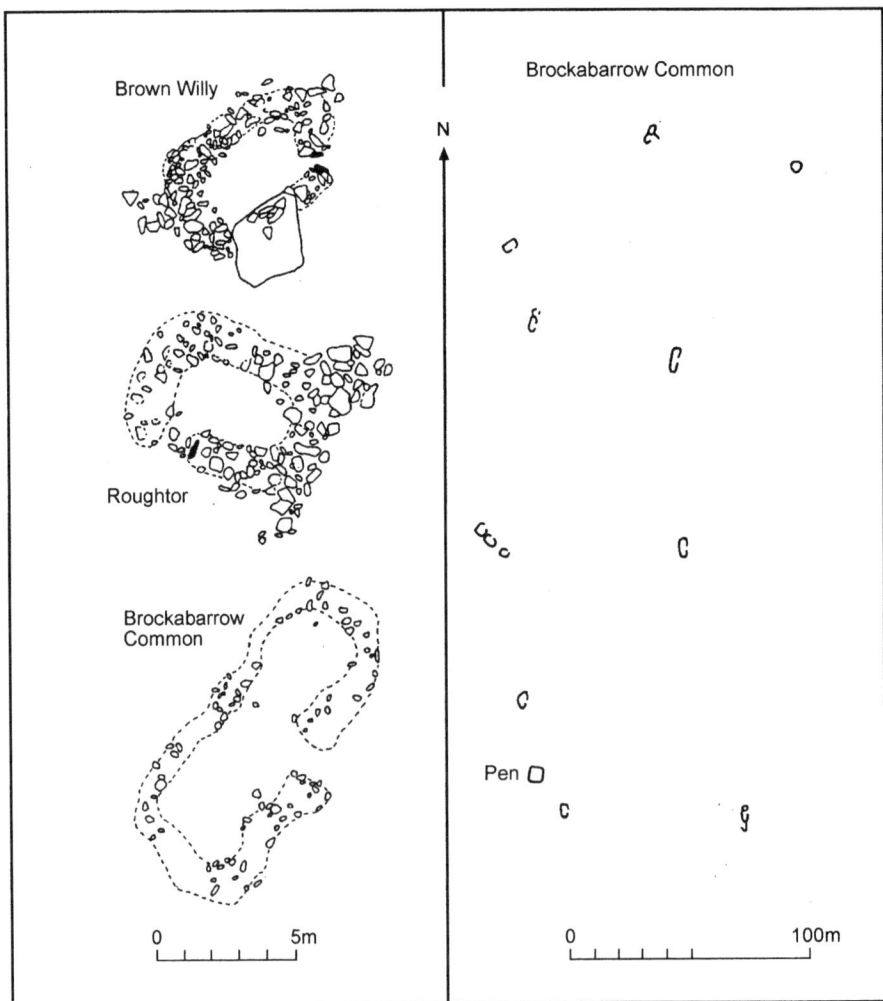

Figure 20 Possible summer occupation huts on Bodmin Moor (after Herring 1996, Fig. 111.2)

The management of a large area like Bodmin Moor, which had no long-range pasture boundaries, would have required care: rights needed to be established, cattle identified, trespassers recognized, round-ups organized, and authority mobilized to adjudicate and evict as necessary. As Herring shows, following similar work on summer grazing links and commote boundaries in north-west Wales,[86] four of the probably Roman or pre-Roman[87] territorial districts meet on Bodmin Moor, and three of these have later manorial pounds, enclosures for holding rounded-up stock, of which Stowe's Pound, at least, is certainly prehistoric. In the same area are appropriate place-names and pastoral hut groups, and the likelihood is that pounds were used for stock management in the post-Roman period, and that organizations of the districts produced the necessary governance of the pastures (Fig. 21). The whole of the Cornish land is so divided between the ancient divisions that each embraces a substantial area of upland.

Dartmoor, extending over 1250 sq km at a conservative estimate, is by far the largest high wilderness in southern England and offers a huge summer grazing potential. It sits in the middle of the county of Devon, so that apart from the area east of the Exe, probably always somewhat separate from the rest of the region, nowhere in Devon is more than 50 km from the moor edge and most communities were much closer. Its importance in the changing economy of Devon up to and including

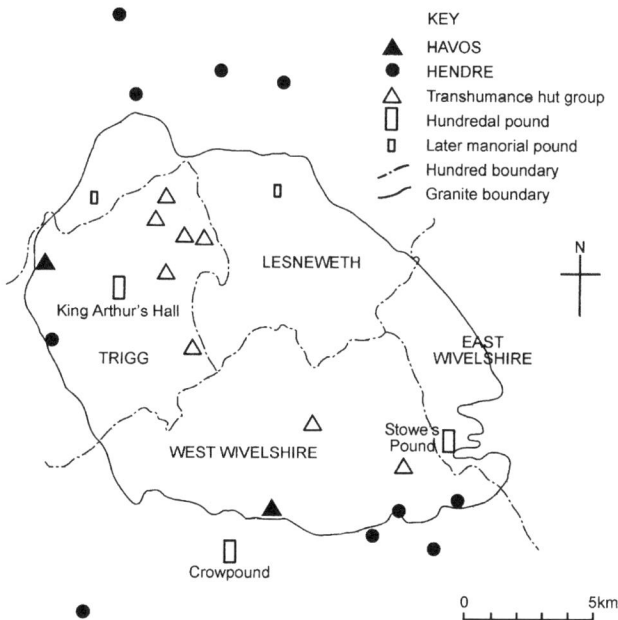

Figure 21 Possible management of summer pasturage on Bodmin Moor (after Herring 1996, Fig. 111.3)

86. G. Jones, 'Post-Roman Wales', in H. Finberg (ed.), *The Agrarian History of England and Wales* (1972), pp. 283–301.

87. See pp. 223–4 for further discussion of these boundaries.

the present century means that the historian is faced with a dense documentation relating to grazing and extraction rights. In the early modern period, it was believed that all the men of Devon had the right to pasture unlimited numbers of animals on the moor; an important document drawn up for the governance of Dartmoor by the administrators of the estate of 'my Lorde Prynce' (Edward, Prince of Wales) soon after 1541 refers to those who 'brought beasts to the Moor', from anywhere in Devon, as 'commoners',[88] and John Hooker in his *Synopsis Chorographical of Devonshire* written about 1599 says,

> And in this dartemore yeldeth iiij speciall commodities, pasture, corne, tynne and turff cole: concerninge pasture it is cheefflye in the sommer: ffor in the winter by rason of the coldenes, continuall stormes and wetness of the grownde there is scarce feedings at all but in the somer tyme the more drye the grownde is the better is theire feedings[89]

These documents seem to reflect the charter of King John, which says that all the men of Devon had customary rights on Dartmoor. Since wholesale rights seem unlikely to have been granted by John or his immediate predecessors, we can be reasonably sure that the access to the common grazing goes back into the period before 1066 (and its continuation into the modern period represents an interesting escape from the imposition of control by manorial lords after *c.* 900 which is probably a result of its dominating size).

No traces of the *havos/hendre* place-names, nor of any possible Anglo-Saxon successors, have so far been identified on or around the moor and, as has already been noted, archaeological evidence is likely to be scanty, although large areas of the moor are, of course, thickly scattered with the remains of prehistoric hut circles and enclosures, and there would have been nothing to prevent medieval pastoralists patching these up and making use of them. However, in 1991 a blue glass bead, with an outside date range of AD 400–700 but probably of the sixth century, was found in an area with extensive occupation remains west of the River Walkham, and a year later a probable shard from a Roman-British flanged dish of gabbroic fabric turned up in excavation at Upper Merrivale.[90] A porphyry bowl of fifth to seventh-century date was found at Chagford[91] and late Roman coins (for what this is worth) have been found at various moorland sites.[92] These stray finds, together with the accumulating evidence for early medieval exploitation of tin,[93] add to our developing picture of the moor.

The best evidence for Dartmoor's seasonal exploitation comes from the records of later West Saxon landholding. The parish boundaries of the south-western flank

---

88.   PRO Rentals and Surveys, SC12/12/39; see E. Fogwill, 'Pastoralism on Dartmoor', *TDA*, 86 (1954): 89–114.
89.   W. Blake, 'Hooker's Synopsis Chorographical of Devonshire', *TDA*, 47 (1915): 345; see also Fogwill, 'Pastoralism on Dartmoor', pp. 89–114.
90.   T. Greeves and P. Newman, 'Tin working and land use in the Walkham Valley: a preliminary analysis', *PDAS*, 52 (1994): 199–219. Excavations, as yet unpublished, by Sandy Gerrard at a hut circle site at Teigncombe, have produced a small sherd of early Roman Samian pottery (information Henrietta Quinnell).
91.   T. Greeves, 'Visions in the fog – Dartmoor in the 1st Millennium', *DAS News*, 76 (2000): 10–11.
92.   Devon Sites and Monuments Register.
93.   See pp. 237–9.

of the moor show a pattern in which the shape of Tavistock and Whitchurch reflect an economic balance of lower (relatively) arable and access to upland grazing, but that of Buckland Monachorum seems truncated on the moorland side. The Meavy charter of 1031 defines an area to the north of the River Meavy and one of its boundary clauses refers to 'the hay wagon way of the dwellers of Buckland', that is to say, a road used by the Buckland men, and this must be more or less the modern B3212 which runs parallel to the Walkhampton/Meavy boundary, and was, therefore, perhaps taken into account when the boundaries were drawn up after 1031 (Fig. 22). In any case, a 'way' important enough to be mentioned in a charter, and to represent a right of way of the men of one estate along the edge of another, must have had considerable economic importance, and obviously this was its function as a road by which cut hay could be brought down, and probably the Buckland beasts could be taken up, onto the high moor.[94]

Other records take a similar story. The undated (but probably late) boundaries of *Peadingtun* have not been satisfactorily identified, but clearly primarily take in the manor of Ashburton and some additional moorland to the north-west, including

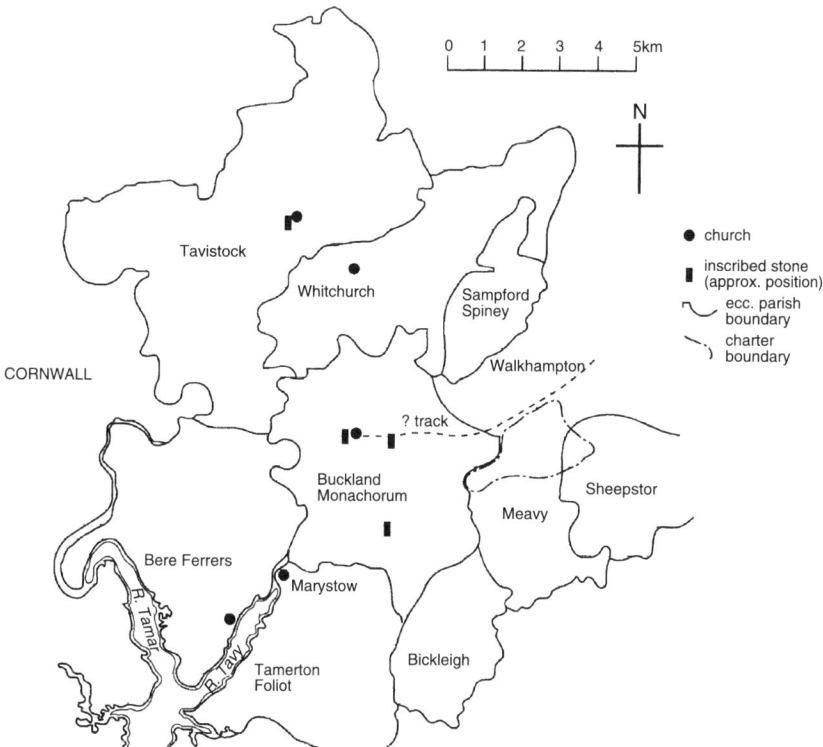

Figure 22 Pre-Norman patterns of land use on south-western Dartmoor (after Pearce 1982a, Fig. 2)

---

94.   S963; S. Pearce, 'Church and society in south Devon AD 350–700', *PDAS*, 40 (1982): 1–18.

perhaps most of what became the parish of Widecombe in the Moor (Fig. 23). Fox[95] has suggested that *Peadingtun*, which cannot be related to any known name in the moorland area, is a reference to Paignton, *Peinton* in 1086, on the south Devon coast. Ashburton follows Paignton in Domesday Book,[96] both held by the Bishop of Exeter, and taken together the references suggest that originally Ashburton was the summer resource of the arable land at Paignton.

Once these links have been recognized, other arrangements seem to fall into place. Domesday also tells us that *Dewdon*, probably Jordan in Widecombe, is a dependent member of the manor of Cockington on Tor Bay, held by William of Falaise, and Kenton in the Exe Valley, held by the king, was linked to Chagford in the south Teign Valley, both probably recording upland areas attached to lower estates. The Abbot of Tavistock held Houndtor, one of the places on Dartmoor which eventually had a permanent settlement;[97] and the manors of Torbryan and Denbury had detached portions in Woodland.[98] The place-name Manaton, *Magnetona*, which eventually

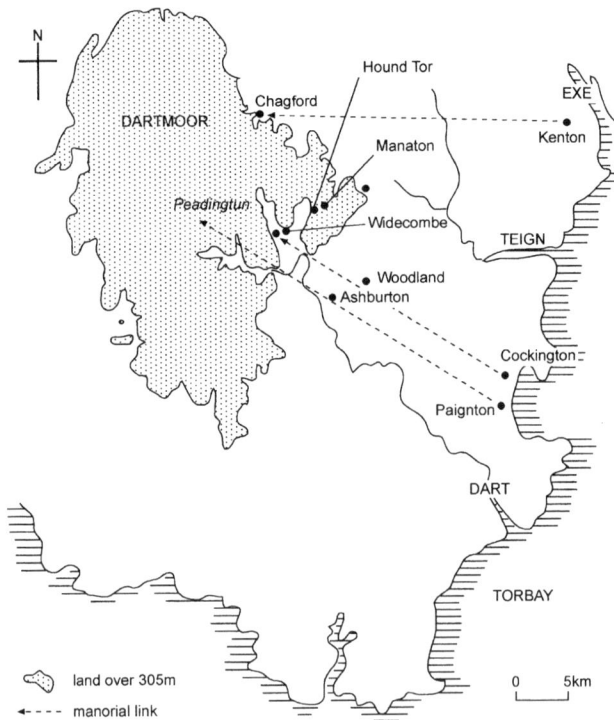

Figure 23 Dartmoor in its local context (after Hooke 1998, Fig. 64)

95.   Hooke, *Pre-Conquest Charter-bounds of Devon and Cornwall* (1994), pp. 190–2.
96.   For what follows see C. Thorn and F. Thorn (eds), *Domesday Book: Devon* (1985), under individual manors.
97.   G. Beresford, 'Three deserted medieval settlements on Dartmoor: a report on the late E. Marie Minter's excavations', *Med. Arch.*, 23 (1979): 98–158.
98.   Hooke, *Pre-Conquest Charter-bounds*, 1994, p. 223

formed a parish extending over a considerable area of the high moor, incorporates the Anglo Saxon *(ge) mæne*, 'common', perhaps suggesting an area used by several lower settlements. The evidence is not conclusive, but these records hint at a substantial and well-recognized system of linked arable and upland pasture of the kind that appears on Bodmin Moor, although whether the tenth/eleventh-century Dartmoor arrangements reflect earlier customs, or whether they represent a new level of organization imposed upon what had been a looser system, remains an open question.

There is a further indication which may take the broad scope of these arrangements back to the late or post-Roman period. The line of the right of way already referred to in the Meavy charter seems to pass by an inscribed stone of that date, standing now in what may have been its original position in what must have been open moorland.[99] The parish of Buckland Monachorum has a similar stone, found in 1804 serving as a gatepost in a field near Roborough, Devon, and perhaps originally standing nearby in what was then moorland.[100] A further inscribed stone appeared recently at Sampford Spinney beside what was certainly in the later medieval period a major route over the River Walkman.[101] In Ilsington at Crownley Parks stands a possibly inscribed stone, now part of a gatepost beside a track leading up to the moor. An unidentified boundary in the *Peadington* charter refers to 'from the spring to the *Writelan* stone', a rare use of the Anglo-Saxon adjective *writol*, which may relate to a sound like babbling which the stone made when the wind set in a particular direction, but which might (given a little confusion somewhere in the transmission) mean 'stone with writing'; in any case, the reference is instructive.[102] Early medieval carved stones seem to have had an important role in the marking of boundaries,[103] and their employment as marking the rights of way which were naturally used to define estates is similarly likely. Among other features, this explains their character, so different from that of, for example, Gaulish cemetery grave slabs, as long, narrow fingers of stone, visible from a distance and effortlessly dominating their surroundings, just as local prehistoric standing stones had done.

The Audetus stone still stands on Sourton Down, and its original position, unknown but in the immediate vicinity,[104] is close to the parish boundary between Okehampton and Sourton, and to the Roman road now known[105] to have run north-east/south-west here, on its way round the flank of the moor. A number of small lanes and field paths which cross the road and give routes up onto the high moor survive; the relationship of some of these to the field systems suggests[106] that they may be of prehistoric date (Fig. 24). Another early medieval monument comes from East Linnacombe on the north-western edge of Sourton Down, and there is a cross-slab carrying a circled cross above a possible stylized representation of Christ

99.   Devon Sites and Monuments Register, information from T. Greeves.
100. E. Okasha, *Corpus of Early Christian Inscribed Stones of South-West Britain* (1993), pp. 79–81.
101. Devon Sites and Monuments Register, information from T. Greeves.
102. Investigation by T. Greeves and the writer; personal communication on *Writol* and *Writelan* from Margaret Gilling, 26 March 1981.
103. T. Charles-Edwards, 'Boundaries in Irish law', in P. Sawyer, *Medieval Settlement: Continuity and Change* (1976), pp. 83–7.
104. Okasha, *Early Christian Inscribed Stones*, p. 260.
105. P. Weddell and S. Read, 'Excavations at Sourton Down, Okehampton, 1986–1991: Roman road, deserted medieval hamlet and other landscape features', *PDAS*, 55 (1997): 71–81, 133–4.
106. *Ibid.*, pp. 128–33.

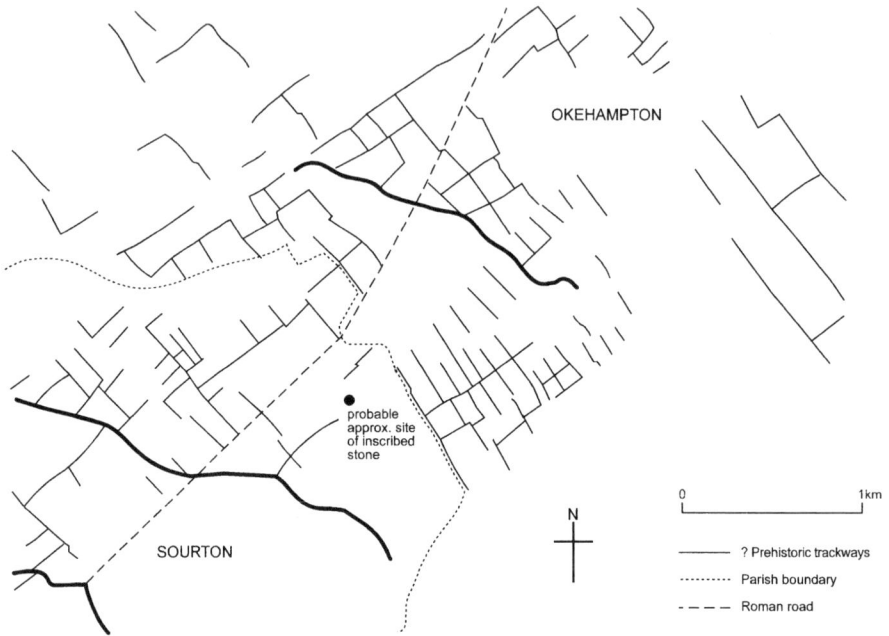

Figure 24 Sourton Down, Devon (after Weddell and Reed 1997, Fig. 4.5)

crucified[107] in Belstone churchyard (see Fig. 105). In the south, the Ivybridge inscribed stone seems to have stood near a route to the moor and there are other similar stones rather further from the edge of the upland.[108] The ring of early inscribed and decorated stones around Dartmoor is very striking. These stones were profoundly embedded in all the imaginative and social practices which constituted regional post-Roman Christian society, and will have served as legitimating monuments to the customs which they witnessed, gathering authority with every passing generation and producing a founding narrative which justified the exercise of rights.

We have to ask if anything in Devon suggests the regional layer of organizational and adjudicating authority, which appears in the Welsh commote system and the Cornish hundreds. The age of the Devon hundreds is an open question. They do show some signs of convergence on the moor, and Wonford, in particular, spans the area from the Exe Valley to the upland. There are four streams on Dartmoor called

---

107. For these, see Fig. 105 and Devon Sites and Monuments Register. Two further decorated slabs are marked as stones on the boundary between Belstone and Sampford Courteney parishes on OS sheet SX 69 (2½ inch) at SX63859415 (Ladywell, Sticklepath) and SX63209480 (Bude Lane). These are illustrated in Phillips, 1987, pp. 244–8: the Ladywell stone has a Latin cross on one face and a series of crosses and curved lines on the other, the Bude Lane stone has a circle and St Andrew's cross on the north face, curved lines on the south face, and a circle and curves making possibly a highly stylized human figure on the east face. The date of these two slabs remains uncertain, but they could be at least pre-Norman.

108. See also N. Edwards, 'Early medieval inscribed stones and stone sculpture in Wales: context and function', *Med. Arch.*, 45 (2001): 15–40.

'Wallabrook', one of which runs into the east Dart just above Dartmeet, the second into the north Teign on Gidleigh Common, the third into the Tavy just above Tavistock and the fourth, a small stream, into the Avon. If these names come from *wealh*, 'Briton', then presumably they imply that the streams meant something distinctive in the economy of the moor when West Saxon authority became effective there, probably in the second half of the seventh century. The authors of *The Place-Names of Devon* were willing to accept only the Dart tributary as a genuinely ancient British name,[109] but subsequently the Tavy tributary 'walla' name has been taken back to 1613,[110] which may have a bearing on the genuineness of the other two names. There are three possible place-names in *wealh* around the edge of the moor.[111]

The Dart Wallabrook forms the boundary of Widecombe parish, and a fair proportion of what, by at least the seventeenth century, were known as the 'ancient tenements' were near it, and in the neighbouring valleys. These 'ancient tenements' were the only permanently settled farms on the moor, and their numbers gradually increased during the late medieval centuries. The inquisition of 1300 mentions 25 tenements,[112] but only two ancient tenements existed in 1260, those at Babeny and Pizwell, both on the Dart Wallabrook.

In the late medieval period, the moorland grazing (with its many legal complications) was managed through the division of the moor into three parts, north, east and west, with a south division added after readjustments in 1404. The roll of appropriate payments for 1346–7 lists the best pasturing locations, called *predas* or lairs, according to their division, which enables us to estimate where the division lines ran.[113] Each ancient division also held a cattle drift (the local name for a round-up) each summer, and each entailed the use of a pound, probably at Dunnabridge for the east, Creber for the north and Erme Pound perhaps for the west; Dunnabridge and Erme, at least, were reused prehistoric enclosures. Other sites may also have been important. Brentor had a well-documented cattle fair in the fifteenth century[114] and several terraces showing the remains of rectangular foundations on the hill below the church which would repay investigation.[115] It was the task of the people at the ancient settlements to organize the drifts, and each division had an official in charge. The testimony to this management structure is, of course, very late, but the existence of the *weahl* place-names, and the reuse of prehistoric enclosures, may be suggestive. The tripartite division of the grazing, particularly if the north-western extension between Tavistock and Lydford was included in the system, produces a roughly equal allotment which slightly favours the northern part, the area with the greatest lower hinterland (Fig. 25).

The substantial areas of rough grazing west of the Exe outside the two biggest

109. Gover *et al.*, *Place-names of Devon* (1931), pp. xxii–xxiii, 16.
110. P. Reaney, *The Place-names of Cambridgeshire and the Isle of Ely* (1943), p. iv.
111. Lost *Walford* in Plympton, Walreddon in Whitchurch and possibly Wallover in Buckfastleigh: Gover *et al.*, *Place-names of Devon* (1931), pp. xxii–xxiii.
112. J. Somers-Cox, 'Saxon and early medieval times' in C. Gill (ed.), *Dartmoor: A New Study* (1970), pp. 76–99. See also A. Fleming and N. Ralph, 'Medieval settlement and land use on Holme Moor, Dartmoor: the landscape evidence', *Med. Arch.* 26 (1982): 101–37; Gover *et al. Place-Names*, (1931) pp. 191, 196; F. Wilkinson, 'The Dartmoor husbandman', *Devon Historian*, 14 (1977): 5–10; H. Fox, 'Medieval Dartmoor as seen through its account rolls', *PDAS*, 52 (1994): 149–72.
113. S. Moore, *Short History of the Rights of Common upon Dartmoor* (1890), pp. 32–47.
114. Fox, 1996b, p. 15.
115. Greeves, 'Visions in the fog', pp. 10–11.

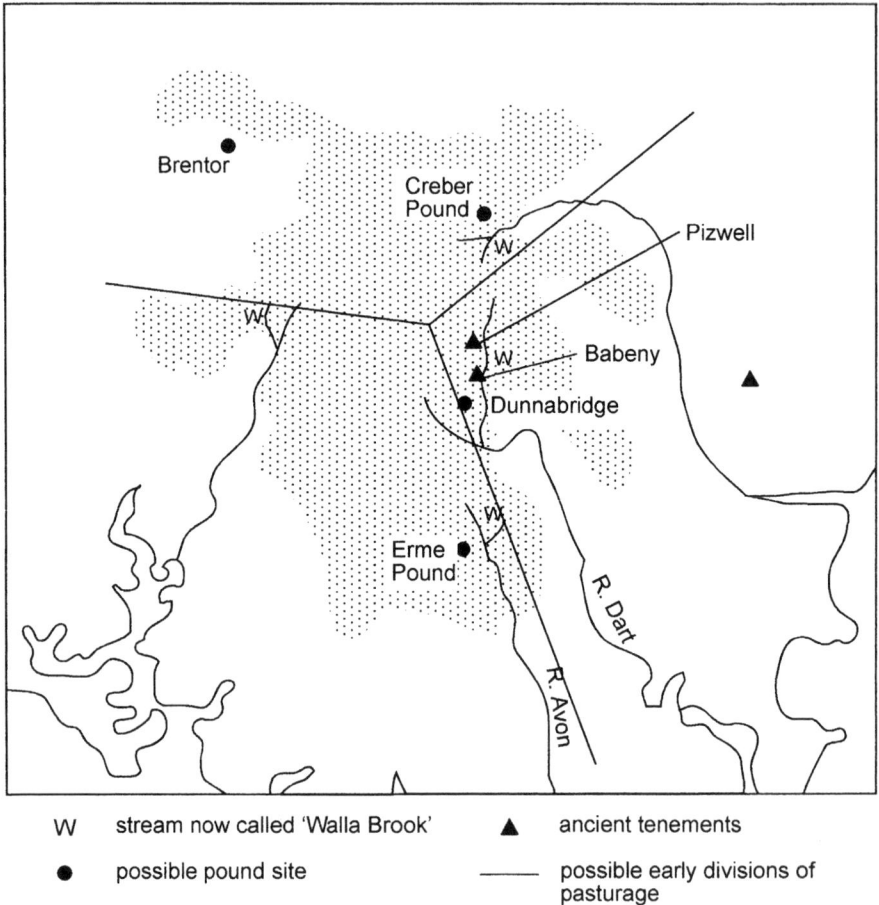

W   stream now called 'Walla Brook'   ▲   ancient tenements

●   possible pound site   ——   possible early divisions of
pasturage

Figure 25 Dartmoor pasturing: possible organization

granite moors are likely to have been used in broadly similar patterns. In Penwith the
Rialbranus inscribed stone stands on Menscryfa (= 'written stone') Moor, marking an
ancient trackway. Less is known about pasturing on Hensbarrow and Carnmenellis,
but it seems unlikely that they were not exploited. Place-names in both Old English
and Celtic which refer to occupations by young people of either sex may point to
the seasonal management of stock in pasture and woodland.[116] There is a Cornish
example in the Lizard Peninsula,[117] a Maiden Hill near the central, highest ground in
southern Dartmoor and a Maidenwell on the south-western edge of Bodmin Moor.

The early medieval exploitation of Exmoor is likely to have been similar. The
Caractacus stone stands beside a track over Winsford Hill, Exmoor, and is mentioned
as a boundary stone in the Exmoor Forest Perambulations of 1219 and 1270 under
the name Langeston. The Cavudus stone stands on the moor's northern edge;
there may have been a third stone at Parracombe, a cross-decorated stone of early

---

116.   A. Smith, *English Place-name Elements* (1956), sv *maegden*.
117.   Padel, *Cornish Place-name Elements*, p. 124.

Christian type comes from Culbone and the Long Stone, East Worlington, carries five incised crosses.[118] The pattern of parish boundaries, particularly that of Braunton, shows a concern for access to the moor; Braunton possesses an estuary for salmon fishing, arable and a salient giving a route on to the higher ground (see Fig. 85). In the sixteenth century tenants at Porlock had the right to pasture sheep on 'Porlock Moor', the high Exmoor hills above the shore.[119] These details are suggestive, rather than conclusive, but the better-documented practices across other parts of early medieval Britain give them weight. The same applies to the heathland commons of east Devon and south-west Dorset, where again the pattern of parish boundaries are suggestive, and to the Dorset chalklands.

The Somerset Levels[120] and the surrounding higher lands, including Mendip, formed a system as large, as complex and with roots as ancient, as that of Dartmoor (Fig. 26). The settlement, Somerton, which eventually gave its name to the county, has a place-name which means 'farmstead used in the summer' and, although this is wholly Old English, it is inconceivable that it is describing a practice which only ran back to around AD 650. The Polden Hills form a relatively high ridge which divides the eastern and western Levels. A charter of 729, in which King Æthelheard gave 60 hides to Glastonbury, shows that the earliest known form of 'Polden' was *Pouelt* or similar, probably from Celtic *go gwelt*, 'cattle pasture',[121] and Glastonbury seems to already to have held land in the area. When the documentation becomes more extensive it appears that most of the settlements on the ridge possessed detached parts of what is now Sedgemoor to the south, while to the north their parish boundaries extend into the wetlands of the Brue system. It seems likely that *Pouelt* originally included both the whole length of the ridge and large tracts of, or perhaps customary access to, the wetland flanks, all of which would be exploited as grazing when local conditions allowed, with the Levels, of course, chiefly in use in summer.

In the same way, tenants from a series of settlements along the coast of the British Channel also had rights of common pasturage on the wetlands, as did those on the marsh islands of Meare, Wedmore, Edington Burtle, Westhay and Godney in the north-east, and Chedzoy, Westonzoyland and Middlezoy to the south-west. Smaller areas could be very important, too. In Cheddar, an area leading up to common grazing rights linked eventually with those of Compton Bishop parish was called 'milkway', at least as early as 1068. The hills north of Chew Magna, where the hill-fort of Maes Knoll occupies the highest point, have the place-name Maidenhead.[122] A *buell waye*

---

118. L. Grinsell, *The Archaeology of Exmoor* (1970), pp.104–6. The third stone seems to have been near Holwell, south of Parracombe; if so it was built into the bridge at Parracombe and was washed away in the 1952 Lynmouth Flood disaster. For Langeston, see E. Rawle, *Annals of the Ancient Royal Forest of Exmoor* (1893), p. 39.

119. Corcos, *Medieval Settlement* (2002), p. 142.

120. See for a general account, M. Havinden, *The Somerset Landscape* (1987), and also M. Williams, *The Draining of the Somerset Levels* (1970). For place-names, see A. Mills, *A Dictionary of English Place-names* (1998), p. 318.

121. S253. C. Thorn and F. Thorn, *Domesday Book: Somerset* (1980), see under appropriate entries; N. Corcos, 'Early estates on the Poldens and the origin of settlement at Shapwick', *PSANHS* (1983): 47–54.

122. For Cheddar, V. Russet, 'Cheddar, Milkway, ST454530', *PSANHS* (1988): 216; for Maidenhead, Corcos, *Medieval Settlement* (2002), p. 128. The suggestion that 'head' comes from *hafod* is interesting but lacks any proof.

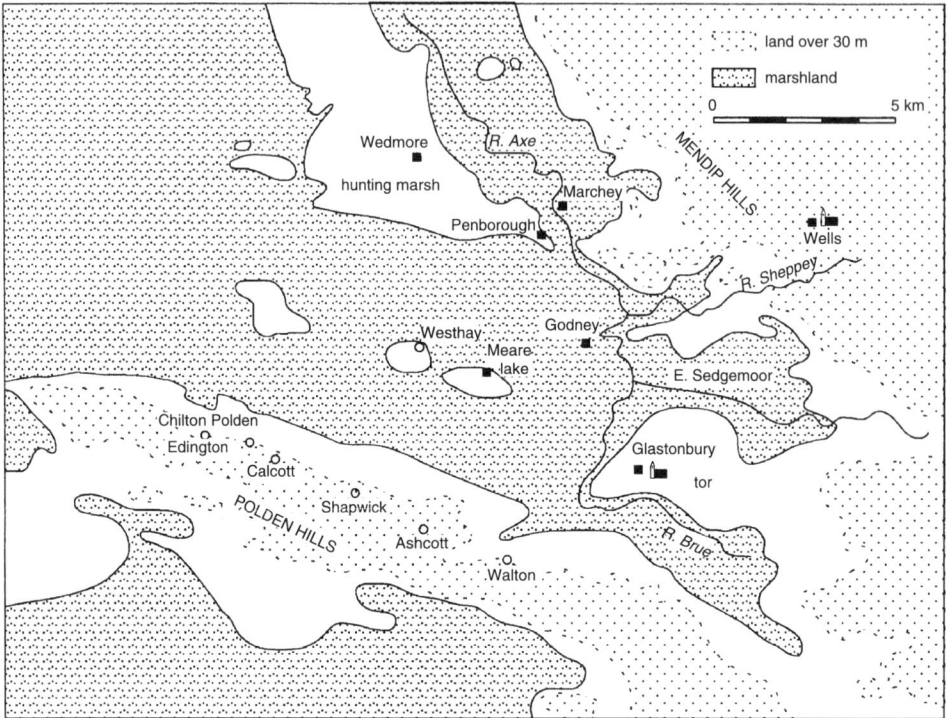

Figure 26 Polden Hills and Levels, Somerset (various sources)

'cattle way', appears in 1570, apparently an earlier name for Babylon Hill, which runs into the high ground between Ham Hill and South Cadbury.[123]

A recent survey of place-names in the Black Mountains of South Wales, which may be linked with such pastoral practices, found that the picture had been clouded by 'fossilisation' and 'antiquation' and urged caution in the formation of 'idealised socio-economic models' since the landscape was undoubtedly used for a large range of activities with variable consequences.[124] However, if the model of a lifestyle marked by a strongly rhythmic movement between winter and spring comes even close to lived reality in the post-Roman period, then its implications are fundamental for every area of life. The seasonal movement of cattle (primarily, but perhaps some sheep) and herders onto broad open pasture by way of other peoples' farms and land resources must have generated the need for a series of regional-level authorities who were trusted to act as repositories of oral traditions about rights and obligations, who could demonstrate, probably publicly, that they had these capacities and who were possessed of sufficient force to carry out their decisions: this force may well have depended upon the perceived justice of their judgements. The alternative would have been an endless series of cattle raids and vengeance killings linked to a male

123. K. Barker, 'Pen, Ilchester and Yeovil: a study in the landscape history and archaeology of south-east Somerset', *PSANHS* (1986): 36.
124. A. Ward, 'Transhumance and place-names: an aspect of early Ordnance Survey mapping, on the Black Mountain commons, Carmarthenshire', *Studia Celtica*, 33 (1999): 346.

honour code, of which we hear a good deal in the native literature and early modern records of highland northern Britain and Ireland (but less from Wales) and from the transhumance lands of the Mediterranean, but not very much from south-western Britain (although the seventeenth-century stories of the Doones on Exmoor, for example, while very late, fit into this general picture). We can perceive in the needs of summer cattle management the matching requirement for the enforcement of regional rights, and for other adjudications, too, if, as seems likely, the summer pasturing was also an opportunity for a range of other transactions.

The upland huts suggest occupation by only one or two people rather than families, and the thrust of later evidence[125] from the western and northern British Isles suggests that it was the young, unmarried women who accompanied the cows up to the hills, there to spend the summer taking responsibility for the beasts, milking and cheesemaking, and spinning yarn. A few men may have accompanied them to act as guards and drovers, but many of the men, and therefore their wives, had to stay on the farmsteads to plough the arable which the cattle had left well dunged. This must have split families, although no doubt there was a certain amount of toing and froing throughout the summer. This gendered division of labour, with the dairymaids out of easy reach of seniors and males, cannot fail to have acted as a powerful stimulant on all concerned. Judging by later descriptions,[126] the girls saw it as the best days of their lives, of which, as married women, they cherished the fondest memories. It created for the women a strongly bonding network of shared responsibilities, difficulties and memories, which may have been the equivalent of those the young men had from war and hunting, and equally supportive and affective in later life. The poetical relation of young women, milk, cows and whiteness, and the powerful erotic charge of desire and distance, came to have a strong emotional resonance in society and culture.

The strongly marked seasonal character of the year would have its parallels in matters like times of marriage, and the likely birth month of a woman's first child. It is unlikely to be coincidental that the two festivals of 'Beltane' (the spelling selected by Sir James Frazer), which took place around 1 May, and 'Samhain', which happened on 1 November, are among those few which Hutton is prepared to allow to predate the early modern (or later) development of seasonal festivals and customs. Of Beltane, Hutton says,

> None the less, enough has been salvaged to permit certain conclusions to be drawn. First, that all over the ancient British Isles summer was reckoned as beginning around the time which was to become the opening of May. Secondly, that in a pastoral economy, this was the period when livestock, penned in folds, byres, and home fields during winter and spring, could be driven out to the new grass of the pastures. Thirdly, that rituals were conducted at that moment to protect them against the powers of evil, natural and supernatural, not merely in the season to come but because those malign powers were supposed to be particularly active at this turning-point of the year.
>
> Nevertheless, the word 'Celtic', when applied to the Beltane tradition, remains in inverted commas. This is not a map of ethnic or linguistic divisions, but a

---

125. See A. Fenton, *Scottish Country Life* (1976), and refs there, esp. pp. 124–46; E. Davies, 'Hafod and Illuest: the summering of cattle and upland settlement in Wales', *Folk Life*, 23 (1984–5): 70–81.

126. C. O'Danachair, 'Summer pasture in Ireland', *Folk Life*, 22 (1983–4): 30–44.

chart of those areas of Europe which, like Ireland and western and northern Britain, had a pastoral economy involving season transhumance.[127]

In relation to Samhain, he concludes

> Thus, there seems to be no doubt that the opening of November was the time of a major pagan festival which was celebrated, at the very least, in all those parts of the British Isles which had a pastoral economy. At most, it may have been general among the 'Celtic' peoples. There is no evidence that it was connected with the dead, and no proof that it opened the year, but it was certainly a time when supernatural forces were especially to be guarded against or propitiated; activities which took different forms in different regions.[128]

Neither feast was ever completely successfully Christianized, and they mark, of course, the two days traditionally associated with the movement up to and finally down from the summer pastures. What connection this has, if any at all, with the well-known Mayday (and November) customs of some areas in the south-west is extremely doubtful, since there is no reason to date any of these earlier than the early modern period.[129] What is pertinent here is the likelihood that early medieval society did mark the two most significant moments of the pastoral year.

Goods from the earth

The upland areas of the peninsula are also rich in mineral resources, providing special opportunities for the exploitation of deposits of tin, copper and lead ores, high-quality stone, and of clays containing particular mineral characteristics which mean that they produce good quality pottery, especially the gabbroic clay deposits of the Lizard peninsula and the granitic clays of the southern Dartmoor flanks. The exploitation of the Mendip lead during the Roman period is well attested by a range of structural archaeological evidence[130] but, elsewhere, for a potentially large variety of reasons, the working sites outside domestic occupation, for the range of processes which must have been involved, have proved extremely elusive, and, if sites have been observed, very difficult to date. So far, no substantial deposits of non-ferrous slag, recognizable ore-crushing sites, obvious large manufacturing sites for metal objects, kilns or dumps of pot wasters have been found with indications of an AD 300 to 700 date range.

Tin is a relatively rare element in the earth's crust, and normally occurs as tin oxide, or cassiterite, a durable mineral which appears in the south-western granite as heavy black or brownish-purple pebbles. It also occurs as sulphide stannite, a steel-grey or bronze coloured mineral with a metallic lustre, and this also occasionally crops up as pebbles on the granite lands. The south-west is the only known sub-stantial source of tin in the British Isles. The tin minerals occur in a broad belt about 120 km long and up to 30 m wide, and are associated with the massive granite

---

127. R. Hutton, *The Stations of the Sun* (1997), p. 225.
128. *Ibid.*, p. 369.
129. See whole thrust of discussion in Hutton, *Stations*.
130. H. Elkington, 'The Mendip lead industry', in K. Brannigan and P. Fowler (eds), *The Roman West Country* (1976), pp. 183–97.

intrusion which gives the principal granite moors and a number of much smaller bosses, together with the surrounding zone of mineralization (see Fig. 1). The area, however, is not uniformly mineralized: the tin-bearing veins are largely restricted to specific 'emanative areas' which may be near the centre of a granite boss, at its margins or some distance away in the surrounding hills of the mineralized regions.

The tin stone appears as large or small veins in the living rock, and as alluvial gravel deposits, which have been weathered out of the veins and deposited in stream beds and on the lower ground. It is these alluvial deposits which were worked, by the simplest hand-and-bag collection, during the Roman and early medieval periods (and probably had been in prehistory). Deposits like these occur in pockets throughout the region, but particularly important areas are likely to have been those around Birch Tor, the upper branches of the West Webbern and the Walla Brook and the Bovey basin on Dartmoor, the twin granite cusps of Kitt Hill and Gunnislake, the eastern margin of Bodmin Moor, Goss Moor and the Pentewan Valley, Carnmenellis and the bosses of Carn Brea and Carn Marth with the Red River and Carnon Valleys, Penwith near Morvah and Sancreed and the Godolphin boss.

Direct archaeological evidence for tinning activities during the Roman period in the shape of extraction installations is lacking, but indirect evidence comes from the relatively substantial pewter industry (see below). The five Cornish Roman 'milestones', indicating an official statement of imperial interest in transport systems and what they transported, have often been interpreted as linked with an official policy of tin acquisition. Of these, three, from Breage, Gwennap and Trethevy, date to the mid-third century, and those from Tintagel and St Hilary from the early fourth.[131] Exactly what road system those stones relate to, whether it was linked to any kind of official depot and how the tin collection was managed – assuming that tin was indeed involved – remain unclear.

Roman Duckpool,[132] near Bude, seems to have been a settlement site with the normal range of subsistence activities, but also the additional economic activities of purple dye extraction from dog whelks and metalworking, in which the inhabitants processed lead, tin and copper ingots and scrap into lead alloy and copper alloy goods. This seems to have been a specialist industrial community served by a small harbour, but what happened here in the fifth and sixth centuries presents the usual problems. In the post-Roman period the direct evidence for exploitation amounts to the probably sixth-century blue glass bead from the Walkham Valley (already mentioned) and the abraded sherd perhaps from a Roman-British style flanged dish of gabbroic fabric found with tin slag, some worked flints and small stones from an apparent clearance cairn at Upper Merrivale, which cannot be described as a particularly secure dating.[133] The extent of evidence for earlier working from medieval or early modern/modern workings like those at Colliford may have been underestimated.[134]

---

131. R. Collingwood and R. Wright, *The Roman Inscriptions of Britain 1. Inscriptions on Stone* (1965), pp. 694–7. As Henrietta Quinnell suggests (personal communication), these may not be 'milestones' but some form of imperial dedication with no direct relevance to road systems; they may, however, still have a bearing on tin-winning.

132. J. Ratcliffe, 'Duckpool, Morwenstow: a Romano-British and early medieval industrial site and harbour', *Corn. Arch.*, 34 (1995): 81–171.

133. Greeves and Newman, 'Tin working and land use in the Walkham Valley', pp. 199–219.

134. Quinnell, 'Cornwall during the Iron Age', p. 130. See also D. Tew, 'The origins, rise and decline of free mining customs in England and Wales: a legal standpoint' (2000).

Small-scale metalworking is found on several domestic sites of the broad fourth to sixth-century period, as has already been mentioned. At late fourth-century Trethurgy, this production evidently involved tin working, since the debris included a tin ingot. Rough, oval, usually plano-convex tin ingots of this type have been found in excavation of occupation sites at Chun Castle,[135] with its fifth to sixth-century material at Praa Sands, Breage, which produced associated radiocarbon dates in the seventh century, and at Par Beach, St Martins, Scilly, as part of a late Roman deposit in a house.[136] Smelted tin weighing 1 kg was found in 1935 in Porthmeor in House 2 and another piece in House 1 with a piece of 'doubtful slag', in 1935.[137] Other sites – Reawla,[138] Carvossa,[139] Goldherring,[140] Castle Gotha[141] – conventionally dated to the Roman period have produced evidence of metalworking on site.

Finds like these are difficult to date with any accuracy, but they reinforce what the minimal evidence from the granite lands suggests, that low-level but important tin stone smelting was happening throughout the period, and at the 'dirty-hands' level it was being carried out by large numbers of men (presumably) who belonged to a sizeable proportion of the substantial lower land hamlets. The direct organization of the craft was at the 'man and boy' level, but the quantity of tin produced in aggregate was relatively considerable because of the numbers of people involved. This model fits the nature of the surface resources, particularly the tin ores, which are widely but thinly scattered.

It could also fit in with the cycle of the farming year, which would allow men to take summer trips to the upland. The ore may have been smelted on the moor, but the tin stones may have been taken back to the farms to be smelted at leisure, conceivably during the winter; the scanty evidence is mixed, and perhaps both were done. This, at any rate, seems to have been the pattern when farms began to be established in the late medieval period further up the moorland flanks.[142] By the twelfth century both Cornwall and Dartmoor had well-established stannary systems to manage the production of tin.[143] For Dartmoor this involved dividing the moor into four areas based on Ashburton, Chagford, Plympton and Tavistock, and it is worth noting that the boundary between the Ashburton and Chagford stannaries crossed Crownley Down near Ilsington, a possible early boundary. Tin was probably significant in the construction of the post-Roman social superstructure, a topic to be pursued in Chapter 5. The important point here is that the collecting of the ore and the smelting of the tin, apparently into the oval ingots, seems to have been done by a large number

---

135.   E. Leeds, 'Excavations at Chun Castle in Penwith', *ARCH*, 76 (1926–7): 238–9.

136.   Praa Sands, L. Bick, 'Tin ingots found at Praa Sands, Breage, in 1974', *Corn. Arch.*, 33 (1994): 57–70; Par Beach, M. Todd, *The South-West to AD 1000* (1987), p. 232. The tin ingot from Carnanton, Cornwall, with fourth-century imperial stamps is described in Frere *et al.*, *Roman Inscriptions* (1990), p. 67.

137.   R. Penhallurick, *Tin in Antiquity* (1986), pp. 219–21.

138.   Appleton-Fox, 'Romano-British round', pp. 106–13.

139.   Carlyon, 'Finds from Carvossa', pp. 103–41.

140.   A. Guthrie, 'Excavation of a settlement at Goldherring, Sancreed 1958–1961', *Corn. Arch.*, 8 (1969): 5–39.

141.   A. Saunders and D. Harris, 'Excavations at Castle Gotha, St Austell', *Corn. Arch.*, 21 (1982): 109–53.

142.   P. Newman, 'Tinners and tenants on south-west Dartmoor: a case study in landscape history', *TDA*, 126 (1994): 199–238.

143.   S. Gerrard, *The Early British Tin Industry* (2000), pp. 32–9.

of local people operating at the 'home workshop' production level according to their own plans and methods.

Among the local population, the tin was made up into a range of small personal or family objects. Poorly dated tin spindle whorls are said to have been found at Bussow, Trevelgue promontory fort, Glastonbury Lake Village and Corbridge, south of Hadrian's Wall.[144] The tin vessels of probable fourth-century date, like the bowls from St Neot,[145] a largely tin flagon from Goodrington on Torbay[146] and the tin bowl with fitting lid from Treloy, St Columb Minor,[147] made in the same style as some of the stone bowls, presumably belong within the local applications, rather than official ones, to which the tin was put, and are part of the lifestyle of socially superior local inhabitants. We do not know if such pieces went on being made, or being used, after *c.* 400.

To produce bronze, tin must be alloyed with copper in the proportion of roughly 10 per cent tin to 90 per cent copper. Copper ores are as common in the peninsula as tin ores and occur generally in the same areas, together with important deposits around North Molton, on the western flanks of Exmoor.[148] Since copper ores are relatively common in western Britain and Ireland and also in central Europe, Iberia, Cyprus and the high plateau behind the eastern Mediterranean coast, the copper deposits of the south-west have never achieved the importance (either economically or imaginatively) enjoyed by the tin. We do not know if the local copper ores were exploited between *c.* 300 to 700, although if they were, the best guess is that it was in the same general style as the tin stone. The surviving range of bronze objects from the later part of the period is very thin, and the only site which has produced evidence of specific bronze working is Glastonbury Tor.[149] We do not know where the metals involved came from, and we should not forget that in the post-Roman period, at least, working may have involved old scrap.

Tin can also be alloyed with lead in varying proportions to produce pewter. Pewter was much in demand in the later Empire for a range of serving and eating dishes which took the place of silver vessels used by the very rich, and imitated their forms. In the south-west lead is associated with the extensive remains of Roman processing on Mendip, where both the lead itself and silver extracted from it by cupellation were important, the silver for plate and coinage, the lead for coffins, large vessels, water pipes and cisterns, all important in the fourth century, and for building – great sheets of it were used for lining the Great Bath at Bath.[150] However, lead is also found in smaller deposits elsewhere in the south-west, on the western flanks of Dartmoor and at various sites in Cornwall: in the St Issey district, north of St Columb Major, for example, it was mined in the nineteenth century.

Fourth-century industrial material from Camerton, Lansdown near Bath and Nettleton Shrub in Wiltshire show that these sites were all manufacturing pewter vessels in the fourth century: all are on the Fosse Way, and well placed to receive tin from the west and lead from Mendip, and send on the finished products eastwards.[151]

---

144. Penhallurick, *Tin*, p. 214.
145. Penhallurick, *Tin*, p. 219.
146. Natural History Society Museum, Torquay.
147. Penhallurick, *Tin*, p. 219.
148. R. Tylecote, *Metalurgy in Archaeology* (1962).
149. P. Rahtz, 'Excavations at Glastonbury Tor', *Arch. J.*, 127 (1971): 1–81.
150. Elkington, 'Mendip lead industry', pp. 183–97.
151. *Ibid.*

Finds, like the group of seven pewter flagons found in the well or shaft of the Brislington villa in Somerset, probably came from one of these centres, although there were two small mould fragments also in the shaft. At the complicated site at Gatcombe (perhaps a small town, or a specially defended settlement) were furnaces and substantial quantities of lump pewter.[152]

There was also some manufacturing further west. The set of stone moulds from Leswidden, St Just,[153] would have produced two dishes and a bigger, shallow dish from one casting, possibly of tin but more likely of pewter which has a better 'flow', and the granite mould from Halangy[154] seems likely to have produced a rectangular lanx-type dish. A similar mould fragment has come from the Indian Queens site near Penhale. Killigrew near Truro appears as a small round-style site with a furnace, perhaps for smelting tin, and work areas but no evidence for domestic occupation. It produced a simple plate of 90 per cent tin of uncertain date and a greison weight with a lead plug for a hook. The pottery was dominated by a mix of dishes and storage jars with few cooking pots, and suggested a date of around AD 200.[155] Although production on a commercial scale generally seems to have ceased soon after 400, it would be rash to suppose that local manufacture for relatively local use came to an abrupt stop, but the paucity of the evidence, and the dating difficulties it presents, must be recognized.

Pottery, like metalworking, is an extraction industry and dependent upon the exploitation of suitable clays, preferably those with natural inclusions which mean they fire well, and which give what is considered to be an attractive appearance. The granitic clays of the southern Dartmoor flank and the gabbroic clays of the Lizard work very well but the geology of the south-west has produced a number of small deposits capable of producing good results which could have been worked on a small scale. This, together with the difficulties of producing dated sequences in circumstances where sites seldom produce good stratified sequences or associated datable artefacts, and where tastes in pot styles changed slowly, produces a very complex situation.

The assemblage from Reawla[156] may or may not be typical, but it illuminates the mixed range of wares a single site can produce (Table 4). The Reawla material, in conjunction with that from Duckpool and Trethurgy, and from Exeter, enables a tentative sequence of the main types to be drawn up, which further excavation may well modify, perhaps particularly in relation to pottery use in east Cornwall/Devon. The inhabitants of Reawla had a very small number of fine ware sherds, chiefly Oxfordshire wares, which also crop up at Stoke Gabriel, Carvossa and Scilly. The ware also occurred at Exeter, where forms after c. 325 were only 9 per cent of the assemblage and at Colliton Park, Dorchester, also 9 per cent, and Ilchester (excavations 1974–5), where they formed 33 per cent. The implication is that late

152.   K. Brannigan, *Gatcombe: The Excavation and Study of a Romano-British Villa Estate 1967–1976* (1977). Further pewter moulds come from Cold Harbour Farm villa, Wick (Som), and from the Bath spring; see N. Beagrie, 'The Romano-British pewter industry', *Britannia*, 20 (1989): 169–91, and B. Cunliffe, *The Temple of Sulis Minerva at Bath Vol. II: The finds from the Sacred Spring* (1988), p. 24.
153.   Brown, P. D., 1970, pp. 107–10.
154.   Ashbee, 'Halangy Down', p.102 and fig. 49.
155.   Penhale, Killigrew, Henrietta Quinnell, personal communication.
156.   H. Quinnell, 'The pottery', in Appleton-Fox, 'Romano-British round', pp. 94–106.

Table 4 Range of pottery from Reawla

Fabric	Sherd numbers	Percentage*
Samian	1	0.05
Rhenish?	1	0.05
Oxfordshire	12	0.6
Rough-cast beaker	5	0.2
Other colour coat	1	0.05
South-east Dorset BB1	31	1.5
South-east Dorset BB1 variant	143	7.0
Exeter micaceous Grey ware	1	0.05
Other micaceous Grey ware	1	0.05
South Devon	84	4.0
Hard-fired south Devon	26	1.2
Local granitic	9	0.34
Gabbroic (including coarse)	1787	85.6
(Coarse gabbro)	(210)	(10.1)
	2089	100

Note: *Fabric percentages based on count of sherds over 1 cm across
Source: N. Appleton-Fox, 'Excavations at a Romano-British round, Reawla, Gwinear, Cornwall', *Corn. Arch.* 31 (1992), Table 5 (some of the figures are approximate)

Oxfordshire wares were not a significant element in south-western material culture west and south of southern Somerset.

A special type of black pottery, in which the outside of the pots were buffed up, or 'burnished' with a soft leather or something similar, was produced in the Poole Harbour area of Dorset,[157] one of a number of sites in Britain producing such wares. It gradually became the main ware in use in third- and fourth-century Exeter (80 per cent of fourth-century coarse wares), and it appears at both Reawla and Trethurgy and, in small quantities, at Hayes Farm (fourth century) and Rewe (third century). In Somerset, the Poole Harbour pottery is found in some density at sites on or near the Ilchester–Dorchester road, and its extension along the Polden ridge to the Parrett estuary. This looks like an export route from Bush Marsh, where warehouses have been recognized, by sea northwards. Elsewhere, in Somerset, however, it is less common: 25 per cent of the pot at Norton Fitzwarren, scarce at Maylands and Woodford near Taunton, and absent from Syndercombe on the edge of the Bredon Hills.[158] It does, however, appear on the highly Romanized sites in east Devon, at Otterton Point, Seaton, Woodbury, Holcombe and Membury. Its typical fourth-century forms are double-strap-handled beakers, cooking pots, storage jars with rope rim and pierced neck holes, and a range of bowls and plates. A variant of the ware, which includes large fragments of rounded slate, may have been produced in the Wareham/Poole area of Dorset. This fabric is generally dark grey and the dishes, bowls and pots are slipped: it has not yet been recognized at Exeter, Dorchester or any Cornish sites other than Reawla.

South Devon ware becomes common in Exeter in the third and fourth centuries.

---

157. N. Holbrook and P. Bidwell, *Roman Finds from Exeter* (1991), pp. 16–19.
158. R. Leech, 'The medieval defences of Bristol revisited', in L. Keen (ed.), *Almost the Richest City: Bristol in the Middle Ages* (1997), fig. 142.

It appears from the late Roman occupation sites at Carwarthen and Trethurgy, while at Kilhallon and Carvossa, sites which seem to end in the third century, there are only a few sherds in the assemblage. South Devon ware was probably made in the Dart Valley, and seems to have been well made, but hand thrown. A variant of the ware but with much smaller grits comprised probably wheel-thrown but bonfire-fired cooking pots, fragments of which appear in late Exeter contexts. During its heyday around the mid-third century, production had developed from humble beginnings to an enterprise which shipped products to London and to Cornwall but evidently was still available locally throughout the fourth century. Typical forms are, like those of the black burnished wares, rimmed dishes, bowls and cooking pots.

The gabbroic wares form by far the largest groups from Reawla, as they do from most contemporary Cornish sites like Trethurgy and Carvossa. A small amount has appeared in Exeter, and one flanged bowl was found at Mount Batten,[159] but at present its importance in Devon seems to have been fairly limited. Despite some argument, it still seems likely that it was made from clays weathered out of rocks in the St Keverne area of the Lizard peninsula. The pots seem to have been basically handmade, but using simple turntables to start and finish off the modelling. The clay contains large quantities of gritty white feldspar and small quantities of equally gritty black tourmaline and other minerals. It has sometimes been suggested that grit filler was added to the clay, but it seems rather more likely that gritty clay was usually deliberately selected.[160] It is clear that sometimes the clay was puddled very carefully to eliminate air bubbles and sometimes this care was neglected. The probable bonfire-firing usually produced red-brown pots, with a burnished black coating over their outside and on the inner side of the rim often worn by use. The range included the usual selection of bowls and dishes. There was also a coarse variety, with large grits, rough finish and no coating, which has been found at Carnoon and Trebaveth. It seems to represent large vessels used for processing purposes not directly related to cooking and serving food.

These potting industries do not exhaust the areas where some potters seem to have been at work. A kind of black burnished ware may have been made in the Brue Valley,[161] where mounds flanking the Brue have produced large amounts of debris.[162] Recent excavations at Woodbury in east Devon have produced large quantities of late third to mid-fourth-century storage jars in a grey fabric, and wasters demonstrate that these, and possibly other types too, were made on the site. Similar storage jars seem to have been made in a range of Somerset sites,[163] one of which may have been at Norton Fitzwarren, apparently operating during the third century.

One of the most sophisticated studies of late Roman pottery production yet published has been devoted to the black burnished wares of south-east Dorset,[164] and work along these lines on the other south-western wares (to go no further) would unquestionably add much to our knowledge. This intensive study shows that the

159.   Holbrook and Bidwell, *Roman Finds*, pp. 177–83.
160.   The occasional sherd has a glittering appearance which derived from processes which had concentrated small quantities of naturally occurring micaceous amphibole particles on the surface.
161.   R. Farrar, 'The techniques and sources of black burnished ware', in A. Detsicas (ed.), *Current Research in Romano-British Coarse Pottery* (1973), pp. 63–103.
162.   Holbrook and Bidwell, *Roman Finds*, p. 90.
163.   *Ibid.*, p. 175.
164.   J. Allen and M. Fulford, 'The distribution of south-east Dorset black burnished Category I pottery in south-west Britain', *Britannia*, 27 (1996): 224–81.

large-scale infrastructure and production/supply management needed to support an industry of this size and complexity ceased around the end of the fourth century, and this seems to be the case with all similar production centres. At its peak, production of the ware seems to have been based upon individual workshops of perhaps six to eight potters, each of whom came from a different family, together with seasonal workers, or part-time help through the year.[165] However, the site at Ower, on Poole Harbour, suggests that small-scale production of black burnished pots continued on a seasonal basis into the fifth, or even the sixth centuries, and this may be the source of the fifth-century ware found at Exeter, Bath and Dorchester.[166] In the pottery producing centres west of the Exe, the level of operation may always have been seasonal or part-time (indeed, the present connotations of the word 'pottering' may have applied to the craft in the long term), and after *c.* 400 there is no obvious reason why their production could not have continued on a more limited scale.

Dating is difficult but radiocarbon dates suggest that occuption at Reawla may have run on to late in the sixth century, and gabbroic pottery seems to continue in use at Trethurgy until around 500. Recent work at Heliggy near Trelawaren on the Lizard has produced a typical group of fourth-century-style gabbroic sherds together with fragments of an African red slipware bowl, dated to the fifth century.[167] This evidence is slight, but it suggests that some, at least, of the local potting industries, including those in the Lizard, carried on into the fifth or even sixth centuries, perhaps at a reduced level, with part-time potters making the kinds of pots which people still felt they needed, in very traditional styles, which would be difficult to differentiate from earlier material, given that the potting had always been based upon an unsophisticated technology. This, in turn, raises the possibility that sites deemed to have been abandoned in the fourth, or even third, centuries on the pottery evidence alone could have continued to be occupied.

In addition to metal goods and pots, some of the inhabitants had access to a range of stone artefacts, chiefly mortars, larger bowls, called Trethurgy bowls from the site where they were first singled out, and weights. A further more miscellaneous group includes moulds and other pieces like the 'toggle' from Grambla. Almost all the artefacts were made from elvan (the local name for quartz-porphyry), which is a cream-coloured rock sometimes shading to pink or grey, or greisen, a silvery or yellowish grey rock which derives from granite. Elvan occurs in dykes, which cluster between Penwith and Carnmenellis, and to the north of Carnmenellis, with a few occurrences further east in Cornwall. Greisen occurs patchily around the granite areas, with a density which increases westwards in Cornwall.[168] The Trethurgy bowls have skeumorphic handles and are obviously meant to mimic similar bowls in metal.

The Trethurgy evidence showed that all the types were in use – and presumably manufactured – in the fourth, fifth and probably sixth centuries, utilizing manufacturing styles which emerged in the second or third centuries, and a long local tradition of comparable stoneworking. The stone artefacts have so dense a distribution on and around Penwith as to make it clear that each settlement there had some, and the distribution continues eastwards, growing proportionately thinner

165. D. Peacock, *Pottery in the Roman World* (1982), pp. 13–25.
166. N. Sunter and P. Woodward, *Romano-British Industries in Purbeck* (1987).
167. For Reawla, see Quinnell, 'The pottery', pp. 94–106; see also H. Quinnell, 'Cornish gabbroic pottery: the development of a hypothesis', *Corn. Arch.*, 26 (1987), pp. 7–12; Quinnell, *Excavations at Trethurgy Round* (forthcoming); Heliggy, Quinnell personal communication.
168. Quinnell, 'Sense of identity', pp. 69–78.

with distance from the main sources. Nevertheless, Trethurgy bowls got as far as Lydney,[169] London (one from a fourth-century context) and Richborough. Like the tin and copper alloy goods, although there is clear community link to the Penwith/Carnmenellis communities, these stone goods seem to have been made, used and exchanged at the level of individual craftsmen and the farmsteads to which they belonged.

More mundane commodities were also needed by the farming community. Salt workings have been found at Trebarveth in West Cornwall, apparently of Roman date, where stone-built ovens, together with the very poor-quality, rough pottery troughs which have left briquettage remains, were used for evaporating salt water. Similar ovens and briquettage have been found at Carnoon Bank,[170] in the Lizard, where the salt working seems to have been in the Roman period although the structure continued in intermittent use to at least the sixth century. Salt-making debris of Roman date has been found on a number of sites in Somerset along the River Brue, and at Brent the East Huntspill briquettage mound showed that peat had been used as fuel.[171] A small grant of land to Sherborne[172] at probably Uplyme in Devon in 774 was made so that 'salt shall be acquired there . . . for the provision of manifold needs, either in the seasoning of food or even that it may be had for use in the divine offices: which we need many times daily for the sake of the Christian religion.' A further grant of land at Uplyme in 938 mentions a 'salt ford'; the field name 'Salters Land' is about a kilometre to the north-west, and a number of paths in the area climb the cliff to form a salt way running from the coast inland.[173]

Iron was a fundamental material for farming and household tools. Its working involves the two processes of smelting metal from ore, which leaves slag, and smithing the metal by heating, hammering and quenching it into finished products, but in the archaeological record distinctions between the two processes tend to have become blurred, a factor not helped by the rapidity with which iron can rust into a shapeless mass. Around the Somerset Levels iron working is recorded from Roman-period sites at Chedzoy, Lakehouse Farm and West Lane near Lymsham. Slag is recorded at Wint Hill and at the Brean Down temple site. Slag has also been recorded at Clapton Rectory and Weston-in-Gordano, Portisham, Wemberham and Craggie Knoll in Tickenham.[174]

The recognition of iron smelting sites in Twitchen parish on southern Exmoor, where a 'cinder' place-name in documents of 1249 led to the discovery of a mound of iron slag, has prompted a major project on Exmoor, and important iron smelting sites of Romano-British and perhaps later date are appearing at Brayford and Timberscombe.[175] Similar sites have been identified in the Blackdown Hills of east

---

169.   P. Casey and B. Hoffman, 'Excavations at the Roman temple in Lydney Park, Gloucestershire', *Antiq. J.*, 79 (1999): 131.

170.   Trebarveth, Peacock, 'Romano-British salt working site', pp. 47–65; Carnoon, F. McAvoy, 'The excavations at a multi-period site at Carngoon Bank, Lizard', *Corn. Arch.*, 19 (1980): 17–30.

171.   Leech, 'The Roman interlude', p. 277.

172.   S263; Hooke, *Pre-Conquest Charter-bounds*, p. 85.

173.   S442; Hooke, *Pre-Conquest Charter-bounds*, p. 132.

174.   S. Rippon, *The Severn Estuary Landscape Evolution and Wetland Reclamation* (1997), pp. 118–20.

175.   G. Juleff, *Earlier Iron-working on Exmoor: Preliminary Survey* (1997), for broad account; 'New radiocarbon dates for iron-working sites on Exmoor' *Newsletter of the Historical Mettalurgical Society* (2000), pp. 3–4, for dates.

Devon, one of which is of Roman date.[176] Sites further west are more elusive, but there are useful deposits of iron ore (brown haematite and micaceous haematite) on eastern Dartmoor in the Ilsington area, at Haytor, in the south at Holne and at Holne Chase and in the west around Hemerdon and Plympton. Isolated outcrops of ironstone occur west of the Tamar, and, at Trevelgue near Newquay, there are bands of iron ore in the cliffs. The settlement sites at Reawla, Carvossa, Trethurgy, Carlidnack, Trevisker, Castle Gotha and Goldherring all produced iron finds, suggesting that blacksmithing was a normal subsistence-farming activity at every substantial hamlet.

Peat was an important source of fuel, in parts of Cornwall probably the most important source, and rights of turbary, the taking of peat, on Dartmoor, the Levels and the Cornish moorlands generated the usual formidable array of medieval and early modern laws and regulations. The physical remains of peat cutting consist chiefly of the turf platforms now recognized on the Lizard, and on Bodmin Moor in large numbers, particularly the north-west, together with places, particularly on Dartmoor and the Levels, where areas of stripping terminating in peat faces can be recognized. The earliest of the turf platforms are perhaps fourteenth century and were intended to produce turf charcoal from cut turves, which was used for smelting purposes;[177] while a Dartmoor account of 1371 refers to *carbonarii* who are 'digging turves for [making] charcoal in order to sell it'[178] and an order from Henry III (1222) requests that the Devon tinners should be permitted to take turves from Dartmoor as they were accustomed to do in the time of King John (*c.* 1205). By then the complex organization of the stannaries was taking shape, but there is no reason to doubt that taking turf was a part of the ancient rights of pasture and metal-winning on the moor lands. Peat will obviously have been used as necessary for domestic heating and cooking, but it will also have been usable for the pyrotechnology which both potting and metalworking require, and which involves the management of heat to produce temperatures around 1000°C. This can be done with normal fire-building arrangements with both wood and peat without the need for pre-processed charcoal or special hearths, and in an area like the south-west, where both metals and pot clay had been worked for well over two millennia by *c.* AD 500, the accumulated and widespread expertise must have been considerable.

Social frameworks

While bearing in mind all the uncertainties and ambiguities, it is perhaps possible to sketch in a broader view of life in the peninsula during the post-Roman centuries. Overall, the workable lands seem to have been relatively densely settled. In the east, unenclosed hamlets, the 'modern' approach to homesteading around 400, were already the norm, and gradually in the west the enclosed settlements were being replaced by new, unenclosed sites (often denoted by the place-name element *tref* in Cornwall and *ton* in Devon), suggesting changes in lifestyle, but the field systems and other resources continue to be exploited, as far as we can tell, along familiar lines. This may have been accompanied by a slight fall in the number of hamlets, but the

176.   C. Webster, 'Blackdown Hills AONB survey', *PSANHS*, 136 (1993), p. 129.
177.   Quinnell, 1984, p. 12.
178.   Fox, 'Medieval Dartmoor through its account rolls', p. 162.

known sites seem solid, substantial and relatively well equipped. The fields produced mainly cereals and the beasts milk, meat and a range of raw materials. The cows went regularly to traditional upland summer pasture, a practice which contributed a great deal to a yearly cycle characterized by seasonal and probably gendered customs. The impression is of a complex balance between upland and lowland resource exploitation, which sustained a pattern of mixed farming.

We have to ask how successful this was in terms of human experience, and what kind of diet all the careful activity yielded for most people. Querns, which most excavated sities have produced, suggest that some of the cereals were ground and could have been used to make flat breads (rather like pitta bread) cooked on hot stone slabs, but the grains could also have been mixed with water to make the thin gruel or thicker porridge which Romano-Britains knew as *puls*, supplemented by vegetables like peas mashed in a mortar, or perhaps cooked in a pot sunk into the ashes.[179] This basic, although extremely boring, diet was presumably supplemented with dairy products from both cow and sheep milk from the summer yield, including butter and varieties of keeping cheeses.

Slaughtered bullocks and sheep would provide occasional feasts of meat, and could be preserved by smoking and salting, as could the conger eel, bream, mackerel, whiting and ballan basse which formed (unsurprisingly) a major part of the diet at Halangy. The cattle bones at Halangy were mainly from adults, and they had been butchered intensively, with the long bones split for their marrow. Cut marks showed where carcasses had been skinned and jointed.[180] At Cadbury Congresbury over half the cattle bones came from immature animals slaughtered for their meat and hides, rather than old animals whose meat was the final produce of a life spent ploughing or producing wool, suggesting an affluent society.[181] The Halangy sheep were generally like those of the 'modern primitive' Soay breed, and had also been expertly butchered. The Halangy farmers had pigs, which seem to have been effectively feral self-foragers, also chopped and cut. The broader evidence from southern Britain generally suggests a rise in the numbers of both cattle and pigs around 250 to 400, in contrast to large numbers of sheep in the pre-Roman Iron Age and around AD 1000, when sheep were again as common as cattle. The south-west fits into the picture reasonably well.[182]

There were horses at Halangy and Cadbury Congresbury and red deer bones from hunting. There were also cats, like those from Duckpool and Exeter, to help protect the grain stores and to act as companion animals. A dog appeared in the bone record from Congresbury and from Duckpool and we can certainly take their noisy presence for granted, on the hunt and in the yard. Certainly, too, across the peninsula, cultivated crops will have been supplemented by seasonal collections of wild nuts and fruits and various shellfish, as country people still do. A wide range of the fruits and cereals could be fermented into alcoholic drinks, and mead could be made from honey, which is likely to have been relatively valuable, but provided some sweetening. The finds from Duckpool show that domestic fowls and their eggs were a part of the diet. Although the evidence is problematical, every household of substance seems to have had a reasonable range of dishes, bowls and plates, which allowed food to be

179.   Quinnell, 'Cornwall during the Iron Age', p. 126.
180.   Ashbee, 'Halangy Down', pp. 118–26.
181.   P. Rahtz *et al., Cadbury Congresbury 1968–73. A Late/Post Roman Hilltop Settlement in Somerset* (1992), pp. 185 9.
182.   Randsborg, *First Millennium* (1991), pp. 34–9.

presented and then shared out into individual bowls rather than a communal dipping into a common pot. Interestingly, a common south-east Dorset black burnished ware type was a two-handled beaker, perhaps suggesting drinks were passed around. These do not occur in Cornwall and were not copied in the local pots, but maybe here people drank from non-ceramic containers, perhaps of leather.

If this is in danger of sounding like a healthy paradise of home-grown, home-cooked, fibre-rich food, skeletal evidence paints in the darker side of the picture. The two sites which have produced the best evidence from the peninsula are the Henley Wood[183] and Poundbury[184] cemeteries; at Poundbury the numbers of men and women were almost the same, while at Henley the men numbered about 39 per cent of the total and the women about 21 per cent. Figure 27 shows the evidence relating to age at death, and suggests overall that most people died between their late teens and their early forties, always supposing that they survived infancy, although some few survived beyond 70. Henley, at least, suggested that a woman's chances of surviving beyond 35 were poor.

The Poundbury population showed the kinds of jaw development and teeth wear associated with chewing bread made from flour with a high husk content and the evidence together suggested a diet based predominantly on cereals, for all ages. As a diet for children, this is of poor nutritional value, and resulted in children who were

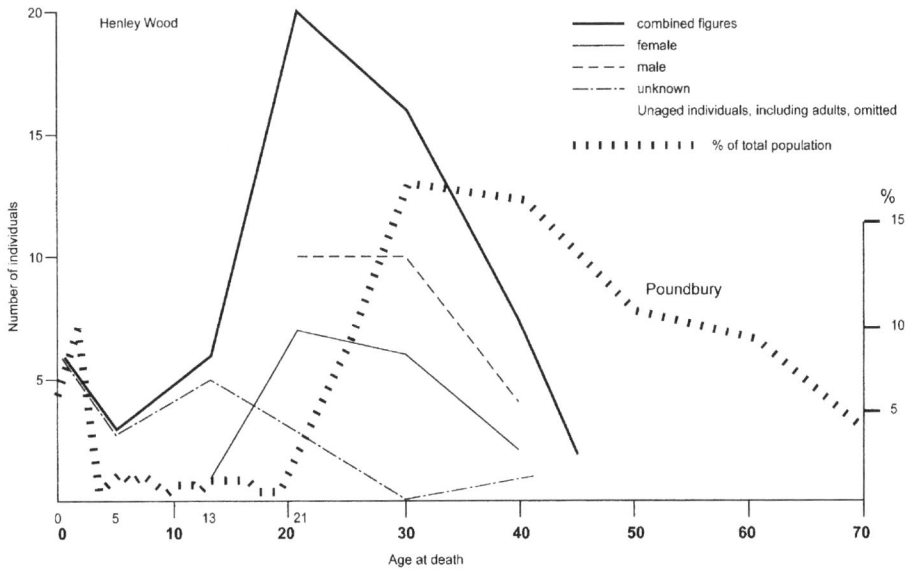

Figure 27 Age at death: Henley Wood and Poundbury (Henley Wood after Watts and Leach 1996, Fig. 44; Poundbury after Farwell and Molleson 1993, Fig. 120). Henley Wood chart shows real numbers, Poundbury percentages, but both show a peak around age 30–40 years

183. D. Watts and P. Leach, *Henley Wood, Temples and Cemetery Excavations 1962–69* (1996), pp. 44–75.
184. T. Molleson, 'Mortality patterns in the Romano-British cemetery at Poundbury Camp, Dorchester', in *Death in Towns* (1992), pp. 43–55.

small for their dental age by our standards, who came to puberty late and who had light bones and poor teeth as adults, although the men were generally 1.62 m to 1.72 m (5′4″–5′8″) in height, and the women 1.58 m to 1.64 m (5′2″–5′5″). Lack of vitamin D from sunlight, essential to those on a largely vegetarian diet, and iron seem to have caused rickets and leg ulcers, while lead poisoning from food preparation and service vessels was common, and could cause chronic ill health. Infectious diseases included tuberculosis and possibly smallpox, but tumours and cancers seem to have been rare.

The Poundbury evidence indicated that infant mortality was high and the birth rate low, suggesting that the living community in Dorchester must have relied upon immigration from the countryside to sustain it. This blurs what otherwise might have been an important difference between the life chances of urban and rural populations. The poor diet and its consequences were probably common to all except the privileged across the peninsula, but infectious diseases may have been much less common where fewer people lived close together. Perhaps lead poisoning plagued only those with a more strongly marked 'Roman' lifestyle, although it is worth mentioning that remote communities, like the settlers at Halangy, or some of them, used pewter dishes from which lead can leak, so it may have been a widespread risk.

The farmstead communities were certainly in touch with pottery and metal producers in the fourth century, and how far this continued into the fifth and sixth centuries is an open question. On present evidence, it looks as if this production was organized on a 'craft' part-time basis, and was carried on very broadly across the population base. A seasonal approach to the collecting of metal ores from the upland, and the processing of it in the homesteads, would fit the model presented here of the farming year (Fig. 28), and its implications for access to raw materials and the gendered division of labour.

The hamlets, both enclosed and open, seem from their numbers, their character and substance, and from the role they apparently played in sustaining the resource linkage between upland and lowland, to have embodied a significant bundle of rights and obligations, which made up the fundamental functioning element in the socio-economic structure. The steady shift, particularly west of the Exe, from enclosed to unenclosed settlements gives us a glimpse of significant local cultural change.

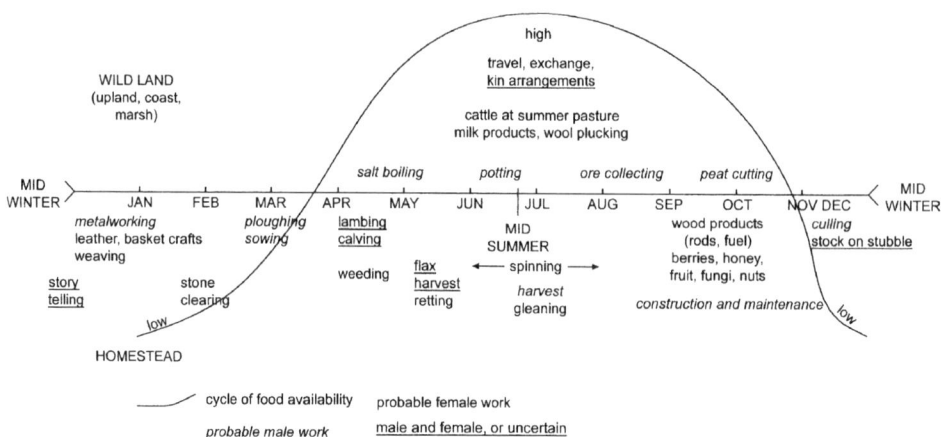

Figure 28 The farming year

3   Christians and pagans

Introduction

At one level, this chapter is concerned with the evidence for 'religious' practices in the Late Antique south-west, that is with the analysis of superficially irrational attitudes connected with the treatment of human remains, objects, buildings and sites within the landscape. At another, perhaps more significant and certainly more interesting, level, the cultural imagination manifested in the evidence for observance and ceremony seems also to have much to do with individual and collective identity, access to resources and the organization and management of those resources. To put it more bluntly, people who responded to the unknown, especially death, together seem also to have come to work, live and think together, a trait which is itself part of the social momentum gathering between roughly AD 300 and 600, which we call Late Antiquity and characterize as emphasizing the personal, the emotional, the small-scale.

How this happened can be investigated from a number of angles: the sensational impact of new and heightened emotion associated with Christian practice,[1] the potential effect of political ramifications[2] or the sociological effects of Christian community life.[3] What appears most clearly is that the gradual emergence of Christian styles must be seen as part of the broader social fabric not as in contrast to it or as a kind of moral progression within it. What we tend to characterize as 'religion', of whatever affiliation, probably did not appear to contemporaries as a distinct or separate activity but one picked up instinctively to express needs and promote social changes.

This chapter analyses what we seem to see as ritual activity in the fourth- and fifth-century south-west. It first discusses the use of Christian symbols and images, and then considers the meanings attached to hoards of coins and other metalwork, the attention paid to wells and other shafts, shrines, temples and ancient hill-fort sites, and the ways in which animal and human body parts were used. Next, it reviews the broader treatment of the human dead and the cemeteries they were buried in, and then analyses the complex histories of Exeter, Ilchester, Dorchester and Bath as focal centres. A key issue is the extent to which Christian belief and practice had taken root in the region by c. 500, and the character of any such Christianity; equally important is the question of how ceremony and ritual of all kinds meshed with broad social organization, and what it meant to people then alive.

---

1.   For a wide-ranging account, see P. Brown, *Late Antiquity* (1998).
2.   See M. Humphries, *Communities of the Blessed: Social Environment and Religious Change in Northern Italy AD 200–400* (1999).
3.   See R. Stark, *The Rise of Christianity. A Sociologist Reconsiders History* (1994).

The British context

In order to put the Late Antique south-west into its broader extent we need to look very briefly at the extent to which the broader British fourth-century community was in any sense Christian, and what character this Christianity took.[4] Four episcopal sees at Lincoln, London, York and perhaps Cirencester were represented at the Council of Arles in 314,[5] and three British bishops, generally (though not necessarily) presumed to be from three of the same cities, accepted the state conference grant to attend the Council of Rimini in 357:[6] these may have represented a larger group of bishops established within a number of British cities. This would mean that there were in these cities groups of believers with the appropriate hierarchy and with somewhere to meet, although the archaeological evidence from Butts Road, Colchester,[7] and at the Minster site at York,[8] and elsewhere at Caerwent,[9] Silchester[10] and possibly Wroxeter,[11] suggests that the potential churches so far identified in these cities are at the earliest late fourth century, and perhaps fifth. The martyrial shrines of St Alban[12] and Sts Julian and Aaron at Caerleon[13] seem to have been significant religious centres from at least the fourth century. We know very little about the Caerleon site, although presumably it was connected with the presence of the army there. Germanus, Bishop of Auxerre, is said to have visited St Albans in 429 and this fits with evidence from north Gaul which shows that martyrial cults were deliberately being cultivated, resurrected from obscurity and indeed created, in the late fourth/early fifth centuries by city bishops with an interest in stimulating a style of spectacular, civic Christianity.

The documentary evidence for a fifth-century British Christian presence is relatively substantial, even though sparse compared with even northern Gaul (not to mention Gaul further south), and significant elements in it come from Gaulish sources, something which may itself be significant. Important records focus upon the visit of Victricius to Britain in 396,[14] the visit of Germanus (and possibly Bishop

4.   For principal accounts, see C. Thomas, *Christianity in Roman Britain to AD 500* (1981), and, for update, see D. Watts, *Christians and Pagans in Roman Britain* (1991); D. Petts, *Christianity in Roman Britain* (2003).

5.   J. Mann, 'The administration of Roman Britain', *Antiquity*, 35 (1961): 316–20; see also Petts, *Christianity* (2003), pp. 38–40 for evidence for other bishops.

6.   C. Morris, *The Age of Arthur* (1973), pp. 13–14.

7.   P. Crummy, *Colchester: Recent Excavation and Research* (1994).

8.   H. Ramm, 'The end of Roman York', in R. Butler (ed.), *Soldier and Civilian in Roman Yorkshire* (1971), pp. 179–99.

9.   V. Nash-Williams, 'Excavations at Caerwent and Caerleon', *Bulletin Board of Celtic Studies*, 15 (1953): 165–70.

10.   Thomas, *Christianity*, p. 169.

11.   R. White and P. Barker, *Wroxeter: Life and Death of a Roman City* (1998), pp. 118–36.

12.   I. Anthony, 'Excavations in Verulam Fields, St Albans, 1963–4', *Hertfordshire Archaeology*, 1 (1968): 9–50; R. Niblett, *Excavation of a Ceremonial Site at Folly Lane, Verulamium* (1999), esp. pp. 417–19.

13.   J. Knight, 'The early Church in Gwent II: the early medieval Church', *Monmouth Antiquary*, 9 (1993): 1–17.

14.   Victricius appears as a name on the late fourth- to fifth-century pewter bowl from Applecross which possibly suggests he was well known in Britain (but could easily refer to somebody quite different), but Bishop Victricius' remark in a letter to Ambrose that he had 'taken the precepts of the martyrs to Britain' is more likely to refer to relics and their implications than monasticism, *pace* K. Dark, *Britain and the End of the Roman Empire* (2000), p. 31.

Lupus of Troyes) in 429 (and possibly again around 435) and the fifth-century career of Patrick in (probably) north Britain, (perhaps) Gaul and Ireland, together with the Irish mission of Palladius. Much of this was underlain by papal anxieties regarding the unorthodox teaching of Pelagius, who may have been British,[15] and it brings a facet of British Christianity within an episcopal, Roman-orientated orbit, which must have coloured perceptions at the time and has probably affected how its record has come down to us. Indeed, we must remember that almost all the documentary evidence relating to the development of Christian practice comes from committed Christians who were usually anxious to stress what were, from their point of view, positive changes, and perhaps to help bring these changes about by writing as if they were more secure than they actually were.

The physical evidence for late Roman Christianity in Britain has depended upon assessment of cemeteries and associated structures like those at Icklingham, Lankhills, Ancaster, York (Railway Station and Bootham Terrace sites) and Butt Road (Colchester); potential church buildings at Richborough, Canterbury, Verulamium, Lullingstone and London, together with those just mentioned; lead tanks, of which at least the six explicitly marked with chi-rho symbols seem to be for baptisms; impressive finds of silverware, notably that from Water Newton which certainly seems to have been for Christian worship as other silver pieces may also have been; place-names; and a range of small objects carrying chi-rhos of varying expertise and a variety of other symbols like fish and palms, the significance of which are debatable.

Density maps for the fourth century embracing this evidence were produced by Thomas[16] and, in revised version, by Watts,[17] and these show the strongest Christian presence in central-eastern Britain and the Thames Valley, and in the north, with less evidence in the areas between these, and very little in the west, outside a certain density in Dorset/Gloucester. It should be noted that both these maps take a cautiously Christian view of the cemetery evidence which will be discussed in detail below. Collectively the evidence presented on these maps is impressive, and informed Thomas' view that in Britain 'some measure of survival, of continuity ... is an explanation for what we encounter in the sixth and seventh centuries; and an explanation preferable to another in which Christianity in Roman Britain was extinguished ... and subsequently indemonstrably, re-introduced'.[18] Searches for the survival of southern British Christianity into the fifth and sixth centuries are looking at areas like the possible continuities in the boundaries of later parishes and dioceses, and the identification of cult places. All this, together with excavation, add to the sum of our knowledge of Late Antique Christianity in Britain. But while this kind of approach succeeds in documenting the probable incidence of Christian practice, it does not look at the evidence for other kinds of practices which were taking place during the same period, and it does not greatly help us understand what some practices labelled 'Christian' may have been like.

---

15. See Thomas, *Christianity*, pp. 53–60. A useful survey of the documentary evidence has been provided by Thomas Snyder, *An Age of Tyrants: Briton and the Britons* (1998).
16. Thomas, *Christianity*, fig. 16.
17. Watts, *Christians and Pagans*, fig. 28.
18. Thomas, *Christianity*, p. 351.

Christian images and symbols in the late Roman south-west

No lead tanks, marked with Christian symbols or otherwise, are known from the area.[19] Equally there is no direct, unambiguous, evidence of buildings which seem to have been used as fourth- or early fifth-century churches, and no ecclesiastical place-names which seem to be so early. The only find of relevant buried or concealed silverware which parallels those from eastern Britain is that from Somerleigh Court, Dorchester, which appears to have come from a ruined building.[20] It contained a hoard of some 50 silver coins (*siliquae*) deposited apparently about 400, with a silver 'prong' and five silver spoons (Fig. 29), one of which is incised with AUGUSTINE (?) VIVAS and another with a fish.[21] Neither reference is necessarily Christian. Objects with VIVAS and an engraved fish are known from the Thetford treasure[22] which may be essentially pagan, with special reference to Faunus and with only incidental Christian connotations in a few of its elements.[23] 'Prongs' of this general type, perhaps like the one engraved with a chi-rho from the small Canterbury silver hoard, may have been used to take bread out of wine (like the well-known strainers) during the liturgy[24] and, if this is true, then not merely is the Christian character of the pieces established, but the likelihood that they came from some kind of church, and although this need not have been in Dorchester, it seems probable that it was. These pieces have

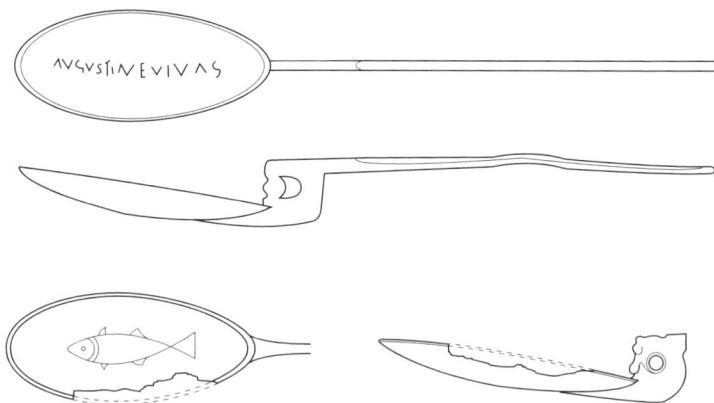

Figure 29 Two of the silver spoons from the Dorchester find (after Mawer 1995, p. 118)

19.   The lead casket, inscribed and with a *chi-rho* which Petts (pp. 105–7) describes as East Stoke, Somerset, comes from East Stoke, Nottinghamshire: see Thomas, *Christianity* (1981), pp. 124–5; *JRS*: 1955, p. 147.
20.   Mawer, *Evidence for Christianity in Roman Britain* (1995), pp. 45, 57–8. A. Robertson, *An Inventory of Romano-British Coin Hoards* (2000), p. 372, no. 1523. For comparable material see Watts, *Christians and Pagans*, pp. 204, 208.
21.   For discussion of VIVAS and the fish motif, see C. Mawer, *Evidence for Christianity in Roman Britain* (1995), pp. 23, 275–6.
22.   C. Johns and T. Potter, *The Thetford Treasure: Roman Jewellery and Silver* (1983).
23.   Watts, *Christians and Pagans*, sees these as linked with lapsed Christians, pp. 153–8.
24.   For possible practices, see DeBhaldraitle 1991 in Watts, *Christians and Pagans*, pp. 231–3. For Canterbury pick, see Mawer, *Evidence*, p. 58.

sometimes been interpreted as toothpicks[25] although they are singularly poorly adapted for this use. Perhaps, like many objects in the late Roman world, they could be used either as high-quality tableware or during the celebration of the Eucharist and therefore much depends upon their context and decoration.[26] The Somerleigh piece is plain and the whole group is ambiguous. Viewed from a different perspective, the Somerleigh hoard forms one in a considerable sequence of valuable metal depositions, and we may anticipate its discussion[27] by saying here that these may be primarily social markers, the specific religious allegiances of which are not their most important feature.

Small portable objects with *chi-rho* symbols from the peninsula include the silver pendant from Shepton Mallet, which has the rare developed form,[28] and the stratified sherd from Exeter (although the sherd from Greyhound Yard, Dorchester, thought to have been scratched with a Christian symbol, probably carries an identification mark, and that from Gatcombe should similarly be eliminated[29]). Two silver signet rings, one with an early *chi-rho* and the other a late one and a bird and two branches come from a villa site at Fifehead Neville, Dorset[30]. There are the compasses (Fig. 30) from Dorchester[31] and a doubtful *chi-rho* scratched on a now lost flat shale roundel from Colliton Park.[32] To this group should be added the fourth-century votive lead tablet from the sacred spring at Bath which reads:

> Whether pagan or Christian, whosoever, whether man or woman, whether boy or girl, whether slave or free, has stolen from me, Annianus, son of Matutina, six silver coins from my purse, you, lady goddess, are to exact them from him.[33]

---

25. C. Johns, 'A late Roman silver toothpick with the Christian monogram', *Antiq. J.*, 72 (1992): 179–80.

26. Mawer, *Evidence*, pp. 57–8.

27. See pp. 89–92 below.

28. Doubts have sometimes been expressed about the authenticity of this amulet because its silver composition is unlike Roman metal but very like that of modern sterling silver; see P. Leach, 'The Roman site at Fosse Lane, Shepton Mallet', *PSANHS*, 134 (1990): 47–55, and 'Shepton Mallet, Mendip Business Park, Fosse Lane, ST632427', *PSANHS*, 135 (1991): 148–50; and also C. Johns in P. Leach *et al.*, *Fosse Lane: Excavations of a Romano-British Roadside Settlement at Shepton Mallet, Somerset* (2001), pp. 257–60. However, its stratigraphy seems secure. The simple punched *chi-rho* can be compared with that on a silver cross-bow brooch *c.* 400, said to be from Sussex: Mawer, *Evidence* (1995), pp. 79, 129.

29. Mawer, *Evidence*, pp. 37, 38. A few star forms are also known, which have been seen as variants of sacred monogram forms. These include the symbol on the tombstone from Sea Mills (J. Bennett, *Sea Mills: The Roman Town of Abonae* (1985), pp. 61–3), probably a simple ornament, the disc with a compact cross, pierced for suspension from a grave at Camerton (J. Brenan, *Hanging Bowls and their Contexts* (1991), p. 194), probably Christian, the pewter bowl from Bath, see p. 92 note 82, and the Wemberham pavement, see p. 86, Fig. 32.

30. *Proc. Soc. Antiq.*, Series 2 (1881–3): 68; a gold ring from Suffolk has a bird pecking a bush and an early *chi-rho*, see Petts, *Christianity*, 2003, pp. 110–11.

31. M. Henig, 'A probable chi-rho stamp on a pair of compasses', *PDNHAS*, 105 (1983): 159.

32. Mawer, *Evidence*, p. 38.

33. R. Tomlin, 'The curse tablets', in B. Cunliffe, *The Temple of Sulis Minerva at Bath Vol. II: The Finds from the Sacred Spring* (1988), pp. 232–4. Similar formulae without the pagan/Christian reference are used on many of the tablets. Many of these are [very] fragmentary so it is possible that this was not the only use of the phrase.

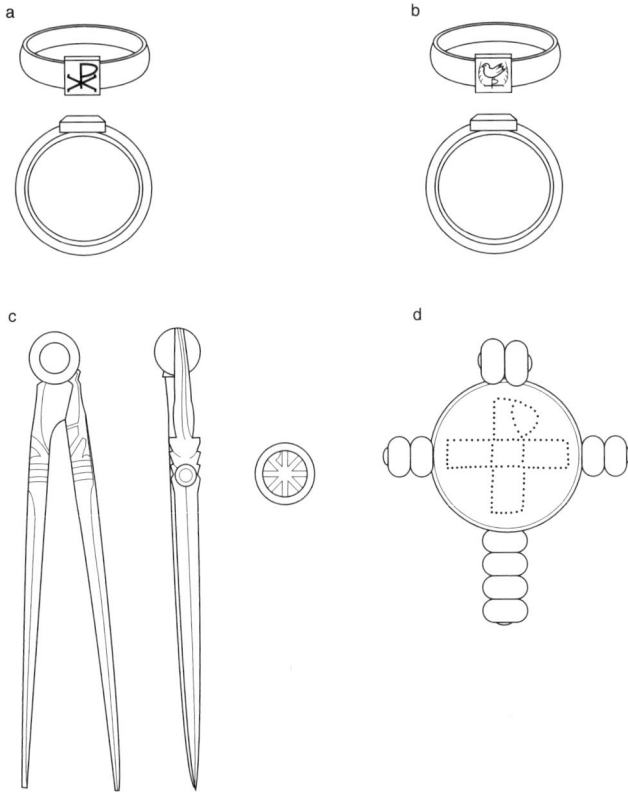

Figure 30 Small objects with chi-rho symbols: two finger-rings from Fifehead Neville, Dorset (after Mawer 1995, p. 127); bronze compasses from Dorchester (after Henig 1983, Fig. 4); and silver pendant from Shepton Mallet (after Leach *et al.* 2001, Fig. 73.2)

The juxtaposition of GEN[TILI]S meaning 'pagan' and CH[R]ISTIANUS, the first recorded use of the word in Roman Britain, is intriguing and, with its use of terminology derived from the New Testament, testifies at the least to the recognition in fourth-century Bath of widespread Christian identity.[34]

The Shepton Mallet pendant (Fig. 30), with its developed form of the chi-rho symbol, fits in with other evidence from contemporary Britain which suggests the presence of committed self-conscious groups of Christians practising their religion in a way recognizably like those attached to churches in Gaul or northern Italy, about whom we are better informed. The Bath tablet suggests the same, not because it itself comes from a Christian context – the sacred spring was a pagan centre – but because its standard ritual gabble demonstrates how normal a part of the social scene both Christians and pagans were. For the rest we have no way of knowing whether the pieces represent a public statement of special allegiance or simply a vague hope of good luck. In general, such pieces have little weight alone, and can only operate as a supporting cast for more substantial evidence.

---

34.   Mawer, *Evidence*, p. 85.

This leaves us with the vexed question of the interpretation to be placed upon the clearly expensive and important mosaic pavements discovered at a number of villa sites in the eastern area of the peninsula, particularly that at Hinton St Mary. If our understanding of villa mosaics is to develop, this can only be by considering each villa as a whole entity, as well as 'the changing historical context of the production of both the villas and the mosaics',[35] because architecture objectifies, but also influences, changing cultural patterns of human thought, feeling and action, and provides a way of bringing together ideas about human identity, with symbolic expressions of meaning drawn from mythological or philosophical representations. It seems clear that, by the fourth century, villas had become the most important stage for exhibitions of social power, following the move away from the cities in the third century, and that (perhaps increasingly insecure) economic surplus was now invested here in personal and familial rather than community display: hence the desire to have impressive suites of rooms situated to operate as formal, semi-public reception areas, and to spend resources on mosaic floors. Lines of the site and access across a villa could be operated to create separate zones centred on a great room with a major mosaic pavement, itself intended to express the control and harmony which, it was hoped, the villa as a whole complex would achieve in the living social sphere.[36]

This is the background against which the pavements at Hinton St Mary and Frampton should be seen (Fig. 31a, b). The larger, square part of the Hinton

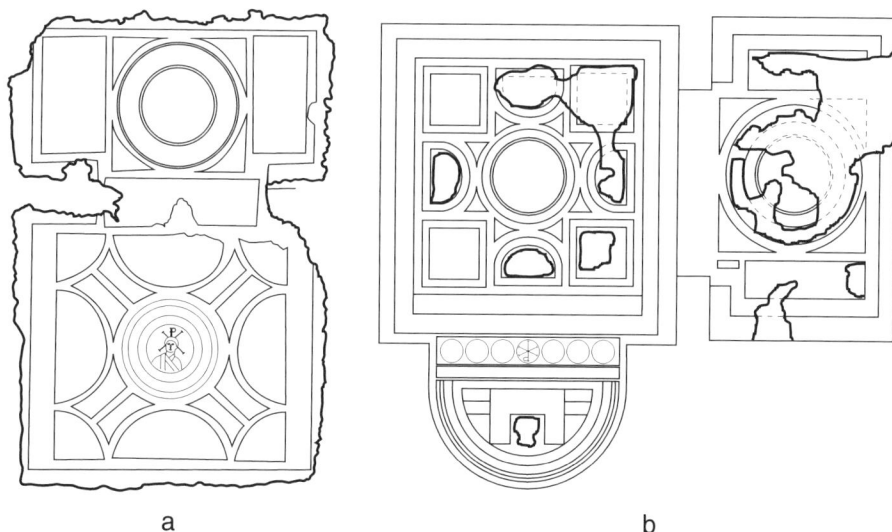

a   b

Figure 31 Simplified plans of the mosaic pavements at (a) Hinton St Mary (after Toynbee 1968, Plate 1); (b) Frampton (after Toynbee 1968, Plate 2, 1813)

---

35.   S. Scott, 'Symbols of power and nature: the Orpheus mosaics of fourth-century Britain and their architectural contexts', *TRAC*, 2 (1995): 105. See also 'A theoretical framework for the study of Romano-British villa mosaics', *TRAC*, 1 (1992): 103–14; *Art and Society in Fourth-century Britain: Villa Mosaics in Context* (2000); and J. Smith, *Roman Villas: A Study in Social Structures* (1997).

36.   As suggested by Scott in her analysis of the layout at Woodchester, Gloucestershire. Scott, 'A theoretical framework', and *Art and Society*.

Figure 32 Wemberham (after Reade 1885, opp. p. 68) showing layout of principal elements (not to scale)

pavement carries the famous central roundel with the head and shoulders of a figure almost universally interpreted as Christ, with a *chi-rho* behind his head and flanked by two pomegranates, set within four registers of geometric ornament; the four corner sections show four similar busts, variously interpreted, but perhaps meant to be the Evangelists in the guise of the four winds;[37] and the four lunettes on each side show scenes of hounds and harts which may be interpreted as allegorical hunts.[38] The pavement floored a space of 6 m by 9 m, divided into two unequal parts by short cross walls. The smaller, rectangular, part shows in its roundel a scene of Bellerophon slaying the Chimera, flanked by two broad rectangles showing more hunting scenes, and it is connected to the main square by a geometric panel.

Continental parallels may be instructive. At Aquileia the important double church built by Bishop Theodore early in the fourth century featured, among other scenes, a magnificent seascape with Jonah and the Whale across the eastern end of the floor of the southern hall; and within the seascape is a clypeus with an inscription referring to Theodore in laudatory terms, and a *chi-rho* monogram placed above his name.[39] It is worth noting that Theodore attended the Council of Arles in 314, where we know there were British bishops. A number of imperial contexts are known, including the column of Arcadius at Constantinople, the diptych of Probus showing Honorius and, most significantly, the *Genera Missorium* depicting Valentinian I or II, where the *chi-rho* fills the nimbus around the emperor's head.[40] Clearly, all these

---

37.   J. Toynbee, 'The Christian Roman mosaic, Hinton St Mary, Dorset', *PDNHAS*, 85 (1964): 116–21; 'A new Roman pavement found in Dorset', *J. Roman Studies*, 54 (1964): 1–4.

38.   R. Eriksen, 'Syncretistic symbolism and the Christian Roman mosaic at Hinton St Mary: a closer reading', *PDNHAS*, 102 (1980): 43–50.

39.   M. Humphries, *Communities of the Blessed: Social Environment and Religious Change in Northern Italy, AD 200–400* (1999), pp. 74–9, 164–5.

40.   Humphries, *Communities of the Blessed*, p. 164, note 107.

representations of the emperor were part of an iconography which fused Christian and imperial authority,[41] and that at Aquileia showed a bishop claiming similar power. The floor position of the Hinton bust, something often noted as strange, is matched by iconic pavements like that at Aquileia, and there may be another example at the church of St Helen-on-the-Walls, Aldwark, York. The cult of St Helen there relates in some way to the fourth-century mosaic, with a female head, on the site.[42] Helen was, of course, a member of the Constantinian imperial family which had special links with York. All these parallels demonstrate the complexity of symbolism, of both content and position, which Late Antique iconography could embrace, and they remind us that contemporary viewers may have seen the Hinton bust as a 'Christian imperial' image rather than a simple image of Christ.[43]

Similar arguments apply to the pavement from the site at Frampton, which may not have been a 'normal villa', but rather an outbuilding of some kind, or even a shrine (which was Lyson's view in 1813), given the reported find of a very large column fragment which could derive from a Jupiter Column.[44] As at Hinton,[45] assessment is bedevilled by the lack of any plan of the site, but Lyson's 1813 drawing of the mosaic shows that it covered a smaller rectangular room opening onto a larger, squarish one, and, at right angles to this larger room, an apse picturing a cantharus and a *chi-rho* in a roundel on the chord. The pavement as a whole features Neptune and dolphins, Venus and Adonis, Bacchus, hunting scenes and various verse texts together with an apparently important scene showing Bellerophon and the Chimera. A second mosaic seems[46] to derive its pictures from Ovid's *Metamorphoses*, perhaps from an illustrated copy owned by the master of the villa. In a general cultural sense, this fits in with the similar literary pavement from Low Ham[47] featuring the *Aeneid*.

In 1818, John Bellamy gave a rather confused account of a mosaic pavement at Halstock which he said featured a circle in each corner 'each containing a head of a warrior in his helmet, the back of which is represented having a double cross in an oblique position from right to left, extending far over the shoulders'.[48] A drawing made by Thomas Rackett in 1818 (Fig. 33) of these corner features does not show the symbols behind the heads very clearly; they may just be decorative motifs, but until

---

41. See P. Brown, *Society and the Holy in Late Antiquity* (1982), pp. 13–14.

42. J. Magilton, *The Church of St Helen-on-the-Walls, Aldwark, York, The Archaeology of York*, 10 (1), pp. 6, 16 (1980).

43. K. Painter, 'Villas and Christianity', in G. Sieveking (ed.), *Prehistoric and Romano-British Studies* (1971), pp. 156–75. The *chi-rho* stamps on some of the ten pewter ingots (? from Mendip) from the Thames, together with the name Syagrius, presumably the owner/shipper, also hint at an 'official' use of the symbol, see Frere *et al.*, *Inscriptions* (1990), pp. 68–70. The Christian belt sets (Petts, *Christianity*, 2003, pp. 112–13), the signet rings and the cross-bow brooch, probably an 'official' piece, suggest the same.

44. R. Farrar, 'The Frampton villa, Maiden Newton', *PDNHAS*, 78 (1956): 81–3; M. Henig, 'James Engleheart's drawing of a mosaic at Frampton, 1794', *PDNHAS*, 106 (1984): 143–6; C. Green, 'The "Frampton Villa", Maiden Newton: a note on the monument and its context', *PDNHAS*, 116 (1994): 133–5. For a gnostic view of the Frampton main pavement, see Perring (2002), pp. 74–83.

45. C. Taylor, 'The later history of the Roman site at Hinton St Mary, Dorset', *British Museum Quarterly*, 5 (32): 31–5 (1967).

46. Henig, 'James Engleheart's drawing', pp. 143–6.

47. J. Smith, 'Villas as a key to social structure', in M. Todd (ed.), *Studies in the Romano-British Villa* (1978), pp. 149–85.

48. J. Bellamy, 'Tesselated pavement near Halstock, Dorset', *Gent's Mag.*, January (1818): 5–6.

Figure 33 Thomas Rackett's 1818 drawing of the Halstock mosaic (after Lucas 1991, Plate 3)

(unless) the pavement reappears, we cannot know what the symbols really were.[49] It is worth noting that we do possess a plan of the Halstock villa (Fig. 34), and that Room 1.9, the most likely original site of the pavement, measures approx. 9 m by 5 m, belongs to a suite of rooms on an alignment different from that of the rest of the building and is situated where this suite joins the main line. Room 1.9 may have begun as part of a bath block, which could explain the original odd alignment, but it had undergone at least two revamps in its lifetime. At Wemberham, Yatton, Somerset, another old excavation produced a mosaic pavement featuring a central equal-armed floriate cross within an elaborate pattern of squares and circles, not overtly Christian, but capable of being viewed by its owners as of Christian significance (Fig. 32). Wemberham was a very substantial, wealthy site on the Somerset Yeo, which produced iron slag and may even have had a wharf on the river. An inhumation in a stone coffin was found nearby in Great Wemberham Meadow.[50]

With this villa group, it is worth mentioning the Fifehead Neville site. Fifehead seems to have been a large courtyard villa with mosaics, one apparently with four dolphins placed concentrically around seven fishes, a central cantharus and what seem to be pomegranates, suggesting another series of equivocal symbols with links to the mystery religions, but capable of a Christian interpretation. The coin sequence ran up to 400.[51] The *chi-rho*-marked rings, together with 'a silver necklace or girdle-

49. Apparently inspired by these cross-forms, Bellamy went on to speculate that the central head had 'a sort of irregular ruff or crest' and 'if this has an analogy to our Lord's thorny crown on the cross, it is most certainly an awkward representation'. R. Lucas, 'The Halstock mosaic found in 1817', *PDNHAS*, 113 (1991): 133–8, has published a drawing made by Thomas Rackett in 1818 of this pavement which shows Medusa in the centre, together with a note on the drawing saying 'The head of Medusa should have been placed with the chin towards the North', suggesting that his drawing was not particularly accurate. The key issue is not the central portrait, but the symbols behind the three surviving corner heads.

50. R. Reade, 'The Roman villa at Great Wemberham in Yatton', *PSANHS*, 31 (1885): 64–73; R. Scarth, 'The Roman villa at Wemberham', *PSANHS*, 31 (1885): 1–9.

51. *Proc. Soc. Antiq.* (1881–3): 68; *PDNHAS*, 24 (1903): 74–6, 172–7; 49 (1928): 92. For the mosaics, see D. Smith, 'The mosaic pavements', in A. Rivet (ed.), *The Roman Villa in Britain* (1969), figs 3.30, p. 119, and refs there.

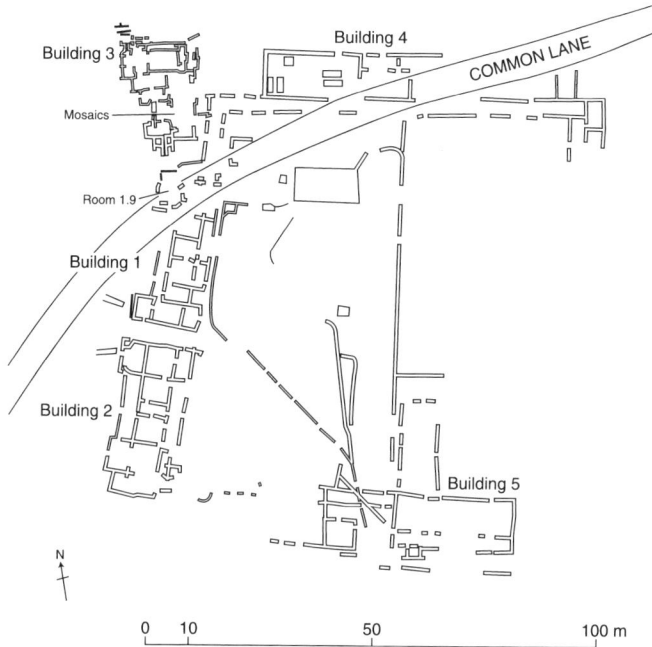

Figure 34 Plan of Halstock villa (after Lucas 1991, Plate 3)

fastener, and nine bronze bracelets with fragments of others' were hidden under a stone in a small hollow cut in the concrete floor at the west end of the main block. The rings are quite simple and do not suggest anything episcopal, but seem to be Christian signet rings of the kind Clement of Alexandria, Cyprian and Jerome recommended.[52] The purpose behind the deposit of what seems to be a mixed collection of jewellery is unclear, and the cultural links represented by the hoard may have as much to do with those surrounding other deposits at villas and elsewhere, as with any specifically Christian purpose.

Encouraged by the apparent capacity demonstrated at Hinton and Frampton on the part of the local gentry to review scenes drawn from classical mythology, particularly that related to the mystery cults, in a Christian light as representing the triumph of good and the future bliss of Paradise, some commentators have drawn into the discussion the Bellerophon pavements known from the western provinces and the famous British series of Orpheus mosaics.[53] The now partially reconstructed early fourth-century pavement from a villa at Newton St Loe, north-west of Bath, has a central feature showing Orpheus playing his lyre surrounded by lively animals and trees. Another apparently Orpheus pavement has been recorded at Whatley near

---

52.   Mawer, *Evidence*, pp. 66–8.
53.   Painter, 'Villas and Christianity', p. 171. For a strong discussion, see especially M. Henig, 'The Lullingstone mosaic: art, religion and letters in a fourth-century villa', *Mosaic*, 24 (1997): 4–7; for south-western Orpheus mosaics, and Newton St Loe in particular, see A. Beeson and M. Henig, 'Orpheus and the Newton St Loe mosaic pavement in Bristol City Museum', in L. Keen (ed.), *Almost the Richest City: Bristol in the Middle Ages* (1997), esp. pp. 1–3, figs 1 and 2.

Newton St Loe, and these form part of the famous group of similar pavements concentrated in the Cotswolds. The origin of the Orpheus depicted on the mosaics may lie in the Hunter-God who also appears on stone statues and reliefs which formed a prominent feature of these villas. Orpheus seems to symbolize the control the landowning class were able to exercise over nature, and over their estates, including the peasants tied to the land and the slaves, who worked it.

Also relevant is the question of the 'house churches' which have been identified at villa sites in Britain, primarily at Lullingstone, on the basis of its layout, the mosaic inscription containing cryptic Christian messages and *orans*-style wall paintings;[54] and conceivably at Woodchester[55] and Littlecote.[56] The *nymphaeum* at Chedworth may have been Christianized by the addition of *chi-rho* carvings for use as a baptistry, and this has prompted the suggestion that the octagonal pools[57] known from south-western villas, particularly Dewlish (Dorset), Lufton (Somerset) and Holcombe (Devon) were also for Christian use, given that they were entered separately rather than through the usual sequence of rooms. However, this is very tentative. The well-attested redesignation of villas as monasteries in Gaul and Italy belongs mainly to the fifth and sixth centuries not to the fourth, whether or not it is relevant to Britain.[58]

On balance, and with the possible exception of Lullingstone, these villa plans and pavements seem to present a complex, sophisticated picture which cannot be interpreted as a straightforward presentation of Christian belief (and even at Lullingstone we find the use of word games). The layouts at Hinton, Frampton and elsewhere which have been seen as suggesting a church form, either in their shape or in their separation from the main villa block, can figure equally well as grand reception areas offering different levels of access and privacy, intended to emphasize the status of the villa owners. Church plans were coming to be used in the same way as members of the clerical hierarchy began to see themselves as separate from their flocks, and it may be the similarity of the role of senior clergy and laymen which accounts for the similarity of plan across churches and villas.

The villa pavements seem to represent an upper-class, and probably genuine, interest in metaphysical speculation and the spiritual life. This draws on the range of refigured mythologies, particularly featuring Bellerophon, Orpheus and mystery religions, including Christianity, to produce statements, the precise elements and emphases of which will differ from place to place, and which in any case had much to do with assertions of control and status. The plate and personal ornaments, which presumably belonged mostly to members of the same class, may have been used in the same way. Perhaps they should be seen with rather than, as is usual, separate from the parallel range of pieces with Orphic, Bacchic and similar 'pagan' motifs, and all of these be regarded as the portable spiritual equivalents of the pavements.

---

54.   G. Meates, *The Roman Villa at Lullingstone, Kent Vol. 1: The Site* (1979); Henig, 'The Lullingstone mosaic', pp. 4–7.

55.   G. Clarke, 'The Roman villa at Woodchester', *Britannia*, 13 (1982): 197–228.

56.   Watts, *Christians and Pagans*, pp. 130–40, and refs there.

57.   For Cledworth see Thomas, *Christianity*, pp. 219–20; for octagonal pools, see Perring, *Roman House* (2002), p. 182.

58.   J. Percival, 'Villas and monasteries in late Roman Gaul', *J. Ecclesiastical History*, 48 (1): 1–21 (1997).

Ritual and ceremony: hoards of coins and pewter ware

Religious activity without an obvious Christian focus was a force to be reckoned with in the late Empire. The Dionysiac cult, with its strong mystery character, was important, and a thyrsus-like shaft of the kind used in its ceremonies was found at the hill-fort site of Dinorben (Denbigh) in a building of Roman date.[59] Similarly, the end of Mithraic worship and the relationship of this to Christian activity is a very complex subject.[60] For Britain, and for the south-west particularly, the notion of a late Roman 'pagan revival' has been challenged[61] but this is probably the wrong way to look at the evidence. Rather, the period of transition from Roman to post-Roman saw some significant approaches to the meanings which material culture could be used to generate, which drew on earlier, indeed perhaps ancient, traditions, but used them to help to reshape contemporary social life. Metal objects and lower status (presumably) things, such as leather goods and pottery, and bodies treated as material culture were brought into the frame, and both their immediate and their broader contexts seem to be important. The same ceremonial or ritual activity seems to be represented by at least some – perhaps many – of the deposits of coins, even if some of these represent uncollected personal savings or similar commercially based deposits.[62]

The recording of coin hoards is often very poor, but it seems that some of the hoards, particularly the bronze ones, contained coins of very mixed dates. From Weymouth,[63] for example, came a solid mass of some 4400 bronze coins of dates ranging from 260–269 to 393–423, while the coins from Horton[64] (Dorset) had dates between 138–161 and 364–378. This suggests either that coins were deposited over a lengthy period of time, or that they could be retained for decades before they were

---

59. V. Hutchinson, *Bacchus in Roman Britain: The Evidence for his Cult* (1986), p. 117.
60. For broad discussion, see E. Sauer, *The End of Paganism in the North-western Provinces of the Roman Empire: The Example of the Mithras Cult* (1996).
61. K. Dark, *Civitas to Kingdom* (1994), pp. 32–6.
62. The nature of the coin and other material group finds, conventionally but usefully called 'hoards', has been much debated: see M. Millett, 'Treasure: interpreting Roman hoards', in S. Cottam *et al.* (eds), *Proceedings of the Fourth Annual Theoretical Roman Archaeological Conference, Durham 1994* (1995), pp. 100–5; R. Reece, 'Interpreting Roman hoards', *World Archaeology*, 20 (2): 261–9 (1988); N. Aitchison, 'Roman wealth, native ritual: coin hoards within and beyond Roman Britain', *World Archaeology*, 20 (2): 270–84 (1988); C. Johns, 'Romano-British precious-metal hoards: some comments on Martin Millett's paper', in Cottam *et al.*, *TRAC Proceedings 1994* (1995), pp. 109–17; C. Johns, 'The classification and interpretation of Romano-British treasures', *Britannia*, 27 (1996): 1–16; and, very cogently, M. Fulford, 'Links with the past: pervasive "ritual" behaviour in Roman Britain', *Britannia*, 32 (2001): 199–218. Johns ('Classification and interpretation') has produced a strongly reasoned paper making the 'rational case' and suggests a classification system for treasure hoard character which can be summarized as: personal, family or institutional banking resource; temple or church wealth; storage of thefts; workshop/craftsman's stock; votive wealth at a temple; official pay chests; and accidental loss. Against this can be briefly urged that there is no reason why 'treasure', i.e., found groups of gold and silver whether ingot, made-up goods or scrap, should necessarily be distinguished from similar groups of base metals, not to mention other materials. When the broader range of depositions is taken into account the picture looks different. To me the issues look very similar to those confronting Bronze Age specialists (S. Pearce, *The Bronze Age Metalwork of South-western Britain* (1983); R. Taylor, *Bronze Age Hoards* (1993)) or indeed within contemporary hoarding and collecting (S. Pearce, *Collecting in Contemporary Culture* (1998)). It is hoped to revisit these issues.
63. Robertson, *Inventory of Coin Hoards*, p. 372.
64. *Ibid.*, p. 340.

deposited (or both), which means that giving a final date for the practice is difficult, and could run late into the fifth century. The group contains the well-recognized run of some 20 hoards of silver *siliquae*,[65] but these are accompanied by around 40 bronze hoards which have attracted less attention.[66] There are also a few gold coins, four from the cult site at Maiden Castle, two from the St Agnes, Cornwall area, and singles from the hill-fort at Carn Brae (from which come scattered bronze coins also), from Newton Abbot and from east Devon which it is hard to believe were either simple losses, or personal savings which it was intended to recover, given the status of gold coins.[67]

The extent to which a genuine money economy operated in the late Western Empire generally and in south-western Britain in particular is difficult to estimate, but the relative lack of, especially, small denomination bronzes from local settlement sites suggests that it did not. Gold and silver coins seem to have been used primarily as counters for tax reckoning, and for giving to soldiers and bureaucrats; since we know that large gold coins were minted to act as imperial gifts to senior personnel, it is possible that other coin distributions had been coming to be viewed generally as 'donatives' rather than 'pay'. Equally, at a period when objects such as officers' belt buckles were being used to create visible hierarchies, and pictures of the emperor conveyed the sense of his real presence, the imperial icons on both sides of the coins of all three metals may have had a compelling significance which it is difficult for us to recapture. The *romanitas* which the coins embodied would have enabled the local groups, many of their members, perhaps, belonging to the upper class, to see in the depositions which they made a powerful way of uniting the idea of the universal Empire with local needs and ceremonies.

Pewter, which was usually made up into dishes and bowls which match the designs of those in silver, may have been regarded as a kind of base silver, particularly since the Mendip lead, used in the south-western pieces, yielded small amounts of silver in the first century through the cupellation process. Sometimes coins and pewter were brought together, as at Carhayes and Carnon, Cornwall, where vessels[68] accompanied large amounts of the poor-quality third-century *antoniniani*, which may, or may not, have been buried as early as around 280. Groups of fourth-century pewter ware are known from Brislington,[69] Bossens[70] and Bath,[71]

65. A. Burnett, 'Clipped *siliquae* and the end of Roman Britain', *Britannia*, 15 (1984): 163–8.

66. For Romano-British coin hoards in general, Robertson, *Inventory of Coin Hoards*, is indispensable. For Cornish finds, see Robertson, *Inventory*, p. 482, Devon p. 483, Dorset p. 488. See also S. Archer, 'Late Roman gold and silver coin hoards in Britain: a gazetteer', in P. Casey, *The End of Roman Britain* (1979), pp. 29–64, and S. Pearce, 'Late roman coinage in south-west Britain', *TDA*, 102 (1970): 19–33.

67. S. Cleary, *The Ending of Roman Britain* (1989), pp. 95–8.

68. N. Beagrie, 'The Romano-British pewter industry', *Britannia*, 20 (1989): 169–91, and refs there. See also Frere *et al.*, *Roman Inscriptions*, pp. 68–70 for details of a pewter ingots find from London.

69. K. Brannigan, 'The Romano-British villa at Brislington', *PSANHS*, 116 (1972): 78–85.

70. A. Fox, *South-West England* (1973), p. 182; M. Green, *The Religions of Civilian Roman Britain* (1976), p. 198 (St Erth).

71. B. Cunliffe, *The Temple of Sulis Minerva at Bath Vol. II: The Finds from the Sacred Spring* (1988), pp. 9–21, plates 8, 9, 13, 14, 15. Well-documented recent pewter finds like that from a peat mire at Abercynafon, Powys, underline the ritual or ceremonial nature of some pewter deposits, C. Earwood, H. Cool and P. Northover, 'Two pewter bowls from a mire in south Wales', *Britannia*, 32 (2001): 279–85.

and the two silver finds, from Fifehead Neville and Dorchester, have already been discussed.

The contexts of these groups are as significant as their contents, although sadly all too often we have very limited contextual information. West Hill, Corfe, Dorset, produced over 20 fourth-century coins running down to Gratian (367–383),[72] for example, and Holway (near Taunton) yielded over 400 coins running down to the very late fourth century;[73] these presumably mark significant sites. Many of the *siliquae* hoards seem to have been buried on or near Roman roads,[74] like perhaps that from Honiton, Devon (Fig. 35), and 'Holway' hints at a similar situation. Some of the *siliquae* finds from central Somerset may have come from watery or boggy sites, classic contexts in European prehistory for social acts of material deposition. In the Somerset Shapwick area have been found, apart from a *siliquae* hoard, a repaired bronze hanging bowl, a wooden stave tankard with bronze fittings which would be at home in the late Iron Age, various pewter vessels associated with more silver coins and a hoard of bronze coins mostly minted in the late fourth century.[75] Collectively, all this suggests a sacred site in the peat bog. A significant run of coin finds largely of bronze come from ancient barrows[76] which seem to have offered upstanding monuments in the landscape where the present could be linked with the ancestors.

A further run of coin finds come from hill-fort sites where they form part of the evidence that hill-forts were significant in the late fourth/fifth centuries.[77] Poundbury hill-fort had 90 coins, mostly bronzes of Constantius II under a flat stone in the south-west corner of the enclosure;[78] a large hoard of late third/fourth-century bronze

Figure 35 Two silver coins (*siliquae*) of the eighteen found at Honiton, Devon, in a natural hollow nodule of ironstone: left, *siliqua* of Arcadius (383–408), with a reverse showing a figure representing the Virtue of Rome, minted at Trier; right, *silique* of Valens (364–78) with the reverse indicating the mint of Siscia. Exeter City Museum (photo, author)

72.   Robertson, *Inventory*, p. 350.

73.   *Ibid.*, p. 391.

74.   St. J. O'Neil, 'A hoard of late Roman coins from Northamptonshire, its parallels and significances', *Arch. J.*, 90 (1933): 290–305.

75.   Robertson, *Inventory*, pp. 258–9, 364, 390–1.

76.   L. Grinsell, 'Somerset barrows: Part I, west and south', *PSANHS*, 113 (1969): 1–43; 'Somerset barrows: Part II, north and east', *PSANHS*, 115 (1971): 44–132; 'The barrows of north Devon', *PDAS*, 28 (1970): 95–129; *Dorset Barrows Supplement* (1982); 'The barrows of Dartmoor', *PDAS*, 36 (1978): 85–180.

77.   See pp. 94–6.

78.   A. Robertson, 'The Poundbury hoard of Roman fourth-century copies and their prototypes', *Numismatic Chronicle*, 11 (1952): 87–95; Robertson, *Inventory*, pp. 238–9, 364.

coins was found in a pot inside Kings Castle, Wiveliscombe;[79] Cadbury Tiverton had a humble hoard of eight poor-quality third-century coins; and a coin find from Blaise Castle ran up to AD 353.[80] Ham Hill had a complex sequence of at least six hoards, running from Domitian (AD 81–96) to the fourth century.[81] All these finds may represent community efforts to contact the 'other worlds' and to express group solidarity.

Wells, shafts, shrines and hill-forts

Some pewter finds, sometimes accompanied by coins, come from deliberately dug shafts which, as a class, seem to have been regarded for a very long time as entrances to the underworld. Amongst the wealth of mixed finds from the Sacred Spring at Bath were coins, pewter pieces and a mould for casting amulets of pewter and lead, and, of course, the lead/pewter curse tablets,[82] also known from Pagans Hill.[83] At Bossens, St Erth, a shaft some 36 ft deep was found in 1756 and from it were taken a pewter jug and disk, which had been cut down from a larger piece and which carried a scratched inscription dedicating it to Mars by Aelius Modestus, with a central 'R' in another script; the shaft had stone weights and other objects.[84] At the Brislington villa (Fig. 36) the well shaft behind the house produced seven pewter vessels, together with pottery, iron objects, both human and animal bones, building material, personal items and a single coin of Constantine II, all in a stratification[85] which seems to be not a tidying-up of rubbish, still less a clearing-up of destruction following the Amianus Marcellinus' (dubious) account of the great barbarian raid of 367, but rather the ritual offerings of significant material of the kind well known in Iron Age and Roman religious contexts, but often contemplated only with reluctance at Romanized sites like forts and villas.

Similar shafts with similar material have been found at Cadbury hill-fort (Tiverton),[86] where a shaft 54 ft deep produced many bronze bracelets, rings, beads, human bones, horse teeth and pottery; and, at Pagans Hill, a well contained building

---

79.   H. St. J. Gray and H. Mattingley, 'A hoard of late Roman coins found on Castle Hill, Wiveliscombe', *PSANHS*, 92 (1946): 65–75. Robertson, *Inventory*, p. 364.

80.   P. Hill, 'The Cadbury Castle hoard', in A. Fox, 'Roman objects from Cadbury Castle', *TDA*, 84 (1952): 113–14. Robertson, *Inventory*, p. 139 for Cadbury. For Blaise, G. Boon, 'Roman coins from Blaise Castle, Bristol', *Proc. U. Brist. Spel. Soc.*, 3 (1957): 7–8; Robertson, *Inventory*, p. 422.

81.   I. Burrow, *Hillfort and Hill-top Settlement in Somerset in the First to Eighth Centuries AD* (1981), pp. 268–77. Robertson, *Inventory*, pp. 115, 132, 146, 188, 413.

82.   Cunliffe, *Sacred Spring*, coins pp. 281–358, pewter pp. 9–21, mould pp. 24–5, tablets pp. 59–277. The Sacred Spring also produced a bowl made of pewter pieces soldered together, decorated with an interlace cross dating ?*c.* 500. If Christian, this hints at an ambivalent view of the spring, and it may link with the concealing of a relief of Diana's hound by placing the block upside down during repaving at the site, but this may be post-500; see B. Cunliffe, *Roman Bath* (1995), pp. 115–17.

83.   P. Rahtz and L. Watts, 'Pagans Hill revisited', *Arch. J.*, 146 (1989): 346; Cunliffe, *Sacred Spring*, pp. 60–1.

84.   Fox, *South-West England*, p. 182; Green, *Religions*, p. 198.

85.   R. Poulton and E. Scott, 'The hoarding, deposition and use of pewter in Roman Britain', *TRAC*, 2 (1995): 115–32. A similar broadly contemporary pattern appears at Chew Park villa, where the well had a mass of material including a copper jug, a pewter jug, two ox-skulls and the wooden fragments recording a legal transaction; P. Rahtz and E. Greenfield, *Excavations at Chew Valley* (1977), pp. 57–64.

86.   Fox, 'Roman objects', pp. 105–14.

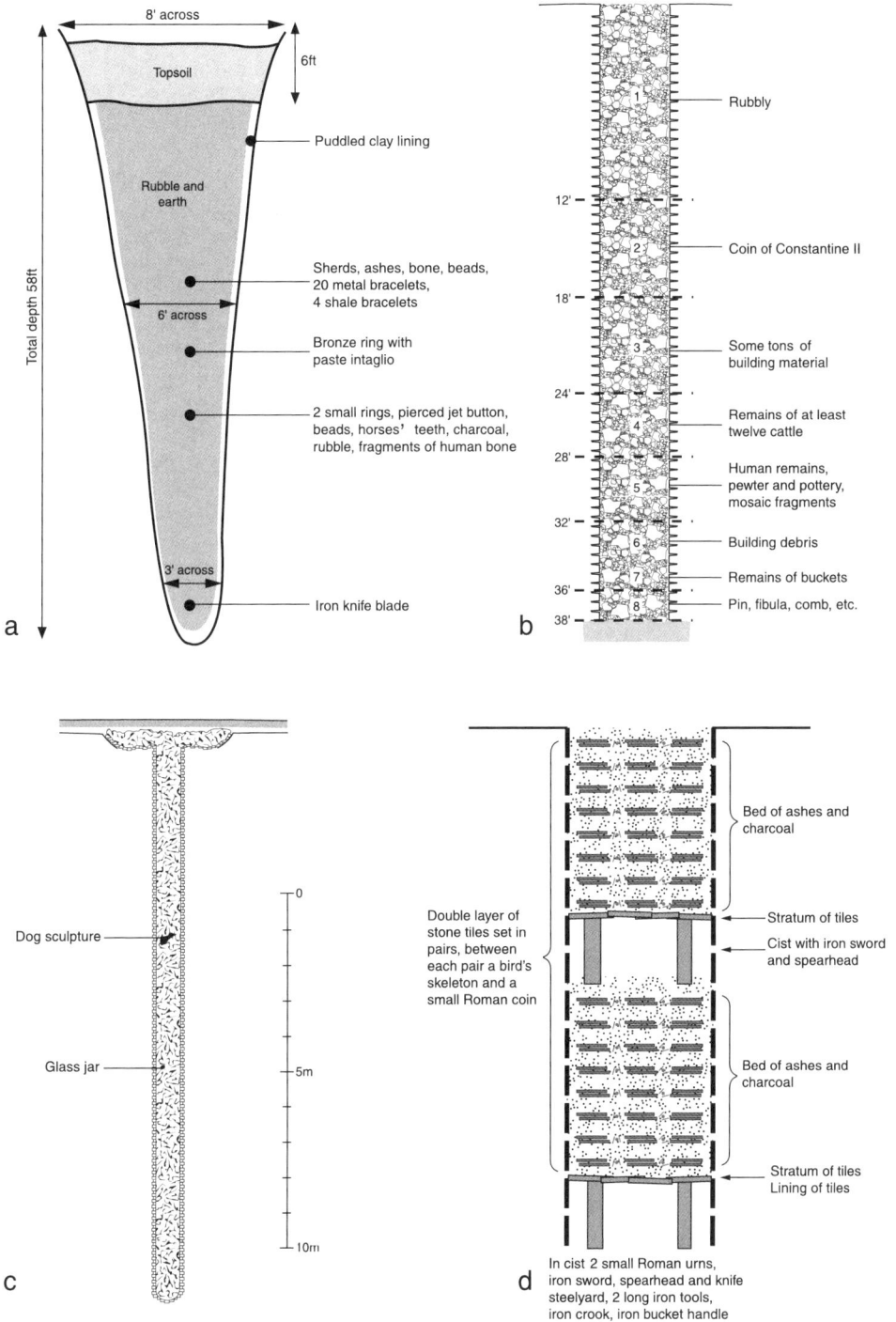

Figure 36 Shafts and their contents at (a) Cadbury Tiverton (reconstructed from descriptions); (b) Brislington villa (after reconstruction by Poulton and Scott 1995, Fig. 21); (c) Pagans Hill temple site (after Boon 1989, Fig. 2); and (d) Jordan Hill (after Ross 1968, Fig. 64). Scales various

debris together with the sculpture of a dog, of third- or fourth-century date and probably part of a cult statue, and a fine glass jar of the seventh century, which may or may not suggest that the well continued as a ceremonial site up to this time.[87] At Jordan Hill, Weymouth, a similar shaft had careful deposits of pottery, weapons, ironware, ashes, coins and bird bones. These give a context for apparently humbler sites, like Soldier's Well at Woodbury hill-fort, Devon, from near which came a piece of fourth-century beaker. One of the Ilchester cemeteries also had a shaft, filled with domestic animals. There may have been similar shafts at Sturminster Marshall (in the common field of the parish) and at Littleton near Blandford, and within the hill-fort at Maiden Castle, all Dorset, although dating evidence for these is poor. Two shafts at Winterbourne Kingston, Dorset, seem to have been part of a shaft-and-pit complex, and one shaft had a characteristic range of probably fourth-century material.[88]

It is quite possible, too, that caves[89] were regarded as similar entrances to the underworld, and that some, at least, of the generally poorly recorded material from caves, which has appeared in all the areas where caves exist, is part of this broad ceremonial activity. At Kent's Cavern, near Torquay, the poorly recorded finds included a spoon. The two levels of Gough's Cave in Cheddar Gorge both seem to have had large quantities of pottery and other material including a fine zoomorphic pin, and people seem to have been leaving objects there at least up to *c.* 400. The adjacent Long Hole, together with the Slitter, a large dump of material immediately below it, had impressive decorative bronze work, and well over 350 coins, some of fourth-century date. Wookey Hole, also on Mendip, had large quantities of pottery, large numbers of coins, some of the fourth century, including a possible hoard, and lead or pewter bars. Interestingly, the fourth chamber was used as a burial ground. Wookey, with its entrance in the cliff face and its underground river, is an extremely impressive site, and the finds from it strongly suggest its importance as a sacred place.

These sites must be seen as part of the tally of certain or potential shrines which were attracting attention in the fourth, and possibly into the earlier fifth, centuries. Of these, some in Dorset, like Duncliffe Hill, Maiden Castle and Jordan Hill, Weymouth,[90] or in Somerset, like Lamyatt,[91] Brean Down,[92] Pagans Hill, Bury

87. G. Boon, 'A Roman sculpture rehabilitated: the Pagans Hill dog', *Britannia*, 20 (1989): 201–19; Rahtz and Watts, 'Pagans Hill revisited', pp. 330–71.

88. Woodbury, H. Miles, 'Excavations at Woodbury Castle, east Devon, 1971', *PDAS*, 33 (1975): 183–208; Dorset, Green, *Religions*, pp. 200–2.

89. K. Brannigan and M. Dearne (eds), *Romano-British Cavemen. Cave Use in Roman Britain* (1992), esp. pp. 98–106. White Woman's Hole, on Mendip, had evidence that the counterfeiting of coins was being carried out there in the third century; the lead/pewter bars from Wookey have been noted, and coin copies with evidence of metalworking also comes from Camerton (see pp. 104, 109). The Mendip sites were obviously well placed to forge coins. It is usually assumed that counterfeiting was carried out for 'normal/modern' reasons, i.e., to create spendable money, but perhaps the coins were mainly, or largely, needed in order to carry out the depositions of coin hoards which are a feature of the late third century, and their manufacture was less a subversive economic activity than a necessary ceremonial one.

90. H. Henig and L. Keen, 'Figures from Duncliffe Hill', *PDNHAS*, 106 (1984): 147–8; Green, *Religions*, p. 201.

91. R. Leech, 'The excavation of a Romano-Celtic temple and a later cemetery on Lamyatt Beacon, Somerset', *Britannia*, 17 (1986): 259–328

92. A. ApSimon, 'The Roman temple on Brean Down', *Proc. U. Brist. Spel. Soc.*, 10 (1964–5): 195–258.

Hill,[93] Brent Knoll[94] and Cadbury Tickenham,[95] tended to have structures, presumably formal temple buildings. There are fewer further west, although Trevelgue[96] had structures of some kind, and Nor'nour[97] on the Scilly Islands had very rich offerings. Most of the known sites produced coins and pottery, although dating is exceptionally difficult because, among the usual problems of poor recording, much hinges also on the extent to which we are seeing the reuse of material which was already old, sometimes very old. Cadbury Congresbury[98] produced small quantities of first-century Samian ware, and similar material may have featured at other sites, judging by early records, but the stratigraphy at Congresbury where the Samian sherds were concentrated in one area suggested that this represented the deployment of heirloom-type pot when it was already reduced to sherds. The common finds of early and later coins may, for all we know, represent the same kind of thinking, and coins, or pottery, could have carried on being used like this well into the fifth, or even the sixth centuries. Samian sherds also came from a barrow at Melcombe Horsey, Dorset, with a coin of Antoninus Pius, and another in Dorset at Pamphill had an iron object, oyster shell and 'Romano-British potsherds',[99] but putting a date on their deposition is hazardous.

What is conspicuous about the run of sites reasonably seen as shrines on other grounds is the number which were sited within prehistoric hill-forts, and many of those which were not are on prominent hilltops. The equation can be put the other way: in Somerset, which has seen the most detailed work, of the 28 recognized hill-forts, fifteen have produced late Roman material. This brings into the frame the large number of hill-fort sites from which have come finds of Roman material, usually pot and coins, and suggests that these may be the equivalent sites to the built temples among communities who could not afford, or, and perhaps more probably, did not wish, to associate their activities with Roman-style buildings. There is not much evidence in the south-west that such sites were being refurbished as defensive positions, or as centres from which rule could be exercised, earlier than *c.* 450, in contrast to Ireland or Scotland,[100] and the Rhine/Danube frontiers[101] and northern Gaul;[102] and where, as at Lydney, Gloucestershire, earthworks do seem to have built in the Roman period, the context was clearly religious.[103]

The hill-forts themselves are very mixed, ranging from very large and impressive earthwork circuits like Maiden Castle, Ham Hill and Cadbury Castle, which are assumed to have been tribal or subtribal centres in the Iron Age, to relatively humble

---

93. *Proc. U. Brist. Spel. Soc.*, 3 (1929): 8–24.
94. Page, *VCH Somerset*, Vol. 1, p. 482.
95. I. Burrow and J. Bennett, 'A Romano-British relief from Cadbury Camp, Tickenham (Avon)', *Rescue Archaeology in the Bristol Area* (1979), pp. 1–5.
96. C. Andrew, 'Trevelgue Head promontory fort', *JRS*, 30 (1940): 175.
97. D. Dudley, 'Excavations at Nor'nour in the Isles of Scilly 1962–6', *Arch. J.*, 124 (1967): 1–64.
98. Burrow, *Hillfort*, esp. pp. 280–90.
99. Grinsell, *Dorset Barrows Supplement*, pp. 119, 122.
100. B. Raftery, 'Freestone Hill, Co Kilkenny: and Iron Age hillfort and Bronze Age cairn', *Proc. Royal Irish Academy*, 68C (1969): 1–108.
101. H. Petrikovits, 'Fortifications in the north-western Roman Empire from the third to the fifth centuries AD 1971', *JRS*, 61 (1971): 178–218.
102. Knight (1999c), p. 44, and refs there; see also Whightman, *Gallia Belgica* (1985) for general account.
103. See P. Casey and B. Hoffman, 'Excavations at the Roman temple in Lydney Park, Gloucestershire', *Antiq. J.*, 79 (1999): 81–144.

enclosures like those at Daws Castle, Somerset, and Stoke Hill (Exeter), which presumably had only ever had a local significance; but what they share is the sense of ancient presence in the landscape.[104] The number of such sites is large (some 30 in Cornwall, over 40 in Devon and nearly 30 in Dorset enclosing an area of over 3 acres) so evidence of more late/post-Roman activity probably awaits discovery, although the incorporation of the interior of the fort at Bathampton into a field system, for example, demonstrates that not all such sites were held sacred.[105] Nevertheless, the character of the activity at the hill-forts, and some hilltops, suggests that they were recognized as significant places which were the proper sites for collective, local ritual activity when social developments needed such embodiment. There may be a regional dimension to these developments, since a similar level of activity on hill-fort sites is known from the area of Gloucestershire,[106] and also, but apparently with fewer numbers of sites involved and perhaps some important differences in date and character, in the Welsh Marches.

Ritual use of animal and human body parts

The finds of metal and other objects, and their relationship to shafts, temple sites and, more broadly, hill-forts and hilltops, collectively suggest that groups of any kind of material found in any circumstances should probably not be taken at their face value. Nails have a widespread symbolic dimension related to their power of 'fixing' things, as in Christian tradition they did at the Crucifixion.[107] They were used to 'fix' material within temples, where curse tablets and sheet metal offerings, like the bronze plaque from Maiden Castle depicting Minerva, were hammered up, and this dimension may cast a new light on the hobnails used in the boots sometimes buried with the dead in the west, as at Fordington (Dorchester), Todbere (Dorset) or Little Spittle (Ilchester),[108] and also upon the nails used in wooden coffins at Ilchester and Poundbury; such coffins were a new fashion in the area, and coffin nails have not yet lost their imaginative power.

This, linked with the bone remains in the shafts, suggests that the manipulation of animals and humans formed a part of the ritual practice. Animal sacrifice certainly, and human sacrifice very probably, was part of the Iron Age mindset throughout western Europe, including Italy. Although the killing of humans for ritual purposes alone was forbidden under Roman law, the ceremonial, indeed spectacular, public

---

104.   A factor perhaps most obviously visible at Treryn Dinas (Corn) where the site encloses an impressive landscape focusing on the Men Amber (the balanced Logan Rock), if Herring ('The cliff castles and hillforts of West Penwith in the light of recent work at Maen Castle and Treryn Dinas', *Corn. Arch.*, 33 (1994): 40–56) is right in identifying Roman/post-Roman activity here.

105.   The enclosure at Kingdown (Som) may have been built, and the ramparts at Stokeleigh (Bristol) altered, during the Roman period, but the dating evidence is susceptible to various interpretations. See I. Burrow, 'Roman material from hillforts', in Casey, *End of Roman Britain*, p. 217.

106.   See Burrow, 'Roman material', pp. 212–29.

107.   D. Dungworth, 'Mystifying Roman nails: *clavus annalis, defixiones* and *minkisi*', in C. Forcey, J. Hawthorne and R. Witcher (eds), *Proceedings of the Seventh Annual Theoretical Roman Archaeological Conference, Nottingham, 1997* (1998), pp. 148–9.

108.   R. Philpott, *Burial Practices in Roman Britain. A Survey of Grave Treatment and Furnishing, AD 43–410* (1991), pp. 305–9.

execution of condemned criminals was considered proper, and evidence is growing from post-Roman Britain to suggest that here too the line between execution and sacrifice was a very thin one, since both involved a ceremonial death and special treatment of the remains (something which remained true in England until the early nineteenth century): we shall never know if the Brislington human body parts arrived in the shaft in this kind of way. The burning of the Great Room at Keynsham villa, with one human 'victim of the event' left in the debris, and the burnt human bones associated with mid-fourth-century coins at West Park villa and with ash and charcoal at Bowood (six skeletons), may not be so very different.[109] The building inside Ham Hill hill-fort, whether a 'villa' or part of some shrine complex, had a coin series running down to Valentinian II (375–392) and two decapitated burials with the skulls missing. On the northern spur, a hoard with coins running up to 306 was found with a female skull and 'weapons'.[110]

Conceivably, the conspicuous number of infants' bodies which were buried in and around villas, as at Churchie Bushes (Bawdrip, Somerset), found inside a third-century building,[111] or at other kinds of sites, like the eleven infants found buried in the inner ditch at Kingsdown hill-fort, have a similar ritual purpose, not necessarily involving infanticide, rather than the manipulation of the bodies of those who had died. The same may be true of the severing of the head after death but before burial, as at Long Sutton, Sea Mills and Ilchester (all Somerset), and the occasional burial with a dog, as again at Ilchester, and at Alington Avenue (Dorchester; two, one also decapitated).[112]

This may be the broad context of the adult burials which have appeared within ancient barrows, often known only from very confused records, particularly in Cornwall. Two cremations were inserted into barrows at Wimborne St Giles, one with a coin of Valentinian I and the other with iron nails in a cist, and one inhumation in a possible stone coffin in one at Winterborne Monkton, Dorset.[113] The Clandon Barrow, Dorset, is recorded as having two intrusive skeletons in stone-lined graves high in the stratigraphy, but these had no direct dating evidence.[114] A barrow near Corfe Castle had nine extended skeletons, seven in stone-lined graves, one near Handley a burial in the ditch with traces of coffin and coffin nails, one at Bincombe, which had a man, women and child covered 'with large stones', and one at Tyneham which had seven skeletons, one with a cup and one apparently with the head severed from the body.[115] In Somerset, intrusive Roman inhumations may have come from a number of barrows including two of the Stone Easton barrow group, with extended inhumations of a youth and young child in one and two adults, possibly with a coin of Constantine I, in the other. The style of these burials does not suggest that they were executed criminals, but rather seems to show the developing desire for connection with the past.[116]

109.   K. Brannigan, 'Villa settlement in the West Country', in K. Brannigan and P. Fowler (eds), *The Roman West Country* (1976), esp. p. 137.
110.   Burrow, *Hillfort*, esp. pp. 280–90.
111.   Leech 1980, p. 354 and refs there.
112.   Philpott, *Burial Practices* (1991), pp. 360–3.
113.   L. Grinsell, *Dorset Barrows* (1959), p. 40.
114.   *Ibid.*, p. 152.
115.   *Ibid.*, pp. 103, 114, 138.
116.   Grinsell, *Somerset Barrows*, 1971, pp. 119–20.

The evident interest in human bodies and body parts,[117] and in practices which treat them in particular, special ways, provides links with the spread of Christian practice and belief, since these depended significantly upon the manipulation of martyrial body parts, which, in the cases of some of the most famous early martyrs, came from spectacular contexts in which they, like Christ, had died as condemned criminals. If much of this body-based ritual had been semi-secret before the fourth century, then the chance of its open practice within some smattering of Christian sentiment helps to explain its greater visibility after *c.* 300, and also bears on the attractiveness of the Church as an institution.

Some social implications

We do not know who was responsible for gathering the deposited material and resourcing the shrines, or how this was undertaken, and we can only speculate about reasons. The transitional circumstances of which the deposits and the shrines are a part suggest that they were intended to help social transformations by using material, some of it, at least, like the imperial portraits on the coins, capable of expressing continuity, in new ways to make legitimate new social and political conditions. Community surplus, in the hands of important families which during the fourth century had been devoted to villas, mosaic floors and the hospitality which went with them, began to be used as the fifth century progressed to promote new kinds of local recognition and interdependence. We might go even further and see in these practices the creation of relationships which were intended to be local and socially vertical, to take in all conditions of people, rather than geographically wide and focused upon just the upper class, and to link them with a new emphasis on kinship (actual or supposed) rather than economic ties, and on the embedding of economic relations within networks of shared kin and shared ideology.

The number of villas which seem to suffer lower-status occupation around the turn of the fourth/fifth centuries is notorious (Fig. 37). Keynsham saw reoccupation, but both here and at Kings Weston large hearths were built on main corridors; at West Coker occupation was in a poorly built structure; at Whittington, where the coins run down to Honorius, the latest people put a hearth in a room and used old roof rafters; at Dewlish, an inserted hearth built of reused tiles from the roof had a coin of Honorius.[118] Similar events happened at Lufton (Fig. 38), Kings Weston and Brislington. Traditional explanations of this destruction and 'squatter' activity invoke raiders, flights to the cities and accidental fires, which are indeed a serious possibility but seem to have been suspiciously frequent, if they were not the action of hostiles. A different kind of explanation suggests a desire on the part of elite families to live more in the 'squalid' style of the surrounding local communities.

---

117.   For general discussions of these issues, see H. Williams, 'The ancient monument in Romano-British ritual practices', in Forcey *et al., Proceedings, Seventh Annual TRAC* (1997), pp. 71–86; C. Holtorf, 'Megaliths, monumentality and memory', *Arch. Review from Cambridge*, 14 (2): 45–65 (1997); K. Dark, 'Roman period activity at prehistoric ritual monuments in Britain and the Armorican peninsula', *Conference of Theoretical Roman Archaeology*, 1 (1993): 134–46; R. Isserlin, 'Thinking the unthinkable: human sacrifice in Roman Britain', in K. Meadows, C. Lemke and J. Heron (eds), *Proceedings of the Sixth Annual Theoretical Archaeology Conference, Sheffield, 1996* (1997), pp. 99–100.

118.   Brannigan, 'Villa settlement', pp. 120–4.

Lufton

Kings Weston

gravelled court

N

0 10 20 30 40 50 m

0   110 m N

Brislington   ○ well

N

0 10 20 30 40 50 ft

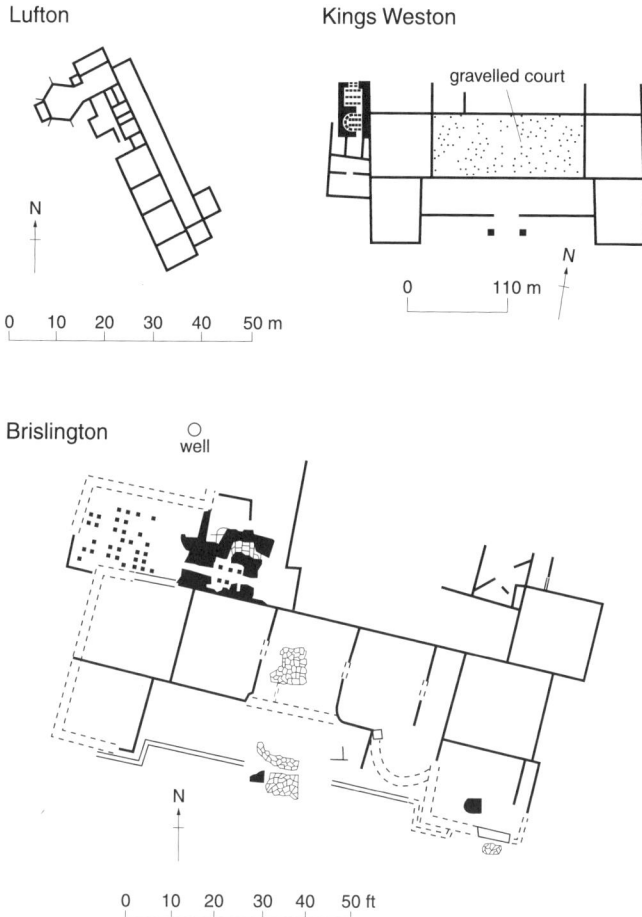

Figure 37 Late occupation at villa sites: Lufton, where small rooms were inserted just beyond the six-sided bathhouse (after Hayward 1972); Kings Weston, where hearths were built in the main areas (Brannigan 1976, Fig. 25); and Brislington, which was burnt down with bodies thrown into the well (after Brannigan 1972, pp. 78–85)

This would presumably require a very powerful motive, which might have been provided by the need to retain a grip on the loyalties of local people which, given the collapse of any central authority, could only be achieved at the hearts-and-minds level represented by 'lower' living, and by visible devotions of wealth which we see in the hoards and shrines. Related to this may be tendency to put in cheap partition walls to create more, smaller spaces, as at Lufton, Bratton Seymour and perhaps Spoonley Wood. These are reminiscent of similar reorganizations of the space in the temples at Pagans Hill, Lamyatt and Maiden Castle.

Regional differences may be perceptible (Fig. 39). The pewter finds[119] are mostly

119. Beagrie, 'Romano-British pewter industry', pp. 169–91.

Figure 38 General view from the west of the villa at Lufton, Yeovil, during excavation in 1946. In the foreground is Room 1 with mosaic pavement, and behind it the octagonal plunge bath. Ovens and low-grade buildings were inserted into the area behind the bath in the late fourth/fifth centuries (photo: L. Hayward)

south of a line from the Wash to the Severn, with concentrations in East Anglia and Somerset. The hoards of silver and those of gold have a very similar distribution with an even more marked concentration in Somerset,[120] and both are strikingly similar to that of group finds of copper alloy and ironwork.[121] Although in the south and south-west this could be linked with the activities of the villa-possessing class, this cannot be true of East Anglia,[122] where the concentration of treasure hoards also appears. Conceivably, the eastern finds may represent the activities of relatively few very wealthy people (including perhaps senior imperial officials?), while what we see in the south and south-west is a scaled-down version matching the larger number of relatively wealthy landed proprietors whether 'villa' owners or not, where coins take the place of plate, although the group finds of everyday materials are perhaps very similar in spirit. The same point appears in the distribution of hilltop and hill-fort shrines and related sites, which are again concentrated in the west. All this, in turn, may be pointing towards some of the reasons why the landholding class in the south-west was able to resist 'Germanic' political pressure, represented by the gradual expansion of what became Wessex, for as long as they did.

120.   Archer, 'Gold and silver hoards', pp. 29–64.
121.   W. Manning, 'Ironwork hoards in Iron Age and Roman Britain', *Britannia*, 3 (1972): 246–9; A. Ross, 'Shafts, pits, wells – sanctuaries of the Belgic Britons?', in J. Coles and D. Simpson, *Studies in Ancient Europe* (1968), pp. 256–85.
122.   M. Millett, 'Treasure', pp. 100–5.

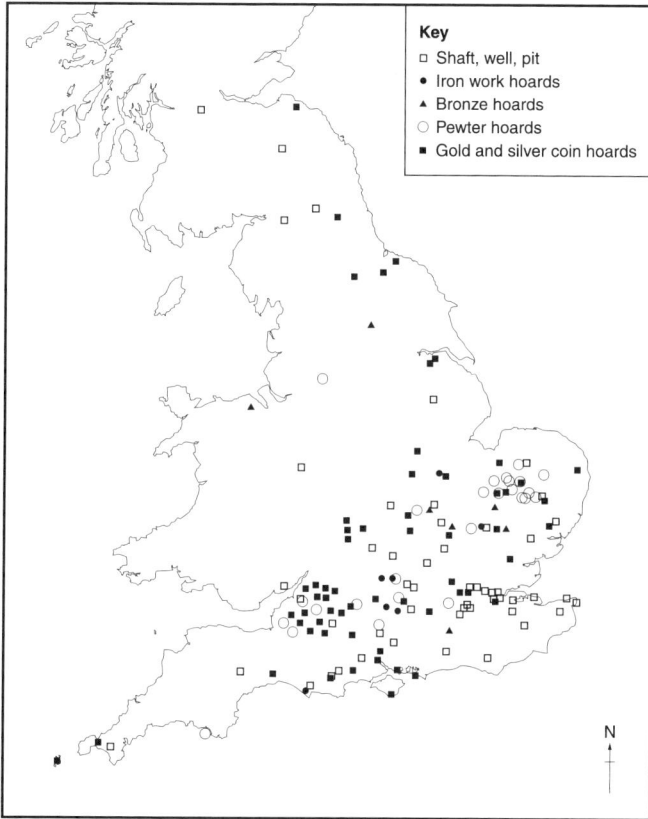

Figure 39 Regional distributions of shafts/pits/wells with deposited material (after Ross 1968, Fig. 67), ironwork hoards, bronze vessel hoards (both after Manning 1972, Figs 2, 4), pewter hoards (after Beagrie 1989, Fig. 3) and later fourth-century hoards of gold and silver coins (after Archer 1979, Fig. 1)

Different although they may be in detail, the coin and other hoards, the material deposited in ancient barrows, the shafts and shrines and the emphasis on hilltops and hill-forts, underline the creation of new focuses in the landscape in the fourth and possibly fifth centuries, away from villas where these existed. The importance given to human bodies similarly created a range of new focal sites, all with roles in the new society which was emerging.

The living and the dead

The disposal of the dead in any society is likely to take us to the core of that society's social and symbolic structure, not necessarily as a one-to-one reflection of its 'normal' or diurnal concerns but nevertheless as a profoundly instructive light on its vision of itself. Moreover, as most of us have experienced, death and disposal in each individual instance seems to happen very quickly in the perspective of those who remain, and engenders a heightened state of emotion and confusion in which the observance of traditional and perceived 'right' forms becomes very important. This makes for conservative practices, and means that any major change, whether very slow or relatively speedy, is likely to be a part of fundamental changes in the social fabric.

During the third century in Gaul and in Britain, richly furnished burials ceased, as inhumation rather than cremation became the general burial rite.[123] This involved extended burial in an earth-dug grave equipped with only a few simple objects like pottery vessels, coins, combs and personal ornaments such as bracelets and hair pins which, it appears, the corpse was often wearing. As the fourth century progressed, even these became rarer, so that, by about 370, 'unfurnished extended inhumation was the burial rite of the vast majority of Romano-Britains'.[124] The dead were often coffined in stone or lead sarcophagi if the family was important enough, or in wood, and stone-lined burial 'cists', perhaps regarded as the cheap equivalent, became fashionable especially in areas with suitable stone. Buried bodies take up a good deal of space and are upsetting if disturbed too soon, so large, organized cemeteries developed in places with substantial populations. This kind of development, allowing for local and regional variations, took place generally across the western imperial provinces in Late Antiquity, and it forms the crucial context for British, including south-west British, developments.

Long-cist cemeteries of this broad kind are relatively common in western Britain, and seem to have their roots in the local Iron Age traditions.[125] As a result, and in view of their character, they are exceptionally difficult to date: in default of dating evidence, any specific cemetery could belong anywhere within a range running from the late Iron/early Roman period to the later Middle Ages, and efforts to create regional chronologies based upon the details of cist shape are not very convincing. A further complicating factor revolves around the difficulties of obtaining useful data from parish churchyards which are still in use and have been for centuries. It may be that those cemeteries which are discovered by chance and can be reasonably fully excavated are those which 'failed' for whatever reason, and information from them may skew our picture. Some dating is forthcoming from Welsh sites. At Capel Eithin, Anglesey,[126] a large cemetery of full and partial cists and dug graves was dated *c.* 400–700. A cist grave cut into the rampart of a small, apparently Iron Age enclosure at Caer Bayvil, Dyfed, shows a C14 date of AD 665±60.[127] In Scotland, the numerous cemeteries of this type are seen as belonging within this broad date range, and, at Midlothian, the inscribed Catstone in association with a cist cemetery supports this date.[128]

West of the Tamar, some 28 cemeteries of this broad type are known,[129] but most have sparse excavation and dating details. Some are clearly full medieval – at Porthminster Beach, St Ives, for example, 'two stone coffins' containing leaden

---

123.   Philpott, *Burial Practices*, pp. 222–6.
124.   *Ibid.*, p. 226.
125.   R. Whimster, *Burial Practices in Iron Age Britain* (1981), esp. pp. 104–8.
126.   H. Jones, 'Early medieval cemeteries in Wales', in N. Edwards and A. Lane (eds), *Early Medieval Settlement in Wales AD 400–1100* (1992), pp. 90–103.
127.   Jones, 'Early medieval cemeteries', pp. 99–100.
128.   E. Alcock, 'Burials and cemeteries in Scotland', in Edwards and Lane, *Early Medieval Settlement* (1992), pp. 125–9, esp. p. 126.
129.   A. Preston-Jones, 'The excavation of a long-cist cemetery at Carnanton, St Mawgan, 1943', *Corn. Arch.*, 23 (1984): 157–79.

chalices were found, while those on the Towans, Lelant, may have been of Iron Age date, although they were at the chapel site.[130] At Tresco Abbey (Scilly), three cist graves, one perhaps with a small cross-marked stone, were found near an inscribed stone, and on Samson a number of graves 'of Christian type' with a tiny seventh/eighth-century stone building in which there was a large stone bowl or mortar, and a timber hut were found on the beach, while, on Tean, a sixth/seventh-century cemetery of fifteen graves was dug into an abandoned hut and rubbish heap where, again, a small stone chapel was built around 700.[131] Possibly pre-Norman cemeteries are also known from Hugh Town (St Mary's) and St Agnes. These are presumed to predate the formal Christian presence on the site, and it is noticeable that relatively few of the sites matured into full parish churches.

Some 56 relevant sites are known in south Somerset/north Dorset,[132] and seven further sites largely concentrated in east Somerset.[133] The complex site at Charlton Mackrell has produced at least 50 burials from an extensive distribution which included a range of alignments, one burial in a lead coffin, one in a wooden coffin, cist graves and associated structures and finds running into the fourth century.[134] A 'Romano-British' cemetery 'was destroyed' just south of the church at Portbury, Avon, in 1972, and at least 43 east–west burials post-dating fourth-century pottery turned up on the opposite side of the Gordano Valley at Portishead.[135] Broadly similar sites appear at West Camel, Queen Camel, West Harptree near Pagans Hill[136] and Long Sutton: all these are in Somerset and the list tells its own story of how common this kind of site was, even though dating is difficult. Eastbury Farm, Carhampton,[137] some distance from the church, produced evidence of an extensive graveyard. Radiocarbon dating suggested a later medieval focus but some of the remains may be earlier.

Similar sites are known in Dorset at, for example, Bradford Abbas and various locations in the Sherborne area. At Langham near Gillingham at least a hundred east–west burials, with two brooches and 'rough pottery' (apparently Roman), were

---

130. *Ibid.*, pp. 157–62.
131. C. Thomas, 'Hermits on islands or priests in a landscape?', *Cornish Studies* (1980): 28–44.
132. For full list, see R. Leech, 'Religions and burials in south Somerset and north Dorset', in W. Rodwell, *Temples, Churches and Religion in Roman Britain* (1980), pp. 329–68. They will continue to be recognized for example at Longford Budville, Somerset, see Corcos, *Medieval Settlement*, 2002, p. 39.
133. P. Rahtz, 'Sub-Roman cemeteries in Somerset', in M. Barley and R. Hanson, *Christianity in Britain, 300–700* (1968), pp. 193–5.
134. Burials of a broadly similar type have been found at Holway, Doulting, Western Zoyland, Puckington, Chillington, Shepton Beauchamp, Currel Rivel, Catsgore and Larkhill; see Leech, 'Religions and burials', pp. 329–68, and Rahtz, 'Sub-Roman cemeteries', pp. 193–5.
135. Rahtz, 'Sub-Roman cemeteries', pp. 193–5.
136. As recorded by Revd J. Skinner in his MS of 1830: 'In this bank the quarrymen have found upwards of 100 bodies interred side by side, generally speaking, with their heads to the West, but some North and South . . . I observed a skull . . . of a child not above eight years of age, and a woman afterwards told me she had seen the skull of an infant who had died before its teeth were cut. Small discs of iron have been found near the skeletons . . . the mode of internment . . . the hands crossed on the pudenda. They have also met with a brass fibula or ring with a tongue to it.' Skinner drew this fibula, but with insufficient detail for identification. See Rahtz and Watts, 'Pagans Hill revisited', pp. 334, 338.
137. P. McCrone, 'Carhampton, Eastbury Farm, ST011427', *PSANHS*, 137 (1993): 144.

poorly recorded,[138] and a similarly thin account covers the burial site at Great Down Quarry, Marnhill, where there were over 20 burials, fourth-century coins and a lead coffin.[139] Devon is still sparsely represented, but now at least has the site at Kenn, and the Victorian find of a stone coffin at Branscombe.[140]

If some of the inscribed stones do indeed belong in the late fourth century, then they, and the graveyards with which some of them were associated, belong within this range of cemeteries. Possible candidates would be Beacon Hill, Lundy, where the OTIMI and RESTEUTA inscriptions may be this early, and Lewannick, where both stones have Latin formulae.[141] The mass of sites demonstrates the dating difficulties which they present and the complex traditions which they embody. Some amongst them went out of use at various points between the late Roman and the medieval period, while others survived to become eventually the sites of parish graveyards.

Choice of site is likely to have been significant, and so is the special way in which each cemetery was permitted to develop. Mortuary behaviour relating to the character of the grave and the treatment of the body illuminates our understanding of motives and hopes, and above ground cemetery structures and patterns of usage may show the continuing relationship between the living and the dead.

Mortuary practices

The mortuary characteristics of these late Roman and post-Roman cemeteries may focus upon simple extended inhumations with sparse or non-existent grave-goods, set in simple dug graves, sometimes lined with stone slabs to create a cist, but nevertheless the cemeteries show quite a range of practice within these broad parameters. Generally speaking, the body was laid flat on its back and, judging by the finds of fastenings – which often constitute the grave-goods – sometimes fully clothed. Two children at Cannington,[142] who had grave-goods which included an amber bead, a glass bead of seventh-century type, a perforated Roman coin, a copper alloy bracelet and a brooch which could be as late as the eighth century, show how, as time went on, some grave-goods were included. Similarly, outside Camerton,[143] a settlement on the Fosse Way, there was a large cemetery of over a hundred graves with grave-goods which began in the fourth century and ran on into the seventh century. Sometimes the presence of a pin, as at Cannington,[144] suggests that the body was enclosed in a shroud. Coffins of stone, lead and lead-lined stone are often found in the large cemeteries, and for those who could not afford these, iron fittings demonstrate the use of wooden coffins. What stands out is the effort made, as far as resources would

---

138.   RCHM, *Dorset, Vol. IV North* (1972), pp. 35–6.

139.   Sites and Monuments Register, Dorset.

140.   Weddell 2000; Hutchinson MS notes, published in J. Butler (ed.), *Peter Orlando Hutchinson's Travels in Victorian Devon* (2000), pp. 107, 108, 117–18; See notes 201, 202.

141.   See M. Handley, 'The origins of Christian commemoration in Late Antique Britain', *Early Medieval Europe*, 10 (2001): 177–99. For Lundy, see E. Okasha, *Corpus of Early Christian Inscribed Stones of South-West Britain* (1993), pp. 154–70; for Lewannick, Okasha, *Inscribed Stones*, pp. 146–53.

142.   P. Rahtz, S. Wright and S. Hirst, *Cannington Cemetery* (2000), pp. 89, 96–8.

143.   W. Wedlake, *Excavations at Camerton, Somerset* (1958), pp. 96–7.

144.   Rahtz *et al.*, *Cannington Cemetery*, pp. 5–96.

allow, to give loving care to the dead body; we sense an almost Victorian desire on the part of even the humblest to give and receive a decent burial.

The orientation of burials in these cemeteries has received much attention, and an overall east–west positioning of the graves, with the head pointing to the west, has been taken to be one of their defining characteristics. This regular orientation of graves is not characteristic of clearly pagan later Roman inhumations, but cannot either be taken as an exclusively Christian characteristic since east–west, or solar, orientation was typical both of fourth-century (and, of course, all later) Christians, and of contemporary Germanic pagans.[145] Both may have been encouraged to adopt the custom by influential sun cults, or Germanic practice may have influenced Christian customs, subsequently to be explained in eschatological terms. Also, in a cemetery of any size, where grave visiting was the custom, management would necessitate decisions about the siting of graves, and in such matters fourth-century Christian practice seems to have adopted the most appropriate of contemporary forms.

Although there is, within many of these cemeteries, enough consistency of orientation to suggest deliberate siting of graves, many features individual to a particular cemetery could be important. At Cannington,[146] feet tended to be pointed towards the south of east, while, at Henley Wood,[147] they tended to point to the north of east: this may be because at Cannington the uninterrupted view was towards sunrise, while at Henley Wood it was towards sunset.[148] Orientation could also be affected by existing features, like the old temple at Henley Wood, and by the exact alignment of a focal or original grave.

The practice of single inhumation witnesses to an emotional shift which transcends particular questions of cult and belief, even if the move to inhumation is bound up with a different view of the body 'which was about to have a new life'.[149] This may be linked with the greater emphasis on immortality which the mystery cults engendered, the iconography of which is visible in the mosaic pavements of the wealthy in the West Country villas. More fundamental, perhaps, is the contrast of feeling which cremation and inhumation embody. The cremated body is translated quickly and immediately into hard, dry, bone and ash, which is sad to see and handle, but not disgusting and not directly recognizable. The symbolic context is the transforming power of fire that can turn wet, impressionable clay into hard pottery, or dull ore into shining metal: the dross of the body is burned away and the soul set free. With inhumation, the body of the loved person goes, complete and recognizable, into a dark, wet hole in the earth, there to undergo physical transformations from which the imagination shies away. The consolation of such burial is that the dead is still directly present in bodily form within his or her long home, with which direct contact can be made. There is a more tender sentiment, shot through with images of soft horror, which sharpens feelings of individual transience and of the relationship between the dead, the living and the yet unborn.

---

145.   Macdonald (1977).

146.   Rahtz *et al.*, *Cannington Cemetery*, pp. 115–21.

147.   L. Watts and P. Leach, *Henley Wood, Temples and Cemetery Excavations 1962–69* (1996), pp. 69–75, and see Rahtz *et al.*, *Cannington Cemetery*, pp. 115–21.

148.   Rahtz *et al.*, *Cannington Cemetery*, p.117.

149.   J. Macdonald, 'Pagan religious and burial practices', in R. Reece, *Burial in the Roman World* (1977), p. 37.

Choices of cemetery sites

Anthropological analysis (and common sense) suggests that sites for cemeteries were likely to have been selected partly for practical and partly for affective reasons. Both make the choice of a site with old buildings on it likely, because such 'brownfield' sites are agriculturally difficult, they may already be in a convenient place for access to the settled community and they embody the comfort which perceived continuity brings. As we have seen, the graves on Tean were sited within an old occupation site, and this choice is mirrored at sites across the peninsula, particularly visible in the eastern part when the underlying occupation was materially richer.

The grounds and buildings of villas (and similar complexes) were often recorded as suitable burial sites. At Bradley Hill, Somerset, over 50 east–west burials, some stone-lined and one with a stone coffin, were associated with a fourth to fifth-century homestead, with the earlier group, some of which had coins in their mouths, inside the building.[150] The skull fragment from Stanchester (Curry Rival, Somerset) was associated with a possible villa, and at Seavington St Mary there were skeletons apparently within the villa buildings. At Great Wemberham, Yatton, just west of the villa site, a stone coffin with a lead interior was found.[151] The villa site at Somerton was associated with a substantial cemetery, and at Chapel Leazes Field, Wint Hill, Banwell, there were probably over a hundred oriented graves apparently post-400 in date, on the large villa site.[152] From the villa site, deposited against the footings with a glass beaker, came an early fourth-century Rhenish shallow bowl of greenish glass, engraved on the outside with a hare hunting scene and below the rim with VIVAS CUM TUIS PIE Z[ESES] followed by a palm (perhaps meaning something like 'Long life to you and yours; drink, long life to you'). This seems to be a simple 'good wishes' gesture, with the palm used as a full stop.[153] At Ilchester Mead villa, an extended adult inhumation was found in the ruins of Room I of the north-west wing, and the villa site had a lead coffin. Similar evidence from Dorset villa sites is thin, but this may be in part because some of them became parish church/burial ground sites in the post-800 period and so evidence is discounted or unavailable.

Work in Gaul on the reuse of villa house sites as late/post-Roman burial grounds has suggested that this relatively common practice may well have had the psychological and social purpose of underlining the continuing unity of the living and the dead.[154] Although these adult burials should probably be seen as distinct from the infant burials, and in any case their dating is difficult, they show the importance attached to the use of burial rites to stress social, ancestral and locational connections. The same desire appears in the custom of inserting some burials into ancient mounds, and perhaps in the siting of burial grounds upon the sites of temple complexes, most of which we have already visited as part of the late Roman renewed interest in ancient hill-fort sites, and which must now be considered in greater detail.

---

150. R. Leech, 'The excavation of a Romano-British farmstead and cemetery on Bradley Hill, Somerset', *Britannia*, 12 (1981): 117–252.

151. Page, *VCH Somerset*, Vol. 1, pp. 306–7.

152. See P. Rahtz and L. Watts, 'The end of Roman temples in the west of Britain', in Casey, *End of Roman Britain* (1979), pp. 183–201, and refs there.

153. Mawer, *Evidence*, p. 34.

154. See J. Percival, 'Villas and monasteries in late Roman Gaul', *J. Ecclesiastical History*, 48 (1): 1–21 (1997), and refs there.

Temples and cemeteries

The sites about which we know most cluster thickly in the eastern part of the region (Fig. 40). Substantial excavation at Uley[155] (West Hill, Gloucester) shows that it had a long pre-Roman history as a sacred site, and probably early in the second century AD a stone Romano-Celtic temple was built, together with ancillary buildings, all of which saw various phases of alteration. Interestingly, the temple had valley gutters, which would have debouched into tanks of either stone of lead, which stood

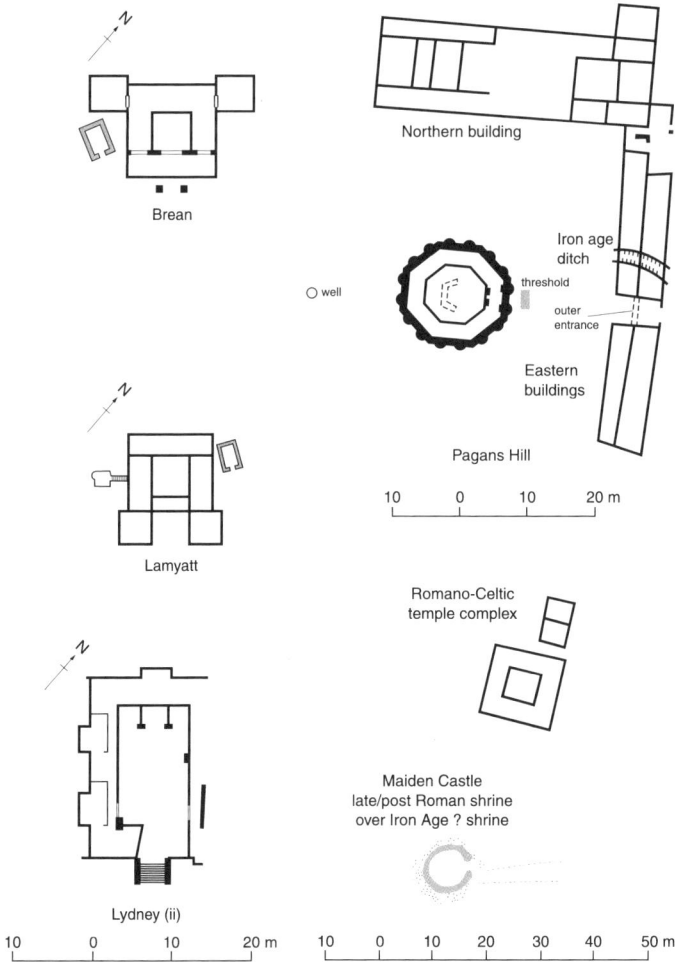

Figure 40 Plans of temples at Brean Down (after ApSimon 1964–5, Fig. 7); Lamyatt (Leech 1986, Fig. 36); Pagans Hill (after Rahtz and Watts 1989, Fig. 2); Maiden Castle temple and circular shrine (after Rahtz and Watts 1979, Fig. 12); and Lydney (Wheeler and Wheeler 1932, Fig. 41)

---

155. A. Woodward and P. Leach, *The Uley Shrines Excavation of a Ritual Complex on West Hill, Uley, Gloucestershire: 1977–9* (1993), for full account.

either side of the temple steps, so evidently such large vessels were used in a range of religious contexts. The principle god was Mercury, whose life-size stone statue stood in the temple, and to whom was offered a wide range of votives, including an interesting fragment of copper alloy sheet, folded in four (as if to 'kill' it?), carrying four Christian scenes, two from the New Testament (Christ healing the centurion's servant, and Christ leading the blind man) and two from the Old Testament (Jonah and the Whale and the Sacrifice of Isaac). The sheet probably dates to the first half of the fourth century.[156]

The religious complex at Henley Wood[157] also saw new activity in the late third-early fourth century where a new temple was built, with a square outer ambulatory surrounding a square cella, and the surrounding ditch progressively filled in. A little later, a second structure was built, possibly of octagonal or polygonal design: this may have been a mausoleum or a shrine, or some combination of the two. Whatever it was, it was dismantled and its site levelled over in the later fourth century, and at the same time the cella entrance was remodelled to make it more impressive. The coin run extended to Arcadius (AD 388–402). The relationship between the temple site and the subsequent cemetery is ambiguous, but it seems that one burial was made on the site when the southern ambulatory wall was still a visible presence, although, thereafter, as more graves were inserted, the wall was robbed for its stone, while the first grave was truncated. It is possible that the final phase of the temple overlapped with the early development of the cemetery, and con-ceivable that it acted as a rather grand focal building for the cemetery, but if so the cemetery continued into the seventh century, by which time the temple had been demolished for at least a century. The Henley burials are presumably of people who lived at or near the hill-fort of Cadbury Congresbury, which itself had a possible late/post-Roman shrine-like circular building, with its bone and copper alloy pendants or 'leaves' and its possibly deliberate burial of amphora handles in the doorway.[158]

The temple complex at Pagans Hill, was built around AD 300 and may have been dedicated to Apollo in his role as healer, with helper-dog. After a hiatus, the site saw a revival in the later fourth century, which involved the octagonal temple and the well or shaft on the cult centre alignment: both shaft and building, perhaps by then in part ruinous, seem to have been used beyond AD 500. Around 380–400, part of the temple collapsed, or had to be demolished, and the worshippers reconstructed and extended what was left to produce an L-shaped building with at least four rooms, and here the cult image may have been venerated for another generation.[159]

This kind of modest construction, involving several relatively small rooms, also appears around the same time at Bath in the small room converted from part of the

156.   *Ibid.*, pp. 107–10; for Uley, see also K. Painter, 'Natives, Romans and Christians at Uley? Questions of continuity of use at sacred sites', *Journal of Roman Archaeology*, 12 (1999): 694–703.

157.   Watts and Leach, *Henley Wood*, esp. pp. 138–44.

158.   Woodward and Leach, *Uley*, p. 141; Rahtz *et al.*, *Cadbury Congresbury 1968–73. Late/Post-Roman Hilltop Settlement* (1992), pp. 242–4.

159.   Rahtz and Watts, 'Pagans Hill revisited'. The superficially suggestive place-name of Pagans Hill seems to be a red herring; it may come from a relatively modern local landowning family called Payne, see Rahtz and Watts, 'Pagans Hill revisited', pp. 335–7. However, Rahtz and Watts believed that 'the building was substantially intact with at least some roofing in position until the thirteenth century' (1989, p. 333). This opens up a range of possibilities.

portico to the reservoir[160] and possibly at Lydney,[161] where reinterpretation of the coin finds[162] suggests serious deterioration of the structures after the mid-fourth century. Again, at Maiden Castle, Wheeler's 'primitive oval hut' on the southern side of the temple has been reinterpreted as a post-Roman shrine[163] and at Maiden Castle, too, the reinterpreted coin sequence suggests use well into the fifth century, when the oval hut and the 'priest's house', perhaps built in two phases, provided similar additional spaces. The shrine of Apollo at Nettleton, Wiltshire, apparently flourishing well into the fifth century, was restructured internally to produce sealed spaces around a cruciform plan which perhaps stimulated the creation of the room reusing column bases and voussoirs in its north-west area: this seemed to have a continuing pagan use. The other part of the formal cella may be contemporary with this room, and, judging by the Theodosian coins from it, performed a similar function. The object at all of these sites seems to be the new creation of small, private, even secret, spaces, and is reminiscent of what was happening at some of the villas.

Something similar seems to have been happening at Camerton, a small but rather strange settlement on the Fosse Way south-west of Bath. The site had some eleven pits, many containing suspiciously high-quality material; one had the remains of two dogs, one with an elaborate collar of iron links, and another had a third dog with a similar collar. The fourth-century community was manufacturing pewter vessels (for use in ceremonies as much as for tableware?), but one of its buildings, which contained three coin hoards, had been partitioned into three rooms, and had had other rooms added, perhaps during the fourth century. Another building contained a range of reused stone columns and carvings, including a pedestal with the feet of two adults and two children, one of several hints that perhaps before *c.* 300 there had been a shrine in the vicinity. Yet a third building had been subdivided and had had a hearth inserted into the floor, but against the west wall a kind of shrine had been created by placing the statuette of a god(dess) on a reused column which was used as a pedestal.[164]

The Uley[165] stone temple was demolished, and during the fifth century a timber double-aisled building in the style of a basilica was erected on the site. Fragments of the cult statue were built into its floor, as were other stone pieces from a large altar, and a second altar with an image of Mercury had been inserted within the paving of the building's western apse or bay: this can be interpreted as a ritual cleansing on

---

160. B. Cunliffe and P. Davenport, *The Temple of Sulis Minerva at Bath Vol. 1* (1985), p. 74.
161. M. Wheeler and T. Wheeler, *Report on the Excavations of the Prehistoric, Roman and Post-Roman Site in Lydney Park, Gloucestershire* (1932); Rahtz and Watts, 'End of Roman temples', pp. 203–4.
162. Casey and Hoffman, 'Roman temple on Lydney Park', pp. 81–144.
163. Rahtz and Watts 1979, fig 12; dating is difficult, and the hut may be later, not post-Roman.
164. Wedlake, *Camerton* (1958), pp. 50–3, 64–7, 71–5, 98–101, 214–15. In Rowberrow Field near the site an inscribed stone appeared in 1828; it is a squared stone pillar now with a large vertical section missing, with the inscription in horizontal lines and good Roman capitals set within a frame. Its date seems uncertain: see Wedlake, *Camerton* (1958), p. 16 and Plate 15. Camerton has also produced a late Roman propellor-shaped belt stiffener, Wedlake, *Camerton* (1958), pp. 256–7, figs 58, 12, and a contemporary belt buckle, R. Jackson, *Camerton. The Late Iron Age and Early Roman Metalwork* (1990), pp. 31–2, Plates 4 to 46. These are parts of (the same?) late Imperial *cingulum*, official 'badge of office'.
165. Woodward and Leach, *Uley*, p. 318.

the part of Christians. This building has been interpreted as a timber church, on the strength of the comparability of its ground plan with other buildings thought to be churches at Verulamium, Canterbury, St Albans, Richborough and Silchester, and the apsidal extension has been interpreted as a baptistery.

A stone building, again interpreted as a church, replaced, and was smaller than, the timber basilica (Fig. 41). It had a rectangular two-cell plan, soon extended by the addition of an apse at the north-eastern end, and was built around AD 600, making much use of reused Roman building materials, but with new, red-streaked glass, used either for windows or for setting in a special fitting, conceivably an altar or a reliquary. Interestingly, the head of Mercury from the old cult statue was buried in a pit just outside the eastern junction of the chapel and apse. The head had not been weathered, and looked as if it had been carefully preserved, even perhaps venerated, during the lifetime of the wooden building. Do we see here some kind of religious tension, or even a reworking of the narrative of the head in a martyrial context?

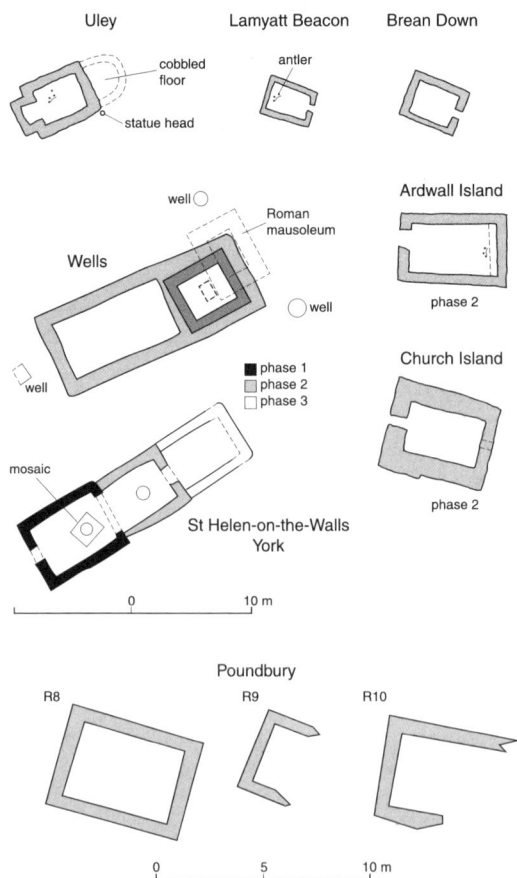

Figure 41 Plans of small late buildings at Uley, Lamyatt, Brean Down and Wells, with those at Ardwall Island, Church Island, St Helen-on-the-Walls. Below, three mausolea from Poundbury (all after Woodward and Leach 1993, Figs 138, 222)

The stone building at Uley should be compared with the little buildings outside the temples at Brean Down and Lamyatt Beacon. At Lamyatt a small east–west rectangular building was built with materials from the derelict temple; its date is uncertain, but it seems to be earlier than the Uley stone building. It had an inner offset or bench wall roughly 1.5 m wide. The floor of the building sealed pits in which some ten antlers had been placed; one of the pits had been cut from an earlier pit, which contained fourth-century pottery. Material finds from the temple suggest that Mars was worshipped there, together with other gods, although the antlers suggest comparison with a British god of Cernunnos type.[166] The Brean Down building is very similar but a little smaller, and was constructed around 400 or a little later. It, too, was built from material robbed from the temple, demolished about 390, and wear on the floor suggested long use. It had a hearth and the remains of domestic clutter, but the creation of a new site, which involved unnecessary work and a different orientation, 'looked like a deliberate rejection of what had gone before'[167] or, at least, a complex relationship to it.

All three of these buildings can be compared to the earliest Christian churches, known from the area of Roman Britain at St Helen-on-the-Walls (York)[168] and Wells,[169] and with two from the north and west at Church Island (Co Wexford)[170] and Ardwall Island, Kirkcudbrightshire.[171] The Christian character of the buildings at York, Church Island and Ardwall is not in doubt, and that at Wells very probable. Brean Down and Lamyatt may be better paralleled by the construction of 'private rooms' as perhaps at Pagans Hill, Nettleton, Maiden Castle and Lydney. Although the new buildings at the old temple sites may represent a change to Christian practice associated with the development of a cemetery at the site, they may also signal a more blurred cultural shift which met the need for a community graveyard with an appropriate focal building where ceremonies could take place, while stressing the continuity both of the site and of the reused building materials.

Uley produced one grave, of a male orientated north–south, without grave-goods, in a nailed coffin, but stray finds led the excavators to consider that a larger cemetery lay within the unexamined area, and the distances involved suggested two burial grounds perhaps of differing date. At Lamyatt there were sixteen west–east findless graves to the north of the temple site, with radiocarbon dates centring on 559 and 782, and Maiden Castle had several of similar type. At Brean Down and Nettleton there were major cemeteries. At Brean Down, some of the graves were formed from limestone blocks and collagen samples gave radiocarbon dates from the sixth to the eighth centuries, although some of the burials may have been earlier. The Nettleton A cemetery of east–west graves may be associated with the two-roomed rectangular building (No. 23) and building 29 may have held a tomb. At Camerton, a cemetery a

166. Leech, 'Romano-Celtic temple', pp. 259–328.
167. ApSimon, 'Roman temple, Brean Down', pp. 231–2. See also M. Allen and K. Ritchie, 'The stratigraphy and archaeology of Bronze Age and Romano-British deposits below beach level at Brean Down, Somerset', *Proc. U. Brist. Spel. Soc.*, 22 (1): 5–48 (2000).
168. Magilton, *St Helen-on-the-Walls, Aldwark*, pp. 16–18.
169. W. Rodwell, 'From mausoleum to minster: the early development of Wells Cathedral', in S. Pearce, *The Early Church in Western Britain and Ireland* (1982), pp. 42–59; *The Archaeology of Wells Cathedral: Excavations and Structural Studies, 1978–1993* (2001) for account of excavation.
170. M. O'Kelly, 'Church Island near Valencia, Co. Kerry', *Procs. Royal Irish Acad.*, 59C (1958): 57–136.
171. C. Thomas, *Christian Antiquities of Cambourne* (1967), pp. 127–88.

short distance from the settlement, which may have begun in the fifth century, began to be used, and continued for some centuries; eventually the focus shifted to what is now the parish church site, which itself has a curious earthwork and has produced late Roman material.

Around 500, and while the timber basilica was still in use, the focal area at Uley was given a perimeter bank, perhaps supporting a fence, with maybe two complex entrances. The surviving traces of the bank can be projected to form a roughly oval precinct. At Lydney, the ancient Iron Age promontory fort bank was refurbished. This contained demolition material from the temple complex, and was splendidly characterized by Mortimer Wheeler as 'some period of recrudescent barbarism after the beginning of the fifth century'.[172] At Nettleton, the Wick Valley bank, running south and west round the building complex, is quite possibly early post-Roman,[173] and Lamyatt also had a boundary bank and ditch, dated by radiocarbon dates from sealed burials to between the fourth and tenth centuries. It is tempting to compare these with the curvilinear banks which surround many Christian sites in western Britain and Ireland, but very few of these banks have attached dates.

Other hilltop sites have produced scraps of evidence which hint at broadly similar processes, particularly if we take the view that conspicuous hilltops partook of the sacred whether or not they acquired temple buildings. At Blaise Castle, Henbury, near Bristol, east–west graves cut across a possible fourth-century temple inside the hill-fort.[174] At Kings Weston, near Bristol, eleven shallow east–west graves were found, placed in a row which ran across the south-western enclosure of a hill-fort.[175] Dawes Castle, Watchet, a probable clifftop Iron Age enclosure,[176] produced evidence of its later role as a *burh* and also 'a quantity of human bones was discovered and others laid bare by the breaking away of a portion of cliff'.[177] They seem not to have had any grave-goods, but their date is uncertain. At Brent Knoll,[178] hill-fort human remains were recorded with Roman pottery and building debris, and Glastonbury Tor[179] produced two extended inhumations aligned north–south. Lamyatt Beacon produced sixteen roughly east–west burials of adults and children from the fourth-century temple complex. Ham Hill has produced a range of burial sites, some of Roman date, and there appears to be a large cemetery of Roman date but unknown end on the south side of Worlebury hill-fort in east Somerset.[180]

On balance, what we seem to see here as the fifth century progressed are sacred sites which experienced a quite gradual transition from 'normal' late Roman temple or shrines, through phases of redefinition of cult buildings – and perhaps some cult furniture – to use as burial grounds, in circumstances which allowed for much overlap and blurring of cultural categories, including some which have a Christian look. This is exactly what we would expect of a society in process of change, and,

172.   Wheeler and Wheeler, *Excavations in Lydney Park*, p. 64.
173.   Woodward and Leach, *Uley*, p. 321.
174.   P. Rahtz and J. Brown, 'Blaise Castle', *Proc. U. Brist. Spel. Soc.*, 8 (3): 147–71 (1957).
175.   C. Goodman, 'Kings Weston Hill, Bristol: its prehistoric camps and inhumation cemetery', *Proc. U. Brist. Spel. Soc.*, 13 (1): 41–8 (1972).
176.   Burrow, *Hillfort*, pp. 232–3.
177.   J. Page, *An Exploration of Exmoor* (1890), p. 241.
178.   Burrow, *Hillfort*, pp. 236–8.
179.   P. Rahtz, 'Excavations at Glastonbury Tor', *Arch. J.*, 127 (1970): 1–81.
180.   Burrow, *Hillfort*, and refs there; P. Fowler, 'Hillforts AD 400–700', in D. Hill and M. Jesson (eds), *The Iron Age and its Hillforts* (1971), p. 209.

assuming that the sites operated with the blessing of the landholding class, who perhaps helped to maintain them, and for whose estates they may have acted as social foci, it is significant that the new approach to identity centred upon a new cemetery, regardless of clear religious affiliation. Shared graveyards had become significant social glue.

Managed and embellished cemeteries

Within the broad late and post-Roman group of cemeteries are a few which stand out because they seem to have been deliberately managed by some overarching authority. These sites are often, although not always, large, the burials are in rows and sometimes within special enclosures, and sometimes the cemeteries were embellished with various buildings. The character of extended inhumation burial meant that settlements with relatively large populations needed to develop the notion of 'planned' cemeteries if characteristics which were evidently considered important, like the continued identification of individual graves and access to them, were to remain possible. It is therefore not very surprising that even the burial grounds relating to smaller settlements seem to show attempts at grave rows, and those of the major settlements were clearly deliberately organized and policed to produce a set design.

At Wembdon Hill, Bridgwater, the cemetery had at least twenty burials arranged in five rows, with possibly other rows awaiting discovery; the bodies had their feet to the east, were apparently without grave-goods and seem to have been associated with settings of sandstone blocks. Here, again, a dog had been buried nearby.[181] Rough rows show up in the densest area of the large cemetery at Cannington,[182] where there were perhaps some five thousand burials, presumably of people who had lived in or near the hill-fort nearby, from which has come evidence of fourth-century settlement. As we might expect, the clearest evidence for a large, deliberately arranged cemetery in the south-west comes from one of the *civitas* capitals: Dorchester.

This is the large cemetery (Fig. 42) at Poundbury,[183] which lay on the north-western side of Dorchester, between the River Frome and the Roman road leading north-west, and skirting the eastern flanks of the relatively small Iron Age hill-fort at Poundbury Camp, although a number of other inhumation cemeteries are known from the western extramural area. Finds from the hill-fort suggest that in the fourth century, or perhaps the fifth, the interior may have been extensively occupied and the defences refurbished, and there was a possible temple on the site in the fourth century. The Poundbury cemetery, which superseded early farms and cemeteries of very mixed character, was in use from at least *c.* 325 to *c.* 400. Some 1114 burials were excavated in the major excavations, with a few more added later,[184] mostly in regimented rows with their heads to the west. Most were in plain wooden coffins, but the rows included

181. C. Hollinrake and N. Hollinrake, 'Bridgwater, Wembdon Hill', *PSANHS*, 133 (1989): 171; H. Woods, 'Bridgwater, Wembdon Hill, ST279278', *PSANHS*, 134 (1990): 222; R. Croft, 'Bridgwater, Wembdon Hill', *PSANHS*, 138 (1988): 221; M. Langdon, 'Wembdon, Wembdon Hill', *PSANHS*, 130 (1986): 151.
182. Rahtz *et al.*, *Cannington* Cemetery, pp. 111–12.
183. D. Farwell and T. Molleson, *Excavations at Poundbury, Dorchester, Dorset, 1966–82: The Cemeteries* (1993), for full excavation account.
184. S. Davies and D. Grieve, 'The Poundbury pipe-line: archaeological observations and excavations', *PDNHAS*, 108 (1986): 81–8.

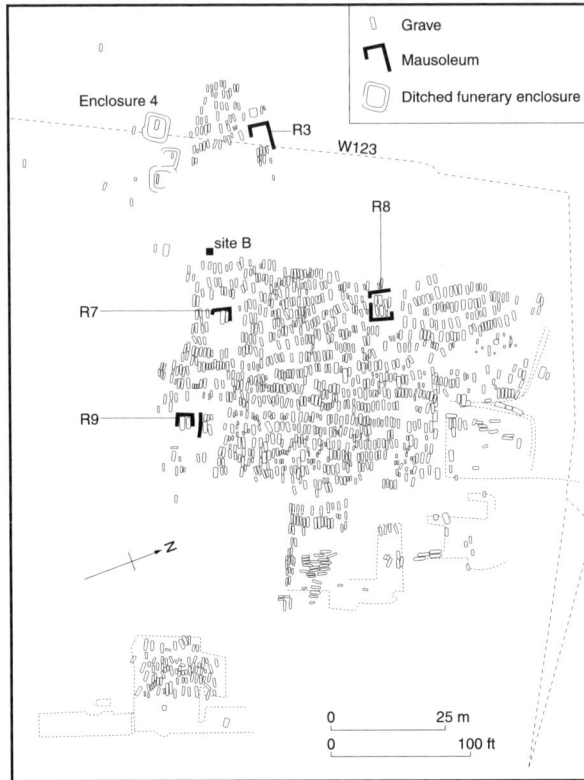

Figure 42 Plan of the cemetery at Poundbury, Dorchester (simplified) (after Farwell and Molleson 1993, Fig. 10)

over twenty wooden coffins with lead linings. Interspersed among the graves in no particular pattern were at least eight mausolea.

This was clearly a cemetery where an overriding authority, which enjoyed sufficient credibility to enforce its views, wished to see this particular order and layout. The burial scheme would have involved formal allocations of uniform plots, enlivened by the occasional burial with a grander coffin, and the even rarer permission to build a mausoleum. The regulation of the burials encourages the supposition that the burial rites and subsequent observances were equally uniform, and equally graded according to the importance of the burial. However, around the edges of the central cemetery were a number of different graves. Those to the east, for example, were aligned north–south and had a range of grave-goods. On the western and eastern sides were groups of often ditched enclosures, and these probably contained most of the stone coffins and some of the lead-lined wooden coffins. Often an enclosure had a single burial, not a family group like the mausolea.

The lead lining to the wooden coffin in one of the central graves (530) carried an inscription in high relief on the inside of the lid. It seems to be complete, though poorly executed, and has attracted a number of efforts to expand the abbreviations and produce something intelligible. Whatever it meant, it was put in an obscure position and 'At best it is only an undeciphered inscription on an object which may be

Christian.'[185] Grave 1339 had a Y-shaped piece of iron nearly 11 cm long in the wooden coffin above the skull of the male burial, which has been claimed as a stylized praying (*orans*) figure or even a 'Cross of Christ', but which is probably part of the coffin fittings.

A number of coffins were packed with plaster or, in a few instances, gypsum, intended as a preservative for the body, and a gypsum burial in what may have been a lead coffin was found on the Crown Buildings site about 500 m away from the Poundbury cemetery beside the Exeter road.[186] Evidence from North Africa, and from the great Rhineland Christian cemeteries,[187] suggests that, although not exclusively a Christian rite, gypsum burial is, particularly in conjunction with other features, helpful in pinpointing Christian burials. In Britain, similar burials have been found principally at York outside the west gate of the city (some twenty, in lead or stone coffins with possible mausolea), with odd examples elsewhere outside the city, at London (twelve in lead/stone coffins on the Colchester Road), and Icklingham, Suffolk, where the south-eastern cemetery, in particular, has produced plaster burials, mausolea and at least one of the lead tanks with a *chi-rho*, surrounded by structural remains.

Nevertheless, the Dunstable group of burials makes one strike a cautionary note. Here were buried five women, one with jewellery and another with a glass beaker, one child with a pottery vase and six men, one apparently coffined and certainly with his head decapitated; all were packed in quicklime plaster, the only group so treated in a large (1112 humans) very mixed cemetery of humans, decapitated humans, dogs and horses.[188] Closer to Poundbury, at Alington Avenue,[189] Fordington (Dorchester), the cemetery (of uncertain date) had two plaster burials, three decapitated burials and two burials with dogs.

One of the most exciting Poundbury finds was the painted wall plaster[190] from Mausoleum R8. The painted fragments came from six different compositions which indicated that the individual walls had different scenes: one showed a townscape and another a group of human figures, one of whom seems to have hands held out in the *orans* position. The ceiling seems to have had a design which included figures and floral zones within a geometric pattern, while remains from the western half of the south wall (Fig. 43) suggested that the whole wall might have held 20–40 painted

---

185. Tomalin (1993), pp. 132–3.

186. C. Green, M. Paterson and L. Biek, 'A Roman coffin burial from the Crown Buildings Site, Dorchester: with particular reference to the head of well-preserved hair', *PDNHAS*, 103 (1981): 67–100.

187. C. Green, 'The significance of plaster burials for the recognition of Christian cemeteries', in R. Reece, *Burial in the Roman World* (1977), pp. 46–57.

188. C. Matthews, 'A Romano-British inhumation cemetery at Dunstable', *Bedfordshire Archaeology J.*, 15 (1981): 4–137.

189. S. Davies, L. Stacey and P. Woodward, 'Excavations at Alington Avenue, Fordington, Dorchester, 1984/5: interim report', *PDNHAS*, 107 (1985): 101–10; see also S. Davies, M. Heaton and P. Woodward, *Excavations at Alington Avenue, Dorchester* (forthcoming), and S. Davies, P. Harding and R. Soames, 'Recent excavations at the Grove Trading Estate, Dorchester 1987: the Wyvern Marlborough site', *PDNHAS*, 109 (1987): 130–3; Davies and Grieve, 'Poundbury pipe-line', pp. 81–8.

190. Poorly preserved plaster from R9 seemed also to show a figural group. For painted rooms at Trier showing members of the imperial family with a *nimbus*, see Weber *Constaninische Deckengemälde* 1984. Painted plaster from Malton, N. Yorks, also showed rods, with cross-shaped terminals and a female figure with a *nimbus*, see Petts, *Christianity* (2003), pp. 107, 115. C. Green, 'The cemetery of a Romano-British community at Poundbury, Dorchester, Dorset', in Pearce, *Early Church in Western Britain* (1982), pp. 61–77; Farwell and Molleson, *Poundbury*, pp. 135–40.

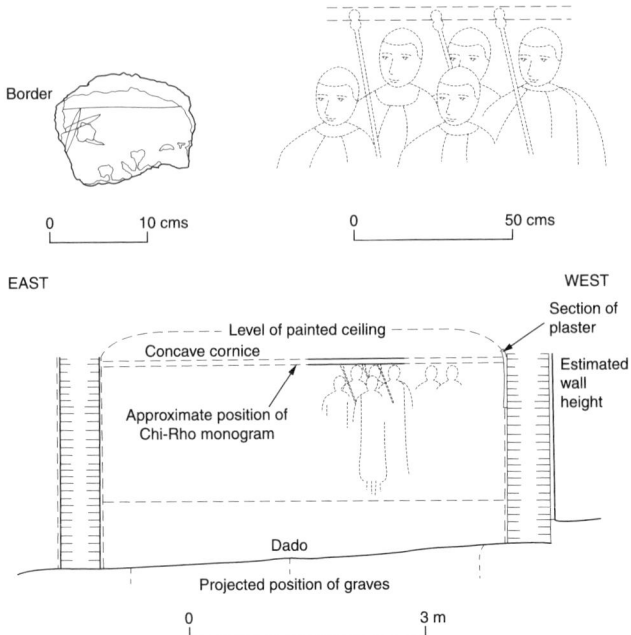

Figure 43 Poundbury mausoleum R8, showing the main surviving section of the wall painting and partial reconstruction of the decorative scheme (after Green 1982, Fig. 6.2)

human figures. Here, also, parts of a *chi-rho* could be discerned as white characters against the blue (sky?) background above and to the right of the first figure. The faces of the figures are turned a little to the east and at least four seem to be carrying rods. The clothing of all the figures was mixed, but much of it colourful and fairly elaborate. The focus of the scenes appears to have been lost, but the intention of the design on the south wall was perhaps to create the effect of people gathered in a sunlit landscape, as if the wall did not exist.

Several successive generations may have been represented in this wall painting. The rods look like staffs of office, and seem to have a certain pagan feel, or at least pagan antecedents. Three of the figures wear purple, with its imperial connotations, and these two features perhaps suggest a provincial representation of civic magisterial status. The whole composition looks like an extended family group, including perhaps some already dead, gathered at a funeral ceremony. One of the figures was semi-nude, and this and at least one other figure were both subject to either vandalism or iconoclasm at some point, a fascinating glimpse of shifting attitudes in Late Antiquity to the human body, and the great classical icon of the nude.

Like so much other relevant material, the figure scene is equivocal. The desire to commemorate the massed ranks of a family across the generations, and to stress its local standing in the imperial scheme of things, is what comes across most strongly, and whatever the precise status of the rods and the purple dress, evidence from the western provinces that bishops wore imperial purple in the fourth century does not seem to be forthcoming. On this line of thought, the *chi-rho* might have more to do with its character as an imperial symbol than as indicating Christian belief and practice. The wall painting must be taken in the context of the cemetery as a whole, and, as we have seen, neither the plaster/gypsum burials nor the lead inscription, and still less the presence of mausolea as such, offer confirmation of Christian character.

The most obvious characteristic of Poundbury is its ordinariness within the late Roman world,[191] particularly its broad similarity to the big Gaulish civic cemeteries. It has a range of characteristic features – managed rows, some grave-goods, upper-class family groups singled out by mausolea, perhaps proximity to a hill-fort and a possible temple site in that hill-fort – together with the equivocal message of the wall painting, and perhaps also of the coffin inscription, ambiguities which are themselves quite usual. A few per cent of the central Poundbury burials produced a range of grave-goods which were chiefly bracelets, rings, pins and similar small items of 'best' wear, but some of the outer graves had coins and a few spindle whorls, apparently deliberately concealed from view at the time of the funeral, and a few funerals departed from the cemetery norm in various ways. The cemetery seems to have stopped being used at the end of the fourth century.

The evidence from the other large urban settlements is less clear. Unfortunately, surprisingly little is known about Exeter's cemeteries, and we have only vague accounts of a few inhumation sites, which does not tell us very much.[192] Little is known in detail of Bath's late Roman cemeteries, but the principal burial ground lay towards the Fosse Way to the north-east of the town: here a number of the burials had simple stone coffins with lids. At Walcott Street, two graves have been excavated, one a woman in a wooden coffin with iron fittings, and one a man in a lead (lined?) coffin; they seem to have been buried in a small plot connected to the neighbouring house, which was derelict by the time the burials were carried out. Roman burials in stone coffins are also reported from Sion Hill near St Winifred's Well, and there may have been a Roman building in the area.[193] Another large cemetery is known in the east at Bathwick, where two burials were found in 1861, of a young woman and an adolescent, in stone coffins packed with sand, perhaps intended to act as a preservative, like gypsum.

Ilchester is bisected by the Fosse Way and cemeteries are known near the Way to the north in the Northover area and on both sides of the road to the south-west; a further inhumation cemetery was found on the western side of the road to Dorchester.[194] The south-western cemetery superseded an area of buildings and ditched enclosures, which were revamped by fresh cutting and, in one place, the erection of a post palisade, to create what might almost be called communal burial plots in which the inhumation burials were aligned according to the boundary ditch orientations. Most of the 40 or so known burials were in wooden coffins, and in one case a dog in its individual coffin accompanied its (presumed) master in the grave. Most of the people were adults, some accompanied by infants, generally extended, but a few face down, or with heads severed, or coffinless and crouched. Most had hobnail boots, and some had bronze ornaments, pottery, food and coins. A fine drystone dressed shaft or well had been filled with the bodies of domestic animals as the fourth century wore on, and perhaps this had some ritual connection with the cemetery. This cemetery is reminiscent of the outer areas at Poundbury.

---

191. Philpott, *Burial Practices*, p. 227.
192. P. Bidwell, *Roman Exeter: Fortress and Town* (1980), for good general account.
193. W. Wedlake, *A North Somerset Miscellany* (1966), p. 7.
194. P. Leach, *Ilchester By-pass Excavations 1975: Interim Report* (1975), for brief account.

In Ilchester at Northover, behind the Fosse Way frontage, lay a large and highly organized cemetery founded within the fourth century in a deliberately created enclosure, extending well into the fifth century, and finally holding at least 1500 inhumations.[195] Most of these had their heads more or less towards the east, and the small amount of excavation suggests the existence of grave rows, with most graves allotted adequate space which was then respected. The graves examined included two adult women, one adult male and three children. Three lead coffins within stone sarcophagi, two in a double grave, were the most expensive kind of burial container on the site, and there were also groups of individual lead and stone coffins, and some were in cist-like arrangements or stone-packed. Northover seems to be Ilchester's equivalent to the central Poundbury site at Dorchester, in terms of extent and broad character.

A similar pattern shows up at Shepton Mallet,[196] which has proved to be a relatively substantial settlement on either side of the Fosse Way, comprising an irregular scatter of homes and workshops which began in the early second century and continued into the fifth (at least). By the later fourth century the settlers had their own cemeteries, concentrated within and to the north of an earlier ditched enclosure on the eastern side of the Fosse Way (Fig. 44). Within the enclosure were a group of east–west aligned graves. One of the bodies had the silver pendant cross with a punched *chi-rho* symbol on the central roundel as already discussed, stylistically of late fourth-century date,[197] and another was in a lead coffin. The other groups were generally aligned north–south. The group to the north of the enclosure seems to have been focused upon a large, rectangular stone-based building which looks like other early Roman domestic properties on the site, apparently turned over to ancillary work and burial use (there were two burials in the middle room) by the time the cemetery was being developed. This cemetery had a rectangular mausoleum containing a single burial with a large stone coffin partly lined with sheet lead. Nearby, another large, rock-cut grave held a lead coffin with a wooden lid. To the north and west of these two groups were burials with ritual decapitation, the remains of hobnail boots, pottery and animal bones.

Other sites, less substantially investigated, have shown similar features. The burial ground attached to the large farming settlement at Chalton Mackrell, Somerset,[198] may also possibly have included mausoleum-type structures. At Wells,[199] where reliable springs to the east of the present cathedral were the attraction and where a number of routes converge, Roman occupation developed as either a small rural town or a villa. Under what is now Stillington's Chapel has been discovered a thirteenth-century Lady Chapel on the site of a small late Saxon chapel which must have been a part of the structures associated with the church of Aldhelm's time and presumably related to the founding of the Saxon church in *c.* 700. This chapel was itself erected partly over an underground tomb chamber built of mortared masonry, apparently

195. P. Leach, *Ilchester Volume 2: Archaeology, Excavations and Fieldwork to 1994* (1994), for excavation report.
196. P. Leach *et al.*, *Fosse Lane: Excavations of a Romano-British Roadside Settlement at Shepton Mallet, Somerset* (2001), esp. pp. 91–7.
197. Leach *et al.*, *Fosse Lane*, pp. 257–60
198. Leach, *Ilchester Vol. 1* (1980), pp. 357–8, and refs there.
199. Rodwell, 'Mausoleum to minster', pp. 49–59; *Archaeology of Wells Cathedral*, for excavation account.

Figure 44 Plan of the cemetery at Shepton Mallet (after Leach *et al.* 2001, Fig. 29).
(1) lead coffin; (2) fine spot of *chi-rho* marked silver amulet; (3) wooden coffins;
(4) stone sarcophagus within mausoleum structure

plastered and painted. An arrangement of timbers in the grave pit suggested some kind of superstructure over the grave, and the grave seems to have originally possessed an inscription on stone. The chamber would have held a pair of coffins orientated north–south, but these had gone. The chamber was within a rectangular building probably of wood, with a chalk floor, and the whole is in the form of a Roman mausoleum. Built into the chapel which superseded the mausoleum was a fragment of a two-line inscription (unfortunately mostly illegible) which seems to have been a funerary inscription. This mausoleum had become the focus of a cemetery of east–west burials believed to be of eighth-century date, and later it was used as an ossuary; its own date is unclear but presumably belongs somewhere between the fourth to sixth centuries.

Another site with mausolea has appeared at Kenn,[200] on the west bank of the Exe, about 1 km from the parish church (Fig. 45). The excavated area contained 120 dug graves, all but four on an east–west axis, which included a significant number of infant burials. Interspersed among the graves – and in one case with three graves –

---

200.   *DAS News*, 'Ancient cemetery discovered', p. 1.

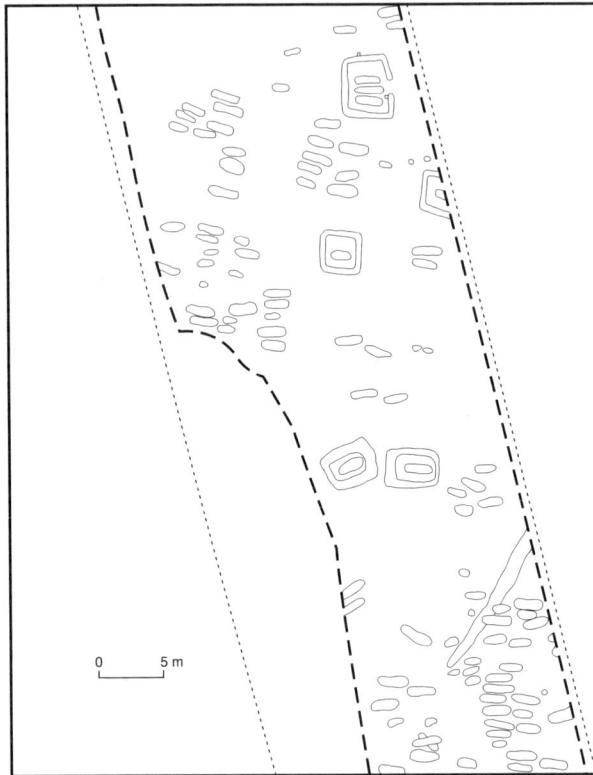

Figure 45 Outline plans of graves and mausoleum at Kenn, Devon (after *DAS News* 1996, p. 2)

were rectangular enclosures. Geophysical survey suggested that the whole cemetery held upwards of 350 graves, and revealed a field system and a possible rectangular enclosure. The number of burials suggests a rural settlement rather than a villa, even if the cemetery continued in use for some time, a suggestion backed up by the large collection of fourth-century pottery, both local and imported wares. The southern graves were cut into the old ground surface dated by fourth-century wares, so the cemetery is presumably largely post-Roman.

A similar settlement, or possibly an undiscovered villa, may be the context of interesting features recorded in the nineteenth century by Orlando Hutchinson at Branscombe, Devon, if indeed they are of Roman/post-Roman date. At Three Acres, Littlecombe,[201] a little back from the sea cliff, was found a stone coffin with inhumed

---

201.   Hutchinson MS notes in Butler, *Orlando Hutchinson*, pp. 105, 107–8; 117–18. The illustration on p. 117 shows a plain rectangular stone coffin, with an internal ledge to take a lid. This is quite different from the two stone coffins in the parish church of Branscombe, one outside and to the east of the south door, the other (fragment) within the arch of a blocked doorway inside the church on the south wall of the nave: these have a figure form cut into the stone and are medieval. These have sometimes been confused with Hutchinson's account and described as 'Roman'. For the record, the 'St Brannoc's Well' set up *c.* 2000 near Branscombe village hall is dedicated to taking voluntary contributions for the nearby car park.

bones, 'some animal', an iron nail and what looks like a possible fourth-century brooch. Near the quarry to the north of Branscombe church Hutchinson records two sides of a square or rectangular enclosure with, at its centre, a 'tumulus', in or near which was 'a slab of stone, about three feet by two by nine inches thick, and under it were bones in a cavity. ... The site is called "Castle Close" '.[202] The quarry site could perhaps be the remains of a cist burial within a special enclosure. The lead coffin from Wiveliscombe, Somerset, and that from Marnhill, Dorset, both seem to have had 'wooden structures' associated with them, but these could have been the remains of outer wooden coffins. The cemetery at Cannington[203] had two focal structures, one the grave of a young girl under a mound, marked by a slab structure and approached by a worn path which produced fourth-century material (Fig. 46), and the other a circular trench on the hilltop with traces of rough polygonal walls enclosing a single grave.[204] It also seems unlikely that the impressive coffins of stone from Northover, Poundbury and elsewhere, together perhaps with

Figure 46 Focal slab-covered east–west orientated grave approached from the north by a worn, stony path area, Cannington cemetery, Somerset. (Photo: Phillip Rahtz)

202.   Butler, *Orlando Hutchinson*, pp. 107, 117–18, 156.
203.   Rahtz *et al.*, *Cannington Cemetery*, pp. 405–15.
204.   See also note 40; *PSANHS*, 92 (1946): 68–9.

some of those which involved sheet lead, were entirely hidden from view.[205] These also may have served as visible markers.

There may also have been a range of markers, including ones of wood, of which we are ignorant, or which may not have been recognized. It is, for example, possible that some of the stone blocks at Brean Down may have served this purpose rather than belonging to a building.[206] All these various grave markers must have performed their function of visibility very well in the inhumation cemeteries of the time. They signalled importance and prestige to the community of the living, and they provided a focus for practices which embodied the imagination and feeling of the day. The resource put into their visual impact seems to have replaced that which formerly had gone into grave-goods and possibly a more elaborate funeral, and the reason for this may be a shift in the ways in which the passing of time was experienced. A single elaborate funerary act, with perhaps some unemphatic annual commemoration, implies a sense of finish: the dead person has completed the good life lived according to the classic precepts of civic duty, restraint, just dealing and proper observance, and has now passed beyond human ken. This may be why children, who could not have achieved these things, were treated differently, and (to our eyes) often callously, before the fourth century.[207] These marked graves suggest something different, which matches the emotional change represented by inhumation: the dead remain, physically and emotionally a member of the community, a continuity across time which stresses the living link between generations, and joins up with – without necessarily deriving from – Christian beliefs about life after death.

The ongoing community of the quick and the dead is symbolized by the grave markers and by the yearly commemorative grave feast which Augustine tells us, in Africa at least, could become very jolly.[208] The cemeteries stress family rather than civic values, and the sense of moving through a life linked with other lives seems at least as important as devotion to the official image of the shining, eternal imperium, so contributing to the tensions inherent in Late Antiquity. The cemeteries also breathe sadness and offer a new overt or expressed tenderness seen most sharply in the frequent inscriptions to dead children which appear at the Gaulish and African sites, and in the formal children's graves in the south-western sites. Even babies, now, have spirits and count as family, past and present, and this may well link up with a desire to position the burial ground on an abandoned habitation site, although, of course, we do not know whether those who were buried on the site had any links with the abandoned home, or how long before it had been abandoned.

Kinship may be an important element in the creation and growth of the burial grounds. The layout at Shepton Mallet, with its three distinct groups which seem to relate to buildings and enclosures, hints at family properties turned over to burial. Examination of bones at Cannington (Fig. 47) showed the scarcely surprising fact that

205.   There is lettering inside one of the Poundbury lead coffin linings which has been interpreted as of Christian significance. However, in Tomalin's view, 'At best it is only an undeciphered inscription on an object which may be Christian'; Tomalin in Farwell and Molleson, *Poundbury*, pp. 132–3.

206.   M. Bell, *Brean Down Excavations 1983–87* (1990), p. 80.

207.   See D. Watts, 'Infant burials and Romano-British Christianity', *Arch. J.*, 146 (1989): 372–83; but note also the earlier discussion of infant burials.

208.   Augustine, *Ep*, 22, in J. Baxter, *St Augustine: Select Letters* (1953), p. 49. See also Augustine, 'On the care to be had for the dead', in *Nicene and Post-Nicene Fathers of the Christian Church* (1978), Vol. 3 (Erdman's Publishing, Grand Rapids).

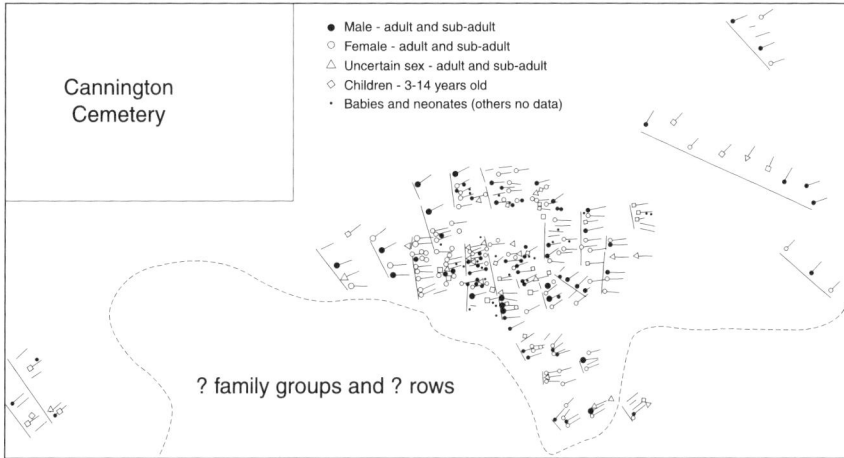

Figure 47 Possible family groups and rows in the cemetery at Cannington (after Rahtz *et al.* 2000, Fig. 252)

members of the same family were buried in adjoining graves.[209] On this line of argument, those buried in the specially marked graves would be the senior members of an extended family, or the ranking family within a ramifying group of kin and dependants, or various combinations of both, depending upon very complex local circumstances.

Dead bodies can be viewed in two broad ways, as either an embodied subject, the remaining trace of the individual who had a social identity and a personal history now part of a group memory, or as a symbolically rich object, a way of expressing cultural markers to do with the local ways of perceiving distinctions in gender, status and so on; all the body manipulations which appear in the record as funerary customs or devotion to relics partake of one or other or (usually) both of these attitudes. What cemeteries like Henley Wood or Kenn seem to suggest is that the human bodies concerned were read as subjects whose individuality was important – hence the carefully separate graves – but whose personal distinctions, of age, gender and detailed local status, were not thought worthy of mark, once the grave had been closed over – hence the virtually identical appearance between the style of the burials and one grave and the next. High status, or upper-class groups, are certainly made distinct, as they are at Poundbury, but within these groups the same rules seem to apply although with perhaps more scope for differential marking. In these burial grounds individuality is important, but it is constructed within a social discourse which did not wish to create distinctions, and a particular individual's grave could usually only be recognized, or visited, with the help of somebody whose memory embraced the personal histories of those concerned, and the details of the ground's layout.

This suggests an overarching conviction that the state of being dead, and perhaps of reaching an afterlife, where others held in memory had gone before, was common to all. It also hints that, here and hereafter, individual distinctions were less important than a collective solidarity likely to be vested in the family. When the members of at least some families went to a cemetery like Cannington they saw, laid out in the rows, the mirror image of their present state, with the added dimension of a time depth

---

209.   Rahtz *et al.*, *Cannington Cemetery*, p. 407, and for biological detail, pp. 131–256.

which reached backwards and would, in due course, move forwards to embrace themselves. In the nature of things, other individuals who lacked but desired similar reassurance, would strive to construct suitable links, successfully or otherwise, depending on the tiny details of local circumstance.

The more specific question of the 'Christianity' or otherwise of those who used these cemeteries is a difficult one. It is possible to draw up a series of internal and external evidential criteria for the identification of late Roman/early post-Roman Christian cemeteries, with relative weightings, which feature Christian inscriptions, east–west orientation, supine and extended position and individual undisturbed burials. The presence of infants and the absence of decapitation also score highly.[210] Against these criteria, a considerable number both of the cemeteries as a whole and of individual graves in the West Country would qualify as Christian. But the separate groups of graves, often with their own enclosures and burial rites, seen clearly at Poundbury, Ilchester and Shepton suggest different customs and, if these were peripheral at the big cities, they may not have been so in the towns and the countryside. The wider perspective suggests that the recognition of kin, status and property was at least as important as any theological alignment. This does not mean that Christian communities did not exist in Dorchester or Ilchester, but it does hint at a broader cultural context. Perhaps what we are seeing is a developing view in Late Antiquity of what constitutes a proper burial, a view which hints at a significant realignment of human experience bound up with the political, economic and cultural shifts which mark the beginning of Late Antiquity, which was already in tune with what Christian belief and practice was in the process of becoming.

Developments in the urban centres

The vital thread which connects the flourishing Roman cities of the earlier Empire with their equally flourishing successors after *c.* AD 1000 in the western provinces generally seems to be the continuing presence of an organized Church, and here the fourth, fifth and sixth centuries were crucial. The question which faces us is the extent to which this is true for the urban settlements of Exeter, Ilchester, Dorchester and Bath, and, if so, what the characters of any connecting threads were. A number of themes are significant: architectural and defensive developments at the cities; the interpretation of settlement evidence; the siting and growth of cemeteries; and the relationship these issues seem to bear to later ecclesiastical developments, for which difficult and largely retrospective arguments have to be considered.

Dorchester,[211] Ilchester,[212] and Bath[213] had all acquired earth bank and ditch defensive systems in the mid/late second century. At Dorchester, fairly soon after 300, a stone wall, in places on a slightly rethought alignment, was added to the banks, and access was by the two major West and South Gates. At Ilchester, the earth rampart was deliberately levelled, certainly in places, to allow the construction of substantial

---

210.   For example, Watts, *Christians and Pagans*, p. 79.
211.   K. Penn, *Historic Towns in Dorset* (1980), p. 58.
212.   Leach, *Ilchester Vol. 2*, p. 5.
213.   Cunliffe, *Roman Bath*, pp. 97–9. Bath never had cantonal capital status, but may, as Cunliffe suggests (*Roman Bath Discovered* (1995), pp. 5–15) have carried out a local government function within its rural area.

dwellings, but sometime in the fourth century a massive stone wall was built fronting the earth rampart and cutting into its face; at the Kingshams Field site, a series of regularly pitched lias blocks butted against the outer face of the wall, perhaps suggesting a later bastion.

Bath (Fig. 48) seems to have had a stone wall built into the front of its bank in the third century or later, and this was fronted by a berm and wide ditch. Along the south-east side of the town possible Roman square block masonry survives to a height of about 2 m, but proof of Roman date of all these structures has not yet appeared, and any Roman wall may not have followed the later wall line. The history of the bank and ditch system at Exeter also remains obscure,[214] but the city seems to have created a ditch system in depth by adding an outer ditch to the existing third-century ditch, and this was associated with a massive wall of local reddish volcanic

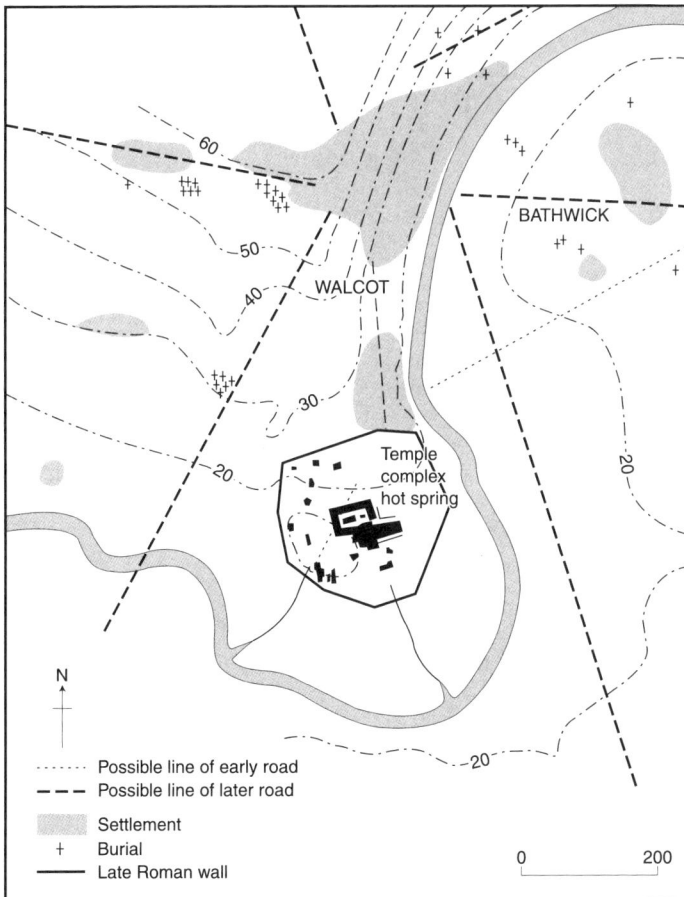

Figure 48 Late Roman Bath (after Cunliffe 2000, Fig. 92)

214. Bidwell, *Roman Exeter*; S. Blaylock, 'Castles in the air at Berkeley House', *DAS News*, 77 (2000): pp. 1–4; Henderson, *South Gate*, pp. 45–124.

trap spalls, perhaps erected around 200–250. The wall was about 6 m high, with a rampart walk and parapet above, pierced by four main gates.

The cultural impact of these impressive stone walls must have been considerable. They presented a much starker, and genuinely more impenetrable, barrier between the urban area and the world beyond than banks and ditches can have done. They provided a strong imperial statement about capacity and control, but also perhaps about defensiveness and secrecy.[215] They made an unmistakable distinction between suburban inhabitants, by the fourth century probably mostly legally inferior *humiliores* and privileged urban dwellers, many superior *honestiores*; these will have included imperial bureaucrats and local officials, either permanent or on visits, any kind of military presence and whatever the place had by way of recognized priests, Christian or otherwise. The actual building of the walls and digging of ditches must have had a disruptive effect upon buildings, rights of way and graves, which can be compared to that produced by a contemporary new motorway. It has been suggested that in Gaul a conscious attempt was made to link the old city and the new by embedding earlier inscriptions and carvings visibly in the new build. At Bath, Leland tells us that he saw carved stones embedded in the wall, and while we cannot tell if these (or some of them) were themselves of Roman date,[216] or if their incorporation in the wall was Roman, it is at least possible that here we have a deliberate Late Antique use of special *spolia* intended to create a psychological impression.

Within the cities, urban affairs seem to have taken the shape we have come to expect. At Bath, the baths and temple complex, where during the fourth century the drainage system had broken down, began to be regularly flooded and silted as the water-table rose, and eventually, perhaps around 400, willingness to clear up and carry out repairs faded. In the temple inner precinct, a small room, reusing old column drums, was constructed out of part of the portico to the sacred reservoir. It was probably built in the late fourth century and timber structures in the same general area survived well into the fifth. By this time the temple was very dilapidated, but the Roman reservoir building was not demolished until at least the sixth century.[217] A final repaving of this area, which lasted long enough to become very worn, was carried out, using limestone slabs robbed from standing Roman buildings, including blocks taken from the temple pediment, and around the same time the great altar was taken apart: the dating of this work is uncertain, and might belong in the seventh century. The precinct area began to be used as a rubbish dump by those still living in the rest of the town unaffected by the flooding. By now the great temple must have loomed as a forlorn ruin over the steaming marsh and surrounding black pools, a sight for which the Anglo-Saxon author of *The Ruin* poem[218] gives us an eyewitness account.

Outside the central complex, however, life in sub-Roman Bath did not come to a sudden end. The house in Abbeygate Street, which by the mid-fourth century was decorated in style and possessed a heating system, collapsed sometime towards 400.

215.   N. Christie and R. Kipling, 'Structures of power or structures of convenience? Exploring the material past of Late Antiquity and the early Middle Ages', in S. Pearce, *Researching Material Culture* (2000), pp. 21–35.
216.   Cunliffe, *Roman Bath*, pp. 6–12.
217.   Cunliffe and Davenport, *Temple of Sulis Minerva, Vol. 1*, esp. p. 74.
218.   The eighth-century poem, known as *The Ruin* written in Anglo-Saxon: M. Alexander, *The Earliest English Poems* (1966), pp. 30–1.

The western part of the site reverted to open ground, but in the east a new building was put up, on a slightly new alignment. Inside was a sequence of occupation levels, linked with a small oven cut into the floor.

At Exeter,[219] (Fig. 49) some areas, like that excavated near St Pancras church, seem to have been turned over to stock and rough timber buildings. Here the final buildings

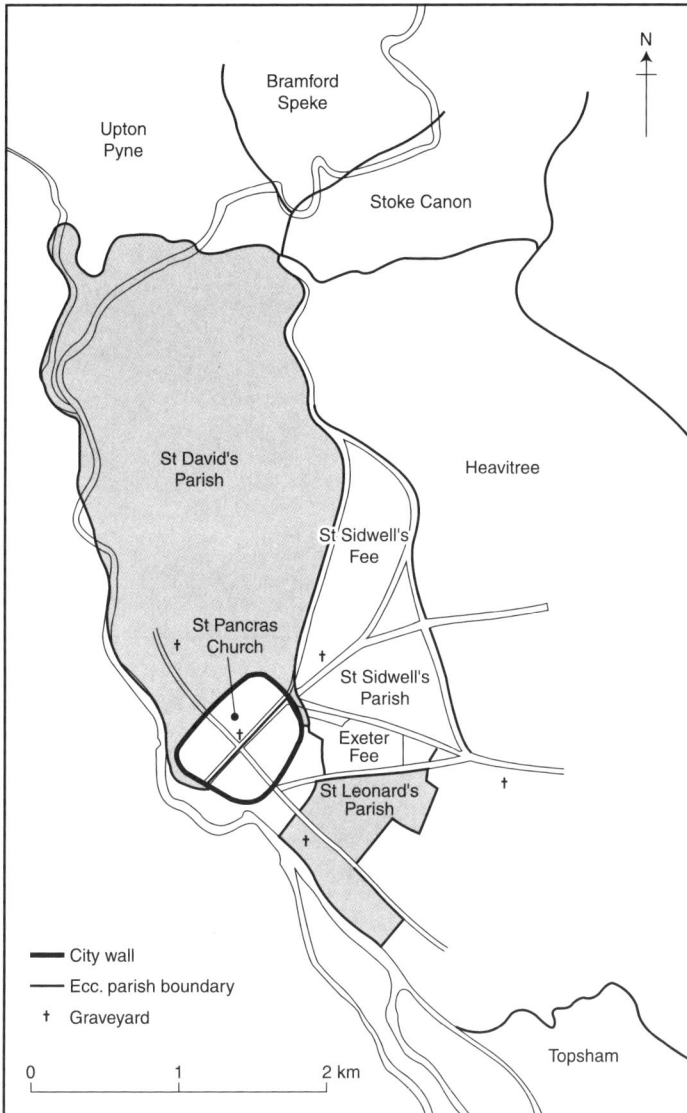

Figure 49 Late Roman Exeter and its possible context (after Pearce 1982b, Fig. 7)

219.   Bidwell, *Roman Exeter*, pp. 69–71.

collapsed, or were cleared away, after 370, and black earth accumulated; this seems to have been the usual sequence within the city. The *basilica* and *forum* at the heart of the city were substantially replanned around 350. At its south-east end the *basilica* was extended, a room identified as the *curia* was enlarged and a possible tribunal added to the *basilica*. A well-worn coin of Valens (364–378) embedded in a relaid *basilica* floor suggests that the buildings continued to be used for some time, but they were demolished before the site was turned over to cemetery use by c. 450. Before the burials started, many small pits had been dug on the *basilica* and *forum* sites; one in the floor of the old *curia* had bronze working debris, and may have been dug as a quarry for the clay needed in metal casting.

The story is similar at Dorchester (Fig. 50) and Ilchester (Fig. 51). At Greyhound Yard, Dorchester,[220] for example, fifth-century occupation included urban field plots and the continued use of only two buildings from what had been a substantial complex, and black earth built up over the site. Colliton Park to the north-west of the city, which had been the governing and landed class quarter, became an area of small-scale industrial development and 'occupation of slum character'.[221] At Ilchester, a building behind the north-east corner of the earlier rampart gave coin and pottery evidence of a series of courtyard resurfacing which probably ran from c. 250 to around 400; some time after this, the building was deserted and collapsed (or the other way round) and subsequently its stonework was extensively robbed.[222]

The problems posed by this kind of evidence, which is widespread in late Roman British cities, require much subtler answers than simple conclusions about 'civic collapse' and 'the end of imperial organization'. Fundamental shifts of outlook and social practice are required to explain why local artisans ceased to make pottery roof tiles, cement for flooring or mortar for repairs, which would at least have kept many buildings going, or why public bathhouses were sometimes turned over to other uses. The 'black earth' deposits seem to be rubbish dumps, suggesting that

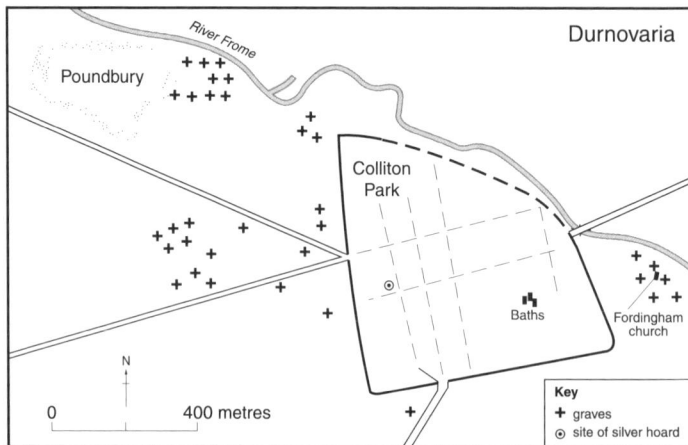

Figure 50 Late Roman Dorchester (after Penn 1980, p. 57)

---

220.   P. Woodward, S. Davies and A. Graham, 'Excavations on the Greyhound car park, Dorchester, 1984', *PDNHAS*, 106 (1984): 99–106.

221.   Penn, *Historic Towns*, p. 58.

222.   Leach, *Ilchester Vol. 2*, pp. 5–12.

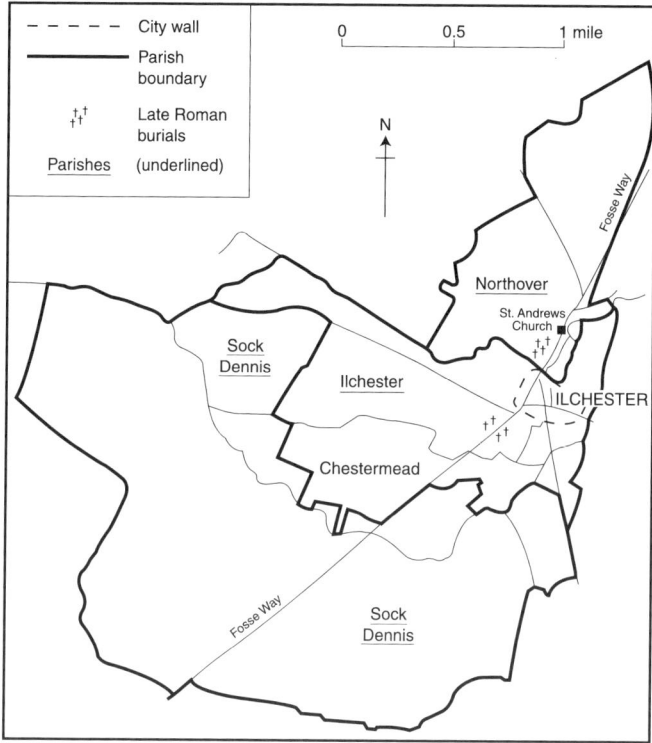

Figure 51 Late Roman Ilchester and its possible context (after Dunning 1975, p. 45)

areas once important to the conception of civic life, like the Colliton Park area of Dorchester and similar once-residential parts of Exeter and Ilchester, were now not significant, so presumably their owners had either moved permanently to country estates or declined severely in status. On the other hand, some central city buildings were reconfigured, as happened at the Exeter *basilica*.[223] It is possible that across Britain the grand civic buildings were coming to the end of working lives, in any case, either through outside factors like the rising water at Bath or because the city authorities had never been willing to produce the investment levels which imperial works, like the Saxon shore forts, had received.

We sense a new mood around 400 which put the buildings, street plan and civic monuments of the old city behind it, together with the classical hierarchies and assumptions which they embodied, including those about personal hygiene, public amenity and civic behaviour. The cities still had their psychologically significant walls and the sense of separateness and centrality which these conveyed, and they had perhaps more inhabitants than has sometimes been supposed, but people were living in them differently, reconfiguring the urban spaces to make different

---

223.   Compare with the substantial rebuilding of the basilica at Wroxeter as suggested by its excavators; see White and Barker, *Wroxeter*, pp. 121–4.

statements about how life should be lived. In northern Gaul (and elsewhere), the new ideas about a lived life focused, of course, upon the Christian Church and its sensational manifestations, primarily emotional display and the profoundly impressive new churches. In south-western Britain, we see in the cities the shift from 'classic' urban values expressed in civic monuments and the life which went with them to 'early medieval' styles which did not value such things; but was it the working of those underlying trends – loss of confidence in earlier public Roman values and their replacement by private, familiar, locally based and experiential values – which helped the Church to success, or was urban Christianity itself a major and active part of the mix?

At Exeter, the central *basilica* site became a probably extensive cemetery, samples from which have produced dates of AD 420, 490 and 1070.[224] The cemetery had a planned layout, with the graves aligned north–west/south–east, an orientation which was governed by elements of the surviving street plan, and possibly hints at alignment on a building, perhaps a surviving late Roman building. The use of the central city site as a burial ground, matched in Britain at Caerwent and Gloucester and further afield at Sabratha in North Africa, suggests a profound shift, in which the buried dead came to be seen as an appropriate settlement focus.[225] This sentiment would gain force if a church, possibly a reused existing building, accompanied the cemetery as at African Lepcis Magna where, in the sixth century, the *basilica* was converted into a church, but there is no direct evidence as yet for such a feature at the Exeter site.

An English monastery seems to have been in existence at Exeter by *c.* 680, and its church may have been on the old *basilica/curia* site, either within the shell of an old building or in a new one. Exeter acquired a church dedicated to St Martin to the east of the early cemetery site, but without supporting evidence this potentially early dedication cannot be given a date. Perhaps more significant is the equally potentially early dedication to St Pancras to the north of the cemetery site; this church evidently predates the medieval street plan as alignments show. Probable fourth/fifth-century churches dedicated to Pancras exist at Canterbury and elsewhere in the Western Empire, and it is just possible that the site, whether or not already a church, or dedicated to Pancras, marked the north-eastern limit of the cemetery or the area associated with it.

No comparable intramural developments are known at Dorchester or Ilchester. At Bath a cemetery developed in the depth of decayed rubbish and soil which had accumulated in the centre of the temple precinct; dating is difficult but this may have started soon after 700, or even somewhat before. The reuse of pagan sculptures in the final effort to repave the northern part of the precinct may relate to the founding of the Christian monastery[226] in Bath by Osric, ruler of the Hwicce in what is now largely Gloucestershire, in 675, around the time when he was making a similar foundation in the old Roman city at Gloucester.

---

224.   For this and what follows, see P. Bidwell, *The Legionary Bath-house and Basilica and Forum at Exeter* (1979), esp. pp. 110–13.

225.   Caerwent, J. Knight, 'Late Roman and post-Roman Caerwent: some evidence from metalwork', *Arch. Camb.*, 114 (1996a), pp. 48, 51, 54; Gloucester, R. Bryant, 'St Mary de Lode, Gloucester', *Bulletin of the CBA Churches Committee*, 13 (1980): 15–18; Sabratha and North Africa, J. Ward Perkins and R. Goodchild, 'The Christian antiquaries of Tripolitania', *ARCH*, 95 (1953): 1–83.

226.   Cunliffe, *Roman Bath*, pp. 207–27.

The continuing use of extramural sites is equally tantalizing. At Dorchester, the Poundbury cemetery came to an end during the course of the fifth century and eventually the site was used for farming, but there was also a major cemetery on the eastern side of the city along the higher ground bordering the river. Its known date range seems to be first to fourth century, the cemetery was not apparently planned like its neighbour on the western side and the orientations were largely north–south. Twenty graves turned up in the garden of the vicarage of St George's, Fordingham,[227] which takes its name from its proximity to an important crossing of the Frome. Fordingham church has Roman remains in its fabric, and may have been an early minster,[228] implying a foundation date in the late sixth/seventh centuries (under a different name and dedication, presumably). Fordingham was a royal manor[229] and its parish wrapped around the city walls on all sides except that of the river, while on the opposite bank stretched the later parish of Frome Whitfield ('the old inhabited land by the Frome') which seems originally to have belonged to the intramural parish of Holy Trinity. It is interesting that it seems to have been the Fordingham cemetery, rather than the Poundbury one, with its important mausolea, which became the site of the minster church.

Extramural Roman cemeteries have been singularly elusive at Exeter, and it is the greatest pity that the post-war opportunity to investigate sites beyond the East Gate was not taken. There was a cemetery here, beside the London road, witnessed by the finds of urns from time to time,[230] and although no Roman inhumations are recorded, these are unlikely to have been differentiated from later medieval burials in the early records. There were also a number of important wells in the area, which contributed substantially to the city's water supply. By the mid-tenth century, at the very latest, the church of St Sidwell, where her body lay, stood some 200 m beyond the gate, since *The Resting Places of the Saints* records, '*Sanctaque Sydefulla Virgo Foras Exanceastre*' ('and Holy Sidwell, Virgin, outside Exeter').[231] The saint's name is very obscure: 70 years ago Max Forster concluded that Sidefulla (= 'full of purity'), a normal English name, is as close to the original as we can get, Latinized as *Sativola*, and subsequently combined with the water supply to give the later 'Sidwell'.[232] The origin of the church can only be guessed at. Sidwell seems to have been English, and, if she really existed, could have been one of the well-known group of high-born ladies who founded minster churches around 700, like Cuthberga at Wimborne or Frideswide at Oxford (of whom equally little is known).

What is clear is that, by 1050, St Sidwell's church was well endowed with St Sidwell's Fee, which covered most of the parish of St Sidwell, the remainder belonging to the city.[233] There is some reason for thinking that the original boundaries of Exeter's three ancient extramural parishes, St David's, St Leonard's and St Sidwell's, can perhaps be traced back to *c.* 670, the traditional date for the founding

227.   *PDNHAS*, (1971): 152.
228.   Penn, *Historic Towns*, pp. 53–65.
229.   *Ibid.*
230.   Devon Sites and Monuments Register.
231.   D. Rollason, 'Lists of saints' resting-places in Anglo-Saxon England', *Anglo-Saxon England*, 7 (1978): 61–93.
232.   M. Förster, 'The etymology of St Sidwell', *DCNQ*, 17 (1933): 243–5.
233.   Pearce, *Early Church in Western Britain*, pp. 10–18.

of the Exeter minster by the West Saxon king, Cenwahl, and it is possible that they represented the territory attached to the Roman city, along the lines which has been suggested at Worcester,[234] although this supposes the survival of at least some administrative arrangements between *c.* 450 and *c.* 670, a gap of over two centuries.

At Ilchester, Northover outside the north gate was a site of the major, enclosed, planned, approximately east–west-orientated cemetery, and within it on the Fosse Way was founded the minster church of St Andrew, with an estate attached to it in 1066 which is more or less the ancient parish of Northover.[235] Ilchester itself had a large parish wrapping round the city and the place-name Chestermead marks water meadows important to the inhabitants. At Bath, evidence for fourth-century extra-mural inhumation cemeteries has been found, at Bathwick and Walcott, but no early churches are known at the sites. The hundred *manentes* granted by Osric to Abbess Bertana for the founding of Bath Abbey are perhaps those parishes north-east of the Avon but within Somerset, which fill the bend of the river, and the ancient boundary of which is marked by the name Marshfield ('boundary area'). This may possibly have been land relating to the urban community at late Roman Bath.

The direct evidence for active or committed Christians in the fourth century and on into the fifth at any of these urban settlements is, therefore, mixed, a situation which perhaps also appears at cities further east in Britain, and is mirrored to an extent in contemporary Gaul, where, by and large, the urban centres of the north-west do not seem to have had active bishops or church-building programmes. What we do see, at all four settlements, are the development of cemeteries, the character of which are consistent with what we know of Christian practice; but these were matched, certainly at Dorchester and Ilchester, and perhaps elsewhere, by cemeteries where the rites seem to have been pagan, or at least more mixed. At two sites – Exeter and Bath – major, indisputably Christian, institutions founded in the later seventh century were sited close to intramural cemeteries, which had a Christian character, and they continued to use them. At Ilchester, Exeter and perhaps Dorchester, extramural cemeteries seem to be the reason why major minster-style churches were founded, perhaps also in the seventh century, immediately outside the walls, not the obvious site for an important church without good reasons for the choice. Linked with this is the pattern of endowment, which at Ilchester and Exeter, and possibly Bath and Dorchester, hints at the endurance into the seventh century of late Roman civic territorial arrangements. Again with many local variations, similar configurations have been detected at Caerwent,[236] Worcester and Gloucester[237] and further east in Britain, and in some of the north Gaulish cities.[238]

---

234.   S. Bassett, 'Churches in Worcester before and after the conversion of the Anglo-Saxons', *Antiq. J.,* 69 (1989): 225–56.

235.   R. Dunning, 'Ilchester: a study in continuity', *PSANHS,* 119 (1975): 44–50.

236.   Knight, 'Late Roman and post-Roman Caerwent', pp. 35–66; M. Redknap, 'A pre-Norman cross from Caerwent and its context', *Monmouth Antiquary,* 10 (1994): 1–6.

237.   S. Bassett, 'Church and diocese in the West Midlands: the transition from British to Anglo-Saxon control', in J. Blair and R. Sharpe, *Pastoral Care before the Parish* (1992), pp. 13–40; 'Churches in Worcester', pp. 225–56.

238.   S. Pearce, 'Processes of conversion in north-west Roman Gaul', in M. Carver, *The Cross Goes North. Processes of conversion in Northern Europe AD 300–1300* (2002).

Culture and society in south-western Britain AD 300–500

The very mixed picture offered by the detail of the evidence suggests a strong desire in the late Roman south-west to express solidarity and identity by focusing upon ritual activity of many kinds at a range of rural sites, especially temples and shrines, shafts, hill-forts and hilltops, by deploying a range of material objects including metalwork. Increasingly, as the fifth century progressed, interest seems to have narrowed, to concentrate upon cemeteries, as at Cannington often on the same sites, and upon bodies as the most potent kind of material deposition. It is possible that this is the ceremonial face of a tightening-up of the social and economic links by upper-class landholders, which helped them maintain their grip upon estates and to extend them to take in new land and new groups, with the ritual sites, and increasing the emotionally powerful cemeteries, providing social cohesion. This would inevitably be a messy process, with a range of local successes and failures.

The reasons behind these shifts link up with the pressures conveniently labelled Late Antique, which include a turning towards the smaller scale, the local, the private and the experiential at the expense of the rational. The idea of kinship seems to have been a significant structuring principle which helped to bring these changes about. Kinship as a way of creating social linkages had, of course, been very powerful before *c.* 300, and the new stress on inhumation burial grounds with their sense of drawing comfort and strength from the past suggests that it was one of the few structuring principles emotionally powerful enough to help shift social patterning towards more cohesive and economically interdependent groupings within the landscape. This helped to produce what we can recognize as early medieval estates.

The extent to which within all this what we see suggests practices which can be called 'Christian' is a difficult and complex question, and may indeed be the wrong question, suggesting as it does clear-cut categories and deliberate choices. Apart from the Bath curse tablet, which talks only, although significantly, in generalities, there are no pieces of documentary evidence earlier than the material in the early *Life* of St Samson which attests directly to Christian activity in the south-west, although the probable bishopric at Circencester, and the martyrial shrines of Julian and Aaron at Caerleon, are geographically close.

On balance, and bearing in mind both the fourth-century evidence of small finds and funerary practice from Exeter, Dorchester, Ilchester and Bath, and the fairly strong suggestion of continuity created by a Christian presence inside Exeter and Bath, and outside the walls at Exeter, Dorchester and Ilchester, it seems likely that there were Christian communities in all of these cities during the fourth and fifth centuries. Presumably they were organized in the usual Late Antique way, with a bishop and a place of worship, although no early urban church buildings have been recognized yet within the peninsula. Characteristically, too, they lavished considerable effort on their cemeteries, which were significant enough to become the sites of later Christian establishments. Perhaps at fourth-century Ilchester and Dorchester Christian practice was the social norm, but this impression should be set beside the obvious pagan interests at Bath, and the burials at Dorchester and Ilchester which show pagan practices.

The ambiguous character of the Poundbury wall paintings fits with the nature of the mosaics at Hinton St Mary, Frampton and, just possibly, Halstock. Within these sophisticated landowning families, interest, perhaps some kind of belief, in Christian teaching is apparent, but it seems to have been a belief in which metaphysical speculation and statements about status combine to create primarily a theocratic ideal of Christ and Emperor. Some rural communities probably closely dependent upon a city, like Shepton Mallet on the Fosse between Ilchester and Bath, or Kenn just across the Exe from Exeter, also seem to have had at least some people who identified themselves as Christians.

Overall, we sense a difference between the cities, and the rural hinterland. This probably does not reflect a distinction between an upper and a lower or labouring class. The Poundbury evidence suggests that the Christian community included the poor people of Dorchester, while out in the country the quality of some of the temple buildings and the metal offerings suggests support from the wealthy.

As the fifth century progressed, there were in Britain active Christians as the careers of Patrick and Germanus attest (and who, it is worth remembering for both Britain and Gaul, were able to influence the written record for future generations). These people were shaping the much more clearly Christian society which would appear as the sixth century progressed. Within this perhaps belong the ambiguous changes at temple sites, such as Uley, Pagans Hill, Lamyatt Brean and Henley Wood, where the temple complexes (or elements in them) seem to have been turned into focal buildings for cemeteries. Conspicuously, however, when these communities finally acquired the unambiguously Christian sites which emerge as parish churches and graveyards, these are on different sites. Perhaps what we see are social and emotional movements in the fourth and fifth centuries which Christian sentiment and practice were able to make their own, as they shaped themselves to the slowly emerging structures of small-scale authority linked with land, and burial grounds expressive of identity and unity.

What this was like to experience, we can only guess. The grey and green dignity, which we are accustomed to associate with ancient religious sites, Christian or otherwise, is very wide of the late and post-Roman mark. Successful Christian centres, in Gaul at any rate, were those where powerful things happened and marvels could be experienced, together with hysterical outbursts, crowds sizable for the time and place, wild rumour, beggars, the sick, penitents and overwrought devotion. Perhaps, sometimes, things like this happened in Exeter or Bath. Outside in the country, matters may have been different. For all we know, fourth-, and perhaps some fifth-century religious observance, whatever its place on some theoretical yardstick of Christian belief, in some parts of the south-west may have been a sort of creole practice, a kind of voodoo featuring graves and even the occasional severed head, providing excitement, comfort and the sense of local togetherness which matched developing economic and legal structures.

4 Cemeteries and monasteries

Introduction

As we have seen, by about AD 500, there were a number of graveyards across the south-west, characterized by east–west findless inhumation burials, and a few, perhaps, marked by inscribed stones, but otherwise very varied in character and background. By the year 1000 (to take a good round date), we see in the peninsula a large range of unambiguously Christian sites. In Cornwall there were eventually to be nearly 200 parish graveyards with churches, the original sites of many of which were in existence by 1000; other sites of similar antiquity did not achieve parochial status but were used as chapels. Beside these were some twenty endowed religious houses. East of the Tamar, the character and diversity and probable dates of origin were similar but the sites were larger in number, reflecting the greater geographical extent. Devon eventually had some 480 parish sites, Somerset about the same and Dorset just under 300. By the time of our arbitrarily chosen terminal date, the majority of these sites encompassed a burial yard, a church building and sometimes important carved stones, all within a clearly denoted boundary. Most seem to have provided pastoral care, which must often have meant the organization of living quarters. There were also a large number of more ambiguous sites, especially the holy wells, across the peninsula.

The histories of many of these sites are very complex. At the broader level, as each social need or crisis developed, the existing pack of Christian sites was shuffled, so that some new sites were founded, some dropped out of use and many re-emerged with different, or new, functions which were grafted onto old identities, a process which sometimes left traces which help our understanding of how all this happened. Locally, the process was likely to have been piecemeal, subject to sudden bursts of enthusiasm and comparable *longueurs*, involved with family arrangements, which might have come to fruition slowly, and characterized by failures and exploitations as well as long-term success.

These sites need accounting for at all levels – chronological and developmental, social and economic, and cultural, in terms both of the broad phenomenon and of why we are faced with the different kinds of sites. The evidence needed to bear on these thorny issues embraces excavated and observed features, place-names, carved and inscribed stones, and hagiographical traditions, all of which have their own specialist literatures. We will take a peninsula-wide view of the development of local Christian graveyards and endowed religious houses, treating, particularly, the Cornish monasteries and the West Saxon minsters as similar manifestations of a western European-wide, broadly contemporary impulse.

In view of the immense literature which attempts to delineate the distinctions between the way Christian institutions operated in western Britain and Ireland on the one hand and the Anglo-Saxon kingdoms on the other, this may seem to be a risky strategy. However, as the cool voice of serious scholarship has urged on all the key issues – the calculation of the date of Easter, the position of bishops, the shape of the tonsure and the 'saintly' and 'eremitical' nature of the British and Irish church – the whole of the western Church up to perhaps 800 was characterized by the considerable diversity we might expect from an institution which had had a range of roots and contrasting influences and which was finding its own way to uniformity, a process which was never finally completed.[1] Particular observances which surfaced from time to time in western Britain and Ireland seem to be a part of this much broader process, and the most which can be said is that in some areas, especially Wales, a certain conservative spirit is perceptible.

All these issues are, of course, bound up with the 'Celticity' of the west, and also with the increasingly better understood effects of Bede's sympathies and prejudices. Our direct evidence for belief and practice among the British in the south-west is tiny, and the frequent assumption that it was the same as that in Wales cannot be effectively demonstrated; in any case, no region had a single 'practice' across its area through time. What does seem to be true in the south-west is that there was a considerable period during which Christian institutions and practices could be established by the local British-speakers, running perhaps to 530/550 in the east, and gradually, in piecemeal fashion, extending to perhaps 800 or even later in the west. These initiatives on the part of British-speakers interfaced in a complex fashion, with those of English-speakers and with the developing power and policies of the West Saxon kingdom.

This chapter will first examine in some detail the crucial evidence presented by the range of relevant place-name elements which refer to Christian sites in the post-Roman period. It will then assess the development of the local, non-monastic graveyards. A similar discussion of the monastic sites will follow, and the final section will assess the social implications of these developments.

The implications of place-names

*lann

The place-name *lann* (where the asterisk indicates that the word does not occur in contemporary records apart from place-names) is one of an important series of place-name elements which have been used as part of the name-creating process at a range of sites, including what became parish churches with their own graveyards, religious houses and the sites of medieval chapels.

In 1985, Padel defined *lann* as the Old Cornish equivalent of Welsh *llan*, widespread in Wales, and Breton *lann*, all meaning 'enclosed cemetery'.[2] About fifty

---

1.   Most recently by W. Davies, 'The myth of the Celtic Church', in N. Edwards and A. Lane (eds), *The Early Church in Wales and the West* (1992), pp. 12–21. See also N. Merriman, 'Values and motivation in pre-history: the evidence for the "Celtic spirit" ', in I. Hodder (ed.), *The Archaeology of Contextual Meanings* (1987), pp. 111–16; P. Sims-Williams, 'The visionary Celt: the construction of an ethnic preconception', *Cam. Med. Celtic Stud.*, 11 (1986): 71–96.
2.   O. Padel, *Cornish Place-names Elements* (1985), pp. 142–5.

of the Cornish parish churches out of 199 (Fig. 52), are known to have names in *lann*.[3] There are two such parish names in north Devon at Landcross[4] and Landkey,[5] one in Somerset at Leigh-on-Street, earlier *Lan-to-kai*, near Glastonbury,[6] and one in north Dorset at Sherborne, earlier *Lanprobi* (or similar).[7] Sites which appear to have a name in *lann* but which, as far as is known, have always had a secular character should be treated with caution because of great confusion with *nans*, 'valley', but it is often impossible to say whether a particular name contains one element or the other.[8] Non-parochial chapel or enclosed cemetery sites are seldom associated with apparent *lann* names: of known medieval chapels the only ones with *lann* names are St Mawer (*Lavousa*), St Michael's in Padstow (*Leveals*) and Lellisick, and of cemeteries Halland ('the old cemetery') and Lanvean. All together, Padel estimates that 'the number of names in *lann* [in Cornwall] cannot be less than 60 (including those of

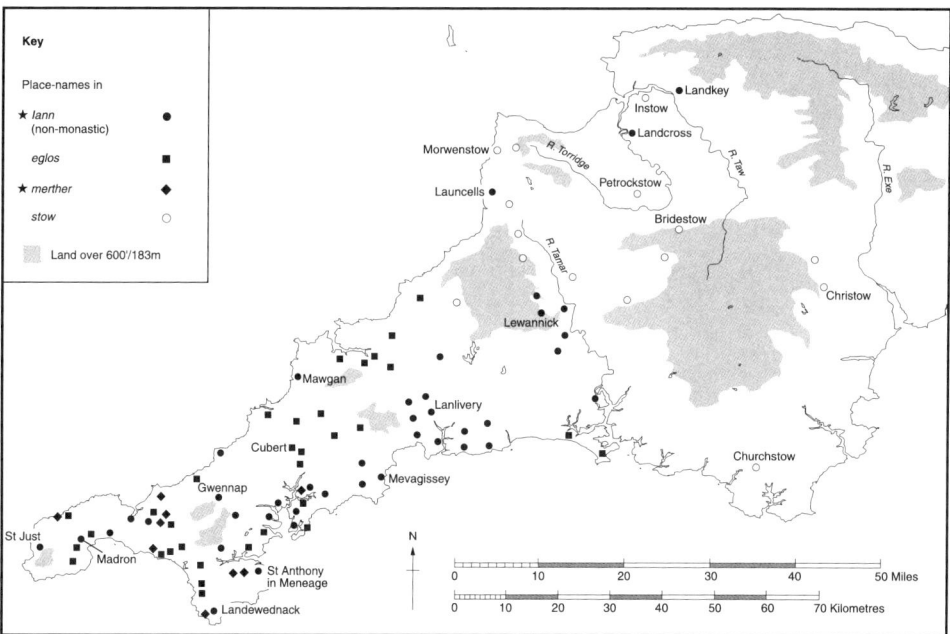

Figure 52 Location map of parish churches with names with element *lann* (monastic sites omitted) and *eglos*, and place-names with element *stow* and *merther* (some doubtful examples omitted; modern names are used)

3. O. Padel, 'Cornish language notes: 5. Cornish names of parish churches', *Cornish Studies* (1976–7): 15–27.

4. O. Padel, personal communication; H. Meade, *Archaeological Check-List of Landcross Parish* (1979).

5. J. Gover, A. Mawer and F. Stenton, *The Place-names of Devon* (1932), pp. 341–2.

6. A. Turner, 'Some Somerset place-names containing Celtic elements', *Bulletin Board of Celtic Studies*, 14 (1952): 113–19; see also A. Robinson, *Somerset Historical Essays* (1921), p. 48.

7. K. Barker, 'The early Christian topography of Sherborne', *Antiquity*, 54 (1980): 229–31 and refs there.

8. Padel, *Cornish Place-name Elements*, p. 144.

parish churches) and it is most unlikely to be as many as 140. The true figure is probably not more than 100.'[9]

Of the south-western *lann* names, 21 in Cornwall are compounded with a personal name which is that of the saint to whom the church is dedicated; of those outside Cornwall, Sherborne seems to recognize Probus as a significant local saint. Of the 21, some eleven had, or may well have had, religious communities before *c.* 1050, and this is also true of Sherborne. Some of the 23 Cornish parish names involve *lann* + a personal name which is not that of the dedication, as do Landkey in Devon and *Lan-to-kai* in Somerset.[10] Three have topographically descriptive names: Landraith ('the enclosed graveyard on the strand', not a parish until 1845), Lawithick (incorporating middle Cornish *gwithek* 'wooded') and Landcross ('the enclosed graveyard on the marsh'). Finally, Lannived looks as if it incorporates earlier British *nemeto*, 'sacred place, sacred wood, sanctuary'. In physical terms, the 'enclosure' element of the place-names in *lann*, and Welsh *llan*, is taken to refer to the roughly round or oval banks which surround the ancient cores of those sites which possess this feature.

Given that *lann* appears to become more common towards western Cornwall, it may not have gone out of use here as an element in the formation of a new name until *c.* 1200, or even later. The surviving *lann* names in northern parts of the peninsula east of the Tamar suggest that *lann* was in active use as a place-name element from perhaps the fifth/sixth centuries to the early eighth century; it seems unlikely that new names in *lann* would be created for significant social sites east of the Tamar after *c.* 710 (even if special pleading were to be mounted for both Sherborne and the Glastonbury area), but this does not, of course, mean that new *lann* names were not created in Cornwall after this time.

The majority of the eleven sites with religious communities seem to have been founded between *c.* 500–*c.* 700, and it is likely that the saints whose dedications they bear had often been involved in their foundation.[11] These names in *lann* are correspondingly likely to have been in place by the same date. Nevertheless, the earliest definite use of *lann* place-names in the south-west occurs in tenth-century charters, and the earliest list which gives the impression of a widespread network of churches and saints, that in the Vatican List,[12] also dates from the tenth century. Much depends here on the Welsh evidence, and in particular on the status of the material in the *Book of Llandaff.*[13] What purport to be the earliest dated charters, if they can be trusted, in the *Book of Llandaff* would date the *llan* names they contain to the late sixth century, and some, at least, of their forms may bear this out: but *llan* was still being used to form place-names post-1066, as *Llanthomas* in Mitchell Troy parish demonstrates.[14] Overall, the use of *lann* meaning 'enclosed Christian cemetery' in the south-west seems to have begun in the post-Roman period and to

9. Padel, *Cornish Place-name Elements*, p. 154.
10. This does not take into account the fact that dedications have changed over the centuries. We do not know what the original dedications of Landkey or Leigh were.
11. See below, pp. 106–75.
12. L. Olsen and O. Padel, 'A tenth-century list of Cornish parochial saints', *Cam. Med. Celtic Stud.*, 12 (1986): 33–71.
13. K. Dark, *Civitas to Kingdom: British Political Continuity 300–800* (1994), pp. 140–8; K. Maund, 'Fact and narrative fiction in the Llandaff Charters', *Studia Celtica*, 31 (1997): 173–93.
14. D. Brook, 'The early Christian Church in Gwent', *Monmouth Antiquary*, 5 (1985–8): 69.

have continued to 1200 at the outside, but 'it may well be that it was largely out of use by an earlier date than that'. This dating matches the Welsh evidence, and it allows a considerable time frame for the creating of the names and of the sites they signify.

*merther

As far as Latin loan words are concerned, no south-western place-names have been found which derive, directly or indirectly, from *basilica*, or from *memoria*. *Merther* has been long recognized as a Cornish place-name cognate with Welsh *merthyr* and Breton *merzher* meaning 'saint's grave; place holding the body of a saint'.[15] The Irish word, *martrae*, was in use by the eighth century meaning 'physical relics, bones', but although all these terms derive from the Latin *martyrium*, meaning 'place possessing a martyr's remains', in the British Isles the terms came by extension to mean 'church or cemetery, holding the physical remains of a named saint or martyr'.[16] Only a small proportion of the sites which claimed named relics of this kind ever had a name in *merther* or *merthyr*, so plainly processes of choice were at work in its usage.

The south Welsh evidence demonstrates that the *merthyr* element could be lost: the Llandaff charters mention ten such place-names presumably in existence by *c.* 950, but many, like Merthyr Tecmed which appears as early as *c.* 750, were named in *llan*, as Llandegveth by 1254, and Llanvaches has a similar history.[17] In several cases *merthyr* was replaced by *llan* or *eglwys*: Llangaffo and Llanfeirian, both in Anglesey, were also called, perhaps originally, *Merthyr Caffo* and *Merthyr Meirion*, this last eventually a chapel in the parish of Llangadwaladr.[18] Dingestow, in the form *Merthyr Dingad*, is not recorded until 1119, although of course this may have been its name in local speech well before.[19] The Merthyr place-names in Wales are concentrated in the south-east, and include '*Merthir Julian et Aaron*', the burial place of the (presumed genuine) martyrs Julian and Aaron outside Caerleon.[20] This might suggest that here the term is early, and has some link with late Roman Christianity, but it might also hint that Julian and Aaron's site influenced local nomenclature in the period after *c.* 450. Ten Cornish sites are known to involve the element *merther*. These sites are concentrated in south-western Cornwall for no very apparent reason, and it is possible that this is the result of some local influence or fashion.

What emerges from this is a mixed picture. Two sites, *Mertherderwa* in Camborne parish and Merther Uny in Wendron, were never fully fledged parish graveyards. At St Martin-in-Meneage the place-names recording two different holy names were attached to adjoining estates, not to the church itself, by the fourteenth century; something similar is true of Merther in Morvah, *Merther Heuni* in Redruth, and Ruan

15. Padel, *Cornish Place-name Elements*, p. 164 and refs there. The equivalent in France, *martres*, occurs as the name of a variety of sites, as at Martres-de-Veyre, near Clermont Ferrand; it often coincides with a large medieval cemetery, J. Knight, *Roman France* (2001), p. 129.
16. C. Thomas, *The Early Christian Archaeology of North Britain* (1971), p. 89.
17. Brook, 'Early Christian Church in Gwent', p. 69.
18. M. Richards, 'Ecclesiastical and secular in medieval Welsh Settlement', *Studia Celtica*, 3 (1968): 15.
19. Brook, 'Early Christian Church in Gwent', p. 69.
20. *Ibid.*

Major and Landewednack, where the **merther* name appears in a boundary. Only at Merther and *Merthersithney*, now Sithney, are there parish names in **merther*, and William of Worcester records the belief that Sithney was buried in the church. Both the Redruth and Wendron sites claimed the relics of Euny.[21]

Most known *merthyr* sites in Wales seem to have some special historical or archaeological feature.[22] For Cornwall, apart from the intrinsic interest of the names themselves, and the claims to holy burials just mentioned, this is true only in a limited way. 'Meneage' had a monastic character[23] and Merther Euny, Redruth, had a standing cross of *c.* 1000, but none of the sites possesses early inscribed stones. Charcoal and Bronze Age pottery were found in a pipe trench near Merthyr Cynog[24] but the only **merther* site excavated in the south-west is Merther Uny, Wendron (Fig. 53). This seems to have started as a first century BC/first century AD roughly oval domestic round of usual local type. By around AD 1000, a date given by the bar-lug pottery, the enclosure had been enlarged and equipped with a sunken wheel-head granite cross; worked stone fragments suggested that a chapel stood here by around 1150. Associated with the site were 'an extensive series' of dug graves orientated

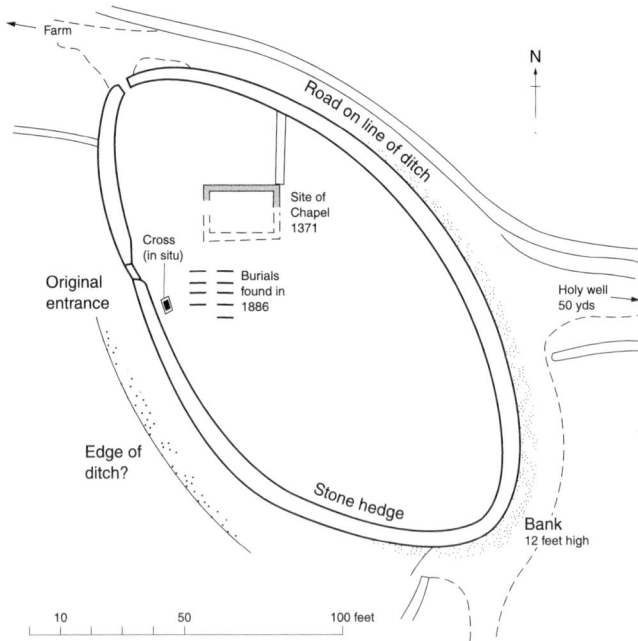

Figure 53 Merther Uny, Wendron (after Thomas 1967, Fig. 9)

21.   S. Pearce, *The Kingdom of Dumnonia* (1978), p. 62; Padel, *Cornish Place-name Elements*, p. 164.
22.   Brook, 'Early Christian Church in Gwent', p. 69.
23.   See below pp. 178, 209–10.
24.   RCAHMW, *An Inventory of the Ancient Monuments in Brecknock (Brycheiniog): The Prehistoric and Roman Monuments. Part I Later Prehistoric Monuments and Unenclosed Settlements to 1000 AD* (1997), p. 72.

roughly east–west, but direct evidence dating of what seemed the earliest phase of the burials was lacking; however, Thomas concluded that these belonged with the bar-lug pottery and cross.[25]

The site suggests that **merther* names could come into being very late, unless the earliest phase of burials was earlier than thought and represented a phase of use at the site which succeeded the farming round but preceded the refurbishing of the enclosure and the erection of the cross: in this case the **merther* name could be of an earlier date. Taken with the south Welsh evidence, the picture overall could suggest that **merther* was an early element in local Christian nomenclature, and that at least some of the relevant sites preceded the establishment of the full parochial system, in which case the name stood a good chance of being supplanted at the church site itself, to survive only in ancillary place-names. At other places, the use of the name was evidently considerably later.

eglos

Cornish *eglos*, meaning 'church', derives from Latin *ecclesia*, like modern Welsh *eglwys*, but place-names which relate to these later forms must be kept carefully separate from the group of place-names in *eccles* (also from *ecclesia*) which may indicate Christian communities in late or sub-Roman Britain: there do not seem to be any of this type in the peninsula.[26] As Padel points out, 'when the word *eglos* occurs as a first element of the name of a church, it is usually followed by the name of the patron saint, or else by a topographical element.'[27] He lists 21 cases where *eglos* occurs with the patron's name, one of which, *Eglosseynney*, replaced an earlier *Merthersithney*, although the *eglos* form is not recorded until 1623. There are five sites with descriptive elements, including *Eglosmerther* (1201) as an alternative to Merther. The remaining four have topographical elements. Two further instances – *Eglos-Withiel* (1692) and *Eglospenbro* (1284) – refer to district names, respectively Withiel and Breage, and the last is an alternative name for *Eglosbrek* (1181). Two names incorporate **lann* and *eglos* at Lanteglos by Camelford and Lanteglos by Fowey, and two *eglos* names apparently belong to chapel sites. Finally, a group of five cases have *eglos* as a more general qualifying element.

The period through which *eglos/eglwys* was used in name formation has been hotly debated. In Wales there is never more than one *eglwys* name in a commote, which may be a pointer to antiquity.[28] There are also more *eglwys* names in eastern Wales than in the west, a fact capable of suggesting either that the name has some (unknown) link with very early, even sub-Roman, ecclesiastical arrangements, or that it represents new or renamed sites through some reflection of the use of *ecclesia* in the developing post-800 bureaucracy. The same broad argument applies equally to the south-western sites, and the name element alone does not give much help in dating.

25. C. Thomas, 'Excavations at Crane Godrevy, Gwithian, 1969: interim report', *Corn Arch.*, 8 (1969): 81–2.
26. C. Thomas, *Christianity in Roman Britain to AD 500* (1981), pp. 262–5.
27. Padel, 'Cornish language notes, 5', p. 19.
28. T. Roberts, 'Welsh ecclesiastical place-names and archaeology', in N. Edwards and A. Lane (eds), *The Early Church in Wales and the West* (1992), pp. 41–4.

stow

The cluster of place-names incorporating the English element *stow* is so noticeable a feature of the nomenclature of ecclesiastical place-names in north-west Devon and north-east Cornwall that it demands an explanation. OE *stow* can be defined as 'assembly place' or 'holy place' and examples are known from across the country.[29] The word can be used very generally as at Plaistow, Sussex, and elsewhere, where it means 'place for play or sports', or Chepstow, Gwent, 'ceapstow' where it means 'market place'.[30] The original essence of the word seems to concentrate upon the notion of people coming together to carry out a special, corporate activity, and there is broad agreement, from the generally wide but fairly thin distribution of names in *stow*, that religious observance was the right kind of activity to generate a *stow* name.

What makes the occurrence of the element in the peninsula particularly noteworthy is the number of times it appears in a very small area, quite unlike the generally dispersed distribution, although there are also in the south-west a number of relevant names scattered outside the main concentration. Within Cornwall, there are Davidstow (*ecclesia S. Davidi alias Dewstow*, 1269), Jacobstow (*Jacobstowe*, 1270), Michaelstow (*Mighelstowe*, 1302), Morwenstow (*Morwestowa*, 1201), St Neot (*Nietestow*, 1086),[31] Padstow (*Eldestowe*, 1086; *Padestowe*, 1347), Warbstow (*capella S. Wergerge, c.* 1180)[32] and St Martin by Looe attested as *Martistowe* in early records.[33] The first reference to the Grenville estate known as Stowe by the seventeenth century is the licensing of a chapel called Stowe in the parish of Kilkhampton in 1368. Some worked stones from the chapel survive,[34] and by 1519 it was dedicated to St Christina de Stowe.[35] To these should be added Mixtow,

29.   A. Mills, *A Dictionary of English Place-names* (1998), pp. 274, 406.

30.   M. Gelling, 'Some meanings of Stow', in S. Pearce, *The Early Church in Western Britain and Ireland* (1982), pp. 187–96.

31.   The hagiography of Neot is extremely confused. He is patron of St Neots, or Eynesbury, in Huntingdonshire, as well as St Neot in Cornwall. 'The list of saints' resting places in Anglo-Saxon England' (see D. Rollason, *Anglo-Saxon England*, 7 (1978): 61–93), in what is probably a late tenth-century section of the list, says Neot rests at the Huntingdon site, although the church of St Neot's (Cor) has the remains of a fourteenth-century relic shrine. By 1100, St Neot's (Hunts) was a daughter house of Bec, and so was Cowick near Exeter, which may have helped various confusions and transferences of the cult to Cornwall. However, a saint called Nioth (or Kioth) appears in the tenth-century list (Olson and Padel, 'List of Cornish parochial saints', pp. 49–51) and this may also have been involved in the various transfers; see N. Orme, *English Church Dedications* (1996), p. 107.

32.   J. Gover, *The Place Names of Cornwall* (1948), pp. (in order of reference) 53, 3, 72, 18, 284, 356, 89.

33.   O. Padel, *A Popular Dictionary of Cornish Place-names* (1988), p. 116.

34.   D. Harris and R. Heard, 'Hundred of Stratton 2: parish of Kilkhampton', *Corn. Arch.*, 19 (1975): 99. Harris and Heard also record 'Penstowe' as an alternative name for Winswood Castle, a 'round', i.e., ?domestic enclosure, in Kilkhampton parish, p. 99. There is also Lestow, see p. 255 note 10.

35.   W. Wilson-North, 'Stowe: the country house and garden of the Grenville family', *Corn. Arch.*, 32 (1993): 113.

Mixtou alias Middlestou (1587)[36] on the Fowey estuary and Stowe Hill on Bodmin Moor.

These Cornish sites are clearly a mixed bunch. The first record of the name tends to be late and, with the exceptions of Padstow, assumed to refer to Petroc, and Morwenna at Morwenstow, who was drawn into the hagiography of the Children of Brychan, the saints referred to belong to pan-Christendom (James, Martin, Michael) or come from outside the traditions of the region (David) or from English traditions (Werburga[37]), while the status of a chapel like Stowe in Kilkhampton is uncertain. The original English name of Padstow, 'the old *stow*', is purely descriptive, and reflects the history of the monastery of St Petroc.

The cluster of *stow* names in Devon is rather larger. Some of the sites emerge as parish churches dedicated to regional saints post *c.* 1000, as Petrockstow (*Petroc (L)estoua*, 1086), to pan-Christian saints, as Jacobstowe (*Jacop-stoue*), and Marystow (*Ecc. S. Marie Stou*, 1266–78), or to traditions from beyond the region as at Bridestowe (*Bridestou*, 1086) and Virginstow (*Virginstowe*, 1174–83), both dedicated to Bridget. Maristow in Tamerton Foliot is *Capellam S. Martini* in the reign of Henry II, *Martinstowe* in 1346 and *Martynstowe al Maristowe* in 1550. There is also Maristowe in Abbotskerswell, which may be very recent. Two names simply mean 'holy gathering place' (*Halestou*, 1086; *Halstowe*, 1244);[38] and Christow, which is not recorded until 1244, probably reflects the Kilkhampton dedication to Christina,[39] while Churchstow (*Churechstowe*, 1242) means what it looks like, intimating that the site had a church building at the time it received its name. Cheristow, a chapel site in Hartland, also means 'Church-stow' (*Chircstoua*, 1167) but retained its dedication to St Wen, another name brought into the Brychan traditions, (*cappelam sancte Wenne de Chirestowe*, 1198).[40]

There is also Stowford, a parish site, deemed to mean 'ford marked by staves or posts', a conclusion plainly suggested by its appearance as *Estaveforda* and *Staveford*, 1066.[41] 'Stowford' is a common Devon place-name with at least thirteen

---

36. Gover, *Place Names of Cornwall*, p. 271.
37. Werburga was a Mercian princess, said to be daughter of Wulfhere and granddaughter of Penda according to Goscelin of Canterbury (*c.* 1090) and Florence of Worcester (d. 1118): if this is true she flourished *c.* 680. She is said to have been a nun at Ely and to have been buried at Hanbury (Staffs) *c.* 700. About 900 the nuns of Hanbury transferred her relics to the church of St Peter and St Paul, Chester; *c.* 1093 a Benedictine abbey was founded in Chester dedicated to Werburga, which evidently became the cathedral. There were dedications to her also at Bristol, Henbury and Bath. For details of the Bath site, see P. Greening, 'St Werburga's by Bath', in W. Wedlake, *Excavations at Camerton, Somerset* (1966), pp. 20–4.
38. Gover *et al.*, *Place-names of Devon* (1931, 1932), pp. 105, 116, 199, 177, 212, 242, 434, 313.
39. Gover *et al.*, *Place-names of Devon* (1932), p. 430, suggest derivation from *cristene-stowe* because 'the church is not dedicated to St Christina and we have no evidence for her cult in England', but see above reference to St Christina de Stowe in Kilkhampton. The Grenvilles held land in Bideford and further research might produce a link with Christow.
40. Gover *et al.*, *Place-names of Devon* (1931, 1932), pp. 295, 72. Some versions of the *Laws of Edgar* (mid-tenth century) and the *Laws of Æthelred* (1014), which regulate payments to churches, use the word *legerstow* for 'graveyard'. This compound word is obviously not the earliest usage for either element, but given that it is the possession of a burial ground which distinguishes between the two smaller classes of churches in the *Laws*, the compound may have been a relevant factor in nomenclature; see F. Liebermann, *Die Gesetze der Angelsachsen*, Vol. 1, pp. xxx, 196, 197, 264 and 282.
41. Gover *et al.*, *Place-names of Devon* (1931), p. 41.

occurrences across the county[42] and the names relate to a water crossing, but the position of Stowford parish is complicated by the fact that the churchyard possesses an early inscribed stone. Stowford in Swimbridge had a chapel dedicated to St Hieretha (or similar), a saint whose principal church was at Chittlehampton in north Devon.[43] Brimpts in Lydford was *Birmstestowe, Brimestow* in 1199, where the first element is *bremel*, 'bramble-grown', and lost *Gorandestowe* (1279) in Weare Gifford seems to embody the family name Gurand, known in the area in the thirteenth century, and if so it must be a post-Conquest formation.[44] Finally, a farm and a headland on Batson Creek at Salcombe are called Ilbertstow and Ilbertstow Point, presumably an English compound, and a farm in Paignton is Tavistowe, perhaps a modern coinage.[45]

No *stow* names seem to be recorded for Dorset, but several are known from Somerset. Bristol derives from English *brycg* and *stow* but whether the bridge is the assembly place, or whether an assembly place acquired a bridge is not clear; if the former then perhaps the oldest Bristol church was meant. Stowbarrow Hill is just south-east of the large parish churchyard of St Ethelreda at West Quantoxhead. It was part of the deer park attached to St Audrie's manor, adjacent to St Audrie's Bay, and seems always to have been rough hunting and grazing land. In Yatton there is Stowe Farm and Stowey, Stowley in Luxborough and Westowe in Lydeard St Lawrence, but no recent work has been done on these. There is also *Wodestow*, perhaps 'holy place in the wood', in Batcombe which, if it does have a religious significance might belong to an early phase of local English speech. Interestingly, Glastonbury is described by the word *stow* by Bishop Æthelwold in the later tenth century.[46]

It seems clear that on the Welsh–English linguistic border *llan* and *stow* were sometimes used interchangeably, or *stow* was used as an English translation of *llan* if the English speakers encountered a Welsh place-name for which they needed an English version. So in Herefordshire Marstow is recorded as *Lann Martin c.* 1130 and Martinstowe in 1277, and Peterstow as *Lannpetyr c.* 1130 and Peterstow in 1207; Herefordshire also has Stowe (*Stowa*, 1193) and Bridstow (Old Welsh, *Lann san Bregit*).[47] Most interestingly, Gwent has Dingestow, dedicated to the local saint Dingad. The same area also has Dewstow and Wonastow. There is a comparable example from St Martin in Looe, which is referred to as *Martistowe* as well as *Lancoff.*[48]

42.   Also in Cornwall e.g. between Lifton and Lewtrenchard and near Marystow.

43.   Orme, *Dedications*, p. 144.

44.   Gover *et al.*, *Place-names of Devon* (1931), p. 192, and P. Reaney and A. Smith, *The Place-names of Cambridgeshire and the Isle of Ely* (1943), 'Addenda and corrigenda', under Vol. 8.

45.   OS maps of Devon. The element continues to be used in the formation of place-names: 'Bishopstowe' just above Redgate Beach in St Marychurch was chosen by the Bishop of Exeter when he built his country home in the later nineteenth century.

46.   See J. Hill, *The Place-names of Somerset* (1914), pp. 89, 354–5; G. Grundy, *Saxon Charters and Field Names* (1935), p. 88. For Glastonbury, see 'Æthelwold's Old English account of King Eadgar's establishment of minsters', in D. Whitelock, M. Brett and C. Brooke, *Councils and Synods with Other Documents relating to the English Church* (1981), pp. 142–54, no. 33.

47.   A. Smith, *English Place-name Elements* (1956), p.160; B. Coplestone-Crow, *Hertfordshire Place-names* (1989); Padel, *Dictionary of Cornish Place-names* (1988), p. 116; A. Preston-Jones, 'Decoding Cornish churchyards', in Edwards and Lane, *Early Church in Wales and the West* (1992), p. 109.

48.   Preston-Jones (1992), p. 109.

Clearly, all this represents a complex situation. The older name for Padstow, *Eldestowe*, 'the Old Church', presumably refers to the move made by the monastery of St Petroc to Bodmin, which is generally dated to around the Scandinavian raid on Padstow, in which case the place-name as it stands is presumably later ninth century. This fits with the dedication to Werburga at Warbstow, and perhaps also the dedication to Ethelreda at West Quantoxhead. Equally, dedications to Bridget, to David in Cornwall and Petroc in Devon may not be earlier than *c.* 800. The dedications to James, John, Mary, Martin and Michael (and Peter in Hereford) are to pan-Christian saints and impossible to date, although they would be characteristic of post-700 dedicating practices, and of course some of them may not be the dedication a site had originally. Equally, some of the *stow* elements are joined to names of apparently genuinely local holy people like Morwenna (and Dingad in Monmouth) or to traditions like those of Wenne at Cheristow, unless these two were produced during the creation of the Brychan traditions. The 'Petroc' element in Padstow seems to have been a late name for a place whose original name, in any case, was *Lanwethenek* or similar.

A model to account for this suggests that in the border lands, where British and English speakers mixed, *llan/*lann* and *stow* could be used interchangeably to describe an ecclesiastical site, and that *stow* became particularly fashionable on the Devon/Cornwall border. In some cases, English speakers may have used the word to describe a Christian site, which existed when they arrived in the area, a process which took place in east-central Devon around *c.* 650, and in north-west Devon/north-east Cornwall around *c.* 700 possibly giving Cheristow and Morwenstowe (and in Gwent around the same time, giving us Dingestow). However most of the ecclesiastical place names in *stow* look later, some much later, and are probably post-700, suggesting either a dedication change in some way associated with the English name, or the construction and consequent naming of such sites in English or in both Welsh and English after *c.* 700. *Gorandestowe*, Devon, demonstrates how late place-names in *stow* could go on being formed.

stocu, circe and 'saint'

The English place-name element *stoc*, which is extremely common across the country, gives names with *stock*, normally as a suffix, and *stoke* as a prefix, and its interest here is that it could be used to indicate a religious place, as well as the more common 'outlying or dependent settlement'. In this sense we have Halstock, Dorset, 'holy place/settlement', which came to possess a religious house; Halstock to the north of Dartmoor (Okehampton), where there was a chapel dedicated to St Michael by at least 1240; and Halstock Wood just west of the parish church at Belstone, also on Dartmoor.[49] The same religious associations appear in Tavistock and Frithelstock, an Augustinian priory (both Devon) and in Kewstoke (Somerset).[50] A number of

---

49. Gover *et al.*, *Place-names of Devon* (1931), p. 203; E. Fogwill, 'Pastoralism on Dartmoor', *TDA*, 86 (1954): 99. Halstock seems to bear some relationship to rights on Dartmoor, and so perhaps Halstock Wood may also have done.

50. Although a number of similar formations from river names – Culmstock, Plymstock – do not seem to have any particular ecclesiastical significance. For relevant sites, see A. Smith, *Place-names of the East Riding of Yorkshire and York* (1939), p.1i.

parish names take the form 'stoke' plus dedicatory names, such as Stoke St Gregory, Stoke St Mary, Stoke St Michael (Somerset) and Stoke Gabriel, and Stoke St Nectan (Devon).

There are some twenty place-names in Devon which embody the Old English element 'church',[51] *circ(e)*, a similar number in Somerset and few, like Marhamchurch, in Cornwall. Not all of these refer to parishes, rather than chapels, but many, like St Mary Church near Torquay, do. Evidence from Herefordshire shows that 'church' could also be used as an equivalent for *llan* in the Welsh border. Kenderchurch was called *Lann Crue* in 1045–1104, *Lanncinitir lana icruc* in 1066–87, *Santi Kenedri c.* 1200 and *Kend(er)-Church(e)* in 1397, an interesting series which includes both a holy name, Cynidr, and a topographical description, *cruc*, 'hill-shaped like a burial mound', in its nomenclature. Similarly, Kentchurch was *Lan Cein* in 1045–1104, *Sancta Kaenae* about 1100 and (*ecclesia de*) *Keme* in 1194, and Whitchurch was *Lann Tiuinauc* in 1054–1104 and *Wytechirche* in 1320.[52]

The prefix 'saint' linked with a personal name as the name of a parish is notoriously widespread west of the Tamar and occurs, for example, in Devon at St Giles in the Wood and in Somerset at Stoke St Gregory. Both the Cornish *Sen*, *Synta* (used as a title), and the English 'saint' are, of course, versions of the Latin *sanctus*, holy. Similarly formed place-names occur across the Christian world.

The purpose of this brief discussion of these three place-names is to draw attention to the fact that relatively large numbers of the names for parishes, and especially in the eastern part of the peninsula for the central villages within parishes, are drawn from the name and existence of the ecclesiastical site, rather than from a natural feature, or habitative name, or some kind of personal name. The creation of these place-names is obviously part of the process by which the early approaches to the establishment of religion and to pastoral care changed and developed into the full parish system.

Bound up with all of this are the local dedications and hagiographical traditions. These, as those of western Britain and Ireland generally, present a terrifyingly complex pattern of religious history and fantasy.[53] Somerset has fourteen or so religious sites,[54] including later parish churches, dedicated to saints with British or Irish names and affiliations. A few of these, like Cai at Street, have early support, but most do not. Some, like the dedications to Bridget at Beckery, seem to be part of Glastonbury's hagiographical activity. Nevertheless, given the likelihood of early monastic activity in sixth-century Somerset, some, at least of the local-looking dedications are probably the only surviving evidence of the contemporary development of Christian graveyards. We possess a tenth-century list of Cornish parochial saints, which gives 48 names of Cornish or pan-Britannic saints, which can be related to particular cult sites in Cornwall.[55] This need not mean that the cults were in place much before 900,

51.   Gover, *et al.*, *Place-names of Devon* (1932), p. 659.
52.   Coplestone-Crow, *Hereford Place-names* (1989), pp. 109–10, 205–6.
53.   They will be considered in more detail in Ch. 6.
54.   See S. Pearce, 'The dating of some Celtic dedications and hagiographical traditions in south-western Britain', *TDA*, 105 (1973): 95–120; M. Costen, *The Origins of Somerset* (1992), pp. 100–10; I. Burrow, *Hillforts and Hill-top Settlement in Somerset in the First to Eighth Centuries AD* (1981), fig. 30; for analysis of Culborne parish, see H. Riley and R. Wilson-North, *The Field Archaeology of Exmoor* (2001), pp. 88–9.
55.   Olson and Padel, 'List of Cornish parochial saints'.

although some may have been. Llansadwrn in Anglesey has an inscribed stone commemorating the blessed Saturninus and 'his saintly wife', where Saturninus, clearly not a monk, seems to be the personal name referred to in the place-name, which shows that non-monastic cemeteries with founders or early names attached existed by *c.* 600 at the latest; but instances where this can be traced are very rare, and Saturninus may have been special, perhaps a bishop, as his epithet *beatus* ('blessed') suggests.[56]

Place-names considered collectively

One of the few points which emerges reasonably clearly from the place-name evidence is the way in which the categories were not distinct, but on the contrary were used as equivalents of one another, depending upon the context, and the language which the writer, and perhaps local informants, were using. Wonastow (Gwent) was presumably what the English speakers of south-east Wales called the church site in the tenth/eleventh century, but in the Latin perambulation it is *ecclesia Gurthebiriuc.*[57] *Eglwys Cain*, like a number of names in *eglwys* in the *Liber Llandaff*, has seen *eglwys* replaced by *llan* to become Llangain.[58] *Eglwys* can also be represented or replaced by English place-names now beginning 'Saint', as at St Bride's, Netherwent, probably called *Eccluis Sant Breit* in the *Liber Llandaff*, and *Egglis Guunlui* mentioned in the *Vita Cadoci*, now St Woolos, Newport.[59] The switches between *eglwys* and *merthyr* have already been described. Most telling of all is Dingestow, which was *ecclesia Dingad* in the ninth century, *Merthyr Dingad* in 1119, *Llandingat* in the twelfth century with Giraldus Cambrensis and Dingestow by 1610.[60] All this is, of course, from south Welsh evidence, where the more substantial documentation gives a bigger picture, but should be relevant to the south-west.

Given this, it would be unwise to suppose that the site name used in any particular piece of documentation is necessarily the only one by which the site has ever been known; what we see in each case is a single moment in an unstable world, and this makes any listing of 'sites named in *merther*' or similar venture very hazardous. The large number of names in **lann* west of the Tamar suggests that here this was the normal prefix for Christian burial grounds, and that these were normally enclosed (or why the name?), but although some of the names may be early, the evidence from Llanthomas shows that this cannot be taken for granted. Similarly names in **merther*, and *eglwys* may be early but could be post-800, depending upon the individual history of the site, which usually we do not have. Names which appear as 'saint', 'church' or 'stow' may have had earlier, different names, particularly in those areas where both English and British (broadly) were spoken for several generations.

56. R. Bromwich, *The Beginnings of Welsh Poetry. Studies by Sir Ifor Williams* (1972), pp. 16–25, esp. p. 19.
57. W. Davies, 'Unciae: land measurement in the Liber Landavensis', *Agricultural History Review*, 21 (2): 116—17 (1973).
58. Richards, 'Ecclesiastical and secular', p. 11.
59. Brook, 'Early Christian Church in Gwent', p. 82.
60. *Ibid.*, p. 69.

It seems that, firstly, place-names viewed generically probably cannot at the moment offer much help towards dating: only evidence from individual sites can inform ideas about their historical development. Secondly, arguments that, for instance, virtually every *merthyr*-named site in Wales 'has some special feature, either historical or archaeological'[61] do not stand up in Cornwall, and suggest that here, and perhaps in Wales too, the precise meaning of a name mattered less to each generation of contemporaries than we sometimes think; or, to put it differently, contemporary notions of significance, smart fashion or conformity may have influenced name choice as much as, or more than, any known earlier history of the site.

The local graveyards: some archaeological evidence

Archaeological work has begun to show us some of the graveyards, many of them quite humble, where most ordinary people were probably buried, although it is usually difficult to separate them chronologically from the fourth- and fifth-century sites discussed in the last chapter, and perhaps also from later sites. Many, probably, were in use for a long time.

Excavations in Wales give some useful parallels. A large (at least 22 graves) unenclosed inhumation cemetery at Plas Gogerddan, near the site of Bronze Age barrows used as an early Roman cemetery, which had wooden coffins and three special graves enclosed in timber structures, gave a radiocarbon date of AD 263–636. Stone-lined pits suggested grave-goods. Llandegai, near Bangor, produced a broadly similar site, and Tadderwen (Clwyd) had square ditched graves (Fig. 54), one of which produced a date of AD 433–680: both Tadderwen and Llandegai were on ancient prehistoric sites. Cist graves from Caer, Bayvil, an Iron Age enclosure, gave a date of AD 640–883, and those from the Atlantic Trading Estate, Barry, within an enclosure, a date range from the earlier Roman period to perhaps the tenth century.[62] This pattern is broadly repeated across Wales and suggests a significant range of cist-grave cemeteries whether unenclosed, newly enclosed or using ancient enclosures, sometimes with focal structures, and sometimes spanning the Roman – post-Roman period.

Evidence from south-western Britain fits into the picture Wales presents. In 1987, seventeen dug and slate cist graves were excavated, part of a more substantial cemetery which ran in three distinct phases or sections for over 400 km beside a trackway running from Wadebridge to Delabole. The cemetery was on both sides of the St Kew and St Endellion parish boundary which zigzags at this point to respect part of the cemetery area. The Norman parish church of St Endellion[63] was built on the opposite side of the Wadebridge–Delabole road (Fig. 55). Dating is difficult, but the cemetery could have been in use during late and post-Roman and/or pre-Norman/post-Norman times.

At Carnsew, on the Hayle estuary (Fig. 56), probably the earliest of the south-western inscribed stones seems to have been associated with an east–west cist grave,

---

61.   *Ibid.*
62.   James, (1992), pp. 95–103.
63.   P. Trudgian, 'Excavation of a burial ground at St Endellion, Cornwall', *Corn. Arch.*, 26 (1987): 142–52.

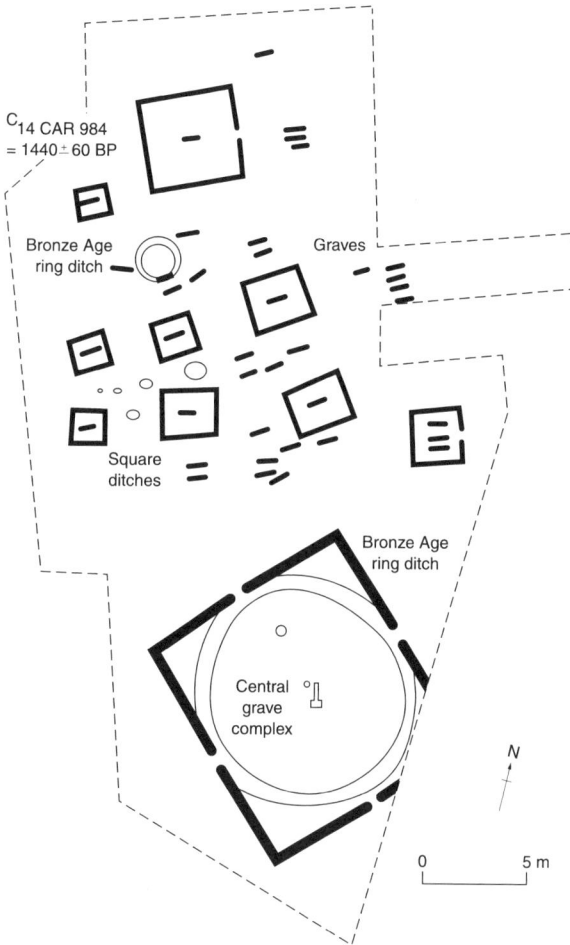

Figure 54 Site at Tadderwen, Clwyd (simplified) (after James 1992, Fig. 10.3)

the cap slabs of which were covered by a mound of stones. Upon opening in 1843, the grave contained sand, ashes and charcoal that presumably had filtered into what was an inhumation from nearby. Carnsew is a small enclosure situated on the eastern side of the Hayle River estuary and commanding a clear view out to sea. It is presumably historic, but no evidence has emerged of its Late Antique use; it is intriguing that the apparently sole burial was placed *outside* the enclosure.

The parish churchyard of Phillack is on the opposite side of the estuary, on the north bank of East Pool. Burials have been found at different times 'outside but close to the churchyard', north of the church with stone bowls and antlers 'in stone graves', north of the churchyard with east–west orientated burials in rows, in the rectory garden and in the church town. A fragment of African slipware was found in the churchyard entrance way during road-widening works but this does not necessarily date the creation of the site's enclosure. The church also possesses a small slab with an early *chi-rho* form, which, if it is genuinely ancient, matches the Carnsew grave

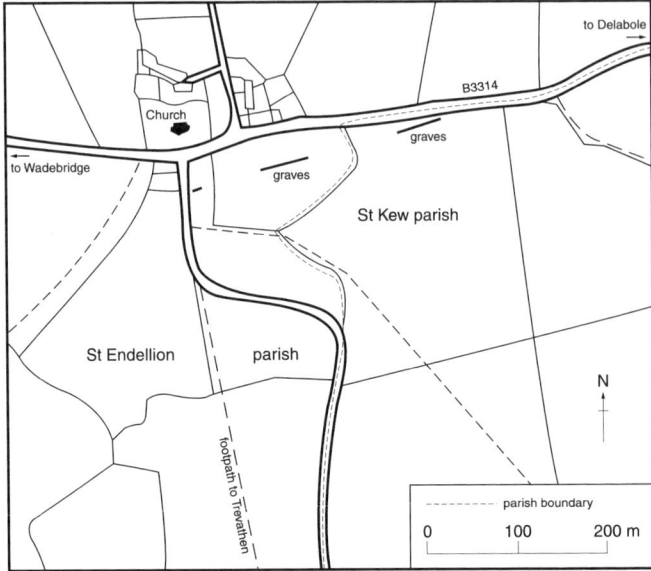

Figure 55 The site at St Endellion, Cornwall (after Trudgian 1987, Fig. 1)

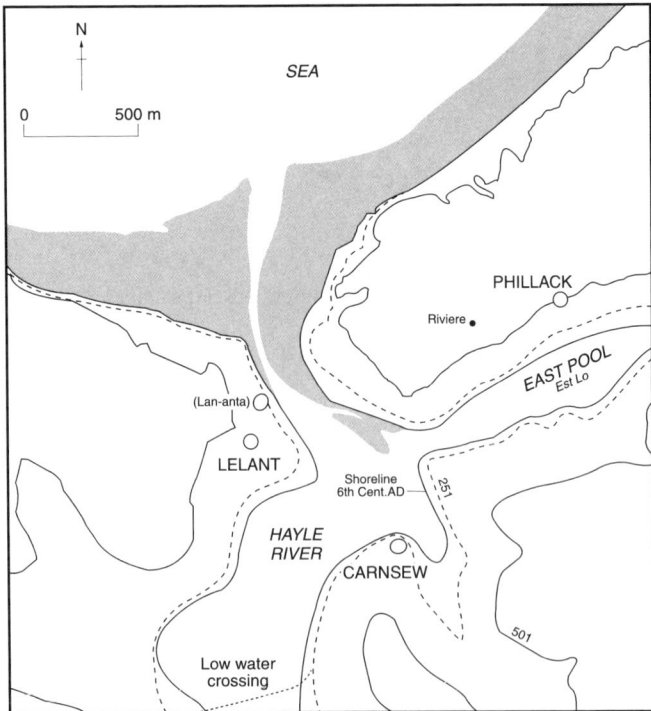

Figure 56 Sites in the Hayle estuary, Cornwall (modern coastline simplified) (after Thomas 1994, Fig. 12.1)

in suggesting there were Christians here before 500.[64] Clearly Phillack was an extensive burial ground, or series of burial grounds, with an extended date range, which seems to have included the post-Roman centuries. The chapel site of Lan-anta on the Lelant towans, which stands on the western edge of the Hayle estuary, also had 'rude graves built and covered with flat stones'.[65] Tintagel, to be discussed in a moment, may have had a similar history to that of Phillack and St Endellion, and so may Crantock, although this became a monastic site.[66] We do not know how many other sites may have been similar.

Other potentially early long-cist sites have been recognized in Cornwall. At Trebelsue, St Columb Minor, Penmaine, St Minver, Constantine and St Merryn the graves were found near disused chapel sites: this was also true at Trethillick and Trevone, Padstow and St Julitta, Tintagel.[67] Several broadly similar sites are known from Scilly, at St Helen's church, Tean, Samson and Tresco Abbey, where three cist burials were found near the inscribed stone.[68]

An important group of graveyards, including Lady St Mary (Wareham), St Helens (Lundy), East Ogwell, Yealhampton (both Devon), Madron and Lewannick (both Cornwall), possess associated inscribed stones which demonstrate that the sites were in use, almost certainly as a graveyard, by 600 if not earlier, although the stones do

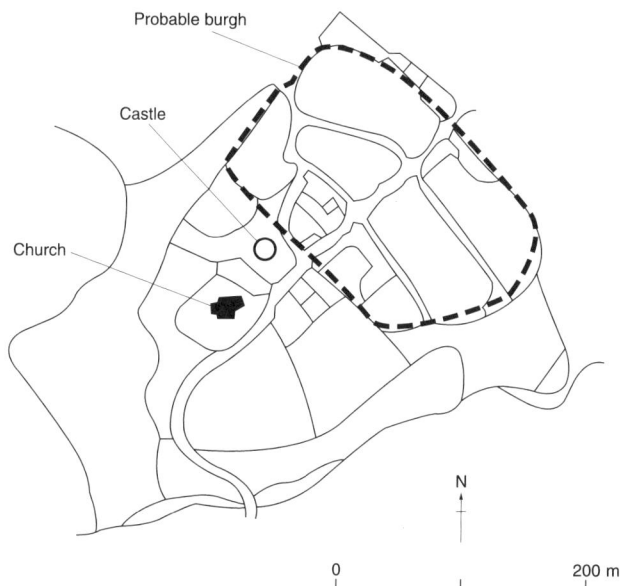

Figure 57 Plan of Lydford, Devon (after Tithe Map 1848)

---

64. C. Thomas, 'Parish churchyard, Phillack', *Corn. Arch.*, 12 (1973): 59; C. Thomas, *And Shall These Mute Stones Speak?* (1994), pp. 190–4.
65. Thomas, 'Parish churchyard, Phillack', p. 59.
66. See p. 169.
67. A. Preston-Jones, 'The excavation of a long-cist cemetery at Carnanton, St Mawgan, 1943', *Corn. Arch.*, 23 (1984): see esp. pp. 175–7. The sites at Carnanton, Lanvean and Mawgan Porth are perhaps not earlier than the eighth century.
68. C. Thomas, 'Hermits on islands or priests in a landscape?', *Cornish Studies*, (1980): 28–44 and refs there.

not, of course, date any enclosures the site may have had. A fragment of an imported bowl is known from Lydford, but not from the church site, although the topography of the presumably tenth-century road into the *burh* respects the churchyard enclosure which seems to predate it (Fig. 57). Somewhat differently, the Lundy grave-yard seems to have succeeded to domestic occupation. The dating evidence is just enough to suggest that some of those sites with inscribed stones, at least, began early enough to link up in general date and character with some of the perhaps late Roman burial grounds, like Kenn, Devon, discussed in the previous chapter.

The local graveyards: physical forms and dating

Cornwall has a range of graveyards, many now belonging to parish churches, which are enclosed by a substantial earth and stone bank taking a subcircular or oval form: it is, of course, to this enclosure that the place-name element **lann*, discussed earlier, refers, and similar sites are common in Wales, where they have related place-names. They also occur, although much less frequently, in Devon and in Somerset and Dorset, and some have been recognized in Cumbria. Similar sites sometimes appear in Dorset (Fig. 58), and further east in England, where, for example, four clear examples have been identified in Northampton deep in the English shires.[69] This hints that

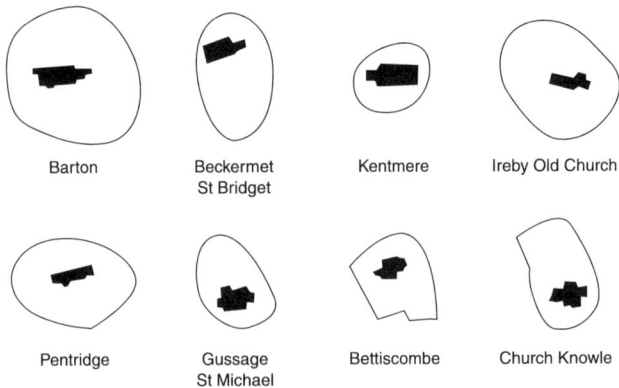

Figure 58 Graveyards with roughly circular or oval enclosures. Cumbria: Barton, Beckermet, Ireby Old Church, Kentmere (after O'Sullivan 1980a, Fig. 1). Dorset: Church Knowle, Pentridge, Gussage St Michael, Bettiscombe (after Hall 2000, Fig. 80)

69. The key sources for this, and much of what follows, are the OS 25-inch pre-1910 map series, the Tithe Map collections held at the various County Record Offices and fieldwork. Also for Cornwall, see Preston-Jones, 'Decoding Cornish churchyards', pp. 105–24; for Dorset, T. Hall, *Minster Churches in the Dorset Landscape* (2000); for Wales, H. Jones, 'Early medieval cemeteries in Wales', in Edwards and Lane, *Early Church in Wales and the West* (1992), pp. 90–103; for Cumbria, D. O'Sullivan, 'Curvilinear churchyards in Cumbria', *Bulletin of the CBA Churches Committee*, 13 (1980): 3–5, and 'A reassessment of the early Christian archaeology of Cumbria' (1980). For Northampton, see C. A. Markham, 'The churchyards of Northamptonshire', *Northampton and Oakham Architectural and Archaeological Society*, 39 (1930): 134–40 (I am grateful to Harold Fox for this reference). The discussion of Devon, and of sites in Cornwall and Somerset, draws on research in progress.

there is no necessary link between the western concentration and some particularly western view of Christian practice, or that sites of this type need be particularly early.

As we shall see shortly, a variety of circular (and other) enclosures were created around monastic churches and burial grounds in early medieval western Europe, and evidently these non-monastic enclosures are part of a deeply rooted cultural impulse to surround Christian sites with a clearly marked precinct. It may also have expressed a complex relationship with the foregoing Roman tradition of angles, and appealed because a 'circle' was capable of deeply significant metaphorical construction.

A tradition of circular enclosures is likely, also, to reflect the local surface geology in a direct way, and in stony areas it is not surprising to find turf and rough stone used in this way, partly because curved angles are easier to create with such materials than difficult joins, partly because the stone was available and building with it well understood, and partly because the fields needed regular clearance: all this is certainly one reason why such sites appear in western Britain. There is a cluster of roughly circular enclosed graveyards, for example, in Penwith, and in Devon, Lydford and Lustleigh, both on the Dartmoor granite, have substantial banks of stone and turf incorporating trees and shrubs. These are all of the kind known locally as 'Devon' or 'Cornish' 'hedges', and which were also the normal type of local enclosure for the older fields and farmyards.

It is probably important that the enclosed graveyards appeared at roughly the same time as the enclosed farmyards, the 'rounds' or sites with the place-name 'ker' (see Chapter One), were being abandoned. There are hints that sometimes old rounds were reused as Christian sites: the church of St Buryan seems to be an example, and the fragment of imported pottery at Phillack might be the remains of secular occupation at an enclosure which was then turned over to Christian use. If this was true on a substantial scale, then the enclosed churchyards may simply be mapping, at least in part, the western area where rounds survived longest before being abandoned, as they had been earlier in the east, rather than any specifically Christian development.

We do not know the extent to which the shape of graveyard enclosures may have been altered down the centuries. Late medieval arrangements at Morebath, in Devon, on the edge of Exmoor, made each farm responsible for maintaining a specific number of feet of the churchyard enclosure.[70] Morebath churchyard is now quite small and its perimeter is about 66 per cent circular, but when and how it reached this shape and size is an open question. We do not know how usual maintenance arrangements of this kind were, or the extent to which they may have encouraged the cutting of corners.

The enclosed western sites are only part of the non-monastic, local burial ground tradition. Squarish or irregular sites are also known west of the Tamar and in Wales and the north-west, and are common in Devon, Somerset, Dorset and further east in England; they create a complementary distribution to the round enclosures in very complex ways. The dovetailing of the two styles can be shown very easily within the peninsula. Figure 59 shows the distribution of non-

---

70. E. Duffy, *The Voices of Morebath* (2001), pp. 50–1. Similar arrangements were made for minster churches; see p. 179 for Chew Magna.

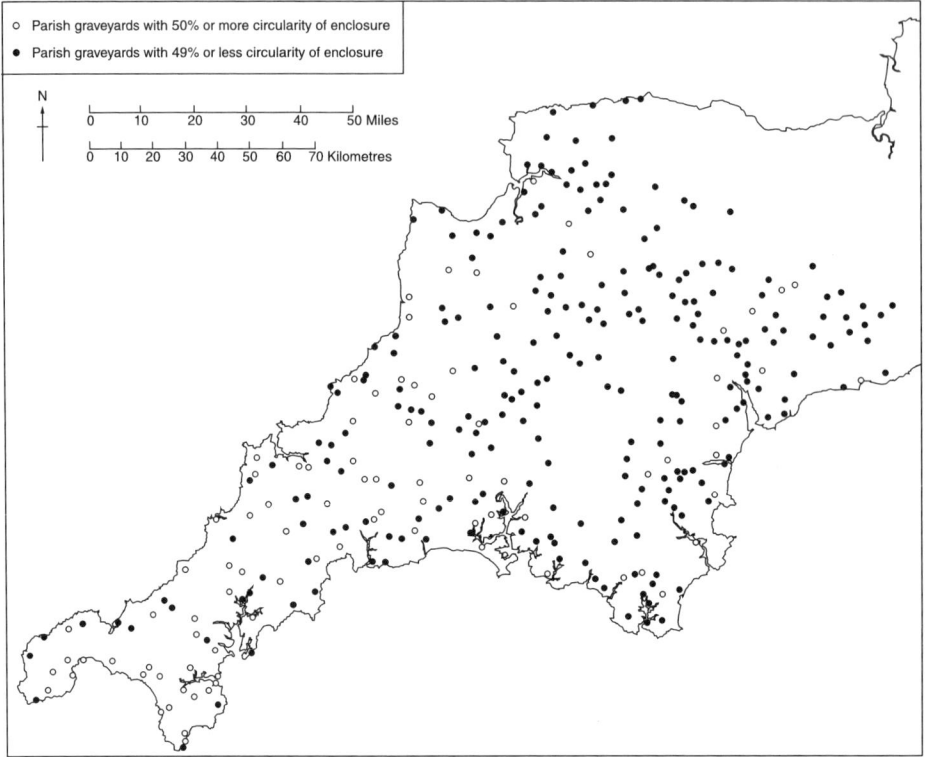

Figure 59 Distribution in Devon and Cornwall of substantial circular and non-circular graveyards (Pearce forthcoming)

curvilinear and curvilinear enclosures, all parish church sites, and all with claims to be considered as having been created before *c.* 1000. It is doubtful if the pattern shows anything like simple chronological horizons, or range of functions, based upon enclosure character. The sites at East Ogwell and Stowford (Devon), St Clement, Lewannick, Lustleigh and St Just in Penwith (Cornwall), for example, all have inscribed stones, but the first three have squarish, unimpressive enclosures and last three what have come to be seen as classic **lann*-style features (Fig. 60). Moreover, with some clear and important exceptions, like these three, Sancreed and Madron, the curvilinear group includes conspicuously mostly sites with rather small churchyards in an area of life where size seems to count, and to which are attached relatively little in the way of stone embellishments suggesting an important site. A number of sites which are embellished, like Cardinham, Phillack and St Helens (Lundy), although they may have (or have had) strong enclosing banks, are not strongly curvilinear.

The sites with place-names in **merther, stow* and *eglos*, already discussed, show a similar mixed picture. The **merther* place-names seem to belong to sites which are often curvilinear, but not of a particularly impressive size, and, as we have seen, the use of the name in Cornwall does not seem to be particularly early (Fig. 61, where some Welsh sites are included for comparison). The *eglos* sites are more

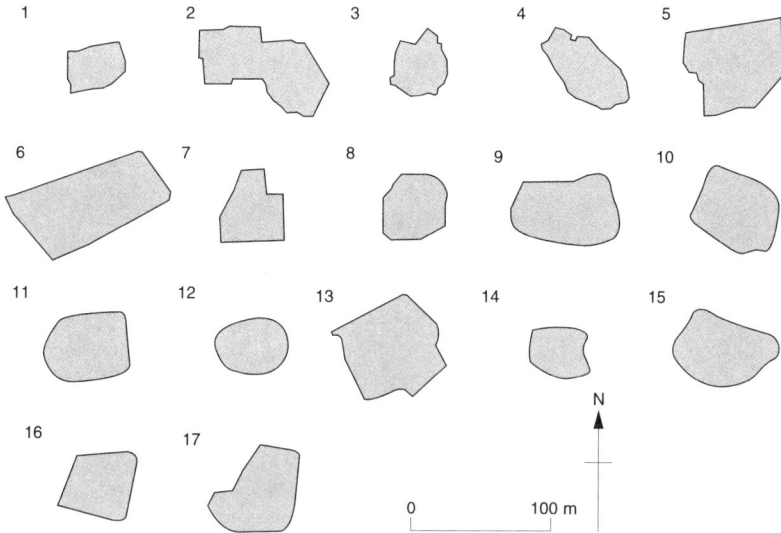

Figure 60 Parish churchyards in Devon and Cornwall with associated inscribed stones. 1. East Ogwell, 2. St Helens Lundy, 3. Lustleigh, 4. Stowford, 5. Yealhampton (all Devon), 6. Phillack, 7. St Just in Penwith, 8. Madron, 9. Cardinham, 10. St Hilary, 11. Redruth, 12. Sancreed, 13. St Kew, 14. St Clement, 15. Lewannick, 16. Cubert, 17. Lanivet (all Cornwall). Tavistock and Tresco are excluded because they have been much altered by later medieval ecclesiastical development. St Kew, although monastic, is included for the sake of comparison. Images reproduced with kind permission of the Ordnance Survey; see Preston-Jones 1992, Fig. 11.1, for Cornish sites

impressive but very mixed (Fig. 62a, b) and the exact constitution of the place-name does not seem to make much difference. The plotting of those sites with names in *lann* which do not seem to belong within the group of endowed religious houses shows a very mixed picture, particularly considering the relationship of the word to the topography of sites. Figure 63 sets out those sites which include *lann* followed by a personal name different from the dedication name of the church, and shows that they are very mixed and that, while some, like Luxulyan or Lanlivery, have a curved character, others do not. Interestingly, the sites with *lann* plus the name of their patron as their place-name includes a number of the smallest and least impressively shaped sites, like St Anthony in Meneage, St Michael Caerhayes and Lamorran. Even after allowance is made for alterations to churchyards over the centuries, the inference from this evidence seems to be that a substantial bank of broadly circular or oval form is not necessarily a criteria either for a wider importance or for great antiquity within the system of south-western Christian sites. This fits in reasonably well with the dating evidence for the unenclosed or lightly enclosed graveyard sites which was reviewed earlier, and which suggested that some sites, perhaps many sites, did not acquire their enclosures until relatively late, possibly after 800, although this does not mean that some enclosures are not considerably earlier.

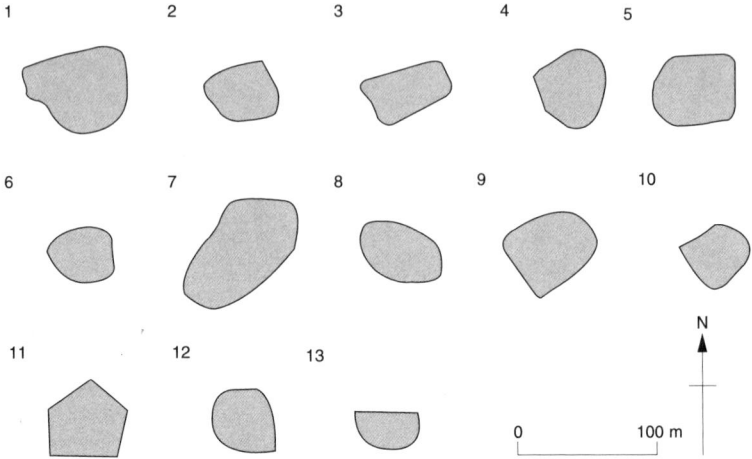

Figure 61 Ecclesiastical enclosures with, or associated with sites with, place-names in *merthyr* (Wales) or **merther* (Cornwall) 1. Morvah, 2. Merther, 3. Ruan Major, 4. Landwednack, 5. Redruth, 6. St Martin in Meneage, 7. Sithney (all parish churchyards, Cornwall), 8. Merther Uny (Chapel in Wendron, Cornwall), 9. Merther Cynog (Brycheiniog, Wales), 10. Landegveth, 11. Mathern, 12. Dingestow, 13. Llanvaches (all Gwent, Wales, see Brook 1985–8). Images reproduced with kind permission of the Ordnance Survey; see Preston-Jones 1992, Fig. 11.1, for Cornish sites

The local graveyards: social character

Important indications of the character of some of the graveyards, both enclosed and unenclosed, can be gleaned from the inscribed stones associated with them (Table 5). Clearly, such comparisons can only take account of sites where stones survive, an unknown proportion of the original total, and the numbers involved (only 24 sites) are relatively small, but the plot does contain some interesting hints (Fig 60). Only one monastic site, St Kew, is known to have possessed an inscribed stone in association with its churchyard, which suggests that these monuments meant something not directly related to monastic ideals. Of the ten parish church names with the element *eglos*, four have surviving stones, a relatively high proportion (although no stones are known from the other seven sites with names in *eglos* which are not parish churches). Of these four sites, two, Cubert and Madron, also have names in **lann*, which may hint at some kind of shift in character. Six of the non-monastic sites with stones come from sites with known names in **lann* (including Cubert and Madron), a surprisingly small number. The rest have a variety of names, including some in 'saint', or, in the case of the eastern sites, have lost their (presumed) British names.

Several of the inscribed stones carry features, particularly the Latin formulae of the HIC IACET variety and variants on the *chi-rho* monogram which seem to show clear Christian intentions by those who erected them, and therefore (broadly speaking) of the graveyard as a whole from, at least, the time when the stone was erected. The Madron stone, for example, came from the vicinity of the churchyard,

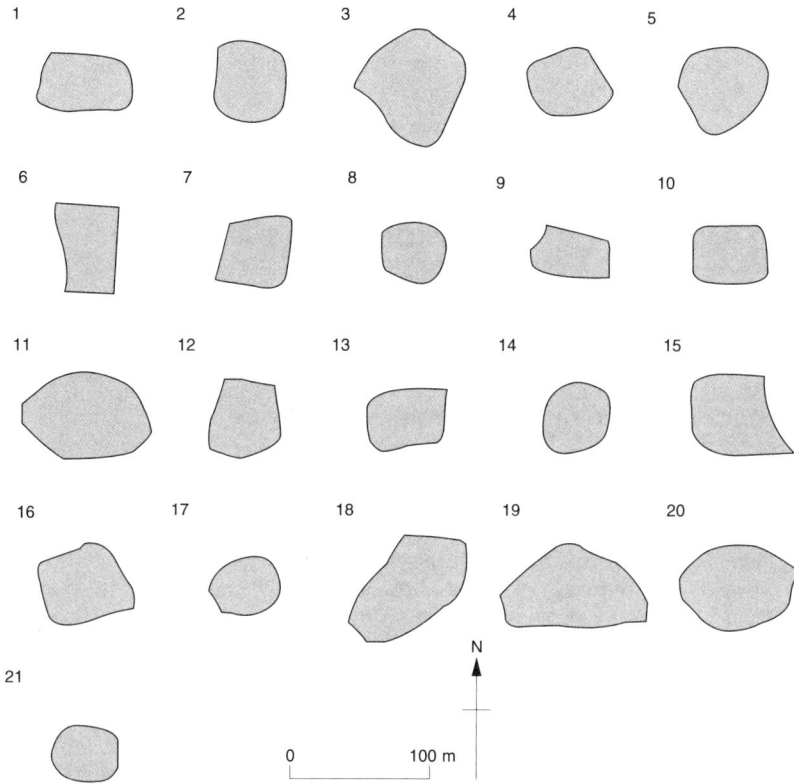

Figure 62a Cornish parish churchyards with the place-name *eglos* as the first element, followed by patron's name. 1. St Allen, 2. Breage, 3. St Breock, 4. Budock, 5. St Buryan, 6. Crowan, 7. Cubert, 8. Cury, 9. Egloskerry, 10. St Enoder, 11. St Erme, 12. Gerrans, 13. Ladock, 14. Madron, 15. Mullion, 16. Newlyn, 17. Sancreed, 18. Sithsey, 19. St Teath, 20. St Tudy, 21. Zennor

and carries a probable *chi-rho*, and the inscribed stone found in the church fabric at St Just in Penwith has both a clear *chi-rho* and an inscription intended to read something like SELVS IC IACIT ('Selus lies here', with IACIT for IACET). Occasionally, as at Lewannick where one of the stones carries MEMO[RI]A, one of other technical phrases in use among the Christian communities of the Late Antique west is employed.

The majority of the stones apparently from churchyards, however, carry a filiation formula ('X son of Y', or 'the stone of X son of Y'), or some simple similar form. Interestingly, several of the stones with this style came from sites which did not mature into full parish churchyards. Those from Bosworgey and Trevarrack came from later chapel sites, and that from Nanscow Farm, St Breock, was associated with signs of burning, although of what is not clear. This is reminiscent of the cist inhumation grave covered with a stone mound at Carnsew, Hayle, which also had some burnt material and was accompanied by an early inscribed stone; Carnsew, equally, never became a parish site. The FILI style stresses the family connections, especially the paternity, of the man commemorated and suggests that what mattered

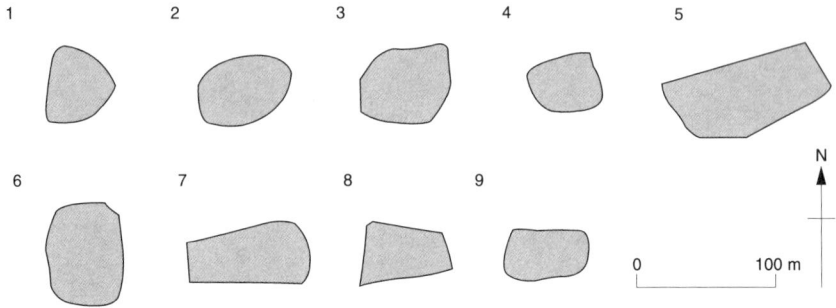

Figure 62b Cornish parish churchyards with the place-name *eglos* as the
first element followed by descriptive element. 1. Egloslayle, 2. Illogan, 3. St Issey,
4. Merther, 5. Phillack, 6. Philleigh, 7. St Stephen in Brannel, 8 Wendron,
9 Withiel. Images reproduced with kind permission of the Ordnance Survey;
see Preston-Jones 1992, Fig. 11.1, for Cornish sites

was the public statement of his ancestry which presumably conveyed the legitimacy
which gave him and his monument authority and dignity.

The strong sense of pedigree as social dynamic which comes from the stones may
be reinforced by the focal graves which seem to have been important in many of
the related graveyards. Excavations at St Helen's, Lundy (Fig. 64), showed that the
graveyard was sited on a late prehistoric/Roman settlement system with fields, a
circular house and the remains of salt working. The stone slabs from this house were
used to make a rectangular surround for a short cist grave roughly on an east–west
orientation, and the whole interior of the surround filled in with loose lumps of
granite, presumably from the wall-fill of the old hut. This may be a *cella memoria*,
and the area gradually filled with at least 30, and probably over a hundred, cist
graves.

The site possesses a section of enclosing bank, but the chronological relation of
this, the hut complex, the *cella* and its grave, and the cist graves in general, remains
unclear. The site also produced no less than four inscribed stones, two of horizontal
form and two with vertical inscriptions, one with a circled cross; the original sites of
these stones is unknown but they seem to have been set up in the cemetery, and they
confirm its Christian character from early in the sixth century or even earlier. On
present evidence, the site could be interpreted as originally a cemetery of cist graves
situated on a domestic site which had gone out of use, which featured a cultural
'special' grave with *cella* and mound, and to which more cist graves, Christian
inscriptions and an enclosure were added.[71] The occupant of the special grave is
often interpreted as a religious man of some type, but he could equally have been
regarded as the founding ancestor of the farming community which used the burial
ground, and whose family members were further commemorated in the four
inscribed stones.

Excavation in Tintagel parish churchyard (Fig. 65) yielded a number of cist graves
and dug graves, orientated east–west, some of the earliest of which seem to have

---

71.   Thomas, *Mute Stones*, pp. 164–5.

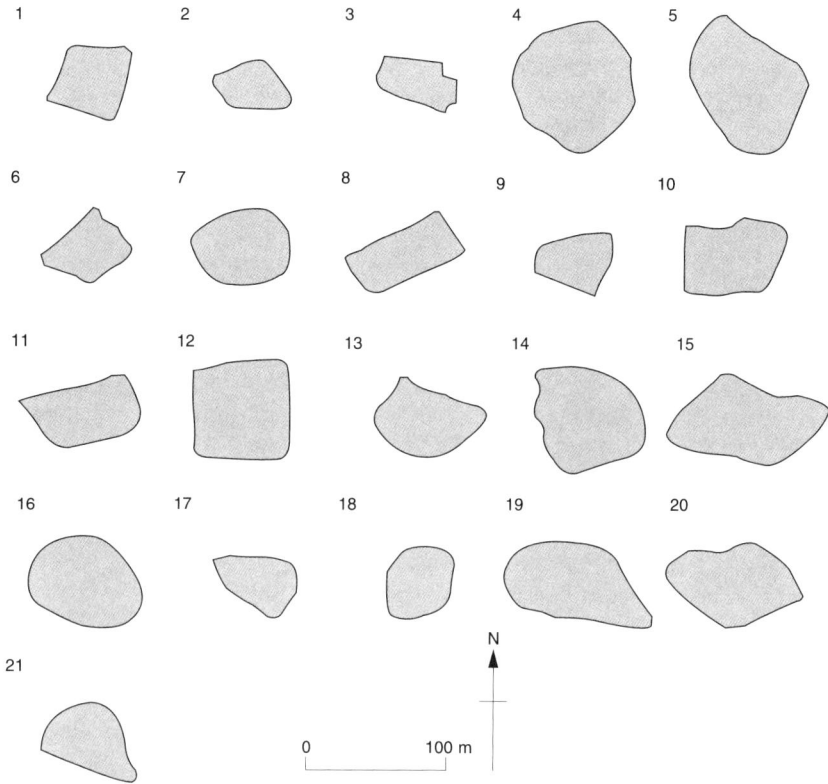

Figure 63 Parish churchyards with the place-name **lann* as first element, followed by a personal name not that of the patron, excluding monastic sites. 1. Cubert, 2. St Erth, 3. Fowey, 4. Gulval, 5. St Just in Roseland, 6. Laneast, 7. Lanlivery, 8. Landreath, 9. Lansallos, 10. Launcells, 11. Lawhitton, 12. Lelant, 13. Lewannick, 14. Lezant, 15. Linkinhorne, 16. Luxulyan, 17. Mabe, 18. Madron, 19. St Mawgan in Pydar, 20. Mevagissey, 21. Ruan Lanihorne. Images reproduced with kind permission of the Ordnance Survey, see Preston-Jones 1992, Fig. 11.1, for Cornish sites

been aligned on an apparently uninscribed, standing granite pillar.[72] This cist grave cemetery is known to have extended beyond the present churchyard, which 'suggests that the burial ground ... was open and not enclosed'.[73] On the old ground surface were stones carrying numerous incised cross forms, presumably individual grave markers. A small (? originally separate) enclosure to the north-west contained a mound (A) and this may have extended to contain other mounds in the Old Churchyard; mound A may have been intended to mark early cist graves placed near the pillar, but some of the other mounds seem to be builders' dumps. The site

---

72. If uninscribed standing stones were used in much the same way as inscribed ones, we can never even guess how many of these there once were, now used as building material.

73. C. Thomas, *Tintagel: Arthur and Archaeology* (1993), p. 105; 'The context of Tintagel: a new model for the diffusion of post-Roman Mediterranean imports', *Corn. Arch.*, 27 (1988): 7 26.

Table 5 Ecclesiastical sites and inscribed stones

Ecc. site associated with inscribed stones	*Filiation or simple formula*	*Latin formula*	*Monastic site*	*Eglos name*	**lann name*	*Stow/ stoc name*	*Notes*
Bosworgey	×						? from chapel site
Buckland Monachorum	×						
Cardinham	×						
Cubert	×			×	×		
East Ogwell	×						
Lanivet	×				×		
Lewannick	×	×			×		2/?3 from site
Lundy	×	?					4 from site
Lustleigh	×						
Madron	×			×	×		
Phillack	×			×			
Redruth	×						
St Clement	×						
St Columb Major	?						
St Hilary	×						
St Just in Penwith	×				×		
St Kew	×		×		×		
Sancreed	×			×			
Stowford	×					?	
Tavistock	×					×	
Tregony	×						
Tresco	×						
Trevarack	?						from chapel site
Wareham	×						5 from site

produced evidence of imported wine jars and bowls, and of fires, which may link with the bowl fragment from Phillack (also apparently from the entrance) and the evidences of fires at Beacon Hill and elsewhere. All of these look like the kind of graveside family commemoration feast which was common in the Late Antique world.

This may link up with the entitlement of children, as family members, to formal burial in the same place as adults. At the Atlantic Trading Estate, Barry, cemetery, genetic links between skeletons have been recognized, and the graves look like those of an extended family group.[74] The Irish legal phase 'heir of a gravestone, which lies about the lands', and the relationship between gravestones, graves, and boundary markers, hint at the legitimization which all this could give to the transmission of landed property.[75] If this can be translated, even in general terms, to the south-west

---

74. C. Price, Atlantic Trading Estate, Barry', *Archaeol. Wales*, 27 (1987): 60–1.
75. T. Charles-Edwards, 'Boundaries in Irish law', in P. Sawyer (ed.), *Medieval Settlement: Continuity and Change* (1976), pp. 83–7.

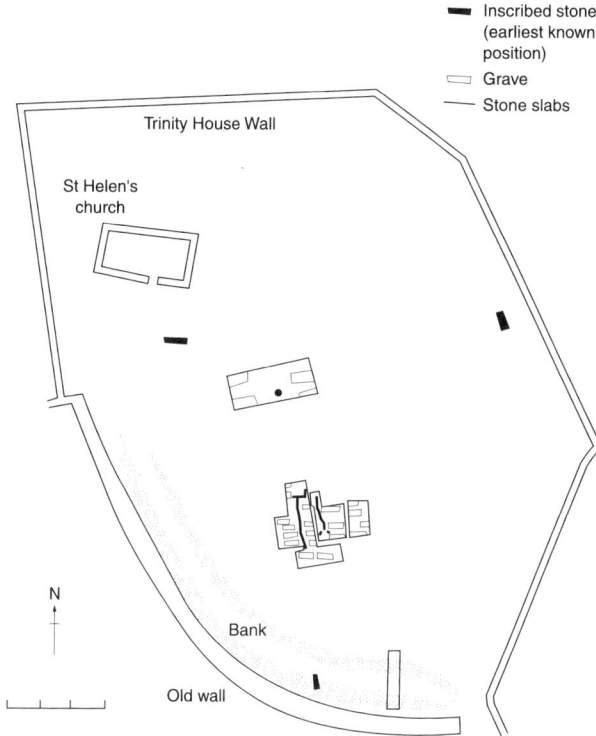

Figure 64 Beacon Hill site, Lundy (after Thomas 1994, Fig. 10.2)

(and Wales) it reinforces the probable kin significance of the burial grounds. It also directs attention to the inscribed stones, like those around Dartmoor already discussed, and others like that now at Indian Queen's church which may have marked what became the boundary between the parishes of St Columb and St Enoder, or that in St Endellion parish which seems to have marked what became the boundary of Roscarrock Barton; these were apparently never in burial grounds, but may, in some cases at least, have marked lone burials, and have had great significance as markers of possession or of boundary.[76] At St Mawgan in Meneage,[77] an inscribed stone marks what seems to be an important point on a larger enclosure surrounding the enclosed burial ground (Fig. 66).

Ideas about kinship and continuity may link up with what sometimes appears as a desire to site churchyards in a relationship to significant elements in the landscape, perhaps elements which had a pre-Christian significance. Knowlton church in Dorset is within a prehistoric henge monument. The church of St Denis is built within a hill-fort, and a number of other churches – Brent Tor, Brent Knoll, St Michael's Mount, Glastonbury Tor – are obviously deliberately sited on impressive hilltops. The churchyard at Ashbrittle, Somerset, incorporates a low mound, possibly a barrow, on

---

76.   OS 25-inch series.
77.   Preston-Jones, 'Decoding Cornish churchyards', fig. 11.11a.

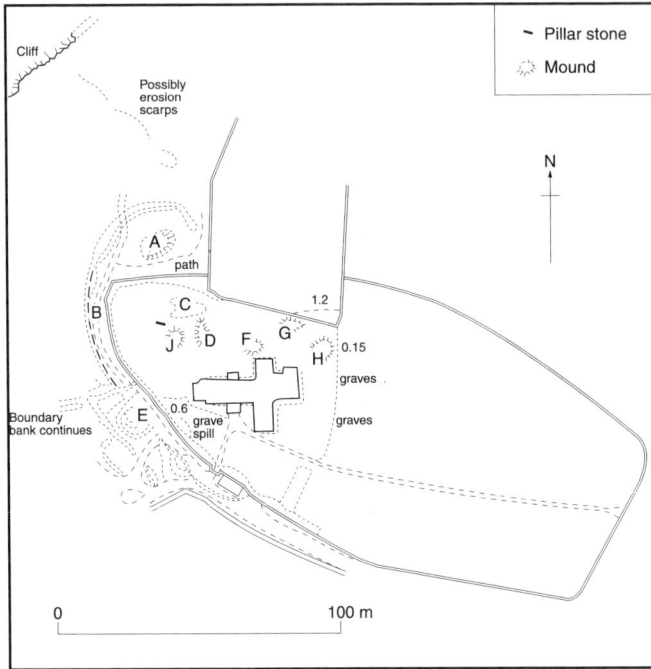

Figure 65 Tintagel churchyard site (simplified) (after Thomas 1988b, Fig. 33)

which stands an enormous, ancient yew tree, conceivably the offspring of an even older tree.[78]

The story in his *Vita* of Samson adding a cross to a standing stone in Cornwall is well known, but no such monument has been identified west of the Tamar, and even though some of the inscribed and cross-decorated stones might be standing stones reused, the writer of the *Vita* seems more likely to have transposed some of the well-known Breton examples to the south-west. However, the East Worlington Long Stone (Somerset) had five incised crosses added to it at some point, and the cross-inscribed stone at Culborne (Somerset) seems to have been originally one of the terminal stones of a prehistoric stone row.[79] Another stone in the row has a faintly inscribed cross,

78.   R. Morris, *Churches in the Landscape* (1989), pp. 78–80. The south-west also has a reference to *Nemet Statis* (Devon) in *The Ravenna Cosmography* (A. Rivet and C. Smith, *The Place-Names of Roman Britain* (1979), p. 254) which incorporates the place-name *nemet*, 'sacred grove', and which has given rise to a cluster of place-names in central Devon, and Lanivet (Cornwall) meaning 'church site (**lann*) at Neved' (Padel, *Dictionary of Cornish Place-names*, p. 106). Padel considers that 'Neved meaning "pagan sacred place", must have been a pre-existing place-name in the area.' The place-name element, and the sacred groves presumably, were widespread in the Celtic world, although what, if any, significance still attached to these in Britain after *c.* 500 is uncertain; consequently it is unclear whether the church site was linked to the sacred wood, or merely took a pre-existing name of no particular significance. However, topographical names linked with **lann* are not very common.

79.   L. Grinsell, (1970b) p. 106, for East Worlington; Riley and Wilson-North, *Exmoor*, pp. 89–99 for Culborne.

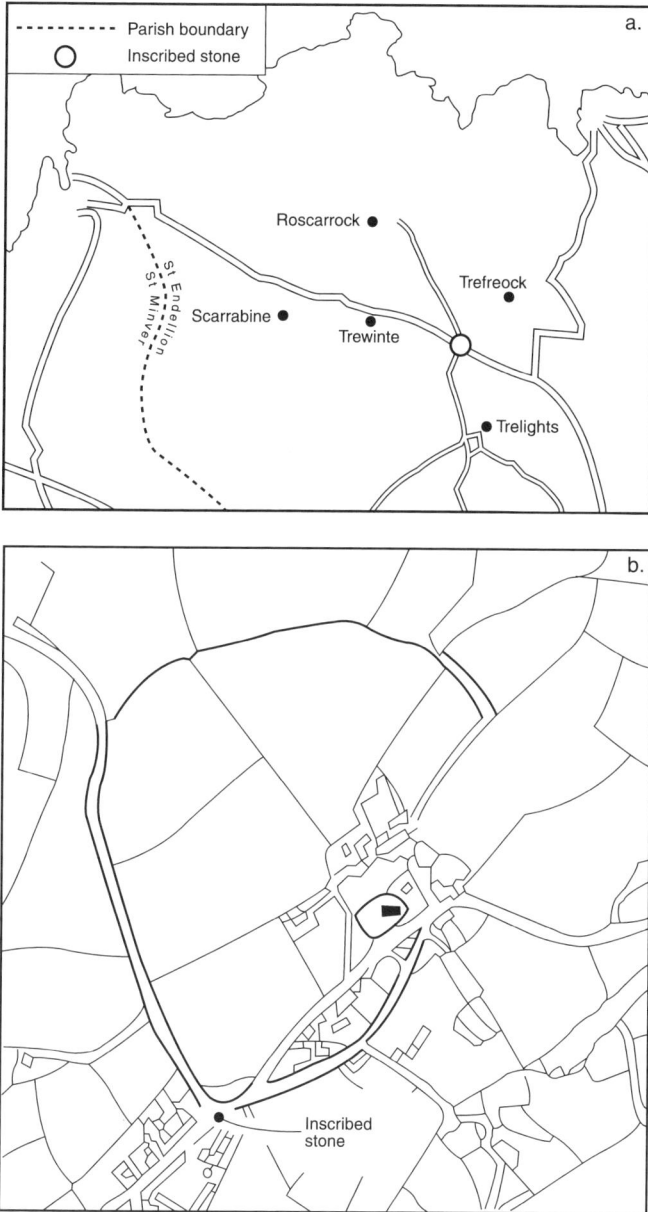

Figure 66 Inscribed stones in context at (a) Roscarrock, (b) St Mawgan in Meneage (after Preston-Jones 1992, Fig. 11.11c)

and the parish boundary follows the row very closely, suggesting a link between the Christianization of the stones and the creation of the parish.

The 'bell stone' referred to in the place-name Belstone, Devon, seems to be incorporated in the south-eastern side of the churchyard enclosure, which itself forms part of a hedge field boundary with a trackway beside it.[80] Belstone is on the northern edge of Dartmoor where prehistoric standing stones are common, and perhaps the 'bell stone' was originally one of them. Similarly, Stanton Drew, Somerset, has an important megalithic complex, and the church was built in close proximity. Perhaps in late Roman Armorica,[81] ancient sites were part of organized or formal pagan observance, while in Britain they belonged within an underbelly of superstition which ran beneath both recognized pagan and Christian practice[82] and that this is the reason why ancient Armorican monuments had to be specifically 'baptized', while not many British ones were considered important enough.

Some of the later parish church sites in the eastern part of the peninsula have a relationship to an earlier Roman settlement site. At Gussage St Andrew, which never became a full parish church, there is Roman material in the fabric.[83] At Combe Down, Somerset, the church is immediately north-west of a 'fair-sized' masonry building and adjacent burials. At Whitestaunton, Somerset, a villa is about 80 m away from the church of St Andrew,[84] and Roman material comes from the area of the church-yard at Chedzoy, Somerset.[85] At Studland, a 'Roman inhumation' was found during church rebuilding and stone-lined cist graves are reported from Worth (both Dorset). Charlbury and Piddletrenthide, also in Dorset, both have Roman remains under the church.[86]

In similar vein, some churches have an evidently deliberate reuse of Roman monumental pieces. Compton Dando, Somerset,[87] has a corner of the sacrificial altar from the temple of *Sulis Minerva* at Bath built into its south-west chancel buttress, and Godmanstone, Dorset, has a Roman altar remodelled and reused in the chancel arch.[88] Both of these seem to represent a conscious attempt to tame and reframe the pagan past. The six inscriptions at Lady St Mary, Wareham, were all cut into Roman architectural fragments, brought either from a nearby villa or temple, or from Dorchester, and a Roman milestone (Fig. 67) was apparently reused in the same way

---

80. This is the version now told in Belstone. Gover *et al.*, *Place-names of Devon* (1931) p. 131, refer to an account featuring the bell-stone as 'a remarkably fine logan stone [i.e., a large stone naturally balanced on another, or on a crag] that looked like a ship in a gale . . . it has been thrown down and broken up by quarrymen'.
81. Giot, Guigon and Merdrignac, *British Settlement* (2003), especially pp. 231–2.
82. C. Holtorf, 'Megaliths, monumentality and memory', *Arch. Review from Cambridge*, 14 (2): 45–65 (1997). Dark 'Roman period activity' (1993): 134–46.
83. Somerset Sites and Monuments Register.
84. *Ibid.*
85. Page, *Victoria County History Somerset*, Vol. 1, p. 259.
86. R. Morris and J. Roxan, 'Churches on Roman buildings', in W. Rodwell, *Temples, Churches and Religion in Roman Britain* (1980), pp. 175–209; D. Hinton, 'Some Anglo-Saxon charters and estates in south-east Dorset, *PDNHAS*, 114 (1994): 19. Hall, *Minsters*, p. 21.
87. Eaton, *Plundering* (2000), pp. 85–6, 88, 91, fig. 26; however, for an alternative view, see Beeson 'The Unknown Deity' (2002), pp. 10–13.
88. In spite of its appearance, given this phenomenon at the church, Mills (*English Place-names*, p. 152) gives Godmanstone as OE personal name Godman + *tun*, 'farmstead'. T. Eaton, *Plundering the Past* (2000), p. 110, suggests the altar may have been transferred from neighbouring Grimstone, where it was in non-Christian use; Mills, *English Place-names*, p. 157, cites examples where Grim-stone means 'farmstead of a Scandinavian man called *Grimr*'. A Scandinavian name would be odd so far south although possible, but as Eaton points out, Grimr is an Old English alias of the god Woden (p. 110).

Figure 67 Roman milestone from St Hilary, Cornwall, reused as an early Christian inscribed stone (after Langdon 1988, p. 414)

at St Hilary, Cornwall.[89] Nonetheless, fewer than 30 such sites with earlier references are known out of a total of over 1400 medieval parish graveyards in the peninsula, and several of the known sites were only ever chapels. It is, of course, highly likely that some of the later church sites have Roman (or earlier) antecedents that we are not in a position to discover, given that they are still in use, and this remains one of the great unknowns, but as matters stand, the number is not striking.

Holy wells may also be the spiritual heirs of the earlier wells and shafts where offerings were made. Some were developed into significant sites although they do not seem to have been used for burials.[90] The site at Fenton-Ia, Cornwall, 'Ia's Fountain', seems to have taken the holy well as its starting point, and to this were added an enclosure, a chapel and a cross, perhaps by 1000.[91] Something similar appears to have happened at Chapel Porth, which possesses a cross pit[92] and at Chapel Jane (Fig. 68).[93]

89.   D. Hinton, 'The inscribed stones in Lady St Mary Church, Wareham', *PDNHAS*, 114 (1992): 116; Eaton, *Plundering*, pp. 79–82.
90.   For overviews see H. James, 'The cult of St David in the Middle Ages', in M. Carver (ed.), *In Search of Cult* (1993), pp. 105–12; G. Jones, 'Holy wells and the cult of St Helen', *Landscape History*, 8 (1985): 61–75; J. Rattue, *The Living Stream: Holy Wells in Historical Context* (1995); P. Quinn, *Holy Wells of Bath and Bristol Region* (1999); A. Lane-Davies, *Holy Wells of Cornwall* (1970).
91.   C. Thomas, 'The rediscovery of St Ia's Chapel, Cambourne', *Corn. Arch.*, 2 (1963): 77–8.
92.   R. Warner, 'Rediscovery of the chapel at Chapel Porth, St Agnes', *Corn. Arch.*, 4 (1965): 41–3.
93.   V. Russell and P. Pool, 'The excavations of Chapel Jane, Zennor', *Corn. Arch.*, 7 (1968): 43–60.

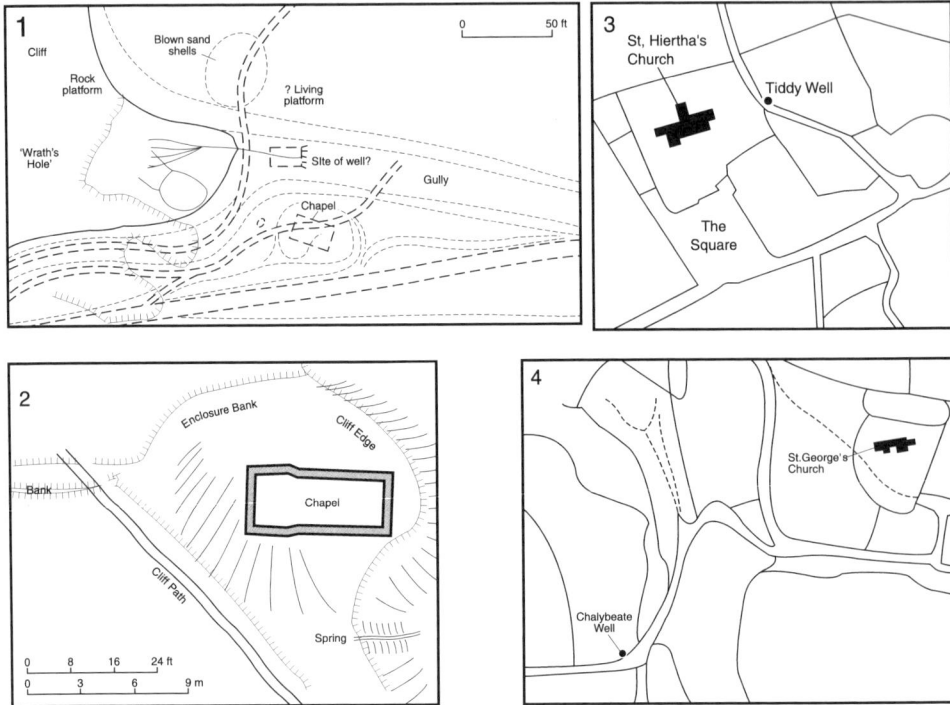

Figure 68 Holy Wells: 1. Chapel Porth, St Agnes (after Warner 1965, Fig. 13), 2. Chapel Jane (after Russell and Pool 1968, Fig. 9), both Cornwall; 3. Tiddy Well, Chittlehampton, 4. Chalybeate Well, Morebath, both Devon. Images reproduced by kind permission of the Ordnance Survey

In Devon an eye-curing well associated with (the highly obscure) St Gudula, which possessed a stone cross, was known in the parish of Ashburton. Morebath had the well referred to in 1249 as *halgewell* ('holy well'), probably that later known as the Chalybeate Well, and Chittlehampton had Tiddy Well near the church, which carried a version of the name of the unique local saint, Hieretha (or similar).[94] It is interesting that local traditions often made wells into Christian holy sites, but not standing stones, and the folklore connected with stones tends to stress rule-breaking and its punishment.[95] Perhaps this reflects the use of water in Christian liturgy.

Monastic developments

In the sermon he gave to mark the arrival of new relics at Rouen in (probably) 396, Victricius was able to refer proudly to the large number of monks 'emaciated by

---

94.   For surviving material relating to Hieretha/Urith, see James, 'St Urith', 1901–02.

95.   E.g. the many stories which suggest that the stones are petrified wrongdoers, as at the Hurlers (three stone circles near Cleer, Cornwall) and Stanton Drew, Somerset. See L. Grinsell, *Folklore of Prehistoric Sites in Britain* (1976).

their privations' who were present.[96] Gildas, writing somewhere in Britain and around the middle of the sixth century, seems to have taken the existence of British monks, and presumably monasteries, for granted. It looks as if men in Britain had adopted the monastic life in some numbers somewhere between *c.* 400, when the inspiration of Martin's example was gathering momentum in Gaul, and the 550s. We know very little directly about this development, either from archaeology or from documents. The best documentary source is the first *Vita* of Samson, probably written in the early eighth century but possibly drawing on older (perhaps oral) material. Samson was organizing monastic affairs at Dol (Brittany) by the mid-sixth century, and the *Vita* suggests that by the early sixth century there were monastic communities in south-east Wales and on the north Cornish coast.[97] These fit into a developing pattern of such communities in Gaul, Ireland, western Britain and northern Britain, within which the complex threads of influence have not yet been satisfactorily unravelled, but which produced a growing number of communities within the south-west.[98]

We may usefully start with a deliberately broad view of the kind of monastic institution (Fig. 69) which had appeared across the peninsula by about 750 and envisage it as having a central church and associated burial ground, together perhaps with additional churches, served by a group of monks (occasionally and/or nuns) whose precise style of commitment or adherence to any particular Rule of life was not considered especially important. The group will have included a superior to whom allegiance, perhaps outright obedience, was due, and at least one adequately ordained priest who could celebrate mass, and perform baptisms and burials.[99] Members of the community were expected to live the Christian life of prayer and contemplation, and in some individual cases this might lead to a solitary existence or extreme ascetic practices, for which individual huts or cells might be required.[100]

Monasteries in Cornwall

Olsen[101] has examined in detail the credentials of the sites west of the Tamar in the light of surviving indications – chiefly concerned with landholding – to be considered established monastic houses. The earliest group included the monastery called *Docco*, now probably represented by the church at St Kew, and 'the southern monastery', probably St Samson in Golant where the author of the earliest *Vita* of Samson had

---

96. R. Herval, *Origines chrétiennes de la Lyonnaise gallo-romanie à la Normandie ducale* (1966); G. Clark, 'Vitricius of Rouen: praising the saints', *J. of Early Christian Studies* (1999): 365–99.

97. See R. Fawtier, *Vie de Saint Samson* (1912); T. Taylor, *The Life of St Samson of Dol* (1925), pp. 34, 47.

98. See, for example, J. Knight, 'The early Christian Latin inscriptions of Britain and Gaul: chronology and contexts', in Edwards and Lane, *Early Church in Wales and the West* (1992) and refs.

99. J. Blair, 'Anglo-Saxon minsters: a topographical review', in J. Blair and R. Sharpe, *Pastoral Care before the Parish* (1992), pp. 226–66; E. Cambridge and D. Rollason, 'Debate: the pastoral organisation of the Anglo-Saxon Church: a review of the "Minster hypothesis"', *Early Medieval Europe*, 4 (1): 87–104 (1995).

100. See especially Cambridge and Rollason, 'Pastoral organisation of the Anglo-Saxon Church', pp. 87–104.

101. L. Olson, *Early Monasteries in Cornwall* (1989), esp. pp. 105–6. The word 'monastery' will be used in much of what follows even though, for reasons described on p. 191, note 101, it may not always be strictly accurate.

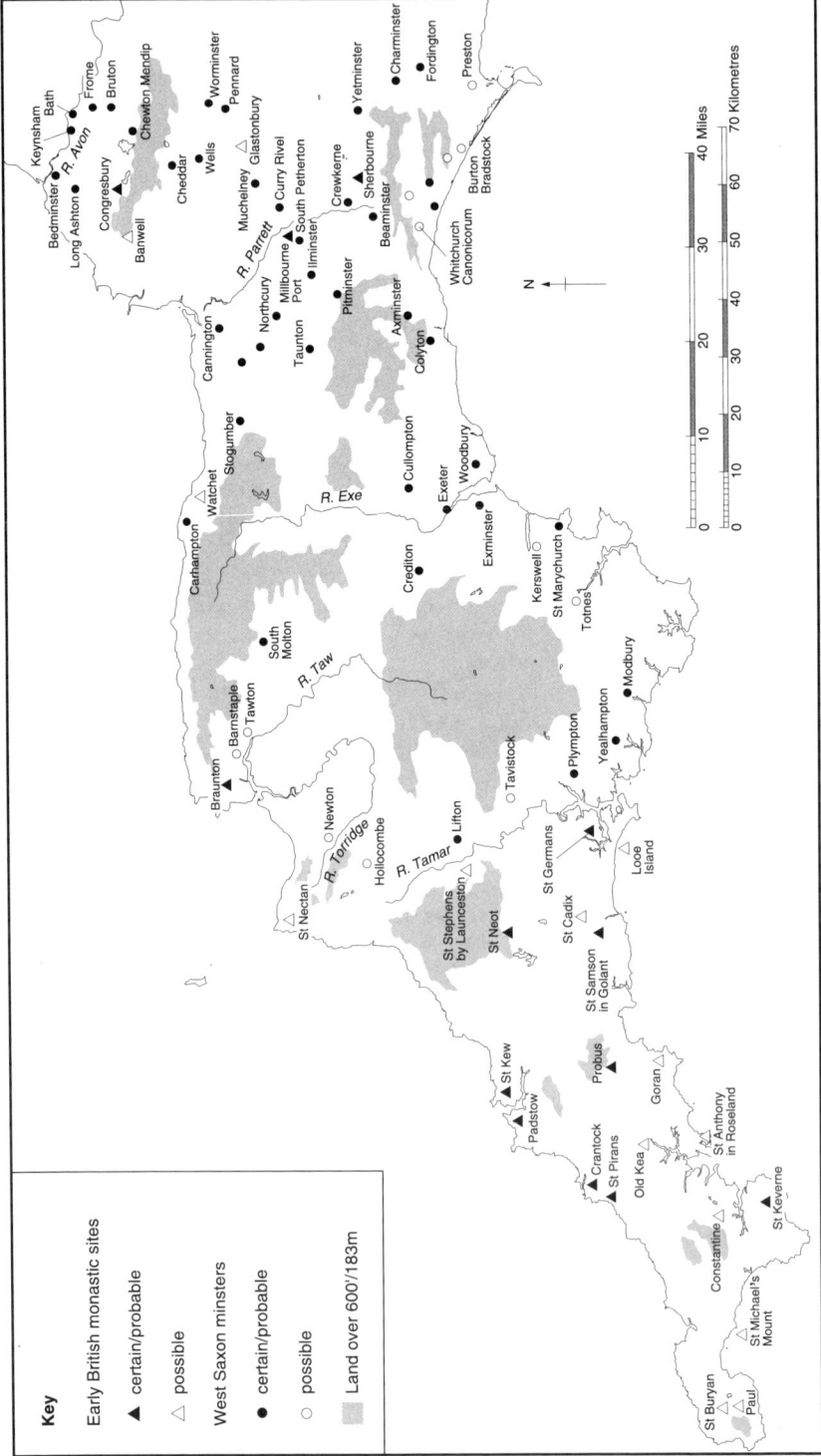

Figure 69 Location map of monastic and minster sites.

lived. In the same group probably belonged *Lan Wethinoc* (Padstow), *Langorroc* (Crantock), which like others had a complex site history, *Lanpiran* (St Piran's Oratory at Perranzabuloe), *Lannachebran* (St Keverne) and *Lanalet* (St Germans). These are attested in various ways to have been in existence by the ninth century, but were indeed probably founded during the sixth.

Possibly as early, but some perhaps later, are the houses of *Lanbrabois* (Probus), *Lammana* (Looe Island), *Ecglosberria* (St Buryan), and St Neot, where the recorded form of the dedication name and associated hagiography is later Saxon but replaced a local saint.

Perhaps Lansallos, which received the estate of *Lanlawren* (Lanteglos) from 'Count' Maenchi in the early tenth century, may belong with this second group. *Dinuurin*, perhaps situated at Bodmin, was in existence by the mid-ninth century. The houses of religious communities at *Lanscauetone* (St Stephen by Launceston), *Langustenyn* (Constantine), *Landighe* (Old Kea) and *Langoran* (Gorran) cannot be dated before the eleventh century. Any early character and date for the establishments at St Carroc (St Cadix, Veep), St Anthony in Roseland and St Michael's Mount are obscure.

In many ways this presents the kind of picture which we would have anticipated. We can see the largest series of sites founded in the full flush of early monastic enthusiasm and admiration, probably in the sixth century, or very early seventh. Thereafter, the records suggest what we would expect, that the local western monastic movement had its own history in which some houses were founded after *c.* 700, perhaps some time after. Equally, some houses have hints of internal histories: the place which was later called Padstow seems to have started as *Languihenoc* (1068) or similar, and St Germans was *Lannaled* (*c.* 950) or similar. The house at St Buryan seems to have taken over a secular 'round'.

A series of confused reports from Crantock (Fig. 70) show that the area of burials is considerably larger than that encompassed by the Old Church Yard, and extended into two fields on the western side of the churchyard. The character of the graves was mixed, and some seem to be prehistoric, but others were possibly Roman or post-Roman. The two fields are called Langurrow and Higher Langurrow,[102] which may suggest that originally the seemingly early monastic site at Crantock (presumably concentrated upon the roughly circular feature focal to the site plan) had an enclosure substantially larger than the later Old Church Yard, embracing these two fields which were the cemetery area. This is possible, but it is also possible that here the burials represent an early cemetery phase which was non-monastic and even not very Christian, which was unenclosed and larger than that later enclosed to form the formal Christian site. Crantock hints at the kind of complex history many sites may have had.

Sites along the north Devon and Somerset coasts

The creation of religious houses which were regarded as founded by men with British names did stop short at the Tamar; along the north coast of Devon and Somerset and southwards into the Somerset hinterland are a string of possible

---

102. L. Olson, 'Crantock, Cornwall, as an early monastic site', in S. Pearce, *The Early Church in Western Britain and Ireland* (1982): 177–86.

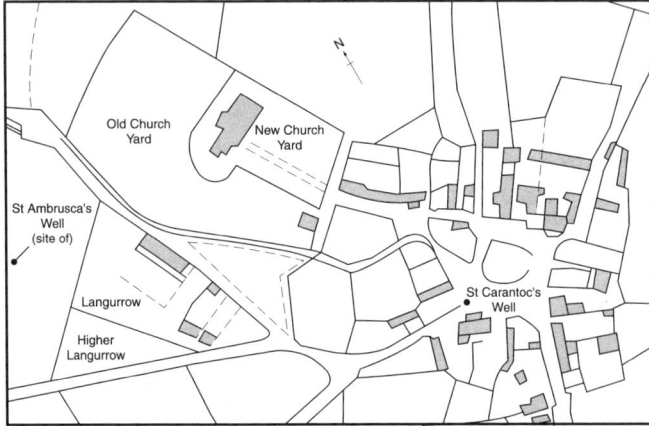

Figure 70   Crantock (after Olson 1982, Figs 11.1, 11.2)

candidates for inclusion. If the sketchy details which we possess of these sites do indeed suggest the existence of a monastery then we have to suppose from the British personal names attached to them that either they originated within the period before each area came under West Saxon control, which means before *c.* 680, or that men with such names were able to found religious houses within eighth-century Wessex (or later) or perhaps that the houses in question acquired their British personal nomenclature at some later 'Celticizing' period, possibly the tenth or twelfth centuries. None of these views is impossible; however, given the lack of firm evidence, the most economic approach is to allow that if the details attaching to a site east of the Tamar suggest that it was a 'British' monastery, then it was founded before 700 at the latest.

In 1086 the manor of Hartland, an area of rocky coast and upland grazing with a coastal strip of workable farmland, evidently comprised at least the later parishes of Hartland and Welcombe: the area is bounded on the north and west by the sea, and on the south by the Cornish/Devon border. The manor was held by the king and within it the holding of Stoke St Nectan was in the hands of twelve canons, and this seems to reflect the broad arrangements in existence when in about 881 Alfred bequeathed the estate to Edward, his eldest son. It seems clear that by then Stoke St Nectan was operating as a West Saxon minster, but the firmly 'Celtic' name of the dedicatee, and the 'Celtic'-orientated accounts of the history of the monastery generated (at considerable length) within the earlier house or its successor abbey founded in 1169 as a house of Regular Canons, suggest that the monastery was founded before *c.* 700 by Nectan, whose relics remained on the site, apparently until the Dissolution. Perhaps the monastery had originally held the whole of the Hartland estate.[103]

In the far north-east of Devon, the parish of Braunton occupies a large area of sand dune and marsh, with a fertile belt along the River Caen where lies the surviving

---

103.   For Harland, see S. Pearce, 'The early Church in the landscape: the evidence from North Devon', *Arch. J.*, 142 (1985): 263–72. The place-name Kismeldon, *Cristelmael-dun*, south-east of Wool-fardisworthy, indicates the earlier existence of a standing cross which may have marked the south-east edge of Hartland's estate. I am grateful to Sam Turner for this reference.

Great Field and Braunton itself, and with access to the Exmoor upland. In 857 the estate, probably more or less the ecclesiastical parish, was called *Brannocminster* and was granted to Glastonbury; the grant included the minster church and whatever holding it had had. Again, the British name of the founding saint, whose body both William of Worcester and John Leland tell us lay in the church which still carries his name, and the subsequent history of the site, suggest a pre *c.* 700 foundation.[104]

Along the Somerset coast are a run of sites where the indications of pre *c.* 700 monasteries are thin or very thin, but not entirely negligible and should be mentioned. In the Watchet area are the clifftop enclosure at Daws Castle, apparently used as a post-Roman cemetery, and Watchet itself, the probable site of the tenth-century *burh*, outside which is a parish church dedicated to St Decuman. Decuman is a British name, and presumably the saint was also British. The general impression is that the name, which is rare and not the object of extended, general hagiography (although a late *vita* was current in Somerset[105]) is likely to be a genuinely pre-700 attachment to the site. A field adjacent to Daws Castle is called Old Minster, which suggests that St Decumans was the site of a minster church until, perhaps superseded by a church in the *burh*, conceivably Holy Cross, which however survived only as a chapel (in 1369), while St Decuman re-emerged as the focal parish church even though outside the urban area.[106] At the end of the twelfth century it was worth being presented to the cathedral church of Wells as a prebend by Simon Briton[107] which may be the context for the *vita*.

The site at Carhampton mirrors the Watchet complex to a certain extent: here too are a parish church with a British dedication, albeit to Carantoc who has an extensive hagiography, and a hill-fort called Batts Castle, which was without known burials but conceivably originally possessed of the name *Dindrathou* which appears in the *Life of Carantoc*. It is difficult to know whether the 'British' dedication and tradition at Carhampton came from the desire to create the kind of 'British' past then being developed at Glastonbury, helped by the coincidence of the place-name and the name of the famous pan-Celtic saint, or whether they point to some kind of genuine pre-700 foundation, by no means necessarily monastic.

Kewstoke, the name of which includes a British personal name added to *stoc*, is first recorded in 1086 as *Chiwestock*. Although in terms of post-Roman Christian developments this is not particularly early, it does suggest a potentially early site, conceivably with pre-Saxon links, but there seems to be no supporting evidence and, if such a site did exist, its nature remains obscure. Keynsham has even more slender grounds for early claims. The name, *Cainesham* in 1086, seems to come from an Anglo-Saxon personal name.[108] It was probably the site of a minster, since Bishop Heahmund of Sherborne was thought to be buried there in 871, and characteristically it was refounded as a house of Augustinian canons in 1166.[109] By the time the traditions of the Children of Brychan were being worked up, *Caine* had been identified with the Cornish St Keyne of the famous well, drawn into the lists of Children,

104. For later material relating to Brannoc, See Grant, 'Lost Life of St Brannoc' (2002), pp. 21–7. For Braunton, see Pearce 1985, pp. 263–72.
105. G. Doble, *The Saints of Cornwall, Part Two: Saints of the Lizard District* (1997), pp. 25–33.
106. I. Burrow, *Hillforts*, p. 294.
107. Doble, *Saints of Cornwall, Part Two*, p. 29.
108. Mills, *English Place-names*, p.195.
109. R. Leech, *Small Medieval Towns in Avon* (1975), pp. 35–43.

and fitted out with a *vita* which embodies local detail, especially the story in which the saint turns snakes into stones found as ammonites, a piece of folklore from the Avon quarries. However, there was apparently no cult of Keyne at Cainesham, and any notions of a pre-Saxon origin for the ecclesiastical site can probably be discounted.

Congresbury, Banwell and Sherborne

The remaining sites belong in a quite different category. In the valley of the Somerset Yeo is the hill-fort of Cadbury Congresbury from which has come a range of evidence demonstrating late Roman/sub-Roman occupation, and close by is the cemetery complex of Henley Wood, presumably the burial ground of those who used the hill-fort (or some of them). On the southern side of the river lies the church now dedicated to St Andrew (the saint of Wells) but to which was apparently attached the British named Congar or Cyngor from whose name + *burh* the parish takes its name.[110] The *Resting Places of the Saints* (*c.* 1000) tells us that 'resteth Congarus, Confessor, on Cungresbyrig', but the most important reference is that in Asser's *Life of King Alfred*. Asser tells us that one Christmas Eve, probably that of 886, the King sent for him and 'he presented me with two documents in which there was a lengthy list of everything which was in the two monasteries named Congresbury and Banwell in English. On that same day he granted these two monasteries to me, with all the things that were in them.'[111] The documents were presumably inventories of material such as relics, church furnishings, books and vestments, and also resources like livestock. The estate of Congresbury, presumably the old monastic endowment, went through a number of vicissitudes after Asser's death in 909 but seems always to have been recognized as church property, first probably of Sherborne, then of Wells. Asser as a Welshman would, of course, have been interested in the fact that, as he implies, Congresbury and Banwell had (lost) British names. This makes it distinctly possible that the site of a monastic house associated with Congar founded before 700 was in the Congresbury area, although the relationships between the monastery, the church, the hill-fort and the cemetery remain to be worked out.

Banwell, perhaps meaning 'spring or stream of a murderer, or of a man called *Banna', is across the Yeo on rising land west of Congresbury. It, too, had an early burial ground in the immediate vicinity at Wint Hill and also two villa sites. The passage just quoted from Asser's *Life* gives the evidence for Banwell's candidature as a monastery. The estate was also usually in ecclesiastical ownership and ended up with Wells, although no hagiography relating to it seems to have been cultivated (unless the translation of the place-name as 'Murderer's Spring' is correct; this looks as if it was the site of a story, conceivably connected with a saint).[112]

---

110.   P. Rahtz *et al., Cadbury Congresbury 1968–73. A Late/Post-Roman Hilltop Settlement in Somerset* (1992), esp. pp. 224–33.

111.   S. Keynes and M. Lapidge (eds), *Alfred the Great: Asser's Life of King Alfred and Other Contemporary Sources* (1983), p. 97.

112.   Mills, *English Place-names*, p. 22, but see Parsons *et al., Vocabulary* p. 46. Efforts to link Banwell with the *Bannavem Taberniae* mentioned by Patrick as his home town should almost certainly be discounted, as should the reinterpretation of other local place-names, and local archaeology, along similar Patrician lines, attempted by H. Jelley, *Saint Patrick's Somerset Birthplace* (1998). For *Bannavem Taberniae* see Patrick, *Confessio,* c. 10 (ed. A. Hood, *St Patrick: His Writings and Muicha's Life* (1978), pp. 23, 41).

About 700, Sherborne was chosen as the seat of the second West Saxon bishopric and Aldhelm was installed as the first bishop with responsibilities for the areas west of Selwood. Thereafter, it had a history appropriate to its position as a leading West Saxon house.[113] Two pieces of documentary evidence, a doubtful charter of Centwine (ruled 676–685) which gives the church 100 hides at *Lanprobi*,[114] and papal bulls confirming the Sherborne property in 1145 and 1163 which mention '*Propeschirche*' near the castle, suggest the earlier existence of a monastery founded under British auspices,[115] presumably by Probus, before 700. Whatever the merits of the charter, it is very difficult to see how the place-name *Lanprobi* could have become attached to a site so far east unless it was genuine, and a church dedicated to Probus was evidently well known in the twelfth century; deliberate efforts to create a 'Celtic' background at any period from the tenth century onwards are usually much less skilful, local or restrained.

The later abbey of Sherborne is situated at the western end of the medieval settlement, and the castle at the eastern end. If the reference to *Propeschirche* as 'near the castle' means that this was the site of the early monastery, then it may be connected with the human bones which come from the castle site but which predate the Norman castle,[116] and with the 'small stone building', rock-cut grave on an east–west axis and 'rock-cut ditch with an outer earthen bank' which was found beneath the castle courtyard.[117]

Glastonbury

In spite of considerable excavation[118] and intensive study of the extensive medieval documentation,[119] the origins of the house at Glastonbury remain obscure and controversial. In the late Roman/post-Roman period, Glastonbury was a promontory isolated on all but the eastern side at times of flood and dominated by Wirral Hill and the very impressive Tor (Fig. 71a). Access on foot was by bridge or causeway across the Brue, which linked Glastonbury to Street, presumably a Roman settlement, or on the east via a neck of land crossed by Ponter's Ball, a roughly north–south earthwork

113. Bede *HE* V18 for the date, *AS Chron* sa 705 for location of the see. See also M. O'Donovan, *Anglo-Saxon Charters III, Charters of Sherborne* (1988).

114. H. Edwards, *The Charters of the Early West Saxon Kingdom* (1998), pp. 240–1.

115. K. Barker, 'Sherborne in Dorset. An ecclesiastical settlement and its estate', *PDNHAS*, 129 (1984): 1–33.

116. *PDNHAS*, 77 (1955): 240–1.

117. See *Med. Arch.*, 18 (1974): 195. Malmesbury can probably be deleted from the list of potential pre-Saxon houses, see M. Lapidge and M. Herren, *Aldhelm, the Prose Works* (1979), pp. 6–7. Bede (*HE* V18) thought the monastery took its name from its Irish founder, Maildub, but this need not have been before the mid-seventh century. Recent work suggests a possible Iron Age complex/possible Roman shrine on/near the site. Also, for the early history of Shaftesbury, see E. Murphy, 'Anglo-Saxon Shaftesbury – Bectun's base or Alfred's foundation', *PDNHAS*, 113 (1991): 23–30.

118. M. Aston and R. Leech, *Historic Towns in Somerset* (1977), p. 59. P. Leach and P. Ellis, 'The medieval precinct of Glastonbury Abbey – some new evidence', in Carver, *In Search of Cult* (1993), pp. 119–24.

119. L. Abrams and J. Carley, *The Archaeology and History of Glastonbury Abbey* (1991); C. Pickles, *Texts and Monuments. A Study of Ten Anglo-Saxon Churches of the Pre-Viking Period* (1999).

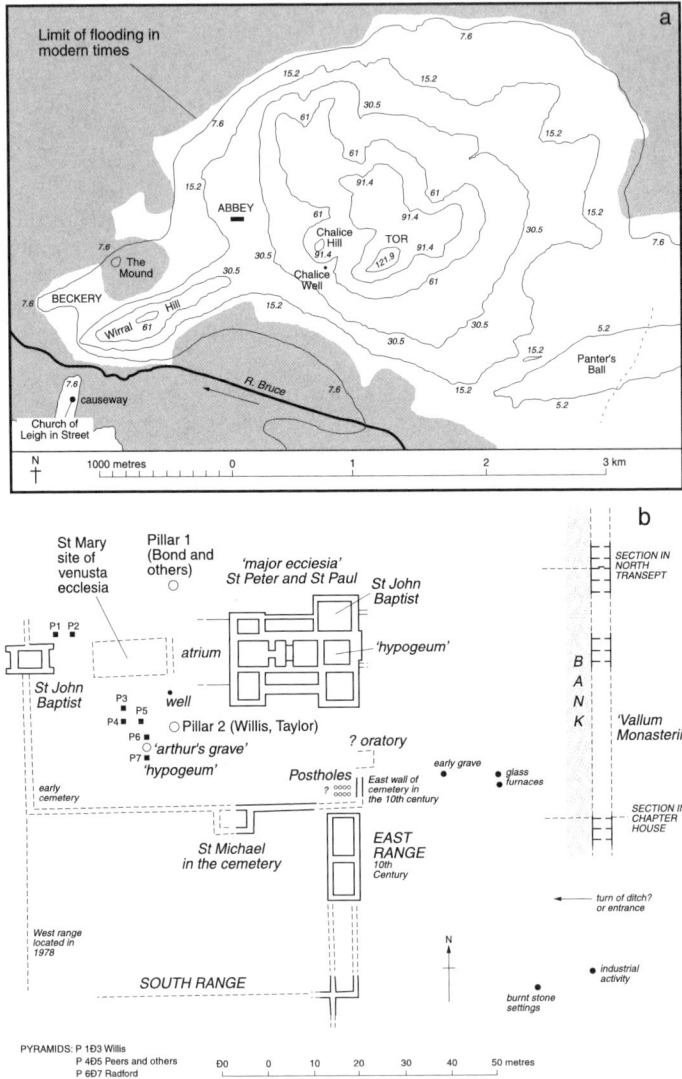

Figure 71 Glastonbury (a) main topographical features, (b) early features on the Abbey site (after Rahtz 1993, Figs 1, 2, 4, 5). Various supposed positions for the 'pyramids' are shown

with a ditch on its eastern side, and of uncertain date.[120] The top of the Tor has produced traces of some kind of occupation dated by sherds of imported ware to the late fifth/sixth century, and similar sherds have come from the Mound, an 'island' of higher ground roughly 1 km south-west of the abbey site.

120.   The bank appears as a substantial Glastonbury boundary by the late twelfth century. For further discussion, see R. Dunning, 'Ponters Ball', *SDNQ*, 25 (2001): 1–2; S. Rands, 'Ponter's Ball or Porter's', *SDNQ*, 35 (354): 55–7 (2001).

In his *De Antiquitate Glastonie Ecclesie* of about 1129, William of Malmesbury described the abbey site as featuring the Old Church, built of wood, and the Old Cemetery, which surrounded this church, and held two 'pyramids', possibly standing crosses.[121] Excavation (Fig. 71b) at the site has demonstrated the probable existence of an early medieval (how early is uncertain) bank and ditch (the so-called *Vallum monasterii*) below the transepts of the abbey church[122] and this has been picked up subsequently under Magdalene Street[123] and possibly Silver Street.[124] Chalice Well could have provided water for the site. A possible reconstruction suggests that an early (? Roman) route may have run from the eastern side of the site to the Tor, and along this, and on the Tor itself, the Saxon churches were built; on the western side the road would have led to the Levels (Fig. 72). Within the *Vallum* Radford believed he had located the possible site of a wattle oratory and of the wooden Old Church, which was burnt down in 1184, together with what may have been the boundary of the Old Cemetery. Within this cemetery he found stone slab-lined graves, two hypogea, or burial vaults, of uncertain date, and traces of wattle buildings. The vault which lay to the east of the first Saxon abbey church may perhaps have been

Figure 72 Glastonbury, Somerset, looking east. The abbey complex is in the centre, with St John's church on the opposite site of High Street. The Tor shows clearly beyond, with St Michael's tower on its summit. (Photo: West Air Photography)

---

121. Pickles, *Texts and Monuments*, pp. 50–6.
122. C. Radford, 'Glastonbury Abbey before 1184: interim report on the excavations 1908–64', in *Medieval Art and Architecture at Wells and Glastonbury* (1981), pp. 110–34.
123. N. Hollinrake and C. Hollinrake, 'Glastonbury, Magdalene Street, ST49803870', *PSANHS*, 129 (1984): 10–11.
124. P. Ellis, 'Excavations at Silver Street, Glastonbury, 1978', *PSANHS*, 132 (1981–2): 24.

arranged to allow a view of the relics within, or offered the ability to let down objects which could come into contact with the dust. Within the cemetery was also a large hole interpreted as the site of one of the two 'pyramids', probably of Saxon date, while the other, it was thought, perhaps marked the sacred burial vault; a further hole perhaps marked the exhumation of 'Arthur's bones' in the late twelfth century.

William gave details of a supposed grant of five *cassates* of land in a place called *Iniswitrin* interpreted as Glastonbury, by a British King of Dumnonia, involving a Bishop Mawron (or Mauuron) and Wogret, Abbot of Glastonbury, in a year said to be 601. William also recorded details of benefactions undertaken by Centwine and by Ine, who built the first Saxon church on the site, perhaps close to the Old Church. Any account of Glastonbury can be challenged in most of its details, particularly those relating to the Old Cemetery and its contents,[125] where the interpretation of excavated evidence has been heavily influenced by William's account, but this sketch shows how Glastonbury (Fig. 71b), though more complex, can be seen to belong in its broad features within what is gradually emerging as a better understood range of pre-Saxon monastic sites. It is an account, however, which may be expected to change, perhaps radically, as archaeological opportunities are exploited.

The eastern minsters

Bede knew relatively little about affairs in what became Wessex, and even less about any formal processes of conversion in the western part of its eventual area, apart from a few stories connected with the difficult early history of the see of Winchester. Consequently, our understanding of how and by whom any such formal Christian initiatives were undertaken in Dorset and Somerset remains dim, and this impinges upon the issue of the extent to which the people of this area had already had any experience of Christian practice, a question reviewed in detail in the previous chapter. What we do see is a pattern of minster churches across this area by about 750, about the founding of which we know very little,[126] and which probably include institutions of widely varying date, origin and subsequent history.

A number of attempts have been made to separate out a range of economic, documentary and archaeological features which can be used as criteria against which minster churches can be recognized and distinguished from lesser establishments. The criteria embrace the existence at the site of pre-Conquest saintly and royal burials, a place-name in 'minster' or 'church'[127] (and 'bury' may also be relevant), large parish size, the existence of a large cruciform church preferably with Saxon fabric and/or embellishment, records of receipt of churchscot and evidence of dependent

---

125.　Pickles, *Texts and Monuments*, pp. 49–50.

126.　Although minsters may sometimes have occupied the sites of earlier Roman buildings, this is not to suggest a continuity between them and any earlier establishment; still less, *pace* Dark, *Civitas to Kingdom*, pp. 161–2 and fig. 12, is there any evidence that the use of the place-name *minster* has any relationship to 'ecclesiastical sites with a British background, perhaps British monasteries' (p. 162).

127.　For criteria, see C. Radford, 'The pre-Conquest Church and the old minsters in Devon', *The Devon Historian*, 11 (1975): 2–12; Pearce, *Dumnonia*, pp. 97–8; Hall, *Minsters*, pp. 4–8. On the difficulties of the place-name *mynster*, see S. Foot, 'Anglo-Saxon minsters: a review of terminology', in Blair and Sharpe, *Pastoral Care*, 223. See also, Blair, 'Anglo-Saxon minsters' (1992), pp. 226–66.

chapels or churches. To these should be added a history of royal or ecclesiastical ownership, and a high value in the *Taxatio* of 1291 (although this is admittedly very late). The post-1066 establishment of a house of Augustinian canons at the church, whose Rule required pastoral work, can hint helpfully at earlier similar, but less regular, activities.

All these criteria do, indeed, seem to be pertinent, but, given that we are dealing with human institutions, it is doubtful if a formulaic approach will catch more than those candidates which will be obvious whatever approach is used. Their differing characters also make this kind of approach unsatisfactory. Some minsters, like that at Bosham (Sussex), were founded to house contemplatives, some, like Wimborne, to be double houses of nuns and monks and some may have been wholly pastoral. Most were founded by kings, sometimes as a result of broad policy, sometimes for a favoured churchman or family member, and some were founded by the diocesan bishop.

Some minsters were from the beginning very substantial, with important early churches and large estate endowments to match, like Wimborne and Bath; others had perhaps only a few monks or priests, or even only one priest, with much more modest parcels of land, like Carhampton in Somerset, and not all of these necessarily had all of the classic (later) payments due to a minster. Payments of tithe, churchscot, hearthpennies, soulscot (burial fee) and plough-alms are not listed fully until Athelstan's time (925–939) and even if this simply codifies much earlier practice, it also allows plenty of time for movement and development. Also, these establishments could, and did, change considerably over time, and there was plenty of scope for false starts, and refoundings, as well as the problems of fake monasteries founded by nobles for the security of tenure which they might offer, and the legitimate family interests which were involved in the affairs of others. Moreover, what we see when we scrutinize surviving (and very scanty) evidence is usually the end product of a lengthy history in which the successful survivors are unduly prominent.

A range of relevant sites can be identified by the existence of a place-name in *minster*. In Devon there are Axminster and Exminster; in Somerset, Ilminster, Bedminster, Pitminster, *Pennardminster* (East Pennard) and *Ceoddormynster* (Cheddar); and, in Dorset, Sturminster, Sturminster Marshall, Yetminster, Iwerne Minster, Charminster, Beaminster and Wimborne Minster.[128] At Bruton (Somerset), the minster of St Peter was founded by Aldhelm, and on the opposite side of the River Brue are the place-names Godminster, (sometimes found as Godmanstow), Holyfather and Holywater.[129] Most of these places with names in *minster* seem to have been major sites, and to have had the kind of subsequent histories which support the suggestion that they were important parts of the original pattern. Royal burials, for example, were carried out at Wimborne and Axminster, as they were at Sherborne and Gillingham, and episcopal burials at Wimborne, Sherborne, Gillingham and Keynsham. Founders' relics were held at Wimborne.[130]

Nevertheless, the existence of a *minster* place-name is not a guarantee either of antiquity or of the earlier existence of a substantial church unless other characteristics are in place. Lytchett Minster (Dorset) appears to be a more recent name, and

---

128. See Mills, *English Place-names*, under entries.
129. Aston and Leech, *Towns in Somerset*, p. 20.
130. For Dorset sites, see Hall, *Minsters*; for Axminster, *AS Chron* sa 755; for Keynsham, R. Leech, *Towns in Avon*, p. 35.

Misterton (Somerset)[131] may originally have been attached in some way to a minster church, but does not itself seem to have been one. Worminster, a hamlet in the Wells parish of St Cuthbert, which was recovered for Wells by Bishop Giso, perhaps owes its name to its episcopal possession. Buckminster in Swimbridge (Dorset) and Buckminster Wood (East Anstey) on the Somerset/Devon border similarly show no signs of genuine minster status, although whether their names refer to a personal name, or to land held by charter, is unclear. The field name Norminster in Abbotsham (Devon) is equally difficult, since there is no known minster nearby with which it might have been connected.[132] Some, at least, of these obscure sites perhaps relate to the more or less 'fake' private minsters which we know were sometimes set up by estate holders to take advantage of the opportunities for tax evasion which they offered, and which tended to be short-lived.

The element continued in use to form place-names. The church at Braunton was called *Brannocminster*, and here a British personal name became attached to English 'minster'. Watchet also apparently acquired a *minster* name. In Cornwall, Porthminster (in the parish of St Ives) was recorded in the fourteenth and fifteenth centuries but with no very obvious ecclesiastical reference,[133] and Minster was recorded as 'ecc. Sante Methaine de Laminster' in the later twelfth century, which relates to the priory attached to Angers founded *c.* 1200.[134] Manaccan was referred to as 'church of Ministre' in 1259, and 'church of Santa Manaca in Menstre' in 1309; there does not seem to have ever been a monastic church here, but Manaccan is within the district of Meneage, meaning 'monkish land'.[135] Equally, the use of the term 'minster' became very flexible as time went on, and by the tenth century it had come to denote a church of superior status, a church of any status or simply a church building.[136]

A similarly significant place-name is 'church' (see earlier, pp. 145–6) provided that the church in question has further indications of ancient high status. St Mary Church, Devon, and Whitchurch Canonicorum, Dorset, are good candidates. 'Bury' from OE *burh*, meaning 'enclosure', was also used at sites beyond the south-west such as Aylesbury (Bucks), Charlbury (Oxon) and Bury St Edmonds (Suffolk), presumably to signify the bank and ditch used to delimit the church and its immediate surroundings, although of course this word had a large remit. Woodbury and Sidbury, both Devon, are two examples, and Congresbury another, although all are close to Iron Age sites which would have carried this kind of name in any case.[137]

A fair number of the likely or possible sites do not have a special type of place-name, but do possess other significant features. Cullompton, Devon, had five

131.   There is also Lyminster Farm in Misterton; both are just south of the Minster at Crewkerne and may refer to it.
132.   The Tithe Apportionment for Abbotsham gives TA 387 Norminster Meadow on the map and in the Apportionment the farm names Goodings, North Middletons, South Middletons, North Minster and Kingland Minster. In the Domesday record, Abbotsham was held by the Abbot of Tavistock, which presumably accounts for the name of the parish, and may have a bearing on the names in *minster*. I am grateful to Tom Greeves for giving me this reference.
133.   Gover, *Place-names of Cornwall*, p. 629.
134.   *Ibid.*, p. 74. Curiously, the family of Blancheminster held Week St Mary around 1300; see A. Preston-Jones and P. Rose, 'Week St Mary, town and castle', *Corn. Arch.*, 31 (1992): 143–5. For Welsh usage, see G. Pierce, 'The Welsh mystwyr', *Nomina*, 23 (2000): 121–40.
135.   Padel, *Cornish Place-Names* 1988, pp. 114, 118–19.
136.   R. Morris, *The Church in British Archaeology* (1983), p. 128.
137.   And Glastonbury is another. Radford suggested that Sidbury Church possessed a Saxon hypogeum like that at Glastonbury; C. Radford, 'Sidbury: church of St Giles', *Arch. J.*, 114 (1957): 166–7.

prebendal holdings, and was given to Battle Abbey soon after 1066; one of the holdings was called *Hineland*, embodying the element Old English *higna*, signifying probably a religious community. The same element appears in the parish of Hollocombe, where either Hollocombe's own priests[138] or the house at Bodmin held a virgate free of geld. In the Domesday record the church at Carhampton, Somerset, had 1½ hides, of which part supported a priest, and at Yealhampton, Devon, we are told the clergy of the settlement held one hide.

Colyton, Devon, had evidence of a Saxon cruciform church plan, a feature shared with Gillingham, Canford, Bere Regis and Beaminster, all in Dorset. This may not be very significant, but more general architectural features may be indicative. Huish Episcopi, Somerset, had a particularly splendid new church built *c.* 1130, possibly replacing a Saxon building: Huish was the mother church of Pitney, and, judging by the shape of its parish, of Langport too, originally, and it became the prebend of the Archdeacon of Wells. Muchelney had a continuous history from the eighth century, and here there was certainly a Saxon church, with an apse plan that has been compared to Reculver, given to Bassa *c.* 680.[139] The minster character of churches like Crediton and Wells is plain from their choice as bishop's sees, and the same is true of major episcopal holdings like Taunton.

It seems likely that the royal endowment policy towards cathedral and major monastic churches involved an intention to combine economy and good practice by giving to these churches the lands – and the surviving responsibilities – of earlier minsters, and, used with caution, this can help to suggest where early significant churches once existed. The gift of Corfe to Shaftesbury around 948 adds to the other evidence for the early status of Corfe church. Powerstock and Yetminster, both given to Sherborne,[140] may belong to this group, and so may Halstock, Dorset, which belonged to Sherborne from an early date and has a place-name meaning 'holy place'. The church of Pitminster, Somerset, in the head manor of a hundred, was given to Winchester by Hardicanute, and by 1066 Ilminster was held by Muchelney.

A number of churches probably demonstrate their ancient minster status by the payments they received from other churches, and the networks of dependent chapels they headed: Burton Bradstock, Puddletown and Cranborne (Dorset) enjoyed this status, and Bere Regis (Dorset) received churchscot. Stokenham in south Devon had a large parish with dependent chapels, and possibly even had its own unique patron. In the seventeenth century the vicar of Chew Magna (Somerset) was receiving tithes and mortuary fees from a range of churches in Chew Hundred.[141] Many, or most, minsters evidently possessed these *parochia*,[142] extents of territory from which they

138. Hollocombe, *Geld Inquest*; Bodmin, *Exeter Domesday*.
139. C. Radford, 'Pre-Conquest minsters', *Arch. J.*, 130 (1973): 120–40.
140. For Corfe, see Hinton, 'Anglo-Saxon charters and estates', pp. 11–20; for Sherborne, see O'Donovan, *Charters of Sherborne*.
141. St Humbeorht/Humbert; for this intriguing possibility see Orme, *Dedications*, p. 205. Stoke Fleming, Devon, also seems to have had a unique saint, Ermund: Orme, *Dedications*, p. 204. For Chew see Corcos, *Medieval Settlement* (2002), p. 54.
142. Usefully mapped for Somerset in M. Aston, 'Post-Roman central places in Somerset', in E. Grant, *Central Places, Archaeology and History* (1986), p. 56; for Dorset, discussed in Hall, *Minsters*, pp. 31–48, and for South Devon by Oscar Alred (personal communication). The earliest use of parochial in this sense seems to be in AD 417 when a dispute between the south Gaulish churches of Ceyreste and St-Jean-de-Garguiet over their respective parochiae, evidently a substantial area, involved the bishops of Marseilles and Aix: J. Knight, *Roman France* (2001), pp. 162, 166.

were entitled to receive dues and towards which they had certain obligations, like the provision of burial (for only some?), and within which they had families of dependent lesser churches (Fig. 73). These are presumed to be either of later foundation than the minsters, or early sites 'captured' by them, and some of them eventually became independent parish churches, or chapels.

What this might mean, and how late it might persist, is vividly shown by a 1752 entry into the Vestry Book at Chew Magna. Charles Wallis, sexton, 'appeared at the vestry and being strictly examined touching the bounds of the churchyard do acknowledge and declare to the best of his memory that: "the west gate with part of the wall as far as a particular upright stone in the said wall, between the said gates and the standing stile and steps belongs to Chew Stoke and is repaired by the parishioners thereof; the other part home to the poorhouse is repaired by the parish of Chew Magna; the east side is repaired and half of the wall and stile by the parish of Stowey; the other by the parish of Norton; the gate and stile except which belongs and is repaired by ... [gap, original rubbed out] Mrs Smith. The North side is repaired by the parish of Dundry." '[143] The extent to which, during their early history, minsters had clearly defined territories of this kind is debatable; they may have emerged as an administrative way of sorting out the inevitable clash of interests between an old established foundation and often new churches established

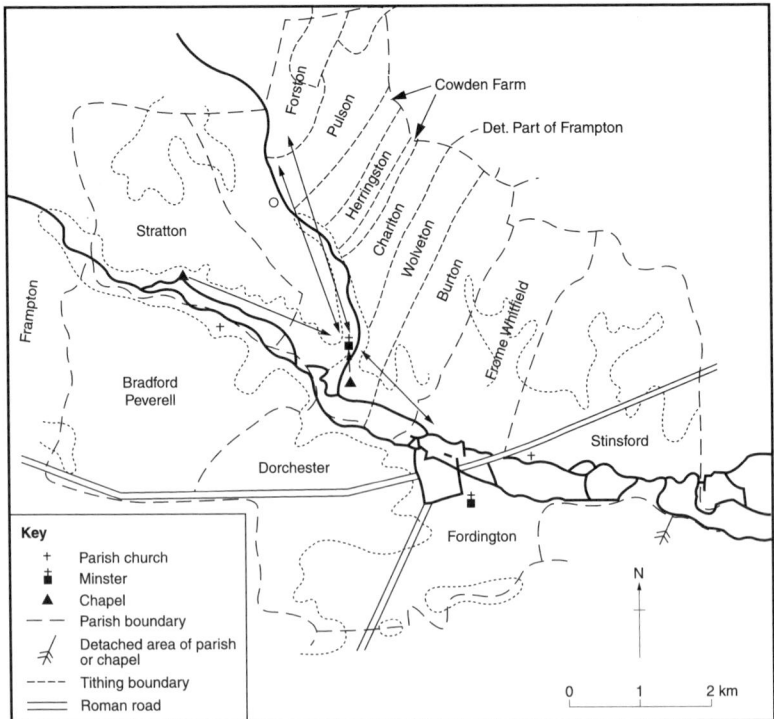

Figure 73 *Parochia* of chapels possessed by Charminster, Dorset (after Hall 2000, Fig. 70)

---

143.   Quoted in Aston, 'Post-roman central places', p. 58.

on estates, something which seems to have happened over the long term, although it did not gather momentum until the tenth century.

The urban centres had, of course, their own arrangements, as we saw in Chapter 2, with possible extramural minster-style churches at St Michael Northover (Ilchester), Fordington (Dorchester) and St Sidwell's (Exeter). Within the walls both Bath and Exeter had major monasteries, both on the sites of earlier cemeteries, founded at Bath by Osric, King of the Hwicce, around 675, and at Exeter, believed to have been founded about 670 by Cenwalh, and certainly in existence by around 675 in time for Boniface to receive his early education there. Nothing substantial is known about the plans of these monasteries.[144]

There are also the churches attached to sites which were developed as defensive points (for which the Old English word was *burh*) in the late ninth/tenth centuries, as St Decumans was at Watchet. The status of these churches has been the subject of considerable debate, and only if we know enough about an individual history can we tell if an existing church and its local settlement, together with its established character as a place for gathering, and perhaps small-scale exchange, seemed the obvious place to fortify or if fortified sites were sited primarily for strategic reasons, and populations, and therefore churches, were drawn to them. Similar arguments apply in the seventh/eighth centuries to the siting of royal palaces, at Cheddar and presumably at Corfe. Sometimes, it is clear, the significant religious site came first, as at Wareham, where the inscribed stones attest to the presence of a late or post-Roman cemetery, which seems to have generated the foundation of Lady St Mary church before *c.* 900.[145] By contrast, at Langport the pre-fortification settlement seems to have belonged to Huish and to have acquired its own church after *c.* 900. At Totnes and Barnstaple it is difficult to see which institution was the first. It looks as if, ecclesiastically speaking, the fortified sites show a mixed pattern.

Monastic precincts

Virtually nothing is known of the internal plans of monastic houses across the peninsula, but it seems probable that some, perhaps many, of them were within substantial enclosures intended to emphasize the practical, legal and psychological distinctions between the monastery and the outside world. This seems to have been the normal response to the establishment of monasteries across the western world, and many examples (Fig. 74) are known from Ireland, where Hurley has illustrated some for County Cork,[146] from northern Britain, as at Dacre, Cumbria,[147] and from Scotland,[148] Wales[149] and Gaul.[150]

144. C. Henderson and P. Bidwell, 'The Saxon minster at Exeter', in Pearce, *Early Church in Western Britain*, pp. 145–77.
145. Okasha, *Corpus of Early Christian Inscribed Stones of South-West Britain (1993)*, p. 348; C. Radford and K. Jackson, 'Early Christian inscriptions', in *An Inventory of Historical Monuments in the County of Dorset, II South-East*, Part 2 (1970), pp. 310–12.
146. V. Hurley, 'The early Church in the south-west of Ireland: settlement and organisation', in Pearce, *Early Church in Western Britain*, pp. 297–332.
147. O'Sullivan, 'Curvilinear churchyards', pp. 3–5.
148. Thomas, *Early Christian Archaeology*, pp. 35–44.
149. Macquarrie (1992), pp. 110–33.
150. Blair, 'Anglo-Saxon minsters', pp. 227–35.

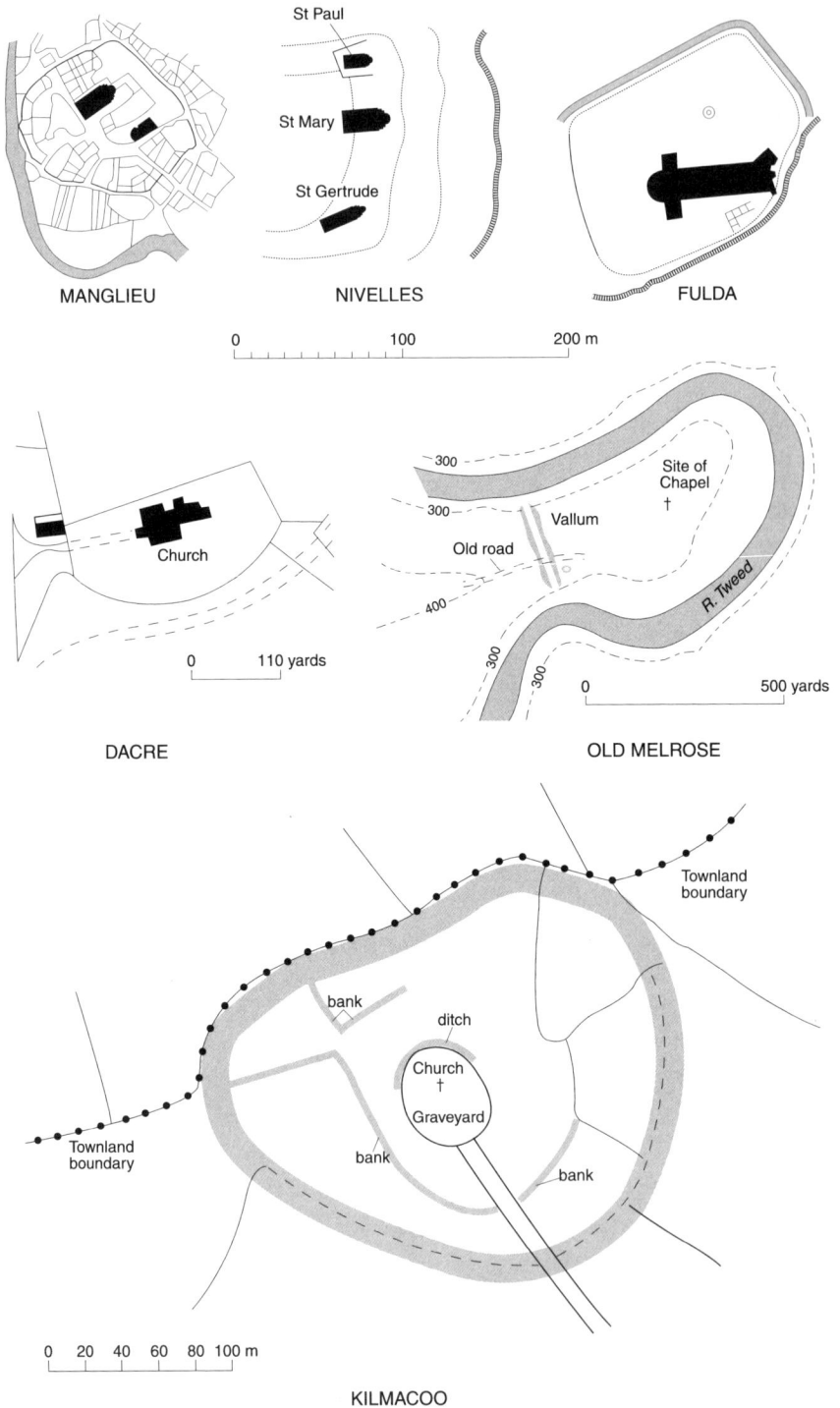

Figure 74 Early monastic precincts. Manglieu (after Blair 1992, p. 229), Nivelles (after Blair 1992, p. 228), both Gaul; Fulda (after David Parsons), Germany; Kilmacoo (possibly monastic) (after Hurley 1982, Fig. 18.7), County Cork, Ireland; Dacre, Cumbria (after O'Sullivan 1980b, Fig. 1); *Mailros* (Old Melrose) (after Thomas 1971, Fig. 11)

The differences in size, shape and construction among the monastic boundaries are probably less important than their role within this broad tradition. The religious houses founded in the sixth century which seem to have had the **lann* ('enclosure') element in their original names, as at St Germans, presumably had original enclosures, which sometimes survive as the characteristic oval or near circular Cornish hedge banks around what are now parish churchyards, although what is now visible is the accumulating development of centuries.[151] They need not originally have been so substantial, and in any case, as Figure 75 suggests, the monastic enclosures were mixed in character, and there is a poor fit between name type and enclosure type.[152] Sometimes, as at Padstow[153] or Stoke St Nectan, churches had a complex of enclosures (Fig. 76).

Further east, the topography of Yetminster, Gillingham, Sturminster Marshall, Beaminster and Cranborne, all in Dorset, suggests that these churches lay in curvilinear enclosures, part of which were often marked by streams, and which were around 300 m or more across their long axis. A similar layout appears conceivably at Ilminster, Somerset, and fairly clearly at Axminster, Devon (Fig. 77, 78). Sometimes churches also had complex outer enclosures, as further west. This matches evidence from further east in England[154] and the circular or subcircular form seems to represent the founding layout of the site, enclosing church, living quarters and graveyard.[155] A number of Dorset minster[156] sites like Bere Regis, Iwerne Minster, Burton Bradstock and Wimborne show a rectilinear plan (Fig. 79), and this may relate to Aldhelm and his possible knowledge of Roman, even Roman military, prototypes. The same plan shows up elsewhere, at, for example, Wareham Lady St Mary and Gillingham in Dorset, and at Bedminster and East Pennard in Somerset. The difficulty is that we usually do not know to what extent these grid formations represent the foundation of the site, or various reworkings, as the churches concerned attracted settlement, and trading and/or defensive characteristics, perhaps by natural accretion, perhaps helped by ambitious planning.

This is a convenient moment to mention the curvilinear boundaries which seem to have been constructed at some point around the complexes at the temple sites in the eastern part of the peninsula at Uley, Lydney, Nettleton, Brean and Lamyatt at dates which may relate to the use of these sites as burial grounds, and perhaps with the small post-temple buildings which have been interpreted as churches.[157] If any of the

151. Ordnance Survey 25-inch series and work in progress.
152. I intend to publish further on this topic in due course.
153. Preston-Jones, 'Decoding Cornish churchyards', p. 121, fig. 11.11.
154. Blair, 'Anglo-Saxon minsters', pp. 227–35.
155. The early topography of Sherborne, with its possible pre-Saxon origin, has been the subject of dispute (Barker, 'Topography of Sherborne', pp. 229–31; Barker, (1984); D. Hinton, 'The topography of Sherborne – early Christian', *Antiquity*, 55 (1981): 222–3; L. Keen, 'The topography of Sherborne, Dorset – *Lanprobus*', *PDNHAS*, 103 (1981): 132–5) and the original site of St Probus's church may have been either at or near the later chapel dedicated to St Thomas à Becket or in the vicinity of the later castle where *Propeschirche* was; it is worth noting that the castle site is associated on its east with Romano-British settlement, with the place-name *Stocland*, and, on the castle site, with early burials, cut through by a curving ditch, earlier than the castle and running underneath it (Keen, 'Topography of Sherborne', pp. 132–5).
156. Hall, *Minsters*, pp. 66–77.
157. A. Woodward and P. Leach, *The Uley Shrines Excavation of a Ritual Complex on West Hill, Uley, Gloucestershire: 1977–9* (1993), pp. 321–2.

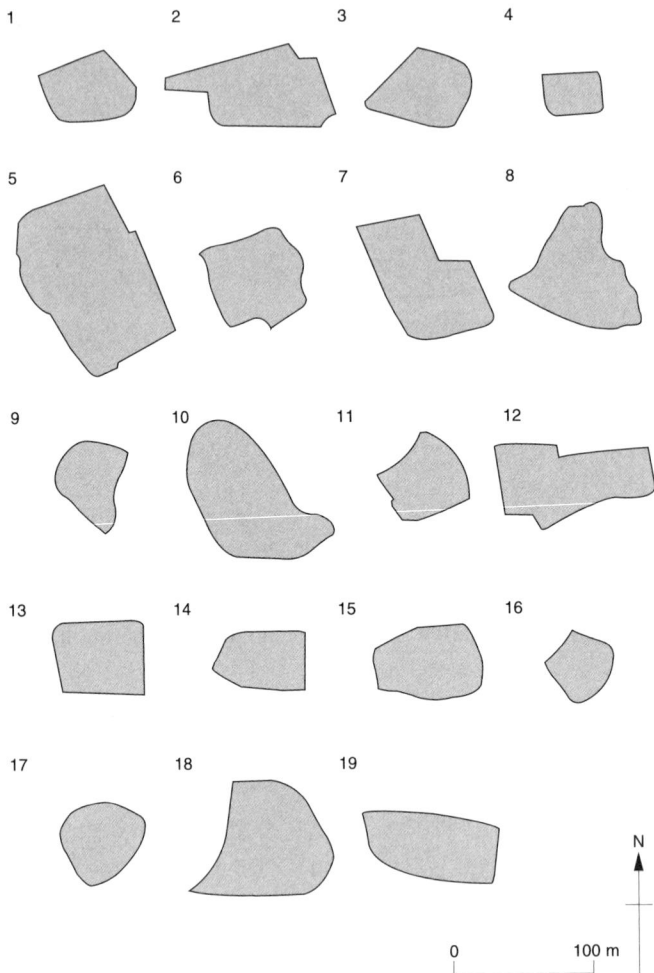

Figure 75 Parish churchyards in Devon and Cornwall apparently the sites of early religious houses. 1. Veep, 2. Padstow, 3. St Neot, 4. St Samson in Golant, 5. Crantock, 6. St Kew, 7. St Stephens-by-Launceston, 8. Bodmin, 9. St Germans, 10. Probus, 11. Gorran, 12. St Anthony-in-Roseland, 13. St Martin by Looe, 14. Old Kea, 15. St Keverne, 16. Constantine, 17. St Buryan (all Cornwall), 18. Braunton, 19. Stoke St Nectan/Hartland (both Devon). (St Piran's Oratory, Perranzabuloe and St Michael's Mount have been omitted, and the location of any site at Looe is uncertain.) Images produced with kind permission of the Ordnance Survey; for Cornish sites, see Preston-Jones 1992, Fig. 11.1

elements at some or all of these sites were Christian in character, these perimeter constructions would fit with that character, although whether the sites were simple graveyards or conceivably had some kind of monastic character is unclear. What may be significant is that, if this Christian usage dates before *c.* 600, then these sites close the geographical gap between the south-western sites and the Welsh sites in an interesting way.

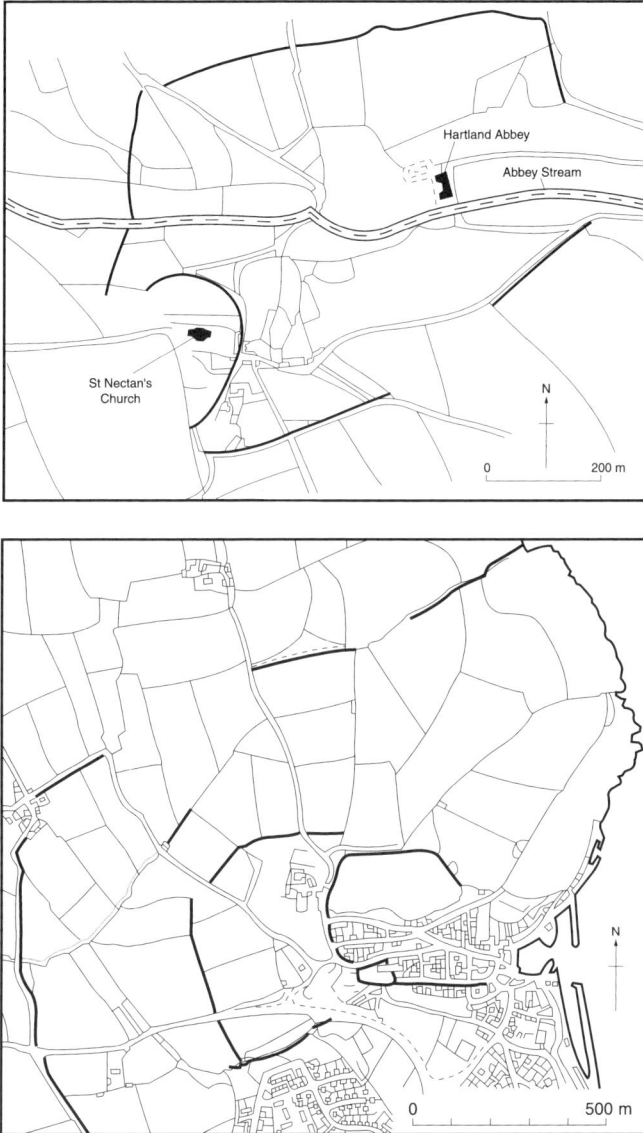

Figure 76 Probable patterns of complex enclosures at Hartland (after Tithe Map of 1844) and Padstow (after Preston-Jones 1992, Fig. 11.11c)

Monastic character

As what finally emerged as the West Saxon royal dynasty gradually established its power westwards, so it and its clergy came into contact with those monastic houses, which had been founded earlier through the initiative of British-speakers. Sherborne and the Somerset sites must have experienced this around the middle of the seventh century, the north Devon sites perhaps after 650, and the east Cornish sites after

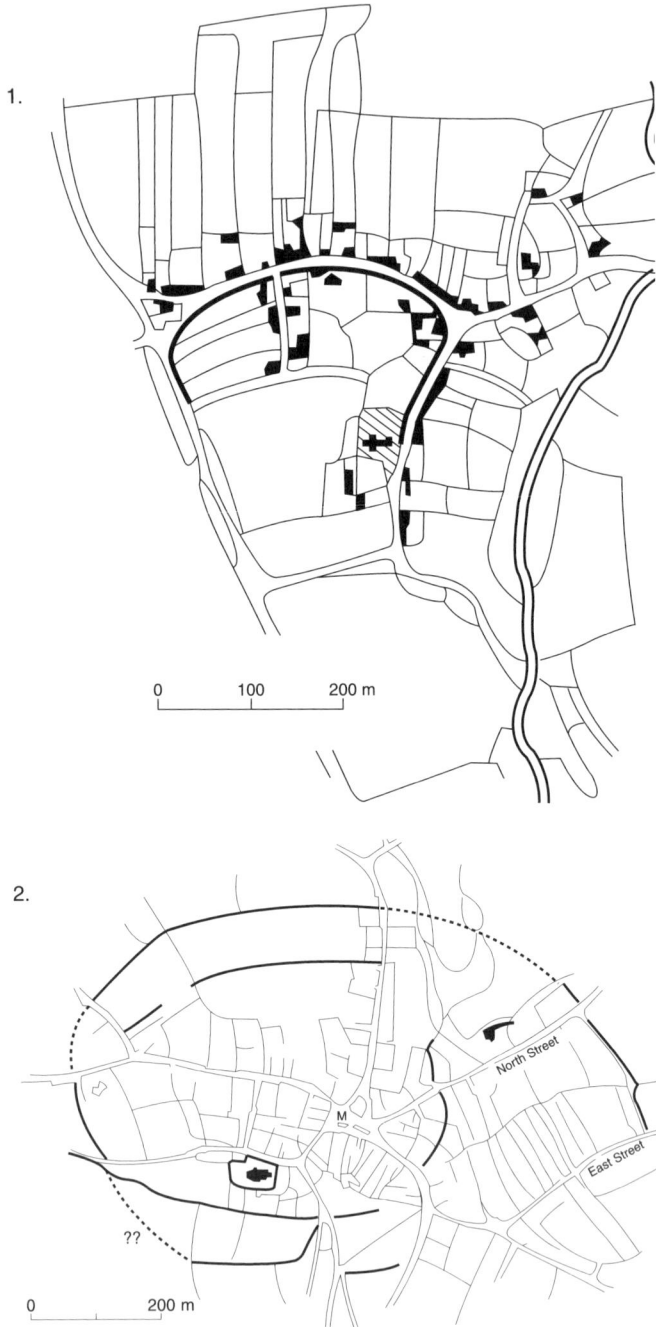

Figure 77 Enclosures around minster churches. 1. Yetminster; 2. Beaminster with apparently an inner, earlier enclosure and an outer, enclosing North and East streets and the area laid off as urban strip-plot development. (1,2 after Hall 2000, p. 63, Fig. 39.)

Figure 78 Enclosures around minster churches: Axminster (from Title Map)

c. 700. To a considerable extent, these houses took their natural places in the overall system, receiving normal respect, retaining their rights and properties and continuing in their pastoral and religious roles, allowing for individual differences of success and failure, which equally affected the eastern churches. Sherborne seems to have had its holdings confirmed and augmented, and in 705 became the seat of the bishop with responsibility for the area west of Selwood; Glastonbury was similarly generously treated, and ultimately was able to develop the narrative of its origins and turn itself into a major attraction. The list of small western houses surviving with a landed endowment in Domesday speaks eloquently of the integration of two groups of institutions with a separate history but common ancestry, and of the success of the system and its hold on the sympathies of the local communities.

One avenue into the mindset of those who saw the need for, or tolerated the creation of, the monastic foundations is to consider the local contexts into which they were set, and the relationship these had with the past. Roman bricks and tiles were reused in the fabric of the minster churches at Whitchurch Canonicorum and (possible minster) Fordington, and thorough fabric surveys would probably reveal more, given the general incidence of examples across the country.[158] The broader context includes the reuse of Roman columns in some of the Roman, southern

---

158. W. Rodwell and K. Rodwell, *Historic Churches: A Wasting Asset* (1977), fig. 30. For example, at Newnham Abbey site, Axminster, the floor make-up contained Romano-British tiles, and Totnes Castle site has produced RB box tiles, see P. Bidwell, *Roman Exeter: Fortress and Town* (1980), pp. 11, 58.

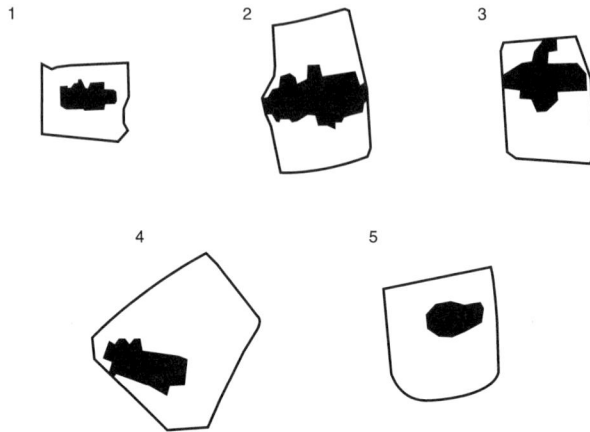

Figure 79 Rectilinear enclosures at minster churches. 1. Burton Bradstock, 2. Wimborne, 3. Gillingham (all Dorset). 4. Bedminster, 5. East Pennard (both Somerset). Images produced by kind permission of the Ordnance Survey

Gaulish and northern Italian churches, and although, of course, there is the obvious practical motif, there may well be an emotional reason as well. This reuse of material looks back to the visible reuse of *spolia* from public (and perhaps private) buildings and tombstones in the late defences of Roman cities, especially where the building of the city wall obliterated earlier landmarks, and looks like an effort at psychological reassurance linked with a clear effort to present continuity. Something of the same may be operating in the minsters, in the south-west and elsewhere.

The reused bricks and tiles seem often to have come from the site where the monastic church was built, or, to put it the other way round, minsters were built on the sites of Roman buildings, something which happens too frequently to be coincidental. Again the practical motive is obvious – the availability of useful supplies and the utilization of a previously well-chosen site, which was now difficult for normal agriculture – but psychological motives may also have been important. All kinds of ex-imperial sites were absorbed, including relatively recent military installations like Caer Gybi near Holyhead, north Wales, used as the site of the monastery, or Burgh Castle in Suffolk which was turned over to Fursa for religious use.

Villa sites are relatively conspicuous in this reuse, in part, no doubt, because villas, especially those sufficiently well appointed to have conspicuous remains, were relatively common in southern Britain, and particularly common in the areas around Ilchester and Dorchester. There is a mosaic pavement under the nave at Wimborne Minster (which may be Saxon reuse of Roman tesserae),[159] a substantial Roman building under the church at Tarrant Crawford,[160] a pavement at Lenthay Green adjacent to the church at Sherborne with further remains said to have been found on the site of the abbey[161] and remains under Fordingham church. At Glastonbury, scatters of Roman pottery have appeared on the abbey site, including within the Old

---

159.   See Penn, *Historic Towns* (1980), p. 121.
160.   This is one of the potential/possible minsters.
161.   See Penn, *Historic Towns* (1980), p. 91.

Cemetery,[162] and from Silver Street;[163] also two tenth-century glass furnaces on the abbey site had a number of Roman box flue tiles included in their construction.[164] This suggests a late Roman building, perhaps a small villa, and also shows how late the reuse of Roman building material could continue.

With this group goes another, equally widespread, where the Roman building was a short distance away from the present church site. There appears to be a substantial late Roman site, possibly a villa, at Bedminster.[165] At Cheddar the church is about 40 metres from a possible villa, which produced possible fifth-century material, and there are substantial Roman remains at Wareham and in the bend of the River Brit at Beaminster. These may fit with what appeared at Deerhurst, Gloucestershire, one of the very few excavated minster sites. Here hypocaust material and a head of Jupiter Amon suggested a villa on the site of Odda's Chapel. The first phases of the stone building on the site, which eventually became that of St Mary's church, seem to have originated in a Roman building made over in various ways, and apparently associated with burials. Reuse of villa sites for monastic purposes was widespread in Gaul, giving us both the range of place-names in -*acum* and, in the courtyard plan, a possible source for the style of the monastic cloister.[166] The incidence of reuse of materials, or reoccupation of site by minsters, seems to be particularly high in the south-west;[167] it is socially and psychologically interesting in its own right, but it also, of course, has a bearing on the possible transmission of villa estates, a point pursued in the next chapter.

A number of minster churches seem to have been built within already existing graveyards, some probably the burials of Romano-Britons associated with nearby occupation sites, and others perhaps who lived after these sites had gone out of habitation. The cemetery and mausoleum at Wells may relate to a villa site, as may that at Banwell, where a villa site is known at Wint Hill. The inscribed stones at Wareham attest to an important late or post-Roman cemetery, which may have spanned a considerable period, although there is no hagiographical or tenurial evidence associated with the probable minster church of Lady St Mary site to suggest its existence as a pre-700 monastic foundation. Wareham looks like the Saxon minster sites in Devon which, judging by the inscribed stones probably associated with their cemeteries, were deliberately built within existing graveyards: Yealhampton, and perhaps Tavistock if the later house succeeded to a minster as is possible.

Similarly, some of the monastic sites west of the Tamar, such as Crantock and St Buryan, may have been set up within existing graveyards. Other sites were close

---

162. Woods *et al.*, 'Glastonbury Abbey' (1995), p. 129.

163. Ellis, 'Excavations at Silver Street (1981–82), pp. 17–38.

164. Woods *et al.* 'Glastonbury Abbey', (1995), pp. 7–73.

165. K. Brannigan, 'Villa settlement in the West Country', in K. Brannigan and P. Fowler (eds), *The Roman West Country* (1976), pp. 221–7. A further number of minsters also seem to have had a villa in the relatively near vicinity: Corfe (M. Hughes, 'A Romano-British sacred well at Norden, Corfe Castle', *PDNHAS*, 94 (1972): 76–7); Charminster, Iwerne Minster (Hall, *Minsters*, p. 21); and doubtless more. This may not mean much, or if it does may be more relevant to continuity of estates than of specific sites.

166. P. Rahtz, *Excavations at St Mary's Church, Deerhurst* (1976); for Gaulish villas, see J. Percival, 'Villas and monasteries in late Roman Gaul', *J. Ecclesiastical History*, 48 (1): 1–21 (1997).

167. Blair, 'Anglo-Saxon Minsters' (1992), pp. 140–1; suggests that since three out of the four known villa sites that acquired names in -*ceaster* ('chester') also have churches on top of the villas, *ceaster* also sometimes denoted a monastery. The three are Frocester, Gloucestershire; Woodchester, Gloucestershire; and Castor (*Cyneburge Caestrel*), Norfolk; the odd one out is Yarchester (Salop).

to old burial grounds, as at Padstow, where the religious site of Lanwethineck (or similar) may have superseded the burial ground at Trevone on the opposite side of the River Camel. At Cannington, a possible minster, the church seems to have succeeded the post-Roman cemetery in function, and the same is true at Congresbury and at Watchet, although the church and cemetery sites are at some distance from each other.

It is possible that, if other minster sites could ever be investigated, instances of fourth/fifth/sixth-century burial sites might appear. Meanwhile, the indications are sufficient to show us a palpable continuity, and the desire to sustain a workable social framework by connecting contemporary stories with the past. When the monastic precincts were laid out, with an old burial ground perhaps embraced within it, a church and monastic buildings put up, and adequate endowment arrangements made for the men who operated the complex, the shock of the new on each local community, west and east, must have been considerable. Sometimes we can guess why a particular site was chosen, although often we cannot, and presumably, in part at least, the choice depended upon the mix of local and superior complexities of power-broking and all the tensions which this encapsulates.

When the precinct at Probus or Stoke St Nectan was drawn out, it made a cosmological statement about the relationship between God and Man, creating a dedicated area of consecrated Christian holiness, a force field which the older burial sites had lacked. How were the monasteries able to create this shared cosmology? How could they impose themselves as a new ideology within a social system which had managed quite well without them, and consolidate their hold on the substantial resources of land, offerings and muscle power for digging and building, and on the attendance which they required? How could they maintain their presence after the first impact had worn off so that they stood a chance of attracting pilgrims, small gifts, large donations and recruits? Clearly, the active intervention of individuals possessed of effective political power was crucial, and without them the enterprise might not have succeeded, but political decision alone is not enough to create so great a shift within hearts and minds.

The answer must lie in the thaumaturgical powers which the monasteries were able to deploy. In part, these lay in the sacraments their priests dispensed, in which baptism was magically perceivable as ritual cleansing by water and the Mass as an especially powerful form of blood sacrifice. In part, also, they depended upon the powers attributed to the saintly relics which monasteries possessed. The founder and all subsequent members of the community were buried in the monastic graveyard, and in due course most houses – Congresbury with Congar, Glastonbury with Indract and others, Petroc's house with Petroc – produced the bodies of their saints in truly theatrical style with special tombs, Masses and customs, and with written accounts to provide the plot. The manipulation of sacred body parts, local and imported, in relation to the bodies of ordinary people, both while alive through touching and kissing and when dead through proximate burial, struck a profound psychological note within individuals and the community. What gave the holy bodies their holiness were the lives which they had led on earth, which entitled them to a privileged status in Heaven and made contact with them valuable.[168]

---

168.   The fundamental work here is Peter Brown's on the holy man in Late Antiquity; see P. Brown, 'The rise and function of the holy man in Late Antiquity', *J. of Roman Studies*, 61 (1971), and *Society and the Holy in Late Antiquity* (1982).

We lack early accounts of the lives and deeds of those who founded the post-700 eastern houses; traditional wisdom says that their notion of religious experience was less extreme than that cultivated within the pre-700 western houses, but how correct this is we do not know. Samson's *Vita* depicts him wrestling with demons, seeing off a murderous sorceress, defeating leprosy and conquering serpents (three times, something of a speciality). The crucial practices which gave him this spiritual power were his 'keener and stricter fasts', the time when he lived as a hermit and had 'seven days fast from food and drink' and when 'he stood wakeful till dawn at the altar alone' and lost consciousness in an ecstatic vision.[169] Local excitement and veneration were aroused by the sight, presumably known and visible to all, at least from afar, of an individual aflame with the conviction which enabled him to subdue bodily needs to the point where he could induce visionary experiences. Such people belong to a well-recognized psychic type, and were, on the whole, poorly regarded in earlier classical times, but became socially powerful in Late Antiquity with its emphasis on ideology constructed through presentation of the body.

None of this fits particularly well with the mentality or the routines of pastoral care, and the extent to which the various kinds of monastic establishments wished, or were expected, to undertake the pastoral duties of local missionary work and the cure of souls is a vexed question. The sense from sources like Samson's *Vita* is that, while Samson longed for the life of prayerful contemplation, he felt obliged to take up the administrative tasks of a bishop, which were, and were to continue to be, discharged from his monastery at Dol. The same kind of tension, and one possible solution, perhaps appears in the foundation charter of Breedon on the Hill (Leicester) which says 'a *monasterium* and oratory of monks serving God should be founded ... and also a priest ... instituted, who should bring the grace of baptism and the teaching of the Gospel to the people committed to his care'.[170] One of the many things we are not clear about is to what extent religious houses, perhaps just of priests, were founded specifically for pastoral work, or how quickly an originally monastic establishment could become what later generations would think of as a house of canons.

However it witnessed to the Christian life, the institution had to be endowed with adequate resources, either a landed estate and/or the right to receive specified payments from particular communities. Houses differed considerably in size, and in the fluctuations of their fortunes, but the resourcing arrangements made for them became so embedded in society that many survived as traces into the late medieval period, or even later, and it is investigation of these traces which often enables the institutions to be identified. It should, however, be noted that the ancient nature of these traits is the effect of hindsight: when the institutions were founded they were a novel element in both the psychology and the resource consumption of the countryside. The picture was probably very mixed, in this as in everything else, but it may be that during the early period only members of the highest lay class, and monks and clerics, normally received the sacraments, including burial within a monastic precinct. The chances of ordinary people receiving baptism are likely to have been dependent upon spasmodic local initiatives, and perhaps many died unbaptized. Most continued to be buried in local, possibly unconsecrated graveyards.

---

169.   T. Taylor (ed. and trans.), *The Life of St Samson of Dol* (1925), pp. 26, 31, 37, 40, 46, 50–1, 53, 56–7.
170.   S72, trans. F. Stenton, 'Medehamstead and its colonies', in J. Edwards, V. Galbraith and E. Jacobs (eds), *Historical Essays in Honour of James Tait* (1933), p. 316.

Some implications

Whatever Christian, quasi-Christian or parallel Christian practices may have been followed in the fourth and fifth centuries in the south-west, the foundation of the first monasteries – St Kew, St Keverne, perhaps Stoke St Nectan, Sherborne and the rest – seems to mark a major shift. A network of religious houses in the peninsula and in Wales (with conceivably the activity represented by the latest phases at Uley, Lydney and Pagans Hill closing the geographical gap) had been created, not apparently by the mix of evangelizing city bishops and monks as in contemporary north Gaul, but by monks alone, with their sensationally impressive version of the Christian life. They represented an essentially new presence, intrusive and in some ways alien, but exciting, powerful and capable of promoting major social change. The charismatic power developed by their spiritual leaders seems to have impressed everybody at all social levels, and contemporary continental accounts stress the popular element in their appeal. However, later British accounts usually stress the royal or noble connections of the leaders, and no house could have survived as an institution without formal access to resources, suggesting a symbiotic link between developing monasticism and emerging central power. This underlines the likelihood that serious direct benefits, like burial in the monastic graveyard, were available only to the elite few.

The religious houses which looked back to founders with British names were founded on sites with mixed backgrounds. Some, like Crantock, seem to have used existing burial grounds; some like Sherborne (and just possibly Banwell) were planted on or near old villas; and some, like St Buryan (although the foundation of this house may have been relatively late), on old enclosed settlements. Many of the early houses were clearly deliberately founded on or close to the sea, and must have been given formal rights over resources, chiefly land. It seems probable, judging from evidence in Ireland and elsewhere, that the monasteries were enclosed with a bank and ditch, from the beginning or from an early stage. We know virtually nothing about ancillary buildings, or the early monastic churches, although (with all its difficulties) the image of the little wooden church at Glastonbury rings true. We may suppose that within each enclosure there were one or more such churches, together with the burial ground.

The man looked back to as the founder (in many cases probably rightly so) was buried in this graveyard, often in the focal grave, but not one apparently normally marked by an inscribed stone. The monasteries have a tendency to possess a name in **lann* and, where they have this, also to have the name of their patron and presumed founder as the personal name following **lann*: so Constantine appears as *Langustentyn* (1367), St Keverne as *Lannachebran* (1086) and Crantock as *Langorroc* (1086). The same seems to be true of Sherborne, where Probus, whose name appears in *Lanprobi*, survived as patron of a chapel in the castle.

In the eastern part of the peninsula something similar happened, but with a time lag. In Dorset, south Somerset and southern Devon, the tide of West Saxon control was marked by the founding of a series of minster churches beginning probably fairly early in the seventh century. From these pastoral care may sometimes, in varying arrangements, have been extended over local communities, and the religious life lived, although possibly less dramatically than in western and northern monasteries, at least in their early days. As a group, these eastern and southern monasteries differed greatly in social status, size of community and general magnificence, as the western ones probably did too. Allowing for these differences, the two groups of foundations may often have looked very similar: the minsters had living quarters, a church, or churches, and a burial ground, sometimes containing the grave of the founder, usually surrounded by an enclosure, often roughly circular.

Like the western houses, the eastern monasteries were planted on a mixture of sites. Some, like Keynsham, Axminster and perhaps Wimborne, seem to have been deliberately placed on or very near Roman occupation sites, probably villas. Some may have taken over existing graveyards; the evidence here has particular difficulties, but Lady St Mary (Wareham), Gillingham and Wells all succeeded to old burial sites, at Wareham and Wells already marked by important focal burials: the same is true further west at Yealhampton and possibly Tavistock. We sense the power of decision at work which could select sites considered appropriate against a range of factors such as economic possibilities, relationship to other administrative arrangements existing or potential, personal wish and sense of special place. All of this must have determined why, for instance, the late Roman graveyard at Wells eventually became the heart of a cathedral, while those at Shepton Mallet or Kenn went out of use. Authorities at the four urban centres seem, in their different ways, to have felt that late Roman civic burial grounds were the appropriate setting for a new minster, but here also choices were made: at Dorchester the Fordingbridge cemetery site probably continued but that at Poundbury did not; at Ilchester the Northover site continued but on a reduced scale, while at both Bath and Exeter the principal concentration seems to have been on the intramural sites.

Meanwhile, ordinary people were dying, and their survivors needed to give their bodies burial in a recognized place. Local community graveyards clearly came into, and went out of, use as very local circumstances directed, some with usage running back into the fourth century and some later, and, as we would expect, their history is very complex and varied. Some, like Shepton Mallet, Kenn, Camerton, Cannington and some of the Cornish long-cist sites stopped being used, and were presumably superseded by what became the parish churchyard. Others became themselves the parish churchyard, most obvious in the west where sites like St Endellion or Tintagel church had an apparently pre-parish phase, and presumably also sometimes in the east. Some survived as local chapel sites. Some were sited on old occupation sites, which in the east often meant derelict villas, and in the west un-Romanized dwellings, as at Beacon Hill, Lundy. This, like the reuse of Roman masonry, may have helped to foster the sense of continuity and legitimacy, but, as at the monastic, so at the much humbler, local level, the choice of site balanced a range of practical, emotional and individual circumstances.

Some of the later parish graveyards had an apparently calculated relationship with a visible ancient landscape feature, as at Ashbrittle or Knowlton, but these are few, and perhaps represent just the odd place where such sites continued in use long enough to become eventually part of the parish network. Dating is, as always, difficult, but the impression received is that the reuse of ancient barrows and the like as burial places, relatively common in the fourth and fifth centuries, no longer commanded the collective imagination in the sixth. Similarly, the depositing of metalwork and other goods in shafts and at ancient sites of all kinds (with the exception of small personal gifts to healing and holy wells, perhaps) was not something ·which the generation coming to maturity in the early part of the sixth century apparently wanted to do, and this is another hint of significant social changes around that time.

The characteristic British ecclesiastical place-name elements seem to have been used with much less precision than we would wish, and sometimes their usage looks suspiciously like the effects of fashion, ecclesiastical snobbery and a general careless looseness. Many of them, like the Anglo-Saxon place-name element *minster*, were used early on, but continued to be used for a long time to create new names for new sites, not necessarily the same kind of sites as the earlier ones. The same seems to apply to the substantial curvilinear enclosures, which, like the **lann* element which describes them, perhaps also had a long period of use; also important, perhaps were the example of the enclosed monasteries, the workings of local pride and the reuse of disused 'round' settlement sites, which itself hints perhaps at a relatively late date for some of these sites, as 'rounds' went progressively out of use during the early medieval period. Indeed, part of the psychological drive behind the enclosed burial grounds may have been the sense that the dead should have the kind of home that the living were now leaving.

If the place-names and the enclosures cannot indicate late Roman or post-Roman non-monastic graveyards with any security, the inscribed stones probably can. The overwhelmingly male and pedigree orientated nature of the inscriptions has already been noted, and the sense they give is that we are looking at the burial grounds of kin groups, where the men mentioned in the inscriptions, probably buried in focal graves, and probably also bound up in the names and hagiographies of the sites, were regarded as the founding fathers of an extended lineage with all the legitimization to rights of inheritance, use of resources and burial which this implies. Quite possibly many of the sites where we lack dating evidence also began with, or acquired, this character, and many of what subsequently became parish church sites may have begun as kin burial grounds.

Some, admittedly limited, evidence suggests that the filiations (and similar) inscriptions show us another face of the changes in the years leading up to *c.* 600. The *c.* 500 inscription from Carnsew which emphasizes Christian burial, gives the age of the deceased and commemorates a woman,[171] matches a well-known range of Late Antique western inscriptions very closely, in all three characteristics. The RESTEUTA stone from Lundy also probably records a woman.[172] This tender tone, stressing intimate, personal hopes, is outweighed by stones proclaiming ancestry and all the powers and practicalities which pedigree can involve, and, judging by the Wareham stones, this style may not have been confined to the western part of the peninsula. Perhaps it also demonstrates the developing combination of interests between landholders, church leaders and the newly emerging power structure. Some-times, as with Justus at St Just or Creed at Sancreed, where the place-name and the dedication name are the same, we are presumably seeing a perpetuation of the man the local, proprietorial family looked back to as its founding father, just as at the monasteries the same pairing reflects the honour paid to the spiritual father. Some-times, where they are different, as is often the case, we are perhaps seeing more than one generation, or more than one tradition (or even shifts in estate possession), and the addition of more names on inscribed stones reflects similar local histories.

Across the peninsula as a whole, during the period up to *c.* 600–700, the network of minsters/monasteries, especially if some, at least, of these were not very interested in pastoral care, and early kin group or local community burial grounds does not seem to have been sufficient to maintain a Christian society, even at the level of limited access to the sacraments which the period seems to have envisaged. These gaps may be one important reason why we see just enough to suggest chronological depth to the picture. In the east, some of the later foundations which emerge as 'mother' or

171.   Thomas, *Mute Stones*, pp. 164–75. Presumably similar arguments might apply to Wales.
172.   *Ibid.*, p. 166.

'major' churches did not apparently have the full range of minster characteristics (whatever these may really have been in the early period) but did have dependent churches, like Stogursey or Wellington, both Somerset, or Churchstow, Devon, which emerges after 1066 with a cluster of five dependent chapels.

It is just conceivable that some of these church sites are marked by place-names in *stock* and *church*, although this idea needs great care, as both names can relate to what were originally 'ordinary' minsters. Tavistock, where the inscribed stone suggests an origin as a family cemetery, seems to have come to have had a more public character which preceded its transformation by Ordulf into a major Benedictine house in the later eleventh century. Halstock in Dorset and Kewstock in Somerset, are candidates, and so are Churchstow and Whitchurch, both in Devon. These seem to have had a primary pastoral role, with perhaps a few canons or a single priest, rather than monks, and are better considered as 'secular minsters'; many of them may have not seemed very different from some of the more substantial kin or estate churches, but they were 'public' churches rather than those whose cure of souls was limited to a particular kin group or estate.

Similar public, but non-monastic churches, may be visible west of the Tamar. Thomas has plotted out the churches with dependent churches for west Penwith[173] from which eight major churches emerge, all of which seem to have acquired enclosed cemeteries (Fig. 80). Of these, four, possibly five, had *eglos* names, with St Buryan as one, and three names with **lann*. Some 31 churches with names in *eglos*

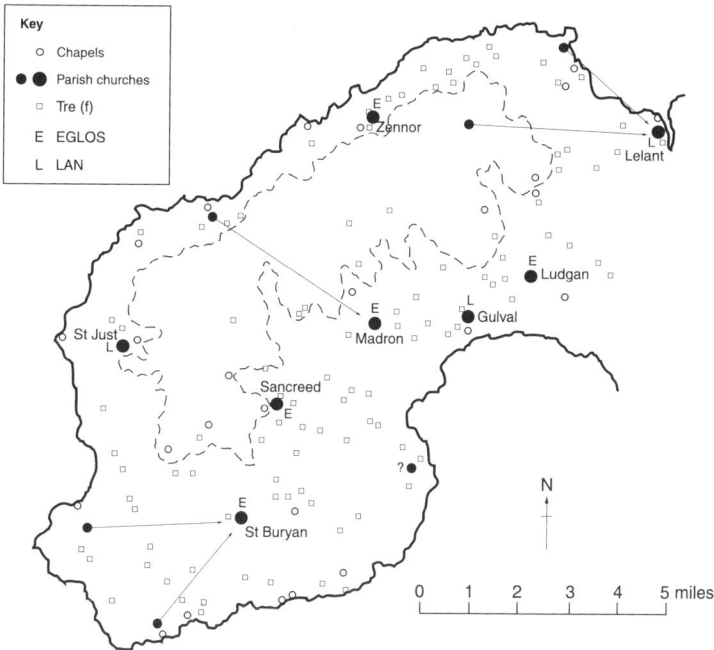

Figure 80 Ecclesiastical sites in West Penwith (after Thomas 1989, Fig. 1)

---

173. C. Thomas, 'Christians, chapels, churches and charters – or, "proto-parochial provisions for the pious in a peninsula" (Landsend)', *Landscape History* (1989): 19–26.

are known from Cornwall, and of these 21 have *eglos* linked with the name of the church's patron, presumably the one who established the site. The remaining *eglos* names are mostly coupled with a descriptive element, including *Eglosmerther* (1201), now Merther, perhaps suggesting a later site. It is possible that some, at least, of the *eglos* names represent a pattern of community cemeteries which, while they too probably had a range of burial or domestic antecedents, were established as formal Christian sites in the period following the foundation of many or most of the monastic sites. This could be any time up to perhaps *c.* 900. *Eglos-Withiel*, the 'church of Withiel district', and *Eglospenbro*, the 'church of Breage district', both have names which suggest a public responsibility to a well-defined and recognized community. It is clear from Lelant that some sites with names in **lann*, which never acquired an *eglos* name, were brought into this network, just as was St Buryan, an endowed religious house, with perhaps an earlier, different site history.

The complexity of the ecclesiastical picture cannot be overstated, and we should not expect unduly clear-cut categories to emerge, either at a single moment in time or during the historical progression. In the late and post-Roman period, the local burial grounds became steadily more formally Christian, demonstrated by the number of burial grounds which eventually became the sites of parish churches; these perhaps began, gradually, as the cemeteries of kin groups and local, perhaps estate-based, communities. From around 500 in the west and north of the peninsula, and 630 in the east, a very significant impetus came from monastic energy combined with elite support which created a pattern of endowed houses. Eventually, perhaps, gaps in the pattern were filled by public rather than monastic churches of the kind which appear as 'mother' or 'major' churches across the peninsula. The sixth, seventh and earlier eighth centuries saw a profound shift, in which people gradually began to see themselves as Christian folk,[174] and to feel the need for local and wider Christian institutions which could constitute their identity.

---

174.   Although in the late twelfth century Bishop Barthomew Iscanus of Exeter was prescribing a penance for 'those who keep the New Year with heathen rites', quoted in R. Hutton, *Stations of the Sun* (1997), p. 7.

5   People, places and power

Introduction

Chapter 1 set out what seems to have been the working lives of most of the inhabitants of the peninsula during the early medieval centuries. This lifestyle was based upon a seasonal cycle of arable farming and cattle grazing and it had its roots in prehistory. Chapter 2 discussed the character of this lifestyle during the later fourth and fifth centuries, as it appears at sites like ancient hill-forts, temples and shafts dug into the earth, and at burial grounds. All this suggests that, although there were probably Christian communities in and near Dorchester and Ilchester and probably in Exeter and Bath, most people of the peninsula were only slightly touched by Christian beliefs and practices. In Chapter 3 we traced how, during the sixth and seventh centuries, the foundation first of the British monasteries and then of the West Saxon minsters provided important elements in the spread of Christian practices, which also appear in the gradual developments at the local graveyards.

This chapter considers how the society in which these developments were taking place was organized, and how this changed from *c.* 400, when imperial government collapsed, to soon after 700, when the peninsula was divided between two post-Roman kingdoms, those of the West Saxons and the south-west British. It discusses the legal position of the individual, and the possible character of landholding and what this may have implied about social changes during Late Antiquity. It considers the nature of the cultural mix and the meanings which can be attributed to indications of Irish or Germanic character, and to connections with Brittany. The chapter then considers administrative structures, and the emergence of centres of power like Tintagel and South Cadbury. The lords of these centres seem, at least in part, to have sustained their authority by their trading and religious links with the Mediterranean world and may have expressed it through the foundations of monasteries. When the Mediterranean connection collapsed, towards the end of the sixth century, power seems to have eventually consolidated into what became the two, probably quite similar, early medieval kingdoms of the peninsula, with the British on the defensive and the West Saxons territorially aggressive.

Individuals and families

The position of the individual within the system as it developed through the early medieval centuries illustrates the social complexities. In public life men might be legal persons, required perhaps to turn out to fight public enemies or to denounce a manslayer; on their home estates many were tied labourers; and in the eyes of the Church they, and women and slaves too, were Christian souls capable of salvation.

The fissures and fusions which could be generated from these contradictions go a long way towards explaining the course of western political thinking.

Virtually the only specific south-western references to the legal condition of individuals before the Domesday record are the tenth-century marginal notes in the Bodmin Gospels[1] which record the freeing of slaves. These show us a few people who, on the evidence of Late Antiquity in general, were probably members of the large class who were legally slaves, a status which, at least in the classical world, did not necessarily mean a depressed economic position but did involve important disabilities including being put to work in any way the master chose. The late Empire had recognized two states outside the slave class. The *honestiores* had included all soldiers, imperial officials, holders of Church offices probably at least down to deacon, landholders, members of the city curial (roughly 'council') families and probably, in practice, anybody substantially prosperous, while the *humiliores* embraced all the rest, including those who seem to have been becoming increasingly soil-bound serfs during the fourth century. The terms themselves ceased to be used as the imperial structures collapsed, but the old legal distinction remained influential.

Within free families, it seems likely that rights of access to resources also passed through patrilinear inheritance, with perhaps the descendants of a common great-grandfather entitled to a share: a system like this would produce the relatively stable distribution of hamlets which fieldwork suggests (irrespective of the morphology of the settlement). What we know of burial practices in the late Empire in the south-west, as elsewhere, suggests that only the relatively socially superior received formal burial in a properly recognized cemetery. This seems to have been true of the possible family burial grounds marked by the inscribed stones and to have continued with the foundation of monastic/minster graveyards. In one sense, the history of the Church, here as elsewhere, is the progressive way in which Christian burial was gradually provided for all, through the creation of new sites or (and perhaps more often) the hallowing of old ones in what eventually became the parish network.

It is worth making the point that in the post-300 period a clash of interests generated tension between Church authorities and family-based society.[2] Churchmen required land grants which might cut into traditional rights, and needed bequests, which could best be made by those with individual property rather than rights in kin resources. As a result, widows were encouraged not to remarry, so that the Church could benefit from their devoted service and eventually from their property at their deaths. Such women might be built into a spiritual force, like that Bishop Victricius of Rouen could call upon around 380. Godparenthood was encouraged, as when Oswald of Northumbria stood godfather to Cynegils of Wessex in 635, in order to provide an alternative Christian parentage, and eventually the Church barred first-cousin marriage in order to encourage the movement of property outside a single family line. Not much of this is likely to have been a live issue in most of the south-west, but perhaps the family burial grounds, which the inscribed stones seem to mark, represent in part an assertive local response to these and similar tensions.

---

1. For the Bodmin Gospels marginalia, see O. Padel, 'Cornwall around the year 1000', *Cornwall Association of Local Historians Journal*, 37 (1999): 5–6, and refs there.
2. For general discussion of all these issues, see J. Goody, *The European Family: An Historical Anthropological Essay* (2000).

Recent work[3] has suggested that the basic publicly recognized unit within Cornwall was the Cornish acre, a unit which goes back at least to the time of the Domesday record, but is probably earlier. Cornish acres seem to have been reckoned in groups of threes, conceivably in relation to the arable, local pasture and meadow, access to all of which was necessary for viable, substantial production. It is possible that three-factor units were a way of reckoning the larger farmsteads, although it is unclear whether an acre was a real and consistent area of land, or whether it was an assessment based on quality and quantity and so presumed yield. Both Helston tithing and that of Penryn Trerose were reckoned at 30 acres, which suggests that either the Helston acres were much larger to take into account the upland nature of much of the area, or a given acreage does not take rough common grazing into account. This is perhaps likely, and in that case the two tithings give a very crude idea of the area an acre represented. Most of what we know about Cornish acres comes from the records relating to Cornish tithings, the assessment of which seems to show a strong relationship with triple acre units.[4]

Detailed work on western Cornwall has produced tentative maps of the local tithing pattern (Fig. 81), and further work could probably extend the pattern to the Tamar. When the tithing system emerges into view in the thirteenth century, it appears as a territorially based framework intended to bring every adult male inhabitant into a public, centrally organized regime of law and order, backed by the tax, known as smoke silver, to be paid by each tithing through a proportionate levy on every household. It may not be too fanciful to see the triple acre units which seem to be embodied in the tithing territories as the households liable to make payment.

The age of this system is extremely difficult to estimate; many of the records are very late but there are hints that it may have been operating in the early medieval period, although, if so, we should be prepared for new work to reveal changes across time. If the system is genuinely ancient and was effective in some guise in the late Roman/post-Roman period, then there is no particular reason why it should have stopped short at the Tamar. Elements of a territorial organization are visible in other parts of the West Country, where, for example, in Dorset tithings were used within hundreds to arrange the assessments of land tax compiled in 1780 and 1832. The later medieval parish of Charminster, Dorset, was divided into seven parallel strip tithings (Fig. 73), all but one of which, interestingly, had a name in *ton*. In Devon, part of the boundary of the Sandford charter of 930 follows the tithing boundary between East and West Sandford as recorded on the Tithe Map for the parish, although the relative dates of the boundaries are not known.[5]

It is possible that here we are seeing the remnants of a genuinely ancient system, originally like that in Cornwall. This brings the hide into the discussion, the unit of

3. D. Harvey, 'The evolution of territoriality and societal transitions in west Cornwall', *Landscape History*, 19 (1997): 13–23; 'The tithing framework of west Cornwall: a proposed pattern and an interpretation of territorial origins', *Cornish Studies*, 5 (1997): 30–51.

4. D. Harvey, 'Providing a territorial framework for studying medieval settlement patterns; using later material to uncover the nature of early systems of landscape organisation', *Medieval Settlement Research Group Report*, 11 (1996): fig. 5.

5. Dorset Archives Service; T. Hall, *Minster Churches in the Dorset Landscape* (2000); D. Hooke, *The Pre-Conquest Charter-bounds of Devon and Cornwall* (1994), p. 119; Devon County Record Office. For a useful discussion of tithings and related matters, see R. Kain and R. Oliver, *Historic Parish of England and Wales* (2001), pp. 12–19.

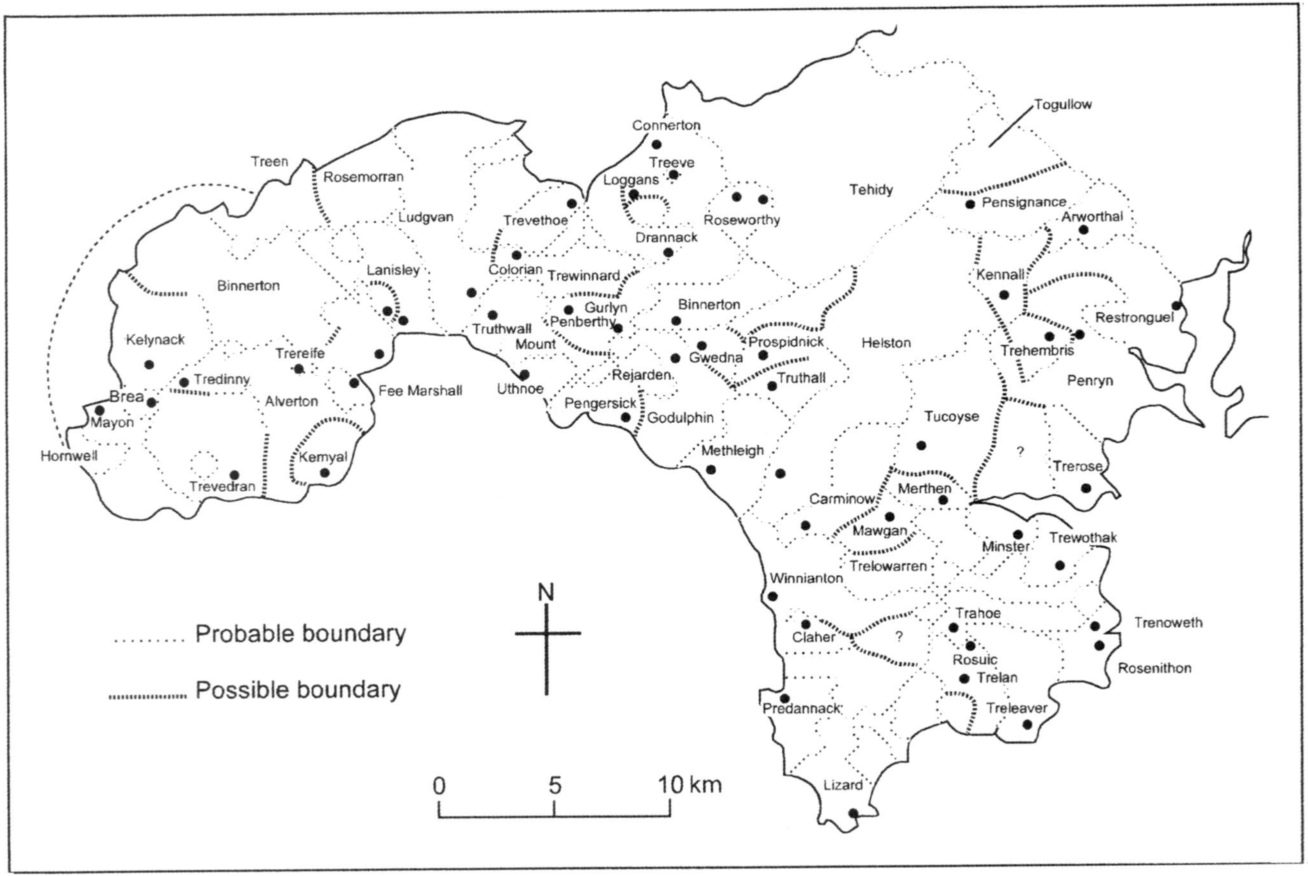

Figure 81 Basic tithing pattern in west Cornwall (slightly simplified) (after Harvey 1997, Fig. 4)

land, varying according to quality of soil but often covering about 120 English acres, considered sufficient to support a family. It has been suggested that the hide was, at root, the fundamental unit of northern European social organization embracing the notion of the freeman and his nuclear family and the land, which could be worked by one (his) plough for the upkeep of that family.[6] Such a freeman would have some un-free dependants, and he would himself be a part of the 5-hide unit (theoretically) which supported a noble: the system embodied, and was sustained by, complex kinship arrangements which created the allocations of land upon which status depended.

Ine's Laws show that, already in seventh-century Wessex, the hide had become a unit of tax assessment, for here the food render required from every 10-hide unit is defined. By 1086, it was used across southern England, with characteristic entries like that for Bishopsteignton, held by the Bishop of Exeter, which 'paid tax for 18 hides' or Stockleigh, held by Alfred the Butler from the Court of Mortain, which 'paid tax for 1 hide'.[7] Cornish lands are treated in the Domesday record in the same way so that Helston, for example, is rated at 6½ hides; it was held by the king and probably had boundaries more or less coterminous with those of the tithing. Any simplistic relationship between the 30 Cornish acres of Helston's tithing and the 6½ hides of its Domesday estate tax assessment should certainly be eschewed on a number of grounds (and would also involve presumptions about rough grazing), but possibly future work in illuminating the significance of both hide and acre may clarify the relationship between the two.

What does emerge from this is the tentative suggestion that much of the south-west was organized into relatively small territorial units, which bore some relationship to what was considered to be the appropriate landholding of a free family, and to the assessment of land for public tax purposes. These may have been grouped in ways intended to help promote local law and order, deviance from which involved the payment of a fine. Such a system would not be incompatible with what we know of the general circumstances of the late Roman state, and it was presumably some system of this general type which was, in the fourth century, being eroded by the tendency to transfer the responsibility for tax payment (and perhaps law and order) to estate proprietors.

The relationship between Cornish tithing and estate is tricky. In Penwith and Kirrier the tithings, by the time the record is reasonably full, seem to be closely associated, indeed even coterminous, with manors and sub-manors, but there does not seem to be a similar pattern of relationships further east in Cornwall. There are a range of possible reasons for this, but one may lie in the processes through which the hundreds of eastern Cornwall, especially what we now see as Trig, East and West Wivelshire and Stratton, were brought directly under West Saxon control in the years after 815. This may have been rougher and more violent than we sometimes suppose, and have involved the disruption of the local landholding pattern to suit new masters while permitting the continuation of the tithing units because they were a useful mechanism for accountability and control. This line of thought strengthens the possibility that the tithings represent an archaic pattern

---

6.   T. Charles-Edwards, 'Kinship, status and the origins of the hide', *Past and Present*, 56 (1972): 3–33.

7.   See C. Thorn and F. Thorn, *Domesday Book: Devon* (1985), under entries.

of landholding, preserved through their public legal status, which fitted the estate arrangements in western Cornwall but had seen separation between the two further east.[8] In the south-west beyond Cornwall it seems that sometimes, as at Charminster, the tithings were subdivisions of the manor, but beyond this present evidence cannot go. These relationships may come into sharper focus when we consider the nature of landholding.

Roman estates and their possible survival

The late Roman state recognized outright private ownership of land, and this carried with it the right to buy and sell land, but in practice the notion caused uneasiness and the result is the typical confusion between *dominium* and *possessio* which characterized the operation of western law. Landownership was less than total, multiple rights would be recognized in the same parcel of land and allocation to strangers was difficult and had to be carefully registered.[9] The state was also, almost always, ready to take on board the local, traditional arrangements. What these were in fourth- and fifth-century Britain we can only guess, but they seem to have included inheritance, and the recognition of an 'elite' or 'noble' class. To put it in a different way, the discussion of landholding arrangements at the level above that of the individual farm or hamlet is probably the same as looking at the role of a particular class of families who held rank, inherited or acquired.

As far as land in private ownership is concerned, we know that members of the fourth-century senatorial class, like Melania, had estates in Britain, but we do not know if these were in the south-west.[10] What we do see in the east of the region are the Roman-style country house 'villas', some of them clustered around Bath, Ilchester, Dorchester and, to a lesser but increasingly recognized extent, around Exeter. It would be hasty to suppose that villa estates were necessarily based upon private ownership by a single individual, but as the fourth century progressed there was an increasing professional class of officers and civil servants who may have wanted to acquire land, and the document from Chew, Somerset, which apparently shows a land purchase, may show how this could be achieved.[11]

A significant question is whether any villa estates survived to become part of the pattern of early medieval landholding. This must be kept carefully distinct from any continued post-fourth-century use of villa buildings or villa sites and certainly from any supposed continuation of Christian practice; all that is at issue here is the possible survival of some estates attached to villas through the fifth and sixth centuries to emerge in the seventh and eighth as distinct parcels of land, usually the endowments of minsters. Opinion has ebbed and flowed since Taylor and then Bonney[12] drew attention to some features of continuity in boundaries within Wessex, with

---

8.   Harvey, 'Evolution of territoriality', pp. 13–23; 'Tithing framework', pp. 30–51.

9.   E. Levy, *West Roman Vulgar Law* (1951), pp. 19–25, 130–5.

10. G. Clark, *Women in Late Antiquity: Pagan and Christian Life-styles* (1992), pp. 128–30.

11. E. Turner, 'A Roman writing tablet from Somerset', *JRS*, 46 (1956): 115–18.

12. C. Taylor, *The Making of the English Landscape: Dorset* (1972), pp. 72–5; D. Bonney, 'Early boundaries in Wessex', in P. Fowler (ed.), *Archaeology and the Landscape. Essays for L. V. Grinsell* (1972), pp. 168–75.

Davies[13], Pearce[14] and Dark[15] taking a more positive view, and Todd[16] a negative one.

Bristol Avon Valley shows the problems as well as any.[17] The minster churches at Henbury, Westbury, Bedminster and Keynsham, together with the (?later) major church at Bristol, are distributed within a pattern of later medieval parish boundaries in a way which suggests that these must reflect the broad outlines of their minster *parochiae*, and the distribution of villas fits into this (Fig. 82). Henbury first appears

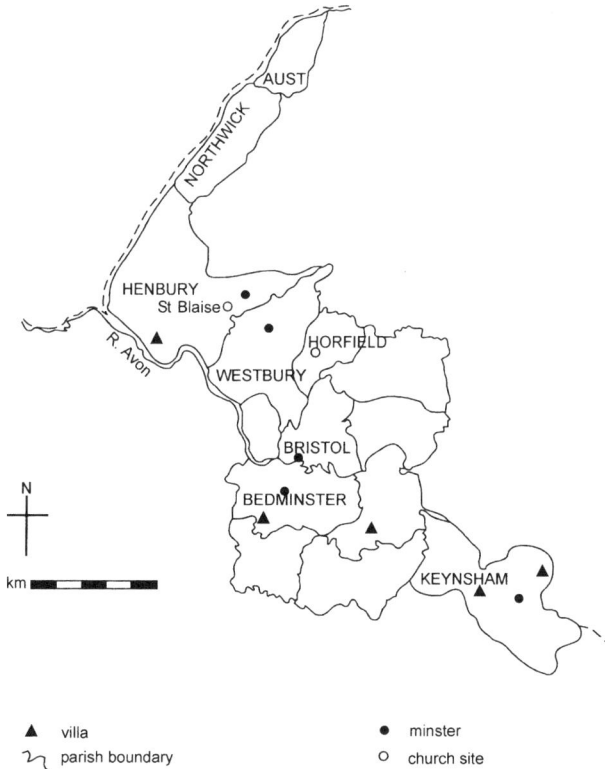

Figure 82 Pattern of villas, minsters and parish boundaries in the Bristol Avon Valley (after Pearce 1982b, Fig. 8.8)

13. W. Davies, 'Roman settlements and post-Roman estates in south-east Wales', in P. Casey, *The End of Roman Britain* (1979), pp. 153–73.
14. S. Pearce, 'Estates and church sites in Dorset and Gloucestershire: the emergence of a Christian society', in *The Early Church in Western Britain and Ireland* (1982), pp. 119–38.
15. K. Dark, *Civitas to Kingdom. British Political Continuity 300–800* (1994), pp. 159–63.
16. M. Todd, *The South-West to AD 1000* (1987), pp. 236–48. The story goes on: recent work by Simon Draper (*http:www-users.york.*) suggests that Bonney's claims for ancient origins for the parish boundaries of Wiltshire cannot be sustained, but work in Somerset by Costen and Corcos, and in Kent, has re-opened the debate, as has new work on the place-name element *wic*; see Corcos, *Medieval Settlement 2002*, pp. 6–47.
17. For what follows, see Pearce, 'Estates and church sites', pp. 119–38.

in a grant of Æthelred of Mercia in 691 as 30 *cassati* at Henbury and Aust described as 'with the ancient bounds and the fishery' in which Aust was probably the fishery.[18] In this area as early as 691 it seems that the ancient bounds may refer to a surviving fourth- or fifth-century estate, which may have reflected that of the villa. Perhaps it focused upon the fourth-century temple within the hill-fort on Blaise Castle Hill, which became the site of a late fourth-century inhumation cemetery and eventually a chapel to St Blasius; the Henbury (meaning 'old enclosure') minster was established a short distance down the hill. Horfield church may also be on an ancient site. Westbury was the subject of a grant between 716 and 757.

The information for the Henbury area may suggest some continuity of estate boundaries from *c.* 380 to *c.* 700, but the evidence is far from conclusive. In south-east Dorset the opposite interpretation has been suggested. At Bucknowle, the villa is very close to the boundary line referred to in two charters (although villas frequently do seem to have been on the edges of their lands), and an argument that it once 'controlled the whole of the west part of the area south of Corfe gap could not be sustained on medieval evidence'.[19] What seems to be clear is that arguments about this kind of continuity conducted at the level of sweeping statements are unhelpful; only through very detailed, local work are we likely to squeeze out clearer indications. The importance of the question may go beyond issues of continuity in the landscape to those of the production of social relationships. In the Ilchester area, for example, the villas are so dense it is difficult to believe that most or all of the available land was not shared out among them. These are very much the kind of estates where we would expect that those living upon them were experiencing the fourth-century drift[20] towards a blurred distinction between public and private obligation, and the emergence of a serf/landlord pattern which then continued.

Multiple estates

This brings us to the vexed questions surrounding what has become embedded in the literature as the 'multiple estate' hypothesis following the work of Jones[21] and others, who recognized estates of comparable type in the northern 'shires', the eastern 'sokes' and the arrangements expressed in medieval Welsh law. As a critic of the hypothesis has put it, the essential features of the multiple estate idea 'are a network of service obligations supervised by a ministerial group, which linked a spatially scattered hierarchy of functionally differentiated settlements and supported a non-producing aristocracy'.[22] Jones has also suggested that such estates sometimes had

18.   D. Hooke, 'Pre-Conquest estates in the West Midlands: preliminary thoughts', *J. Historical Geography*, 8 (3): 228 (1982), quotes other similar places, e.g., Wootton Wawen, early eighth century 'with the boundaries constituted by the ancient possessors'.

19.   D. Hinton, 'Some Anglo-Saxon charters and estates in south-east Dorset', *PDNHAS*, 114 (1994): 19.

20.   See, for a general account, A. Jones, *The Decline of the Ancient World* (1966), esp. pp. 291–5; S. Williams and G. Friell, *Theodosius. The Empire at Bay* (1994), pp. 103–15.

21.   G. Jones, 'Some medieval rural settlements in north Wales', *Trans Institute Brit. Geographers*, 9 (1953): 51–72; 'Multiple estates and early settlement', in P. Sawyer, *Medieval Settlement: Continuity and Change* (1976), pp. 15–40.

22.   N. Gregson, 'The multiple-estate model: some critical questions', *J. Historical Geography*, 11 (1985): 339–51.

their roots in the pre-Roman Iron Age because they quite often seem to focus upon a hill-fort as centre, and indeed, that they may have been the organization by which the labour needed to dig the hill-forts was originally mustered.

The suggestion can be divided into two elements. Firstly there is the idea of large estates, which were multiple in the sense that they had a range of separate settlements, field systems and home pastures and were presumed to have had an internal governance capable of maintaining local peaceful production and support for the local proprietor(s); and, secondly, the notion of large estates which were also, often, the same as the legal and administrative units – sokes, 'shires', possibly hundreds – which appear in the record, and from which a range of services – food rents, transport duties, work on public building projects, military service – were due to the king and which, among other things, demonstrate how public and private rights and obligations were bundled together. Our understanding is bedevilled by the fact that by the time (post-850) our records start to be even relatively full, the system, if it had existed, had begun to fragment. Our evidence for these early multiple estates frequently involves later but suggestive-looking patterns of smaller estates which may have been carved out of them, and information about tenurial and other legal arrangements within groups of such smaller estates which may (but may not) reflect an older, more integrated system.

In the south-west a search for pre-800 estates, multiple in their occupational and productive foci, produces several candidates. Hoskins[23] originally suggested that early land arrangements in Devon were focused upon river valleys: he cited Tawton with Tawstock on the Taw, Plympton with Plymstock on the Plym, Taviton with Tavistock on the Tavy and Cullompton with Culmstock on the Culm. The pair of names are sometimes several miles apart and may show how far the original estate extended; it was named originally from its river, and the two suffixes, with *tun* meaning 'estate centre' and *stock*, outlying 'stock-farm', were given later. On this model, early grants like that of 729, by which King Æthelheard gave 10 hides *in Torric*, that is 'on the Torridge', to Glastonbury, and that of 739 by which he gave 20 *cassati* at *Cridie*, 'on the Creedy', to Crediton, represent an early stage of this process.

The area immediately to the east of the Exe estuary provides an example of this kind of landscape (Fig. 83). It offers three principle natural advantages, the fertility of the lower Otter Valley, the coastal strip with its potential arable and marine food and the adjoining sandy heathland for rough grazing. The heathland was eventually divided among the local parishes as common land, and is collectively known as Woodbury Common. The pattern of the ancient parish boundaries hints at an original estate to the west based on the lower Otter incorporating the modern Otterton, Ottery St Mary, Sidmouth, two small parish/landholdings at Harpford and at Newton Poppleford (which were originally just river crossings), Aylesbeare and Rockbeare (whose *beare* elements, from Old English 'wood', suggest the original place of these parts of the estate). The grant by Edgar to his thegn Wulfhelm in 963 of Ottery St Mary and the Domesday record which shows that, in Edward the Confessor's reign, St Mary, Rouen, held Ottery and Mont St Michele, Otterton, suggest that the whole estate may have been a royal possession, but was being broken up in the tenth and eleventh centuries.

---

23. G. Hoskins, 'The making of the agrarian landscape', in G. Hoskins and H. Finberg (eds), *Devonshire Studies* (1952), pp. 302–3.

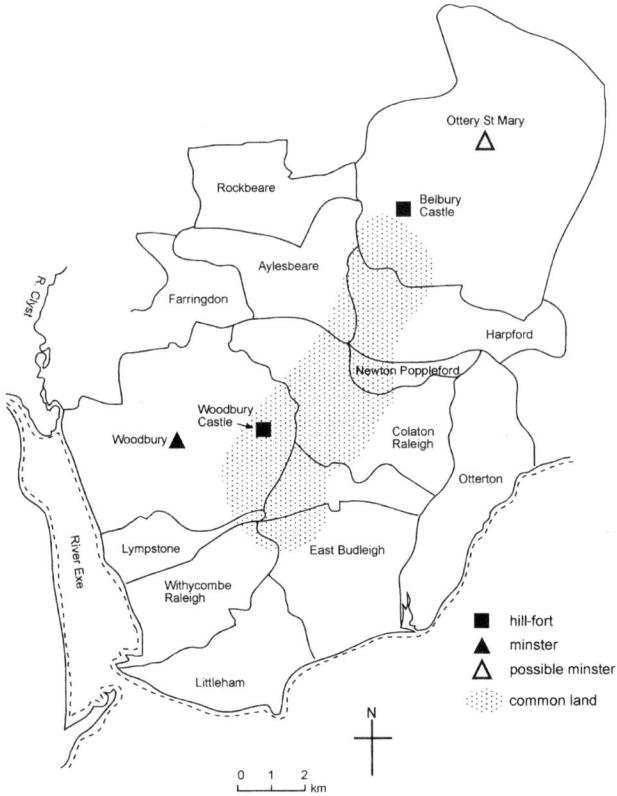

Figure 83 Parishes and topographical features east of the lower Exe Valley, Devon

Another possible estate emerges in the area incorporating the large parishes of Woodbury and East Budleigh, both of which were apparently old royal estates in 1066, Littleham and the adjacent parishes. The hill-forts of Woodbury and Belbury provide two ancient centres on the pasture/arable margin. Woodbury church was an ancient minster; we have no direct evidence that Ottery was and, although its later donation to Rouen could be a likely consequence of early minster status, the Rouen grant is late eleventh century. Similar neighbouring ancient large estates may be visible based on Sidbury, again with a minster, a stretch of rough country and a hill-fort, and in the Clyst Valley.

Similar suggestions – they are no more than that – could be made for Brent and Congresbury in Somerset. A charter of 693[24] grants to Glastonbury an estate at Brent defined as 'having on the west the Severn, on the north the Axe, to the east the Ternuc and to the south the Siger'. This defines the area of the later parishes of East Brent, Brent Knoll (originally South Brent), Lympsham, Barrow and Brean. Brent is a British place-name, and the area has a major hill-fort at Brent Knoll and a minor enclosure at Brean Down. Burrow employed a polygonal 'nearest neighbour' approach starting from the distribution of hill-forts in north-east Somerset to define possible territories

---

24.   S238; H. Edwards, *The Charters of the Early West Saxon Kingdom* (1988), pp. 23–5.

and produced the outline of an early estate centred on Cadbury Congresbury (Fig. 84) which embraced a typical mix of landscapes, and followed closely the amalgamated parish boundaries of Brockley, Congresbury, Puxton and Yatton; Congresbury was a minster church and possibly had been a British religious house before that.[25] The area of Cannington may be another, with its hill-fort occupation, and relationship to the Quantock Hills, and there are other possibilities.[26] The Hartland peninsula in north-west Devon may preserve in some of its parish boundaries[27] the estate of *Heortigtun* which Alfred left in his will, and which, judging by the holding within it of the possible British religious house at Stoke St Nectan, came to him from the earlier period.

The possibilities can be viewed from a rather different, earlier and larger, perspective, by plotting the evidence for late and post-Roman occupation in the major areas of upland. The role of the early inscribed and decorated stones as waymarks which legitimized the passage of people and beasts onto the upland has already been discussed, but they are also likely to represent a further dimension of territoriality. On Exmoor the distribution of certain and possible inscribed stones, and of the early Christian graveyards which are likely to be pre-750, should indicate not just use of the land, but may give some indication of how the land was organized. What this

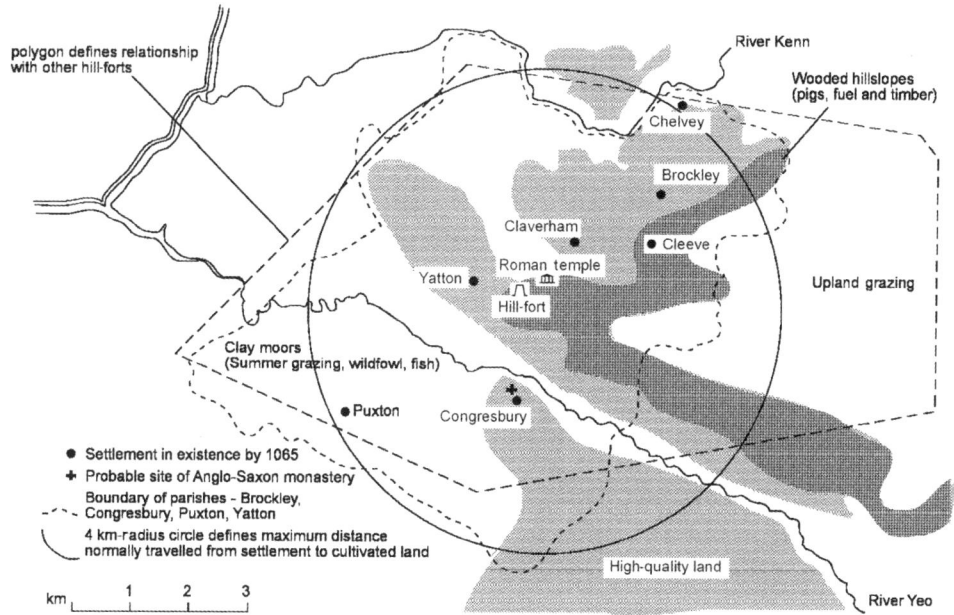

Figure 84 Possible territory around the settlement at Cadbury Congresbury (Ian Burrow in Rahtz *et al.* 1992, Fig. 9.15)

25.   P. Rahtz *et al.*, *Cadbury Congresbury 1968–73. A Late/Post-Roman Hilltop Settlement* (1992), fig. 162.
26.   M. Costen, *The Origins of Somerset* (1992), pp. 50–79.
27.   S. Pearce, 'The early Church in the landscape: the evidence from north Devon', *Arch. J.*, 142 (1985): 255–75; see also p. 170.

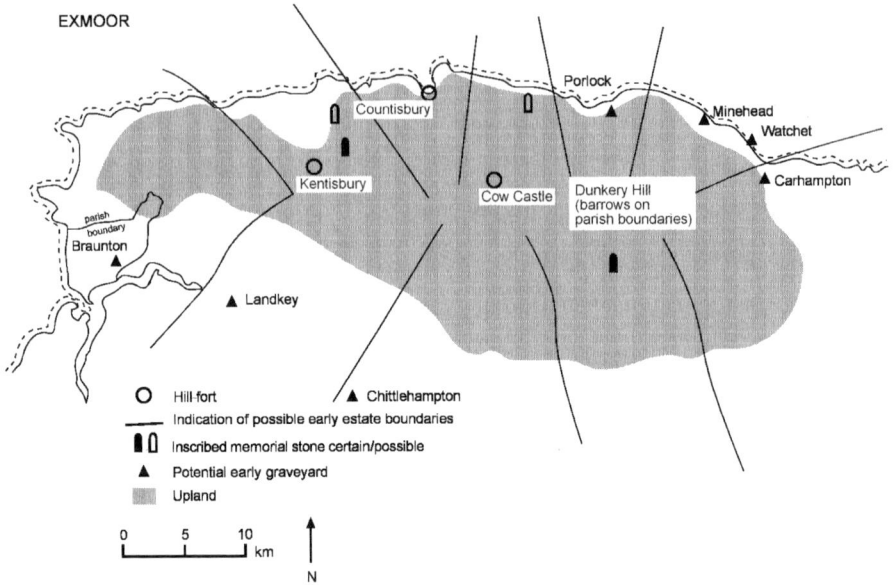

Figure 85 Pattern of possible post-Roman land allotment around Exmoor

organization might have looked like in skeletal form is suggested in Figure 85. The same kind of pattern shows up on Dartmoor (Fig. 86), where the stones, early graveyards and later parish boundaries together suggest where the land divisions could have run.

The arrangements made in the tenth-century Meavy charter (see p. 55) suggest an earlier larger estate based on what is now Buckland St Mary, an area with a concentration of early inscribed stones. Attention has already been drawn (p. 56) to the relationship between lowland estates in Kenton and Cockington with specific Dartmoor pastures. We do not know whether what we see here are the remains of early, once very large, consolidated estates stretching from the coast to the moor which were later dismembered, or ancient estates of the kind in which the parts were not geographically compact. The arrangements may, of course, reflect later circumstances in which, as settlement developed, some lords could arrange for what had been common, or at best custom-linked, pasture to be recognized as belonging to a particular estate.

A similar pattern can be seen on the Bodmin Moor and this raises the difficult question of the existence or otherwise of the large early estates in Cornwall. Several inscribed stones, like that at Boslow close to the junction of several lanes, that at Indian Queens perhaps originally on the boundary between what became the parishes of St Columb and St Enoder, or that at St Endellion on the boundary of what became Roscarrock Barton and St Endellion church, seem to be marking the edges of early land units. Some of the stones apparently originally set up by streams may have been doing the same.

The persistence of the Cornish tithing as the public unit in a way not generally pertinent to the English tithing may suggest that the history of institutions took a different course in Cornwall, something not surprising in conquered territory. An argument could be made which suggests that, in early medieval Cornwall, public

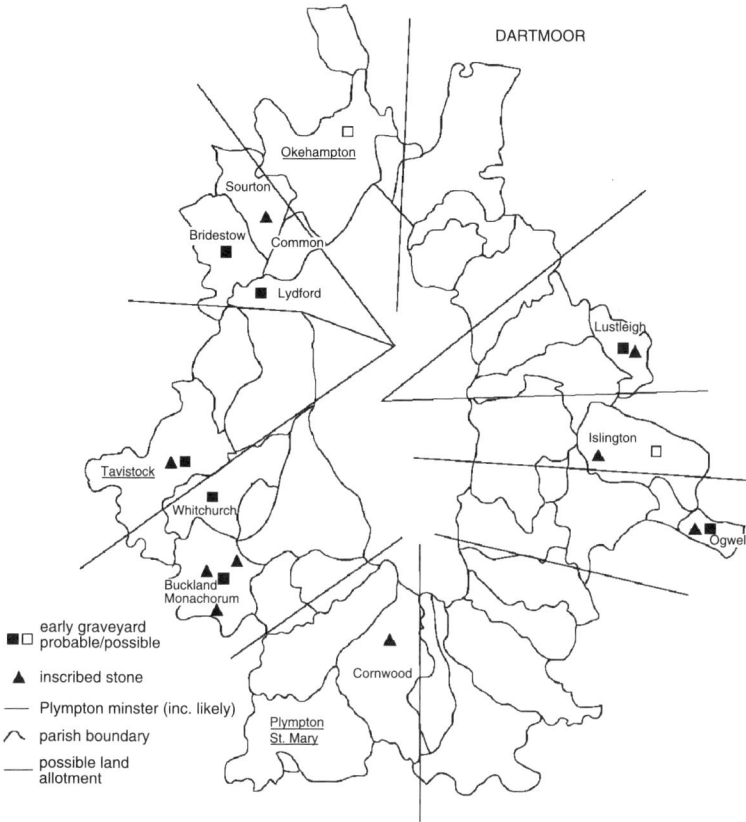

Figure 86 Pattern of possible post-Roman land allotment around Dartmoor

liabilities remained with the free farmers in their membership of territorial tithings because here the creeping fourth-century tendency to allow landholders to turn local people into serfs had not progressed far; there are virtually no villas in Cornwall. Nevertheless, early estates seem to have operated in the British-speaking areas of northern England and Wales, suggesting that it is worth seeing what some of the Cornish evidence offers.

In the far west, units like Tebiddy and Helston might repay further investigation. If, as seems possible, the place-name *lis* often refers to an ancient monument rather than to a contemporary element in the administrative pattern,[28] then some of the later manorial names with this element, such as Arrallas, Cornwall, and Charles, Devon, may be appropriating a perceived ancestral feature as a way of creating self-identity and even perhaps as a meeting point, just as happened with English names in *bury* which refer to ancient hill-forts, and hint that they were once old estates focused upon the monuments.

Other areas where large estates may have existed appear in the Lizard peninsula. The territory known as Meneage attested in 967, meaning 'monkish land', where the

---

28.   O. Padel, *Cornish Place-name Elements* (1985), pp. 150–1.

three parishes of St Antony, St Mawgan and St Martin are all said to be 'in Meneage', together with the adjacent parishes of St Keverne and Manaccan (a place-name either from a dedication name or meaning 'place of monks') may hint at an early large religious estate[29] focusing on the fertile coastal strips and the Goonhilly Down pasture. If this is the case, the estate was broken up by small, secular land grants in the later tenth century at the latest.[30]

Padel[31] has suggested that *Bridanoc*, 'the British one', was the name of the Lizard Point from perhaps the fifth century onwards and that it was the name of a large territory which formed the hinterland of the Point and which presumably included at least the present parishes of Landewednack and Mullion and perhaps a substantial part of the Lizard peninsula, although, as Padel admits, the manorial evidence for the hypothesis creates difficulties. The shift from hamlets enclosed within rounds to open settlements often associated with the *tref* place-name element may be of importance here. The move away from prestigious, perhaps defensible, enclosed farmsteads to open ones hints at a loss of status within what had once been independent farming families. It suggests some at least of these basic units of production were now becoming dependent upon superior landlords, who may have been able to establish control over several such hamlets to build up a larger estate.

The linking of these suggested early large estates across the peninsula generally with specific tenurial and dues-gathering arrangements is very difficult. We should seek evidence[32] for a social hierarchy comprising a lord, his representatives charged with estate management, perhaps freemen holding land and bondmen linked with the land who, together with the slaves, did the actual work. This could, as a collective unit, produce the renders and services due to the lord and king as the central authority characteristic of later arrangements, but presumably broadly also required in Late Antiquity. Suggesting a possible model is not so difficult. The inscribed stones, with their overwhelming, indeed overweening, desire to record one individual with his pedigree and to associate him, often, with the power of Christ, the related capacity to designate land for Christian burial with which the proprietor's name may sometimes survive as the associated saint and the likely centrality of this to the early land units all point to the self-commemorating class as the local lords.

The inscriptions on the stones (Fig. 87) give us, for the first time, the names of some of this class, and also information about how they wished to be seen.[33] Of the 62 names which can be read with some certainty on the stones (excluding the Wareham group), eighteen are Latin names of normal Late Antique type, 33 seem to be British and perhaps eleven have Irish affiliations (although some of these may actually be British). Moreover, of those seventeen stones where two names, normally expressed as father and son, can be read, seven are both British, four have Latin-named fathers and British-named sons, two sons with Latin names and fathers with British names, and four involve Irish names, while none are both Latin. It is clear that Celtic names were the most favoured, with a hint that this preference became more

29.   *Ibid.*, p. 118.
30.   D. Hooke, 'Saxon conquest and settlement', in R. Kain and W. Ravenhill (eds), *Historical Atlas of South-West England* (1999), p. 99.
31.   O. Padel, 'Predannack or Pradnick, in Mullion', *Cornish Studies*, 15 (1987): 11–14.
32.   Gregson, 'Multiple-estate model', pp. 339–51.
33.   Names recorded on the inscribed stones, see E. Okasha, *Corpus of Early Christian Inscribed Stones of South-West Britain* (1993), pp. 171–3, 224–8.

Figure 87 Early Christian inscribed stones. (a) the 'Audetus' stone, Sourton, north-west Dartmoor, showing (?later) cross-shaped head (the H visible on the face is a relatively modern addition). (b) stone reading SABINI FILI MACCODECHETI, an inscription with Irish characteristics, originally from near churchyard, Buckland Monachorum now in Vicarage Garden, Tavistock. (c) stone commemorating Enabarr (or similar) originally from Roborough Down now in Vicarage Garden, Tavistock. (d) stone reading NEPRANI FILI CONBEVI, originally near abbey site, Tavistock, now in Vicarage Garden, Tavistock. (e) inscribed stone from site of churchyard, Lustleigh, Devon. (f) inscribed stone from churchyard of St Clement near Truro, Cornwall, with primary inscription reading VITALI FILI TORRICI, secondary inscription above first reading IGNIOC and cross-decorated head (?added later). (a,b,c,d,e, photo: author, f, photo: Charles Woolf)

marked as time went on. If Cunliffe is right in suggesting from the Bath curse tablets that before *c.* 400 people with British names were socially inferior to those with Latin ones,[34] then the stones may show an effort on the part of the elite to create a common identity between themselves and their dependants, which is also bound up with the promotion of kinship as the social glue and the creation of local focal centres. Names like the Celtic *Rialbranus*, 'Royal Raven' (Madron), and the Latin *Cumregnus* (South-hill), which apparently embodies the idea of 'royal', suggest the heroic light in which the stone-erecting gentry wished to appear.

Inscribed stones as elite markers peter out in the east of the peninsula (with the exception of Wareham), as they do east of what became the Welsh border, suggesting that the equivalent class here felt the need to create different markers to register their distinctive position, perhaps through making use of what must have been very large quantities of Roman building and domestic material scattered across the eastern landscape, in contrast with that further west. This, in turn, suggests a slightly different mental emphasis, in which, perhaps, a higher degree of earlier 'Roman' cultural loyalty was gradually transmuted into a loyalty towards the West Saxon kingdom, seen as more like an imperial successor than the authorities which existed further west. Equally, of course, the West Saxon kingdom found it easier to take this stance because its elite had a Romanizing tendency.

A number of factors – the lack of an obviously socially superior class of home-steads, the clear interest in ancestry, the provision of graveyards where kin could be together at death as they had been in life – hint at the central significance of the free kinship group from whom were drawn the superior people who set up the stones, the landed proprietors, and perhaps the various managers. It would not be too difficult to see how, in a system of this kind within a large area of mixed countryside, the creation and transport of all the mixed resources due to the kin could be fitted into the rhythm of the farming year. Equally, Vitalis in the St Clement area, Cavud in north Devon and their peers, each in their area and generation, would be responsible for seeing that the local 'king' received what custom said he was due, either by taking it to him, or by allowing him to consume it on the estate.

A number of hints in the Domesday record suggest the relationship between estates and royal obligation. Some of the royal Somerset manors[35] like North and South Petherton and Curry Rival had never been assessed for tax, but had to be paid for by one night's revenue for the king and his followers. At South Petherton, we are told that before 1066 'a customary due was paid every year to this manor for Cricket (St Thomas); that is six sheep with as many lambs, and each free man [paid] one bloom of iron'. South Petherton was a large manor with dependent land units in 1066, and the arrangements at Crewkerne were similar. These might be regarded as the royal dues in kind surviving from an earlier period; and indeed the estates themselves may have passed to the West Saxon king directly from preceding British landholders.

In Devon, Walkhampton, Sutton and Kings Tamerton are listed separately but we are told that 'these three manors paid one night's revenue with their dependants' and

---

34.   B. Cunliffe, *Roman Bath* (1995), p. 135.
35.   See C. Thorn and F. Thorn, *Domesday Book: Somerset* (1980), under each manor. These arrange-
      ments must have related to the countrywide administration system centring on royal villes, where
      dues and services were collected for the king, and which may be very early. Again, the distinctions
      between rents due to the king from his own land and taxes liable generally are unclear.

that all three 'belong in Walkhampton', now a large parish on the south-western Dartmoor edge.[36] The situation inland of Bigbury Bay, Devon, suggests two early land units based on the Erme and Avon Valleys. In 847 Æthelwulf, in his South Hams charter,[37] seems to have reserved to himself the best coastal land in this area, including the later parishes of Kingston, Ringmore and Bigbury, so cutting off the estuaries of the Erme and the Avon,[38] both of which had been significant points of an earlier exchange network which we shall discuss shortly. However, the Domesday record for Ermington tells us that it was a royal manor to which belonged the customary dues from five dependent units.

It must be stressed that the notion of the early large estate remains no more than a working hypothesis, which cannot be demonstrated beyond all reasonable doubt in any particular instance. It is likely, too, whatever the status of the hypothesis, that the variety of landed arrangements in the post-Roman south-west was large, and included some small freemen on their own land, and others who were only loosely attached to a larger landlord. These are hard to see, but should never be allowed to drop out of the equation. There is a lurking suspicion, too, that some of the putative large estates, far from being an Iron Age inheritance, were newly formed in the fourth/fifth centuries. The development of temples, the burial grounds and the reworking of hill-fort and villa sites during this time, together with the possible dedications of metalwork and coin and the interest in manipulating body parts, all of which were discussed in detail in Chapter 2, may be the material face of the effort to create emotional and social stability within developing landholdings. They look like the emergence of local focal places, perhaps the ceremonial centres of new or fairly new consolidated estates, where communal rituals could help to cement new social and economic relationships. Perhaps they represent the strivings of the local Late Antique elite to consolidate their position in a world where larger loyalties and opportunities were shrinking, but where this very fact encouraged people to exchange some freedoms for the greater security which dependence on a large landlord represented.

We might expect this to be patchy, and this may be why the situation in parts of Cornwall (and also elsewhere) may be different. It is also, however, likely to link up with the steady abandonment of enclosed farmsteads for open sites. The new subdivided rectangular buildings which start to appear at this time, which seem to be similar to the subdividing carried out at some temple buildings, also perhaps have their roots in the Late Antique emphasis on privacy and close family, witnessed by the formal burial of children. It is not difficult to see how estate focal places of this very mixed kind could gradually come to take on a more specifically Christian character, sometimes on the old site, sometimes on another old site which also had emotional connotations, and sometimes on a new site. These newly defined sites were usually Christian burial grounds, which appear embellished with inscribed stones and other characteristic features.[39]

---

36. S298; Thorn and Thorn, *Devon*, under each manor.
37. Hooke, *Charter-bounds*, pp. 105–12.
38. Unless defence was on his mind; if so, perhaps the Oldaport site on the Erme estuary played some part in his thinking; see M. Farley and R. Little, 'Oldaport, Modbury: a reassessment of the fort and harbour', *PDAS*, 26 (1968): 31–6; P. Rainbird, 'Oldaport and the Anglo-Saxon defence of Devon', *PDAS*, 56 (1998): 153–64, and p. 231.
39. Discussed in detail in Ch. 3.

The cultural mix

While perhaps large estates were being consolidated in parts of the south-west during the fourth and fifth centuries, the social character was changing. It is difficult to estimate the role played by the appearance in the south-west of exotic elements which look as if they came from those parts of northern and western Europe which were never formally part of the late Empire. Much work on material culture has made it clear that the appearance of exotic material cannot be equated in a simple way with foreign settlers: a woman buried in late fifth-century Britain with a 'Germanic' necklace[40] may have been a first-generation immigrant, or a second or third-generation settler or the result of complicated marriages and/or shifts in social standing; equally, she may have been somebody who was disliked, or who lacked important kin, and so was sent to the grave with an object everybody considered embarrassing and wanted to be rid of. Fashion and feeling governed (as it still governs) object use at least as much as ethnic, or any other, rules. More specifically, evidence has been accumulating for some time[41] to suggest that fashions people saw as 'German' or 'barbarian', like hairstyles, jewellery and clothing, especially trousers, were modish in western Late Antiquity and were contributing to social change.

It has become clear that the Rhine frontier, like presumably those within and around Britain were, and by *c.* 400 had been for generations, also permeable zones crossed and recrossed at every imaginative, social and economic level. Within this the position of the army was equivocal. By the fourth century it had a large proportion of Germans, and perhaps other incomers including Irish,[42] serving at every level and in a range of technical relationships to central government. It is clear that the late imperial army in the west did genuinely fight, and eventually fail to contain, war-bands from across the Rhine, whose leaders then set up the western successor kingdoms. However, it also seems likely that the frontier troops, together with their hugely expensive and often state-of-the-art military bases, like that of the Second Augusta Legion at Cardiff built (or rebuilt) in the later fourth century, were a politically crucial pressure lobby whose chief interest was the maintenance of military lifestyle and esprit.[43]

Irish elements in the south-west

This is the context within which indications of the exotic in the south-west must be examined. A body of much-discussed evidence can be marshalled to suggest that the western seaboard of Britain, particularly Wales and Argyll, which takes its name from the Irish kingdom of Dalriada, saw an influential influx of settlers from Ireland

---

40.   'Germanic' is used throughout as a very general term implying real or perceived affiliations with the area east of the Rhine and north of the Danube.

41.   E.g. in R. White, *Roman and Celtic Objects from Anglo-Saxon Graves* (1988).

42.   Irish soldiers in fourth-century Britain are suggested by the Wroxeter inscription and the possible ogham inscription in Silchester. R. White and P. Barker, *Wroxeter: Life and Death of a Roman City* (1998), p. 106, Plate 13; M. Fulford and B. Sellwood, 'The Silchester Ogham Stone: a reconsideration', *Antiquity*, 54 (211): 95–9 (1980); M. Fulford and A. Clarke, 'Silchester and the end of Roman towns', *Current Archaeology*, 161 (1999): 176–80, for Silchester.

43.   J. Drinkwater, 'The "Germanic threat on the Rhine frontier": a Romano-Gallic artefact?', in R. Mathisen and H. Sivan, *Shifting Frontiers in Late Antiquity* (1995), pp. 31–44.

in the post-Roman centuries. Irish characteristics are most visible in the fifty-plus British inscriptions in ogham script, which may have originated in the Waterford region of Ireland in the fourth–fifth centuries but could have been invented in south-west Wales.[44] These go with occurrences of clearly Irish names in Latin inscriptions, which are distributed in western Britain, with the main concentration in south-west and south-central Wales and the south-west, and a range of Irish place-names and place-name elements which have been identified in Wales.[45]

The inscriptions and the place-names have been linked with Irish traditions, chiefly those relating to the wanderings of the Munster Déisi who are said to have settled eventually in south-west Wales, and those in the ninth-century compilation known as *Cormac's Glossary*, which refers to the forts of *dun Tredúi* ('the fort of Tredúi') and *dind map Lethain/dún maic Liathán* ('the fort of the sons of Lethain') which is said to be in the land of the Cornish Britons. Neither has been identified, but it may be significant that the name of the second is given twice, in Irish and British. The úi Lethain were an Irish group, who, like the Déisi, belonged to south-east Ireland.[46] The difficulties of dating these relatively late traditions, and their probable bias, means that they cannot be taken as simple statements of genuine historical fact.

The south-west has eight inscriptions in ogham like those from Lewannick (Fig. 88), and several more giving Irish names in Latin-type lettering, like that reading SA[B]INI FILI MACCODECHETI from near the churchyard at Buckland Monachorum, where the father's name, which includes the element 'mac', is an Irish one, but the son's, Sabinus, is Roman. Dating is difficult, but the use of ogham script on such stones in Britain perhaps ran from the late fifth/sixth century to the eighth, although the sequence may begin earlier, since the Irish ogham stones seem to begin in the fourth century. In all cases in Britain, the ogham is matched by an inscription in Latin obviously intended to convey the same information, and this contrasts with most of the Irish examples which carry only ogham inscriptions. The inscriptions show that Irish continued to be understood in the relevant parts of the south-west until the end of the sixth century[47] but the stones show a clear desire to make their point not only in the vernacular but also in the language of church and literary exchange.

The roles of the stones with Irish characteristics seem to show the same pattern that the stones do overall. The Lewannick pair, and the stones from Buckland Monachorum, St Kew and perhaps St Clement, seem to be associated with grave-yards, and those from Roborough Down and Fardel with rights of way to high grazing, while those from St Endellion and Worthyvale were boundary markers. This suggests that those responsible for the stones were like other local landholders, and

44. D. McManus, 'Ogham: archaising, orthography and the authenticity of the manuscript key to the alphabet', *Erin* (1991): 1–31.

45. M. Richards, 'The Irish settlement in south-west Wales: a topographical approach', *J. Royal Society of Antiquities of Ireland*, 90 (1960): 133 52.

46. For *Cormac's Glossary*, see K. Meyer, *Anecdota from Irish Manuscripts* (1912), p. 75; for *Tredúi*, see C. Thomas, (1964b); 'Irish colonists in south-west Britain', *World Archaeology*, 5 (1): 78 (1973); for discussion of these issues in general, see H. Jenner, 'The Irish immigration into Cornwall in the late fifth and early sixth centuries', *J. Royal Cornwall Polytechnic Society*, 2 (1917): 38–85; J. Sheehan and M. Monk, *Early Medieval Munster* (1998; Thomas 1972, 1973a).

47. K. Jackson, 'Notes on the ogham inscriptions of southern Britain', in C. Fox and B. Dickins, *The Early Cultures of North-West Europe* (1950), pp. 199–213.

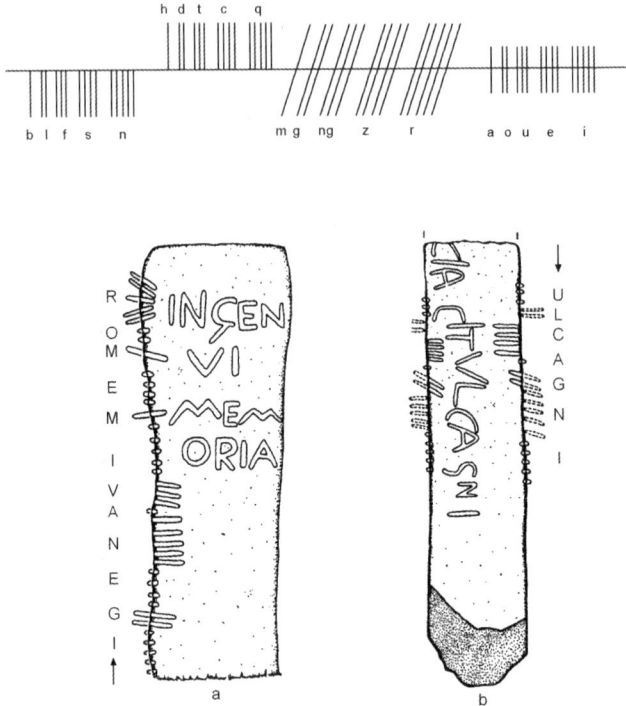

Figure 88 The ogham alphabet (after Okasha 1993, Fig. 1.3) (a)(b), the stones from Lewannick, Cornwall with ogham inscriptions, one, now inside church, reading INGENUI MEMORIA ('the memoria of Ingenuus'), the other, now in churchyard, reading [HI]C IACIT VLCAGNI ('here lies Ulcagnus'); there are two versions of the name Ulcagnus in ogham on this stone on the left and on the right (a)(b) (after Thomas 1994, Fig. 16.2)

that their holdings fitted into the local pattern of large, early estates possessed of summer grazing rights and, often, a linked burial ground.

The stones of Irish character provide some of the best examples of the ways in which the type seems to have been used to embody the rights of kin and inheritance. One of those from Lewannick has three texts, one in Latin and two in ogham, all of which feature the name Ulcagnus (or similar). These may commemorate several people of the same name or be multiple commemorations[48] intended to express group descent from a man looked back to as the common ancestor, who conceivably may indeed have been the founding father of the local elite family. The same kind of possibilities arise with the Ivybridge stone (Fig. 89) which has two Latin inscriptions, and one, or if they were intended to be read separately, two ogham inscriptions. Altogether, the stone commemorates five named individuals.

The surviving distribution of the stones with Irish elements shows them concentrated in the Tamar Valley and the adjacent north Cornish coast, suggesting an immediate link with southern Ireland or the tip of south-west Wales, where again

---

48.   See Okasha, *Inscribed Stones*, pp. 274–7. The left-hand ogham inscription may be simply an incorrect attempt, corrected on the right.

a   b

Figure 89 Inscribed stone from Ivybridge, Devon, showing two faces, one inscribed FANONIMAQUIRINI and the other SAGRANI, with ogham around the outside edge of one face. Now in the British Museum. (Photo: British Museum Photographic Department)

such stones are concentrated, or both. This could suggest a high-level, military influx from Ireland, perhaps through a kind of domino effect, to south Wales, and from either or both into the Tamar Valley, at (say) around 500 which succeeded in grabbing land, setting up elite networks and, in Wales, founding kingdoms: this is how the Irish tradition was later shaped, and how it was broadly interpreted by the earlier generation of scholars who, for example, looked for evidence of Irish raiding in the late fourth/early fifth centuries in the 'destruction' of the Somerset villas.[49]

It is, however, at odds with some recent interpretations, which suggest a revisionist view of the nature of the kingdom of Dalriada in south-western Scotland, and see the 'Irishness' of the kingdom as the invention of the later medieval political class. On

---

49.   K. Brannigan, 'Villa settlement in the West Country', in K. Brannigan and P. Fowler (eds), *The Roman West Country* (1976), pp. 136–41.

this view, the Irish Gaelic speech, which was certainly the main language of the area during the medieval period (and later), is the result of a shared language on both sides of the northern Irish Sea in late/post-Roman times. Similar links could be behind what appears in later medieval record as the 'Irish' kingdom of Brecknock in south-central Wales, and also the Irish inscriptions in south Wales and the south-west. An alternative view suggests that some of the Irish character in western Britain may be the result of the settlement of federated troops, *foederati*,[50] during the fourth century through the official imperial action of the kind known from elsewhere in the Empire.

Little work so far has been put into assessing the evidence for broad, perhaps quite humble, contacts across the western sea.[51] These are difficult to perceive anyway in a period when most commodities seem to have been in perishable form, but they have left their traces in Patrick's record of his early experiences, and in a few oddments like the beads from Cannington or the pin from Long Sutton, both in Somerset. Within this mix, too, belongs the display metalwork, particularly penannular brooches with animal decoration, pins and the hanging bowls. The brooches may have been developed in the late fourth century in the Severn Valley, but they rapidly became highly desirable across the western British/Irish world and the field for much artistic and fashion innovation. Two of the most fashionable types came from Cadbury Congresbury and others from Bath and St Kew.[52] Hanging bowls are another controversial subject, but may have been widely manufactured across western Britain.[53]

A permeable cultural province of this kind in the late Roman/post-Roman period seems likely. It could produce a number of people in the south-west, and south Wales, who chose to see themselves as Irish, or even bring a number of Irish settlers, whether officially or not, into western Britain (settlers in the other direction remain elusive), some of whom could acquire property rights through normal mechanisms of marriage and inheritance. Influence from Ireland and from Irishmen may also have helped to encourage the rich mix of post-500 Christian practices in the south-west.

Britons and Brittany

An element in the mix and movement of individuals in the late and post-Roman south-west is represented by the existence of Breton speech in the Amorican peninsula, almost universally taken to have resulted from the settlement there of

50. For a 'deconstructed' view, see E. Campbell, 'Were the Scots Irish?', *Antiquity*, 75 (2001): 285–92; for *foederati*, see P. Rance, 'Attacotti, Deisi and Magnus Maximus: the case for Irish federates in late Roman Britain', *Britannia*, 32 (2001): 243–70.
51. The various attempts to produce landscape evidence for Irish settlements in the south-west are not convincing; see P. Rahtz, 'Irish settlements in Somerset', *Proc. Royal Irish Academy*, 76C (1976): 223–30; I. Burrow, 'Possible Irish earthworks in Somerset', in Rahtz, 'Irish settlements', pp. 228–9; C. Newman, 'Fowler's Type F3 early medieval penannular brooches', *Med. Arch.* 33 (1989): 7–20. Settlement evidence from pottery is also ambiguous, see C. Thomas, 'The Irish settlements in post-Roman western Britain: a survey of the evidence', *JRIC*, 4 (1972): 251–74.
52. T. Dickenson, 'Fowler's Type G renannular brooches reconsidered', *Med. Arch. 26* (1982): 41–68.
53. J. Brenan, *Hanging Bowls and their Contexts* (1991). There is a mould for making their decorative escutcheons from Seagrey, Wiltshire, of possible early sixth-century date.

families from Britain, although, in the light of fresh thinking on the Irish question, perhaps the suggestion that Breton is a local Gaulish Celtic development should not be ignored.[54] On the basis of linguistic study, Jackson[55] saw a relatively small move-ment to Amorica from southern Britain in the second half of the fifth century followed by a more considerable one in the second half of the sixth century from Devon and Cornwall, which swamped the existing local dialect and ensured that Breton and Cornish remained mutually intelligible. It is significant that the two major divisions of the Amorican peninsula were called Domnonée and Cornouaille. As we would expect, in the later medieval period these events attracted a large super-structure of origin narrative and hagiography which obscures our understanding of what was beginning in late Roman/post-Roman times. The best documentary evidence for links between Amorica and Britain is provided by ecclesiastical notices relating to two Breton priests with (possible) British names, Lovocat and Catihern, who were admonished by Melanius, Bishop of Rennes in 511–520, and the story of how Samson came from south Wales and founded the abbey-bishopric of Dol in the *Vita Prima*.[56]

From the point of view of south-western Britain, the most interesting feature of British influence in Brittany rests in the place-names. Names in *plou* and variants, from the Latin *plebs*, 'people', later interchangeable with *gui/guic* (Latin *vicus*), are very common. Seventy-five per cent of them are compounded with a male personal name, about 60 per cent of which were counted as saints as the areas denoted by names in *plou* became parishes, but it is far from clear that the names represent the establishment of parish communities by incomers from Britain. By the tenth century, the *plou* in its social sense seems to have been a lay community rather than one primarily associated for religious purposes, a role which fits its apparent identifica-tion with the *vicus*. It may be that the original *plou* structure emerged as the appropriate way to create local communities with mixed origins which could deliver the public obligations of order and tax, and only later (?ninth century), as the parish system developed, became the obvious territorial expression of a parish. If this turns out to be the case, then social organization in Brittany appears as similar to, but in some ways simpler than, that of the south-west.

Breton *tré* (equivalent to Welsh *tref* and Cornish **tref*, all meaning 'an unenclosed hamlet') appears as an element in the place-names of settlements and parish sub-divisions. It is often found linked with the same personal names that are joined to *plou* hinting, perhaps, at an early (even settlement period) organization in which a sub-stantial farmstead and its satellites formed a *plou* community, which came to look back to a named founder, and which eventually became the local ecclesiastical unit. Interestingly, as Breton settlement expanded, its characteristic place-name element was *ker*, equivalent to Welsh *caer* and Cornish **ker*, meaning 'enclosed hamlet'. In the east, at least, *ker* replaced *tré* from the tenth century onwards, a nomenclature pro-cess which reverses that in Cornwall, and reminds us that social practices, including naming, are seldom translated to a new territory in a simple fashion.

54.   See discussion in P. Galliou and M. Jones, *The Bretons* (1991), pp. 143–7. For a comprehensive – but flawed – discussion of British settlement in Brittany, see Giot *et al.*, *British Settlement* (2003).

55.   K. Jackson, *Language and History in Early Britain* (1953), pp. 20–6. For the possible similar but smaller-scale movement to Galicia, see E. Thompson, 'Britonia' in M. Barley and R. Hanson, *Christianity in Britain, 300–700* (1968), pp. 201–5.

56.   For this and what follows, see Galliou and Jones, *Bretons*, pp. 122–47.

Brittany has a range of place-names in *lan* (Welsh *llan*, Cornish **lann*) and some of these, as at *Landevennec*, clearly represent major churches. A number of parish names in *lan* appear along the north coast, but in some cases the element seems to have retained its earlier sense of 'land', an area of open or common land, or an estate. Further work is necessary before we can hope to unravel the significance of these place-names, but it seems that, like *plou*, the ecclesiastical early nature of Breton *lan* cannot be taken for granted. *Loc* (Latin *locus*) also appears as a place-name element, apparently as a later form for new sites, as at Loctudy ('the place, i.e., church of St Tudy'). Brittany also has an important sequence of inscribed and decorated stones, which parallel those of western Britain.[57]

The Germanic presence

From at least as early as 200, there were in Britain people whose origins, directly or a generation or so back, lay in the area east of the Rhine. These arrived as ordinary soldiers, senior military officers, perhaps, as has sometimes been argued for the later fourth century, privately hired militia, and presumably assorted traders and settlers. They were a part of the cosmopolitan Empire and its great Rhine frontier institution, and they seem to have inspired local fashions, like perhaps that of women wearing their hair in plaits rather than classical curls,[58] and indeed the whole trend to flashy jewellery and equipment which must have seemed so vulgar to those of the old school, and which is reflected uncertainly in the material culture and renders 'Germans' hard to spot in the record during the later fourth and fifth centuries. Official symbols of rank were often in the Germanic taste. The propeller-shaped belt stiffener from Sixpenny Handley (Dorset) which came from a later imperial official uniform belt, and the similar belt fittings from Camerton,[59] give welcome confirmation that such officers were present, and presumably conducting imperial business in the rural south-west; we do not know if these men were actual Germans but many such were.

Apart from these, a scatter of early objects in Hampshire and Wiltshire extends geographically to two fifth-century Germanic-style brooches and a roughly contemporary, culturally similar, spearhead, all from Hod Hill.[60] Another spearhead of *c.* 500 comes from Worlebury, Weston-Super-Mare, and another, possibly a little later, from Badbury Regis, Dorset.[61] There are two from Cadbury Congresbury,[62] and a

57. See W. Davies, Graham-Campbell and J. Handley, *The Inscriptions of Early Medieval Brittany* (2000); for specific parallel to south-western and Welsh decorative forms, see pp. 131–6.

58. H. Cool, 'The parts left over: material culture into the fifth century', in T. Wilmot and P. Wilson (eds), *The Late Roman Transition in the North* (2000), pp. 47–65.

59. C. Green, 'A late Roman "propeller" belt fitting from Handley, Dorset', *PDNHAS*, 108 (1986): 184–5. For Dorset, W. Wedlake, *Excavations at Camerton, Somerset* (1958), pp. 256–7, fig. 58.12; R. Jackson, *Camerton. The Late Iron Age and Early Roman Metalwork* (1990), pp. 31–2, Plate 4.46.

60. B. Eagles and C. Mortimer, 'Early Anglo-Saxon artefacts from Hod Hill, Dorset', *Antiq. J.*, 73 (1993): 132–40.

61. B. Eagles, 'The archaeological evidence for settlement in the fifth to seventh centuries AD', in M. Aston and C. Lewis (eds), *The Medieval Landscape of Wessex* (1994), pp. 13–32.

62. Rahtz *et al.*, *Cadbury Congresbury*, pp. 118–27.

further similar spearhead is known from Spotisbury, Dorset.[63] Ham Hill (Fig. 90) has produced a shield boss of around 500.[64] These pieces are all associated with hill-fort sites, which helps to underline their focal position in local communities, and perhaps suggests that they were linked with the operation of small military units during the fifth century, rather like those that seem to have protected London, Lincoln and Circencester. Earlier Germanic material found at some of the western villa sites, such as Chedworth, Barsley Park and Spoonley Wood, suggests that villa sites could also act as military posts.[65] Of course the soldiers concerned need not have been 'German', just carrying what was seen as appropriate military gear.

By the sixth century, evidence for Germanic occupation was widespread throughout Berkshire, Hampshire and much of Wiltshire, where it was 'a significant part of the emergence of the kingdom of the West Saxons',[66] or, to put it differently, notions about 'Germanness' were beginning to harden. Further west such material is still sparse. A harness mount is recorded from Wor Barrow, Dorset, which may link

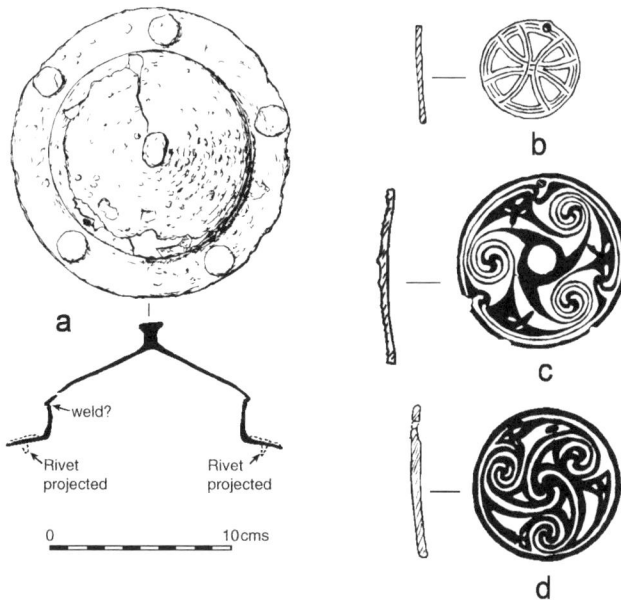

Figure 90 Objects from Ham Hill and Camerton. (a) Shield boss, Northern Spur, Ham Hill (after Burrow 1981, Fig. 34), and (b)–(d) three enamelled discs, probably from a hanging bowl, from the grave of a young girl, cemetery, Camerton. The smallest disc has been bored for suspension (?round the neck) and seems to have been used as a Christian symbol (after Brenan 1991, pp. 193, 194)

63.   Eagles, 'Archaeological evidence for settlement', pp. 13–32.
64.   I. Burrow, *Hillfort and Hill-top Settlement in Somerset in the First to Eighth Centuries* (1981), pp. 198–200, 268–77.
65.   Brannigan, 'Villa settlement', pp. 120–41; Pearce, 'Estates and church sites', pp. 119–38; K. Dark, *Britain and the End of the Roman Empire* (2000), pp. 51–3.
66.   Eagles, 'Archaeological evidence for settlement', p. 16.

up with the general ambivalence towards ancient burial sites, and which produced the feeling that they could be evil, together with their use as meeting places and boundary marks.[67] Sixth-century Germanic material in burials comes from Oakley Down,[68] Hardown Hill, both Dorset[69] and Bargates (Christchurch).[70] Ilchester[71] produced two sixth-century square-headed brooches, presumably worn as a pair in the German fashion, and a possibly Germanic-type spoon bowl comes (unprovenanced) from Lamyatt Beacon;[72] somewhere here belongs the intriguing animal-style decorated bronze ring with a make-over pin, and the button brooch and drinking service mount from South Cadbury.[73] From as far west as Clovelly Dyke comes a dark blue glass bead of Germanic type.[74]

Further pagan-style burials belong to the seventh century. A cluster centring on Dorchester includes 'The Trumpet Major' cemetery[75] just outside the city, where one grave had an elite-style silver wire ornament, and small groups of burials at Maiden Castle[76] and the prehistoric earthwork at Mount Pleasant.[77] Similar cemeteries have been found at Bradford Peverell, Long Crichel and Hambledon Hill.[78] Further north, the large Camerton cemetery[79] had graves with Germanic material including culturally ambivalent fragments of a hanging bowl,[80] and others are known from Buckland Dinham. The slightly earlier metalwork material from South Cadbury possibly belonged with the seventh-century group of burials from Compton Pauncefoot and that from Queens Camel. An inhumation at Huish Episcopi had a pair of bronze tweezers, and a rich grave with beads and a gold pendant has been found at Burnett, Keynsham.[81] The grave-goods at Cannington, particularly those which accompanied the burials of two children, show a high level of cultural fusion.[82] One striking feature of all this material is the cultural mix which it often reflects. Another

---

67.   See, for example, L. Grinsell, 'Barrows in the Anglo-Saxon land charters', *Antiq. J.*, 71 (1991): 47–63; A. Meaney, 'Gazetteer of hundred and wappentake meeting-places of the Cambridge region', *Procs. Cambridge Antiquarian Society*, 82 (1994): 67–92; S. Semple, 'A fear of the past: the place of the prehistoric burial mound in the ideology of middle and later Anglo-Saxon England', *World Archaeology*, 30 (1): 109–20 (1998); D. Bonney, 'Pagan Saxon burials and boundaries in Wiltshire', *Wilts ANHM*, 61 (1966): 25–30.

68.   Eagles, 'Archaeological evidence for settlement', pp. 13–32.

69.   V. Evison, 'The Anglo-Saxon finds from Hardown Hill', *PDNHAS*90 (1969): 232–40.

70.   Eagles, 'Archaeological evidence for settlement', pp. 13–32.

71.   P. Leach, *Ilchester Volume 1. Excavations 1974–5* (1982).

72.   R. Leech, 'The excavation of a Romano-Celtic temple and a later cemetery on Lamyatt Beacon, Somerset', *Britannia*, 17 (1986): 259–328.

73.   L. Alcock, *Cadbury Castle, Somerset: The Early Medieval Archaeology* (1995), pp. 67–74.

74.   A. Fox, 'Sixteenth report on the early history of Devon', *TDA*, 81 (1951): 85–8.

75.   C. Green, 'Early Anglo-Saxon burials at the Trumpet Major public house, Alington Avenue, Dorchester', *PDNHAS*, 106 (1984): 149–52.

76.   M. Wheeler, *Maiden Castle, Dorset* (1943), pp. 77–8.

77.   J. Schweise, 'The Anglo-Saxon burials', in G. Wainwright, *Mount Pleasant, Dorset: Excavations 1970–1* (1979), pp. 181–3.

78.   P. Rahtz and P. Fowler, 'Somerset AD 400–700', in P. Fowler (ed.), *Archaeology and the Landscape*, pp. 200–17.

79.   Wedlake, *Camerton*, pp. 96–8.

80.   Brenan, *Hanging Bowls*, pp. 193–4.

81.   Rahtz and Fowler, 'Somerset, AD 400–700', pp. 200–17.

82.   White, *Roman and Celtic Objects*, p. 412.

is the continuing significance of hill-fort sites, and the areas immediately around them.

The recognition of settlements to match these objects has proved controversial. Grass-tempered pottery has sometimes been culturally linked but grass-tempering as a potting technique seems to have been used widely during the fifth and sixth centuries and crops up for example, at Cadbury Congresbury, and at various sites within Dorchester, where its cultural significance could be interpreted in a number of ways. House forms and building styles are equally difficult to pin down, and late fourth/early fifth-century buildings with 'sunken floors', often seen as 'Anglo-Saxon', like those at Alington Avenue, Dorchester, need not have been built or occupied by people who thought they were Germanic.[83] Another fifth-century settlement was established just outside Dorchester within the old civic cemetery at Poundbury, and whatever its precise cultural affiliations, it shows that at least part of the old cemetery, including its mausolea, was not considered worth preserving. The timber buildings and pottery from Dorchester and its vicinity do suggest that, as at Gloucester, Wroxeter, Circencester and Caerwent, people were still living there after *c.* 400, whatever their exact backgrounds.[84]

What emerges most clearly from all apparently exotic material in the post-Roman south-west, as from similar material throughout the British Isles, is the extent to which it does not seem to represent the clearly defined, formal movements of groups or individuals of older interpretations. It looks much more the flexible, indeed opportunistic, efforts of culturally mixed people to assert their chosen identities.

Administrative structures

The collapse of the overarching imperial authority in the west in the early fifth century may not have been traumatic, given the likely existence of a black economy of tax avoidance and increasing local self-sufficiency which evaded the imperial command economy,[85] but the fluid political conditions of the fifth century, about which for the south-west we know very little, must have offered opportunities to the local mix of large landholders, local magistrates and regional bureaucrats. We can go some way towards recognizing some of the legal and administrative structures through which such people were probably able to create social organization and exercise power after *c.* 400 (Fig. 91).

We would expect regional divisions to have existed in the peninsula, given the need for an overarching arrangement to manage the very large areas of common grazing, and the fact that the Roman authorities normally divided tribal units into *pagi*, which we might translate into 'rural districts'. There are cogent reasons for believing that the Cornish districts known eventually (and conventionally) as hundreds (Fig. 92) were in origin probably six substantial divisions, Penwith, Kerrier, Pydar, Powder, Trigg (in its modern form) and the area known since at least the eleventh century by

---

83. C. Green, 'Early Anglo-Saxon burials', pp. 149–52.

84. Dark, *Britain*, pp. 105–9, and refs there.

85. See, for example, Williams and Friell, *Theodosius*, pp. 103–15. Although the specific conditions are obviously very different, the long-term weaknesses in the USSR system, followed by its sudden complete collapse and the emergence of post-imperial structures, gave us an object lesson in how the processes of decline and fall can operate.

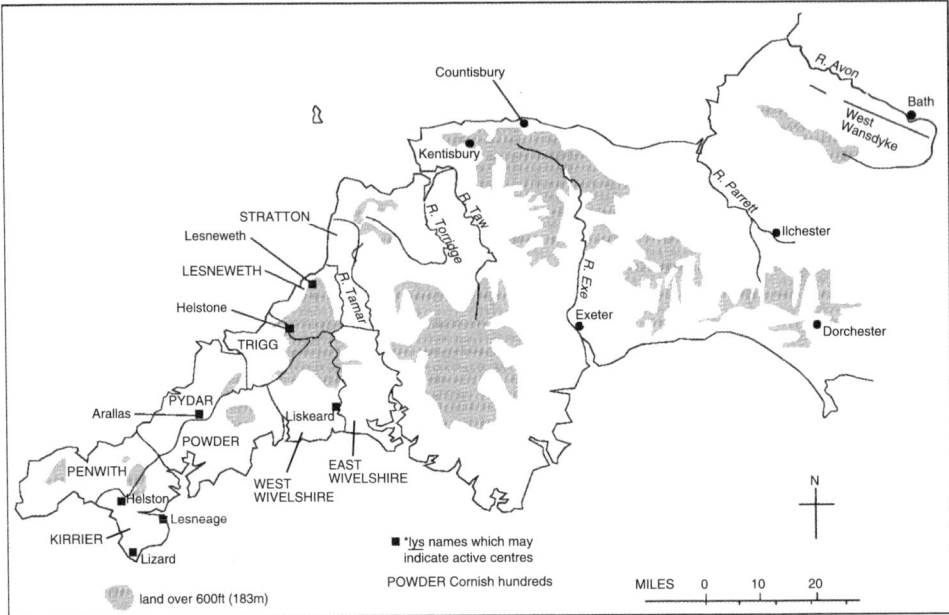

Figure 91 Some potentially significant boundaries and administrative centres in the post-Roman south-west

its English name, Wivelshire. These divide Cornwall between them in a way which provides a sensible allotment of the upland grazing, and the late Cornish name for them, *keverang*, suggests a link with 'meeting, battle', hinting at an early military function, so they probably represent divisions of Roman, or indeed pre-Roman date.[86]

The first element in Powder seems to be Old Cornish *pou*, 'land, country', which in post-Roman records was regarded as the equivalent of *pagus*. Trigg, which originally included the later separate divisions of Stratton and Lesneweth, is from British *try*, 'triple' or 'very', and **cor*, 'clan, family', meaning something like 'three armies', a triple division which may be reflected in the later tripartite arrangement. In the *Vita* of St Samson the name is rendered *pagus Tricurius*.[87] Kerrier may mean 'place of the *kers*', suggesting a specific relationship to the enclosed settlements and therefore an origin when they were the dominant form of farmstead.[88] Leland noted that the name

---

86.   C. Thomas, 'Settlement-history in early Cornwall, I: the antiquity of the hundreds', *Corn. Arch.* 3 (1964a); Padel, *Cornish Place-name Elements*, p 56; K. Jankulak, *The Medieval Cult of St Petroc* (2000), pp. 116–24. Thomas also suggests that Pydar, given its position in relation to the four western hundreds, may refer to British **petuar-ija*, 'fourth quarter', and if so this would support the proposed antiquity of the system. However, Jankulak saw Pydar as deriving from 'Petroc's shrine' and representing broadly the lands of the monastery of St Petroc.

87.   We do not know if the word *pagus* here is an echo of imperial usage or the later use of what seemed to be an appropriate word. The use of *pagus* did sometimes survive into later place-names as Powys from *pagenses*, cf. W. Davies, *Wales in the Early Middle Ages* (1982), p. 87. For a general discussion of land divisions, see P. Jenkins, 'Regions and cantrefs in early medieval Glamorgan', *Cam. Med. Celtic St.*, 15 (1988): 31–50.

88.   Dark, *Britain*, p. 151.

for Breage (or part of it) which lies within Kerrier was Pembro, and the local church was called *Eglospenbro* around 1207. This is apparently from *pen bro*, 'the head place of the region/district', and the actual centre may have been the hill-fort at Tregonning, perhaps Leland's Pencair (*pen caer*, 'head enclosure').[89] The Cornish divisions may reflect pre-Roman arrangements, and perhaps served as *pagi* during the imperial period.

Otherwise, the picture is largely blank. There is the faintest hint that the management of the Dartmoor grazing involved a tripartite division of (most of) Devon, but, if so, these divisions would have been a much larger than the Cornish hundreds.[90] The element **cant*, 'boundary',[91] may lie behind the first part of the name Kentisbury, and also perhaps of Courtisbury, both major hill-forts and perhaps strategically placed in relation to the Exmoor upland. It is possible that major names in British *pen* ('head, top, end, headland') may be associated with early boundaries.[92] We have already noted Pembro, and another possibility is Penbury Knoll (Dorset), with a hybrid British/Saxon name, and the settlement name Pentridge from *pen* and **crouk-a*, 'hill'.[93] Names in Old English *torre*, 'rock, hill',[94] may also sometimes have had territorial significance: the upland tors have almost always been important landmarks.

Some of the major earthworks, which have also been associated with the specific phases of the expansion of the West Saxon kingdom, also seem to have been boundaries, and obviously these two functions are quite compatible. Bokerley Dyke's complex history may have begun as a Bronze Age boundary marker and it still marks a stretch of the Dorset/Hampshire boundary.[95] West Wansdyke, which runs to the south of Bath and onwards to Maes Knoll on Dundry Ridge (and further on incorporates Stantonbury hill-fort), may relate to a region centred upon Bath.[96] Some such territory is implied by the *Anglo-Saxon Chronicle* entry under 577, alleging that three named British kings were killed and the three cities of Bath, Gloucester and Circencester were captured in that year; but the authority of such annals is very uncertain.

In east Cornwall, the Giant's Hedge,[97] of uncertain date, cuts off a large block of land between two rivers, and the Bolster Bank[98] a much smaller area of rich tin ground in St Agnes. *Dic* ('dyke', usually a ditch and bank) is a common reference point in Anglo-Saxon charter boundaries and in several such references from

89. Padel, *Cornish Place-name Elements*, p. 32, for Breton Broërec; Galliou and Jones, *Bretons*, p. 135.
90. See pp. 58–9, Fig. 25.
91. J. Gover, A. Mawer and F. Stenton, *The Place-names of Devon* (1931), pp. 49, 62–3; see M. Higham, 'Names on the edge: hills and boundaries', *Nomina*, 22 (1999): 61–74; forms of *cant* occur in Cornwall at Cant and possibly elsewhere, and in Somerset in the Quantock Hills; see Padel, *Cornish Place-name Elements*, pp. 37–8.
92. Higham, 'Names on the edge', pp. 61–74; Padel, *Cornish Place-name Elements*, p. 177.
93. A. Fagersten, *The Place-names of Dorset* (1933), p. 103; see A. Rivet and C. Smith, *The Place-names of Roman Britain* (1979), pp. 436–7.
94. A. Mills, *A Dictionary of English Place-names* (1998), p. 406.
95. See C. Bowen, *The Archaeology of Bokerley Dyke* (1990).
96. P. Fowler and P. Rahtz, 'Somerset AD 400–700', in Fowler, *Archaeology and the Landscape*, pp. 200–17.
97. The Giant's Hedge earthwork runs some 10 miles across country east of the northern end of Fowey estuary; its date is uncertain.
98. N. Johnson, 'The Bolster Bank, St Agnes: a survey', *Corn. Arch.*, 19 (1980): 77–88.

Somerset the dyke is described as 'old', as at Pitminster, Rimpton, Taunton and High Ham, suggesting that, at the very least, they predated the gift the charter recorded.[99] Many of these local dykes were relatively small and probably marked estate rather than regional boundaries, but, given fluctuating political circumstances, obviously could be used at different social levels at different times.

Other regional or local centres of administration may be indicated by some of the place-names embodying the element Old Cornish *lys (Welsh, *llys*; Breton, *lez*), 'court'. Names including this element occur quite frequently in Wales, and are known in Brittany and northern Britain.[100] There are some twenty instances in Cornwall, unevenly distributed with more known in Pydar but at least six in Kirrier, and two in north Devon.[101] The use of *lys as a place-name element seems to have covered a considerable time-span, perhaps from the Roman/post-Roman period to the later Middle Ages, and had a number of applications. Where *lys is qualified by words meaning domestic animals or natural features, it evidently means 'ruins' of any date, in much the same way that later in England 'castle' came to be used for prehistoric earthworks. Lezerea ('flock court'), Leskernick ('rock-pile court'),[102] perhaps Lestrainess ('thorn court') and, in Devon, Charles ('rocky court') and perhaps Breazle (?'court at the bridge or ford') would come into this group.

Some of the *lys place names seem to be associated with what are now deemed earthworks of the broad 'round' type, as at Arallas ('silver court')[103] and Liskeard.[104] Lestowder ('court of Teudar'), in the parish of St Keverne, has an extensive bivallate fortification with a large central enclosure,[105] and this presumably is the site associated in later legend with the supposed Cornish King Teuder. Helsbury and perhaps Hesingey seem to refer to hill-forts. Whether the sites themselves had such names when they were going concerns, or whether the names were given (much) later in the antiquarian spirit is not clear, but perhaps the latter is the more likely.

Nevertheless, some of the places with a *lys name, such as Liskeard, Helstone in Trigg ('ancient court'), Lesneweth nearby ('new court' and presumably Helstone's replacement), Helston in Kirrier Arallas and Lizard ('court on a high place'), were important Domesday manors. Helston and Lizard were both royal manors, and Lesneage ('monks' court) was presumably the administrative centre for St Keverne's estate. It may be that some of these places were important administrative centres in the period before *c.* 900, but if so they seem to be operating at the estate, rather than the wider regional level.

There may perhaps emerge from this a general sense that the south-west did have a structure of regions which occupied a position between individual estates (of

99.   M. Costen, 'Settlement in Wessex in the tenth century: the charter evidence', in Aston and Lewis, *Medieval Landscape* (1994), pp. 97–114.

100. Padel, *Cornish Place-name Elements*, pp. 150–1, for what follows; for a useful discussion of such sites in Wales, see D. Longley, 'The royal courts of the Welsh princes in Gwynedd, AD 400–1283', in N. Edwards, *Landscape and Settlement in Medieval Wales* (1997), pp. 55–70.

101. Gover *et al., Place-names of Devon* (1931), pp. 61, 174.

102. Leskernick Hill, for example, is high on Bodmin Moor near a stone circle, but also near a field system; see B. Bender, S. Hamilton and C. Tilley, 'Leskernick: the biography of an excavation', *Corn. Arch.*, 34 (1995): 58–73.

103. K. Dark, *The Early British Court: Place-names and Archaeology* (1998).

104. A. Jones, 'Liskeard', *Corn. Arch. Soc.* Newsletter, Sept. (1996), n.p.

105. M. Tongye, 'Lestowder, St Keverne: a previously unidentified stronghold', *Corn. Arch.*, 34 (1995): 176–81.

whatever size and scope) and the larger units which eventually became shires within Wessex, but, if so, apart from the Cornish hundreds, the evidence for them is very scrappy. The social level at which a boundary functioned is usually unclear, and so, correspondingly, is their role in the generation of wider political authority unclear, although in the east, presumably, it was in part their amalgamation which contributed to what finally emerged as the Wessex heartland.

Major centres

A small range of excavated sites has produced evidence suggesting that they were major centres for perhaps a century or so after the late fifth century. Their candidature rests largely on the activity levels dated by imported pottery, but they were generally originally chosen for investigation because they are the foci of later medieval legend, and the extent to which they represent the total of such sites in the southwest is not clear. They do, however, fit into a sequence of broadly similar sites, like Dinas Emrys and Dinorben (Wales), and Dunbarton and Dunadd further north, along the western seaways.

At Cadbury Congresbury,[106] the Contour Rampart was refurbished perhaps in the later fourth century and a little later the inner circuit was reconstructed, with the creation of the Diagonal Bank (although this may have been earlier) which formed a flattish platform rather than a strong military defensive work, although it eventually incorporated a bastion or watch tower (Fig. 92a). Later still, perhaps in the sixth century, this went out of use and the new Perimeter Bank was constructed. There are a range of structures in the interior which remain undated. Work at Cannington hill-fort[107] produced evidence of timber structures associated with Roman pottery behind one of the southern ramparts, suggesting refurbishment, or even new work, in the late Roman/post-Roman period.

The construction at Cannington and Cadbury Congresbury may have been mostly to assert authority but the building at South Cadbury,[108] which included Rampart E (the 'Stony Bank') built from dug stone and timber and a south-western gate with a timber tower or gatehouse, suggest a desire to create a formidable-looking stronghold (Fig. 93). A concentration of imported amphora sherds suggested a special 'high status' area in the interior (Fig. 94), perhaps the site of a postulated large rectangular 'hall'. The site also produced a low-tin bronze ingot suggesting metalworking, a fifth or sixth-century Roman-style crossbow bolt and Germanic metalwork.

Glastonbury[109] is included in this group chiefly on the strength of its immensely impressive Tor (Fig. 92b). The Tor was not apparently fortified but did produce evidence for a range of structures, a small bronze alloy human head, presumably a mount from an import object, metalworking, imported pottery and the remains of large numbers of joints of beef, with some mutton and pork. This heavy eating argues against a monastic character for the Tor settlement, although the grave-sized

106. Rahtz *et al.*, *Cadbury Congresbury*, for summary see pp. 214–23.
107. *Ibid.*, pp. 11–14, and esp. pp. 225–53.
108. For an account of Cadbury excavations see Alcock, *Cadbury Castle* (1995). John Davey is carrying out a major study of the hill-fort's environs in the post-Roman period; it seems to have been the centre of an estate, perhaps created in the third century (*www-users.york.ac.uk/~rc132/*).
109. P. Rahtz, 'Excavations at Glastonbury Tor', *Arch. J.*, 127 (1971): 1–81.

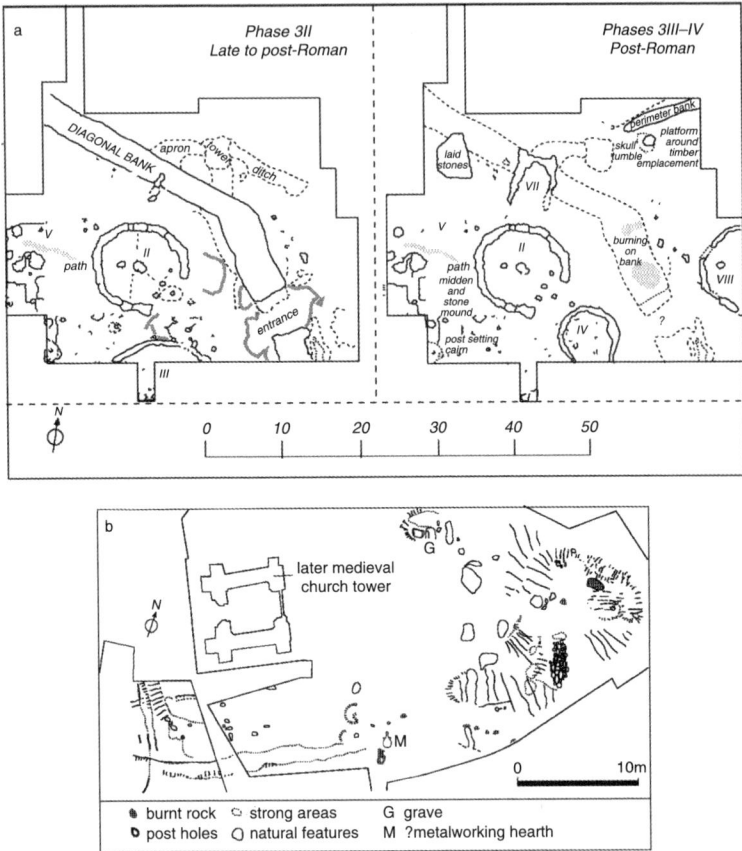

Figure 92 Plans of a post-Roman occupation at (a) Cadbury Congresbury (after Rahtz *et al.* 1992, Figs 158, 159) and (b) Glastonbury Tor (after Rahtz 1991, Fig. 6)

cairn remains a puzzle. The Mound, a high 'island' about 2 km west of the Tor, has also produced imported pottery.[110]

All these sites were concentrated in the relatively small area of eastern Somerset, and on the (large) assumption that they all continued to flourish during the late fifth and sixth centuries and that their possessors were all of equal consequence, it is possible to suggest the territories which they might have dominated. These embrace other hilltop sites, like Brent Knoll, Worlebury and Maes Knoll, which, judging by their late Roman material, seem to have been of significance in the fourth and perhaps the earlier fifth centuries. A possible model to account for this would suggest that South Cadbury, Glastonbury, Cannington and Congresbury were the centres of important estates or territories which by the later fifth/sixth century had absorbed smaller areas of importance in the fourth and earlier fifth centuries, many with hilltop foci. This absorption may have been achieved through the manipulation of

110. P. Rahtz, *Glastonbury* (1993), pp. 109–11.

Figure 93 The hilltop of South Cadbury, Somerset, looking north-east, showing the prehistoric defences and the present settlement clustered beneath the hill. The Somerset lowlands lie to the north-west. (Photo by West Air Photography)

kinship, marriage and inheritance or it may have resulted from a local desire to 'keep up with the Joneses', and some genuine naked aggression may have featured.

Ham Hill, with its imported amphorae,[111] and Hod Hill, with its Romano-British material, fourth-century (or later) quarry pits associated with the rampart and Germanic metalwork,[112] may be part of the same pattern further south. Strategically important Badbury Regis has produced Germanic spearheads, and the pre-castle bank at Corfe and the pre-*burh* massive bank at Wareham,[113] which might be linked with the group of inscribed stones there, have both been suggested as post-Roman centres, although dating evidence is lacking. If the early Germanic material from Cadbury Congresbury, Badbury Regis, Dolebury,[114] Worlebury, South Cadbury, Ham Hill and Hod Hill represents soldiers in the employ of local leaders, then these, too, look like local strong points and centres, although whether the solders were employed to fend off Germanic aggression or to defend local British leaders against each other, is not clear.

Across Devon, our ability to distinguish 'major' sixth-century centres distinguished by construction work, from 'minor' ones marked only by other indications

---

111. Burrow, *Hillforts*, p. 269, fig. 34 lower; E. Campbell, 'Imported goods in the early medieval Celtic west: with special reference to Dinas Powys' (1991), p. 404.
112. Burrow, *Hillforts*, pp. 268–77.
113. Dark, *Britain*, p. 146.
114. *Ibid.*

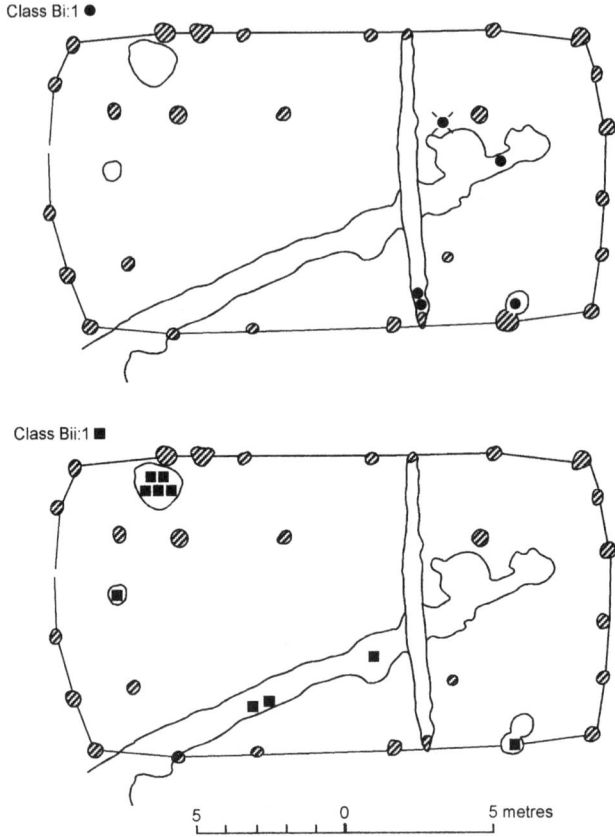

Figure 94 Site L1 at South Cadbury, showing distribution of sherds of amphorae attributed to class Bi/1 and Bii/1 (after Alcock 1995, Fig. 2.24).

of fourth or fifth/sixth-century occupation, falters, partly because excavation has not been so extensive. However, new evidence from the hill-fort on Raddon Hill, Stockleigh Pomeroy,[115] backed by radiocarbon dates, suggests that the west enclosure had been recut in the post-Roman period, and that several pits, some containing granite trimmings from quern production, some charred grain and some perhaps to be interpreted as graves, are roughly contemporary. Another possible site is the coastal hill-fort at High Peak, which produced occupation debris and imported amphorae sherds: the layout of the site as a whole looks Iron Age but some of the sherds came from the small rampart outside the ditch suggesting some possible post-Roman construction.[116] A pit fill from Haldon Hill near Exeter has also given a

115.   T. Gent and H. Quinnell, 'Excavation of a causewayed enclosure and hillfort on Raddon Hill, Stockleigh Pomeroy', *PDAS*, 57 (1999): 1–76, esp. pp. 24–7.

116.   S. Pollard, 'Neolithic and Dark Age settlements on High Peak, Sidmouth, Devon', *PDAS*, 23 (1966): 23–35; 'Radiocarbon dating, Neolithic and Dark Age settlements on High Peak, Sidmouth, Devon', PDAS, 25 (1967): 41–2.

calibrated date of AD 595–690.[117] Another candidate is the enigmatic site at Oldaport, Modbury. Investigations at the site have been distinguished by very few finds and the date(s) of the fortifications are uncertain, but 'a much abraded sherd of probable Samian ware' from the topsoil suggests post-Roman use of the site (since a Roman site would have produced more material), and re-examination of the sherd might be illuminating. The Oldaport site dominates the Erme estuary.[118]

It seems that whoever possessed these sites dominated substantial areas of the very large hinterland of Devon. The potential local or 'minor' centres in Devon are a mixed bag. They include Countisbury, Kentisbury and Denbury, a two-phase hill-fort whose name means 'the fort of the men of Devon'[119] and from which comes Germanic-style metalwork.[120] A number of other hill-forts have a British place-name element followed by OE *burh* ('fort, enclosure'), including some already discussed, like Cadbury Tiverton and Maesbury, which were of some significance in the fourth century. The fragment of imported ware from the Lydford Castle area, given the probable pre-750 existence of its churchyard, hints at a focus in the area, conceivably in or around the castle site. As far as we can see from the distribution of hilltops with imported wares, the structure of power in Devon was patchy, something conceivably reflected in the lack of a grand legendary status at any of the sites.

West of the Tamar, the late fifth-to-sixth-century situation seems to have been complex in a different way. Here Tintagel (Fig. 95), with its late Roman, possibly official or quasi-official background, dominates the scene by virtue of the much larger quantities of imported ware found here than anywhere else in the British Isles so far. Tintagel Island covers much the same area as South Cadbury, and its natural strength was enhanced by the post-Roman digging of the Great Ditch. Finds include spindle whorls made from imported amphorae bits as at Bantham, and a possible Gaulish ring ornament. There is also a range of undated, worked slate pieces, one depicting a warrior with a perhaps sword and small circular shield, another a stag and a third a ship.

Analysis of the post-Roman finds suggests important areas of occupation on the landward side of the ditch and just above the Iron Gate rocks. These are flanked by some of the assorted rectilinear huts of which there are over a hundred at the site, some on artificial terraces, amongst which the post-Roman buildings are difficult to distinguish from later medieval hutments (Fig. 96a). There is some evidence for metalworking but, the imported pottery apart, little signs of the rubbish which substantial or continuous occupation would generate, and this suggests that Tintagel was visited occasionally. This offers the attractive proposition that it functioned as the summer meeting place at which the local ruler met lesser men, transacted business and fostered the important personal relationships upon which, in part, his power

---

117.   T. Gent and H. Quinnell, 'Salvage recording on the Neolithic site at Haldon Belvedere', *PDAS*, 57 (1999): 77–104, esp. pp. 102.

118.   Farley and Little, 'Oldaport, Modbury', pp. 31–6; the sherd is apparently lost: could it possibly be red-slip ware (below pp. 234–7)? See Rainbird, 'Oldaport', pp. 153–64, for a discussion of the possibly eleventh-century date of the second phase at Oldaport.

119.   Gover *et al., Place-names of Devon* (1932), p. 253, Introduction xiv note 1. Dinas Dinorwic in north Wales means 'the fort of the Ordovices' but may reflect an earlier level of nomenclature; Dark, *Britain*, p. 173.

120.   S. Probert and C. Dunn, 'Denbury Camp, Torbryan Parish: a new survey', *PDAS*, 50 (1992): 53–9; Dark, *Britain*, p. 164.

Figure 95 The headland of Tintagel, Cornwall, looking south-west. Remains of the later medieval castle can be seen either side of the narrow neck. Imported pottery fragments have been found scattered over the terraces on the headland, but the dating and character of the groups of buildings are uncertain (photo: Cambridge University Collection of Art Photographs, copyright reserved)

depended.[121] It is possible that the broadly similar Somerset sites, and for that matter the dimly seen Devon sites, functioned in the same way.

As further east, Cornwall has also produced a range of what may have been lesser centres, or, at times perhaps, independent centres as political fortunes fluctuated between roughly 450 and 600. It must, though, be admitted that our ability to recognize such centres rests on the proposition that hill-forts, or hilltops more generally, were 'high' socially as well as geographically: candidates are Chun Castle, Trevelgue and Killibury, all of which have archaeological evidence, and sites like Pencair (Treggoning Hill) with (difficult) documentary evidence. Recent finds of imported pot and traces of defensive bank found in survey together with the significance which seems to have surrounded the site with its unique physical qualities, suggest that St Michael's Mount[122] may have been an important centre (Fig. 96b), even conceivably acting as the southern equivalent of Tintagel.

---

121.   See C. Thomas, 'Tintagel papers: special issue', *Cornish Studies*, 16 (1988), and Thomas, *Tintagel* (1993), for general discussion. For recent excavation, see C. Morris and R. Harry, 'Excavations of the Lower Terrace, Site C, Tintagel Island, 1990–1994', *Antiq. J.*, 77 (1997): 1–43.

122.   P. Herring, *St Michael's Mount Archaeological Works, 1995–8* (2000), pp. 120–4. Trevelgue seems to have fourth-century coins, and a ?Bii ware amphora handle amongst its old finds (information: Henrietta Quinnell).

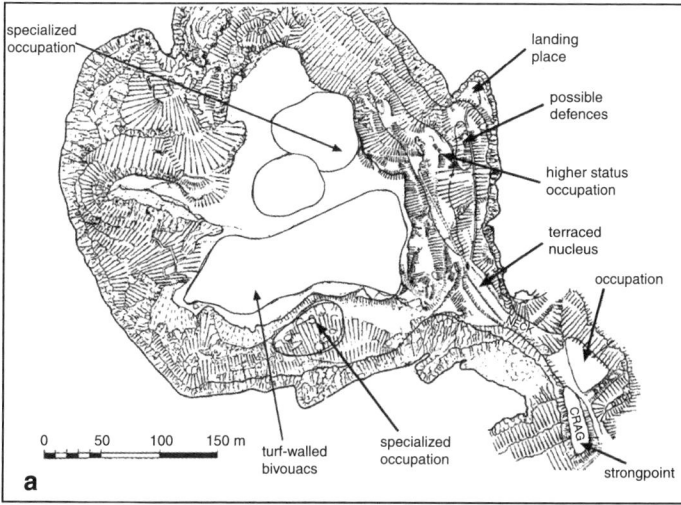

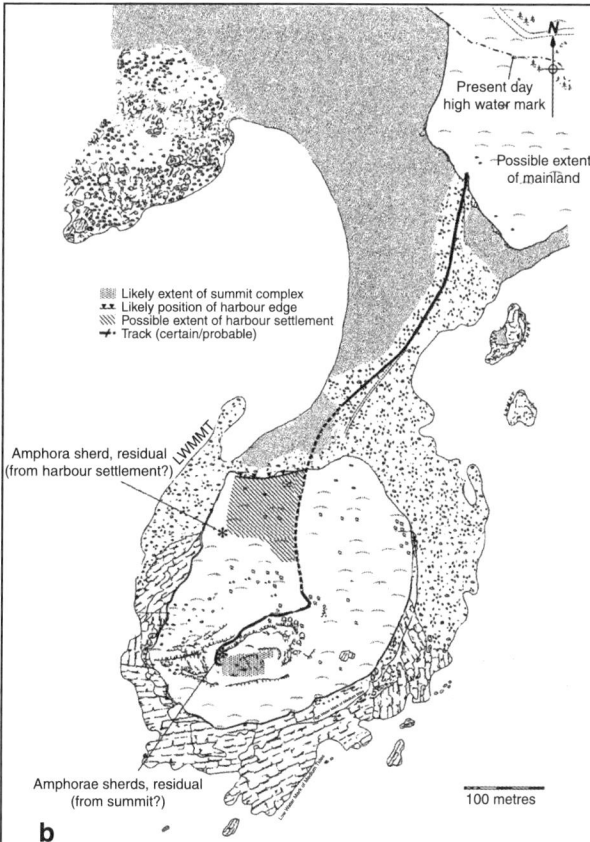

Figure 96 (a) Plan of post-Roman occupation at Tintagel (after Thomas 1993, Fig. 68, showing hypothetical model of use). (b) Plan of post-Roman occupation at St Michael's Mount (after Herring 2000, Fig. 49, copyright Cornwall County Council)

A working hypothesis sees the fifth-century south-west as a patchwork of land-holdings, some small, some large enough to be called estates. The dominant men in these were at pains to foster local ceremonial centres as places for the imagination to fix upon, taking up an old villa site, a hill-fort or hilltop, or perhaps a prominent burial mound, all as landmarks around which emotions already clustered. Some-times, the significant site may have been a Christian burial ground. If some men emerged as superior, their triumph was too short-lived to make any mark upon the record, but by around 480 some differences were beginning to crystallize, and these are what we see as the major sixth-century sites most of which were based at similar ancient sites. Such centres appeared in Somerset, at Tintagel in Cornwall and perhaps at potential sites in Dorset. In Devon, the picture is less clear. Perhaps several families achieved local importance, but none emerged as major regional powers. However, the quantity of Mediterranean pottery found at Bantham suggests a major authority in or around the Erme Valley, and it is to the Mediterranean link that we must now turn.

Connections with the Mediterranean

Two developments were probably bound up in these changes: the institutional establishment of the Church, to be discussed in the next section, and the contacts with the Mediterranean which appear chiefly as the finds of sherds of late fifth- and early sixth-century imported pottery, mostly amphorae, which were the all-purpose containers of the ancient world. A trade between the Mediterranean and Britain involving wine and some olive oil carried in amphorae of various types can be traced back to before the Roman conquest of Britain and continued at a modest level during the later fourth and perhaps earlier fifth centuries as material from Exeter and Gloucester shows.[123] The finds of imported pottery sherds of later fifth- and sixth-century date distributed along the western coast of Britain and across Ireland, suggesting that during this time it was these areas which were in touch with the Mediterranean world. Tintagel has overwhelmingly the largest share of the pottery, representing nearly 50 fine, red slip bowls and dishes, and over 130 coarse ware amphorae and similar containers, all from various areas of north Africa and the eastern Mediterranean. The other sites have much smaller quantities, usually just a handful of amphora sherds, or the odd fragment of a red slip bowl, although material is appearing in some quantity from Bantham on the Avon estuary.[124]

The Tintagel assemblage, with its east Mediterranean coarse ware pots suggest that entrepreneurs sailed out of eastern Mediterranean ports into Atlantic waters since

---

123.   D. Williams and C. Carreras, 'North African amphorae in Roman Britain: a reappraisal', *Britannia*, 26 (1995): 231–52, esp. pp. 250–1. The Byzantine–Western connection has recently been reviewed by Harris in *Byzantium, Britain and the West* (2003), who suggests that to exchange goods represents a 'Late Antique Byzantine commonwealth' (p. 194); this is interesting but, in default of texts, not really provable either way.

124.   For Tintagel, see C. Thomas, 'The archaeology of Tintagel parish churchyard', *Cornish Studies*, 16 (1988): 79–91, 'The context of Tintagel: a new model for the diffusion of post-Roman Mediterranean imports', *Corn. Arch.*, 27 (1988): 7–26, and 'Tintagel papers'; for Bantham, see 'Secrets of the sands', *DAS News*, 79 (2001): 1, 8–9. For details of classes and dating of the range of imported wares, see pp. 17–20.

otherwise they would have carried similar but easily locally available vessels from, for example, Carthage, and, indeed, similar arguments may apply to the eastern Mediterranean red slip bowls. Perhaps some were smaller enterprises[125] in which modest ships like that found wrecked off western Sicily tramped the Eastern and North African ports buying and selling mixed cargoes as they went. A model like this would account for the range of vessels and for the 'mixed batches' of amphorae which the major British sites tend to show, and also perhaps for the African and Eastern red slip fine wares. These seem to have been carried as 'extras' pushed into the spaces of the main cargoes, but were included, perhaps, because they could be offered as flattering specials to especially discriminating (and rich) customers. Amphorae were regarded as throwaway containers in the Mediterranean world, but if some of this trade was in the hands of individual ship captains, then it is possible that the collection of empty amphorae (or amphorae full of some local product – salt?) along the British and Irish coasts and their recycling formed part of the exchange system. This would help to account for the range of the coarse ware types found at insular sites. It also opens up the possibility that the level of trade was more substantial, and contacts more frequent, than the pottery finds suggest.

It is likely that we are looking at a trade in which foodstuffs were of major importance at the British/Irish end, although pending further analysis of amphorae residues, quite what these commodities were remains unclear. The current view favours olive oil, which would point unmistakably to a continuing desire among the elite in western Britain for a Mediterranean cuisine, based presumably upon bread, vegetables, pulses, herbs, fish and seafood and small quantities of meat, preferably lamb, perhaps served in individual helpings in bowls like the red slip ones and their local equivalents. Perhaps a little of the oil was used for lighting on special occasions and even for the occasional rub-down.

Some amphorae may have contained what counted locally as luxury foods like dried fruit or fish sauce (the brown sauce of the Roman world). It is hard to believe that wine did not feature at all, and indeed we might expect wine to have been a major stimulus, especially at the British end of the trade. It is also possible that the amphorae themselves were only fillers for other, bulky goods, which did not need such solid containers and were presumably perishable. The *Life of St John the Almsgiver* tells, in the context of a miracle story, of a corn carrier which ended up in Britain, but this does not carry much conviction as regular traffic.[126] Is cheap wine travelling in skins or barrels a possibility and so did some of the amphorae contain the contemporary equivalent of chateau bottled?

While it is true that the known quantity of imported pottery could have travelled as a single shipload, it seems improbable that what we see is indeed the result of a one-off effort on the part of a particularly intrepid sea captain (Fig. 97). The amphorae fit into a context of what seem to have been regular sailings between

---

125.   Thomas, 'Tintagel papers' (1988c); P. Arthur, 'Amphorae and the Byzantine world', in J.-Y. Empereur and Y. Garlan (eds), *Recherches sur les amphores grecques*, Supplément 13, *Bulletin de Correspondence Hellénique* (1996), pp. 655–60; see also M. Fulford, 'Byzantium and Britain: a Mediterranean perspective on post-Roman Mediterranean imports in western Britain and Ireland', *Med. Arch.*, 33 (1989): 1–6; H. Wooding, Communication and Commerce (1996); Holbrook, 'Coastal Trade' (2001), pp. 149–58.

126.   The text is quoted in full in R. Penhallurick, *Tin in Antiquity* (1986), p. 245.

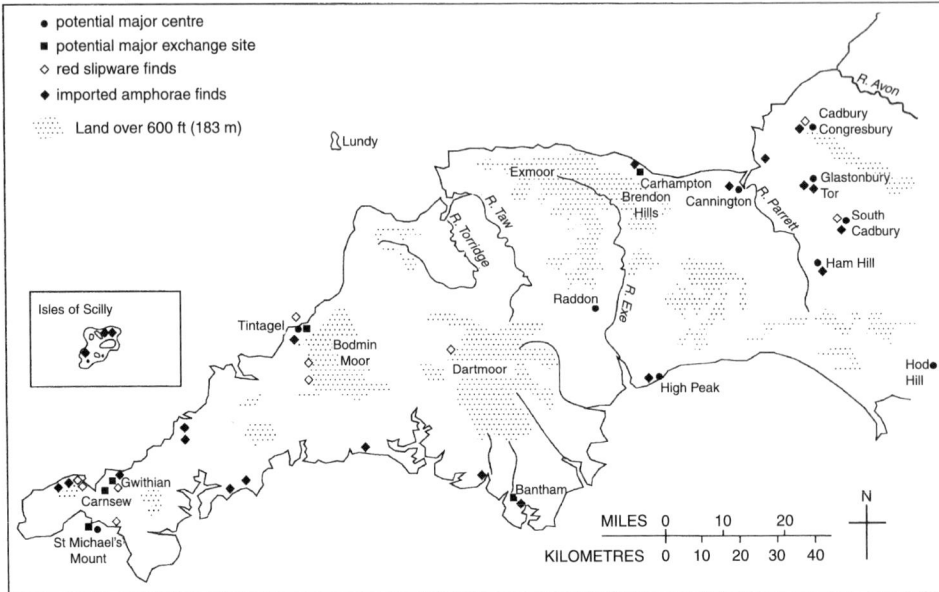

Figure 97 Major occupation sites, exchange sites and Mediterranean imported pottery

Ireland, northern Britain, the south-west, Brittany and ports like Rouen, Nantes and Bordeaux, for which there is an ample range of fifth- and sixth-century evidence. For sailing ships which depended upon the stars for navigation and whose captains probably preferred to maintain sight of land as much as possible, British/Irish waters, with their strong currents, tides and poor weather, were a difficult environment.[127] This suggests that sometimes, at least, the risks of the open channel crossing may have been reduced by using particularly suitable beaches with relatively short passages to the Continent as landing and departure points for the crossing. Bigbury Bay, where both Mothercombe and Bantham have produced evidence of exchange activity, is an obvious possibility.

The heart of the trading voyage would then have been a coastal trip around the peninsula, stopping at local outlets (and possibly further north up the Irish Sea, but the system here may have been different). It is also possible that somewhere – Bordeaux might be a good place to look – served as a transition point at which Mediterranean goods were transferred to fresh ships which took them north, although the lack of identifiably Frankish goods remains a problem. A direct link with the Mediterranean seems likely, and presumably it appeared in the *Life of St John the Almsgiver* set in Alexandria, and perhaps in a handful of other pieces, like the sixth-century Byzantine censor from Glastonbury and conceivably some, at least, of the Byzantine coins found at Exeter, Ilchester and in the rural area of the

---

127.   For full discussion of technical sailing problems, see P. Davis, 'Some navigational considerations of pre-medieval trade between Cornwall and north-west Europe', *Corn. Arch.*, 36 (1997): 129–37.

south-west (and elsewhere)[128] which may have arrived with the consumables (Fig. 98). The prominent churches in Constantinople dedicated to Ia and Madron[129] (Madonna) may link up with the south-western cults of the saints with these names, and represent a facet of the same link.

Whether oil principally, or wine also, stimulated the British end of the trade, tin, smelted and offered in ingot form, seems likely to have been the lure from the Mediterranean end, although the other traditional British goods – slaves, dogs and woollen clothes – need not be ruled out. The evidence for the working of tin streams in Late Antiquity is beginning to accumulate and includes the tinner's oak shovel from Boscarne[130] tin stream with a C14 date of between AD 635 and 1045. At Chun Castle amphorae sherds were associated with a crude furnace and an oval block of smelted tin, similar ingots came from Penwithick, and from Trethurgy (Fig. 99) which also produced a mould cover, matched by one from Pencair (Tregonning Hill); comparable evidence of tin working is also known from Killigrew, Halengy Down and Penhale.

The fascinating find by divers of 40 tin ingots (Fig. 99) on the landward side of the rocky reef at the mouth of the River Erme in Bigbury Bay, South Devon, may take us closer to the operation of the exchange, although a post-Roman date from the find remains conjectural.[131] The Erme may have been navigable up to a harbour at Oldaport in the post-Roman period but passage of the river mouth is difficult and the safest berth is the small, sandy Mothercombe beach, from which comes occupation debris and sherds of imported pottery. Some of the ingots were badly corroded, but

a   b

Figure 98 Copper forty nummia piece, (a) obverse, head of Justinian, Emperor of the Eastern (Byzantine) Roman Empire *c.* 527–538; (b) reverse, mint mark for Constantinople (C-N). Found at top of Foregate Street, Exeter, in 1810. Exeter City Museum (photo: author)

---

128. For censor, P. Leach and P. Ellis, 'The medieval precinct of Glastonbury Abbey – some new evidence', in M. Carver (ed.), *In Search of Cult* (1993), pp. 119–24; for coins, G. Boon, 'Byzantine and other exotic bronze coins from Exeter', in N. Holbrook and P. Bidwell, *Roman Finds from Exeter* (1991), pp. 38–45; Metcalf, 'Byzantine Coins' (1995), pp. 253–61. A Byzantine coin weight is also known from Somerset: Entwhistle, 'Coin Weight' (1994).
129. Dark, *Britain*, p. 163.
130. For what follows, see Penhallurick, *Tin*; A. Fox, 'Tin ingots from Bigbury Bay', *PDAS*, 53 (1995): 11–23. A tin ingot has also emerged among the finds from Castle Dore, although of uncertain date: see Fox, 'Tin ingots', p. 22.
131. *Ibid.*, pp. 21–2.

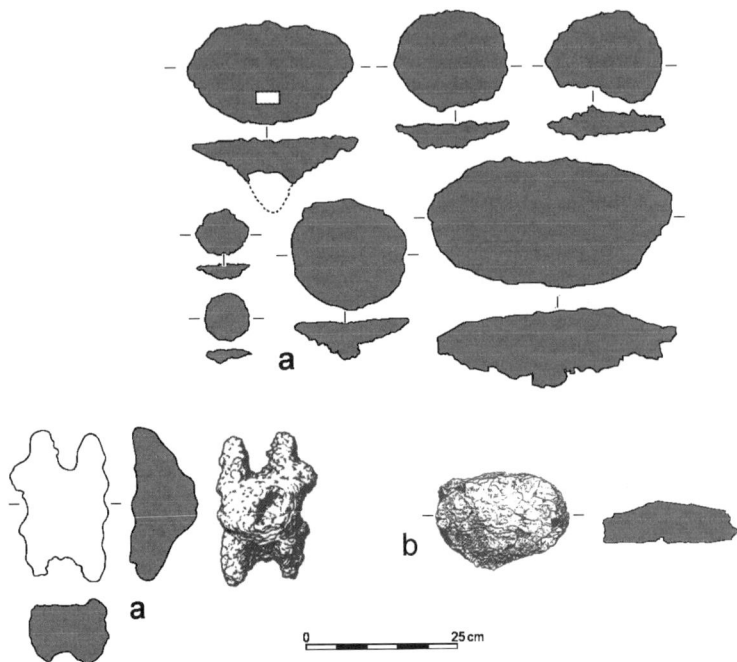

Figure 99 Tin ingots from (a) Bigbury Bay (after Fox 1995, Figs 5, 6), (b) Trethurgy (after Penhallurick 1986, Fig. 128)

clearly they differed considerably in size, weight and shape, suggesting a range of origins and little interest in uniformity. Most are plano-convex, or bun-shaped, and may be the direct result of tin from smelting ore dripping onto the bottom of a basic bowl furnace, but one large heavy ingot is rectangular and perhaps came from a stone mould. One H-shaped ingot invites comparison with the much larger but similarly shaped ingot found off St Mawes in 1812.[132] More directly comparable in size and shape are the four ingots found together at Prah Sands (Germoe), together with timbers which yielded a radiocarbon date of 666 ± 70.

Further east, the corresponding lure for traders was presumably the availability of lead from Mendip, either as such or possibly already made up into pewter, although there is no direct evidence of exchange in either pewter wares or blocks.[133] It may be added that the trade goods on offer further north, from Ireland, Wales and northern Britain, are rather obscure; Irish gold and Welsh copper are possibilities but evidence is lacking, and both could probably have been found more easily in the Mediterranean world. Perhaps tin was, from the Mediterranean point of view, the key for the whole enterprise. It is possible that, after the accession of Justinian I to the Eastern Empire in 527, his wars of reconquest stimulated an increased need in Constantinople for

---

132. N. Beagrie, 'The Romano-British pewter industry', *Britannia*, 20 (1989): 169–91.
133. Unless the group of three known pewter vessels from Goodrington Sands, Torbay, found at different times buried in the sand, was part of such an exchange. They seem to be of fourth-century date. Torquay Museum and Devon County Sites and Monuments Register.

metals, especially bronze, and that imperial encouragement supported the connection at least until his death in 565.

In the south-west, the finds seem to come from a mixture of high-status sites, like Tintagel and South Cadbury, local sites and landing beaches. It seems to have been at these beaches that the exchanges of ingot tin, foodstuffs and small temptations took place, conducted in vulgar Latin, under the eye of representatives of the elite group at the 'high site', to which most of the imported wares went. The coastal sites are rather mixed, but this may be the result of unevenness in our knowledge. Bantham Ham[134] had copious food waste suggesting heavy meat-eating, iron work (undated), quern stones and wool-processing equipment including spindle whorls worked from old bits of Samian ware. Over 500 imported amphorae sherds have been found (Fig. 100), and combs, (Fig. 101) which may also have been textile-working tools. The squarish enclosure on the site seems to have been part of earlier Roman (or earlier) occupation of an ordinary subsistence kind, but this need not completely rule out its later use by

Figure 100 Handle of late fourth–early fifth-century imported coarse ware amphora from beach at Bantham, Devon. Torquay Museum (photo: author)

---

134.   F. Griffith, 'Salvage observation at the Dark Age site at Bantham Ham, Thurlston, in 1982', *PDAS*, 44 (1986): 39–58; F. Griffith and S. Reed, 'Rescue recording at Bantham Ham, south Devon, in 1977', *PDAS*, 56 (1998): 109–32. The lack of evidence of bits of jewellery as part of the exchange is odd.

Figure 101 Composite bone combs of early medieval type from beach at Bantham, Devon. Torquay Museum (photo: author)

those who accumulated the rubbish associated with the imported pot, and whose use of the site may have run on as late as *c.* 700. There were also a number of open-air hearths. Bantham may even have served as a nodal point in the north-western end of the exchange network. Carhampton[135] had occupation debris and traces of metal-working. Gwithian had the remains of buildings.[136] The beach by St Enodoc[137] church has produced a piece of Bi ware and a broadly contemporary penannular brooch. These places could have been seasonally occupied trading sites; some of them, like Bantham, Gwithian and Carnsew, seem to have involved enclosures close to the beach, although these may have been living and trading quarters rather than coastal forts.[138]

Early reports mention human bone at Bantham and there are burials adjacent to the beach at Carnsew (one), Phillack, Carhampton and St Enodoc (now the parish churchyards), so graveyards may also have been a feature.[139] Probably one of the reasons why Tintagel has so large an accumulation of broken imported pottery is because its character enabled it to be both a 'high-status site' and a point of exchange, so that access and dispersal could be more tightly controlled; it would be equally true

---

135. C. Hollinrake and N. Hollinrake, 'Carhampton, Eastbury Farm ST01127', *PSANHS*, 140 (1997): 149–50; 1995 p. 177: the material need not imply that the site was monastic.

136. See C. Thomas, *Gwithian. Ten Years' Work* (1958).

137. Dark, *Britain*, p. 167, citing illustration in W. Page, *A History of the County of Cornwall* (1924), Part 5, illustration on p. 6.

138. Mount Batten remains another coastal possibility although excavations have not produced any imported wares; for general discussion, see B. Cunliffe, *Mountbatten. A Prehistoric and Roman Port* (1988).

139. Dark, *Britain*, p. 167. The Falmouth estuary is another area where work might be fruitful; a fragment of Phocean red slip has turned up at Trenogh, Penrhyn, near Falmouth (information: Henrietta Quinnell).

to suggest that Tintagel developed its pre-eminent position because a local leader, perhaps aware of the site's possible late Roman background, realized its considerable potential and emphasized its special position by the digging of the Great Ditch. St Michael's Mount had a similar position, and similar potential.

The contents of the amphorae, and any other goods, could have been dispersed through a series of personal encounters within each area which produced what we see as the rubbish of consumption at places of local importance like the hill-forts of Killibury or Chun, or substantial hamlets like Trethurgy and Gramblas. These may have been functioning as the significant or central places within landholding arrangements, which appear, at least in some places, as early, large estates. The tin seems to have been gathered on an individual basis and probably during the summer; some of it was used at the home settlement but we may not be far wrong in suggesting that local landlords took a proportion (although whether this took the form of rent, tax or was part of a local system of exchange is uncertain), some of which went to the area lord as his trading surplus. This is, of course, an idealized sketch, and must, at each actual time on each actual beach or centre, have involved an infinity of ramifying negotiations and side deals. Not all the goods which probably changed hands would have involved overseas connections. The pattern of stone bowls, mortars and weights suggest complex inter-area exchanges which could run eastwards and these may have been matched by perishable goods.

Whatever commodities actually changed hands, the social implications are likely to have been more significant than just economic. Participation in the exchanges could give access to the controlling group of those who intermarried, debated, decided and dined: the emphasis on oil and probably wine suggests civilized meals in the Late Antique manner, sufficiently refined to match Christian sensibilities. The very special glassware, much of it conical drinking vessels, imported from north Gaul during the fifth and sixth centuries, and continuing into the ninth century, appeared in some quantity at Cadbury Congresbury, and in much smaller quantities at Tintagel (where there was also a flagon of Spanish glass), Trethurgy and South Cadbury. It seems to represent the sophisticated service of wine, just as the red slipware bowls may do of food.[140] Exclusive parties are an excellent way of producing superior social networks, especially if, as here, they capture the nostalgia and affirmation of better, bygone days and perhaps offer a place to the women of the landed class. Other reciprocal exchanges may have been in place. More or less competent stonecutters must have been available to create the inscribed and decorated stones, and the inscribed slab from Tintagel which mentions an 'Artognou',[141] whatever its full significance (Fig. 102), looks like a trial piece and hints that such cutters were available at centres such as Tintagel, as may have been high-class bronze smiths and perhaps other craftsmen.

Such services would not come free, and the resulting web of obligation, even debt, can easily be imagined. Large numbers of labourers would have been needed to dig earthworks and shift stone and timber, and to produce, deliver and prepare the food to sustain all concerned. The leader at each centre must have had a troop of bully boys (or, in more dignified language, a 'retinue' or 'war-band') and they were probably

---

140.   Campbell, 'Imported goods', pp. 41–9, 197–9; for Tintagel flagon, see C. Morris, 'Tintagel', *Current Archaeology*, 159 (1998): 87–8.

141.   Photographs of this piece have appeared in the press, e.g. Morris, 'Tintagel', pp. 86–7, but it has not yet been fully published.

Figure 102 Slate from post-Roman context, Tintagel, carrying several inscriptions of which one features the personal name ARTOGNOU (photo: Paul Johnson, Dept. of Archaeology, University of Glasgow)

at least as concerned with harassing each other as they were fighting people who thought of themselves as Germanic. Finally, the opportunities offered by the Mediterranean link probably acted as an important catalyst to the emergence of the whole system. Energetic individuals could exploit the early generation of the traffic and the emotions it aroused to produce the social and political system which the finds suggest.

Christian establishments

Interestingly, a detectable pattern suggests that most of the chief hilltop centres were paired with a major Christian site, linking the new early sixth-century impetus represented by the monasteries with the new elite and authority structure. Cadbury Congresbury seems to have been associated with the probable monastery associated with Congar, the Tor with the possible centre at Glastonbury and South Cadbury perhaps with Sherborne, which was certainly some six miles away, but easily accessible along a ridgeway. We may suspect a similar pattern at St Michael's Mount, although the nature of the Christian presence is unclear. The linked site was not necessarily monastic. At Cannington the adjacent cemetery seems to have served the local community and the focal grave did not develop into a local cult centre. Tintagel was paired with what became the parish churchyard on the cliff beyond the headland, which has itself produced imported sherds, the granite pillar, cross-marked slates and several enigmatic mounds. The pattern may be detectable at some of the apparently lesser hilltop sites: Denbury, for example, is relatively close to East Ogwell parish churchyard which has an inscribed stone.

Something similar appears at the coastal sites too often to be entirely coincidental. Some, like Padstow, Looe and Perran Sands, were monastic sites and others, like Carhampton, Phillack and some of the sites on Scilly, seem to have begun as community burial grounds. This underlies the importance of the coastal sites in the balance of the system, and suggests, not that churchmen were managing the traffic, but that ecclesiastical and secular authorities were together embedded within it. The traded commodities point to links with the eastern Mediterranean and Frankish Gaul, where Christian institutions were firmly embedded. Contacts with Auxerre, Lyon and the Rhone Valley, all important Christian centres, and south to the highly influential monastery at Lérins, can be traced in the transmission of key texts and ideas involving men like Faustus and Riocatus in the fifth century and Columbanus in the sixth. Archaeological work is now turning up long-cist and earth-grave cemeteries like the British ones in western Gaul at sites such as Chinon, Civaux and across the Vendée.[142] The British inscriptions need not be direct borrowings from these areas, but rather witness to a common western late and post-Roman culture of which Britain was a part.

A small number of south-western inscribed stones, whether their dates turn out to be in the late fourth or fifth centuries (or for some, even later), carry inscriptions and symbols linking them with contemporary continental Christianity. The Carnsew stone with its REQUIEVIT . . . HIC TUMULO ('may he/she rest . . . this tomb') formulae can be linked, for example, with more elaborate memorials at Ecully in the Gaulish province of Lugdenensis I and several from Lyons itself[143] and inscriptions from further north at Amiens and Paris carry similar wording.[144] All these can be linked with a few inscriptions further north in Britain, like those from Kirkmadrine and Yarrow. The MEMOR (roughly 'memorial') formula, which appears on one of the Lewannick stones,[145] and at the Castell Dwyan 'Vortipor' stone, belongs with similar inscriptions from the central Mediterranean. An inscription from Lake Alban in central Italy, for example, reads AELIUS MARCUS QUI VIXIT ANN VIII IULI A VALERIA FILIO MEMORIA FECIT IIIX KI IUNIAS,[146] and of the relatively large number from Africa, one from Satafi reads MEMORIA IULIAE DONATE VIX ANIS III ('the memorial of Julia, she lived for three years'): noticeably, many of the African stones with MEMORIA are for children.[147] The word also appears at Tours as part of the inscription on St Martin's tomb. The British HIC IACET series[148] belongs within the same milieu, and the form occurs widely in Gaul, in the Lyons area, the Bordelais, Aquitaine and the Vendée.

Inscriptions with the longer formulae have shown themselves to be susceptible to analysis intended to elucidate word puzzles in the text, associated with the so-called

---

142.   For links with Gaul, see N. Chadwick, 'Intellectual contacts between Britain and Gaul in the fifth century', in N. Chadwick, *Studies in Early British History* (1954), pp. 189–263; for cemeteries, see J. Knight, 'The early Christian Latin inscriptions of Britain and Gaul: chronology and contexts', in N. Edwards and A. Lane (eds), *The Early Church in Wales and the West* (1992), pp. 45–50.

143.   E. Le Blant, *Inscriptiones Chrétiennes de la Gaul* (1856), pp. 38, 88–9, 151–2.

144.   *Ibid.*, pp. 282–3, 431–3.

145.   It is possible that *memoria* in the form MIMORI appears on the stone from Rialton Barton, St Columb Major, perhaps linked with BO[N]E to mean 'of good memory', a phrase common on Gaulish monuments. See Okasha, *Inscribed Stones*, pp. 220–3.

146.   E. Diehl, *Inscriptiones Latinae Christianae Veteres* (1925–31), pp. 245–8, no. 3600. It reads something like 'Aelius Marcus who lived eight years. Julia Valeria made this memorial for her son on the seventh day of the Kalends of June.'

147.   *Ibid.*, pp. 245–8, nos 3615, 3626.

148.   J. Knight, 'Seasoned with salt: insular-Gallic contacts in the early memorial stones and cross slabs', in K. Dark, *External Contacts and the Economy of Late Roman and Post-Roman Britain* (1996), p. 111; relevant here may also be the Roman pillar from St Lawrence's Church, Jersey, with an inscription of *c.* 600 (and later interlace carving), see C. Stevens *et al.*, 'The Roman pillar in St Lawrence's Church, Jersey: a stocktaking', *Bulletin de la Societé Jersaise*, 21 (3): 343–57 (1975); Davies *et al.*, *Inscriptions*, pp. 298–306.

'biblical style' of Latin composition.[149] The fourth-century mosaic inscriptions from Lullingstone show that such puzzles were part of British (and presumably generally western) late classical culture as they were of broadly contemporary Ireland, and, whatever the eventual verdict on the potential complexities of the inscriptions on stone, it seems that the sophistication (not to say, donnishness) of the Latin-educated elite in Late Antique Britain should not be underestimated.

A similar broad context is the frame for the symbols found on the south-western stones (Fig. 103). Two *chi-rho* crosses of Constantinian form are known on slabs at Phillack and Cape Cornwall (lost): if these are indeed genuine, they fit with similar *chi-rho*s from, for example, Pisa, Paris and Amiens.[150] The later, monogram, form appears, at St Just, Sourton, St Endellion and perhaps Southill: this seems to have been current in Gaul from about 400 to *c.* 550 or later, and is distributed up the western seaway and along the western Irish coast.[151] The inscribed stone from Madron church carries a complex cross form.[152] Plain crosses within circles appear on two of the Lundy stones, and a third Lundy stone perhaps has a circle which may once have held a painted symbol.[153] A similar cross form appears on the 'Vortipor' stone. The stone from Culborne Hill (Somerset)[154] has a circled cross but no known

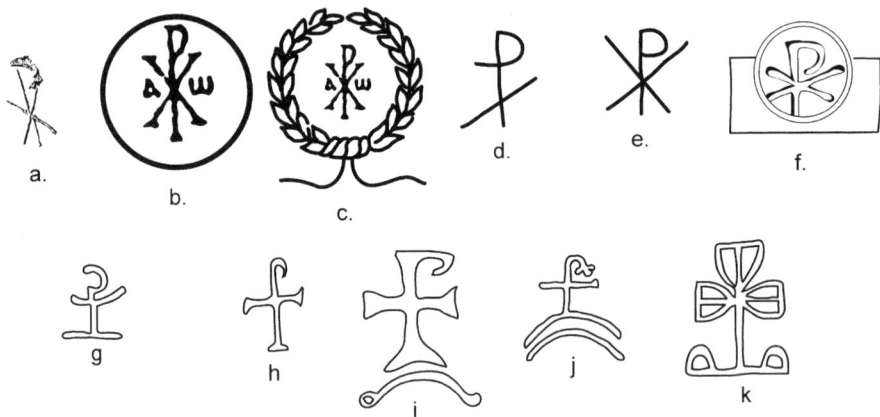

Figure 103 Chi-rho symbols from (a) Pisa (after Gabba 1977, Plate 30), (b) Amiens, (c) Paris (both after Le Blant 1856, pp. 431, 277), (d) Exeter, (e) Cape Cornwall, (f) Phillack, (g) Sourton, (h) St Just, (i) St Endellion, (j) South Hill, (k) Madron (not to scale)

149.   C. Thomas, *Christian Celts: Messages and Images* (1998); D. Howlett, *Celtic Latin Tradition of Biblical Style* (1994); M. Henig, 'The Lullingstone mosaic: art, religion and letters in a fourth-century villa', *Mosaic*, 24 (1997): 4–7; see also G. de la Bedoyere, 'Carausius unveiled', *Current Archaeology*, 153 (1997): 358. For a deconstructive argument, see McKee and McKee, 'Counter Arguments and Numerical Patterns' (2002), pp. 29–40.

150.   Le Blant, *Inscriptiones*, pp. 282–3, 431–3; C. Gabba, *Camposanto Monumentale di Pisa: Le Antichità* (1977), p. 69.

151.   A. Hamlin, 'A chi-rho-carved stone at Drumaqueran, Co. Antrim', *Ulster J. Archaeology*, 35 (1972): 22–8.

152.   Okasha, *Inscribed Stones*, pp. 16–18, 178–81.

153.   C. Thomas, *And Shall These Mute Stones Speak?* (1994), pp. 165–7

154.   Grinsell, *Exmoor*, (1970), p. 106.

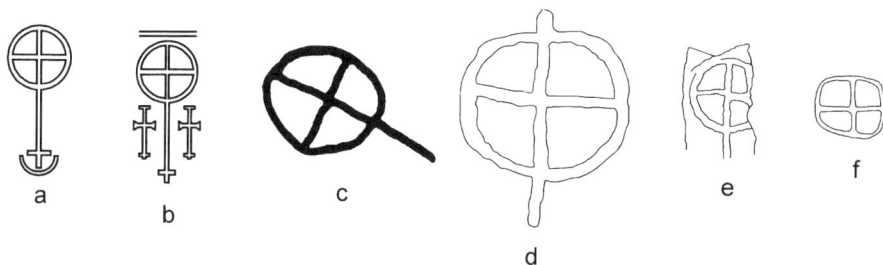

Figure 104 Symbols from (a) Newport (Pembs), (b) Llantrisant (Gwent) (both after Nash-Williams 1950, Fig. 5, nos 15, 16), (c) Culbone, (d) Abergwili, (e) Llanllyr (both after Nash-Williams 1950, Figs 106, 98, no. 124), (f) Beacon Hill, Lundy (not to scale)

inscriptions, and similar stones are known from a number of sites in Wales (Fig. 104). These are difficult to date, but there is no good reason to doubt that the sequence begins at the latest in the sixth century.[155]

The same probably applies to the Belstone stone[156] with its cross within a ring surmounting a stylized crucifixion, which has common elements with stones from Llantrisant (Gwent) and Newport (Pembroke), and more generally with some from northern Gaul, Ireland and southern Scotland (Fig. 105). The stone from East Linnacombe, near Sourton, Devon, with its design of cross forms and circles, belongs within a wide class of designs and may be broadly compared with that from Llanfihangel (Anglesey).[157] All of these cross forms link up in a broad way with the cross symbols found stamped on the red slipware bowls (Fig. 106), of which the most distinctive from the south-west are those from Tintagel[158] and that with a probably elongated, decorated cross from Cadbury Congresbury.[159]

Collectively, all this attests to a surprisingly cosmopolitan society in Late Antique western Britain and Wales, linked at a range of levels in a network running across Ireland, much of Gaul, the Atlantic façade and the Mediterranean as far, probably, as Constantinople. Within this society, from at least the fourth century, the monastic life was one of the big ideas, and may indeed have gathered some adherents in later fourth- to fifth-century eastern Britain, but, by c. 650, the western and northern areas of the peninsula, like the whole of Wales and Ireland, were studded with a network of monastic houses which had taken root within the space of a couple of generations.

Houses of monks need lay protection, especially in their vulnerable early years,

---

155.   V. Nash-Williams, *The Early Christian Monuments of Wales* (1950), pp. 17–27. See also J. Knight *et al.*, 'New finds of early Christian monuments', *Arch. Camb.*, 126 (1977): 60–73; T. Gwyn, 'An early monument in Caernarvonshire', *Arch. Camb.*, 141 (1992): 183, for groups of broadly similar sites in Wales. There is also a damaged cross head from Throwleigh, SX67808905, which has incised an equal-armed cross within a circle; M. Phillips, 'Supplementary notes on the ancient stone crosses of Devon (fifth paper)', *TDA*, 85 (1959): 90, Plate 24. Compare the undoubted early Christian inscribed stone from Sourton which also at some point acquired a cross head; Okasha, *Inscribed Stones*, pp. 260–3; compare also the decorated stones from East Linnacombe (see below), Sticklepath and Bude Lane, p. 58 note 107.

156.   Devon Sites and Monuments Register, Belstone, SX61939350.

157.   Nash-Williams, *Early Christian Monuments*, pp. 55, 138, 200, figs 5/16, 5/15, 20.

158.   Thomas, *Tintagel*, p. 94.

159.   Rahtz *et al.*, *Cadbury Congresbury*, p. 164.

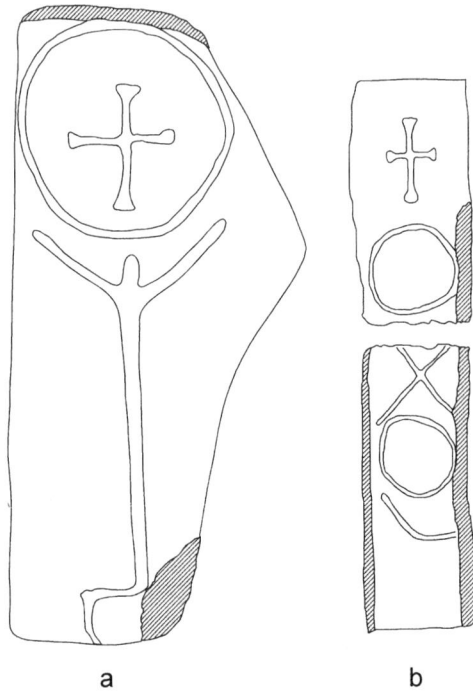

Figure 105 Decorated stones from (a) Belstone churchyard and (b) East Linnacombe, Devon (not to scale)

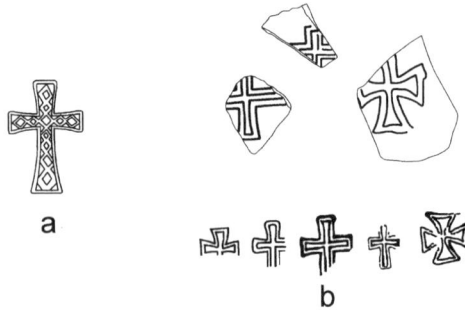

Figure 106 Cross forms on imported pottery from (a) Cadbury Congresbury, African red slipware (after Rahtz *et al.* 1992, Fig. 116) and (b) Tintagel Phocean red slipware (Thomas 1993, Fig. 75) (not to scale)

and they need provision, which meant a landed endowment. The first *Vita* of Samson says that, before he left south Wales, Samson and other members of his family turned their family estates into monastic houses, an approach to the religious life well recognized in the west generally, and which provides a possible model for some monastic origins in the south-west. Another possibility is the diversion of what had been imperial land to monastic support. The identification of these lands in the south-west is difficult, but the lead-producing Mendip area had originally been under direct imperial control, and in the first century was leased to a firm called the Novaec Company (*Novaec Societas*). Lead extraction continued until at least the fifth century, on what legal and administrative basis we do not know,[160] but it is worth mentioning that Sherborne claimed two early grants, from Ine *iuxta Predie* ('next to Priddy') and from Cenwalh a large estate of 25 hides *apud Menedip* ('at Mendip').[161] Clearly by *c.* 700 the West Saxon kings were in a position to grant Mendip lead concessions, and it is possible that Sherborne already had interests in the area. There may have been a Latin charter tradition in western Britain (and Ireland and Brittany) with its roots in the post-Roman world;[162] and William of Malmesbury indeed believed he had found at Glastonbury a document which recorded the gift of land to the Church in 601 by a man he described as *rex Domnoniae* ('King of Dumnonia'), whose name was no longer legible, but who used the British name (*Yneswitrin*) for Glastonbury. The date may be wrong, and it is not clear that the document William saw actually said the donor was a king, but possibly it might have recorded the kind of transaction which must have taken place.[163]

Land transactions of this kind suggest how the monastic movement in the south-west, as elsewhere, succeeded in creating a significant relationship with the elite class. This is also seen in the clear Christian character of some (but by no means all) of the inscribed stones, and in the long-distance exchange with its significant social and political dimensions. We sense a tacit social contract, which allowed relatively peaceful monastic acquisition and possession of important resources, but also involved a similar recognition of the family landed rights which we see most clearly in the inscribed stones. Sometimes the relationship may have been even closer. The title *princeps* which occurs on the Sourton stone (and also on that from Yarrow)[164] perhaps reflected the usage of the word in Ireland to mean the head of a church, a status not incompatible with marriage and children. Thaumaturgical glamour linked up with social opportunity, so that the negotiations which gave monastic leaders their resources could help to transform the position of local lords. Through the support they gave to monks, such lords could enhance their legitimacy; where earlier this had depended on local loyalties and local ceremonies at estate centres, it was now bound up with a universal Church and its impressive holy men.

Kings and kingdoms

The middle years of the sixth century seem to mark a number of interrelated changes, perhaps sharpened and complicated by the poor environmental effects of volcanic activity, and the great bubonic-type plague which affected the eastern and

160. H. Elkington, 'The Mendip lead industry', in Brannigan and Fowler, *The Roman West Country* (1976), pp. 183–97. For details of the finds of Mendip lead pigs see Frere *et al.*, *Roman Inscriptions* (1990), pp. 38–50.
161. S228; H. Finberg, *Early Christian Charters of Wessex* (1964), pp. 113, 116.
162. W. Davies, 'The Latin charter tradition in western Britain, Brittany and Ireland in the early medieval period', in D. Whitelock, R. McKetterick and D. Dumville (eds), *Ireland in Early Medieval Europe* (1982), pp. 258–80.
163. H. Finberg, 'Ynyswitrin', in *Lucerna* (1964), pp. 83–94.
164. RCHMS, *The County of Selkirk* (1957), p. 112; D. Petts, 'Burial and gender in late and sub-Roman Britain', in C. Forcey, J. Hawthorne and R. Witcher (eds), *Proceedings of the Seventh Annual Theoretical Roman Archaeology Conference, Nottingham, 1997* (1998), pp. 112–24.

western worlds in the 540s.[165] The death of Justinian in 565 and the run-down in the reconquest programme may be an important reason why the exchange link with the eastern Mediterranean seems to have petered out by *c.* 570 at the latest.[166] We sense that the political importance of South Cadbury, Cadbury Congresbury and Tintagel faded at around the same time (although this need not mean that they were entirely deserted).

The rulers, whom Gildas was able to list (and berate), may be integral to these changes, which hint at consolidations of power in western Britain that gelled into what were to become the early medieval kingdoms of the region, functioning more or less like every other contemporary imperial successor western kingdom, but on a much smaller scale. Gildas here includes the famous reference to 'Constantine the tyrant whelp of the filthy lioness of Dumnonia', and, as Jackson put it, in Gildas' eyes, 'Constantine was conspicuous for perjury, sacrilege, the murder of two boy princes, adultery and sodomy',[167] so evidently his relationship with the monastic community was strained. We know nothing of any predecessors Constantine may have had, or of any successors until the ruler called Gereint surfaces in the record around 700.

The scatter of pre-600 material of 'Germanic' character found in the south-west does not, as far as the difficult sources take us, suggest any kind of local substantial central authority which saw itself as in any sense immigrant or 'German'. When cultural pressures encouraged the emergence of such authorities, perhaps not long before 600, it happened in the Hampshire basin and the Isle of Wight, whose rulers saw themselves as 'Jutes', and in the upper Thames Valley. These were members of the group of the king-based proto-states,[168] whose chief men were interested in building a unified, insular cultural identity based on the use of material culture. The Hampshire group may possibly have been sufficiently numerous – although this is contentious – to have included enough women and children to begin the linguistic change from British to Old English. By *c.* 600 they may have established themselves within an area defined on the north and west by a series of substantial earthworks, like Wansdyke and Bokerley Dyke, the complex sequences of which may represent various frontiers negotiated during the later fifth to sixth centuries.

The upper Thames community[169] turned out to be vulnerable to attack from Midland rulers making their way in the same processes of kingdom consolidation, and as an element in this, in 635 Cynegils was baptized by Birinus at Dorchester-on-Thames, which became the bishop's seat. This rise in the power of Mercia, which blocked northern expansion on the part of the Germanic community in the upper Thames Valley, coincided with the beginning of the western expansion of this community, which came to adopt the name West Saxon; the name expresses the political

165.   For volcanic activity, see p. 247; for bubonic plagues, see, for example, A. Cameron, *The Mediterranean World in Late Antiquity AD 395–600* (1993), pp. 111, 123–4.

166.   For full account, see Campbell, 'Imported goods'; see also C. Thomas, ' "Galuci Nantae de Galliarum Provinciis." A sixth/seventh-century trade with Gaul reconsidered', *Med. Arch.*, 34 (1990): 1–26; see also J. Maddicott, 'Trade, industry and the wealth of King Alfred', *Past and Present*, 123 (1989): 3–51. See p. 2.

167.   M. Winterbottom, *Gildas. The Ruin of Britain and Other Works* (1978), pp. 29–30; K. Jackson, 'Varia: II. Gildas and the names of the British princes', *Cam. Med. Celtic St.*, 3 (1982): 31.

168.   H. Geake, *The Use of Grave-goods in Conversion-period England c. 600-c. 850* (1997).

169.   For this and what follows, see B. Yorke, *Wessex in the Early Middle Ages* (1995), pp. 52–60.

realities of the seventh century and was probably a useful way of creating a kind of unity among what had been disparate groups. By the mid-sixth century, Cenwalh, followed by Centwine, succeeded in organizing a power base in Wiltshire and west Hampshire with its bishopric at Winchester (*c.* 661). Cenwalh was claimed as a benefactor of Sherborne, and Centwine granted land both to Glastonbury and to Malmesbury, suggesting that the British landed elites who had sustained the political units based on the major Somerset hill-forts had recognized the West Saxon rulers by the mid-seventh century, or had been overwhelmed by them.

The sequence of events which brought western Dorset and the whole of Devon under the control of Wessex are still extremely obscure. Older efforts[170] to produce an historical reconstruction based on annals recording West Saxon victories in the Anglo-Saxon Chronicle are now regarded as unacceptable, given the lack of real, early, information in the Chronicle.[171] It is possible that a successive breaching of the earthworks at Bokerley Dyke, Coombs Ditch and Battery Banks represents a successful West Saxon sweep through Dorset, which had been completed by the end of the seventh century. The *Life of St Boniface*[172] implies that Exeter was under West Saxon control by about 680, and Cenwalh may indeed have founded the minster there, as the later traditions of the house claimed.[173] How and when the very large area which includes Dartmoor and the fertile lands to its south and north came into West Saxon hands cannot be traced; the most that can be said is that, when Ine came to the throne of Wessex in 688, the south-western British kingdom was still a major force, and may well have included substantial areas of western Devon.

For Ine and his West Saxon contemporaries, the south-western kingdom represented the principal area of potential expansion, and this is the context for Bishop Aldhelm's correspondence,[174] pointing out the British 'errors' in the calculation of the date of Easter and the shape of the tonsure, addressed to King Gereint and his bishops, probably soon after 710. The letter suggests that Gereint, Ine's contemporary and defeated opponent in *c.* 710, had normal early medieval powers much the same as Ine's own, and indeed the south-west British had a military success *c.* 730 at an unidentified place called *Hehil*. What does seem to be clear is that by *c.* 700 in both Wessex and Cornwall a conjunction of kings and churchmen had produced a more sharply stratified society in which 'Germanness' and probably 'British Romanness' were reduced to origin myths, to be made use of by emerging kingdoms.

Ine's kingdom was clearly culturally extremely mixed. His Laws show that Wessex included those who identified themselves (or were identified by others) as British (or Welsh) in which the Welsh counted for less in legal matters but in other respects led normal lives, including the holding of land. Here we see Ine acting as the king of a self-consciously sovereign state, both in the creation of higher justice through the

---

170. Notably by W. Hoskins, *The Westward Expansion of Wessex* (1960).

171. D. Dumville, 'The Anglican collection of royal genealogies and regnal lists', *Anglo-Saxon England*, 5 (1976): 23–50; 'Kingship, genealogies and regnal lists', in P. Sawyer and I. Wood (eds), *Early Medieval Kingship* (1977), pp. 72–104; 'The West Saxon genealogical regnal list and the chronology of early Wessex', *Peritia*, 4 (1985): 21–66.

172. W. Levison (ed.), *Vitae Sancti Bonifatii, MGH Scriptores Rerum Germanicarum* (1905), Ch. 1, trans. in C. Talbot, *The Anglo-Saxon Missionaries in Germany* (1954), p. 28.

173. Pearce, *Early Church*, esp. pp. 14–15.

174. M. Lapidge and M. Herren, *Aldhelm, the Prose Works* (1979), pp. 155–60.

issuing of dooms, and in the vision to produce a collective system within which people of different origins could live together. Probably some substantial British-speaking communities survived, and one may appear in the Wareham/Purbeck area, where the large seventh-century cemetery at Ulwell (Swanage)[175] in the isle of Purbeck south-west of Wareham was in use throughout the seventh century, but belongs within the group of findless, east–west orientated row-organized burial grounds previously discussed; the Wareham inscribed stones may belong in a similar context, and remind us that across the peninsula such cemeteries were continuing to be used by many communities.

It is possible that one reason why we have no narrative of any seventh-century conversion of what was becoming Wessex is because most of the inhabitants were already in some sense Christians. It is not inconceivable that the British churchmen Augustine met around 600 included some from the south-west as well as (presumably) Wales and the south-west Midlands, and the fact that we know about this meeting at all hints that Bede had ironed out his story much of whatever he knew about a surviving post-Roman Church east of the Wye/Severn line. Very few cemeteries with 'pagan' material goods are known from west Dorset or east Devon, suggesting that people who thought of themselves as German were nevertheless willing to be buried in the local cemeteries.[176] Society in the area may have been open to the firmly Christian influences radiating from the ministers at their elite level, and these moved formal conversion in the countryside a step further.

By *c.* 700 the time was ripe for the statesman-like vision which informed Ine's dealings with the Church, as it had his predecessors like Cenwalh and Centwine, and would do his successors in the eighth century. Astute kings like Ine could mobilize the possibilities for legitimizing central authority, which church institutions offered through the new kind of educated elite and the opportunities for control and stability in the long term. In practice, this meant supporting whatever Christian institutions already existed in the newly absorbed lands, as Centwine and then Ine did at Glastonbury (if, indeed, the Christian presence predated them) and Cenwalh may have done at Exeter. Cenwalh may also have granted land to Sherborne, and when in 705 the kingdom of the West Saxons was big and secure enough to need a second, western bishopric, Sherborne was chosen as its seat, and Aldhelm was appointed.

The same kings were concerned in the direct funding of, and the general encouragement given to, the minster churches which gradually came to stud the landscape, and to occupy an important role in relation to the royal centres at which dues were collected and justice dispensed, and in the generation of royal and saintly spectacle. Ine's sister Cuthburga founded the important minster at Wimborne, Dorset, and significant kinship networks emerge in the positions held by a family like that of Lul, some of whose members were associated with Boniface in the German mission, and one of whom, Cyneheard, became Bishop of Winchester in 756.[177] The minsters provided new opportunities for ambitious families, and careers for able high-born women, interwoven with the royal authority, in which old pagan

175.   P. Cox, 'A seventh-century inhumation cemetery at Shepherd's Farm, Ulwell, near Swanage, Dorset', *PDNHAS*, 110 (1988): 37–41.
176.   For an analysis of the cemeteries, see L. Quensel von Kalben, 'The British Church and the emergence of the Anglo-Saxon kingdoms', *Anglo-Saxon Studies in Archaeology and History*, 10 (1999): 89–97.
177.   Yorke, *Wessex*, p. 187.

allegiances and the places and practices associated with them were gradually rendered obsolete.

New Christian cult centres, with their permanent substantial communities, buildings and endowments, fostered a faith which offered notions of moral struggle, obedience and a progressive view of time and history as normative. The Church legitimized social inequality as God-given, and offered David as the model of a king transcendently different from other men in a style very helpful to royal dynasties, but it also preached that goodness and salvation were open to all, a comforting way to relieve and mask social tension: Ine's Laws assume that all children would be baptized and that even slaves would not work on a Sunday.[178] The Christian monopoly gave a model for the state which drew together fruitful ideas of the Christian king, the imperial successor, and the royal family as possessors of the land. The tradition notion of the royal pedigree was harnessed to domesticate the old gods as royal ancestors, creating the sense of historical depth, and ancient inheritance, and fostering the sense of cultural unity. We can see why both Caedwalla and Ine wished to make the pilgrimage to Rome, and both seem to have died there.[179]

As any capable soverign authority must, the kings of the West Saxons were able to levy taxes, grant land and sustain warfare, all interlinked activities. The landed possessions of the dynasty, viewed broadly as personal property, were clearly extensive as, for example, the long list of evidently old royal estates in the Somerset Domesday record shows and presumably chiefly represented appropriation through conquest. They enabled men like Ine to endow minster churches, to reward followers and to sustain the royal household in its movements from one royal estate to another, there consuming the food renders due to the king, a necessary practice which meant that a central 'capital' did not develop until much later. Whether all free men were obliged to perform military service (some as support corps rather than as fighters), or whether this obligation only applied to those specially commended to the king, remains a matter of debate.[180] The West Saxon army seems to have been bound up with the shire organization which emerged in the seventh century and which presumably represents the reorganization of earlier units into blocks of a suitable size to field an army and to be commanded and governed by an ealdorman who owed his authority to the king.

By Ine's time, Wessex had effectively solidified into one principal kingdom of Anglo-Saxon England, together with Mercia, East Anglia, Northumbria and Kent. It was based firmly on its four shires of Hampshire, Wiltshire, Dorset and Somerset, and possessed of at least the eastern part of Devon. We know of no named successors to Gereint in the western part of the peninsula, but, as we shall shortly see, the south-western British kingdom remained a power to be reckoned with, and an opportunity for West Saxon kings, throughout the eighth and ninth centuries.

---

178.   *Ibid.*, p. 190.
179.   *Ibid.*, p. 98.
180.   *Ibid.*, p. 91.

6 Shifting frontiers

Introduction

As we saw in the previous chapter, the later sixth century seems to have seen the amalgamation and consolidation of earlier political structures. Eventually, these changes created what became visible as the kingdoms of the south-western British and the West Saxons. The record is too poor to allow us to trace the process in detail, particularly in the west, but probably mutual hostility helped both kingdoms to develop their powers. By 700, the south-western British were ruled by figures powerful enough to emerge into the record, Gereint in the west, and Ine in Wessex.

The first part of this chapter considers the political relationships between the two kingdoms, and then traces the administrative arrangements through which Cornwall was absorbed into Wessex. The next section analyses the changes in the flow of goods. The shift in the late sixth century away from the Mediterranean towards Gaul may well have helped Gereint's immediate predecessors to consolidate their power, and was certainly important to Ine and his successors.

The chapter then assesses social changes, the earlier Viking attacks and the developing relationship of Church and state in Wessex. The relationship between minster churches, hundreds and royal estates is discussed, and the significance of the boroughs.

A substantial part of this chapter considers a broad range of changes in the landscape, which created in many areas new patterns of estates, settlements, fields and homes. Changes in the organization of the Church and the Christian presence matched those in the landscape. The chapter continues with a discussion of the emergence of the parish network, and the significance attached to saints and their symbols. It concludes with an assessment of the broader impact of the changes.

Wessex and Cornwall

The warfare between Wessex and the west British in 710 seems to have ended in some success for the West Saxons. Around the same time, Gereint seems to have given 5 hides of the Tamar to Sherborne, and Ine was in a position to grant land to Glastonbury also on the west side of the river. It seems that Wessex had effectively managed to acquire territory within eastern Cornwall, although this was cast in the form of grants to churches probably recognized to have had British pasts, which was perhaps intended to soften the stark realities of power.

However, *Annales Cambriae* record a British victory in 722 at 'Hehil apud

Cornuenses', evidently a Cornish river estuary.[1] Cuthred of Wessex is said in the *Anglo-Saxon Chronicle* to have fought against 'the Welsh', presumably the south-west British, in 743 and 753, and the same source tells us that Cynewulf (757–786) was frequently engaged against the Welsh. In one of his charters, dated around 770, he gave land on the River Wellow in Somerset to St Andrew for the minster at Wells 'in expiation of my sins, and also, which is sad to say, on account of any vexation of our enemies, the Cornish people'.[2] Quite what this means it is difficult to say, but Cynewulf may be alluding to a deplorable payment which he had had to make to the Cornish in order to buy them off. It seems reasonably clear that the eighth century saw much fighting between the two kingdoms in which the south-west British were weakened but not finally defeated.

By whom, and on the basis of what organization of men and material, the British were led during these wars we do not know. Even allowing for the lopsided account presented in the English sources, the trend of events is clear. By 802, Egbert, a descendant in the fourth generation from Ine's brother Ingild, achieved power in Wessex, and in 815 he invaded Cornwall and harried it, we are told, from end to end. In 825 the men of Devon, by now clearly regarded as a normal West Saxon shire, repulsed a Cornish raid at *Gafulford*, perhaps Galford in Lewtrenchard, and finally, in 838 the Cornish made common cause with a Danish army but were defeated by Egbert on Hingston Down near Launceston. This seems to have been the final defeat: after 838 there are no further reliable references suggesting Cornish rulers or independent Cornish action.[3]

The administration of Cornwall *c.* 800–1086

Alfred's will of *c.* 881 and the Domesday record show the very substantial Cornish estates which accrued to the West Saxon kings, providing both new direct wealth and opportunities for creating the various landholding arrangements which we see as grants to royal officials during the tenth century (Fig. 107). Alfred's will[4] bequeathed to Edward, his elder son, the lands in *Tricorscire*, 'Trigg-shire', which were *aet Straetneat*, and to his younger son, Æthelweard, *Liwtune* (Lifton) 'and all the lands belonging to it, that is all I have among the West Welsh except Trigg'. *Straetneat* is usually taken to be Stratton in north-west Cornwall, and Trigg is the Cornish hundred of Trigg, presumably all three divisions of it, which is called Stratton in the Exeter Domesday. In 1086,[5] the Crown still held Kilkhampton, Brisland, St Kew and Trevalga in Stratton, and the hundred manor of Stratton was held by the Count of Mortain:

1.   *Annales Cambriae* s.a. 722.
2.   S262 and B. Yorke, *Wessex in the Early Middle Ages* (1995), p. 67.
3.   *Annales Cambriae* s.a. 875 (perhaps to be corrected to a few years earlier) note a Dumgarth king of the West Welsh who was drowned, who has sometimes been identified with the man whose name *Doniert* is inscribed on a late eighth/earlier ninth-century cross fragment near Redgate, Cornwall, but he was probably a ruler in south-west Wales. The Hywel, King of the West Welsh, who, with other Welsh kings, submitted to Athelstan at Eamont Bridge in 927, probably also ruled in this area. The recent rereading of the Penzance cross shaft rules out reference to 'King Riocatus'; see C. Thomas, *Christian Celts: Messages and Images* (1998), pp. 186–92.
4.   S. Keynes and M. Lapidge (eds), *Alfred the Great: Asser's Life of King Alfred and Other Contemporary Sources* (1983), pp. 173–8, 313–26.
5.   C. Thorn and F. Thorn, *Domesday Book: Cornwall* (1979), under relevant landholders.

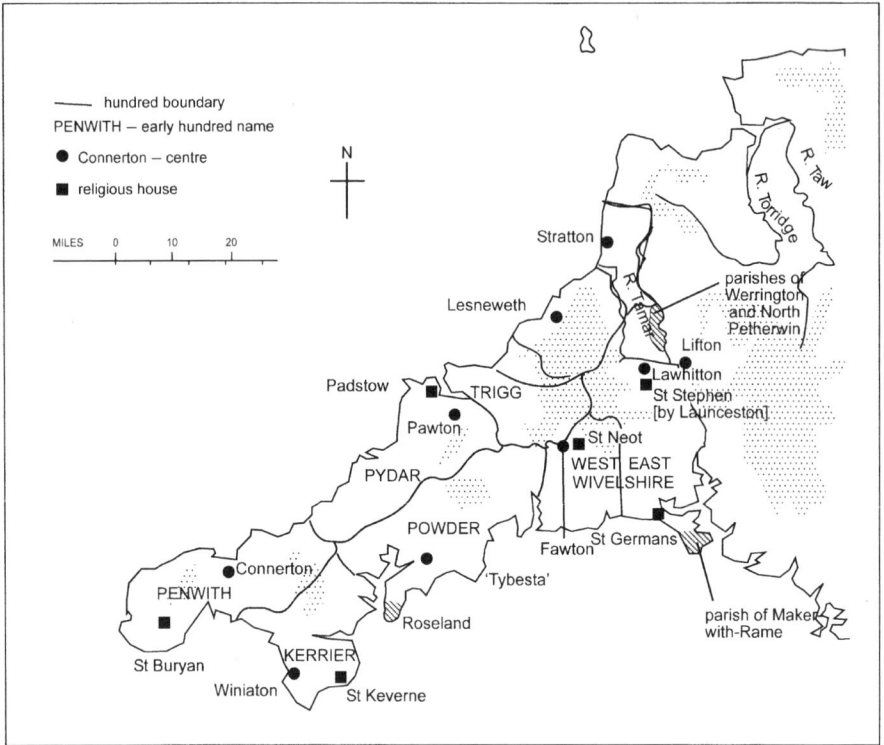

Figure 107 Administrative framework in Cornwall (Trigg, Lesneweth and Stratton were earlier all within Trigg)

probably these lands had already been in royal hands by 880, administered and exploited from Stratton itself.

Lifton, in Devon, is likely to have been the comparable centre for the royal estates in East and West Wivelshire. This pair of hundreds seems to be named from a single region whose name is not evidently Celtic. In the Exeter Domesday the two hundreds are called respectively *Rielton* (Rillaton) and *Fawiton* (Fawton). In all these place-names, the *ton* element is conspicuous and these arrangements probably originated soon after 838. In 1086, the king had Callington in Rillaton but the two hundred manors, like much else, were in the hands of the Count of Mortain. The king also had Werrington, which by 1086 apparently embraced the parishes of North Petherwin and Werrington west of the Tamar and St Giles in the Heath east of the river, so forming the conspicuous western bulge of the Devon/Cornwall county boundary which lasted until 1966 when the west Tamar parishes were finally transferred to Cornwall. By the eleventh century, the hundred boundary followed the river, so the estate was divided between Stratton and (Black) Torrington, but arrangements in Egbert's day were presumably simpler.

Further west, the place-names below the social level of major royal centres suggest that there was little or no West Saxon settlement. In 1086, the king held the substantial estates of Connerton, the hundred manor of Connerton/Penwith hundred, and Winiaton (or Winnington), that of Winiaton/Kerrier hundred, which presumably served as royal administrative centres for the collection of dues. In 1086, Pawton, the hundred manor of Pawton/Pydar, was held by the Bishop of Exeter, and Tibeston, that of Tibeston/Powder, by the Count of Mortain. It would be extremely interesting to know what these places were like before the West Saxon conquest. Were they existing major estates from which the regional government was exercised? Or were they separate holdings, then grouped together to make the kind of centre the West Saxon rulers needed? The name 'Winiaton' has an English suffix (-ton) added to an existing Celtic name which appears also in the nearby headland of Pedngwinian. The Celtic name possibly referred to an earlier territory or estate, which may have embraced a substantial part of the south-western Lizard peninsula.[6] Winiaton would then have been created to act as the administrative centre for the estate and the hundred. Connerton[7] may embrace an earlier name for the Red River plus *tun*: its site was centred on Gwithian, with its claim to have been a small *emporium*, but the extent of its attached estate is difficult to judge.[8]

Doubts, real or contrived, about the orthodoxy of south-west British church practices had featured largely in Aldhelm's official correspondence with Gereint of Cornwall,[9] and we might expect that the West Saxon conquest would have been followed by the stripping of land from Cornish churches either to be given to eastern churches or to be retained in royal (or other lay) hands. Some of the major estates of 1086 were immediately adjacent, or very close, to land in religious hands, as Winiaton was to St Keverne's, and Fawton[10] to St Neot's. Egbert seems to have made two large grants to Sherborne, of 12 hides at *Kelk* (Kilkhampton) and 18 at *Ros* and *Maker* (Roseland and Maker) to the community, and *Polltun* (Pawton), *Caellwic*[11] and *Landwithan* (Lawhitton) to the bishop. Sherborne may itself have been a British monastery in origin, although it is unlikely that this would have been much consolation to the Cornish whose lands it acquired. Like Winiaton and Fawton, Pawton in St Breock, situated between Bodmin and Padstow, both in the hands of St Petroc's, lay close to a major religious house, and, less convincingly, Finberg argued that *Landwithan* (Lawhitton) and Werrington divided between them an existing

---

6.   See O. Padel, 'Predannack or Pradnick, in Mullion', *Cornish Studies*, 15 (1987): 11–14.

7.   O. Padel, *A Popular Dictionary of Cornish Place-names* (1988), pp. 71–2.

8.   The ninth/tenth-century cross not now in its original position, but always on Connor Downs, may relate to this estate, perhaps to its boundaries; see A. Langdon, *Old Cornish Crosses* (1988), pp. 306–8.

9.   A. Haddon and W. Stubbs, *Councils and Ecclesiastical Documents* (1869–71), Vol. 3, pp. 268–73.

10. Interestingly, near Fawton there is the place-name 'Lestow' (of uncertain age), now a farm, at SX16606750, and also a 'round' earthwork at SX17106775.

11. In spite of many efforts, *Caellwic* has not been satisfactorily identified. O. Padel, 'Kelli Wic in Cornwall', in H. Miles *et al.*, 'Excavations at Killibury hill-fort, Egloshayle 1975–6', *Corn. Arch.*, 16 (1977): 115–19, suggests that the two most plausible suggestions for the Anglo-Saxon manor are Callington and Kelly in Egloshayle. Callington is not near a pre-Saxon religious house, but Kelly, like Fawton, Pawton, Winnington and Lawhitton, is close to St Kew, and the parishes of Egloshayle and St Kew are neighbours. The *Caellwic* of Anglo-Saxon sources is probably, but not definitely, the same as the *Kelli Wic* of *Culhwch and Olwen* and the Welsh Triads, and this site is probably to be identified with the hill-fort at Killibury ('fort at Kelly'), which sits on the St Kew/Egloshayle parish boundary and produced two sherds of Bi ware (Miles *et al.*, 'Excavations at Killibury hill-fort', p. 115): Killibury was perhaps the centre of a large post-Roman estate with its religious focus at the church site of Egloshayle.

ecclesiastical estate subsequently represented by North and South Petherwin.[12] *Landwithan* was also very close to land held by St Stephen-by-Launceston.

Nevertheless, the long run of estates held in 1086 by St Petroc's and the substantial list of small houses which still had endowments, including St Stephen's, suggests that in the ninth, and later in the tenth, century local churches were allowed to hold on to at least some of what they had, and charter evidence suggests that the major depredations of the Cornish church was in the tenth century. There may have been a policy in the early ninth century of linking royal administrative and hundred centres with major religious houses, but we do not know if, or to what extent, this involved seizing ecclesiastical land, or if it were largely a continuation of the previous governmental system.

A significant hint of the nature of both the conquest and the religious settlement is provided by the profession of obedience to Ceolnoth, Archbishop of Canterbury (833–870) made by Kenstec 'bishop elect for the Cornish people in the monastery, which is called in the British language Dinurrin'[13] sometime in the mid-ninth century. Kenstec's succession as Bishop of the Cornish was apparently sufficiently routine to make it desirable that he should acknowledge that his see was now subordinate to the province and metropolitan of Canterbury. In other words, while a man with a British name was allowed to succeed to the see, it was being made clear that the Cornish church was henceforward incorporated into the Anglo-Saxon hierarchy. Kenstec's episcopal seat was in a monastery, as many others had been and were to be in southern England, but we do not know how the bishop's responsibilities related to those of the community there. The location of *Dinurrin* remains unsolved but likely candidates are St Petroc's at Padstow (on the assumption that it had not yet shifted to Bodmin) or St Germans, later chosen as the bishop's seat. The implication is that, for some decades, routine ecclesiastical affairs among the Cornish continued much as they always had.

There seems no reason to doubt that, during Egbert's reign, Cornwall was treated like a conquered kingdom, with some rough exploitation, and a substantial dispossession of local landholders, including presumably lands held by the ruling family. A West Saxon determination to hold the key estates in each hundred is likely

---

12.   H. Finberg argued that *Polltun* (Pawton in St Breock) 'lay midway between Bodmin and Padstow, the two great centres of the cult of St Petroc, whose monks had until then dominated a vast territory on both sides of the Camel' ('The making of a boundary', in Lucerna (1964), p. 164), and that therefore Pawton was land transferred from the Cornish church to a West Saxon one. This may be true, but there seems to be no evidence, only inference drawn from topography. Finberg argued that as *Landwithan* (Lawhitton) included North Petherwin, the two Petherwins represented a Cornish ecclesiastical estate belonging to the church of St Paternus which was appropriated and divided between the king and the bishop. Presumably a large estate known as Petherwin, which took its name from St Paternus to whom both parish churches are dedicated (Padel, *Dictionary*, pp. 137–8), originally embraced a substantial block of land immediately west of that held by St Stephen's at later Launceston, but no real evidence survives of a landholding religious house dedicated to Paternus, as opposed to a local cult of the saint, and the nature of the putative estate remains unclear. W. Picken ('Cornish place-names and fiefs in a twelfth-century charter', *Cornish Studies*, 13 (1986a): 55–61) suggests that the church of *Lanwittonia* (Lawhitton) may have been 'a manorial foundation of the eleventh century' (p. 57) and adds that the old manorial capital must have been at the place recorded as *Yolde Lawhitta* in a manor rental of 1538, now Oldwit (p. 57).

13.   See refs and discussion in M. O'Donovan, 'An interim revision of the episcopal dates for the province of Canterbury 850–950: Part I', *Anglo-Saxon England*, 1 (1972), esp. pp. 34–5.

and this enabled the king to get a grip on existing local administration and to enforce West Saxon taxation along the hidage lines recorded in Domesday, together with the other impositions (including presumably Danegeld in due course), quite apart from the renders levied from estates in royal possession.

It is also clear that there was as yet no notion of the Tamar as a major boundary. Finberg calculated that in the southern part of East Wivelshire English names represent 40 per cent, in the north 45 per cent and in the centre 65 per cent overall, rising to over 80 per cent in the parishes of St Mellion, St Dominick, Calstock and Stoke Climsland, while throughout the hundred of Stratton (the eastern division of Trigg) the proportion is over 90 per cent,[14] and Padel makes the same points.[15] English influence, in other words, was as strong here (whether by settlement or culture) as throughout much of west and north Devon, and the language frontier seems to have been well west of the Tamar. As we have seen, west Tamar lands were administered from Lifton and the estate of Werrington probably spanned the river: there was in *c.* 840 evidently no reason why English culture should not continue on down the peninsula, or why the Tamar should be of any greater importance than the Exe or the Dart had been. Together with the south-eastern English kingdoms, to whose resources Egbert also had access, it is possible that the opportunities offered by the Cornish lands was one of the reasons why the ninth-century West Saxon dynasty was stronger and more stable than its predecessors and contemporaries.

Putting this into the context of what continuing life among the Cornish was like is difficult, and involves eschewing anachronistic and emotional concepts of Celtic nationalism. West of Stratton/Wivelshire, Cornish place-names survived (or continued to be formed, depending on the dates of some place-name elements), and English names are correspondingly scarce; similarly, of course, Cornish continued to be spoken well past the Norman Conquest. This might mean that English penetration stopped, but it might have something subtler to do with how Cornish culture was regarded from *c.* 850 (or a mix of the two). In 969, Ælfeah Gerent and Moruurei his wife were the recipient of lands in Lamorran and Trenown from King Edgar. It seems likely that here we have a Cornish noble given an English name, and that a blend of culture (and perhaps some personal ambition) was producing such dual identities. The pattern is echoed by 'Wulfnoth Rumuncant', 'Æthelwine Muf' and Bishop 'Wulfsige Comoere' of Cornwall at much the same time.[16] 'Maenchi the count, son of Pretignor' was able to grant land by charter of his own to St Heldenus[17] (possibly a small religious house at Lanlawren) by attending the royal West Saxon court at Athelney, Somerset, suggesting in his title and his action some possible continuity of local landholding and authority in Cornwall. The people with Cornish names who freed slaves, as recorded in the notes in the Bodmin Gospels,[18] were presumably landholders, and equally those with English names doing the same may in fact have been Cornish.

---

14.   H. Finberg, 'Sherborne, Glastonbury and the expansion of Wessex', in *Lucerna*, p. 106.
15.   O. Padel, 'Place-names', in R. Kain and W. Ravenhill (eds), *Historical Atlas of South-West England* (1999), pp. 88–94.
16.   Picken, 'Cornish place-names', (1986b) pp. 55–61. For Edgar's grant of 969, see S770.
17.   O. Padel, 'The text of the Lanlawren Charter', *Cornish Studies*, 7 (1979): 43–4.
18.   O. Padel, 'Cornwall around the year 1000', *Cornwall Association of Local Historians Journal*, 37 (1999): pp. 5–6.

There are several hints of surviving enclaves of British speech and culture well to the east of the Tamar. The British-style inscribed stones at Wareham have already been discussed.[19] A perch of land called *Hyples eald land* ('Hypel's old land') in central Devon in Treable, itself a place-name incorporating the British element *tref*, was given to Ælfsige in 976; a previous holder of the property had evidently borne the British name, Hypel. A British-speaking community may have survived here into the ninth or tenth centuries.[20] The Devon place-name Walreddon ('community of Britons') near Tavistock[21] hints at a similar British enclave. Asser's chance remarks about some settlements and sites having names in English and British[22] is matched by a reference in the bounds of a grant dated 682 to Glastonbury, the text of which probably incorporated seventh-century material,[23] to *collem qui dicitur britannica lingua cructan, apud nos crycbeorh*, 'the hill which is called in the British language *cructan* but among us (i.e., Old English speakers) *crycbeorh*'. The place is Creech-barrow Hill near Taunton, and the statement suggests a bilingual phase in the seventh century.

Equally telling is the appearance of the Old Cornish *odencolc*, 'lime kiln', in the South Hams charter of Æthelwulf.[24] *Odencolc* is a very different kind of occurrence of an Old Cornish word for a landscape feature than the name of a hill or a (probably pre-Saxon) monastery. The kiln is unlikely to have commanded any traditional significance, or to have been particularly old, and suggests that the Cornish word was its ordinary name among those who worked it and used its products. Altogether we sense a complex cultural situation in which British acculturation to the English pattern, under West Saxon royal dominance and the emergence of an apparently increasingly Anglicized aristocracy, was as patchy and uneven at the grass-roots level west of the Tamar as it had been elsewhere in the south-west.

The flow of goods

One marker for new developments in the late sixth and seventh centuries is the appearance of E ware,[25] the range of wheel-made coarse cooking pots, beakers, bowls and jugs in the late Roman tradition, coming from somewhere in north-central or western France (see Fig. 108). The pot picks up the earlier links with Gaul, witnessed to between *c.* 400 and 600 by a range of documentary influences, the odd object and a few pieces of D ware, a form of Gaulish paléochrétienne grey ware, which were found at Tintagel, South Cadbury and Cadbury Congresbury, Dinas Powys and a few Scottish and Irish sites.

19.   D. Hinton, 'The inscribed stones in Lady St Mary Church, Wareham', *PDNHAS*, 116 (1992): 260, and see Fig. 123.

20.   H. Finberg, 'The Treable Charter', in *The Early Charters of Devon and Cornwall* (1963), pp. 21–32; Padel, 'Place-names', pp. 89–90.

21.   J. Gover, A. Mawer and F. Stenton, *The Place-names of Devon* (1931), p. 248.

22.   Keynes and Lapidge, *Alfred the Great*, pp. 84, 97, 248, 264, but see also pp. 82–3, 245, 246.

23.   H. Edwards, *The Charters of the Early West Saxon Kingdom* (1988), pp. 15–17.

24.   O. Padel, 'Cornish language notes: 1', *Cornish Studies*, 1 (1973): 58–9, for discussion of *odencolc*.

25.   For the British tradition of land-conveying documents, see W. Davies, 'The Latin charter tradition in western Britain, Brittany and Ireland in the early medieval period', in D. Whitelock, R. McKitterick and D. Dumville (eds), *Ireland in Early Medieval Europe* (1982), pp. 258–80; *The Llandaff Charters* (1979), pp. 5–6.

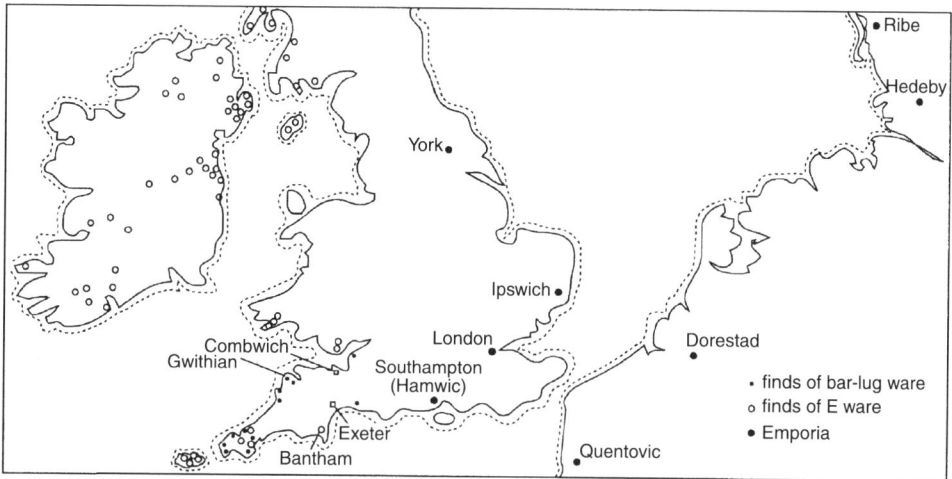

Figure 108 Exchange patterns in north-western Europe, centring upon the seventh century

However, the E ware pottery has a wide distribution along the shores of the Irish Sea and northwards, but does not appear at the south-western hill-fort sites which received the earlier Mediterranean imports. It is possible[26] that the pottery came as a makeweight to the principal Gaulish commodity, wine, travelling perhaps in barrels, together possibly with fine metals and woven cloths, capable together of sustaining the social lifeblood of gifts, fine clothes and convivial hospitality. E ware does not appear east of Dartmoor, and its distribution hints at entry points on Scilly, the Hayle estuary and perhaps Bantham (and a range of harbours further west and north). It may represent a western British/Irish/Gaulish trading network which flourished during the seventh century, but which dwindled as the west British kingdom came under increased political and military pressure from the early eighth century.

An important element in the emerging stability of Wessex as a kingdom during the eighth and earlier ninth centuries, despite dynastic upheavals, seems to have been its capacity to develop a new, small, but probably significant, flow of exchange. This connected it with the major realignment which replaced Mediterranean contacts with those orientated towards north-western Europe and the North Sea (Fig. 108), as a result presumably of Arab pressure upon the Byzantine Empire and its western Mediterranean links from the mid-seventh century.[27] These contacts were not new[28] but Ine's Laws protecting traders and foreigners show that he was actively promoting the new trading centre at *Hamwic*[29] near modern Southampton. *Hamwic* formed part of the network of the so-called *emporia*, many distinguished by the place-name element *wic*, which included Sandwich, *Lundenwic* (the trading bank on the Strand west of the city of London), Ipswich and *Eorfwic* (York) in England, and Quentovic

---

26.   C. Thomas, ' "Gallici Nantae de Galliarum Provinciis." A sixth/seventh-century trade with Gaul reconsidered', *Med. Arch.*, 34 (1990).

27.   For general discussion, see C. Arnold, *An Archaeology of the Early Anglo-Saxon Kingdoms* (1988); R. Hodges and O. Whitehouse, *Mohammed, Charlemagne and the Origins of Europe* (1983).

28.   Thomas, 'Gallici Nantae', pp. 1–26.

29.   A. Morton (ed.), *Excavations at Hamwic: Vol. 1* (1992), pp. 20–77, esp. p. 33.

(north-west France), *Wijk bij Duurstede*, Dorestad (Frisia), Hedeby and Ribe (modern Denmark) overseas.[30]

These *emporia* seem to have developed from the earlier small but significant river and sea trading beaches, perhaps visited every so often by a single ship. They were often commercial camps, for which 'fair' might be the right description, rather than formally established settlements, and many people who dealt there may have been transients, although the craftsmen working in Hamwic seem to have lived in more permanent-looking houses arranged in a street plan.[31] No doubt barter was important, but much of the trading across the system may have taken place in the varieties of silver coins known as *sceatta*. Incoming goods at Hamwic included pottery and glass and outgoing were apparently metalwork, bone-work and textiles, much of the raw material perhaps from the Hampshire royal estates which suggests that the king took a substantial part of the profit.[32]

Evidence from the kingdoms generally suggests that at this time each kingdom only had one significant *wic*, so there may not have been any rival or equivalent to *Hamwic* further west. Combwich on the Parrett estuary is the only local *wic* name, and seems to have been a locally important trading centre since at least the fourth century. Bantham may have continued to be of some importance.[33] Following the lead of York and London, the shelf of rock beside the navigable Exe immediately to the south-west of the city of Exeter might repay further investigation, to see if there is any evidence for development following Exeter's absorption into Wessex in the late seventh century. Exeter, like London and York, was to re-emerge as a leading regional commercial and administrative centre.

No Cornish site appears as a major centre but the appearance of the bar-lug feature is interesting. This was a protected loop added to the locally made grass-marked cooking pots, which seem to have begun in the sixth century. It prevented the suspension string from burning and so permitted pots to be hung over the fire, meaning that households which lacked metal equipment (virtually all) could cook a wide range of stews and porridges, something otherwise very difficult with handmade pottery which was not flameproof (Fig. 109). The bar-lug seems to be a north-Germanic idea, and a few fragments with it came from Hedeby. In south-western Britain it is limited to Cornwall, where it overlapped with E ware and then continued as the dominant local type.[34] This suggests separate Cornish trading outlets, something the political circumstances of the two kingdoms in the eighth century might suggest in any case.

The prime commodity from Devon and Cornwall presumably remained tin. The best evidence for this is the manufacture and distribution of Tating ware jugs and small jars[35] in the decades either side of 800. Tating ware was probably made in the middle Rhineland and was decorated with tin foil applied in decorative patterns.

30.   See Arnold, *Anglo-Saxon Kingdoms*, pp. 103–25.
31.   Morton, *Hamwic*, pp. 20–77.
32.   Arnold, *Anglo-Saxon Kingdoms*, pp. 123–4.
33.   F. Griffith and S. Reed, 'Rescue recording at Bantham Ham, south Devon, in 1977', *PDAS*, 56 (1998): 109–32.
34.   R. Penhallurick, *Tin in Antiquity* (1986), pp. 240–3; G. Hutchinson, 'The bar-lug pottery of Cornwall', *Corn. Arch.*, 18 (1979): 81–103; R. Bruce-Mitford, *Mawgan Porth, a Settlement of the Late Saxon Period on the Cornish Coast* (1977), pp. 74–80.
35.   Penhallurick, *Tin*, p. 240.

Figure 109 Restored bar-lug pot from Gwithian, Cornwall, Royal Cornwall Museum (photo: author)

Judging by its range, which includes Russia, Scandinavia and Dorested, it was very popular. Silver coins contained percentages of tin, and finds of pewter and cheap tinned jewellery, like the two brooches from Long Wittenham, across the northern world, demonstrate the demand.[36] Abbé Raynal, writing in 1782, who may have had access to lost documents, mentions seventh-century fairs and markets established in France by King Dagobert to which came traders from England with lead and tin.[37] If this can be trusted, it points firmly to metals from the south-west. If there really was an international trade around 800 featuring Devon and Cornish tin (and Somerset lead), then this would not only have buttressed West Saxon royal power but also provided an extra reason for the conquest of land west of the Tamar and a further access of wealth when it had been absorbed.

With metals and animal products went human livestock, judging by the prohibition in Ine's Laws against selling slaves overseas, possibly because they might go to non-Christian owners, and the efforts of Bishop Wulfstan II of Worcester in the late eleventh century to end the Bristol slave trade.[38] Slave trading within, and on the northern and western fringes of, the old Roman Empire had been a fact of life for centuries and the slaves recorded on the Domesday manors, where they usually constitute about 10 per cent of the population, show how widespread and normal they were. Slaves could not be made to work on Sundays, and they seem to have had modest opportunities to grow food and sell goods,[39] which suggests the possibility of buying freedom. The tenth- and eleventh-century records of manumissions at Bodmin, Exeter, Okehampton and elsewhere suggest that freeing a slave was regarded as a meritorious act of piety, but also that slaves could be bought, sold and

---

36. *Ibid.*
37. *Ibid.*
38. D. Pelteret, 'Slave raiding and slave trading in early England', *Anglo-Saxon England*, 9 (1981): 91–144, and for general discussion of early medieval slavery in England, see D. Pelteret, *Slavery in Early Medieval England* (1995).
39. Yorke, *Wessex*, pp. 261–4.

bequeathed like any other chattel. Unsurprisingly, the records taken together suggest a social distinction between house or familiar slaves whose careers might be like that of a Roman freeman, and field slaves whose chances of freedom were tiny. The manumissions in the tenth-century Bodmin Gospels show a mixture of Cornish, British and biblical names with one or two Irishmen, demonstrating a broad cultural mix characteristic of the period. Many were presumably slave-born and others fell into slavery through theft, debt or personal disaster, but most of those traded on a substantial scale though the ports had been taken by raiding or warfare, for which the profit to be made on people was always one of the main motives.

Ine's Laws use the word *walh* with the primary meaning of 'British', 'Welsh', and while it certainly came to mean 'slave' in late Saxon Wessex, it may by then have lost its racial connotations.[40] The heavy concentration of slaves in west Devon in the Domesday record, and their relatively heavy concentration across Cornwall, might suggest that locals had been enslaved, as lords who saw themselves as West Saxon replaced those who were identifiably British. There seems to have been a general shift in late Saxon Wessex through which slaves gradually became the *coliberti* of the Domesday record, dependent peasants owing heavy services who were expected to keep themselves from small allowances of land, but this may not have proceeded as far by 1086 in west Wessex as elsewhere. As a result, the number of slaves listed here may simply represent what had been the wider situation rather earlier and need not indicate any substantial geographical distinction. If so, this in turn suggests that slaves had been heavily concentrated everywhere, and raises the question of their origins: possibly they, or some of them, had been the effectively unfree *coloni* of the large fourth-century estates.

Social changes in the earlier ninth century

The opening up of wider contacts seems to have had profound effects upon West Saxon society. While it is not until the tenth century that the charter record begins to show a significant number of land grants to individual laymen (and the occasional laywoman), the social forces which are reflected in these grants seem to begin in the ninth century. The Danish pressures which began to affect Wessex seriously from the 830s certainly helped to produce a class of men in the service sometimes of the king himself, and sometimes of his shire ealdormen, upon whom the crucial work of organizing the matériel of war, of commanding fighting units and of managing complex fortification projects depended. Contemporaries would probably have thought of these men as 'thegns' but this seems to have embraced a considerable range of importance by the time Edgar was granting land in Devon to men like Wulfhelm and Ælfhere,[41] both of whom are described as his 'ministers', a title which, like thegn, carries the fundamental meaning of service. Who men like these were, and whether or not they were 'new' men, we cannot usually tell. Nonetheless, they were an integral part of the fundamental shift away from a kin-based, segmented social structure and towards that orientated upon emerging West Saxon royal power, which

---

40.   M. Faull, 'The semantic development of the Old English walh', *Leeds Studies in English*, 8 (1976): 20–44.

41.   In his grants respectively in 963 at Ottery St Mary, and in 974 at *Nymed* in central Devon, S721, S795.

could mobilize strength from increases in royal land (in Cornwall and south-eastern England) and international commerce. Within the pattern, the Danish troubles, for all their contributions to change, may have been as much a symptom as a cause.

Somewhere in this process, at least in part, may lie the reasons for some of Æthelwulf's actions. The South Hams charter of 847, by which the king granted 20 *hides on homme* to himself in hereditary ownership and exempting himself from all secular obligations except military service and bridge-building, was as far as we know a unique event.[42] It is odd because, if the land was already Æthelwulf's to give, there is no obvious reason why he had to mark his possession in this way. Possible specific explanations include the need to build up Crown lands, to defend vulnerable river valleys or the desire, as Stenton thought, to devote the land 'to the service of religion',[43] although there is no evidence that this happened. It is worth remembering that, whatever the precise boundaries of the land, its owner would be in a position to control river traffic on the Erme, Avon and Dart, all of which are likely to have been used to move whatever tin was being produced from the southern Dartmoor deposits, and that Bantham, conceivably operating as a small *emporium*, was at the Avon mouth. If this traffic was a part of the eighth-century *emporia*-based trade, then Æthelwulf's particular interest in the area, and perhaps his need to regulate and assert ownership in a special way, makes sense as part of an effort to build up royal wealth-based power.

Of more general implication were Æthelwulf's act(s) of decimation by which, sometime in the mid-850s, he 'booked a tenth part of his land throughout all his kingdom to the praise of God and his own eternal salvation',[44] which seems to have meant that the land involved was free of tax and royal services. This may have been primarily intended to benefit the Church as an act of simple piety and to align ecclesiastical interests firmly behind him as he departed for his Roman pilgrimage in 855, but, however it is read, it seems to have benefited secular landholders. The same effort to consolidate the power of the dynasty within an emerging framework of royal land, supportive landholding thegns and income from international trade seems to appear in the careful arrangements Æthelwulf made, between his return from Rome in 856 and his death in 858, for the royal succession. While these offered a role for all his surviving sons, they seem to have been intended primarily to prevent the kind of interkin fighting which had weakened Wessex in the previous century, and to make the rule of a minor in Wessex less likely.

Within this frame belong the substantial series of buildings and enclosures, certainly occupied during the mid-ninth century at Cheddar (Fig. 110), which is interpreted as a royal residence. The site had an impressive Long Hall, some kind of religious complex, objects of personal wealth and a consciously impressive entrance, and although no king is likely to have lived there in any permanent sense, probably most visited it. Cheddar looks like one of several efforts by the West Saxon kings to emulate the dominant polity of the day in north-western Europe, that of

---

42. See S. Keynes, 'The West Saxon charters of King Aethelwulf and his sons', *HER*, 109 (434): 1109–49 (1994), and refs there, and D. Hooke, *The Pre-Conquest Charter-bounds of Devon and Cornwall* (1994), pp. 105–12.
43. F. Stenton, *Anglo-Saxon England* (1947), p. 305.
44. Keynes, 'West Saxon charters', p. 1119.

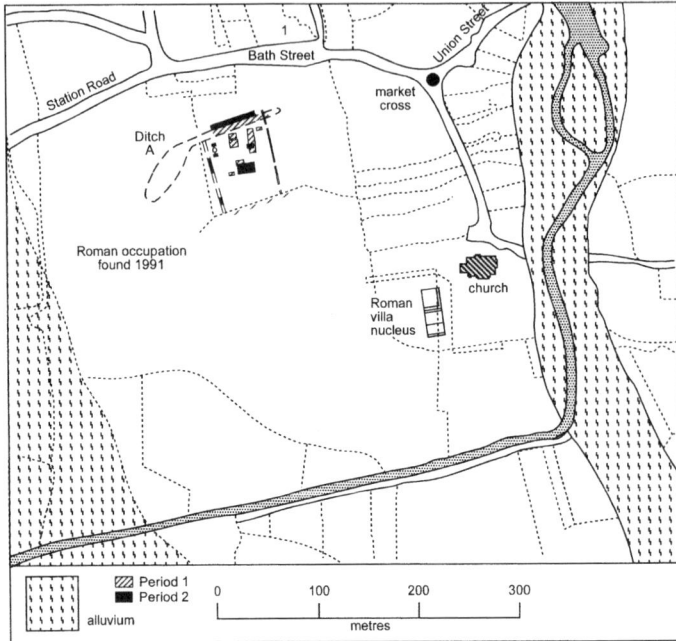

Figure 110 The site at Cheddar (after Rahtz 1979, Fig. 6)

Carolingian Francia.[45] Francia was sustained by the ideology of a Christian empire that consciously presented the king as a sacred ruler; the West Saxons had done the same in the tradition of royal consecration rites, including anointing, which began in the first half of the ninth century. In both states, this meant that rebellion could be cast as sacrilege. It is possible that some of the artwork expressing the unity of king and Church which is conveniently dated to Alfred's reign (or later) may in fact be of the earlier ninth century, just as may an important range of church buildings, including major work at Glastonbury and Sherborne, which embodied similar aspirational statements set in liturgical form. The importance of Boniface and other Englishmen in the Carolingian Empire show that the ideological traffic was far from one-way, just as Æthelwulf's marriage to Judith, daughter of Charles the Bald, in 856 on his way back from Rome, demonstrated a high-level personal alliance.

Viewed in this perspective, the *emporia*-based exchange in animal products, slaves and metals across the seaways connecting the Frankish empire and its penumbra of states takes on a cultural, rather than a simple economic character. Its major participants perhaps intended it primarily to generate the personal links and the flow of material objects which could demonstrate their standing within a world wider than Wessex. For them, perhaps, the accumulation of economic wealth was the welcome consequence of relationships created for emotional and aspirational reasons.

---

45.   P. Rahtz, *The Saxon and Medieval Palaces at Cheddar. Excavations 1960–1962* (1979); R. Hodges and J. Moreland, 'Power and exchange in middle Saxon England', in S. Driscoll and M. Nieke (eds), *Power and Politics in Early Medieval Britain and Ireland* (1988), pp. 79–95.

Something like an early medieval state had emerged in ninth-century Wessex, with its ambition and capacity to absorb Cornwall (and the south-eastern kingdoms), to reorganize its social relationships and to rethink the meaning of a Christian society. This represents the success of the ruling group in harnessing the gifting of lands and goods, spiritual benefits and impressive self-presentations, and by using the wealth which the system itself was generating, to develop crucial loyalties to the king rather than the local community. These loyalties were to work themselves through in the vital test of the Danish wars, so enabling Wessex, and through Wessex, England, to take conceptual shape.

The early Viking attacks

According to the *Anglo-Saxon Chronicle*, the first appearance of the Vikings in England was in the reign of King Beorhtric (789–802) when three Norwegian ships put into Portland, and killed the king's reeve based in Dorchester when he had ridden down to them to carry out normal official business with what he thought were merchants.[46] The story evidently made a considerable impact, as the dramatic prelude in Wessex to what became first a series of raids and then outright war (Fig. 111). The south-west was vulnerable along its northern coast to raids from the Hiberno-Norse who were settling and raiding along the western seaways during the ninth century, and along its southern coast to predominantly Danish fleets operating out of bases established in Francia, which moved back and forth across the Channel as the fortunes of war fluctuated.

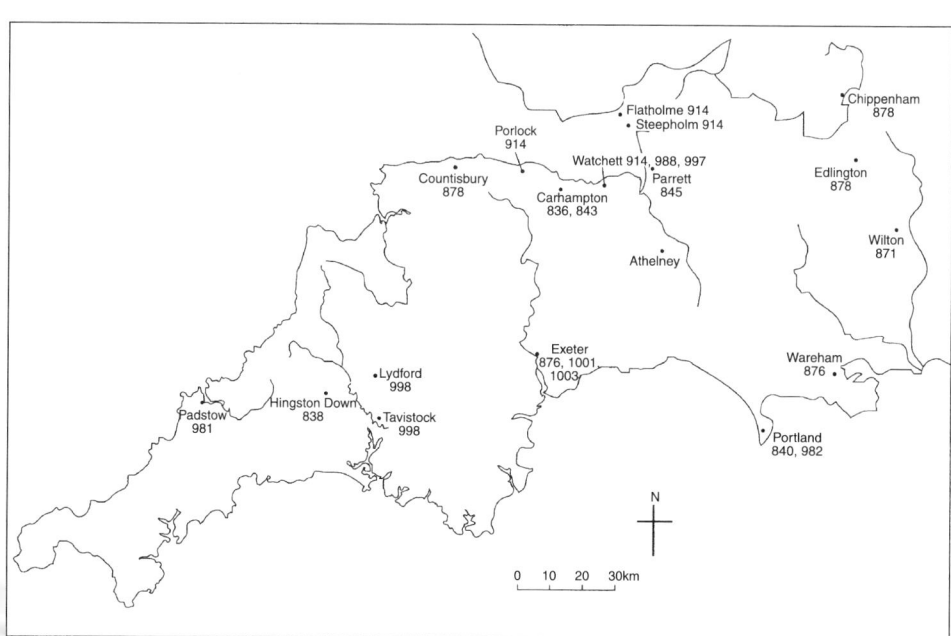

Figure 111 Viking attacks on Wessex, 836–1003

46.   See Yorke, *Wessex*, p. 107, and generally for what follows and refs there.

On the northern coast, Carhampton, presumably chiefly the minster, was attacked in 836 and 843, but Egbert himself defeated a joint Viking/Cornish army at Hingston Down in 838, the men of Somerset and Dorset a Viking one at the mouth of the Parrett, Somerset, in 845, and the men of Devon were victorious at *Wicganbeorg* (unidentified) in 851. In the south, Portland was attacked again, and the earldorman of Dorset killed, in 840, and *Hamwic* raided at least once, while what seem to have been warbands from substantial fleets were driven away from Surrey in 851 and Hampshire in 860. No permanent bases had been created in or near Wessex, and the raiders had been seen off by the shire contingents under their own leaders.

Substantial political threat did not develop until the 'great heathen army' led by Bagsecg and Halfdan and originally based on Thanet, having defeated the royal armies of Northumbria and East Anglia and brought parts of these kingdoms under direct control, turned to Wessex in 870/1, setting up their headquarters at Reading. Fighting at Ashdown, Basing and *Meretun* ended in a stalemate, although the *Chronicle* is anxious to emphasize Alfred's part in the fighting and to depress that of his elder brother, King Æthelred. At this point the Reading Vikings were joined by 'the great summer army' under Guthrum, according to Asser from overseas, and Æthelred died, to be succeeded immediately by Alfred (passing over Æthelred's two young sons). Alfred was quickly defeated at Wilton and made peace which probably involved the payment of substantial tribute.

In 876 Guthrum was back, outmanoeuvring the West Saxon forces to occupy Wareham with its agriculturally rich hinterland and important sheltered harbour, as the 'great army's' winter base for 876–877. Alfred bought the invaders off, but they left to go west not east, and spent the next winter at Exeter. The occupation of a new base every autumn had been the normal pattern of the 'great army' since its arrival in 865, and the practice continued in the early years of Alfred's reign. At Christmas 878 Alfred was at the royal centre at Chippenham, when Guthrum attacked suddenly and Alfred had to flee quickly to Athelney in the Somerset Levels; meanwhile most of east Wessex, including Wulfhere, earldorman of Wiltshire, seem to have submitted to Guthrum. But at *Cynuit* (?Countisbury on the north Devon coast) in 878 the men of Devon defeated a fleet from Wales led by Ubbe brother of Halfdan, on its way to join the main Viking force, and in May 878, with the western thegns and others from further east who rallied to him, Alfred was able to score a decisive victory at Edington, Wiltshire; Guthrum was baptized and bound by a peace treaty which proved lasting.

Sporadic difficulties continued for the next century or so. In 892 Vikings from western France set up bases in eastern England from which over the next four years they raided widely in Wessex. Edward the Elder had to fend off two Viking invasions in 903 and 914 when an army from Brittany camped on Flatholme (and/or Steepholm) in the Severn estuary and Watchet and Porlock were attacked. Significantly, King Eadred (946–955) left money in his will to redeem southern England 'from famine and from a heathen army'. Nevertheless, first Edward the Elder, and then Athelstan, with the prestige of his victory over a combined Scottish-Hiberno-Scandinavian force in 937 at *Brunanburh* (unidentified), was able to establish a military pre-eminence which kept southern England relatively secure until the early 980s.

The national and shire field armies were only half of the response to the Viking problem. The requirement for fortress work, together with road and bridge-building and military service became a regular obligation upon land in Wessex from 855. The system of defensive *burhs* probably grew up piecemeal from the middle of the ninth century, and continued to develop in this way until well into the eleventh century, although with probably several phases of centrally managed effort, one of which was probably responsible for the list known as the *Burghal Hidage*.[47] What has emerged is that here, as probably in his warfare, Alfred's policies[48] were not strikingly different from those of his predecessors and successors, and the long-term attribution to him of the lion's share of the credit owes a good deal to the manipulation of the record during his reign.

Church and state in west Wessex

The creation of the diocese of Sherborne in 705 had been intended to regularize the position of the large area west of Selwood, which included what were emerging as the shires of Dorset, Somerset and Devon. Through some combination of existing reputation and royal choice, Sherborne emerged as the leading church and episcopal see of western Wessex, while Glastonbury and, to a lesser extent, Exeter had important communities. All these had claims (at least) to have originated in the post-Roman world and could offer Ine and his successors prestige in exchange for benefactions; Glastonbury and Sherborne, in particular, began their long English land-gathering careers with grants from Ine. During the eighth and ninth centuries, successive bishops of Sherborne must have been responsible in their area for consecrating the new churches which appear in the record as the minster foundations, for ordaining priests serving these, and any other priests serving private estate arrangements (if indeed, any such yet existed).

For reasons which seem to lie in a characteristic tangle of royal domestic, episcopal and international issues, two major new minsters at Taunton and Creedy (later known as Crediton) were created during the episcopacy of Forthhere of Sherborne, the second bishop (709–*c.* 737). Frithogyth, wife of King Æthelheard (726–740), accompanied Forthhere to Rome in 737, and either before or after she is said to have founded a church at Taunton, where, so the *Anglo-Saxon Chronicle* tells us under 722, her predecessor Queen Æthelburg had 'destroyed Taunton which King Ine had formerly built', a comment Stenton called a 'remarkable but by no means luminous statement'.[49] In 739 Æthelheard gave Forthere an estate on the Creedy in a charter which Frithogyth witnessed.[50] Presumably both Taunton and Crediton served as headquarters for the episcopal administration of their respective shires. The reason for the choice of Crediton as the birthplace of Boniface is probably right, although this is not recorded until the fourteenth century at Exeter, and it is interesting that Forthere, Frithogyth and Boniface were all in Rome in 737 and quite possibly met.[51]

---

47. N. Brooks, 'The unidentified forts of the Burghal Hidage', *Med. Arch.*, 8 (1964): 74–90; 'The development of military obligation in eighth and ninth-century England', in P. Clemoes and K. Hughes (eds), *England before the Conquest: Studies in Primary Sources Presented to Dorothy Whitelock* (1971), pp. 69–84; 'Arms, status and warfare in late Saxon England', in D. Hill (ed.), *Ethelred the Unready* (1978), pp. 81–104; D. Dumville, *Wessex and England from Alfred to Edgar* (1992), pp. 24–7, 48.

48. For Alfred's later cult, see S. Keynes, 'The cult of King Alfred the Great', *Anglo-Saxon England*, 28 (1999): 225–56.

49. Stenton, *Anglo-Saxon England*, p. 70.

50. S254; H. Finberg, *Early Charters of Wessex*, no. 383.

51. F. Rose-Troup, 'The ancient monastery of [St Mary and St Peter] at Exeter', *TDA*, 63 (1931): 197–200; C. Insley, 'Charters and Episcopal scriptoria in the Anglo-Saxon south-west', *Early Medieval Europe*, 7 (1998): 174.

We know from information in his *Life* that Boniface was a schoolboy there in the 620s, so there was a, presumably respectable, religious community in Exeter, which appears in the eighth-century graveyard in the Cathedral Close[52] (even if some or many of the burials were citizens rather than religious), and possibly in the ninth-century gold finger-ring which was found in one of the graves.[53] This community must have had a church, perhaps on the St Mary Major site where at least three poorly dated but pre-Norman constructional phases have been recognized.

The deputy-bishops, *chorepiscopi*, appointed to help Willibrord and Boniface in north-western Europe seem to have encouraged the use of these strictly uncanonical but sometimes necessary arrangements in France and England. Esne, called 'Bishop' in Alfred's will dated 880, by which he was left the same sum of money as the archbishop and the Bishop of Sherborne, and associated with Taunton in a number of roughly contemporary documents,[54] seems to have been a *chorepiscopus* for Sherborne. A similar arrangement may have been repeated in the 880s by which the Welsh Asser, possibly already a bishop, was given by Alfred 'Exeter with all the jurisdiction pertaining to it in Saxon territory and in Cornwall',[55] which may mean simply charge of its dependent lands with all their rights, but may have involved a suffragan function in Devon and Cornwall. If so, it may be significant that no successors to Kenstec are known in Cornwall. Asser himself became Bishop of Sherborne in the 890s, dying in 909.[56]

Once the first major phase of war was ended and the West Saxon defensive system had reached an effective level of development, we sense a certain desire on the part of Edward the Elder (899–924) and then Athelstan (924–939) to put at least some long-standing problems into the kind of order which would reflect well upon kings, who saw themselves as major figures in Britain, and, in Athelstan's case, in western Europe. In particular, Alfred, Edward and Athelstan were all involved at the highest levels in the political affairs of both the Welsh kingdoms and of Brittany. We must, however, beware of exaggerating the effect this may have had on their dealings with

---

52.   J. Allen, C. Henderson and R. Higham, 'Saxon Exeter', in J. Haslam, *Anglo-Saxon Towns in Southern England* (1984), pp. 385–414.

53.   J. Campbell-Graham, 'A middle Saxon gold finger-ring from the Cathedral Close, Exeter', *Antiq. J.*, 62 (1982): 366–7. A roughly contemporary, poor quality strap-end also came from the site of the late Saxon church, see Campbell-Graham (1983), pp. 133–4.

54.   Keynes and Lapidge, *Alfred the Great*, pp. 173–8, 323.

55.   *Ibid.*, pp. 97, 264–5.

56.   John Hooker of Exeter, who may have had access to now lost documents, writing in the second half of the sixteenth century records that 'Werstanus was the first who fixed the episcopal chair at Tawton, a small village about a mile and a half to the south of Barnstapel ... *anno* 905 he was consecrated Bishop of Devon and had his seat at Tawton aforesaid, where, having sat one year he died and was buried in his own church there' (*An orderly Catalogue with Authentic Memoirs of all the Bishops down to 1583*). His successor was Putta who resided at Tawton, but was killed on his way to Crediton to pay his respects to the king or his officials. He was followed, Hooker tells us, by Eadwulf, first Bishop of Crediton, who was installed in 910 (? 909), information (see J. Chanter, 'Tawton – the first Saxon bishopric of Devonshire', *TDA*, 7 (1875): 179–96) which is correct. Bishops Tawton was an Exeter manor in 1066, and it is not wholly impossible that Werstan, and perhaps Putta, were based there in the period before 909 as suffragans of Sherborne in north Devon; alternatively, the story may be a back-formation from the later prefix added to the name of the estate, and the ecclesiastical Putta, in particular, may derive from the 'Putta's post' on the highway/army way (*on herepath on puttan stapul*) which is one of the boundary points listed in Crediton's foundation charter of 739 (Hooke, *Charter-bounds*, pp. 87, 93).

Cornwall, where the fact that it was a part of Wessex rather than a separate polity may have been the most significant factor. Asser's death made the division of the diocese a personal and political possibility, and accordingly it was formally divided into three parts, Sherborne remaining responsible for Dorset, and new sees being created for Somerset at Wells and at Crediton for Devon and Cornwall.[57] We do not know why Wells was favoured over Glastonbury,[58] but Crediton may have been preferred to Exeter because its endowments were greater. In the event, neither choice turned out to be very satisfactory in the long term. Presumably the question of a Cornish bishopric was considered in 910 but shelved, pending a general settlement which William of Malmesbury, our only documentary and somewhat doubtful source,[59] tells us Athelstan undertook.

William thought that Athelstan, 'then fixed the left bank of the Tamar as the shire boundary, just as he had made the Wye the boundary for the north Britons'.[60] This implies that Athelstan recognized the administrative structure represented by the Cornish hundreds (not a great change), and the Tamar line as a formal administrative boundary. We know that the Werrington anomaly was not altered, and land west of the Tamar continued to be linked with Lifton,[61] so if Athelstan did establish a formal shire boundary, it probably did no more than reflect existing arrangements. Athelstan also recognized a Bishop Conan, and apparently gave him, perhaps in 936, 'all the territory of the bishopric, that is, of the blessed St Germans, Bishop of the region of

---

57.   For a full discussion of this reorganization, see A. Rumble, 'Edward the Elder and the churches of Winchester and Wessex', in N. Higham and D. Hill (eds), *Edward the Elder* (2001), esp. pp. 238–47.

58.   Or over other places in Somerset. About 1175 a canon at Wells produced his *Historiola de Primordiis Episcopatus Somersetensis* which claimed that, up to the time of King Ine (*c.* 700), Congresbury had been the seat of the Somerset bishop. This is part of the twelfth-century effort at Wells to establish itself as the natural successor of Congar and of his house and burial place at Congresbury, which includes a *Vita* of the saint produced at Wells; in 1060 Wells had inherited the estate of Congresbury from Bishop Dudoc. The presence of a bishop within a (putative) British monastery at Congresbury cannot, of course, be ruled out in general terms, but it seems unlikely that the canon had access to any specific now lost information; see S. Pearce, *The Kingdom of Dumnonia* (1978), pp. 131–3; G. Doble, 'Saint Congor', *Antiquity*, 19 (1945): 32–43, 85–95.

59.   Dumville dismissed the likelihood that William had access to now lost sources (*Wessex and England from Alfred to Edgar* (1992), pp. 142, 146), but Hill, while remaining cautious about William's claims to have consulted 'a certain very old book', cites Athelstan's stay in Exeter in April 928 and the Athelstan Law Code which says, 'Now I have decided with the councillors who have been with me at Exeter at Midwinter that all (disturbers of the peace) shall be ready to go themselves, with their wives and property and with everything (they possess) whither so ever I wish unless they are willing to cease (from wrongdoing) – with the further provision that they never afterwards return to their native district.' This certainly fits in with William's account, as may the archaeological evidence for work done on Exeter's defences in the earlier tenth century; D. Hill, 'Athelstan's urban reforms', *Anglo-Saxon Studies in Archaeology and History*, 2 (2000): 173–85; S. Blaylock and R. Parker, *Exeter City Defences: Fabric Recording of the City Wall in Northernhay Gardens adjacent to Athelstan's Tower 1993–4* (1994), esp. figs 1–3.

60.   R. Mynors, R. Thompson and M. Winterbottom, *Gesta Regum Anglorum: History of the English Kings* (1998), c 134, pp. 216–17.

61.   The Pipe Rolls under Henry II refer to Cornish manors 'which belong to the farm of Devonshire' (Great Rolls of the Pipe, p. 46, *Pipe Roll Soc*, 34: 156) and in 1275 the Hundred Rolls refer to 'all the run of the county of Cornwall who belong to Lifton (*Rotuli Hundredorum*, 1: 75); see H. Finberg, 'The making of a boundary', in *Lucerna* (1964), p. 166. See also J. Alexander, 'The beginnings of Lifton', *TDA*, 63 (1931): pp. 349–58. For Werrington, see p. 254.

Cornwall'.[62] Presumably Conan served as the bishop for Cornwall with his seat at the community of St Germans. Bishops continued to be based at St Germans, with first Wulfsige Comoere and then Daniel serving there in King Edgar's reign (959–975). The complicated and rapidly shifting arrangements for episcopal provision seem to have caused long-standing disputes over the endowments of churches. A memorandum, drawn up in the name of Dunstan, Archbishop of Canterbury perhaps in the 980s,[63] was produced to assert St Germans' claim to the Cornish estates of Pawton, Callington and Lawhitton which it considered had been allocated for Cornish episcopal support successively at Sherborne, Crediton and, finally, St Germans.

Cornish episcopal affairs do not seem to have been settled until 994 when Æthelred II made St Germans into a diocesan see with Ealdred as its bishop. Recent work at the east end of what is now the parish church of St Germans has revealed fascinating traces of what may have been the pre-Norman cathedral church, the ancient cathedral of Cornwall.[64] The king annexed to St Germans the church of St Petroc at Bodmin in some way which presumably gave the bishop the income from at least some of Bodmin's estates.[65] Probably difficulties over endowing a bishopric adequately and rivalries between religious houses (and perhaps with Crediton) had delayed this move, but as with Wells and Crediton, it is strange that St Germans was ever chosen over well-endowed and much more central Bodmin, unless proximity to the English-speakers of east Cornwall was a factor; two of the bishops of St Germans whose names we have, Ealdred and Burhwold (unlike Kenstec and Conan), have English names, but, as we have seen, this tells us little about their origins. In 1018 Cnut granted immunities to the bishopric and church of St Germans (Fig. 112), probably during Burhwold's episcopate.[66]

Pastoral provision for the south-west was reformed once more in the second quarter of the eleventh century. Both Lyfing (1027–46) and his successor Leofric (1046–72) seem to have held both sees – Crediton for Devon and St Germans for Cornwall – in their care. The inherent instabilities across the system were decisively resolved eventually by Leofric in 1050 when, in spite (presumably) of local opposition at Crediton and St Germans, the two dioceses were merged and moved to Exeter, together with the long list of endowments in both shires listed in Domesday Book.[67] The arrangement was to remain stable for some eight centuries. Leofric's cathedral was almost certainly on the site of the church of St Mary Major in the Cathedral Close, adjacent to the later Norman cathedral, where at least three phases of building have been identified in a large church (Figs 113 and 114).[68]

Athelstan was also later credited with founding (or refounding) the church of St Buryan,[69] which created the kind of substantial religious house in Penwith hundred

---

62.   O'Donovan, 'Revision of episcopal dates', pp. 34–6.
63.   W. Picken, 'Bishop Wulfsige Comoere: an unrecognised tenth-century gloss in the Bodmin Gospels', *Cornish Studies*, 14 (1986b): 34–8. Finberg, *Charters of Devon and Cornwall*, p. 19; D. Whitelock, M. Brett and C. Brooke (eds), *Councils and Synods with Other Documents relating to the English Church I AD 871–1204* (1981), Vol. 1, no. 35 (ii).
64.   Olson and Preston-Jones, 'An Ancient Cathedral' (1989–99), pp. 153–69.
65.   S880.
66.   Finberg, *Charters of Devon and Cornwall*, p. 19.
67.   See F. Barlow, *et al.*, *Leoffric of Exeter* (1972), pp. 1–14, and P. Conner, *Anglo-Saxon Exeter: A Tenth-century Cultural History* (1993), for broad discussion.
68.   Allen *et al.*, 'Saxon Exeter', pp. 385–414.
69.   Finberg, *Charters of Devon and Cornwall*, p. 17.

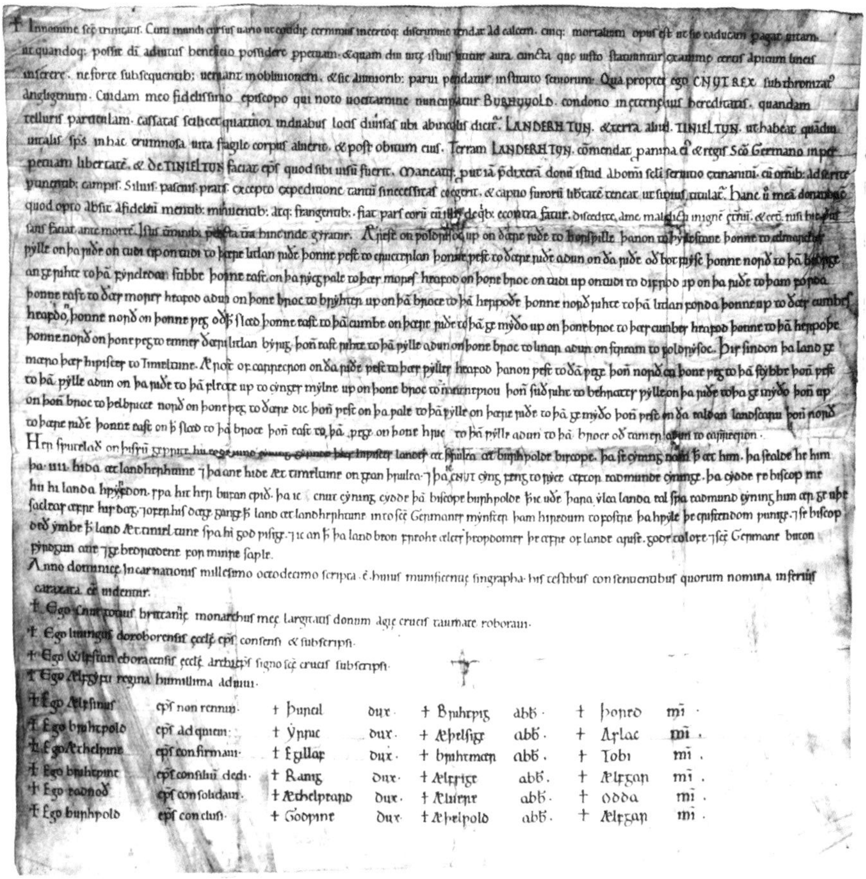

Figure 112 Charter of Cnut to Bishop Burhwold of St Germans, Cornwall, dated 1018. (Photo: Exeter Cathedral Archives, by permission of Dean and Chapter, Exeter)

which that of Kerrier had at St Keverne, a pattern also reflected further east. He was also later believed to have made grants to St Petroc but, as Pedler sapiently pointed out in 1860, the gift of Newton St Petroc, Devon, to Bodmin, made by Eadred *c.* 950 was later credited to Athelstan and a charter concocted to prove it, testifying to the 'prevailing desire in Cornwall to claim an origin from King Athelstan'.[70] Around 963, Edgar booked *Landochou* to St Kew, presumably land the house already claimed and for which felt it was prudent to have royal confirmation. The part played by Edmund (939–946), Edgar and Æthelred in the manumissions recorded in the Bodmin Gospels suggest that all three visited Bodmin, presumably staying in the religious house.[71] In the tenth century, it appears, visits to Cornwall were a relatively normal part of the royal itinerary, just as were stays at Lifton (931), Exeter (928) and Cheddar (941,

---

70. E. Pedler, *The Anglo-Saxon Episcopate of Cornwall* (1860), p. 72n: it is interesting to find such scepticism so relatively early.
71. Padel, 'Cornwall around 1000', p. 6.

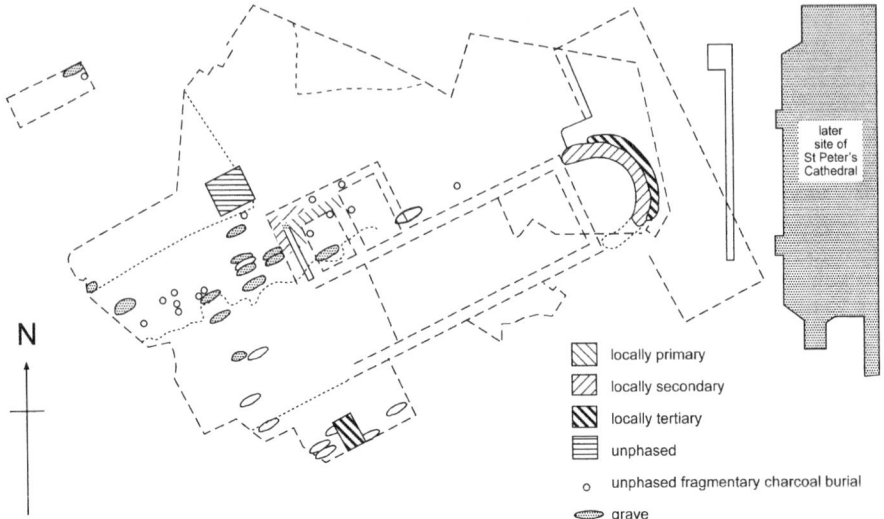

Figure 113 Late Saxon minster, Exeter (after Allen *et al.* 1984, Fig. 125)

Figure 114 Semi-circular robber trench of eastern apse of pre-Conquest church, presumably of the late Saxon minster, on the site of later church of St Mary Major, Cathedral Close, Exeter. (Photo: Exeter City Archaeological Field Unit)

956, 968), where tenth-century kings remodelled the old site, building a new stone chapel and a new West Hall and created a palatial centre[72] from which national and international policy could be conducted.

In sentences either side of his remarks about the Tamar boundary, William of Malmesbury says Athelstan 'attacked [the Cornish] with great energy, compelling them to withdraw from Exeter, which until that time they had inherited on a footing of legal equality with the English ... Having cleansed the city of its defilement by wiping out that filthy race, he fortified it with towers, and surrounded it by a wall of square-hewn stone.'[73] Leaving aside William's interesting anti-Cornish bias, there is nothing inherently unlikely in the suggestion of a recognizable, presumably Old Cornish-speaking, element at Exeter in the early tenth century, since such groups probably still existed across parts of Devon and Somerset. Any such group need not have been the descendants of post-Roman inhabitants[74] rather than related to much more recent commercial interests (since we always tend to underestimate social fluidity and enterprise in the pre-Norman period). However, this is not to say that William had access to genuine information, and still less that Athelstan's control of Exeter involved an episode of deliberate racial cleansing.

The history of the city wall is not yet very well understood, but some late Saxon work[75] has been identified in its northern section (near the structure subsequently known as 'Athelstan's Tower') (Figs 115 and 116). It was clearly strong enough to withstand military action in 1001, 1003 and 1067, which suggests that the old Roman wall and the work associated with the *burh* were further augmented at some (or several) points in the tenth century. There may also have been a substantial ditch

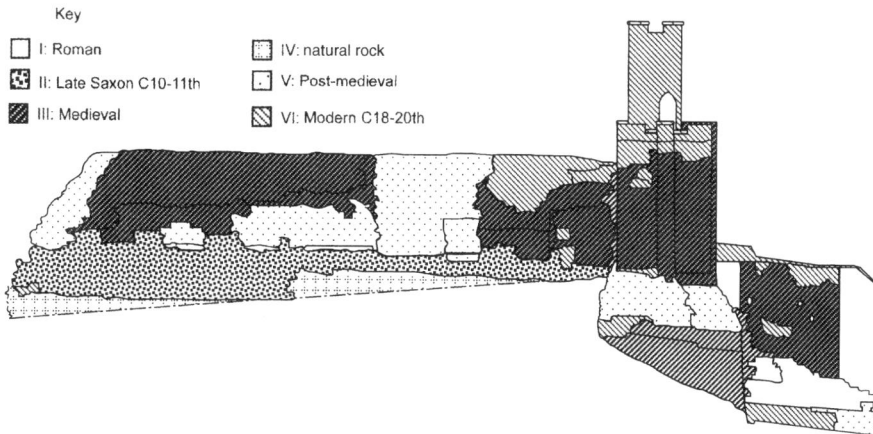

Figure 115 Northern section of Exeter city wall, Northernhay Gardens (after Blaylock and Parker 1994, Fig. 4)

---

72. Rahtz, *Cheddar*, esp. pp. 374–6.
73. Mynors *et al.*, *Gesta Regum Anglorum*, pp. 216–17. See p. 269 note 59.
74. In particular, they need not have been grouped in a 'British quarter' represented by those parishes of the city, especially Petroc and Kerrian dedicated to saints with Celtic names and affiliations, as T. Kerslake suggested: 'The Celt and the Teuton', *Arch. J.*, 30 (1873): 211–25.
75. Blaylock and Parker, *Exeter City Defences*, esp. fig. 103. See Stoyle, *Circled with Stone* (2003), for a comprehensive study of Exeter's walls.

Figure 116 Stretch of northern part of city wall, Exeter, near (so-called) Athelstan's Tower, Northernhay. Visible differences in the work demonstrate the different building phases. (Photo: Exeter City Archaeological Field Unit)

some 33 m in front of the wall. Orderic Vitalis mentions towers in the 1060s, although whether these were post-900 work or surviving Roman bastions, perhaps repaired, is not known. Whether or not William was correct in identifying Athelstan, it seems that some tenth-century authority (or authorities) did take Exeter's defences in hand.[76]

Athelstan was, in the later eleventh century, credited with making four substantial land grants to the Exeter minster of St Mary and St Peter, which were seen as restoring the church to its former major position, and he was also believed to have presented a collection of relics.[77] In 1086, Exeter held two of the estates (Stoke Cannon and Culmstock) and the third, Topsham, seems to have been appropriated by Earl Harold and was in the king's hands, so it is likely that, even if the church's claim to some of these lands was ancient, restoration and confirmation was made at some point in the tenth century.[78] On balance, Athelstan probably did foster Exeter's institutions, probably because of its gaining commercial significance.

---

76.   See Allen *et al.*, 'Saxon Exeter', pp. 385–414, and Hill, 'Athelstan's urban reforms', pp. 173–85, esp. pp. 179–81.

77.   These are Culmstock (S386), *muneca tun* in Shobrooke and Thorverton (S387), Stoke Cannon (S389) and Topsham (S433). See P. Chaplais, 'The authenticity of the royal Anglo-Saxon diplomas of Exeter', *Bulletin of the Institute of Historical Research*, 39 (99): 1–34 (1966). For the relics see pp. 317–18.

78.   See C. Thorn and F. Thorn, *Domesday Book: Devon* (1985), under headings. The fourth estate claimed to have been given by Athelstan was *muneca tun*, 'Monkton', a lost place-name in Shobrooke and Thorverton.

The record of a grant to St Heldenus of property at Lanlowren in Lanteglos by a Cornish Count Maenchi made in the reign of Athelstan at Athelney 'in the land of the Saxons'[79] shows that Cornishmen exercising authority within the region continued to exist, and to have land to dispose of by deed to a native religious house. Why Maenchi was at Athelney is not clear, but perhaps he was attending a West Saxon state function, possibly a council. The word *comes* ('count') appears frequently in Anglo-Saxon charters,[80] and in 977 it is used to describe Æthelweard (who may have been Cornish) when he received what looks like land that had belonged to St Keverne, while Maenchi's rather earlier grant is a private gift to a Cornish religious house. It looks as if a native aristocracy survived in Cornwall until at least the later tenth century, suggesting that here the processes of English acculturation had not gone very deep. In Devon the picture seems to have been much more mixed, while in Somerset and Dorset the processes were virtually complete. Nonetheless, for the practical purposes of governance the whole peninsula had become an integral part of Wessex by the mid tenth century.

The later tenth and earlier eleventh centuries

The developing emphasis on both land lordship and royal service as the structure of social operation ran the obvious risk that individuals might draw into their own lands too much power, creating major imbalances in the system which threatened royal central authority. This risk was reinforced following the death of Athelstan in 939 when Edmund (939–946), Eadred (946–955), Eadwig (955–959) and Edgar (959–975) all came to the throne young and died relatively soon, enabling the two major families of Athelstan 'Half-King' and Ælfhere of Mercia to gather up most of the West Saxon ealdormanries. Open hostilities broke out when, after Edgar's death in 975, rival factions collected round his surviving sons, Edward and Æthelred. This ended with the unsolved murder of Edward at Corfe, Dorset, in March 978. It is probably the familiarity of the English personal and place-names which blinkered earlier historians to the broad similarities between what was happening in southern England and the emerging 'feudal society' of late tenth-century northern France.

Devon offers a telling illustration of how this was happening in the family of Ordgar, who emerged as a charter witness in the 950s and continued to do so until 970, soon after which he seems to have died and to have been buried at Exeter. A late source says that Ordgar was made ealdorman of Devon and Cornwall, which may be true since he was able to marry his daughter Ælfthryth first to Æthelwold ealdorman of East Anglia, and after his death to King Edgar, the kind of marriage which seems to have been the aim of most ambitious lords (including Godwine, whose daughter married Edward the Confessor). It is possible that his son, Ordulf I, was the royal reeve at Lifton, and if so, the family was effectively exploiting royal office and private landholding, witnessed by the large estate probably held by his wife Alfwyn in the Torridge Valley.

The style of Ordulf's efforts is also represented by the building of his monastery at Tavistock in 981, and by the *Martyrology* and the work by Hrabanus which Bishop

---

79.   Padel, 'Lanlawren Charter', pp. 43–4, S1207. A text has been rediscovered in the Petworth House Archives 11601, 134V copy S. XV: I am grateful to Nicholas Brooks for drawing this to my attention.

80.   E.g. Finberg, *Charters of Devon and Cornwall*, p. 19, in a charter of Edward the Martyr.

Ælfwold of Crediton left to him. A second Ordgar, probably a member of the same family, appears as a charter witness in the first half of the eleventh century, and a second Ordulf was still alive in 1066, when the Conquest put an end to what would presumably have emerged (all being well) as a major local magnate English family complete with land, thoroughly privatized royal powers, a family monastery, where appropriately legitimatizing ceremonies could take place for the living as well as the dead, and an hereditary title. Æthelweard, ealdorman of Devon during Cnut's reign and founder of Buckfast abbey in 1018, is a similar figure.[81]

The murder of Edward, which popular narrative attached to his wicked step-mother, Ælfthryth daughter of Ordgar, and its background did not help King Æthelred to cope with Viking attacks of renewed vigour, although our principal source for the region, the material in the C, D and E manuscripts of the *Anglo-Saxon Chronicle*, is hostile to the king, and in particular seems to be biased against the men of the six main Wessex shires (including of course Devon, Somerset and Dorset) who are portrayed as ineffectual.[82] In part, this seems to be bound up with Æthelred's difficulties with his senior noblemen, for when Æthelweard, the king's kinsman and his most senior ealdorman, died in 988, his son Æthelmaer was not appointed his successor in West Wessex and in 1005 he was forced to retire to the monastery at Eynsham.

Whatever the rights and wrongs of the quarrel, it is not surprising that we next see Æthelmaer in 1013 with the Danish Swein as ealdorman of the western shires. In an England-wide emergency, ealdormen could easily be caught between national responsibilities and loyalties to the local men bound to them through lordship, so that as the C, D and E manuscripts say under the year 1010, 'in the end, no shire would even help the next'. This must have helped to solidify local loyalties and the position of regional lords, but, in the shorter term, it also meant that Danish armies could move from shire to shire, as in 1001 when the failure of the Hampshire forces enabled the Danes to move on to Devon, and in reverse two years later when, after the capture of Exeter, the Danes moved on to raid Wiltshire.

The south-west was vulnerable to attack from both the Hiberno-Norse colonies across the Irish Sea and the Vikings settled in Normandy and Brittany. In 981, Padstow – presumably the church of St Petroc – was ravaged and much damage done along the Cornwall and Devon coasts, presumably affecting the religious focuses of St Kew, St Nectan and *Brannocminster*. In 998, Watchet, a *burh* and the site of St Decumans' church, was raided, and there seems to have been fighting in Devon. But in 993/4 the nature of the war changed, with the appearance of a fleet led by Olaf Trygvasson of Norway, accompanied perhaps by King Swein of Denmark. By 988 the Vikings had a base on the Isle of Wight from which they conducted a pattern of serious raids, dubious treaties and the taking of money payments from Æthelred's government. In 997 'the Danes went around Devonshire into the mouth of the Severn and there ravaged in Cornwall, Wales and Devon.' They burnt Watchet again, and then 'went around Land's End again on the south side and went into the mouth of

81. For Ordulf's family see H. Finberg, 'The house of Orgar and the foundation of Tavistock Abbey', *EHR*, 58 (1943): 190–201; 'Childe's tomb', in *Lucerna* (1964), pp. 186–203, for Ælfwold's will, S1492; for Buckfast see Reynolds and Turner, 'Holy Trinity, Buckfastleigh' for an account of work in progress, which is producing evidence of a tenth-century Saxon church and charcoal burials on the church (not later abbey) site, and perhaps earlier material.
82. For this and what follows, see Yorke, *Wessex*, pp. 132–41.

the Tamar, continuing up until they came to Lydford', where the *burh* seems to have stopped them successfully, although 'they burnt down Ordulf's monastery at Tavistock and brought with them to their ships indescribable plunder.'[83] In the following year Dorset was ravaged.

In 1001, having ravaged Hampshire, a fleet sailed up the Exe, following a complex story of treachery on the part of Pallig, a Danish leader recruited by Æthelred who joined the raiders, but although they failed to take Exeter, they ravaged much of the country around. Eventually, in 1003 but apparently only after the treachery of its reeve, Hugh, a Frenchman, Exeter was taken, and it may have been during this that the minster's ancient charters were burnt, as we are told in Cnut's charter to the house of 1019,[84] and that its furnishings were reduced to the single poor vestment which Leofric found when he arrived in 1050.[85] Matters seem to have come to a head when Swein took the submission of east Wessex at Winchester and that of west Wessex at Bath, probably in 1013. After a confused period involving Æthelred's son Edmund and Swein's son Cnut, which may have seen east Wessex supporting the Danes, Cnut became king of all England following Edmund's death in 1016.

Æthelred's reputation has probably suffered unduly,[86] in that much of what he did parallels Alfred's policy in the 870s which commentators have received very differently. Many of the burghal defences seem to have been reinforced during Æthelred's time, including perhaps those of Exeter. The hill-fort of South Cadbury, like others further east, was fortified, and our ignorance of the garrisons provided for the fortified centres should not allow us to conclude that they were necessarily inadequate. The Domesday record suggests that urban settlements like Exeter were able to put their prosperity together again quite quickly. Monasteries complained as much about the amounts levied to pay Danegeld as actual destruction, following experiences like those at Glastonbury, which seems to have had estates confiscated by royal officials, which were later redeemed.[87]

Cnut made few changes to the structure of local English government, but one or two Scandinavian settlers can be traced in the peninsula. A certain Bovi was involved in the refoundation of Horton, and Urk in the founding of Abbotsbury, both men with Scandinavian names. The dedication of a parish church in Exeter to the Norwegian St Olaf may indicate a Norse community in the city. Further west the church of Poughill in east Cornwall is also dedicated to Olaf, but otherwise there seems to be no place-name or linguistic evidence of Scandinavians in Cornwall which cannot be attributed to later influence from further north.[88] There are, however, two recumbent domed gravestones of 'hogback' type at Lanivet and St Tudy, both in the churchyard (Fig. 117), and a probable fragment of a third at St Buryan,[89] all of

---

83. *Anglo-Saxon Chronicle* s.a. 997.
84. Finberg, *Charters of Devon and Cornwall*, p. 14. See also Conner, *Anglo-Saxon Exeter*.
85. Barlow *et al.*, *Leoffric*, pp. 12–13; R. Chambers, M. Forster and R. Flower, *The Exeter Book of Old English Poetry* (1933), p. 28.
86. Yorke, *Wessex*, p. 140.
87. *Ibid.*, p. 141.
88. M. Wakelin, 'Norse influence in Cornwall: a survey of the evidence', *Cornish Studies*, 4/5 (1976–7): 41–9.
89. Langdon, *Old Cornish Crosses*, pp. 410–17. For a discussion of these 'hogback' stones and a distribution map showing a Cornish outlier from the main northern group, see R. Bailey, *Viking Age Sculpture* (1980), pp. 85–100.

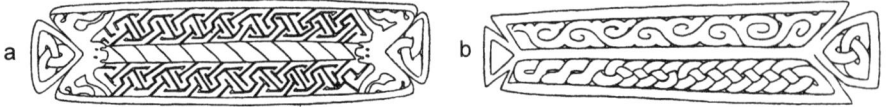

Figure 117 Rubbings taken from the tops of the hogback stones at (a) Lanivet and (b) St Tudy (after Langdon 1988, pp. 413, 415)

which carry interlace and knot ornament, accompanied at Lanivet by animal designs, which are Scandinavian in general style, and suggest the burial of local landholders of some importance who valued what they saw as their Viking links.

Lundy ('Pelican Island') is, like Flatholme and Steepholme, a Norse name, and a case can be made on the basis of early records of grave-goods, for reinstating (some of) the burials on the Bulls Paradise site some 500 m east of the post-Roman graveyard as Viking.[90] Vikings are recorded as having been on Lundy in *c.* 1139/1140, and the island continued to be used as a pirate base well on into early modern times. All this suggests that within the peninsula some men who identified themselves as Scandinavian were settling into the local community at the landholding level, with perhaps a trading community in Exeter, but that there were never enough to affect local nomenclature.

Crucially, Cnut, in disposing the family of Æthelweard, merged the two earl-dormanries of east and west Wessex, and by 1020 had appointed Godwine, a south Saxon, as earl of Wessex and married him to his sister-in-law Gytha. The Godwine family built up the enormous network of estates which can be traced in Domesday Book. West Wessex, however owed them no particular personal loyalty, and Harold was strongly resisted in 1052 by the men of Devon and Somerset when he tried to land at Porlock, following Edward the Confessor's attempt to outlaw them earlier in the year.[91]

The appointment of a stranger as governor of Wessex marks a moment of change. This is matched by the burial of Æthelred in St Paul's, London (where he seems to have been based for much of his time), rather than in one of the traditional churches for the burial of West Saxon kings like those at Winchester or Glastonbury (although Cnut was laid in the Old Minster, Winchester, expressive of his desire to be seen as a legitimate West Saxon king).[92] In the next generation, Edward the Confessor devoted much effort to his building project at Westminster, where he was buried. It was an inevitable consequence of Athelstan's position as king of all England that the balance of regional power would swing away from the west and towards London, with its much superior internal communications and its better access to continental Europe.

---

90.   K. Gardner and M. Ternstrom, 'The giants' graves: a nineteenth-century discovery of human remains on the Island of Lundy', *TDA*, 129 (1997): 51–78.

91.   When Harold's three sons landed on the Somerset coast from Ireland in 1067 they had to defeat the local militia, and, when they landed again in 1069 also in the south-west, they were not able to achieve anything, which suggests a geographical rather than a political reason for their choice. Exeter's stand in 1067 does not seem to have involved any loyalty to the Godwine family although the city had special links with Edward's queen and this may have been influential; Stenton, *Anglo-Saxon England*, pp. 591–4.

92.   Yorke, *Wessex*, p. 147.

Hundreds, minsters and royal estates

No exercise of power can be real unless it reaches down to grass-roots level, and by the tenth century, English kings had produced in the hundred system a reasonably effective mechanism for tax collecting and the maintenance of law and order. Taxes and obligations like army service and fortification work were calculated on the hide, and theoretically each hundred contained one hundred hides, although in southern England reality was usually different.[93] Although the role of the hundreds in collecting tax, by then generally in the form of silver pennies, is clearer in the eleventh century, the practice probably began before this, and the collecting and accounting came to take place at the head estate of each hundred. Peace was maintained (at least to an extent) through obligations to charge thieves and to declare details of the acquisition of goods, especially cattle, and within the hundred and its constituent tithings[94] there operated a kind of compulsory collective bail which imposed stiff penalties for the withholding of information by a member. Two of the tenth-century records of manumissions carried out at Bodmin refer to 'Maccos the hundredsman' and 'Maccosi the *centurio*'[95] presumably the same man, who had a British (or Irish?) name and seems to have been the headman of the hundred, and around the same time we hear of 'the man over the tithing'.[96] These men were manifestations of royal authority at local, indeed humble, levels, witnesses to the reach and effectiveness of the king in his capacity to make an early medieval state work.

The irregular hidage of most hundreds by the time of Domesday Book may reflect a longer history of tax concessions in the form of 'beneficial hidage', that is the grant to favoured nobles or churches of a reduction in the assessment of their estates. This process, which may have begun before the tenth century, also produced 'private hundreds', that is hundreds whose control had passed from the king into the hands of secular or ecclesiastical lords. The *villa*, liberty, or hundred known as Glastonbury Twelve Hides, was one such private hundred, in which the public structure of hide and hundred had been merged with the estate of a great abbey.[97]

A pointer to the age of some hundreds may be their tendency to meet at ancient gathering places. Barrow Hundred met at a barrow in Bere Regis parish, and Longbarrow Hundred at the Pimperne long barrow, both in Dorset. Three hundreds met in the hill-fort site at Ham Hill, Somerset, at least from the seventeenth century, and one at the prehistoric Knowlton henge, Dorset. Four Somerset hundreds – Bempstone, Bulstone, Whitestone and Stone – met at stones.[98] However,

---

93. For the possible early history of Anglo-Saxon institutions, see P. Barnwell, 'Hlafaeta, ceorl, hid and scir: Celtic, Roman or Germanic?', *Anglo-Saxon Studies in Archaeology and History*, 9 (1996): 153–61.

94. For territorial tithings in the south-west and their potential antiquity, see pp. 199–200. There remain intriguing landscape features like those at the farmhouse called Tythingland in Horrabridge parish (Devon) where the OS 1906 edition shows road and field boundaries creating a rough oval immediately NW of the farm, conceivably part of the tithing administration.

95. Hooke, *Charter-bounds*, pp. 77, 82.

96. P. Sawyer, *From Roman Britain to Norman England* (1978), p. 198, citing also laws of Cnut (11 Cn 20).

97. S. Moreland, 'Glaston twelve hides', *PSANHS*, 128 (1984): 35–67; see H. Cam, 'The evolution of the medieval English franchise', *Speculum*, 32 (1957): 428–33.

98. For Somerset, M. Aston, 'Post-Roman central places in Somerset', in E. Grant, *Central Places, Archaeology and History* (1986), p. 63; for Dorset, L. Grinsell, *Dorset Barrows* (1959), p. 68.

this could mean no more than convenience and perhaps a sense of reassurance.[99]

By 1066, hundreds across Somerset, Dorset and Devon usually included several separate estates, but quite frequently these estates may have emerged relatively recently out of the fragmentation of large estates.[100] The coincidence of royal estates and estates whose centres seem to be also the head of a hundred is substantial, amounting in Devon to around two-thirds (Fig. 118) and in Somerset to nearly half.[101] In both shires some of the missing estates, like Crediton, Ottery St Mary (Devon), Wells, Taunton and Glastonbury (Somerset) were in ecclesiastical hands. The coincidence of royal estate and hundred is markedly less in Dorset, with less than one third,[102] perhaps suggesting either that kings had given away more royal land here, or that the circumstances of its incorporation into the West Saxon kingdom had given less opportunity for large-scale royal land taking.

It was clearly administratively sensible to bring together the payment of royal estate dues and public taxes, although as late as 1086 the Domesday record shows that the inhabitants of many manors, like Axminster, Devon, or Bruton, Somerset, did not pay tax but only dues. It may also suggest that the hundred organization as

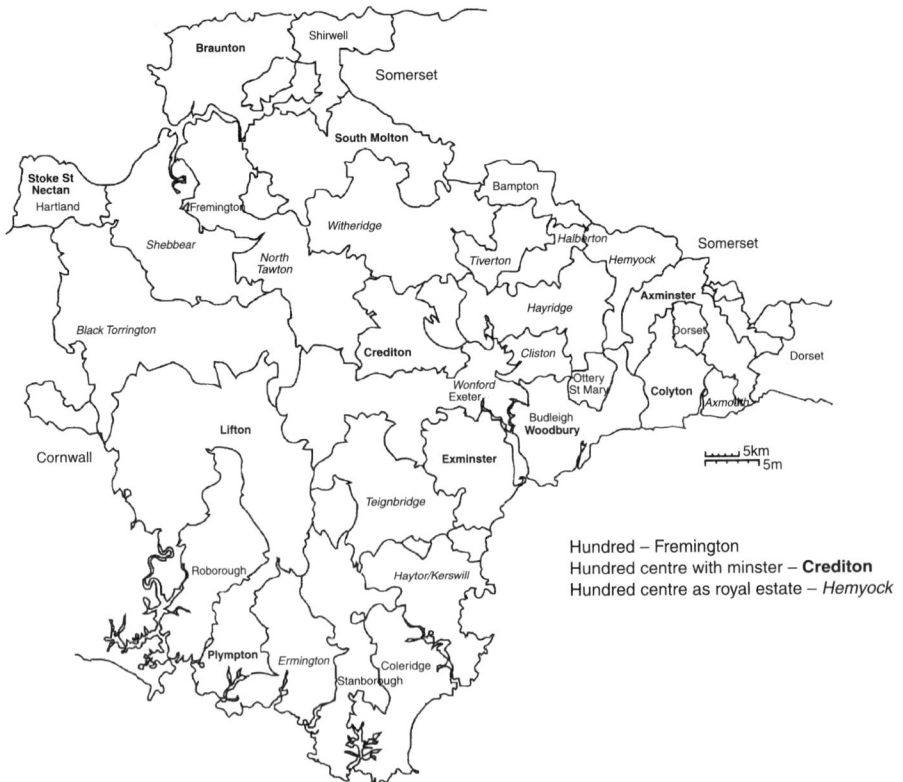

Figure 118 Royal estates, minsters and hundred centres in Devon. (simplified)

---

99.   Links with centuriation are inconclusive, see A. Richardson, 'Further evidence for centuriation in Cumbria', *Trans. Cumberland and Westmorland Antiquities and Arch. Soc.*, 86 (1986): 152–4.
100.   Aston, 'Post-Roman central places', pp. 53–5.
101.   C. Thorn and F. Thorn, *Domesday Book: Somerset* (1980); *Devon* (1985), under place-names.
102.   *Ibid.*, *Domesday Book: Dorset* (1983), under place-names.

we see it in the tenth century arose out of the old, large estates and was in part a mechanism for assuring that, as such estates broke up, the fiscal responsibility to the king of all the new units was retained and enforced.

The frequent coincidence, or close proximity, of royal estates and minster churches has often been noticed, whether they were ancient minsters founded before, say, 775, or later smaller quasi-minsters (or proto-parish churches): in Devon this is true of some fourteen or more places including Yealhampton, Woodbury and Bradstone. It was obviously intended to underline the mutual support generated between Church and king, which was reinforced by the building of a relatively imposing church, sometimes with significant relics, and with the staff of clergy capable of producing appropriately impressive services for visits of royal officials or the king himself. What emerged as the minster's *parochia* would be more or less the ancient royal estate. There is also the sense that it was felt appropriate to have a minster in every hundred, so that, again in Devon, nineteen of the 30 hundreds seem to have had such a church. The Somerset pattern is similar with some 22 out of the 44 hundreds, many like Bedminster, Congresbury, Carhampton or Frome at the hundred centre.

Within this pattern, places which combined the functions of minster, royal (or major episcopal) estate and hundred head, like Axminster, Plympton, Crediton (episcopal) Colyton, all in Devon, Bruton, Taunton (episcopal), Frome, Keynsham and Crewkerne, all Somerset, had particular opportunities. Mid-tenth-century law required the hundred court to meet every four weeks, and people were expected to hear Mass at their local minster at the very least several times a year, while considerable business must always have been transacted at the royal centre. The potential for informal but very important market trading is obvious; most of these centres were not those chosen to be fortified, but they were to emerge as classic southern English market towns.

We sense an interlocking pattern of ancient royal estates, minsters and *parochia*. These had individual, complex, often idiosyncratic histories, which could be exploited, as older land units and *parochia* were replaced by smaller, more intensively managed estates and estate-based parishes, to produce in the hundred (and perhaps also tithing) system a serviceable instrument of government for the post-900 state which had satisfyingly deep roots in the past. The hundred and its meeting centre had a crucial focal role post-900 across the administrative, legal, economic and often religious spectrum. Like the parish, it proved long enduring, and survived to become the background to the administrative arrangements of the nineteenth and early twentieth centuries.

The boroughs

Royal policy, as we have seen, also created the network of fortified boroughs from about 880 (Fig. 119), for which our principal information comes from the document known as the *Burghal Hidage*, and from excavations and fieldwork.[103] Dating of the list is difficult, but it may reflect the situation in the early tenth century. Exeter,

---

103. For the *burh* system in general, and its problems, see D. Hill, 'The Burghal Hidage: the establishment of a text', *Med. Arch.*, 13 (1969): 84–92; 'Athelstan's urban reforms', pp. 173–85, and refs there. For archaeological detail, see M. Aston and R. Leech, *Historic Towns in Somerset* (1977), and K. Penn, *Historic Towns in Dorset* (1980), under individual towns. For a recent paper on Lydford's mint see Allen, 'Anglo-Saxon mint at Lydford' (2002).

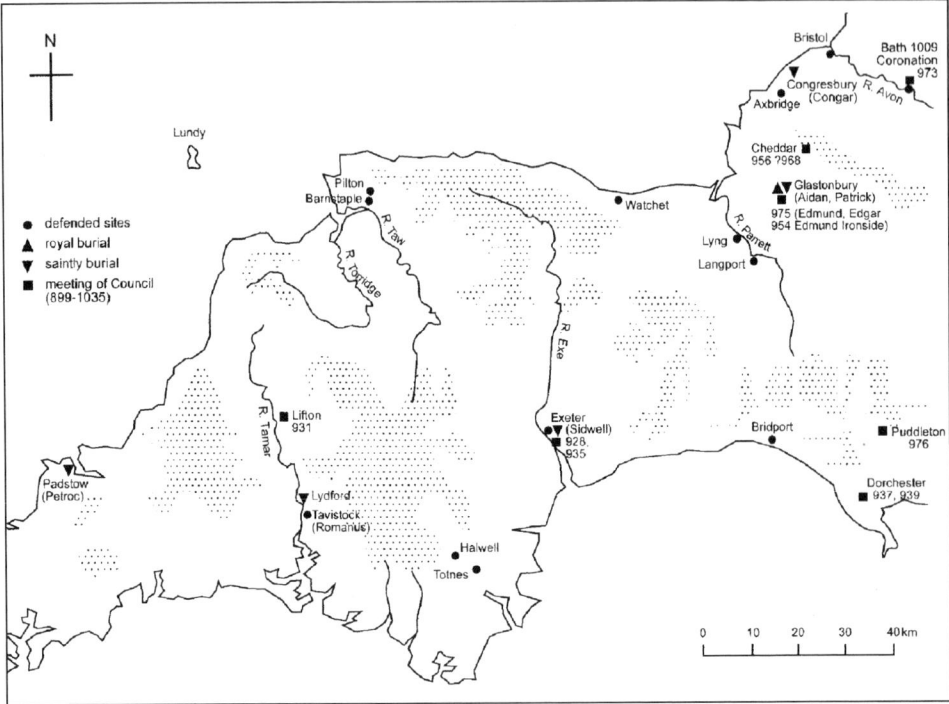

Figure 119 Location map showing *burhs*, saintly burials (after 'The resting places of the saints' ed. Rollason 1978), places where Councils were held and royal burials (after Hill 1981, Figs 54, 2, 63)

with its Roman walls capable perhaps of relatively easy minor refurbishment, was chosen, but apparently neither Dorchester or Ilchester were, their ancient walls notwithstanding. Perhaps the key difference was that Exeter's position on an estuary opening immediately to the sea was important, and so may have been the religious house inside the walls, since the major religious centres at the other two were outside them. Similar considerations apply to Bath, with its large allotment of 1000 hides in the *Burghal Hidage*. The protection of major religious houses, always the target for raiders and also, as we have just seen, already developing as important economic centres, was clearly one factor in the choice of sites: the defences at Wareham, Christchurch and Shaftesbury (all Dorset) all protected religious houses although at Watchet, St Decumans' church seems to have been outside the fortified area, whether this was under the present town or at Daws Castle a little to the west.

Lyng (Fig. 120), listed with a very small assessment in the *Burghal Hidage*, was part of Alfred's old command centre at Athelney in the Somerset Levels and was linked with his early fort and the abbey he founded, so conceivably sentiment played a part in the choice here, as it may have done at Shaftesbury where he had founded a convent for his daughter. The fort at Axbridge may have provided some support for the royal palace at Cheddar,[104] although its exact site is uncertain, just as that

---

104.   E. Blair, 'Palace or minster? Northampton and Cheddar reconsidered', *Anglo-Saxon England*, 25 (1996): 97–121.

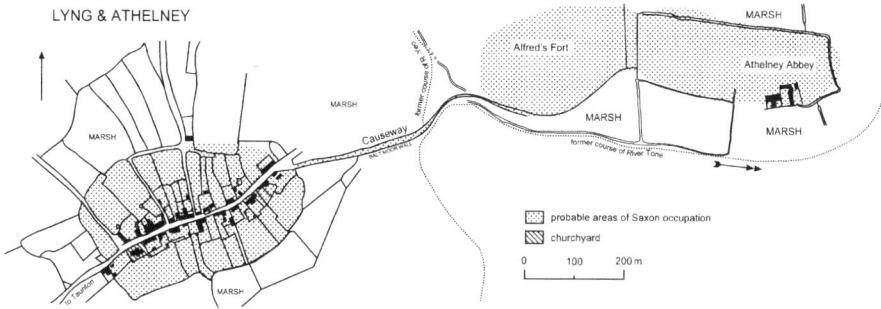

Figure 120 Features at Lyng and Athelney (after Aston and Leech 1977, Map 35)

at Langport[105] may have been placed to protect the royal estate at Somerton, and Watchet that of Carhampton. The site of Halwell in south Devon is also a matter of debate, although there are possible candidates in earthworks at Stanborough and Halwell. The *Brydian* of the *Burghal Hidage* takes its name from a river, the Bride, which has also given rise to the place-names Long and Little Bredy. Little Bredy, which has appropriate topographical features, may have been the site of *Brydian*. The name was later transferred to the new settlement of Bridport which by 1086 had 120 houses and a moneyer.[106]

The borough said to be on the River Lyd is usually taken to mean Lydford, which may already have had a religious site of some importance. The Lydford defences seem to have been fully functioning in 997 when the *Anglo-Saxon Chronicle* tells us the place resisted a Danish attack. The site of the borough listed as 'Pilton' or, in the later version, as 'Pilton with Barnstaple' is also unclear, although it may have been Roborough camp at Pilton. In any case, the urban functions were soon transferred to Barnstaple which had emerged with a mint by at least Æthelred II's reign (979–1016) and a developing settlement, together with defences at least on the western side which was unprotected by rivers.[107]

The boroughs and the other centres were bound together by highways which carry the element *here*, 'army'. Place-names of this kind appear in charters like, for example, that for Monkton in Shobrooke, Devon, dated 925 × 939 and in sites like Harepath in Cheriton Bishop and Harepathstead in St Thomas near Exeter (both Devon). Some of these were probably very old, but others may have been more recent, and together they provided a service network of rights of way presumably backed by watering places, fields where men could camp, and even food depots, which were crucial to the war effort before 900, and continued thereafter to allow the movement of men and goods.

The omissions in the *Burghal Hidage* list are as striking as the inclusions. Quite apart from Dorchester and Ilchester, Sherborne was apparently left without special defences. Taunton, which may have had fortifications of a kind by *c.* 900 and certainly had a major minster and a very large, rich dependent estate, is not mentioned. Edward the Elder seems to have acquired the minster at Plympton by deliberate

---

105. C. Webster, 'Langport, Hanging Chapel ST424267', *PSANHS* (1992): 171.
106. Penn, *Historic Towns in Dorset*, pp. 23–9.
107. H. Miles and T. Miles, 'Pilton, north Devon. Excavations within a medieval village', *PDAS*, 33 (1975): 267–95.

exchange with Asser for land in Somerset, but if defence of the Plym Valley was in his mind, this does not seem to have been put into effect. Equally, no boroughs are listed for the whole of Cornwall in spite of its obvious vulnerability to sea attack. There is, however, evidence from the hidage allocation that Cornish estates contributed to the repair and defence of the Devon boroughs. It looks as if, after the support the Cornish gave to the Danes in 838, they were not to be trusted with their own borough.[108]

The pattern of boroughs in the south-west can be seen, as at Lydford in the greater Tamar Valley or Wareham on the south-east coast, as elements in a wider strategic plan which aimed to protect large tracts of country and secure riverine penetration points. In Somerset, no major settlement in the county was more than 20 miles (32 km) from a fortified centre. However, the impression received from the list of sites is that often their strategic importance was a product of their tactical significance, that is they were often sited primarily in relation to royal resources, of movable wealth tied up in churches, of men, perhaps trained and experienced, and of matériel on the big royal estates. They were intended to protect, but also to act as *foci* for the mobilization and deployment of army groups, and their siting was determined by the historical accidents which had concentrated resources in particular places.

We can also see the development of military thinking through the tenth and especially in the early eleventh centuries. In Somerset, the early group was augmented by the construction of defences on the hilltop at South Cadbury and the establishment there of a small mint early in the eleventh century.[109] Fortifications were built probably at Bristol, in order to protect the royal port, and perhaps also the estate at Barton.[110] In the South Hams (Fig. 121), Halwell[111] had a significant strategic position within a communication system embracing perhaps Kingsteignton in the east, Totnes, Kingsbridge, Plympton in the west and possibly Brent Hill on the south flank of Dartmoor; an additional fort may have been built soon after 1000 at Oldaport[112] (Modbury). The South Hams had been a particular focus of royal interest since at least Æthelwulf's time, and after 900 a policy of land exchange was clearly intended to bring the area into royal control: by 1066, fifteen estates, concentrated along 25 miles (40 km) of coast from the Tamar to the Dart and cutting off access into south Devon by way of the south-flowing rivers, were in the king's hands, a strategy which protected a large swathe of potentially vulnerable farmland, and also perhaps the supplies of tin coming from Dartmoor.

As matters turned out, although bitter fighting against Viking enemies erupted again between 980 and 1016, this tended to be essentially dynastic in character. This may help to explain why the south-western boroughs had mixed fortunes, and why some, like Halwell, possibly Oldaport and Lyng faded away and others, like Watchet, dwindled, as military bases usually do when their *raison d'être* has disappeared.

108.   N. Brooks, 'The administrative background', in D. Hill and A. Rumble (eds), *The Defence of Wessex: The Burghal Hidage and Anglo-Saxon Fortifications* (1996), pp. 128–50, esp. pp. 142–3; for Plympton, S380.

109.   L. Alcock, *Cadbury Castle, Somerset: The Early Medieval Archaeology* (1995), pp. 154–62.

110.   Aston, 'Post-Roman central places', p. 59; L. Keen, *'Almost the Richest City': Bristol in the Middle Ages* (1997), pp. 18–30.

111.   T. Slater, 'Controlling the South Hams: the Anglo-Saxon *burh* at Halwell', *TDA*, 123 (1991): 57–78; see also B. Horner, 'Totnes revealed – new evidence of the early town and its defences', *PDAS Newsletter*, 73 (1999): 1–3.

112.   P. Rainbird, 'Oldaport and the Anglo-Saxon defence of Devon', *PDAS*, 56 (1998): 153–64.

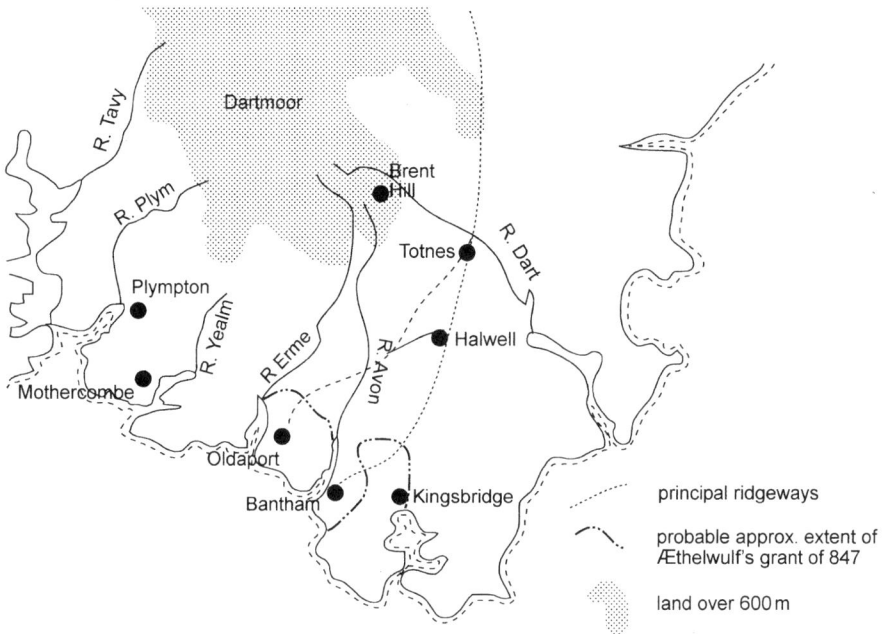

Figure 121 Strategic considerations in the South Hams, Devon

Developing markets

For those settlements well placed to exploit tenth-century economic opportunities, choice as a borough no doubt gave a boost. In 877 Exeter is described as a *faesten* ('fortress') but in 893 it is called a *burh*, suggesting the rebuilding of its walls, which fieldwork is beginning to unravel.[113] It is fairly certain that the four main city gates continued to be on (or very close to) the Roman sites (Fig. 122), and that South Street developed in the post-Roman period as a short cut between the central graveyard and the South Gate. Within its walls the city developed a new street plan which differed from the Roman plan, particularly in the south and west, implying important realignments of property boundaries as the space filled up with craft and service workers. There may also have been an access route all the way round the inside of the walls, a characteristic piece of military planning.

Businesses were springing up in the eleventh-century city. A kiln and wasters of high quality was excavated in Bedford Street, and other finds of pottery show links with Normandy, Brittany and the Loire Valley. Horners were working in Goldsmith Street and Waterbeer Street, judging by the remains of horn cores, and metalworkers there and in the High Street. Presumably buildings were both homes and workshops and most of these were timber-built. The street plan suggests that churches like St George's (South Street) and St Stephen and St Lawrence (High Street) were being built, in stone, with the development of parochial organization which this implies.

---

113. Allen *et al.*, 'Saxon Exeter', pp. 385–414; Hill, 'Athelstan's urban reforms', pp. 173–85; Blaylock and Parker, *Exeter City Defences*.

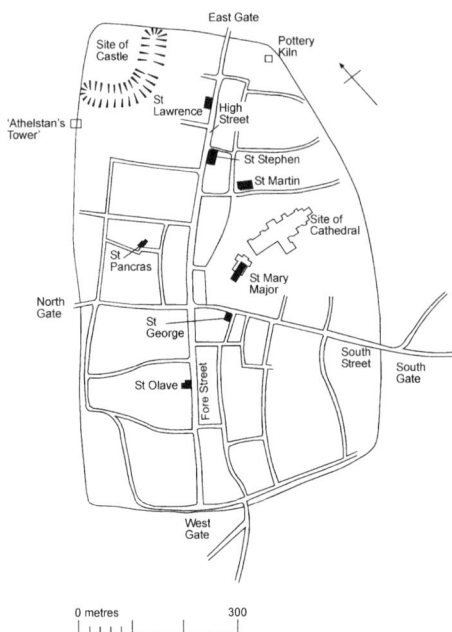

Figure 122 Late Saxon Exeter (Allen *et al.* 1984, Fig. 126; Morris 1997, Fig. 47)

Like Barnstaple, Lydford's surviving town plan seems to show elements of a late Saxon layout, and coins were being minted there by about 973; its development was surely tied to tin-winning activities on Dartmoor (Fig. 123). Axbridge had 36 burgesses in 1086, and Bath was a substantial borough of 20 hides. Bridport, Wareham and Shaftsbury are all listed as boroughs in 1086, and Wareham's street plan, with spine and side roads, may have been laid out in the tenth century, as may those of the other three.

However, centres which did not figure in the burghal list were at least as successful: in 1086 Okehampton had a market and Totnes, where the overall layout of the streets running around the High Street represents the extent and defences of the Saxon town, had over a hundred burgesses, while Tavistock certainly had a market by the early twelfth century. Taunton, similarly, had 64 burgesses and a substantial market. Ilchester, with a newly developing street plan which largely ignored the Roman layout, had 107 burgesses and a market in 1086, and Milborne Port had 56, and a relatively small market. At Dorchester again a new street plan developed in probably the tenth century, and Wimborne had burgesses in 1086.

In Cornwall, too, the Domesday record provides evidence of the development of trading activity. Bodmin is recorded with 68 dwellings and a market, and there were also markets at Launceston, originally at St Stephen's, at St Germans and at Liskeard, and one also at Marazion opposite St Michael's Mount; in Cornwall the importance of a monastic background is particularly clear. Both Bruton and Crewkerne had mints, at least in the early eleventh century, as did the flourishing sites of Barnstaple and Totnes. The rising number of mints through the eleventh century seems to be a sure indicator of increasing trade, operating at centres with a mixed range of back-

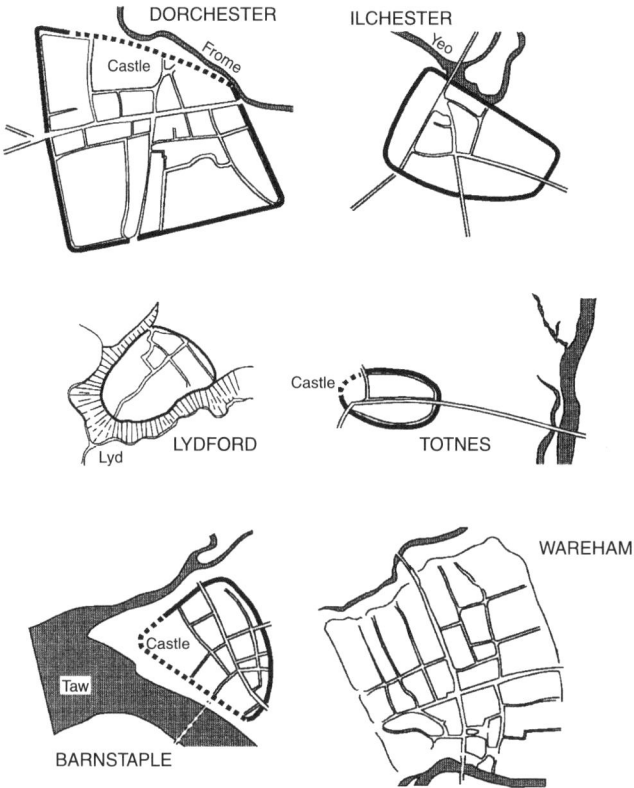

Figure 123 Late Saxon settlement plans at Lydford, Ilchester, Barnstaple, Dorchester, Totnes (after Hill 2000, Figs 2, 5), and Wareham (after Penn 1980, Figs 55, 57, 109)

grounds, suggesting that organic growth embracing a broad range of topographical and entrepreneurial factors were important and that general royal encouragement was at least as important as direct royal intervention.

Probably most of the trade flowing through these developing market towns dealt in locally produced foodstuffs and clothing, or the products of local farming, like the horn spoons available in Exeter. Their significance rests in the slow but steady rise in the range, number and probably quality of the material goods which, as the spiral of prosperity developed, became available to increasing numbers of people. The post-900 towns mark an important stage in the civilizing process which gradually produced the homes, manners and mindset that became characteristic of the middle class.

Within this undramatic but crucial development, there may have been a factor with a different kind of significance. Interesting recent controversy[114] has suggested that

114. J. Maddicott, 'Trade, industry and the wealth of King Alfred', *Past and Present*, 123 (1989): 3–51; J. Nelson, 'Debate: trade, industry and the wealth of King Alfred', *Past and Present*, 135 (1992): 151–63; R. Balzaretti, 'Debate: trade, industry and the wealth of King Alfred', *Past and Present*, 135 (1992): 142 50; J. Maddicott, 'Reply', *Past and Present*, 135 (1992): 164–88.

the wealth Alfred was able to deploy for the payment of fighting men, the building of fortifications and generally for the matériel of war derived to an important degree from the exploitation of Dartmoor tin, and, to a lesser extent, Mendip lead-derived silver. It is possible that the economic strength of the south-east of the kingdom had declined as a result of Viking activities, which destroyed the lucrative cross-Channel continental trade. This tilted the political and economic balance of Wessex away from its relatively recently acquired eastern provinces and back to its western heartland, particularly Somerset, where Alfred turned at the crisis of his reign in 878, and to eastern and southern Devon.

Information about coin minting and the silver flow, together with evidence illuminating 'Exeter's remarkable prosperity'[115] in the late tenth century, may suggest that, even as early as Alfred's reign, the city had sustained a principal role in a three-cornered trade. This may have been based on tin, together with hides, slaves and hunting dogs, the always cited products of the British underdeveloped hinterland, and covered south Devon and Ireland, with Brittany as the continental entry. Lydford may have been an important centre for working tin ore, or, as later, the administrative centre for part of the industry. The remarkable silver hoard containing a scourge, a chalice, various ornaments and coins buried in (former) tin workings at Trewiddle,[116] Cornwall (Fig. 124), perhaps in 868 or 875–877, may suggest that tin was being worked there at the time. After *c.* 1000, as the Irish trade passed to Chester and Bristol, Exeter's significance dipped, and fluctuated thereafter, but it may have played a pivotal role in producing in Alfred's reign the 'wealth which . . . made possible the emergence of England'.[117]

However, although Alfred was indeed rich, much of his wealth took the form of traditional treasure rather than coined silver and the evidence for tin exploitation on a

Figure 124 Silver chalice from Trewiddle (electrotype), Royal Cornwall Museum (photo: author)

115.   Maddicott, 'Trade, industry and wealth', p. 30.
116.   D. Wilson and C. Blunt, 'The Trewiddle hoard', *ARCH*, 96 (1961): 15–122.
117.   Maddicott, 'Trade, industry and wealth', p. 51.

politically significant scale in the ninth–tenth centuries is sketchy.[118] We may wonder, too, if a man like Alfred could have thought in terms of 'managing an economic resource'[119] and, if he could, whether the limitations of ninth-century political power would have made such management possible. When Alfred retreated to Athelney he was above all looking for support in the land where lay the West Saxon royal 'lands and palaces, their family monasteries, their bishops, the tombs of their ancestors and kin'.[120] Nevertheless, early medieval kings did not have to think like modern economists to understand the political advantages which derive from controlling the supply and redistribution of prestige goods or the fiscal advantage to be taken from taxing the flow of exchange, for such manipulation of material culture had been at the heart of power for centuries (if not millennia). Early *emporia* and the tenth to eleventh-century trading towns which succeeded to them, whether West Saxon (and other) kings fully understood this or not, were key in the development of the state. They generated resources outside the traditional sources of land and conquest, and they encouraged a society ordered upon royal law and the mutual obligations it would create, rather than on kinship and blood feud.

Changes in the landscape

The most fruitful way of approaching understanding of what was happening in the allocation and management of the landscape is through concentration upon a few key areas for which we have significant records in the form of monuments and charters as well as Domesday Book, always allowing for the fact that all these are difficult and controversial to interpret.

As we saw in Chapter 2, Dartmoor around 600 seems to show a series of large estates in a rough ring around the moor, each on an axis intended to give access to high grazing at one end and potential arable at the other, most with some visible evidence of elite proprietorship in the shape of carved or inscribed stones and many with a Christian burial ground. Dartmoor revisited towards the end of the tenth century hints at broad social developments (Fig. 125). In 739, Æthelheard had given to Crediton as its founding endowment a large tract of land, the south-western edge of which ran down to the north-eastern area of the moor, and which embraced some ten later parishes. All of these except Drewsteignton and Hittisleigh constituted the hundred of Crediton which, when it surfaces in the record, belonged as a private hundred of the Bishop of Exeter. Further south, the tract of land belonging to Exeter known as *Paedington* was described in an undated set of boundary clauses probably drawn up around 1050. It appears to include the parishes of Ashburton, Woodland, Bickington and Buckland in the Moor in the south, and that of Manaton in the north, but bisects those of Widecombe in the Moor and Ilsington.

The history of these two estates suggests that originally they were much like, although in the case of the 739 endowment, larger than, the kind of substantial, mixed resource estate which seems to have been the pattern of post-Roman settlement in the area. It seems likely that the open moor began at their western edges and that what later became the parishes of Manaton, whose name means 'common

118.   Nelson, 'Debate', pp. 151–63.
119.   Balzaretti, 'Debate', p. 150.
120.   Nelson, 'Debate', p. 163.

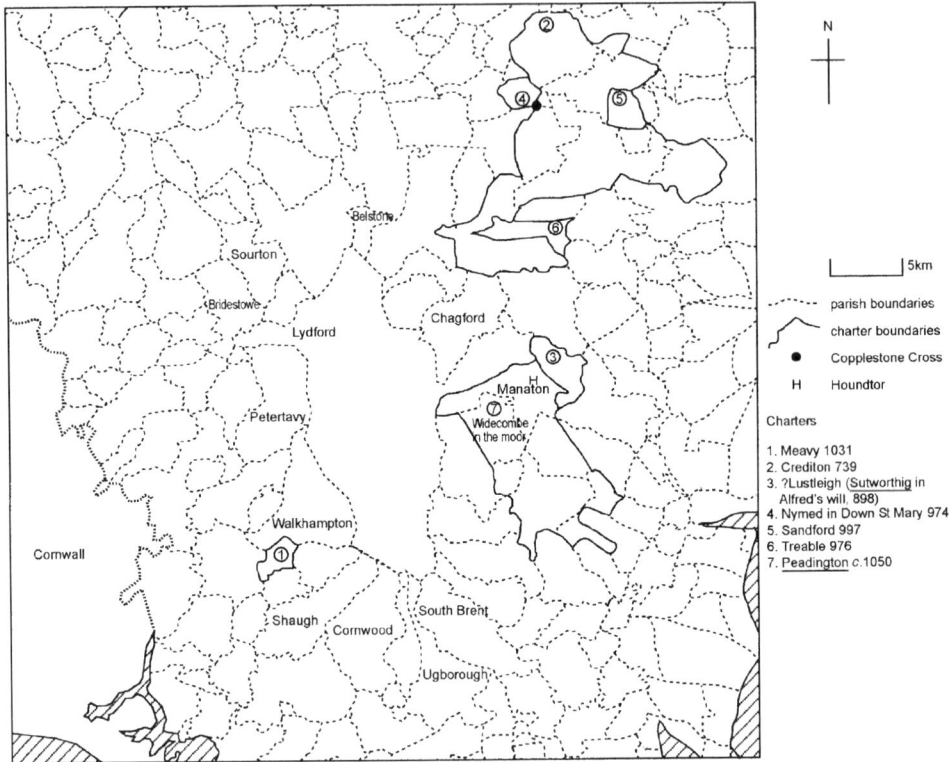

Figure 125 Later Saxon land arrangements in and around Dartmoor

land', Widecombe, Buckland and others to the north, were in the eighth and ninth centuries rough grazing without permanent settlement. The land unit now called Lustleigh (whether or not it should be identified with the *Suthworthig* of Alfred's will) may have shared the common land and access route which came to be Manaton parish.

What we seem to see here are the creation, probably in the tenth century, of a crescent of new settlements on the eastern side of the moor from perhaps Dean Prior to Throwleigh, inserted between the older units and the high moor on what had been open grazing attached to the older settlements. The same seems to have been true on the western side of the moor, where the common lands shared between Sourton and Bridestowe still survive, but where Peter Tavy, Walkhampton and Meavy, for example, seem to have new developments between the old areas and the high moor. The Meavy charter of 1031, with its reference 'thence due east to the hay (wagon) way of the people of Buckland (Monachorum)',[121] seems to record a phase in this process, with the creation of the new estate linked with a desire to ensure continued access to the moor's resources for the people of Buckland.[122] On the

---

121.   Hooke, *Charter-bounds*, p. 199.
122.   Pearce, 'Church and society in south Devon AD 350–700', *PDAS*, 40 (1982): 1–18.

southern flank of the moor evidence is thin, but Ugborough, for example, looks like one of the old units.

By 1086, the area of the Crediton charter included not only the great episcopal manor of Crediton, but, among other units, Kennerleigh ('Cyneweard's wood or clearing'), Sandford, Hittisleigh ('Hyhten's wood or clearing'), Bramford Speke and Upton Pyne, all of which came to be separate parishes. By 1086 both Upton Pyne and Bramford Speke contained various manors. In the south, the land had frag-mented into at least six manors, most very small, with Drewsteignton rather larger. Two grants on the estate's flank at *Nymed* dated 974 and Treable dated 976 show up landholdings similar to that of Kennerleigh, but in neither case were these holdings the whole of their parishes (and in Treable's case, at least, and possibly *Nymed*'s too, these were probably not new farming units, but newly separated from their old estates as legal units in their own right).

Similar processes were at work elsewhere. The land in Meavy parish was held as several manors in 1086. In *Peadington*,[123] both Bickington ('Breocca's farmstead or estate') and Woodland, whose name speaks for itself, became separate parishes. Buckland, whose name shows that it too was the subject of a (lost) charter (*Bocland*, 'land granted by book/charter'), was turned into a separate unit. The large, rough upland areas of Widdecombe and Ilsington were organized into parishes containing a range of holdings recorded in Domesday, and the same happened at Manaton where Houndtor (*Hundatora*) high on the moor is listed. By 1086 all three estates had been lost by Exeter, but when this had happened is unclear.

All this suggests that, in central Devon, long-term trends from perhaps as early as *c.* 780 were working to create new land units, some by turning what had been tracts of marginal upland grazing into productive holdings in their own right and some by fragmenting early, large estates, like that on the Creedy, into similar pieces. The relatively late boundaries of *Peadington* suggest that the process was continuing well up to the Norman Conquest, and probably beyond it. The bald statements in the records veil what must, on the ground, have been a complex series of legal arrange-ments, some intended to protect the rights of the old landlord and others to enhance those of new tenants or owners, and some of the losses which Exeter seems to have suffered presumably featured here.

Similar processes can be seen at work in west Cornwall. Around Bodmin Moor new settlements were being created, signalled by the appearance of Hamatethy in St Breward as a manor in 1066. Its name includes the element **havos* (Old Cornish, 'summer dwelling'), and Hamatethy must have started as a shieling used during the summer grazing.[124] The parishes of St Keverne, St Martin in Meneage, St Antony in Meneage and perhaps Manaccan may all have been the substantial property of the religious house of St Keverne at an early stage, given that 'meneage' is a district name meaning 'monkish land'. If this was so, the estate (Fig. 126) seems to have been deliberately broken up from the mid-tenth century. In 967 Edgar gave estates at Lesneage and Pennare to Wulfnoth Rumuncant, 'his faithful vassal', and in 977 Edward gave Earl (*comes*) Æthelweard grants at Traboe, Trevallack and Grugwith, all in the parish of St Keverne and at Trethewey in St Martin in Meneage.[125]

---

123. Hook, *Charter-bounds*, pp. 217–24.
124. P. Herring, 'Transhumance in medieval Cornwall', in H. Fox (ed.), *Seasonal Settlement* (1996), pp. 35–44; N. Johnson and P. Rose, *Bodmin Moor: An Archaeological Survey Vol. 1. Human Landscape to c. 800* (1984), pp. 78–9.
125. Hooke, *Charter-bounds*, pp. 45–52.

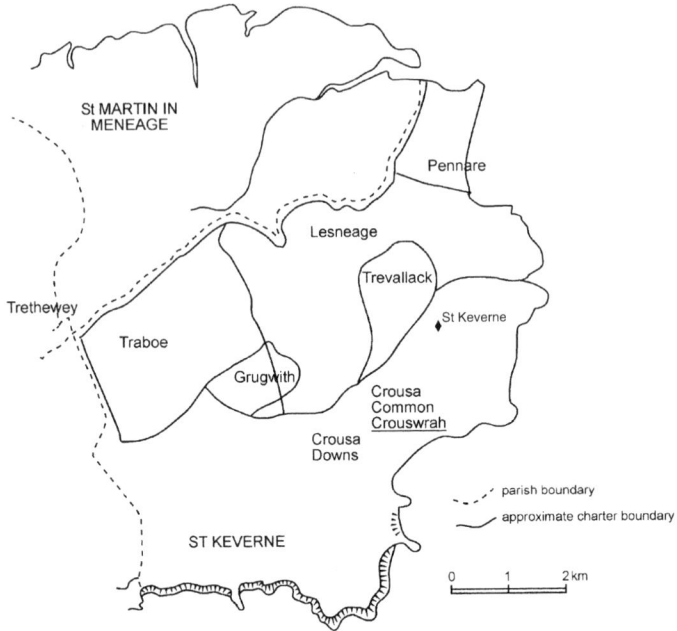

Figure 126 Estates (simplified) in the St Keverne area, West Cornwall (after Hooke 1994 pp. 38, 47), showing the relative positions of Lesneage, Pennare, Traboe, Grugwith, Trevallack, Trethewey and the *crouswrah*

St Keverne had, of course, been an important institution within the defeated Cornish kingdom, and perhaps was treated less respectfully for that reason (although it still held a large estate in 1086), and the Crediton/Exeter lands also belonged to the Church. It is possible that Church lands were being targeted in the tenth and eleventh centuries, partly no doubt, because some houses were so rich in land, but this maybe an illusion created by the higher survival of records relating to Church land, coupled with their corporate nature, which meant that their lands tended to survive en bloc while those in private hands were subject to the usual family vicissitudes.

In Somerset, we see the long list of old estates held by the king in 1086, like Somerton, Cheddar, North and South Petherton and Curry Rival, which 'had never paid tax' but owed 'one night's revenue with its customary dues'.[126] Here any fragmentation of the estates seems to be generally both petty and recent. This attests to the careful way in which successive kings had preserved these lands, which were in many ways the economic and social engine that had enabled Wessex to survive in the 870s. Elsewhere in the shire, things look more familiar. In 729, Æthelheard had given Glastonbury the huge (60 hides) estate at Pouholt and this seems to have included what became by 1086 a 30-hide estate with its centre at Shapwick and another also of 30 hides at Walton. By then Shapwick, still held by Glastonbury, contained five recognized holdings which seem to be amalgamations of the land held by fourteen

---

126.   Thorn and Thorn, *Somerset*, under place-names.

thegns in 1066, and recent history of Walton was similar.[127] At Rimpton we see the opposite process in which the estate left by Brihtric Grim to the Old Minster at Winchester in the mid-tenth century was built up from a unit south of the river, to which were added two further single-hide units, while in the neighbouring parish of Sandford Orcas a single-hide unit maintained a distinct identity until at least 1086.[128]

The history of the Isle of Purbeck in south-east Dorset may have been similar. Corfe seems to have been the centre of a royal estate which originally comprised the area of the two parishes of Corfe Castle and Worth Matravers (and possibly also those of Langton Matravers, Swanage and Studland, that is, the whole hundred of Rowbarrow). A series of charters and later documents cast (some) light on the creation of landholdings within the old estate, and by 1086 Worth contained some six holdings, five in its western part and Swanage in the east, and Corfe Castle perhaps seven, including the large estate of Kingston held by Shaftesbury.[129] These are, of course, only quick snaps taken at limited, and what may turn out to be rather specialized, sites across the region, but perhaps they serve to give the numerous landholdings in the Domesday record a context.

Villages and fields

The nature and history of the units, which show up in the legal record from *c.* 900 as separate, viable holdings with their own capacity to produce surplus and pay dues, is critical, and one of the great areas of debate: were these new land units carved out of (more or less) virgin land within an older estate, or were they existing, perhaps ancient, small, ancillary settlements, newly elevated to become the heads of small but separate estates which perhaps comprised the land which they had worked? Collectively, the evidence suggests that often what had been specialized elements in a larger, older estate – perhaps, as the place-names show, a hamlet where the inhabitants had had particular expertise with sheep or honey bees – became the centre of a new unit carved out of the old one which was now expected to manage its land as a mixed food producer, virtually by itself. Bound up with all this is probably the process by which estates established formal rights to pieces of detached, distant pasture, as did *Peadington* on Dartmoor and various communities on Blackmoor in north Dorset.[130] Other estates acquired subsidiary settlements in small food-rich coastal areas. In south Devon, Haccombe-with-Combe parish had a small enclave of Stokeinteignhead on Babbacombe Bay and Kenton one in Dawlish on the open sea just beyond the Exe estuary sandbar of Dawlish Warren.[131] All the arrangements, as

127. N. Corcos, 'Early estates on the Poldens and the origin of settlement at Shapwick', *PSANHS*, 127 (1983): 47–54.
128. M. Costen, 'Settlement in Wessex in the tenth century: the charter evidence', in M. Aston and C. Lewis, *The Medieval Landscape of Wessex*, (1994), pp. 97–114.
129. D. Hinton, 'Some Anglo-Saxon charters and estates in south-east Dorset', *PDNHAS*, 116 (1994): 11–20.
130. K. Barker and D. Seaward, 'Boundaries and landscape in Blackmoor: the Tudor manors of Holnest, Hilfield and Hermitage', *PDNHAS*, 112 (1990): 5–22.
131. H. Fox, *The Evolution of the Fishing Village: Landscape and Society along the South Devon Coast* (2001), pp. 48–51.

the tangled parish boundaries which record them show, were to have a long and complex future history.

The issue is intimately bound up with the history of what we see in some places as the substantial nuclear village,[132] and of the development of field patterns and other exploitative practices in the landscape. Closely linked to the origins of the village were the origins of its fields, particularly of the so-called 'open field' system. Here the arable was subdivided into ploughlands, which were worked collectively by the peasants of the estate, but where the holdings of individual peasants were in strips, which were not consolidated but rather distributed throughout the whole of the great arable fields.

It is a strikingly odd system which badly needs explanation, both for its origins and, given the length of time it could survive, for the formative effect it must have had on the mindset of the generations who worked it, and on their contemporary descendants. It is important, also, to remember that the broad system differed from place to place in intimate response to soils and climate, types of crops and livestock, technological developments, population profiles and the local inheritance of custom and belief.

Glastonbury's estate at *Pouholt*, granted in 729, had, by 1086, split into the separate holdings of Shapwick, Catcott, Edington, Chilton Polden and perhaps some others too: Shapwick was probably the minster church of the area (Fig. 127). Within Shapwick parish scattered finds of Roman pot and coin hoards, together with the names Abchester, Chestells, Bassecastell and Blackland, all suggest a pattern of late/post-Roman scattered settlement, with their own local, small, squarish fields along lines typical of the time, although these have not been firmly located. Names in the fields, like Shortenworthy, Nitherborgh and Bosehaies, which all suggest enclosures, hint that this pattern continued, sometimes perhaps on the old sites, and perhaps with isolated farmsteads, with attached fields worked by the family and its assorted dependants; most of the settlers' cattle would have gone onto the Levels for the summer grazing.

At some point, in perhaps the tenth century, and possibly at much the same time as when *Pouholt* began to fragment into a number of legally separate estates, Shapwick saw a fundamental reorganization. This recast the arable into two big open fields, East Field and West Field, in which the farming families now had separate strips. Excavated evidence from Bridewell Lane and elsewhere suggests that they probably came to live together in what we call the village of Shapwick, an inevitable part of the creation of the big fields because the scattered old homes would have had to be destroyed to prevent them hindering the plough. Some may have appreciated the move towards neighbourliness and collectivization and encouraged village life, but others must have viewed it with sinking hearts and bitter dissent.

---

132.   Reviews of work on village formation appear in D. Hooke (ed.), *Medieval Villages: A Review of Current Work* (1985), where B. Roberts, 'Village patterns and forms: some models for discussion', pp. 7–25, analyses elements and models, in A. Ellison, *Villages Survey: An Interim Report* (1976), which discusses the methodology of village survey with special reference to Isle Abbots (Som), and in C. Taylor, 'Polyfocal settlement and the English village', *Med. Arch.*, 21 (1977): 189–93. H. Fox ('The study of field systems', *The Devon Historian*, 4 (1972): 3–11) gives a useful analysis of field system management with special reference to Devon; and M. Bird, D. Butler and D. Griffiths ('Landscape archaeology', *DAS News*, 72 (1999): 6) have published guidelines for studying the Devon landscape.

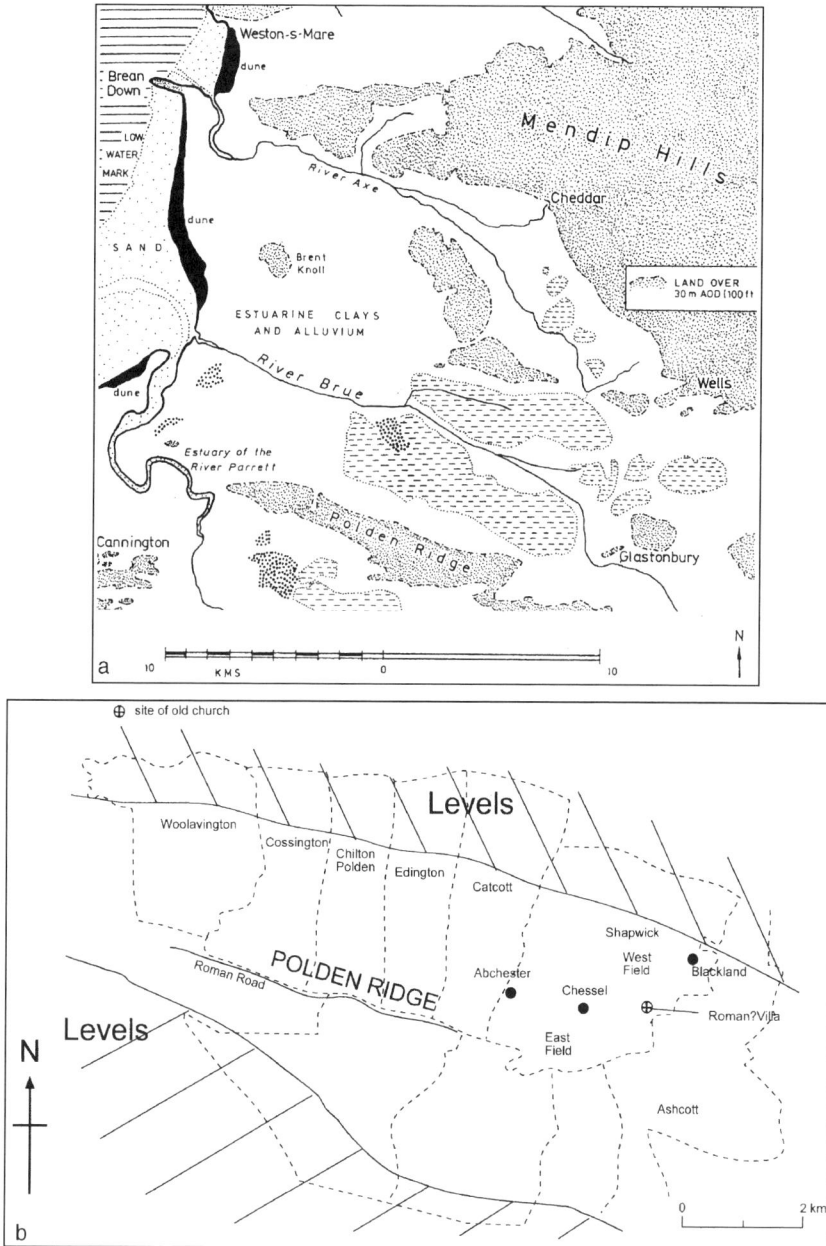

Figure 127 (a) Shapwick in context, (b) landscape features around Shapwick, Somerset (after Costen 1992b)

This need not have been a sudden or catastrophic event, but there are hints that at Shapwick the settlers may have been faced with a *force majeur*, particularly the strong suggestion that the village was deliberately laid out according to a preconceived plan.[133] Similar signs of overarching planning appear in the other settlements along the Polden Ridge, which were also part of ancient *Pouholt*. Shapwick and the rest were owned by Glastonbury, and in the 940s Glastonbury was refounded by Dunstan, the great reforming abbot, who may have given the inhabitants of *Pouholt* short shrift.

Whether or not Dunstan was personally responsible for what happened at Shapwick, or how swift the changes may have been, other Glastonbury estates show signs of what looks like a calculated policy. In 973 King Edgar had acquired Braunton in north-east Devon from Glastonbury, an estate based on an ancient religious house which Glastonbury had acquired in the mid-ninth century. Braunton is unlikely to produce much evidence of Roman settlement and work so far has not yielded information about post-Roman settlement patterns, but the famously surviving open-field layout, which still occupies some 142 ha to the south-west of the settlement, may have been laid out in the tenth century. Braunton Marsh and adjacent Horsey Island were also both carefully divided and managed, at a later date at least, as out-field pasture, which supplemented the excellent access to the Exmoor upland grazing. Within the Great Field (Figs. 128 and 129), the surviving names Lower and Higher Croft and Hayditch possibly hint at settlement sites abandoned as the field

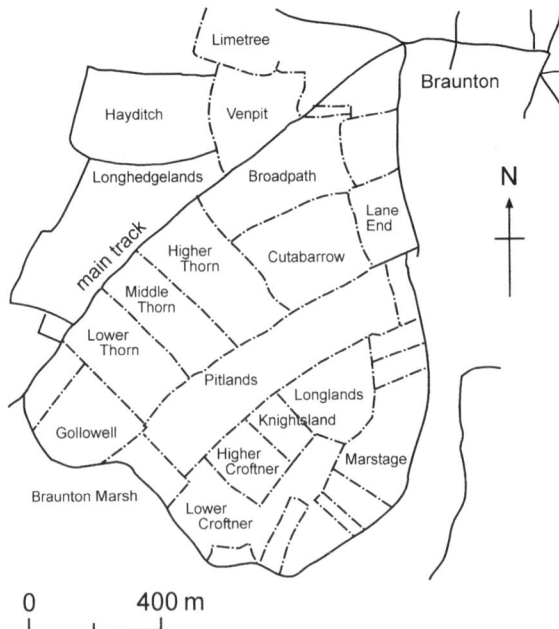

Figure 128 Braunton Great Field, as it survived in the earlier twentieth century (after Slee 1952, Plate 5A)

---

133.   For Shapwick, Corcos, 'Early estates', pp. 47–54; Costen, 'Settlement in Wessex', pp. 97–105; M. Aston, M. Costen and C. Gerrand, 'The Shapwick project', *Current Archaeology*, 151 (1977): 244–54. The planned ladder-like grid at Shapwick and Braunton is known from a number of sites, e.g. Cheddar, Dundon, Carhampton and Hardington Mandeville in Somerset. Blair has suggested (1996) that these originated in the lay settlements attached to minsters, but they might still be part of an arable re-organization.

Figure 129 South-eastern part of Braunton Great Field, looking north, with adjacent fields to the north and part of Braunton Marsh to the south-west. The strips in the Great Field, arranged in bundles, can be seen plainly. (Photo: Crown Copyright 1960/ MOD)

developed.[134] The layout of Braunton village, with its ladder pattern bisected by the River Caen, bears considerable similarity to that of Shapwick (Fig. 130). Podimore, in east Somerset (Fig. 130), owned by Glastonbury between 966 and 1529, may be another example.[135] It is possible, too, that on some, at least, of the crucial Somerset royal estates, like Bruton, Milborne and Queen Camel, similar reorganizations were imposed within a relatively short time-span. Where villages emerged they were also institutional communities through which were arranged the new economic system of tofts, tenancies, royal taxes and church tithes, elements in the wider regularization of life which typified the later ninth century and onwards.

Elsewhere, outside the immediate control of the largest corporate landlords, the movement towards open-field communal agriculture may have been slower and more organic. Most of the 50 or so Somerset parishes lying south-east of the Fosse Way,[136] in an area of clay land which forms a south-western extension of the Midland Plain, have surviving visible and documentary evidence of their open fields, although dating is usually lacking. These parishes show the 'classic' pattern of nucleated villages (and sometimes additional nucleated hamlets too, suggesting that there had been amalgamation of communities at some stage) each with its church, manor house

---

134. *Braunton Great Field and Marshes* (1982).
135. H. Fox, 'Approaches to the adoption of the Midland system', in T. Rowley, *Origins of Open-field Agriculture* (1981), pp. 64–111. For the workings of strip systems, see discussion in H. Fox and O. Padel, *The Cornish Lands of the Arundels of Laherne: Fourteenth to Sixteenth Centuries* (2000).
136. M. Whitfield, 'The medieval fields of south-east Somerset', *PSANHS*, 125 (1981): 17–29.

Figure 130 Plan of villages at Braunton, Devon, from the Tithe Map of 1841, and at Shapwick, Somerset, from that of 1839 (after Aston, Costen and Gerrand 1997, p. 246, Map 1)

and adjacent arable fields, meadow and grazing. This general pattern is also apparent in a number of Dorset parishes. In Devon documentary evidence for the existence of subdivided arable before 1500 suggests that such systems were mostly clustered in east Devon, which is topographically an extension of Dorset, and where again large royal manors, like Axminster, are conspicuous.[137] Perhaps, however, documentary evidence tends to produce material relating to the larger, more elaborate and legally complex field systems, rather than the smaller ones with simpler management processes; or, to put the matter rather differently, it is possible that archaeological work would produce evidence of smaller-scale open strip fields in northern Devon, as it has in Cornwall.

Eventually, subdivided arable was at least as common in Cornwall as elsewhere, although dating is difficult. Carew, writing in 1602, described how the land 'lay all in common, or only divided by stichmeal [the local name for the separate strips] . . . in times, not past the remembrance of some yet living'.[138] Searches of the Tithe Maps have brought to light many examples of late or fossilized survivals of unenclosed strip systems, some, at least, of which may have pre-Conquest origins. On 50 ha at Forrabury Common, Willapark, perhaps originally part of Minster parish, survives an impressive stichmeal strip system with the parish church of Forrabury tucked into its southern side, although settlement patterns in the immediate area have probably

---

137.   H. Fox, 'Field systems of east and south Devon, Part I: East Devon', *TDA*, 104 (1972): 81–136.
138.   Quoted in A. Preston-Jones and P. Rose, 'Medieval Cornwall', *Corn. Arch.* 31 (1986): 151–2.

been much influenced by the founding of Bottreaux Castle in the twelfth century.[139] In many places, as at Treskilling in Luxulyan,[140] the strip systems related to small hamlets, although probably many of these small settlements also had enclosed fields, which were not subdivided or worked cooperatively.

Cornwall and north and west Devon did not as a rule develop the large nuclear villages which are typical of areas further east. The Tithe Maps, though dating from the 1830s and 1840s, give some indication of the character of earlier settlement patterns. For example, those from Inwardleigh and Thornbury, or Broadwood Kelly and Tetcott (all Devon), where the vestigial remains of a strip field system seem to survive (Fig. 131), show how very limited settlement, usually consisting of a few farms and their related cottages, clusters in a disorganized pattern around a focal church, which is often fronted by an open space to which the roads lead.

On a wider focus, a possible model suggests that, over a long period, perhaps beginning in the early eighth century and running on to at least the later eleventh, most farming communities thought it worthwhile to turn, at least in part, to the reorganization of rights, work and productivity which we see as open subdivided arable. This chimes in with what Ine's Laws say about ceorls having 'common meadow or other land divided in shares (*gedal land*)', some of which are clearly fenced while others are not, and which suggests that arable is similarly divided and partially fenced.[141] In some places, this may have been more or less enforced, and involved the

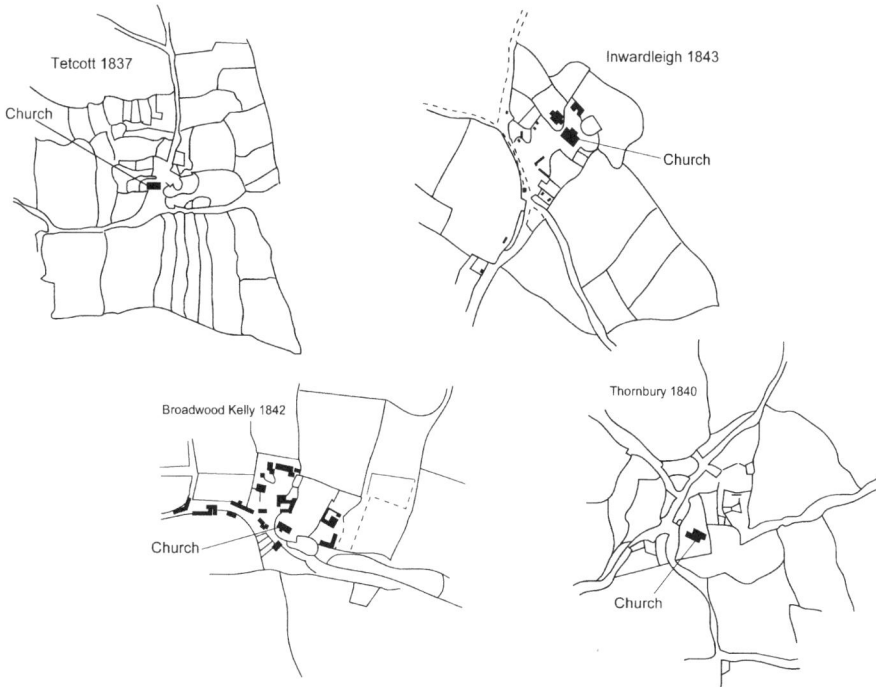

Figure 131 Settlements at Tetcott (from Tithe Map of 1837), Indwardleigh (1843), Broadwood Kelly (1842) and Thornbury (1840), Devon

139.   P. Wood, 'Open field strips, Forrabury Common near Boscastle', *Corn. Arch.*, 2 (1963): 29–33.
140.   Preston-Jones and Rose, 'Medieval Cornwall', pp. 151–3.
141.   Fox, 'Adoption of the Midland system', p. 87.

creation of nuclear villages as part of the process. Elsewhere it developed organically and relatively slowly, producing less regular villages which may be polyfocal and represent the coalescence of several older centres. Sometimes there was apparently virtually no nuclearization but perhaps a sharing of arable between a few hamlets, some relatively close to each other and their church, others more scattered.

Where the change took place cumulatively, it could have worked itself through over several generations who were able to work with the grain of local patterns of inheritance and population profile to create the necessary agreements and put new arrangements into effect. In some places, partible inheritance may have already been splitting up once integrated family holdings into the intermixed landscape typical of an open field, which it had become sensible to tidy up in a mutually operative style of management.[142] The development of the new, heavy ploughs, with furrow-turning mould boards which turn the earth more efficiently and work best when they are used to produce long, narrow strips, are often dragged cumbrously into the argument, but the relationship between material and culture is a complex one in which hearts and minds matter as much as technology. We must not assume that the use of heavy ploughs would have become widespread unless they could further ends which were desired for other means.

Some social implications

Issues like these help to describe the mechanisms through which change was brought about, and may themselves have contributed to the deeper reasons for the shift, but we sense that the fundamental implications behind so profound a change in human relationships to each other and to the land must lie within each community's capacity to produce enough food, particularly cereals. Local blips and the effect of population cycles notwithstanding, there seems to have been a general trend towards population growth in pre-Conquest centuries. Linked to this was the royal political need to satisfy the gentry/thegn class by creating booklands for them. This had an important effect across the countryside, as what had been ancillary settlements in large estates became the centres of their own smaller units. These units now had to generate the surplus needed to feed and clothe their lords who did not themselves directly produce. Since royal tax, levied from most of the estates, old and new alike, was needed to pay for defence and the bureaucratic structure of the medieval state, the burden of requirements probably generally rose. It was clearly necessary to raise the food yield country-wide, and this could be achieved by increasing the land under cultivation (as was done around the moorland edges) or increasing the production power of the cultivated land.

Increasing production of land already under the plough seems to be at the root of communal field systems. In order to keep the land fruitful, it had to be left fallow regularly, and its quality was greatly improved if during this period cattle were allowed to graze and drop manure upon it, something which was only possible if the fallow area was a large one, since small areas were very difficult to fence off in ways which kept the cattle out of any neighbouring areas of sown, and the perpetual irritation caused by straying animals may have been one of the reasons why com-

---

142.   R. Dodgshon, 'The interpretation of subdivided fields: a study in private or communal interests', in Rowley, *Origins of Open-field Agriculture* (1981), esp. pp. 131–2, and refs there.

munities were able to agree to create the large fields of the subdivided systems. It is possible, also, that in areas like south-east Somerset, and parts of Dorset, the considerable density of land exploitation hampered access to the large, traditional summer grazing areas, creating the need to find a large fallow area in which the cattle could be put, and which could then be used to grow food.

Access to open grazing was very important partly because it allowed a local economy to be geared as much to sheep, pigs, cattle and woodland products as to cereals, and partly because it relieved communities of the necessity to manage home pastures and the fallow with all that this implies. Devon, Cornwall and west Somerset all possessed enormous tracts of what is still the unfettered grazing land of the open moors. The patterns of traditional access by droving herds and flocks onto the communal upland, which were traced in Chapter 2, continued to influence the management of farming in the region fundamentally. The moorlands like Dartmoor were accompanied by smaller areas of woodland pasture, like that of Blackmoor between Sherborne and Cerne Abbas where access ways have been traced.[143] Most of the south-west lies within what has been called southern English woodland countryside, like that of Kent, Essex and the Chilterns, characterized in the later medieval period by more scattered settlement, winding lanes, mixed field shapes and often large parishes, rather than the 'champion' landscapes which run from South Yorkshire to Dorset and feature big villages, straighter roads and field boundaries, and uninterrupted vistas, a distinction which is very obvious to the eye both when walking in the countryside and looking at maps.

This contrast seems to be fundamental and suggests that, as the movement towards increased productivity which we call the subdivided arable system gathered momentum, it took a subtly different form in areas like much of the south-west. It helps to explain why the subdivided areas, although common, tended to be smaller and to be attached to hamlets or even single farms, rather than promoting the for-mation of large villages. It also fits with accumulating evidence suggesting that individual holdings, independent in the sense that they possessed their own viable fields and were worked separately, had been a normal part of the scene at least since late Roman times and continued to be throughout the post-Roman period and pre-Conquest periods.

The Law of Ine which refers to the need for fencing described the holding, evidently a socially low or 'peasant' holding, as a *worthig*, an Old English 'habitative' term which could apparently describe a large range of holdings from a tiny plot to a whole estate, but which perhaps essentially expresses possession, and which, judging by its context in Ine's Law, could be used in the sense of a separate farm.[145] Place-names containing *worthig*, often with a personal name attached, occur particularly in Devon and Somerset with a strong cluster in north-west Devon, which has an extension into north-east Cornwall and down the Tamar Valley (Fig. 132).[146]

Their concentration in north Devon, where a large run of both British and Anglo-Saxon place-names describing woodland suggests opportunities for new settlers, hints that perhaps they always tended to be on more difficult land. They may repre-

---

143. Barker and Seaward, 'Boundaries and landscape in Blackmoor', pp. 5–22. The broad way of life survived long enough to be described by Thomas Hardy in *The Woodlanders*.
144. Fox, 'Field systems of Devon', p. 84.
145. Fox, 'Adoption of the Midland system', pp. 86–7.
146. Gover *et al.*, *Place-names of Devon* (1931, 1932), and Padel, 'Place-names', pp. 88–94.

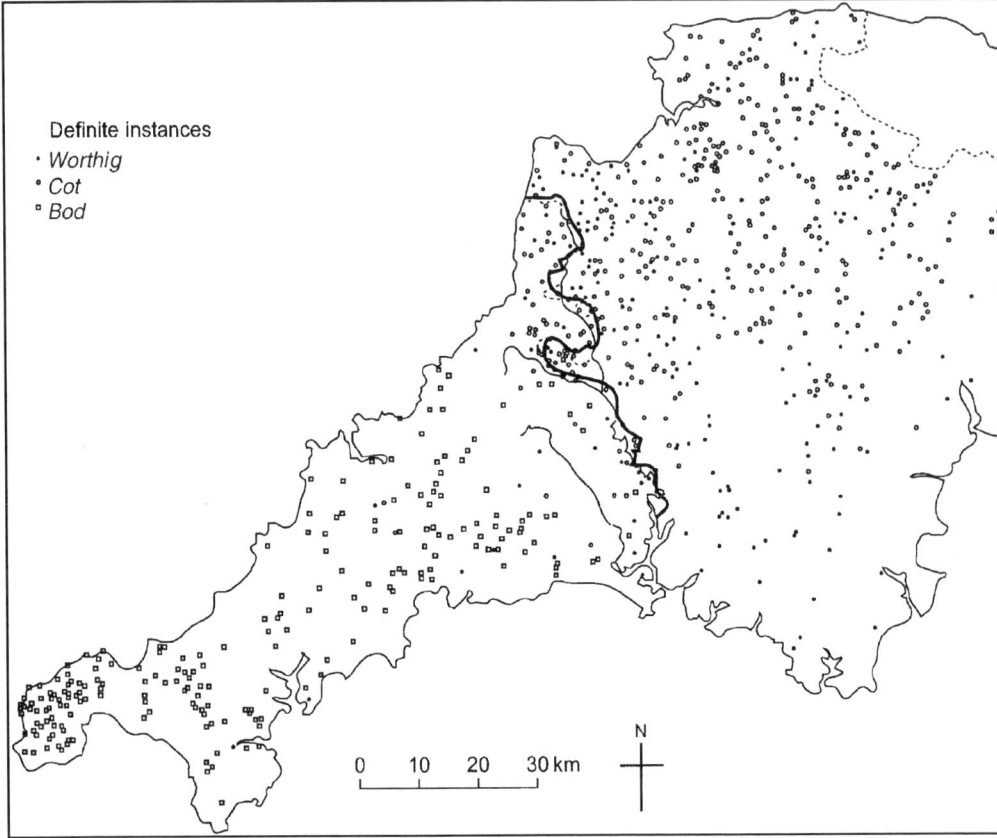

Figure 132 Places-names in *worthig*, *cot* and *bod* (after Padel 1999b, Maps 13.4, 2, 5)

sent self-contained holdings created or taken over from previous British-speaking inhabitants, in the areas between or beyond the bigger established estates.

Similar circumstances may lie behind the perhaps even humbler Old English place-name element *cot*, which has a clear concentration in north Devon. Conceivably *bod* represents the Cornish equivalent, although its concentration in Penwith suggests unexplained complexities.[147] The place-name element *huish*,[148] which derives from the same root-word as 'hide', meaning 'a family', or 'land for a family' and which seems to have been a self-contained unit of around 80 hectares, occurs over twenty times in Somerset in a widely dispersed pattern, and some seventeen times in Devon, and, like *worthig* names, tends to appear in what look like previously under-developed areas. South Huish in the Devon South Hams was a single-hide unit in 1086. The *huish* at Uddens in Dorset, granted by King Eadwig to his *optimas* Alfred, was still being run as a single farm in the eighteenth century, and it seems likely that many of these small areas continued to operate as self-contained farms.[149]

---

147. Padel, 'Place-names', pp. 93–4.
148. M. Costen, ' "Huish", "Worthen": Old English survivals in a late landscape', *Anglo-Saxon Studies in Archaeology and History*, 5 (1992): 65–83.
149. South Huish, Hooke, *Charter-bounds*, p. 111; Uddens, Costen, ' "Huish" ', pp. 65–83.

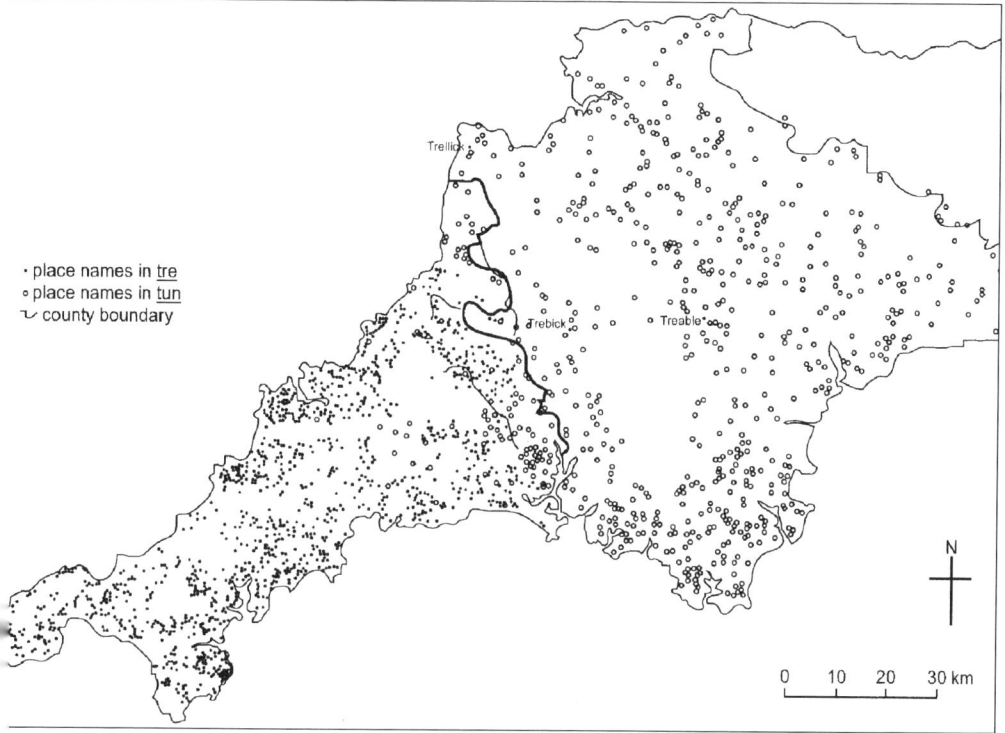

Figure 133 Place-names in *tre*, Old Cornish 'hamlet, farmstead', and *tun*, Old English 'farmstead, settlement' (definite instances) (from Padel 1999b, Figs 13.1 and 13.3)

The Cornish place-name *tre*, 'hamlet, farmstead', and the Anglo-Saxon *tun*, 'farm-stead, settlements',[150] seem to have an essentially complementary distribution west and east of the Tamar, with *tre* common everywhere outside the high upland in Cornwall and *tun* general in Devon, particularly common in the far south and with a distinct presence in eastern Cornwall (Fig. 133). *Tre* names seem to have been formed in Cornwall between the fifth to the eleventh centuries, and to represent the open settlements which superseded the enclosed rounds but which often continued to farm the same land. Whether such names ever existed in Devon and were overlain by Anglo-Saxon ones, whether linguistic circumstances changed before such British names could be formed or whether the older-style round enclosed settlements had been superseded anyway in Devon before we have access to any records telling us what they were called all remain open questions.[151] Names in *tun* may have begun

150.   Padel, 'Place-names', pp. 88–94.
151.   There are only three place-names in Devon with *tre* as their first element: Treable, Trellick and Trebick; and these are widely spread across the centre/west of the shire. Treable is first recorded in 1242 with a *tre* form as *Tryfebel* = *tref* + personal name *Ebel*, but in the charter of 976 the same estate is called *Hyples eald land*, 'Hyple's old estate', and Padel ('Place-names', p. 89) suggests that *Hyple* is an English version of OC *Ebel* and 'old estate' a rough translation of *tre(f)* showing how such place-names could disappear (although, as it happened, Treable hung on). We have no idea how widespread this kind of process may have been, but if it was common, and represents primarily cultural fashion, then it would help to demonstrate how the largely English nomenclature of west/north Devon place-names came about. See also Finberg, *Charters of Devon and Cornwall*, pp. 21–32.

to form as early as the sixth century, and largely seem to have ceased to be created in the eleventh century. Both names represent substantial settlements whose leading members seem to have been 'gentleman farmers' and the settlements themselves probably functioned as local centres for the collection and onwards transmission of various dues, and for localized exchange, a role signalled by the later derivation from *tun* of modern English 'town'.

Charter evidence suggests that holdings with *trev* names had been component parts of large estates from which they could be detached in the tenth century as separate estates, as was done around St Keverne, and perhaps at Trerice in St Dennis.[152] Similarly, holdings with *tun* names could clearly be parts of big estates, but could be separated off, as perhaps at Dunterton, Brixton and Dolton, all in Devon and held in 1086 by various men from Baldwin the Sheriff. This suggests that the farming settlements named in *tre* and *ton* were often substantial parts of large, established units, and were probably centred upon a relatively socially superior family; they were, also, sometimes, separate holdings. For a long period after *c.* 700 they were sometimes part of an estate-wide cooperative movement which eventually produced subdivided common arable, but also, sometimes, they retained some, perhaps ancient, enclosed fields. Often, too, they produced miniature versions of subdivided fields which appear as fossilized strip systems for reasons which may reflect those behind the large estate systems on a smaller scale. Legal arrangements which, especially during the tenth century, created new estates either by out-right gift or by a range of leasing arrangements, cut across a variety of agrarian arrangements in complicated ways, and often turned such settlements into estate centres. The settlements represented by place-names in *worthig*, *huish* and *bod*, many of them probably at a lower social level, seem to have had similar experiences. All of this variety, within a countryside which continued to offer scope to make a variety of livings, including new holdings on the marginal moorland fringes, helped to create the mixed, irregular and delightful landscapes still characteristic of the region.

Settlements and houses

A range of excavations has recovered house plans and material goods which have given us some insight into the patterns of life in the farming hamlets. The long-house,[153] with its living area at one end and an animal byre or shippon at the other, with side entrances and increasingly, probably, divisions sited to provide good access and separate the two functions, became the standard house type in the south-west (Fig. 134), as it was in the wider tradition across Britain. The basic plan allowed for a range of uses at different social levels, and eventually produced the characteristic form of the later medieval hall, with its eating and living end dominated by the dais, and a service end, divided by an open cross-passage. In most of the peninsula it seems that rectangular houses had replaced the earlier native roundhouse tradition by perhaps the fourth century, but the sequence from Gwithian, with its roundhouses of sixth–eighth-century date and its rather tentative, rectangular ninth to eleventh-

---

152.   P. Herring and D. Hooke, 'Interrogating Anglo-Saxons in St Dennis', *Corn. Arch.*, 32 (1993): 67–75.
153.   Preston-Jones and Rose, 'Medieval Cornwall', pp. 146–51.

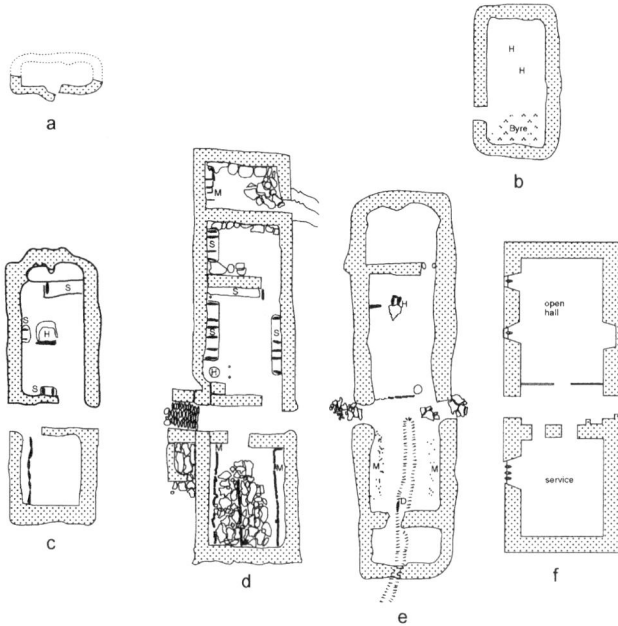

Figure 134 Plans of houses at (a) Gwithian, tenth/eleventh century; (b) Tresmorn stone-built house I; (c) Garrow longhouse of simple form; (d) Treworld longhouse with inner room; (e) Stuffle longhouse with additional room and inner room; (f) Truthall, Sithney, extant fifteenth-century hall house (after Preston-Jones and Rose 1986, Fig. 6)

century building, may give us an insight into the way in which Cornwall moved into the housing mainstream.

The hamlet at Mawgan Porth,[154] of tenth to eleventh-century date, consisted of at least two farms, each with a longhouse and ancillary buildings placed around a courtyard, or farmyard (Fig. 135). The buildings were stone built, and broadly similar structures are known at Tresmorn and Garrow. The better of these houses could be equipped with stone-built hearths and benches in the living area and mangers and drains (essential) in the byre. At Houndtor,[155] similar stone buildings, dated to the thirteenth century, may have been arranged in a similar if less definable pattern. These may have been preceded by turf houses of similar shape, but the excavated traces may just be stake holes for pens and so forth, contemporary with the stone houses. The Hut-Holes[156] settlement at Widecombe in the Moor presents similar issues of interpretation. If these sites are anything like typical of the pre-Conquest period, then we should think in terms of longhouse complexes across the peninsula, grouped a few together in those areas where hamlets prevailed, and clustered, with

---

154. R. Bruce-Mitford, *Mawgan Porth, a Settlement of the Late Saxon Period on the North Cornwall Coast* (1997), for full excavation account.
155. E. Minter, 'Eleven years of archaeological work on Dartmoor', *Trans. Torquay Natural History Soc.*, 16 (1972–3): 112–20; G. Beresford, 'Three deserted medieval settlements on Dartmoor: a report on the late E. Marie Minter's excavations', *Med. Arch.*, 23 (1979): 98–158.
156. Minter, 'Archaeological work on Dartmoor', pp. 112–20.

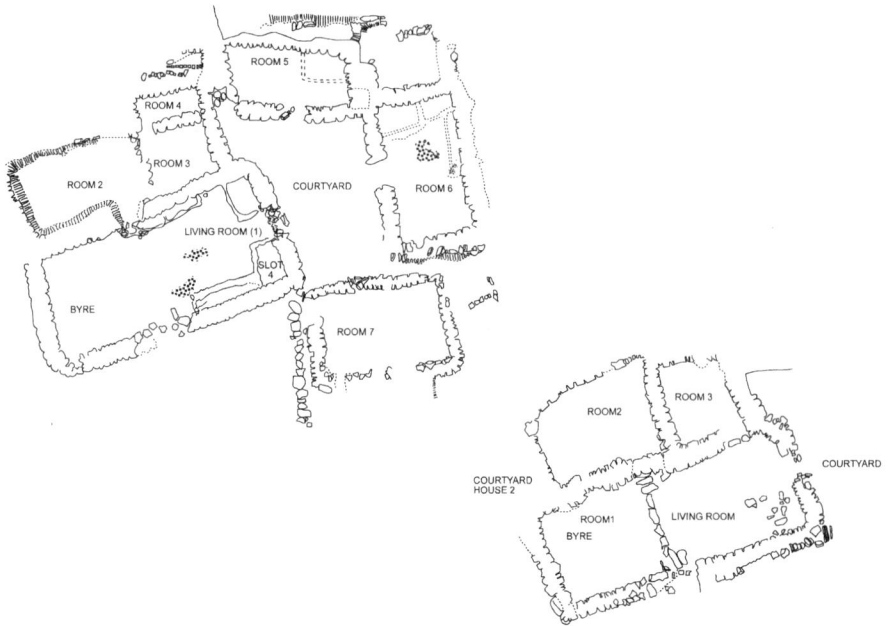

Figure 135 Plan of two courtyard complexes (simplified), Mawgan Porth, north Cornwall (after Bruce-Mitford 1997, Fig. 3)

perhaps an element of collective planning, where nuclear villages had emerged, but only excavation can confirm this kind of picture.

The Mawgan Porth people had small oxen presumably for ploughing, and they also had sheep (or goats), horses, dogs, cats and chickens. Mussels from the beach were evidently a very important source of protein, and numerous quern fragments testify that cereals were grown. The site produced over 2000 fragments of bar-lug pots.[157] Probable loom weights and spindle whorls suggested weaving. Metal was very scarce, and this was essentially a 'stone and bone' economy, based on seafood, sheep, some cereals and tools like hammer stones made from beach pebbles. The settlement was largely self-sufficient, but the silver penny of Æthelred II struck at Lydford between 990 and 995[158] suggests that the inhabitants had something to sell, perhaps hides. The settlers had their own graveyard of cist graves, with separate areas for infants and adults, and no known evidence of clear-cut religious affiliation. The hamlet was stripped of everything useful and abandoned when the inhabitants finally gave up the struggle against shifting sand. They established a new settlement up the valley on the site of the present village, where finds of bar-lug sherd show that life went on, without a break in the settlement's history.

Bar-lug pots continued to be used locally until the eleventh century when they seem to have been superseded by the various forms of Sandy Lane pots which

---

157.   G. Hutchinson, 'The bar-lug pottery of Cornwall', *Corn. Arch.*, 18 (1979): 81–103; Bruce-Mitford, *Mawgan Porth*, p. 80.
158.   Bruce-Mitford, *Mawgan Porth*, p. 85.

may have gradually evolved into the standard English wheel-made, sagging-base medieval cooking pots, but the dating of all these sequences, the relationship of the stylistic types and the sources all need further work. Similar cooking pots seem to have been in general use across the peninsula, but understanding of how production and distribution was managed, and when, is still thin.

The broadly rectangular house plan seems to have its roots in the late Roman villa/farmhouse buildings with their two or three rooms set end-on in a rectangle, together perhaps with continental traditions drawing on a similar background.[159] Its gradual adoption west of the Tamar may link with the shift away from the enclosed settlements with place-names in *caer* ('round') and towards unenclosed settlements with names in *trev* ('settlement, hamlet') and all this signals cultural change. The desire to have a presumably fairly small kin group, together with its oxen and maybe milk cows or a horse, under the same roof suggests that the notion of 'important kin' now meant fewer people living closer together, whose livelihood was directly identified with their own animals. This change may have happened after *c.* 700 in Cornwall and west Devon, and perhaps rather earlier further east.

The Church in the landscape

Related changes in ideas about lordship and how the production of the land should be managed were naturally matched by conceptual shifts in how the Christian nature of the countryside should be expressed. The stress on smaller units represented by the fragmentation of the old, great estates was accompanied by a similar pastoral localization. This appears as investment in churches, priests and their supporting land allotments (glebes) and service payments, which by the twelfth century linked up to become a parish system that had been established across Britain and western Europe. The evidence from excavation and fabric study suggests that stone parish churches were being built from around 970, as the first phase of what has been called 'the great rebuilding' which extended into the middle of the twelfth century, and in which, perhaps, the Norman Conquest was not the significant event it used to seem.[160] Some of these may, of course, have replaced humbler wooden churches, but the building programmes gave very positive expression to the lordship and landscape arrangements which were developing gradually from the eighth century, arrangements which were also able to generate the prosperity to make the buildings and their priests possible.

The congruence between the eastern consolidated estate with its developing nuclear village (of whatever genesis) and its new church is obvious, and created the classic pattern of the English landscape, which can be found in parts of the south-west. East Coker, three miles south-west of Yeovil, has a nuclear village, a manor house with a fifteenth-century hall and a church with probable late Anglo-Saxon

159.   S. James, A. Marshall and M. Millett, 'An early medieval building tradition', *Arch. J.*, 141 (1984): 243–51.

160.   J. Blair, 'Introduction: from minster to parish church', in *Minsters and Parish Churches. The Local Church in Transition 950–1200* (1988), esp. pp. 7–10. For an England-wide overview of the problems of dating the development of the parish system, see R. Morris, *Churches in the Landscape* (1989), pp. 140–67.

fabric.[161] The parish boundary suggests that Todber, Dorset, recorded as a self-contained estate in Domesday Book, began as a secondary settlement of neighbouring Marnhull, but it possesses fragments of a decorated stone cross of *c.* 1000 date.[162] The fragmentation of estates seems to have been a feature of life across the peninsula, but, as we have seen, in the 'woodland pasture' areas of the north and west the patterns of settlement and field seem often to have been either miniature versions with small strip systems and hamlets or (perhaps sometimes) self-contained farms and their fields. This has often suggested that the parochial history of the two areas was fundamentally different, but there is no overriding reason why this should be so. In the west, scattered settlement meant the parish came, quite naturally, to take its name from the church itself by employing the name of its patron, but this is by no means universally true in the west, and it appeared elsewhere too.

Probably the newly emerging parochial-style arrangements mark the time when most people first had access to regular celebrations of Mass, Church baptism and, perhaps most important of all, churchyard burial with prayers from an ordained priest. It is possible, indeed, that its ability to provide these things was one of the reasons why people were willing to accept the dislocations, however slow and carefully considered some of them may have been, which the new landed arrangements involved. Together, the fields, the houses and the church, and the network of paths made by the constant toing and froing, created the combination of habit and physical presence which fuses together as locality. The slow rhythm, and the association of that movement with the crises of life, together with the memories of important events bound up with the place, became a very significant way in which people created meaning and value in themselves, their landscape and their daily lives.

These changes and additions required a fresh configuration of the old pattern. Edgar's *Ordinance* of *c.* 960 on the payment of tithe gives an insight into the ideal the king hoped to impose:

1.1 And all payment of tithe is to be made to the old minster, to which the parish (*parochia*) belongs, and it is to be rendered both from the thegn's demesne land and from the land of his tenants, according as it is brought under the plough.

1.2 If however there is any thegn, who has on his bookland a church with which there is a graveyard, he is to pay the third part of his tithe into his church.

2.1 If anyone has a church with which there is no graveyard, he is then to pay to his priest, from the (remaining) nine parts, what he chooses.

2.2 And all churchscot is to go to the old minster from every free hearth.[163]

Up to a point the position of the 'old minsters' is protected; these are the religious establishments (east and west) whose responsibility for a *parochia*, that is an area

---

161.   Anglo-Saxon sculpture in Somerset churches is listed in S. Foster, 'A gazetteer of the Anglo-Saxon sculpture in historic Somerset', *PSANHS*, 131 (1987): 49–76, who also gives a brief list (p. 66) of Somerset churches with AS architectural masonry; as she justly remarks, the small number reflects 'how paltry are the actual remains' (p. 66); the principal sites are Muchelney, Milborne Port (possibly dubious) and Glastonbury.

162.   RCHM *Dorset, Vol. IV* (1972), p. 114.

163.   D. Whitelock (ed.), *English Historical Documents I 500–1042* (1955), p. 395.

within which they were expected to provide at least basic pastoral care and from which they received dues, is made clear. 'Old' is probably a relative term. Some of them undoubtedly had histories running back to the sixth–seventh centuries, but others probably belonged, perhaps like the Cornish churches with names in *eglos*,[164] to the eighth–ninth centuries, and represented the quasi-minster or proto-parish church arrangements made when a royal or large ecclesiastical estate happened to lack a religious foundation or when such an estate was first broken up into two or three large pieces, themselves later to fragment further.

We can see this process in the Culm Valley (Fig. 136) in east Devon where the church at Cullompton, with its hide recorded in 1086, and its five prebendal holdings given by William to Battle Abbey (one of which was called Hineland including the element *higna*, 'land of the community'), seems to be a substantial early minster whose *parochia* probably included the large royal estate on the upper reaches of the Culm Valley. The royal estate began to break up as early as the mid-eighth century, when Æthelwulf personally gave Uffculme to Glastonbury, and enabled Sulca to give the abbey Culmstock and Culm Davey. Cullompton itself remained in royal hands until Alfred bequeathed it to his younger son. By 1066 all these elements of the old estate were in the hands of thegns except Cullompton (with perhaps Culm Davey), which belonged to Exeter. Culmstock, Cullompton and Uffculme all became separate parishes, with the rebuilt old minster church serving as the parish church at Cullompton. Similar fragmentations of a minster *parochia* linked with the emergence of parishes can be seen across the three eastern shires, and perhaps in Cornwall too,

Figure 136 Patterns of estates in the Culm Valley, east Devon

164. See p. 141.

where parish formations may have accompanied the break-up of the monastic estate in the Lizard, for example.

Edgar's thegn's church with a graveyard which is entitled to support from the estate represents the emerging parish church network. Amongst these were the ancient estate-based burial grounds intended perhaps originally as family cemeteries which had acquired church buildings as time went on. In the west these are often marked by the inscribed stones and they may be hinted at further east by the reuse of Roman material or the site of a Roman building. On the same legal footing were more recently established sites, sometimes completely new, something particularly likely if these had also been realignments in the local settlement pattern, sometimes perhaps existing rather humble sites (see below) given a new meaning. Perhaps sometimes, at some point in this lengthy process, the opportunity was taken to replace an old, possibly slightly ambivalent site, with a new unambiguously Christian one. This may explain why the parish church was sited away from the old burial ground at Cadbury Congresbury and again at Pagans Hill.

The net result of this was a levelling-off in the status and function of churches. Ancient minsters were gradually reduced to the standing of parish churches for what had originally been the core geographical area of their *parochia* and which became their parish, although they retained those surviving indications of ancient importance which help us to recognize them. Estate churches acquired a local, public function, defined by the receipt of tithes, and in some cases, glebe land, which could fund a priest, and burial rights for all who lived within the parish boundaries. The process was the ecclesiastical expression of the greater concentration in sentiment as well as topography, which was driving increased agricultural production through the break-up of large estates and the creation of many smaller ones.

The coincidence across southern England of ancient parish boundaries and the boundaries of tenth- and eleventh-century estates preserved in charters, as at Culmstock, is strong enough to show the essential nature of parish churches as estate churches, and parishes as the ecclesiastical expression of the territorial estate community. However, parish and estate boundaries by no means always coincide, and evidently, in any given parish, its boundaries represent one particular period of landholding arrangements, which may have changed later, while the parish pattern was to show itself long enduring, and clearly capable of achieving a strong grip on local loyalties. Parish boundaries often represent a snapshot of one moment in time, and the tenurial arrangements at that moment which brought them into being.

The thrust of this discussion has been to suggest that similar processes producing a similar outcome were operating across the peninsula, but some Cornish peculiarities need particular consideration. Padel[165] has drawn attention to the incidence of the Cornish *plu*, from Latin *plebs* ('people'), meaning 'community, people living in an area' and so 'parish'. The solitary Cornish parish name in *plu* is Pelynt (*plu* plus perhaps Nonnita, a form of the saint's name Nonna), and this is probably due to Breton influence, where this element in place-names is very common. *Plu* was also used as an element in the formation of parish boundary names. Some boundary stones came to have names which emerge as 'Blue Stone', like that on the Wendron/ Illogan boundary, or that at the point (more or less) where Towednack, Ludgvan and Madron meet. An inscribed stone evidently stood near, and was at some point used

165.   O. Padel, 'Cornish language notes: 3', *Cornish Studies*, 3 (1975): 19–23.

as, the footbridge which marked the Gulval–Ludgvan boundary and which in 1700 was called the Blue (?*Bleu*) Bridge.[166] Collectively, all these records reflect practices general across southern Britain (allowing for the particular approaches taken by the Cornish language), and none need be pre-1000. At Gulval–Illogan we perhaps have a sixth to seventh-century boundary, marked by the inscribed stone, which was later used as the parish boundary.

Similar considerations apply to the important tenth-century list of Cornish parochial saints[167] which gives the names of 48 individuals, of whom half are certainly associated with Cornwall, some very distinctively, and who are listed in an order which has correlations with the actual locations of the saints' dedications in Cornwall. A plot of the dedication names with the parish boundaries added shows their mutual relationship, especially in southern Cornwall, and suggests that the parish system may have been emerging here around or soon after 900 (Fig. 137). Edgar's charter to Ælfeah Gerent and his wife *Moruurei* of 969,[168] which grants to them the estate of *Lannmoren*, Lamorran, 'the enclosed cemetery of Moren', where

Figure 137 Geographical correlation of saints' names in the tenth-century Vatican List, and relevant parish boundaries, Cornwall (after Olson and Padel 1986, Map 2). The saints who relate to the parishes are 1. Salamun, 2. Guenosam, 3. Just, 10. Entenin, 12. Filii, 13. Rumon, 15. Meler, 17. Maucan, 18. Achobran, 19. Berion, 20. Felec, 21. Guidan, 23. Nioth, 24. Probus, 25. Latoc, 27. Pierguin, 28. Geuenenoc, 29. uai (first part of the name is missing), 33. Gernun, 34. Lallu, 38. Elenn, 39. Austoll, 40. Megunn, 42. Crite, 43. Guron, 44. Euai, 46. Memai, 47. Iti

166.   E. Okasha, *Corpus of Early Christian Inscribed Stones of South-West Britain* (1993), p. 108.
167.   L. Olson and O. Padel, 'A tenth-century list of Cornish parochial saints', *Cam. Med. Celtic St.*, 12 (1986): 33–71; for discussion of dedications, see below pp. 321–4.
168.   Hooke, *Charter-bounds*, pp. 41–5.

the church is dedicated to St Moren (not on the tenth-century list) gives a glimpse of the process: the boundaries of their estate seem to be the same as those of the later manor and parish of Lamorran. The dedication names may, of course, have been attached to burial sites before the crystallization of the parish/estate system between the later eighth and the late eleventh centuries, and the people behind the names, who may have been local clerics, assorted holy men or landholders, may have lived at any point from say, the sixth to the tenth centuries. It looks as if the creation, and perhaps often the enclosure, of the smaller and apparently less significant ecclesiastical sites which became parish centres also belongs here.

Edgar's *Ordinance* also refers to churches without graveyards, which appear to lack any public function, although they may be served by priests, and presumably represent private facilities attached to major households, presumably mostly secular. The *Ordinance* does not mention what may have been a large category of sites, the simple burial grounds without churches or any sustained priestly ministry, sometimes of considerable age, in which were buried the humble poor, and which did not emerge into legislation because no resources were needed for their management. Some of the underdeveloped ones seem to have been gradually abandoned as part of the whole process of change, as the outlying settlements which some, at least, of them had served were integrated into larger groupings, and everybody came to feel the need for proper Christian burial. The small mid to late Saxon cemetery at Templecombe,[169] for example, which lay on what became the parish boundary of Templecombe and Abbascombe, Somerset, seems to have been abandoned in the early eleventh century. It apparently served a small community, the remains of whose settlement and its enclosures were cut by the parish boundary which follows one of the enclosure banks. In other places, as an outlying settlement and its land was redefined as a self-contained unit, or a small separate landholding was reconfigured as a thegn's estate, its burial ground became the parish churchyard.

The tensions and satisfactions engendered by these new ecclesiastical arrangements are probably embodied in the new fashion for erecting monumental, stone, standing crosses. Apart from a few stones that have distinctive ornamentation, they are very difficult to date. This is especially true of the simple granite crosses which are relatively common on Dartmoor, and all that can be said is that the sequence seems to begin in the tenth century, when it is part of a British and Irish trend, and to continue, perhaps, until as late as *c.* 1500. Similar difficulties of interpretation arise from the extent to which crosses have been moved about. The functions of the crosses are clearer, and link them with the earlier inscribed stones, whose place, in some ways, they take.

In a charter of 960, King Edgar granted to his *minister* Eanulf an estate which bordered on the land belonging to St Piran: the boundary of the church's land is said to be marked by the *cristelmael* ('crucifix'), presumably a stone cross.[170] Similarly a few years later, when Edgar granted land at Lesneage to Wulfnoth Rumuncant, his *vasallus*, the edge of St Keverne's land was marked by the *Crouswrah* ('Witches

---

169.   C. Newman, 'A late Saxon cemetery at Templecombe', *PSANHS*, 136 (1992): 61–71. The estate of Abbascombe, including Templecombe, belonged to Shaftesbury in 1086. Templecombe was granted to the Knights Templar in *c.* 1184 by Sirlo Fitz-Odo but was presumably in lay hands before this.

170.   Hooke, *Charter Bounds*, pp. 28–9.

Cross'),[171] and, in 974, Ælfhere received an estate at Nymed[172] in Down St Mary in which the bounds start at Copplestone Cross[173] which seems to be a landmark put up by the minster at Crediton. All these crosses look like intentionally charismatic markers set up to mark and protect Church lands at a time when churches may have feared a predatory royal policy towards old estates for the benefit of royal officials, and also wished to defend themselves against local aristocrats. For all we know, some of the cross fragments collected at major sites like Glastonbury, Keynsham and Sherborne once belonged to crosses serving similar purposes, as that at Exeter may have done (Fig. 138).

The crosses in the St Neot area (Fig. 139) formed a rough ring around the religious house,[174] and seem to have been intended to create a space under the special

Figure 138 Cross shaft, probably tenth century, from Exeter. Now in grounds of St Nicholas Priory, Exeter. (Photo: author)

---

171. *Ibid.*, pp. 37–40.
172. *Ibid.*, pp. 172–4, 95, 118.
173. The cross shaft now standing in the garden at St Nicholas Priory, Exeter, is very similar in ornament and date to Copplestone Cross and may have come from the same workshop. The cross appeared when the Exe Bridge was demolished in 1778; the bridge had been repaired in 1539 with stones from the recently demolished priory church and this may have been the cross's site by the sixteenth century. Alternatively, it may have been incorporated in the bridge *c.* 1603 and have stood before that outside the West Gate near the river. Nothing is known of its earlier history; see M. Phillips, 'Supplementary notes on the ancient crosses of Devon (second paper)', *TDA*, 72 (1940): pp. 270–1; 'The ancient stone crosses of Devon: Part II', *TDA*, 70 (1938): 322–3.
174. Personal communication: I am grateful to Sam Turner for this information, which is based on his forthcoming doctoral research.

Figure 139 Crosses at (a) Cardinham churchyard, (b) St Neot churchyard, (c) Temple Moor, St Neot (after Langdon 1988, pp. 356, 388, 407)

protection of the saint. Four Holes Cross probably dates to the eleventh century. It was formerly sited on the St Neot/Blisland parish boundary.[175] In the later Middle Ages, St Buryan, Padstow, Probus and St Keverne all had sanctuary zones around them. Possibly the pre-Conquest crosses and fragments found near Padstow have a place here.[176] The parish of St Buryan has at least 24 crosses and cross fragments of a wide range of dates. Some of the oldest of these, at least, may have been erected to mark religious boundaries.[177] Three Holes Cross lies on the boundary of St Kew parish: St Kew was an important early religious house whose lands were confirmed in a charter of King Edgar.[178]

Some of the virtually undatable Dartmoor crosses which mark routes to Tavistock and Plympton may also have a relationship to traditional access to grazing, as the inscribed stones seem to have done.[179] The cross-shaft section inscribed with Doniert's name seems to be in its original position; it stands near the parish boundary between St Neot and St Cleer on the south-eastern edge of Bodmin moor. It suggests that a major monument like this could create a range of interlinked meanings, all to do with the visible authority which marked and protected special places in a

175. Thomas 1997, p. 224; see also A. Langdon, 'A Cornish cross, lot no 473, going, going, gone', *DCNQ*, Spring (2001): 273–7.

176. A. Langdon, 'Cornish crosses: recent news', *Corn. Arch.*, 31 (1992): 164; *Old Cornish Crosses* (1988), pp. 196, 229, 396–8, 407–10.

177. A. Preston-Jones and A. Langdon, 'St Buryan crosses', *Corn. Arch.*, 36 (1997): 107–28

178. I am grateful to Sam Turner for this information from his forthcoming doctoral research. See also W. Picken, 'The Landchou Charter', in W. Hoskins, *The Westward Expansion of Wessex* (1960), pp. 36–44.

179. A number of crosses on Dartmoor mark routes between the abbeys of Tavistock (founded 981), Buckfast (1018) and Buckland (1280). Some of these, like Siwards Cross (Lydford), mentioned in Buckland's foundation deed and in the 1240 *Perambulation of Dartmoor*, and *Smalacumbacross* (Meavy) and *Yanedonecrosse* (Sheepston), both mentioned in the 1280 foundation deed, may possibly be pre-Norman or on the sites of pre-Norman crosses; see M. Phillips, 'The ancient stone crosses of Devon', *TDA*, 69 (1937): 309, 312, 315.

landscape. Other crosses inscribed with personal names, like that at Tintagel which has an English name and probably the names of the four Evangelists, and seems to belong between the tenth or eleventh century, probably served similar roles.[180]

The same desire to express divinely sanctioned authority and possession seems to lie behind the crosses erected within or close to the smaller minsters which did not have large landed possessions to worry about but which did stand to lose prestige and fees as estate churches developed. Reasoning like this may lie behind the very fine cross carved for Colyton church,[181] and the fragments of the important monuments which survive at Sidbury,[182] Banwell, Frome and Gillingham,[183] all ancient minsters. Similarly, surviving late Saxon stonework at what were in the process of becoming parish churches points up a corresponding desire to express status and permanence, as perhaps at Chew Stoke, Porlock, West Camel[184] (all Somerset), East Stour and Todber (both Dorset).[185]

In Cornwall, standing crosses sometimes enriched existing burial grounds as perhaps at Sancreed,[186] where what may have been an inscribed stone was recarved as a cross, or Cardinham, where an inscribed stone was joined by a cross.[187] Sometimes a cross may have marked the establishment (or further definition) of a burial ground which did not itself survive, if Thomas's[188] reading of the Penzance cross as *Procumbant in foris. Quicumque pace venit hinc, oret,* 'They lie, out in the open. Whomsoever in peace comes here, let him pray [for their soul]', is correct. The same may now be true of the cross bearing the name Runhol which came from what is now a field called 'Chapel Close' at Roseworthy in Gwinear.[189] At their least, all these monuments are intended to signal rights over places and to link this not, as did the inscribed stones, with pedigree, but with Christ crucified and the Christian dead.[190] The pressures of the ninth century seem to have stimulated a new and more intense relationship with Christian teaching at local level, which is seen equally in the potency of the new estate churches, and, higher in the social scale, in what we see as the tenth-century religious reforms and monastic foundation.

Symbols and saints

How truly severe was the disruption to the social fabric, and particularly ecclesiastical life, caused by the two main phases of Viking wars and the intermittent raids

---

180.   Okasha, *Inscribed Stones*, pp. 213–17, for 'Doniert' cross, pp. 290–5 for Tintagel.
181.   M. Phillips, 'Ancient stone crosses Part II', pp. 324–5.
182.   M. Phillips, 'Supplementary notes on the ancient stone crosses of Devon (first paper)', *TDA*, 71 (1939): 332.
183.   Foster, 'Gazetteer of Anglo-Saxon sculpture'.
184.   *Ibid.*
185.   RCHM, *Dorset Vol. IV*, p. 114.
186.   Okasha, *Inscribed Stones*, pp. 251–9.
187.   *Ibid.*, pp. 85–90.
188.   C. Thomas, 'Christian Latin inscriptions from Cornwall in biblical style', *JRIC*, 2 (4): 42–66 (1997); *Christian Celts: Messages and Images* (1998), esp. p. 192.
189.   Under Lanherne, Okasha, *Inscribed Stones*, pp. 133–7.
190.   Perhaps also smaller ?individual grave slabs began to be used as maybe at Ludgvan; C. Thomas, 'A cross-incised slab from Ludgvan churchyard', *Corn. Arch.*, 5 (1966): 86–7.

between them, is a matter for debate.[191] The immediate damage, as at Exeter and elsewhere, is clear, but Exeter apparently retained its relic collection if not much else,[192] and although St Petroc's house seems to have had to move from Padstow to Bodmin, it relocated very successfully.[193] The extent to which west Wessex churches lost lands, appropriated by kings to create resources for the wars, is less clear. The real nature of the internal organization at houses like Hartland, Devon, or Whitchurch, Dorset, or Probus, Cornwall, is equally uncertain. We do not know the extent to which any earlier communal life had fragmented into loose groups of canons living on separate holdings. In the effort to create the new notion of the Christian society, major west Wessex houses like Exeter, Glastonbury, just embarking on the creation of its own version of Christian history,[194] and probably Sherborne were very important. The same enterprise included the harnessing of a Germanic heroic past in the reworking of the *Anglo-Saxon Chronicle* and the royal genealogies, and that of the imperial past represented by the presentation of kings like Athelstan and Edgar. But embracing much of this, as the supreme effort of communal imagination which ran all the way up the social ladder, was the significance attached to the holy saints.

The centrality of the saints expressed a world-view which (unlike our own) did not see a separation between the accessible universe of tangible materiality and that of the supernatural. Rather, it brought the two images together in a single fused vision, which meant that everybody, dead and alive, acted always on both the earthly and the heavenly stage, concentrating human history into an external moment. The profound psychic effect of this single-mindedness created a densely structured world in which everyone, from king to slave, had a symbolic significance and every place was a site where holy power might manifest itself.

Key points, where direct access between the seen and unseen parts of the world was possible, were those inhabited by God's saints, most powerfully in the body as tomb or relic but also as more minor physical trace or through special reverence: the psychic effect created by the materiality of the sacred in real place and time was profound. As a result, what we see, intercutting each other in highly complex ways, are creative efforts across the social levels – king, high nobility, perhaps lesser nobility, estate-holding gentry and working people – to create numerous sites where by making things happen the resident saints can show the truth on which the endeavour was predicated. The raw materials for this effort were drawn from carefully chosen and rethought aspects of the past and its remains, and its authenticity was embodied in a rapidly developing body of physical miracles, visions, elaborate liturgies and the written accounts which enabled these to be continuously enacted and experienced.

The group of documents which gives the resting places of famous saints in

191.   See Yorke, *Wessex*, pp. 192–225.
192.   Conner, *Anglo-Saxon Exeter*, pp. 171–214; unless bones were discreetly replaced.
193.   This is the received opinion of the history of the house.
194.   See essays in volume edited by L. Abrams and J. Carley, *The Archaeology and History of Glastonbury Abbey* (1991); L. Abrams, 'St Patrick and Glastonbury Abbey: *nihil ex nihilo fit?*', in D. Dumville, *Saint Patrick AD 493–1993* (1993), pp. 233–42; M. Lapidge, 'The cult of St Indract at Glastonbury', in Whitelock *et al.*, *Ireland in Early Medieval Europe* (1982), pp. 179–212; and for general discussion, H. James, 'The cult of St David in the Middle Ages', in M. Carver (ed.), *In Search of Cult* (1993), pp. 105–12. For Beckery and its ?Irish links, see P. Rahtz and S. Hirst, *Beckery Chapel, Glastonbury 1967–8* (1974).

England[195] seems to embody a list completed in *c.* 1031, but representing cumulative composition. In west Wessex the list gives Glastonbury (Aidan and Patrick), Congresbury (Congar), Exeter (Sidefulla or Sidwell), Tavistock (Rumon) and *Haegel-mutha*, 'Haylemouth' (presumably intended to mean Padstow) with Petroc. Sherborne is not mentioned but Malmesbury, Shaftesbury and Milton Abbas (Branwalader, Samson) are. When this is mapped with those places where kings chose to be buried,[196] complemented by the places where councils and crown-wearings were held,[197] we can begin to see how the linking together of some (believed) ancient sites, especially Glastonbury, and some carefully considered new ones, like Milton Abbas, shaped emerging cultural patterns. The picture gains in density when the houses chosen as episcopal seats between *c.* 880 and 1050 (including Congresbury which Wells believed had been a see) are added.

All of these places, presumably, had churches substantial by contemporary standards, sanctuary furnishings, books and musical and liturgical expertise to mount impressive services and processions. At all of them access to the virtuous power of the saints was a secret mystery of liturgical space and ritual time controlled by the church priests. All were focal points in the larger sacred landscape, and some like Glastonbury,[198] perhaps Bodmin/Padstow[199] and Hartland,[200] were developing narratives of the immediate surroundings of the church marked by features like chapels, wells and standing crosses. These were written up as *vitae* embodying the standard themes of miracles, monsters killed, hostile kings foiled and title to lands validated which could be perpetually re-enacted as pilgrims walked the story.

The tradition at Exeter was that the relics the church possessed were given by Athelstan, and represented a third of his personal collection. Although the earliest of the surviving Relic Lists (in English) dates to *c.* 1050 or a little before and includes post-Athelstan material, there seems no good reason to doubt the broad substance of the claim.[201] The possession of a formidable relic collection is both a crucial aspect of, and a confirmation of, Exeter's tenth-century reassertion of its ancient status, represented equally by its renewed fortifications, and the probable reworking of its street system, and the building of its first parish church. All are elements in the new presentation of the Christian state.

The Relic List tells us in its preamble that Athelstan gave the relics for 'the deliverance of his own soul' and 'for the eternal salvation of all those who seek out and worship the holy place',[202] a clear reference to pilgrims and to the special character which the relics gave the church. The List continues, 'we shall tell you what the relic-collection contains which is here in this holy minster, and tell you forthwith the writing which reveals without any duplicity what each of the relics in the collection is',[203] so clearly the church mounted a major event, probably annually, in which

195.   D. Rollason, 'Lists of saints resting-places in Anglo-Saxon England', *Anglo-Saxon England*, 7 (1978): 61–93.
196.   Information from Yorke, *Wessex*, p. 103, fig. 26.
197.   D. Hill, *Atlas of Anglo-Saxon England* (1981), figs 154–69.
198.   See essays in Abrams and Carley, *Glastonbury Abbey*; and P. Rahtz, *Glastonbury* (1993); Abrams, 'St Patrick and Glastonbury Abbey', pp. 233–42; Lapidge, 'Cult of St Indract', pp. 179–212.
199.   K. Jankulak, *The Medieval Cult of St Petroc* (2000), esp. pp. 1–53.
200.   G. Doble, *The Saints of Cornwall Part 5, Saints of Mid-Cornwall* (1970), St Nectan, pp. 59–79.
201.   Conner, *Anglo-Saxon Exeter*, pp. 171–214.
202.   *Ibid.*, pp. 176–7.
203.   *Ibid.*

the relics were announced one by one, and probably successively displayed at the same time to pilgrims who were there for this event. Each group of articulated or fragmented human bones, or desiccated piece of body tissue, seems to have been separately wrapped or, in the case of the most important, perhaps housed in a reliquary, and each is likely to have had a written label, from which the List was compiled, and on the strength of which the original acquisition was made. They will have been stored, perhaps behind an altar or in a crypt, in the later Saxon apsed church excavated in the Cathedral Close on the St Mary Major site, which almost certainly was the tenth to eleventh-century minster church and Leofric's cathedral in 1050. Virtually all the great churches must have had similar arrangements.

The belief at Exeter was that, while in the city (he was there in 928), Athelstan had the idea of making a major relic collection, and this was why he afterwards donated relics to the church. He sent out agents to travel the Continent purchasing relic material[204] which had presumably come onto the market either as a direct result of Viking upheavals or indirectly following a need to raise cash for repairs and reorganization, so we cannot be certain that the material listed came directly from the churches which claimed to hold the major relics of the saint concerned, or from existing mixed collections. The general character of the material suggests that most of it was acquired in northern France.

Like every collecting process, Athelstan's was an imaginative effort to impose a vision of order upon the chaos of the world by bringing together specially chosen objects. By being placed in relationship to each other, these could create meaningful location and context by means of which people could move through an organized world; they could also produce an intelligible history, providing an intelligible story of the past, present and future into which an individual life could fit.[205] The pilgrim adoring each piece in Athelstan's gift as it was held up before Exeter's high altar was able to experience his or her personal identity. At a more fundamental level, it is possible that the urge to create meaning by manipulating human bones tends to be a response to social stress and uncertainty, as it had been during the concentration on martyrial and confessional remains in the fourth–fifth centuries.[206] Holy bones, which were once like the living men who revered them, and which had become what the living knew they would be, stimulated in people the mixture of deep excitement and horror which accompanies recognition of the inevitability of personal death and decay, linked with the life of heavenly salvation their holiness offered.

There are 138 relics in the Exeter List, which[207] – whether most of them actually come from Athelstan or not – give an insight into tenth to eleventh-century perceptions. Twelve derive from events in Christ's life, and although these are headed by the more or less obligatory piece of the True Cross, some are distinctly second class; the earth from Mount Olivet, for example, is no more than an ordinary tourist souvenir. Three relics of St Mary follow, and the next big group (some fifteen) are relics of John the Baptist and the Apostles, and the following group (44 plus) of

204.   *Ibid.*
205.   S. Pearce, *On Collecting. An Investigation into Collecting in the European Tradition* (1995), esp. pp. 100–8.
206.   See A. Woodward, 'The cult of relics in prehistoric Britain', in Carver, *In Search of Cult* (1993), pp. 1–7.
207.   Conner, *Anglo-Saxon Exeter*, pp. 171–214.

generally well-known early martyrs, relics of many of whom had been in Gaulish/ Frankish churches since the late fifth–sixth centuries.

There follows a long list of confessional relics (some 48), which include the roll-call of the famous bishops of late Antique Gaul such as Martin of Tours, Germanus of Auxerre, Remigius of Rheims and Evertius of Orléans, pointing clearly to the largely north French network in which Athelstan, his agents and perhaps later collectors were able to participate. Finally, comes a list of women's relics (22), patterned as the male list, in which Mary Magdalene (the female equivalent of the Cross?) comes first, followed by Elizabeth, martyrs like Agnes and a group of confessors and nuns. The last named entry in the martyr's group is 'St Edward the king', showing Exeter was also a link in the promotional policies associated with the reverence paid to royal saints.[208] The interesting point about this collection is the way it succeeds in framing Exeter within the normative view of the Christian past and its practitioners which had been established in fifth-century Gaul.

Welsh saints (or saints believed by then to be Welsh) are conspicuous by their absence, and Irish saints represented essentially only by Bridget, who also had a cult at Glastonbury. Cornish saints are represented by a group of Petroc relics, as we would expect, and there is a striking group of Breton relics, including those of Winwaloe, Wennoc and Melanius. Athelstan's own foundation at Milton Abbas, Dorset, was dedicated to the Breton saints Samson of Dol and Branwalader, and Glastonbury had parts of Samson, Winwaloe and Budoc.[209] Connections between the West Country and Brittany run back, of course, into the Roman period and before, but the Viking impact upon Brittany had brought a number of important relics into north France, as the body of Winwaloe was taken to Montreuil in Picardy, and those of St Paul Aurelian and St Maurus to Fleury-sur-Loire. Both Athelstan and his father Edward were in confraternity with the house of St Samson at Dol.[210] Athelstan was an important force in Breton politics, as befitted his sense of himself as the supreme ruler over British and Norse, as well as English, speakers in the island of Britain and an imperial actor on the European stage. The ability to dispose of significant, exotic holy objects signified the divinely validated power of the king.

Breton exiles brought to Britain key texts[211] relating to what has often been called 'the tenth reformation'. This encompasses the new enthusiasm for the monastic life and the creation of genuine monasteries, often in ancient houses then in the hands of canons, by men like Ælfheah Bishop of Winchester (934 × 5–951), Oda of Ramsbury (909 × 927–941), Dunstan, Abbot of Glastonbury and eventually Archbishop of Canterbury, Æthelwold of Winchester and Oswald of Worcester and York. This is a formidable array, and it is clear, from the acrimony surrounding Æthelwulf's repossession (or, in fact, perhaps acquisition) of the estate of Taunton for

---

208. S. Ridyard, *The Royal Saints of Anglo-Saxon England* (1988), for discussion.
209. For the relic collection at Glastonbury, see G. Doble, 'The Celtic saints of the Glastonbury Relic Lists', *SDNQ* (1994), n.p.
210. These Breton links are discussed in S. Pearce, 'The dating of some Celtic dedications and hagiographical traditions in south-western Britain', *TDA*, 105 (1973): 95–120, and see J. Nightingale, 'Oswald, Fleury and continental reform', in N. Brooks and C. Cubitt (eds), *St Oswald of Worcester: Life and Influence* (1996), pp. 23–45; D. Rollason, 'Relic-cults as an instrument of royal policy c. 900–1150', *Anglo-Saxon England*, 15 (1986): 91–103.
211. Dumville, *Wessex and England*, pp. 156 60.

Winchester,[212] or the upheavals accompanying Dunstan's tenure at Glastonbury, that genuine, painful changes were made.

A different perspective would stress the ramifying family links across the churchmen involved: Dunstan, for example, was kin to Ælfheah, and Oswald was born into a major network of ecclesiastical and lay magistrates.[213] Embedded in their actions was the creation of family-orientated religious houses, at the highest levels of endowment and importance. This was generally done by reworking ancient foundations like Glastonbury or Winchester, where royal support followed, but seems not to have involved houses which were already part of royal self-presentation, like Exeter, and perhaps Sherborne and Bodmin. From this angle, Dunstan's Glastonbury has something in common with Ordgar's foundation at Tavistock, also on an ancient site and primarily intended to act as the family centre for validating ritual continuity, particularly of burial. The reworking of venerable minster and cathedral houses appears as the ecclesiastical equivalent of the emergence of new families (like Ordgar's) providing newly needed royal officials, and struggling to maintain or assert the status which land conveys. It may also represent a way of asserting blood ties in a world where land law and order were steadily becoming embodied in tenurial, rather than kin-based, arrangements.

Part of the desirable power and prestige of these ancient churches was bound up in their relic holdings which were accordingly promoted by the 'new' men, as Æthelwold did that of Swithin, one of his predecessors at Winchester, who was translated into a focal shrine in 971 as part of a major rebuilding programme.[214] The monasticization of the cult of the saints was very significant in post-800 northern France, with all its attendant features of exclusiveness, especially of women, and control, especially of access by pilgrims and the poor.[215] When, for example, the monks of Micy near Fleury were rebuilding their church in the 1020s, they mounted a special search for the sarcophagus of their founder, Maximinus, who had lain there since at least the early ninth century but whose tomb had been lost, a possible context for the relic of Maximinus which appears in the Exeter List. Across west Wessex, as in north-western Europe generally, ancient cults with their reassuringly deep roots were reworked, like that of Sidwell.[216] In its final form this brought together Exeter and Sherborne (and various other interested people and places) to produce a self-authenticating story of the Christian past. These efforts knitted together individual churches in a Christian society, and were embodied in the immense hagiographical production and the gradual construction of new churches with special provision, often below the main level of the church and near its main altar, for sacred remains.

---

212.   E. John, *Orbis Britanniae and Other Studies* (1966), pp. 154–80.

213.   A. Wareham, 'St Oswald's family and kin', in Brooks and Cubitt, *St Oswald* (1996), pp. 46–63.

214.   Biddle (1986), pp.1–13.

215.   Head (1990), esp. Ch. 2.

216.   For the cult of Sidwell, see P. Grosjean, 'Legenda S. Sativolae Exoniensis', *Annalecta Bollandia*, 53 (1935): 359–65; M. Förster, 'The etymology of St Sidwell', *DCNQ*, 17 (1933): 243–5; Förster, 'Die Heilige Sativola oder Sidwell eine Namenstudie', *Zeitschrife für Englische Philogie*, 62 (ns 50): 3–80 (1938); G. Doble, 'The "Vita" of St Sativola', *DCNQ*, 17 (1933): 245–7; G. Rushforth, 'The legend of St Sativola', *DCNQ*, 17 (1933): 249–53; E. Lega-Weeks, 'St Sidwell and her fee', *DCNQ*, 17 (1933): 253–6; F. Rose-Troup *DCNQ*, 17 (1933): 256–7; G. Doble, (1997a), pp. 40–42; E. Lega-Weeks, 'St Sidwell', *DCNQ*, 13 (1924–5): 18–23, 104–6.

Local cults and dedications

This frame of mind, which supported the self-creating royal efforts of Athelstan and his successors, and the similar ones at the noble and *minster* social level, is paralleled at the local level by what emerges as the pattern of dedications and patronage, and associated observance,[217] at what were in the process of becoming parish churches in the south-west, as generally in Britain. It is not until the post-Conquest period that we have a relatively full picture of dedications and related cults across the south-west, and we usually do not know what changes there may have been to patrons in the previous centuries. By then we see a mix of dedications to universal saints and cults, famous early martyrs, founders of early local and religious houses and to those seen as having 'Celtic' connections, together with dedications to patrons which seem essentially unique to the usually single site with which they are linked. Within this there is a clear distributional pattern which shows dedications to saints with local, Breton, Irish or Welsh hagiographical connections concentrated west of the Tamar, with a spread of similar names in Devon and in north Somerset,[218] and a few in Dorset. An estimate of the relative types of dedications of parish churches in Cornwall and Devon is given in Table 6.[219] While this pattern does not follow the linguistic frontier presented by secular place-names in any simple fashion, cultural factors bound up with language were clearly very important. Similar patterns appear in Wales and the adjacent English border counties, and in north-western France.

The dedications to universal saints and martyrs represent normal devotional, tenurial and episcopal links which influenced the landholders, priests and bishops who were involved in the creation of what were becoming parishes and parish churches. The dedications to Andrew, for example, reflect that of the minster, then cathedral church, at Wells, and (some at least of) those to Peter reflect that of Exeter. There are undoubtedly interesting patterns here, like the tendency to associate Michael with hilltops, which are only just beginning to be studied.

It seems likely that the dedications across the peninsula to famous Brittonic saints often regarded as monastic founders are part of the promotion of such cults associated with post-900 interest in Christian devotional historiography, a

---

217. The literature on hagiography is huge, but indispensable for south-western studies are G. Doble, *The Saints of Cornwall Parts One–Six* (1997a, 1997b, 1997c, 1965, 1970, 1997d); N. Orme, *English Church Dedications* (1996), 'English Church Dedications: Supplement No. 1' *Devon and Cornwall Notes and Queries* (2001), Vol. xxxviii, Part X, pp. 305–7, and *The Saints of Cornwall* (2000); Olson and Padel, 'Cornish parochial saints', pp. 33–71; Conner, *Anglo-Saxon Exeter*; O. Padel, 'Cornish language notes: 5. Cornish names of parish churches', *Cornish Studies*, 4/5 (1976–7): 15–27. See also Pearce, 'Dating of Celtic dedications', pp. 95–120. Also central is the Transnational Atlas of Saintly Cults Project (TASC) directed by Graham Jones, which is creating a database capable of analysing all medieval dedications, devotions, fairs and feast days, landscape features, etc. Material relating to south-west Britain, Wales and the Midlands is already available at *http://www.le.ac.uk/elh/grj/tasc*. For an interesting discussion of dedication change see Clark, 'Dedications of Medieval Churches' (1992), pp. 48–60. For Roscarrock's *Lives of the Saints of Cornwall and Devon*, see Orme, *Nicholas Roscarrock* (1992).
218. M. Costen, 'A Celtic saint at Weare', *SDNQ*, 30 (1974–9): 219–20.
219. These figures are based on Cornish parish churches only, from which have been deleted the sites of certain/probably pre-Saxon religious houses, instances where the 'saint' is a back-formation from the place-name, also those where any decision about the character of the saint proved impossible (e.g. Columb). It should also be noted that the calculations are based on dedications, not saints.

Table 6 Relative numbers of types of medieval parochial dedications in Devon and Cornwall

Dedication	Devon	Cornwall
Universal saints	177	35
Universal martyrs	11[1]	7
Local founders e.g., Piran	19[2]	5
Breton links	2	22
Welsh links	1	6
Irish links	3	5
Unique	6[3]	83

Notes:
1. Of which 5 to Pancras
2. Of which 18 to Petroc and 1 to Nectan
3. ?Bramscombe/Brandwell, Chittlehampton/Urith (or Hieretha), Exeter/Sidwell, Landkey/Cei, Stoke Fleming/Ermund, ?Stokenham/Humbeorht.

trickle-down effect created by the royal and noble policy just discussed. They also reflect the stronger role which some of the religious houses concerned were playing post-900. The scattered series of dedications to Petroc[220] probably reflect tenurial and personal factors now not recoverable, together with St Petroc's standing as the seat of a bishop; the same is true of Germanus, and of the Breton Winwaloe, whose considerable popularity probably relates to Athelstan's interest in Breton affairs. The other Breton dedications probably form part of the same complex. The same factors probably apply to most of the dedications relating to apparently Welsh saints, like David, Dubricius, Carantoc, Cadoc and Patern, all of whom have substantial cults in Wales. This is a particularly complex area, partly because, with some exceptions like David, it is usually not clear whether or not the saint in question should be identified with a Welsh saint of similar/identical name, and partly because of the effects of the intense hagiographical activity at Glastonbury.

Similar considerations probably account for the cults of well-known Irish saints like Brendan, Patrick and Bridget who make a strong appearance in north Somerset, which is probably due to Glastonbury's influence, and who have a scatter of dedications across the peninsula. Rather different are the group of patrons mostly in west Cornwall, who, according to notes which Leland made in Breage church from a *vita* of the saint, were listed as coming together from Ireland; there may have been another (?related) list of Irish-derived saints in the *Life* of St Ia which Leland also saw at St Ives. These Irish connections could have been put together at virtually any date, but the identification of the Cornish Piran with Irish Ciaran of Saigher, which may have arisen in post-Conquest Exeter, will have encouraged the creation of Irish-orientated links. It is important to recognize that the hagiographical association with these figures should be kept separate from an assessment of their role as local church patrons, and its implications.

The large group of local or unique patrons is largely concentrated west of the Tamar but with a group in the Hartland peninsula and representatives further east, like Urith/Hieretha at Chittlehampton, Devon, Rayne at Windwhistle Hill and Ernin

---

220.   See Jankulak, *Medieval Cult of St Petroc*, for full consideration of the evidence.

at Wear,[221] Somerset, and St Whyte or Candida at Whitchurch Canonicorum[222] and Juthware at Halstock, both in Dorset. All these are in the vicinity of (probable) pre-Saxon monastic foundations which also have unique local patrons.[223] The tenth-century *Vatican List* has 48 Brittonic names which are evidently principally of saints associated with Cornish churches;[224] of these some are known as founders of religious houses, like Keverne, Buryan and Probus, but most are known only from a unique dedication (and some not even that). The *List* has a distinct concentration in south/south-central Cornwall, with a scatter further afield, and suggests the important fact that, in parts of Cornwall at least, the pattern of parishes with their unique patrons was in place by the early or mid-tenth century. The *Vatican List* is paralleled in many ways by the various *Lists of the Children of Brychan*[225] which similarly name very obscure saints uniquely linked to churches and chapels concentrated in north-west Cornwall/north-west Devon, and which possibly draw on a pre-Conquest source. The list of those saints associated with Ia and seen as of Irish origin may be another example of the genre. The saints on the *Vatican List* may originally have had some kind of connecting legend like those on the Brychan lists.

Archaeological and morphological evidence for the parish churchyards of the peninsula seems, at the present stage of their investigation, to throw some but not much light on the issues of date and origin which the dedication names present.[226] Of those sites with pre-750 origins vouched for by the possession of inscribed stones, six have unique, local saints, one an apparently Breton patron, and two pan-Christendom saints. As yet, analysis does not suggest that any dedication group relates to a particular range of churchyard size or degree of circularity, but that size and morphology cross-cut the dedication patterns.

At present, the unique patrons, like the equally unique names attached to the elements **lann* and *eglos*, seem to be best interpreted as the names of people (often perhaps real people) who played a significant role in the early history of the graveyard, as donors or developers of the site, resident holy men or simply locally

---

221. Costen, 1974–79; 'Celtic saint at Weare', pp. 219–20.

222. Clearly there was a link between the names of saint and church, but which way it leant is not clear. The relics of the saint seem to have been in the church throughout a very long period, and are still there.

223. St Nectan's (Hartland) in NW Devon, Congresbury, St Decumans, ?Glastonbury in Somerset, Sherborne in Dorset.

224. See K. Jankulak, 'Fingar/Gwinear/Guigner: an "Irish" saint in medieval Cornwall and Brittany', in J. Carey, M. Herbert and Ó. Riain (eds), *Studies in Irish Hagiography. Saints and Scholars* (2001), pp. 120–39.

225. The substantial hagiography surrounding the saintly Children of Brychan, eponymous founder of the south Welsh kingdom of Brycheiniog, has a Welsh and a south-western strand. When William of Worcester visited Cornwall in 1478 he found an *Acts of St Nectan*, probably at St Michael's Mount, which gave a list of 24 Children of Brychan; Leland found a similar list at Hartland in 1536 and both seem to derive from a *vita* of Nectan written at Hartland. Nectan is said to be a son of Brychan and the 24 children in the *vita* can be linked with a range of ecclesiastical dedication names in north-west Devon/east Cornwall. Briefly, the south-western Brychan tradition seems to represent an attempt to link the region with the traditional history of south Wales, possibly in the pre-Conquest period; see Pearce, 'Dating of Celtic dedications', pp. 100–4; Doble, *Saints of Cornwall, Part Six*, pp. 98–140; C. Thomas, *And Shall These Mute Stones Speak?* (1994), pp. 131–62.

226. A. Preston-Jones, 'Decoding Cornish churchyards', in N. Edwards and A. Lane (eds), *The Early Church in Wales and the West* (1992), pp. 105–24.

important people, some of whom may have had a recognized focal grave at some stage of the site's history; some may also have been members of a nearby religious house who were particularly involved with the site. The inscribed stones suggest that sometimes this process could begin as early as the fifth (or even the fourth) century, although we do not know what names were attached at this time to those sites which were being set up. Sites as early as this may well have been kin group burial grounds, and many cemeteries of various kinds went on being created as need arose, with perhaps a particular growth in the eighth, ninth and tenth centuries as new estates were carved out of older units. It is this very mixed group which eventually became the parish network, and they all acquired their associated names, sometimes unique, sometimes pan-Christian or pan-Brittonnic, depending upon detailed (and generally irrecoverable) local circumstances. The *Vatican List* and its parochial plot gives us an important glimpse of this process in relation to a group of uniquely named sites at around 900.[227]

This process is in essence not much different from that happening in Devon, and throughout south England, where local burial grounds of various degrees of formality and date (some have late Roman roots, others are later) were brought into the developing parish network (together with new sites as necessary) during the tenth century. The chief distinction seems to be that of nomenclature. In English-speaking areas it was not customary to remember at a site the names of people who were part of its earlier history (although, of course, such must have existed). Rather, the norm was to associate the site, possibly at a late stage in the development of some when they became 'respectable' parish churchyards, with a holy person universally recognized across Christendom as such.[228] In most cases we cannot recover the reasons for the choice, but they will rest among the family and tenorial connections and the devotional fashions, like that represented by Athelstan's Breton relics, which were the bread and butter of medieval life. On this reading, the 'British' dedications in Devon, Somerset and Dorset, once those relating to post-900 cult activity have been stripped away, represent communities of Brittonic speakers following native customs, something which could perhaps have continued to at least 800. Correspondingly, but perhaps largely after *c.* 900, some influential Cornishmen were adopting English practice in having local cemeteries dedicated to universal saints.

The cultivation of the saints ran from top to bottom of tenth-century society. Whether it involved the royal construction of divinely ordained imperial power, the statements of family solidarity and holy patronage made by major landholders and their ecclesiastical kin or hope of participating in holy benefits at local estate level, it operated within a holistic understanding of Christianized history which in itself provided very significant social glue. Fundamental to the inward experience of what this meant were the actual places, the sites and cemeteries, where the saints were reverenced, and those special churches, glowing in the landscape, where the holy bones lay.

227.　How old the attachment of the names to sites was in *c.* 900 or any hagiographical story connecting them we do not know, but it could have been relatively recent; similarly, where the sites themselves were we do not know. Either, or both, may not have preceded *c.* 900 by very long, and there may well be differences between the sites. It is also very important to draw a distinction between local burial grounds, with whatever range of nomenclature they possessed, and the parish system as it emerges post-900, and into which many (but not all) of the existing local cemeteries were drawn.

228.　This does not mean, of course, that there were not some locally significant dedications, outside the Brittonic-speaking areas, which are fossils of the particular history of the site concerned.

Some conclusions

If, as is sometimes said, the period from roughly 850 to 950 seems the true end of 'post-Roman' or 'successor kingdom' society, then in south-western Britain several factors emerge, all contributions to the wider pattern. Exploitation of the landscape intensified in ways which probably required harder, more organized and better sustained work by many people, but which offered the rewards (if that is what they were) of a more intensive community life focused in some places upon a village, in others upon developing hamlets, and everywhere upon a tighter relationship with Christian practice through a local church. This was linked with the larger number of viable estates, created by complex local processes of unit fusion and fission, needed to sustain the class of gentlemanly thegns who could use their essential royal services to extract grants of bookland, and who represent a steady move away from kin-based custom-regulated land management towards lordship operating through royal law.

This reciprocal system, legitimized through the reforming bishops and monks of the tenth and eleventh centuries, enabled the Wessex dynasty, in the persons of an exceptionally able run of kings, to emerge from the 870s and 880s able to exploit relatively powerful mechanisms of law and government. These were funded in part by the improved revenue which new approaches to estate management yielded, and in part by the royal share of the modest prosperity being generated within the new towns. It is impossible to judge to what degree these individual elements were elements of change or symptoms of it. However, local difficulties notwithstanding, the changes which had taken place by the end of the tenth century in south-west Britain, as across northern Europe as a whole, were profound enough to provide the firm basis for the later medieval states.

7 Wider contexts

Introduction

This last chapter has been written to make three important, final points. First, it considers briefly the part the south-west played in the events of 1066 and its immediate aftermath. This seems to be the last time the region was to take a major role in the politics of the kingdom until early modern times. But, secondly, as the military and political, although not the economic, significance of the area faded away, it experienced a second coming through the imaginative significance of its traditional stories. Finally, attention is drawn to the normality of the history of the south-west within the broader western European context.

Political realities around 1066

The coronation of King Edgar on Whit Sunday in Bath Abbey in 973 marked the ceremonial high point of the relationship between the ancient West Saxon royal house and the western shires which had become its homeland and the basis of its power. Thereafter, although as we have seen Cnut was buried in Winchester,[1] and Winchester continued to be of substantial political significance into the mid-twelfth century, royal interest gradually swung away from the West Country, towards London and the Continent.

Exeter continued to be a significant trading centre and, after 1050, the seat of the south-western bishop. Its political and economic importance, and the strength of its defensive walls, are demonstrated by the events of 1067.[2] In December, the men of Exeter openly defied King William, perhaps because he was asking more from them than the customary payments which they were used to making to the Crown. They seem to have refurbished the city walls, and to have persuaded foreign traders within the city to join them. William marched into Devon and besieged the city. Exeter held out for eighteen days, during which time William could neither storm nor undermine the walls. In the end, the citizens surrendered on terms. Rougemont, the highest point in the city, was taken as the site of a castle (Fig. 140), an action which involved the destruction of 48 houses. But the army was kept from plundering, and, as Domesday Book shows, the payments to the Crown were not increased.

By 1086, a series of south-western castles had been built to serve as strong

---

1. See p. 278.
2. F. Stenton, *Anglo-Saxon England* (1947), pp. 591–3 and refs there.

Figure 140 Gatehouse of the Castle, Exeter. This is the principal building surviving from the castle built by William I after the events of 1067–8. (Photo: Exeter City Museum)

points and centres of government. The Domesday record[3] of destroyed houses at Barnstaple, Lydford and Totnes suggests, as we would expect, that these boroughs had castles imposed upon them. Baldwin the Sheriff built his own castle at Okehampton, controlling the northern route around Dartmoor. Robert, Count of Mortain, William's half-brother and the chief landholder in Cornwall, built his principal castle near the religious house of St Stephens-by-Launceston to which the canons' market was transferred. Robert also possessed a castle at Trematon near St Germans' house of canons.

Documentary research and fieldwork[4] suggest that many more castles existed by 1100. The original work at Restormel involved a substantial ringwork. A similar work existed at Dunkerswell, and perhaps at 'The Rings', Loddiswell, both in Devon, although these seem to have been occupied only temporarily. Eventually permanent castles were built at Plympton, Dunster and Stogumber. All of these were, of course, originally intended to dominate occupied country, but their military significance

---

3.   C. Thorn and F. Thorn, *Domesday Book: Devon* (1985), under separate manors.
4.   See S. Pearce, *The Archaeology of South-western Britain* (1981), pp. 205–8, and refs there.

seems quite rapidly to have been overtaken by their capacity to act as centres of government, and as important focuses of social life.

During the medieval period, the south-western shires continued to be of considerable economic importance. This was partly through their production of metals, especially tin, and of woollen textiles. It was also through the steadily increasing significance of the opportunities presented by the sea coasts, and developing enterprises like the trade in fish.[5] However, by the early twelfth century, the region had ceased to play any particular role in the broader political history of the kingdom. It was well away from the north–south routes, and remained relatively unaffected by the intermittent civil wars of the twelfth–earlier fourteenth centuries, or by the wars against the Welsh. But as the region dwindled in real politics into a prosperous, provincial backwater, its legendary history took flight. By the early thirteenth century it was established as the land where the most important events of early British history had taken place.

Legend and romance

Wessex had gradually absorbed the British of west Devon and Cornwall in the eighth, ninth and earlier tenth centuries, and then, as the English kingdom, established an insecure overlordship of the Welsh kingdoms in the tenth and eleventh centuries. These political and economic developments were matched by intellectual and imaginative efforts intended to complement and comment upon political events. This was achieved by the perpetual reworking of legendary, mythological and folkloristic material, in ways which depicted past glories associated with imperial Rome and created a dense network of linkages across the world where Celtic languages were spoken. So detailed were the connections which this pseudo-history created between Wales, northern Britain, south-western Britain and Ireland, that much of the modern historians' endeavours has been directed towards dismantling the system, an enterprise by no means complete. The reworking of the past was well under way in the tenth century. After the Norman Conquest it gathered momentum to become a major element (Fig. 141) in the growth of post-1100 Arthurian and related romance.

The stories used to unite a group of south-western dedication names into the 'Children of Brychan' and another into the 'Irish Companions of Ia' have already been mentioned:[6] there may have been others. These hagiographical developments were part of a very substantial and immensely complex project, intended to produce histories of saints and their churches which would help to establish the rights of religious committees in the face of political pressure, and knit the world of the past into a sacred, coherent, whole. A major centre in the twelfth century was the religious house of Llancarfan in South Wales.[7] Here three blood relations, Lifris, Stephen and Caradoc, all composed significant saints *Lives*, and probably also helped to put together the material in the *Book of Llandaff*. Caradoc seems to have spent part of his later life at Glastonbury where he wrote his *Life of St Gildas* and was probably

5. H. Fox, *The Evolution of the Fishing Village: Landscape and Society along the South Devon Coast 1068–1150* (2001), esp. pp. 51–9.

6. See p. 253.

7. J. Tatlock, 'Caradoc of Llancarfan', *Speculum*, 13 (1938): 139–52; see also J. Tatlock, 'The dates of the Arthurian saints' legends', *Speculum*, 14 (1939): 345–65.

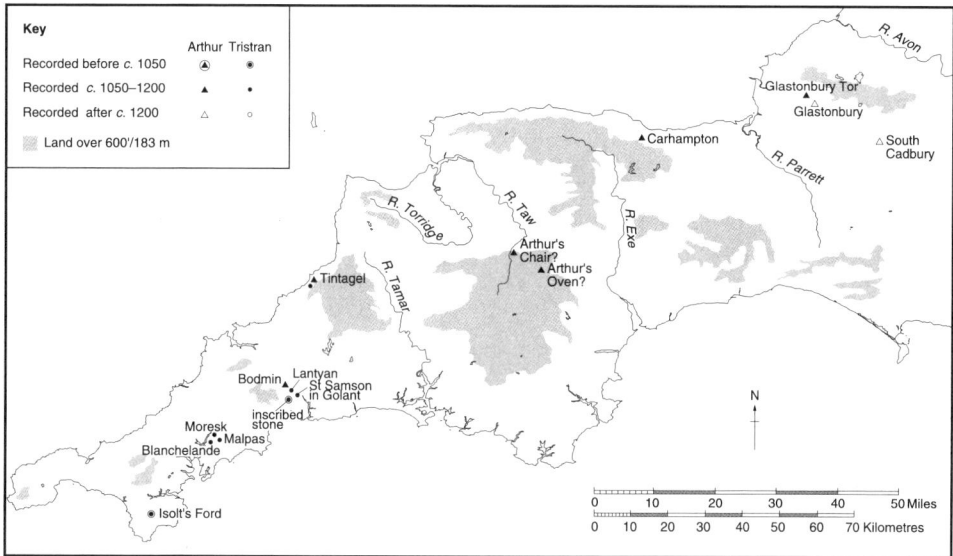

Figure 141 South-western places at which stories related to Arthur and Tristan were located

responsible for a *Life of St Congar*. Lifris's *Life of St Cadoc* had referred respectfully to Petroc and this seems to have fed into the broadly associated *Life of St Petroc*; true to developing form, Petroc is said to have been a Welshman who studied in Ireland before founding his Cornish house.[8]

As the traditions of the Children of Brychan show, much the same people who were composing saints' *Lives* were also working up a mass of very mixed traditional material into a coherent set of royal and hagiographical genealogies. What probably purports to be a pedigree of the south-western British kings appears in Jesus College (Oxford) MS 20 as part of the elaborate pedigree of Morgan ab Owain, King of Gwent and Glywsing, who died in 974.[9] Whether there was any real kinship connection between the shadowy Cornish rulers and kings in south Wales is quite unknown, and there is no reason to think that the pedigree represents any real sequence of Cornish kings, whether related by blood or not. Nevertheless, the pedigree has some importance. Like the saints' *Lives*, it stresses the desire to treat western British supposed traditions as an integral part of the wider whole. It underlines the perceived value of the imperial connection by putting Eudaf Hen, a figure connected in legend to Magnus Maximus, Emperor in Britain and Gaul between 383 and 388, at the head of the genealogy as a origin figure.[10] The pedigree also lists Gereint the son of Erbin, who became a substantial figure in post-1100 Arthurian romance.

---

8. K. Jankulak, *The Medieval Cult of St Petroc* (2001). For analysis of the structure of saints' *Lives*, see J. Picard, 'Structural patterns in early Hiberno-Latin hagiography', *Peritia*, 4 (1985): 67–82, and E. Henken, *The Welsh Saints. A Study in Patterned Lives* (1991).

9. P. Bartrum, *Early Welsh Genealogical Tracts* (1966), esp. pp. 41–6; S. Pearce, 'The traditions of the royal king-list of Dumnonia', *Trans. Hon. Soc. Cymmrodorion* (1971): 128–9.

10. D. Dumville, 'Kingship, genealogies and regnal lists', in P. Sawyer and I. Woods (eds), *Early Medieval Kingship* (1977b), p. 81.

The figure of Arthur

The different views taken of the nature of the figure of Arthur over the last century or so provide an index to historiographical perceptions as they have changed during that time. Arthur has been seen as an aspect of mythology, as a fifth-century British war-leader in south-western Britain, or the whole of Britain, and as an heroic warrior in the poetic traditions of northern Britain.[11] A persuasive view[12] sees him as essentially a figure of pan-Brittonic folklore associated wherever a Brittonic language was spoken with hunting and fighting, magical animals and fabulous weapons; above all, he was linked with natural or ancient sites in the landscape about which stories were told. Some of these were in the south-west. In 1131 some canons of Laon, in northern France, in England on a fund-raising trip, were shown Arthur's Oven and Chair, probably on northern Dartmoor and apparently natural rock features. They were apparently also told that he had one of his courts in the south-west at an unidentified place called *Kelli Wic*, 'the forest grove'.

This folkloristic figure seems to have been historicized into a war-leader, that is he was linked with various traditions of warfare to create part of the received account of the post-Roman history of Britain. This has produced the Arthur who appears in the *Welsh Annals* as victorious at the battle of Badon in 516 (an unidentified site) and as killed at Camlann (also unidentified) under the year 537. It also created the account in the *Historia Brittonum* of Arthur's battles.

By the early twelfth century this complex figure of Arthur had been picked up by a range of Welsh writers. In *Culhwch and Olwen*, an early romance, Arthur's court is a *Kelli Wic* and a terrible wild boar is prevented from ravaging Cornwall. In the early Welsh poem, *The Dialogue of Arthur and the Eagle*, Arthur is addressed as 'chief of the hosts of Cornwall'. Arthur plays a substantial role in Lifris's *Life of Cadoc*, probably written around 1100, although the setting here is Wales. He also appears in the twelfth-century *Life of St Carannog*.[13] Here he is located in Somerset, where he gives to Carannog *Carrum*, Carhampton; when the action shifts to Cornwall, Arthur seems to be in authority there too. Arthur is also located in Somerset in two other Welsh texts, the *Dialogue of Melwas and Gwenhywfar* and Caradog of Llancarfan's *Life of Gildas*, written around 1130, both of which draw in Glastonbury.

It is important to recognize that these texts are either earlier than Geoffrey of Monmouth's writing career, or independent of it, but that Geoffrey was in touch with the Llancarfan circle. His immensely influential book, *Historia Regum Britanniae* ('History of the Kings of Britain'), published in or just before 1139,[14] stresses the Cornish elements in the early history of Britain and sites Arthur's conception at Tintagel and his death at the battle of the Cornish River Camblan. Geoffrey seems to have created his Cornish Arthur by working up hints in the earlier Welsh texts, and by picking up perhaps on local folklore of the kind recorded by the Laon canons. There may also have been local stories about Tintagel which reflected its genuine

---

11.   T. Charles-Edwards, 'The Arthur of history', in R. Bromwich, A. Jarman and Roberts (eds), *The Arthur of the Welsh: The Arthurian Legend in Medieval Welsh Literature* (1991), pp. 15–32.

12.   O. Padel, 'The nature of Arthur', *Cam. Med. Celtic Stud.*, 27 (1994): 1–31, on which the following draws.

13.   Tatlock, 'Dates of Arthurian saints', pp. 345–65.

14.   J. Tatlock, *The Legendary History of Britain* (1950); O. Padel, 'Geoffrey of Monmouth and Cornwall', *Cam. Med. Celtic Stud.*, 8 (1984): pp. 1–20, 28.

post-Roman history as a site of major political importance (whether or not such stories mentioned Arthur), and which Geoffrey knew.

The recently discovered slate[15] carrying a late fifth- or earlier sixth-century inscription which includes the name ARTOGNOU (or something similar) does not refer to an 'Arthur' and does not provide 'evidence' for the activities of 'Arthur' at the site. It is, however, possible that, in some indirect and unknown way, the existence at the site of an inscription carrying what might have been read as the letters ARTOS is bound up with the production of a Tintagel Arthur.

The same mixture of stories drawn from early origins and regional (and possibly more local) folklore about Arthur probably account for most of the other south-western sites which acquired Arthurian legends. In his *De Antiquitate Glastonie Ecclesia* ('On the Antiquity of the Church at Glastonbury') written soon after 1129, William of Malmesbury set out the local view of the very early origins of the church.[16] This was taken up by Caradog of Llancarfan, whose *Life of St Gildas* made Gildas write his history at the monastery and brought Arthur on stage as the regional king. The bad fire at Glastonbury in 1184 made fund-raising necessary, and stimulated the excavation of the supposed bodies of Arthur and Guinevere at the abbey in 1191.[17] The exhumation had had the patronage of Henry II and is recorded by Gerald of Wales, who also mentions the finding in the grave of a lead cross (Fig. 142) recording Arthur's burial. Wherever this cross[18] was made, there is no reason to think that is as early as the sixth century. On this basis, Glastonbury proceeded to work up the steady accretion of Arthurian and Grail stories into the history of the house.

The Arthurian association with South Cadbury[19] is first recorded by John Leland about 1550. He identified the hill-fort with 'Camalate' and said, 'The people can tell nothing there but that they have heard say that Arthur much resorted to Camalat.' The post-Roman significance of South Cadbury has been demonstrated by excavation. The style of Leland's description suggests the possibility that the site may also have attracted Arthurian folklore of the local type already described.

The story of Tristan and Isolt

Although Geoffrey of Monmouth placed significant events in Arthur's life at Tintagel, the site is chiefly associated in romance with King Mark, his wife Isolt (or

---

15.   The inscription has not yet been fully published. Whether or not the juxtaposition of 'Arthur' and of an inscription with a different, but superficially similar, name at Tintagel is simple coincidence remains to be seen. For slate, see C. Morris, 'Tintagel', *Current Archaeology*, 159 (1998): 86–7. For legendary role of Tintagel, see O. Padel, 'Some south-western sites with Arthurian associations', in Bromwich *et al.*, *Arthur of the Welsh* (1991), pp. 230–4.

16.   J. Crick, 'The marshalling of antiquity, Glastonbury's historical dossier', in L. Abrams and J. Carley, *The Archaeology and History of Glastonbury Abbey* (1991), esp. pp. 217–21.

17.   Crick, 'Marshalling of antiquity', p. 220 and refs there.

18.   A lead cross, supposedly that which Gerald said was found in the grave in 1191, was preserved at Glastonbury, but is now lost. An engraving of it was published in the 1607 edition of Camden's *Britannia*. Probably the cross was made at Glastonbury around the time of the excavation, to serve as a 'proof' of the discovery of Arthur's grave.

19.   Padel, 'South-western sites with Arthurian associations', pp. 238–40.

Figure 142 Lead cross supposedly from the grave said to be that of Arthur at Glastonbury in 1191. It reads HIC IACET SEPULTUS INCLITUS REX ARTURIUS IN INSULA AVALONIA, 'Here lies buried the famous King Arthur in the island of Avalon'. Published in Camden's *Britannia*, 1607

similar) and his nephew Tristan, Isolt's lover.[20] Virtually all the medieval narratives of Tristan, whether they are drawing on each other or not, agree that the main action of the story takes place in Cornwall and Mark's court was Tintagel. In the Tristan story narrated in the surviving fragment of Béroul's version, written in Norman French in the twelfth century, parts of the story are set in identifiable Cornish locations. These include *Lanciën*, generally identified with the Domesday manor of *Lantien*, now Lantyan near Fowey, and the church of *St Sanson*, St Samson in Golant, in which parish Lantyan is situated. Béroul's *la forest de Morrois* refers to the manor of Moresk near Truro, which is indeed recorded in Domesday as possessing an area of woodland exceptional in Cornwall. There are also *la Blanche Lande* which seems to refer to the medieval manor of *Blanchelande*, and *le Mal Pas*, a ford, which seems to be the ford of Malpas near Truro.

Béroul's account was very influential in the transmission of the story (or stories) to the Continent. He may well have had special knowledge of Cornwall, but an important piece of evidence shows that tales about one of the characters were being told in Cornwall well before the development of romance narrative. The Anglo-Saxon charter of 967[21] which conveys an estate in the Lizard has as one of its boundary

---

20.   Padel, 'The Cornish background of the Tristan stories', *Cam. Med. Celtic. Stud.*, (1981): 53–81, on which the following draws.

21.   S755, *Ibid.*, pp. 65–6.

points *hryt eselt*, 'Isolt's Ford'. This is the earliest record of Isolt's name, and, as is normal with Celtic place-names, the name strongly suggests that it was linked with a story that told what happened to Isolt at the ford. It seems likely that such Cornish stories fed into Béroul's account of what happened at the ford of *Mal Pas*. We do not know if the early Cornish stories involved a King Mark and a Tristan, but it seems likely. The implication is that stories about the three were part of Cornish folklore earlier than, and independent of, the narrators of romance.

Some, at least, of the elements in the romance narratives were probably parts of pan-Brittonic folklore, like Arthur. 'King Mark' occurs widely, and in his Cornish version he was probably located at Tintagel because it was remembered as an important post-Roman centre. 'Tristan' stories were known in twelfth-century Wales at the very latest, where his name appears as *Drystan*, the Welsh form which lies behind the later version. *Drystan* has also been linked with various Pictish figures called *Drust*, which has suggested a Pictish strand in the composite stones.[22]

The earliest known occurrence of the name is on the probably sixth-century inscribed stone near Castle Dore,[23] Cornwall. This is a particularly large and impressive example (Fig. 143) of its kind. The inscription (Fig. 144), now very worn, seems to have read DRUSTAVS HIC IACIT CVNOMORI FILIVS.[24] If this reading is broadly correct, the inscription translates as 'Drustanus (or similar) the son of Cunomorus lies here'. There is no reason to doubt that both this Drestan (or similar form) and his father Kenvör (or similar) were real people. The father's name was a common one, meaning 'Great Hound'. While the existence of the inscription need not suggest that the Tristan story rests in historical fact rather than folklore, it does seem unlikely, given that the inscription would have been fully legible in the tenth–twelfth centuries (to go no further either way), that it played a part in the development, and the locating, of the story. In particular, it may account for the statement made by the ninth-century Wrmonoc of Landévennec, in Brittany, that King Marcus was 'by another name called Cunomorus'.[25] It also may account for Béroul's interest in the Lantyan area, although whether either man made the connection, or whether it was already a part of local storytelling, is not clear.

Overall, it seems that Mark was originally a figure of pan-Brittonic folklore, and Tristan may have been the same, or stories about him may have originated in Cornwall. Isolt is first recorded in Cornwall in circumstances which suggest stories were told about her as early as the tenth century. Probably a variety of episodes about

---

22. R. Bromwich, 'Some remarks on the Celtic sources of "Tristan"', *Trans. Hon. Soc. Cymmorodorion* (1955): 32–60.

23. Castle Dore is not now thought to have any post-Roman features, and should not be brought into any consideration of the Tristan material; see Padel, 'South-western sites with Arthurian associations', pp. 240–3, P. Rahtz, 'Castle Dore – a reappraisal of the post-Roman structures', *Corn. Arch.*, 10 (1971): 49–54, and H. Quinnell and D. Harris, 'Castle Dore: the chronology reconsidered', *Corn. Arch.*, 24 (1985): 123–32.

24. This reading, with noted uncertainty over the reading of the final three letters of the first name, was accepted by Padel in 'Cornish background of Tristan stories', p. 55 note 8. For a variant reading, see E. Okasha, *Corpus of Early Christian Inscribed Stones of South-West Britain* (1993), pp. 90–6. A version of the same name appears as DROSTEN on a ninth-century Pictish stone from St Vigeans: T. Clancy, 'The Drosten Stone: a new reading', *Proc. Soc. Antiq. Scot.*, 123 (1993): 345–53.

25. G. Doble, *The Saints of Cornwall, Part One: Saints of the Land's End District* (1997), pp. 10–60, esp. p. 16.

Figure 143 The Castle Dore inscribed stone. It is known to have been moved several times, but seems to be close to its original position. It now stands near the junction of the B3369 Fowey to Lostwithiel road and the A3082. The stone now stands some 3 m high. The inscription is on the right-hand side. On the opposite side is a T shape in relief, of uncertain date (photo: Ray Bishop)

Figure 144 The Castle Dore inscribed stone. The first letter is a reversed D, and the reading of the letters immediately after the first T are uncertain. The M of CUNOMORI is upside down (after Thomas 1994, Fig. 17.2)

the three were told in Cornwall, tied to a range of places which included Tintagel, the traditional home of kings, and the Lantyan area, encouraged by the existence of the inscribed stone. Similar stories may have been told elsewhere in the Celtic world (either independently or derived from Cornwall), but it was the Cornish version which shaped the continental narrative.

The story of Arthur and of the British kings as told by Geoffrey of Monmouth, the story of Tristan and Isolt as it came to be told in continental romance, and the Arthurian history of Glastonbury as successfully constructed at the abbey all focus upon the West Country. Collectively, by *c.* 1200, these, and similar narrators, had turned the south-west into the location for what were seen as the defining events in early British history, and for stories which shaped subsequent European literature fundamentally. There seems to be an early level of folklore, both local variants of widely told stories and perhaps some purely local stories, upon which the post-1066 narrators drew. Why they wanted to draw on Celtic lore and legend, what they made of the stories and how they were received belongs to the wider cultural history of taste and feeling. What does seem to have been important was the unique position of the south-west. Here was an unimpeachably 'Celtic' area where the western population still spoke Cornish, but one which, unlike Wales or northern Britain, had been a peaceful, administratively unremarkable, part of the English kingdom since before the Norman Conquest. The character of the region was established as intrinsically romantic, a character it has retained in popular imagination into the twenty-first century.

Continuity and change

This book has tried to trace the course of events in the south-west area over some seven centuries between *c.* AD 350 and 1050. To put the same point in a different way, and allowing the usual three generations to a century, people alive in 1050 are separated from us by 28 generations, and those in 350 by 49 generations, perhaps rather fewer than we sometimes think. What such continuity can sometimes mean was vividly illustrated in Somerset, where a genetic link was demonstrated between early human remains found at Cheddar and a man living nearby.[26]

Similar continuities are written on the landscape. Many of the boundaries which define large territories, like shires and administrative divisions within counties, follow tribal boundaries, tribal divisions like the Cornish hundreds or ancient arrangements for regulating grazing on the moor lands. Some of these certainly go back to the pre-Roman Iron Age, and many even have their roots in the Bronze Age. Perhaps we can also still trace the boundaries of early large economic units, conveniently called estates, fossilized in later arrangements. Some of these may also be pre-Roman, although some perhaps were created in the upheavals of the third century, and others may be later still. Sometimes these units seem to have centred upon important hilltops like Corfe in Dorset or Brent Knoll in Somerset. Major hilltops like Carn Brea, Cadbury Tiverton, Maiden Castle and Glastonbury Tor had been gathering places in the countryside for millennia by AD 300 and reappear in the fourth and fifth centuries as the sites of shrines and communal activity. They still provide comforting landmarks.

Within this enduring framework, however, changes are obvious. As pressures developed particularly, perhaps, externally from the Scandinavians, and internally from the kings and their immediate supporters, it became necessary to divide the landscape into smaller economic units and to make these units more productive. The results are often visible in the parish boundaries which sometimes still follow those the new units created from fragments of older estates. They can be seen, too, particularly in the east of the peninsula, in the villages which were often seen as the best way to manage the new and more intensive approach to farming. The common, subdivided fields, which were created as a crucial part of these changes, must have seemed very stable, but they were to disappear in the modern period, leaving only their traces behind. Increased production stimulated manufacture and trade, creating,

---

26.   See L. Barham, P. Priestly and A. Targett, *In Search of Cheddar Man* (1999).

often on the basis of royal or ecclesiastical centres, the market towns which are still the focus of social and economic life across the West Country.

Dimly and uncertainly, we may be able to see a parallel change in how people lived their lives. It is possible – no more – that the creation of the large estates turned what had been at least some independent landholders into dependants, who now contributed rent to a landlord rather than tax to the central authority.[27] This may have been a feature of the villa estates of the fourth century, where owners seem to have acquired some legal and fiscal powers as well as economic ones, and many people perhaps began to slip from free status to something like serfdom. It may be tied up with the disappearance around the sixth century of the Cornish enclosed settlements (with names in **ker*) and the beginning of the open hamlets (with names in **trev*), a process which seems to have happened earlier further east. The creation of new units out of fragmented parts of earlier, larger ones seems to have encouraged this process, and the development of manorial courts created a mechanism for enforcing local custom and practice.

If the hundred system, or even parts of the tithing system (a substantial 'if'), have their roots in pre-300 arrangements, then presumably they were a part of the organization regulating the lives of relatively free peasant households. Hundreds and tithings, like shires, often remained structures of the central authority, although much entangled in the developing manorial system, and they became major elements in the power of medieval English kings. If these arrangements are, in some cases at least, genuinely ancient, they may originally have been vested with the management of the open grazing (and possibly the other resources of upland, marsh and wood). As the landscape filled up, units were subdivided, and farming became more demanding, access to the resources of the larger areas of upland became more difficult and less free: Dartmoor is the principal area to have retained substantial commoners' rights, perhaps because of its enormous size. In human terms, this seems to have meant that fewer people were able to spend their summers in the freedom of the open upland, although some, like herders and tinners, continued to do so.

The role of Christianity in all this is significant. In the south-west, at any rate, it seems probable that during the fourth and perhaps the earlier fifth centuries, the only significant Christian communities were those in, and in the vicinity of, the cities of Exeter, Dorchester, Ilchester and Bath. Christian practice spread, probably mostly among the elite who had access to special burial grounds during the later fourth (possibly), fifth and sixth centuries. Unquestionably, the carefully managed links between churchmen and kings enabled royal power to set itself up as qualitatively superior to any rivals, just as the need to endow the newly founded monasteries and minsters created ways of conveying land and building up corporate endowments. Probably most people were not able to see themselves as fully Christian folk until the lords of the new, smaller estates began to set up what were to become parish churches, with their graveyards. These provisions may have been a major reason why people were willing to accept the new arrangements. These 'new arrangements' are, of course, now the ancient parish churches and churchyards of the countryside.

---

27.   C. Wickham, 'The other transition: from the ancient world to feudalism', *Past and Present*, 103 (1984): 3–36.

Western European contexts

The history of the south-west during the post-Roman period is, like all regional histories, a sequence of unique events. These derive in part from its particular position in the centre of the seaways between the Continent and western Britain and Ireland, and the geophysical contrast between its coastal lands and its uplands, granite and sedimentary. For most of the period covered by this book, the region happened to become an area of interface between Brittonic speakers and Germanic speakers, with all that this implies. The political success of the Germanic-speaking kingdom of Wessex, and its subsequent transformation into England, made possible the imaginative re-creation of the West Country as the land of Tristan and Arthur, and so its entry onto the stage of European art and literature.

The Arthurian stories, coupled with development of political and emotional 'Celticism' discussed in the first chapter, have coloured the view of south-western post-Roman history to a substantial degree. I wish, finally, to emphasize that, regional twists and quirks notwithstanding, within the wider context of western Europe, the history of the south-west is characterized by its normality. In the later fourth- and fifth-century deterioration of civic amenities at Exeter, or Dorchester, we can see the broad late imperial loss of confidence in city life and its classical values. The same general shift of values shows in the unwillingness to repair villas like Holcombe or Lufton, and the same turn to local and family loyalties appears in the hilltop shrines and the burial grounds. As everywhere else in the old empire, Christian belief and practice, with its emphasis on the body and on special places, came to satisfy emotional, social and political needs.

Everywhere, the Late Antique was characterized by a shifting cultural and linguistic mix out of which, in the later fifth and sixth centuries, kingdoms crystallized. Wessex, Cornwall and the other kingdoms of Britain were dissimilar from those of western Europe in some important ways, especially in their small size (although some others, like that of Suebi in Galicia, were almost as small[28]), probably because of the scale offered by the relatively small island, but there are significant similarities also. Everywhere rulers established their royal credentials by founding monasteries, like those at Wimborne, Bath, perhaps Exeter and probably some of the Cornish houses. Wherever possible they worked with their bishops and founded new sees where these seemed to be helpful, as Ine did at Sherborne. Everywhere, also, kingdoms tried to expand through the aggressive absorption of neighbours, as Wessex did Cornwall.

These processes stimulated production and trade generally in western Europe and seem to have triggered what became the Viking wars and Scandinavian settlement centred on the ninth century. The same processes were also probably producing a larger 'gentry' class and an increased demand for food. The Viking upheavals are not now seen as the sole catalyst for major social change, but as part of complex processes of the longer term which created what is traditionally called 'feudal society' across western Europe. In south-western Britain this appears as the fragmentation of some older large estates into smaller ones, many made viable by the reorganization of their arable into subdivided common fields and their settlements into villages. This helped to lessen the personal freedom of most people, and to create a hierarchy of landlords.

---

28. For Suebi, see M. Todd, *The Early Germans* (1992), pp. 185–8, and generally for the early Germanic kingdoms.

From all this emerged a series of medieval states across western Europe by the eleventh century. England was one of these, albeit with a ruling family more deeply rooted in early medieval history than many, especially those of the counties and dukedoms which made up France. Most of these states, including England, had complex pasts and were culturally mixed. Their rulers were at pains to establish unifying traditions, and in this the notion of a new Christianity with reformed monasteries and an improved network of pastoral care was important, as it was in England. Gradually, regions, which had been politically significant in their own right, became simply parts of the new polities, as the south-west did of later medieval England.

Bibliography

Abrams, L. (1993) 'St Patrick and Glastonbury Abbey: *nihil ex nililo fit?*', in Dumville 1993, pp. 233–42.
Abrams, L. and Carley, J. (1991) *The Archaeology and History of Glastonbury Abbey*. Boydell Press, Woodbridge.
Adkins, R. and Petchey, M. (1984) 'Secklow Hundred Mound and other meeting place mounds in England', *Arch. J.*, 141: 243–51.
Aitchinson, N. (1988) 'Roman wealth, native ritual: coin hoards within and beyond Roman Britain', *World Archaeology*, 20(2): 270–84.
Aitken, G. and Aitken, G. (1990) 'Excavations at Whitcombe 1965–1967', *PDNHAS*, 112: 89–94.
Alcock, E. (1992) 'Burials and cemeteries in Scotland', in Edwards and Lane 1992, pp. 125–9.
Alcock, L. (1972) *'By South Cadbury is that Camelot . . .' The Excavation of Cadbury Castle 1966–70*. Thames and Hudson, London.
Alcock, L. (1973) *Arthur's Britain*. Pelican Books, London.
Alcock, L. (1995) *Cadbury Castle, Somerset: The Early Medieval Archaeology*. University of Wales Press, Cardiff.
Alexander, J. (1931) 'The beginnings of Lifton', *TDA*, 63: 349–58.
Alexander, M. (1966) *The Earliest English Poems*. Penguin, Aylesbury.
Allan, J. (2002) 'The Anglo-Saxon Mint at Lydford', TDA 134: 9–32.
Allason-Jones, A. (1995) ' "Sexing" small finds', in Rush 1995a, pp. 22–30.
Allcroft, A. H. (1908) *Earthworks of England: Prehistoric, Roman, Saxon, Danish, Norman and Medieval*. Macmillan, London.
Allen, J. and Fulford, M. (1996) 'The distribution of south-east Dorset black burnished Category I pottery in south-west Britain', *Britannia*, 27: 224–81.
Allen, J., Henderson, C. and Higham, R. (1984) 'Saxon Exeter', in Haslam 1984, pp. 385–414.
Allen, M. and Ritchie, K. (2000) 'The stratigraphy and archaeology of Bronze Age and Romano-British deposits below beach level at Brean Down, Somerset', *Proc. U. Brist. Spel. Soc.*, 22(1): 5–48.
Andrew, C. (1940) 'Trevelgue Head promontory fort', *JRS*, 30: 175.
Anthony, I. (1968) 'Excavations in Verulam Fields, St Albans, 1963–4', *Hertfordshire Archaeology*, 1: 9–50.
Appleton-Fox, N. (1992) 'Excavations at a Romano-British round: Reawla, Gwinear, Cornwall', *Corn. Arch.*, 31: 69–123.
ApSimon, A. and Boon, G. C. (1964–5) 'The Roman temple on Brean Down', *Proc. U. Brist. Spel. Soc.*, 10: 195–258.
Archer, S. (1979) 'Late Roman gold and silver coin hoards in Britain: a gazetteer', in Casey 1979, pp. 29–64.
Arnold, C. (1988) *An Archaeology of the Early Anglo-Saxon Kingdoms*. Routledge, London.
Arthur, P. (1986) 'Amphorae and the Byzantine world', in Empereur and Garlan (eds) 1986, pp. 655–60.
Ashbee, P. (1996) 'Halangy Down, St Mary's, Isles of Scilly, excavations 1964–1977', *Corn. Arch.*, 35: 5–201.
Aston, M. (1986) 'Post-Roman central places in Somerset', in Grant 1986, pp. 49–77.
Aston, M. and Burrow, I. (1982) *The Archaeology of Somerset*. Somerset County Council, Taunton.
Aston, M. and Costen, M. (1994) *Shapwick Report*, No. 5. Bristol University, Bristol.
Aston, M., Costen, M. and Gerrand, C. (1997) 'The Shapwick Project', *Current Archaeology*, 151: 244–54.
Aston, M. and Leech, R. (1977) *Historic Towns in Somerset*. CRAGS, Gloucester.
Aston, M. and Lewis, C. (eds) (1994) *The Medieval Landscape of Wessex*. Oxbow Monograph 46, Oxford.
Attenborough, F. (1922) *The Laws of the Earliest English Kings*. Cambridge University Press, Cambridge.
Bailey, R. (1980) *Viking Age Sculpture*. William Collins, Glasgow.
Baillie, M. (1999) *Exodus to Arthur*. Batsford, London.
Baker, P., Forcey, C., Jundi, S. and Witcher, R. (eds) (1999) *Proceedings of the Eighth Annual Theoretical Roman Archaeology Conference, Leicester 1998*. Oxbow, Oxford.
Balzaretti, R. (1992) 'Debate: trade, industry and the wealth of King Alfred', *Past and Present*, 135: 142–50.

Bammesberger, A. and Wollmann, (eds) (1990) *Britain 400–600: Language and History.* Carl Winter, Heidelberg.

Barham, L., Priestly, P. and Targett, A. (1999) *In Search of Cheddar Man.* Tempus, Stroud.

Barker, K. (1980) 'The early Christian topography of Sherborne', *Antiquity,* 54: 229–31.

Barker, K. (1984a) 'Institution and landscape in early medieval Wessex: Aldhelm of Malmesbury, Sherborne and Selwoodshire', *PDNHAS,* 106: 33–42.

Barker, K. (1984b) 'Sherborne in Dorset. An early ecclesiastical settlement and its estate', *Anglo-Saxon Studies in Archaeology and History,* 3: 1–33.

Barker, K. (1985) 'Early ecclesiastical settlement in Dorset. A note on the topography of Sherborne, Beaminster and Wimborne Minster', *PDNHAS,* 129: 107–12.

Barker, K. (1986) 'Pen, Ilchester and Yeovil: a study in the landscape history and archaeology of south-east Somerset', *PSANHS,* 130: 11–45.

Barker, K. and Seaward, D. (1990) 'Boundaries and landscape in Blackmoor: the Tudor manors of Holnest, Hilfield and Hermitage', *PDNHAS,* 112: 5–22.

Barley, M. and Hanson, R. (1968) *Christianity in Britain, 300–700.* Leicester University Press, London.

Barlow, F., Dexter, K., Erskine, A. and Lloyd, L. (1972) *Leoffric of Exeter.* University of Exeter, Exeter.

Barnwell, P. (1996) 'Hlafaeta, ceorl, hid and scir: Celtic, Roman or Germanic?', *Anglo-Saxon Studies in Archaeology and History,* 9: 153–61.

Bartholomew, P. (1982) 'Fifth-century facts', *Britannia,* 13: 261–70.

Bartholomew, P. (1984) 'Fourth-century Saxons', *Britannia,* 15: 169–85.

Bartrum, P. (1966) *Early Welsh Genealogical Tracts.* University of Wales Press, Cardiff.

Bassett, S. (1989a) 'Churches in Worcester before and after the conversion of the Anglo-Saxons', *Antiq. J.,* 69(2): 225–56.

Bassett, S. (ed.) (1989b) *The Origins of the Anglo-Saxon Kingdoms.* Leicester University Press, London.

Bassett, S. (1992a) 'Church and diocese in the West Midlands: the transition from British to Anglo-Saxon control', in Blair and Sharpe 1992, pp. 13–40.

Bassett, S. (ed.) (1992b) *Death in Towns,* Leicester University Press, London.

Bastide, T. (2000) *Les Structures de l'habitat rural protohistorique dans le sud-ouest de l'Angleterre et le nord-ouest de la France.* BAR International Series 847, Oxford.

Baxter, J. (1953) *St Augustine: Select Letters.* Heinemann and Harvard University Press, Cambridge, MA.

Beacham, P. (1985) 'The Dartmoor longhouse', *Devon Arch.,* 3: 23–30.

Beagrie, N. (1989) 'The Romano-British pewter industry', *Britannia,* 20: 169–91.

Bedoyere, G. de la (1997) 'Carausius unveiled', *Current Archaeology,* 153: 358.

Beeson, A. (2002) 'The Unknown Deity on the Compton Dando Corner Stone', *Bulletin for the Association of Roman Archaeology* 13: 10–13.

Beeson, A. and Henig, M. (1997) 'Orpheus and the Newton St Loe mosaic pavement in Bristol City Museum', in Keen 1997, pp. 1–8.

Bell, M. (1986) 'Brean Down, Sandcliffe ST296587', *PSANHS,* 102: 218–21.

Bell, M. (1989) 'Brean Down, Sandcliffe ST29565871', *PSANHS,* 133: 159–60.

Bell, M. (1990) *Brean Down Excavations 1983–87.* English Heritage Archaeological Report No. 15, Historic Buildings and Monuments Commission for England, London.

Bellamy, J. (1818) 'Tesselated pavement near Halstock, Dorset', *Gent's Mag.,* January 1818: 5–6.

Bender, B., Hamilton, S. and Tilley, C. (1995) 'Leskernick: the biography of an excavation', *Corn. Arch.,* 34: 58–73.

Bennett, J. (1985) *Sea Mills. The Roman Town of Abonae.* City of Bristol Museum and Art Gallery Monograph No. 3, Bristol.

Beresford, G. (1979) 'Three deserted medieval settlements on Dartmoor: a report on the late E. Marie Minter's excavations', *Med. Arch.,* 23: 98–158.

Bevan, B. (ed.) (1999) *Northern Exposure: Interpretative Devolution and the Iron Age in Britain.* Leicester Archaeology Monographs No. 4, Leicester.

Bick, L. (1994) 'Tin ingots found at Praa Sands, Breage, in 1974', *Corn. Arch.,* 33: 57–70.

Biddle, M. (1986) 'Archaeology, architecture and the cults of the saints', in Butler and Morris 1986: 1–31.

Bidwell, P. (1979) *The Legionary Bath-house and Basilica and Forum at Exeter.* Exeter Archaeological Reports, Vol. 1, Exeter.

Bidwell, P. (1980) *Roman Exeter: Fortress and Town.* City Council, Exeter.

Bintliff, J. (ed.) (1991) *The Annales School and Archaeology.* Leicester University Press, London.

Bintliff, J. (ed.) (1999) *Structure and Contingency.* Leicester University Press, London.

Bintliff, J. and Hamerow, H. (1995) *Europe between Late Antiquity and the Middle Ages.* BAR International series 617, Oxford.

Bird, M., Butler, D. and Griffiths, D. (1999) 'Landscape archaeology', *DAS News,* 72 (Jan): 6.

Black, E. (1995) *Cursus Publicus: The Infrastructure of Government in Roman Britain.* BAR British Series 241, Oxford.

Blair, E. (1996) 'Palace or minster? Northampton and Cheddar reconsidered', *Anglo-Saxon England*, 25: 97–121.

Blair, J. (1985) 'Secular minsters in Domesday Book', in P. Sawyer (ed.) 1985, *Domesday Book: A Reassessment*, pp. 104–44.

Blair, J. (1988a) 'Introduction: from minster to parish church', in Blair 1988b, pp. 1–19.

Blair, J. (ed.) (1988b) *Minsters and Parish Churches. The Local Church in Transition 950–1200.* Oxford University Committee for Archaeology Monograph No. 17, Oxford.

Blair, J. (1992) 'Anglo-Saxon minsters: a topographical review', in Blair and Sharpe 1992, pp. 226–66.

Blair, J. and Sharpe, R. (1992) *Pastoral Care before the Parish.* Leicester University Press, Leicester.

Blake, W. (1915) 'Hooker's Synopsis Chorographical of Devonshire' *TDA*, 47: pp. 334–48.

Blaylock, S. (2000) 'Castles in the air at Berkeley House', *DAS News*, 77 (September).

Blaylock, S. and Parker, R. (1994) *Exeter City Defences: Fabric Recording of the City Wall in Northernhay Gardens adjacent to Athelstan's Tower 1993–4.* Exeter Museums Archaeological Field Unit Report Nos 94, 92, Exeter.

Bonney, D (1966) 'Pagan Saxon burials and boundaries in Wiltshire', *Wilts ANHM*, 61: 25–30.

Bonney, D. (1972) 'Early boundaries in Wessex', in Fowler 1972, pp. 168–85.

Boon, G. (1957) 'Roman coins from Blaise Castle, Bristol', *Proc. U. Brist. Spel. Soc.*, 3: 7–8.

Boon, G. (1989) 'A Roman sculpture rehabilitated: the Pagans Hill dog', *Britannia*, 20: 201–19.

Boon, G. (1991) 'Byzantine and other exotic bronze coins from Exeter', in Holbrook and Bidwell 1991, pp. 38–45.

Boon, G. (1992) 'The Early Church in Gwent, I: the Romano-British Church', *Monmouth Antiquary*, 8: 11–24.

Borlase, W. C. (1872) [1994] *Naema Cornubiae. The Cromlechs and Tumuli of Cornwall.* Llanerch Publishers, Felinfach.

Bowen, C. (1990) *The Archaeology of Bokerley Dyke.* HMSO, London.

Bowen, H. and Fowler, P. (eds) (1978) *Early Land Allotment.* BAR British Series 48, Oxford.

Bradley, R. (1998) 'Ruined buildings, ruined stones: enclosures, tombs and natural places in the Neolithic of south-west England', *World Archaeology*, 30(1): 13–22.

Bradley, R. and Thomas, N. (1984) 'Trial excavation in West Walks, Dorchester', *PDNHAS*, 105: 154–9.

Brannigan, K. (1972) 'The Romano-British villa at Brislington', *PSANHS*, 116: 78–85.

Brannigan, K. (1976) 'Villa settlement in the West Country', in Brannigan and Fowler 1976, (eds): 120–141, Appendix 2: 221–7.

Brannigan, K. (1977) *Gatcombe: The Excavation and Study of a Romano-British Villa Estate 1967–1976.* BAR British Series 40, Oxford.

Brannigan, K. and Dearne M. (eds) (1992) *Romano-British Cavemen. Cave Use in Roman Britain.* Oxbow Monograph 19, Oxford.

Brannigan, K. and Fowler, P. (eds) (1976) *The Roman West Country.* David and Charles, Newton Abbott.

Braunton Great Field and Marshes (1986) Devon County Council, Exeter.

Brenan, J. (1991) *Hanging Bowls and their Contexts.* BAR British Series 220, Oxford.

Bromwich, R. (1955) 'Some remarks on the Celtic sources of "Tristan" ' *Trans. Hon. Soc. Cymmrodorion*: 32–60.

Bromwich, R. (ed.) (1972) *The Beginnings of Welsh Poetry, Studies by Sir Ifor Williams.* University of Wales Press, Cardiff.

Bromwich, R., Jarman, A. and Roberts, B. (eds) (1991) *The Arthur of the Welsh: The Arthurian Legend in Medieval Welsh Literature.* University of Wales Press, Cardiff.

Brook, D. (1985–88) 'The early Christian Church in Gwent', *Monmouth Antiquary*, 5(3): 67–97.

Brook, D. (1992) 'The Early Christian Church east and west of Offa's Dyke', in Edwards and Lane (eds) 1992, pp. 77–89.

Brooks, N. (1964) 'The unidentified forts of the Burghal Hidage', *Med. Arch.*, 8: 74–90.

Brooks, N. (1971) 'The development of military obligations in eighth and ninth-century England', in Clemoes and Hughes 1971, pp. 69–84.

Brooks, N. (1978) 'Arms, status and warfare in late Saxon England', in Hill 1978, pp. 81–104.

Brooks, N. (1996) 'The administrative background', in Hill and Rumble 1996, pp. 128–50.

Brooks, N. (2000) *Anglo-Saxon Myths: State and Church 400–1066.* Hambledon Press, London.

Brooks, N. and Cubitt, C. (eds) (1996) *St Oswald of Worcester: Life and Influence.* Leicester University Press, London.

Brown, P. (1970) 'A Roman Pewter Mould from St Just in Penwith, Cornwall', *Corn. Arch.*, 9: 107–10.

Brown, P. (1971) 'The rise and function of the holy man in Late Antiquity', *J. of Roman Studies*, 61: 80–101.

Brown, P. (1982) *Society and the Holy in Late Antiquity.* University of California Press, Berkeley.

Brown, P. (1990) *The Body and Society: Men, Women and Sexual Renunciations in Early Christianity*. Faber and Faber, London.

Brown, P. (1997) *The Rise of Western Christendom: Triumph and Diversity 200–1000AD*. Blackwells, Oxford.

Brown, P. (1998) *Late Antiquity*. Belknap Press, Cambridge, MA.

Bruce-Mitford, R. (1997) (ed. R. Taylor) *Mawgan Porth, a Settlement of the Late Saxon Period on the North Cornish Coast*. English Heritage, London.

Bryant, R. (1980) 'St Mary de Lode, Gloucester', *Bulletin of the CBA Churches Committee*, 13 (Dec.): 15–18.

Bryant, T. (1984) 'Caratacus Stone – a new interpretation?', *PSAHNS*, 129: 32–3.

Buckton D. (ed.) (1994) *Byzantium: Treasures of Byzantine Art and Culture*, London.

Burnett, A. (1984) 'Clipped *siliquae* and the end of Roman Britain', *Britannia*, 15: 163–8.

Burrow, I. (1972) 'Devon, 300–700 AD', *Archaeological Review*, 7: 46–7.

Burrow, I. (1973) 'Tintagel – some problems', *Scottish Archaeological Forum*, 5: 99–103.

Burrow, I. (1976) 'Possible Irish earthworks in Somerset', in Rahtz 1976b, pp. 228–9.

Burrow, I. (1979) 'Roman material from hillforts', in Casey 1979, pp. 212–29.

Burrow, I. (1981) *Hillfort and Hill-top Settlement in Somerset in the First to Eighth Centuries AD*. BAR British Series 91, Oxford.

Burrow, I. (1985) 'Brean, Sand Cliff ST296587' *PSANHS*, 128: 17.

Burrow, I. and Bennett, J. (1979) 'A Romano-British relief from Cadbury Camp, Tickenham (Avon)', *Rescue Archaeology in the Bristol Area I*. Bristol City Museum, pp. 1–5.

Bursche, A. (1996) 'Contacts between the late Roman Empire and north-central Britain', *Antiq. J.*, 76: 31–50.

Butler, J. (ed.) (2000) *Peter Orlando Hutchinson's Travels in Victorian Devon*. Devon Books, Tiverton.

Butler L. and Morris R. (1986) *The Anglo-Saxon Church*. Council for British Archaeology Report No 60, London.

Butler, R. (ed.) (1971) *Soldier and Civilian in Roman Yorkshire*. Yorkshire Press, York.

Cam, H. (1957) 'The evolution of the medieval English franchise', *Speculum*, 32: 427–522.

Cambridge, E. and Rollason, D. (1995) 'Debate: the pastoral organisation of the Anglo-Saxon Church: a review of the "Minster hypothesis" ', *Early Medieval Europe*, 4(1): 87–104.

Cameron, A. (1993) *The Mediterranean World in Late Antiquity AD 395–600*. Routledge, London.

Campbell, E. (1991) 'Imported goods in the early medieval Celtic west; with special reference to Dinas Powys', Vols 1–3. Unpublished PhD thesis, University of Wales, College of Cardiff.

Campbell, E. (2001) 'Were the Scots Irish?', *Antiquity*, 75: 285–92.

Campbell-Graham, J. (1982) 'A middle Saxon gold finger-ring from the Cathedral Close, Exeter', *Antiq. J.*, 62: 366–7.

Carey, J., Herbert, M. and Ó. Riain (eds) (2001) *Studies in Irish Hagiography. Saints and Scholars*. Four Courts Press, Dublin.

Carlyon, P. (1982) 'A Romano-British site at Kilhallon, Tywardreath: excavation in 1975', *Corn. Arch.*, 21: 155–70.

Carlyon, P. (1987) 'Finds from the earthwork at Carvossa, Probus', *Corn. Arch.*, 26: 103–41.

Carlyon, P. (1994) 'Excavation at Kilhallon', *Corn. Arch.*, 23: 181–3.

Carr, G., Swift, E. and Weekes, J. (2002) *Proceedings of the Twelfth Annual Theoretical Roman Archaeology Conference*. Oxbow, Oxford.

Carver, M. (ed.) (1993) *In Search of Cult*. Boydell and Brewer, Woodbridge.

Carver, M. (ed.) (2003) *The Cross Goes North. Processes of Conversion in Northern Europe AD 300–1300*. Boydell and Brewer, Woodbridge, York Medieval Press.

Casey, P. (1979) *The End of Roman Britain*. BAR British Series 71, Oxford.

Casey, P. and Hoffman, B. (1999) 'Excavations at the Roman temple in Lydney Park, Gloucestershire', *Antiq. J.*, 79: 81–144.

Celtic Inscribed Stones Project Database, University College, London. *http://www.ucl.ac. uk/archaeology/cisp/*.

Chadwick, H. M. and Chadwick, N. (1932–40) *The Growth of Literature*. Cambridge University Press, Cambridge.

Chadwick, N. (1954a) 'Intellectual contacts between Britain and Gaul in the fifth century', in Chadwick 1954b, pp. 189–63.

Chadwick, N. (1954b) *Studies in Early British History*. Cambridge University Press, Cambridge.

Chadwick, N. (1963) *Celt and Saxon: Studies in the Early British Border*. Cambridge University Press, Cambridge.

Chambers, R., Forster, M. and Flower, R. (1933) *The Exeter Book of Old English Poetry*. Lund Humphries, London.

Champion, T. (ed.) (1995) *Centre and Periphery*. Routledge, London.

Chanter, J. (1874) 'Devonshire lanes', *TDA*, 6: 173–96.

Chanter, J. (1875) 'Tawton – the first Saxon bishopric of Devonshire', *TDA*, 7: 179–96.
Chaplais, P. (1966) 'The authenticity of the royal Anglo-Saxon diplomas of Exeter', *Bulletin of the Institute of Historical Research*, 39 (99): 1–34.
Chapman, T. (ed.) (1989) *Centre and Periphery: Comparative Studies in Archaeology*, Routledge, London.
Charles-Edwards, T. (1972) 'Kinship, status and the origins of the Hide', *Past and Present*, 56: 3–33.
Charles-Edwards, T. (1976) 'Boundaries in Irish law', in Sawyer (ed.) 1976b, pp. 83–7.
Charles-Edwards, T. (1980) '*Nau Kynywedi Teithiauc*', in Jenkins and Owen 1980, pp. 23–39.
Charles-Edwards, T. (1991) 'The Arthur of history', in Bromwich *et al.* 1991, pp. 15–32.
Chope, R. Pearse (1902) 'The early history of the manor at Hartland', *TDA*, 34: 418–454.
Chope, R. Pearse (1922–3a) 'St Clare's Well, Hartland', *DNCQ*, 12: 314–15.
Chope, R. Pearse (1922–3b) 'Stoke St Nectan', *DNCQ*, 12: 313–14.
Christie, N. and Kipling, R. (2000) 'Structures of power or structures of convenience? Exploring the material past of Late Antiquity and the early Middle Ages', in Pearce 2000, pp. 21–35.
Christie, P. (1978) 'The excavation of an Iron Age souterrain and settlement at Carn Euny, Sancreed, Cornwall', *Proceedings of the Prehistoric Society*, 44: 309–434.
Clancy, T. (1993) 'The Drosten Stone: a new reading', *Proc. Soc. Antiq. Scot.*, 123: 345–57.
Clark, G. (1992) *Women in Late Antiquity: Pagan and Christian Life-styles*. Clarendon Press, Oxford.
Clark, G. (1999) 'Victricius of Rouen: praising the saints', *J. of Early Christian Studies*, 7 (3): 365–99.
Clark, R. (1992) 'The Dedications of Medieval Churches in Derbyshire', *Derbyshire Archaeological Journal* CXII; 48–60.
Clarke, G. (1982) 'The Roman villa at Woodchester', *Britannia*, 13: 197–228.
Clarke, S. (1997) 'Abandonment, rubbish disposal and "special" deposits at Newstead', in Meadows *et al.* 1997, pp. 56–67.
Clarke, S. (1998) 'Social change and architectural diversity in the Roman period in Britain', in Forcey *et al.* 1998, pp. 28–41.
Cleary, S. (1989) *The Ending of Roman Britain*. Batsford, London.
Cleary, S. (1992) 'Town and country in Roman Britain', in Bassett 1992b, pp. 28–42.
Cleary, S. (1995) 'Review of *Civitas to Kingdom* by K. R. Dark', *Britannia*, 26: 397
Clemoes, P. and Hughes, K. (eds) (1971) *England before the Conquest: Studies in Primary Sources Presented to Dorothy Whitelock*. Cambridge University Press, Cambridge.
Coles, J. and Simpson, D. (1968) *Studies in Ancient Europe*. Leicester University Press, Leicester.
Collingwood, R. and Wright, R. (1965) *The Roman Inscriptions of Britain 1. Inscriptions on Stone*. Oxford University Press, Oxford.
Collinson, J. (1791) *The History and Antiquities of the County of Somerset*, Vols 1–3. Cruttwell, Bath.
Conner, P. (1993) *Anglo-Saxon Exeter: A Tenth-century Cultural History*. Boydell Press, Woodbridge.
Cool, H. (1990) 'Roman metal hairpins from Southern Britain', *Arch. J.*, 147: 148–82.
Cool, H. (2000) 'The parts left over: material culture into the fifth century', in Wilmot and Wilson 2000, pp. 47–65.
Cooper, N. (2000) 'Rubbish counts: quantifying portable material culture in Roman Britain', in Pearce 2000, pp. 75–86.
Coplestone-Crow, B. (1989) *Herefordshire Place-names*. BAR British Series 214, Oxford.
Corcos, N. (1983) 'Early estates on the Poldens and the origin of settlement at Shapwick', *PSANHS*, 127: 47–54.
Corcos, N. (2002) *The Affinities and Antecedents of Medieval Settlement. Topographical Perspectives from three of the Somerset Hundreds*. BAR British Series 337, Oxford.
Costen, M. (1974–9) 'A Celtic saint at Weare', *SDNQ*, 30: 219–20.
Costen, M. (1992a) ' "Huish", "Worthen": Old English survivals in a late landscape', *Anglo-Saxon Studies in Archaeology and History*, 5: 65–83.
Costen, M. (1992b) *The Origins of Somerset*. Manchester University Press, Manchester.
Costen, M. (1994) 'Settlement in Wessex in the tenth century: the Charter evidence', in Aston and Lewis 1994, pp. 97–114.
Cottam, S., Dungworth, D., Scott, S. and Taylor, J. (eds) (1995) *Proceedings of the Fourth Annual Theoretical Roman Archaeological Conference, Durham 1994*. Oxbow Books, Oxford.
Cox, P. (1988) 'A seventh-century inhumation cemetery at Shepherd's Farm, Ulwell, near Swanage, Dorset', *PDNHAS*, 110: 37–48.
Crick, J. (1991) 'The marshalling of antiquity, Glastonbury's historical dossier', in Abrams and Carley 1991, pp. 217–44.
Crittall, E. (ed.) (1959) *Victoria County History: Wiltshire*, Vol 4. Institute of Historical Research, London.
Croft, R. (1988) 'Bridgwater, Wembdon Hill', *PSANHS*, 132: 221.
Croft, R. (1995) 'Ilchester, Northover Church ST524232', *PSANHS*, 138: 179.
Crummy, P. J. (1994) *Colchester: Recent Excavation and Research*. Colchester Excavation Unit, Colchester.

Cubitt, C. (1992) 'Pastoral care and conciliar canons: the provisions of the 747 Council of *Clofesho*', in Blair and Sharpe 1992, pp. 193–211.

Cunliffe, B. (1988a) *Mountbatten. A Prehistoric and Roman Port*. Oxford University Committee for Archaeology Monograph 26, Oxford.

Cunliffe, B. (ed.) (1988b) *The Temple of Sulis Minerva at Bath Vol. II: The Finds from the Sacred Spring*. Oxford University Committee for Archaeology Monograph 16, Oxford.

Cunliffe, B. (1995) *Roman Bath*. Batsford/English Heritage, London.

Cunliffe, B. (2000) *Roman Bath Discovered*. Tempus, Stroud.

Cunliffe, B. and Davenport, P. (1985) *The Temple of Sulis Minerva at Bath Vol. 1*. Oxford University Committee for Archaeology Monograph 7, Oxford.

Curley, M. (1982) 'A new edition of John of Cornwall's *Prophetia Merlini*', *Speculum* 57, pp. 217–49.

Dalton, O. (1922) 'Roman spoons from Dorchester', *Antiq. J.*, 2: 89–92.

Dark, K. (1992) 'Epigraphic art-historical, and historical approaches to the chronology of Class I inscribed stones', in Edwards and Lane 1992, pp. 51–61.

Dark, K. (1993) 'Roman period activity at prehistoric ritual monuments in Britain and the Armorican peninsula', *Conference of Theoretical Roman Archaeology*, 1: 134–46, Avebury.

Dark, K. (1994) *Civitas to Kingdom. British Political Continuity 300–800*. Leicester University Press, Leicester.

Dark, K. (1996) *External Contacts and the Economy of Late Roman and Post-Roman Britain*. Boydell Press, Woodbridge.

Dark, K. (1998) *The Early British Court: Place-names and Archaeology*. Late Antiquity Research Group, London.

Dark, K. (2000) *Britain and the End of the Roman Empire*. Tempus, Stroud.

Dark, K. and Dark, P. (1997) *The Landscape of Roman Britain*. Sutton, Gloucester.

Davies, E. (1940) 'The patterns of transhumance in Europe', *Geography*, 25: 155–75.

Davies, E. (1984–5) 'Hafod and Illuest: the summering of cattle and upland settlement in Wales', *Folk Life*, 23: 70–81.

Davies, S. and Grieve, D. (1986) 'The Poundbury pipe-line: archaeological observations and excavations', *PDNHAS*, 108: 81–8.

Davies, S., Harding, P. and Soames, R. (1987) 'Recent excavations at the Grove Trading Estate, Dorchester 1987: the Wyvern Marlborough site', *PDNHAS*, 109: 130.

Davies, S., Heaton, M. and Woodward, P. (forthcoming) *Excavations at Alington Avenue, Dorchester*.

Davies, S., Stacey, L. and Woodward, P. (1985) 'Excavations at Alington Avenue, Fordington, Dorchester, 1984/5: interim report', *PDNHAS*, 107: 101–10.

Davies, S. and Thompson, C. (1987) 'Archaeological evaluation at Southfield House, Dorchester, Dorset', *PDNHAS*, 109: 126–9.

Davies, W. (1973) 'Unciae: land measurement in the Liber Landavensis', *Agricultural History Review*, 21 (2): 111–21.

Davies, W. (1979a) *The Llandaff Charters*. National Library of Wales, Aberystwth.

Davies, W. (1979b) 'Roman settlements and post-Roman estates in south-east Wales', in Casey 1979, pp. 153–73.

Davies, W. (1982a) 'The Latin charter tradition in western Britain, Brittany and Ireland in the early medieval period', in Whitelock *et al.* 1982, pp. 258–80.

Davies, W. (1982b) *Wales in the Early Middle Ages*. Leicester University Press, Leicester.

Davies, W. (1988) *Small Worlds: The Village Community in Early Medieval Brittany*. University of California Press, Berkeley.

Davies, W. (1992) 'The myth of the Celtic Church', in Edwards and Lane 1992, pp. 12–21.

Davies, W., Graham-Campbell, J. and Handley, M. (2000) *The Inscriptions of Early Medieval Brittany*. Celtic Studies Publications 5, University College, London.

Davis, P. (1997) 'Some navigational considerations of pre-medieval trade between Cornwall and north-west Europe', *Corn. Arch.*, 36: 129–37.

Detsicas, A. (ed.) (1973) *Current Research in Romano-British Coarse Pottery*. Council for British Archaeology Research Report 10, London.

Dickenson, T. (1982) 'Fowler's type G Penannular brooches reconsidered', *Med. Arch.*, 26: 41–68.

Diehl, E. (1925–31) *Inscriptiones Latinae Christianae Veteres*, Vols 1 and 2. Berlin.

Ditmas, E. (1978) 'Breton settlers in Cornwall after the Norman Conquest', *Trans. Hon. Soc. Cymmrodorion*: 11–39.

Doble, G. (1933) 'The "Vita" of St Sativola', *DCNQ*, 17: 245–7.

Doble, G. (1945) 'Saint Congor', *Antiquity*, 19: 32–43, 85–95.

Doble, G. (1965) *The Saints of Cornwall, Part Four: Newquay, Padstow and Bodmin District*. Holywell Press, Oxford. Reprinted 1997, Llanerch Press, Felinfach.

Doble, G. (1970) *The Saints of Cornwall, Part Five: Saints of Mid-Cornwall*. Holywell Press, Oxford. Reprinted 1997, Llanerch Press, Felinfach.

Doble, G. (1994) 'The Celtic saints of the Glastonbury Relic Lists', *SDNQ*, March (not paginated).

Doble, G. (1997a) *The Saints of Cornwall, Part One: Saints of the Land's End District*. Holywell Press, Oxford. Reprinted 1997, Llanerch Press, Felinfach.

Doble, G. (1997b) *The Saints of Cornwall, Part Two: Saints of the Lizard District*. Holywell Press, Oxford. Reprinted 1997, Llanerch Press, Felinfach.

Doble, G. (1997c) *The Saints of Cornwall, Part Three: Saints of the Fal*. Holywell Press, Oxford. Reprinted 1997, Llanerch Press, Felinfach.

Doble, G. (1997d) *The Saints of Cornwall, Part Six: Saints of North Cornwall*. Holywell Press, Oxford. Reprinted 1997, Llanerch Press, Felinfach.

Dodgshon, R. (1981) 'The interpretation of subdivided fields: a study in private or communal interests', in Rowley 1981, pp. 130–44.

Dorset Historical Monuments in the County of Dorset (1972) Vol. 4, *North*. Royal Commission on Historical Monuments, HMSO.

Douch, H. and Beard, S. (1970) 'Excavations at Carvossa, Probus, 1968–1970: preliminary report', *Corn. Arch.* 9: 93–7.

Drew, C. (1947) 'The manors of the Iwerne Valley, Dorset', *PDNHAS*, 69: 45–50.

Drinkwater, J. (1996) 'The "Germanic threat on the Rhine frontier": a Romano-Gallic artefact?', in Mathisen and Sivan 1996, pp. 31–44.

Driscoll, S. (1988) 'The relationship between history and archaeology: artefacts, documents and power', in Driscoll and Nieke 1988, pp. 162–87.

Driscoll, S. and Nieke, M. (eds) (1988) *Power and Politics in Early Medieval Britain and Ireland*. Edinburgh University Press, Edinburgh.

Dudley, D. (1967) 'Excavations on Nor'nour in the Isles of Scilly 1962–6', *Arch. J.*, 124: 1–64.

Duffy, E. (2001) *The Voices of Morebath*, Yale University Press, New Haven, CT.

Dumville, D. (1974) 'Some aspects of the chronology of the *Historia Brittonum*', *Bulletin of the Board of Celtic Studies*, 4: 439–45.

Dumville, D. (1975–6) ' "Nennius" and the *Historia Brittonum*', *Studia Celtica*, 10–11: 78–95.

Dumville, D. (1976) 'The Anglican collection of royal genealogies and regnal lists', *Anglo-Saxon England*, 5: 23–50.

Dumville, D. (1977a) 'Kingship, genealogies and regnal lists', in Sawyer and Wood 1977, pp. 72–104.

Dumville, D. (1977b) 'Sub-Roman Britain: history and legend', *History*, 62: 173–92.

Dumville, D. (1985) 'The West Saxon genealogical regnal list and the chronology of early Wessex', *Peritia*, 4: 21–66.

Dumville, D. (1992) *Wessex and England from Alfred to Edgar*. Boydell Press, Woodbridge.

Dumville, D. (1993) *Saint Patrick AD 493–1993*, Boydell Press, Woodbridge.

Dungworth, D. (1978) 'Mystifying Roman nails: *clavus annalis, defixiones* and *minkisi*', in Forcey *et al.* 1978, pp. 148–59.

Dunning, R. (1975) 'Ilchester: a study in continuity', *PSANHS*, 119: 44–50.

Dunning, R. (2001) 'Ponters Ball', *SDNQ* (March) XXXV, (353): 1–2.

Dymond, C. (1902) *Worlebury*. Weston-super-Mare.

Eagles, B. (1994) 'The archaeological evidence for settlement in the fifth to seventh centuries AD', in Aston and Lewis 1994, pp. 13–32.

Eagles, B. and Mortimer, C. (1993) 'Early Anglo-Saxon artefacts from Hod Hill, Dorset', *Antiq. J.*, 73: 132–40.

Earwood, C., Cool, H. and Northover, P. (2001) 'Two pewter bowls from a mire in south Wales', *Britannia*, 32: 279–85.

Eaton, T. (2000) *Plundering the Past. Roman Stonework in Medieval Britain*. Tempus, Stroud.

Edwards, H. (1988) *The Charters of the Early West Saxon Kingdom*. BAR British Series 198, Oxford.

Edwards, J., Galbraith, V. and Jacob, E. (eds) (1933) *Historical Essays in Honour of James Tait*. Manchester University Press, Manchester.

Edwards, N. (ed.) (1997) *Landscape and Settlement in Medieval Wales*. Oxbow Monograph 81, Oxford.

Edwards, N. (2001) 'Early medieval inscribed stones and stone sculpture in Wales: context and function', *Med. Arch.* 45: 15–40.

Edwards, N. and Lane, A. (eds) (1988) *Early Medieval Settlement in Wales AD 400–1100*. Department of Archaeology, University College, Cardiff.

Edwards, N. and Lane, A. (eds) (1992) *The Early Church in Wales and the West*. Oxbow Monograph 16, Oxford.

Efthymiades, S., Rapp, C. and Tsougarahis, D. (eds) (1995) *Bosphorus: Essays in Honour of Cyril Mango*. Byzantinische Forschungen 21, Verlag Hakkert, Amsterdam.

Elkington, H. (1976) 'The Mendip lead industry', in Brannigan and Fowler 1976, pp. 183–97.

Ellis, P. (1981–2) 'Excavations at Silver Street, Glastonbury, 1978', *PSANHS*, 126: 17–38.

Ellis, P. and McDonnell, R. (1988) 'Salvage operations and recording of Romano-British and post-Roman remains at the Town Hall, Ilchester, 1986', *PSANHS*, 132: 83–8.

Ellison, A. (1976) *Villages Survey: An Interim Report*. CRAGS, Occasional Papers 1, Bristol.

Empereur, J.-Y. and Garlan, Y. (eds) (1986) *Recherches sur les amphores grecques*, Supplement 13, *Bulletin de Correspondence Hellénique*. Athens.

Entwhistle, C. (1994) 'Coin weight from Somerset' in Buckton 1994, 86.

Eriksen, R. (1980) 'Syncretistic symbolism and the Christian Roman mosaic at Hinton St Mary: a closer reading', *PDNHAS*, 102: 43–50.

Evans, J. (1990) 'From the end of Roman Britain to the "Celtic West" ', *Oxford Journal of Archaeology*, 9(1): 91–103.

Evans, J. (1995) 'Roman finds assemblages, towards an integrated approach', in Rush 1995b, pp. 33–58.

Everitt, A. (1977) 'River and Wold: reflections on the historical origin of regions and pays', *J. Historical Geography*, 3: 1–19.

Evison, V. (1969) 'The Anglo-Saxon finds from Hardown Hill', *PDNHAS*, 90: 232–40.

Exeter Archaeology (1996) 'Ancient cemetery discovered', *DAS News*, 65: 1–2.

Fagersten, A. (1933) *The Place Names of Dorset*. Uppsala University Press, Uppsala.

Farley, M. E. and Little, R. I. (1968) 'Oldaport, Modbury: a reassessment of the fort and harbour', *PDAS*, 26: 31–6.

Farrar R. (1956) 'The Frampton villa, Maiden Newton', *PDNHAS* 78: 73–92.

Farrar, R. (1973) 'The techniques and sources of black-burnished ware', in Detsicas 1973, pp. 67–103.

Farwell, D. and Molleson, T. (1993) *Excavations at Poundbury, Dorchester, Dorset, 1966–82: The cemeteries*. *DNHAS*, Monograph 11, Dorchester.

Faull, M. (1976) 'The semantic development of the Old English *walh*', *Leeds Studies in English*, 8: 20–44.

Fawtier, R. (1912) *La Vie de Saint Samson*. Paris.

Fenton, A. (1976) *Scottish Country Life*. University of Edinburgh Press, Edinburgh.

Ferris, I. (1995) 'Shoppers' paradise: consumers in Roman Britain', in Rush 1995b, pp. 132–40.

'Fifehead Neville' (1881–3) *Proc. Soc. Antiq.*, Series 2: 68.

Finberg, H. (1943) 'The house of Orgar and the foundation of Tavistock Abbey', *EHR*, 58: 190–201.

Finberg, H. (1963a) *The Early Charters of Devon and Cornwall*. Dept. of English Local History Occasional Papers 2, Leicester University Press, Leicester.

Finberg, H. (1963b) 'The Treable Charter', in Finberg 1963a, pp. 21–32.

Finberg, H. (1964a) 'Childe's tomb', in Finberg 1964d, pp. 186–203.

Finberg, H. (1964b) 'Continuity or cataclysm', in Finberg 1964d, pp. 1–20.

Finberg, H. (1964c) *Early Charters of Wessex*. Leicester University Press, Leicester.

Finberg, H. (ed.) (1964d) *Lucerna*. Macmillan, London.

Finberg, H. (1964e) 'The making of a boundary', in Finberg 1964d, pp. 161–79.

Finberg, H. (1964f) 'Sherborne, Glastonbury and the expansion of Wessex', in Finberg 1964d, pp. 95–115.

Finberg, H. (1964g) 'Winchester Cathedral clergy, their endowments and their diplomatic crimes', in Finberg 1964c, pp. 95–115.

Finberg, H. (1964h) 'Ynyswitrin', in Finberg 1964d, pp. 83–94.

Finberg, H. (1969a) *Tavistock Abbey: A Study in the Social and Economic History of Devon*. David and Charles, Newton Abbot.

Finberg, H. (1969b) 'Two acts of state', in Finberg 1969c, pp. 11–28.

Finberg, H. (1969c) *West Country Historical Studies*. David and Charles, Newton Abbot.

Finberg, H. (ed.) (1972) *The Agrarian History of England and Wales*, Vol. 1. Cambridge University Press, Cambridge.

Fitzpatrick, A. (1997) 'Everday life in Iron Age Wessex', in Gwilt and Haselgrove 1997, pp. 73–86.

Fitzpatrick, A., Butterworth, C. and Grove, J. (2000) *Prehistoric and Roman Sites in East Devon: The A30 Honiton to Exeter Improvement DBFO, 1996–9, Vol 1: Prehistoric Sites, Vol II: Roman Sites*. Wessex Archaeology Report 16, Wessex Archaeology.

Fleming, A. and Ralph, N. (1982) 'Medieval settlement and land use on Holme Moor, Dartmoor: the landscape evidence', *Med. Arch.*, 26: 101–37.

Fogwill, E. (1954) 'Pastoralism on Dartmoor', *TDA*, 86: 89–114.

Foot, S. (1992a) 'Anglo-Saxon minsters: a review of terminology', in Blair and Sharpe 1992, pp. 212–25.

Foot, S. (1992b) ' "By water in the spirit": the administration of baptism in early Anglo-Saxon England', in Blair and Sharpe 1992, pp. 171–92.

Forcey, C., Hawthorne, J. and Witcher, R. (eds) (1998) *Proceedings of the Seventh Annual Theoretical Roman Archaeology Conference, Nottingham, 1997*. Oxbow Books, Oxford.

Förster, M. (1933) 'The etymology of St Sidwell', *DCNQ*, 17: 243–5.

Förster, M. (1938) 'Die Heilige Sativola oder Sidwell, eine Namenstudie', *Zeitschrife für Englische Philogie*, Vol. 62 (New series Vol. 50): 3–80.

Foster, S. (1987) 'A gazetteer of the Anglo-Saxon sculpture in historic Somerset', *PSANHS*, 131: 49–76.

Fowler, E. (1963) 'Celtic metalwork in the fifth and sixth centuries AD, *Arch. J.*, 120: 98–160.

Fowler, P. (1962) 'A native homestead of the Roman period at Porth Godrevy, Gwithian', *Corn. Arch.*, 1: 61–84.

Fowler, P. (1971) 'Hillforts AD 400–700', in D. Hill and M. Jesson (eds) *The Iron Age and its Hillforts*, Southampton University Archaeology Society, Southampton, pp. 203–13.

Fowler, P. (ed.) (1972) *Archaeology and the Landscape. Essays for L. V. Grinsell.* John Baker, London.

Fowler, P. (1978) 'Pre-medieval fields in the Bristol region', in Bowen and Fowler 1978, pp. 29–47.

Fowler, P. and Rahtz, P. (1972) 'Somerset AD 400–700', in Fowler 1972, pp. 187–221.

Fowler, P. and Thomas, A. C. (1962) 'Arable fields of the pre-Norman period at Gwithan', *Corn. Arch.*, 1: 61–84.

Fox, A. (1951) 'Sixteenth report on the early history of Devon', *TDA*, 81: 85–8.

Fox, A. (1952) 'Roman objects from Cadbury Castle', *TDA*, 84: 105–14.

Fox, A. (1958) 'Twenty-fourth report on the archaeology and early history of Devon', *TDA*, 90: 213–29.

Fox, A. (1964) *South-West England 3500 BC – AD 600.* Thames and Hudson, London.

Fox, A. (1965) 'Twenty-fifth report on the archaeology and early history of Devon', *TDA*, 96: 61–80.

Fox, A. (1973) *South-West England.* David and Charles, Newton Abbot.

Fox, A. (1995) 'Tin ingots from Bigbury Bay', *PDAS*, 53: 11–23.

Fox, A., Radford, C. A. R., Rogers, E. G. and Shorter, A. H. (1948) 'Report on the excavations at Milber Down 1937–8', *PDAS*, 4: 27–78.

Fox, A. and Ravenhill, W. (1959) 'The Stoke Hill Roman signal station', *TDA*, 91: 71–82.

Fox, A. and Ravenhill, W. (1966) 'Early Roman outposts on the north Devon coast, Old Burrow and Martinhoe', *PDAS*, 24: 3–39.

Fox, A. and Ravenhill, W. (1969) 'Excavation of a rectilinear earthwork at Trevinnick, St Kew 1968', *Corn. Arch.*, 8: 89–97.

Fox, C. and Dickins, B. (1950) *The Early Cultures of North-West Europe.* Cambridge University Press, Cambridge.

Fox, H. (1970) 'The boundary of Uplyme', *TDA*, 102: 35–47.

Fox, H. (1972a) 'Field systems of east and south Devon, Part I: East Devon', *TDA*, 104: 81–136.

Fox, H. (1972b) 'The study of field systems', *The Devon Historian*, 4: 3–11.

Fox, H. (1981) 'Approaches to the adoption of the Midland system', in Rowley 1981, pp. 64–111.

Fox, H. (1994) 'Medieval Dartmoor as seen through its account rolls', *PDAS*, 52: 149–72.

Fox, H. (1996a) 'Introduction: transhumance and seasonal settlement', in Fox 1996b, pp. 1–24.

Fox, H. (ed.) (1996b) *Seasonal Settlement.* Vaughan Paper 39, University of Leicester.

Fox, H. (2001) *The Evolution of the Fishing Village: Landscape and Society along the South Devon Coast 1086–1150.* Leopard's Head Press, Oxford.

Fox, H. and Padel, O. (2000) *The Cornish Lands of the Arundels of Lanherne: Fourteenth to Sixteenth Centuries.* Devon and Cornwall Record Society, Exeter.

Frazer, W. and Tyrrell, A. (eds) (2000) *Social Identity in Early Medieval Britain.* Leicester University Press, London.

Frend, W. (1997) 'Altare Subnixus: a cult of relics in the Romano-British Church?', *J. Theological Studies Part I*, 48: 125–8.

Frere, S. (1975) 'The Silchester church: the excavation by Sir Ian Richmond in 1961', *Arch*, 105: 277–302.

Frere, S., Roxan, M. and Tomalin, R. (eds) (1990) *The Roman Inscriptions of Britain*, Vol. 2, Fascicule I. Alan Sutton, Stroud.

Fulford, M. (1979) 'Pottery production and trade at the end of Roman Britain: the case against continuity', in Casey 1979, pp. 120–32.

Fulford, M. (1989) 'Byzantium and Britain: a Mediterranean perspective on post-Roman Mediterranean imports in western Britain and Ireland', *Med. Arch.*, 33: 1–6.

Fulford, M. (2001) 'Links with the past: pervasive "ritual" behaviour in Roman Britain', *Britannia*, 32: 199–218.

Fulford, M. and Clarke, A. (1999) 'Silchester and the end of Roman towns', *Current Archaeology*, 161: 176–80.

Fulford, M., Handley, M. and Clarke, A. (2000) 'The Silchester Ogham Stone rehabilitated', *Med. Arch.*, 44: 1–23.

Fulford, M. and Peacock, D. (1984) *Excavations at Carthage: the British Mission*, Vol. 1(2): *The Avenue du President Habib Bourgulba.* Sheffield University Press, Sheffield.

Fulford, M. and Sellwood, B. (1980) 'The Silchester Ogham Stone: a reconsideration', *Antiquity*, 54(211): 95–9.

Gabba, C. (1977) *Camposanto Monumentale di Pisa: Le Antichità*. Pacini Editore, Pisa.

Gallant, L., Luxton, N. and Collman, M. (1985) 'Ancient fields on the south Devon limestone plateau', *PDAS*, 43: 23–38.

Galliou, P. and Jones, M. (1991) *The Bretons*. Blackwell, Oxford.

Gardner, K. (1999) 'The PRIA tribal boundaries', *DAS News*, 74: 8–9.

Gardner, K. and Ternstrom, M. (1997) 'The giants' graves: a nineteenth-century discovery of human remains on the Island of Lundy', *TDA*, 129: 51–78.

Geake, H. (1997) *The Use of Grave-goods in Conversion-period England c. 600–c. 850*. BAR British Series 261, Oxford.

Gelling, M. (1982) 'Some meanings of Stow', in Pearce 1982b, pp. 187–96.

Gent, T. H. and Quinnell, H. (1999a) 'Excavation of a causewayed enclosure and hillfort on Raddon Hill, Stockleigh Pomeroy', *PDAS*, 57: 1–76.

Gent, T. H. and Quinnell, H. (1999b) 'Salvage recording on the Neolithic site at Haldon Belvedere', *PDAS*, 57: 77–104.

Gerrard, S. (1994) 'The Dartmoor tin industry: an archaeological perspective', *PDAS*, 52: 173.

Gerrard, S. (2000) *The Early British Tin Industry*. Tempus, Stroud.

Gilchrist, R. (1999) *Gender and Archaeology*. Routledge, London.

Giles, M. and Pearson, M. (1999) 'Learning to live in the Iron Age: dwelling and praxis', in Bevan 1999, pp. 217–31.

Gill, C. (ed.) (1970) *Dartmoor: A New Study*. Devon Books, Plymouth.

Giot, P.-R., Guigon, P. and Merdrignac, B. (2003) *The British Settlement of Brittany*. Tempus, Stroud.

Gittos, B. and Gittos, M. (1991) 'The surviving Anglo-Saxon fabric of East Coker church', *PSANHS*, 135: 107–18.

Goodman, C. (1972) 'Kings Weston Hill, Bristol: its prehistoric camps and inhumation cemetery', *Proc. U. of Brist. Spel. Soc.*, 13(1): 41–8.

Goody, J. (1983) *The Development of the Family and Marriage in Europe*. Cambridge University Press, Cambridge.

Goody, J. (2000) *The European Family: An Historical Anthropological Essay*. Blackwell, Oxford.

Gover, J., Mawer, A. and Stenton, F. (1931–2) *The Place-names of Devon*. English Place-Name Society, Vols 8, 9. Cambridge University Press, Cambridge.

Gover, J. (1948) *The Place-Names of Cornwall*, typescript. Royal Institution of Cornwall, Truro.

Graham-Campbell, J. (1983) 'A ninth-century Anglo-Saxon strap-end from the cathedral close, Exeter', *PDAS* 41: 133–5.

Grant, E. (1986) *Central Places, Archaeology and History*. Dept. of Archaeology and Prehistory, University of Sheffield.

Grant, N. (2002) 'The lost life of Saint Brannoc of Braunton', *Devon Historian* 65: 21–7.

Grant, R. (1959) 'Royal forests: Selwood', in Crittall 1959, pp. 414–17.

Gray, H. St. G. (1922) 'Trial excavation at Cadbury Camp, Tickenham, Somerset', *PSANHS*, 68: 8–20.

Gray, H. St. G. and Mattingley, H. (1946) 'A hoard of late Roman coins found on Castle Hill, Wiveliscombe', *PSANHS*, 92: 65–75.

Green, C. (1972) 'Interim report on excavations at Poundbury, Dorchester, 1973', *PDNHAS*, 94: 97–100.

Green, C. (1977) 'The significance of plaster burials for the recognition of Christian cemeteries', in Reece 1977, pp. 46–57.

Green, C. (1982) 'The cemetery of a Romano-British community at Poundbury, Dorchester, Dorset', in Pearce 1982b, pp. 61–77.

Green, C. (1984a) 'Early Anglo-Saxon burials at the Trumpet Major public house, Alington Avenue, Dorchester', *PDNHAS*, 106: 149–52.

Green, C. (1984b) 'A late Roman buckle from Dorchester, Dorset', *Britannia*, 15: 260–4.

Green, C. (1986) 'A late Roman "propellor" belt fitting from Handley, Dorset', *PDNHAS*, 108: 184–5.

Green, C. (1994) 'The "Frampton Villa" Maiden Newton: a note on the monument and its context', *PDNHAS*, 116: 133–5.

Green, C., Paterson, M. and Biek, L. (1981) 'A Roman coffin burial from the Crown Buildings Site, Dorchester: with particular reference to the head of well-preserved hair' *PDNHAS*, 103: 67–100.

Green, J. and Green, K. (1970) 'Excavations at Clannacombe, Thurlstone', *PDAS*, 28: 130–8.

Green, M. (1976) *The Religions of Civilian Roman Britain*. BAR British Series 24, Oxford.

Green, M. and Solley, T. (1980) 'Romano-British pottery from Salmon Lodge, Oldberry on Severn', *Bristol Archaeology Research Group*, 1: 30–4.

Greening, P. (1966) 'St Werburga's by Bath', in Wedlake 1966, pp. 20–4.

Greeves, T. (2000) 'Visions in the fog – Dartmoor in the 1st Millennium', *DAS News*, 76:10–11.

Greeves, T. and Newman, P. (1994) 'Tin working and land-use in the Walkham Valley: a preliminary analysis', *PDAS*, 52: 199–219.

Gregson, N. (1985) 'The multiple-estate model: some critical questions', *J. Historical Geography*, 11(4): 339–51.

Griffith, F. (1986) 'Salvage observation at the Dark Age site at Bantham Ham, Thurlston, in 1982', *PDAS*, 44: 39–58.

Griffith, F. (1988) 'A Romano-British villa near Crediton', *PDAS*, 46: 137–42.

Griffith, F. (1994) 'Changing perceptions of the context of prehistoric Dartmoor', *PDAS*, 52: 85–100.

Griffith, F. and Reed, S. (1998) 'Rescue recording at Bantham Ham, south Devon, in 1977', *PDAS*, 56: 109–32.

Grinsell, L. (1959) *Dorset Barrows*. Dorset Natural History and Archaeological Society, Dorchester.

Grinsell, L. (1969) 'Somerset barrows: Part I, west and south', *PSANHS*, 113: 1–43.

Grinsell, L. (1970a) *The Archaeology of Exmoor*. David and Charles, Newton Abbot.

Grinsell, L. (1970b), 'The barrows of north Devon', *PDAS*, 28: 95–129.

Grinsell, L. (1971) 'Somerset barrows: Part II, north and east', *PSANHS*, 115: 44–132.

Grinsell, L. (1976) *Folklore of Prehistoric Sites in Britain*. David and Charles, Newton Abbot.

Grinsell, L. (1978) 'The barrows of Dartmoor', *PDAS*, 36: 85–180.

Grinsell, L. (1982) *Dorset Barrows Supplement*. Dorset Natural History and Archaeological Society, Dorchester.

Grinsell, L. (1983) 'The barrows of south and east Devon', *PDAS* 41: 5–46.

Grinsell, L. (1991) 'Barrows in the Anglo-Saxon land charters', *Antiq. J.*, 71: 47–63.

Grosjean, P. (1935) 'Legenda S. Sativolae Exoniensis', *Annalecta Bollandia*, 53: 359–65.

Grundy, G. (1935) *Saxon Charters and Field Names of Somerset. SNHAS*, Taunton.

Gunn, J. (ed.) (2000) *The Years without Summer: Tracing AD 536 and its Aftermath*. BAR International Series 872, Oxford.

Guthrie, A. (1969) 'Excavation of a settlement at Goldherring, Sancreed 1958–1961', *Corn. Arch.*, 8: 5–39.

Gwilt, A. and Haselgrove, C. (eds) (1997) *Reconstructing Iron Age Societies: New Approaches to the British Iron Age*. Oxbow Monograph 71, Oxford.

Gwyn, T. (1992) 'An early monument in Caernarvonshire', *Arch. Camb.*, 141: 183.

Haddon, A. and Stubbs, W. (1869–71) *Councils and Ecclesiastical Documents*, Vols 1–3. Oxford University Press, Oxford.

Hadley, D. (1996) 'Multiple estates and the origins of the manorial structure of the northern Danelaw', *J. Historical Geography*, 22: 3–15.

Hall, M., Forsyth, K., Henderson, I., Scott, I., Trench-Jellicoe, R. and Watson, A. (2000) 'Of makings and meanings: towards a cultural biography of the Crieff Burgh Cross, Strathern, Perthshire', *Tayside and Fife Archaeological Journal*, 6: 154–88.

Hall, T. (2000) *Minster Churches in the Dorset Landscape*, BAR British Series 304, Oxford.

Hamlin, A. (1972) 'A chi-rho-carved stone at Drumaqueran, Co. Antrim', *Ulster J. Archaeology*, 35: 22–8.

Hampton, J. (1981) 'The evidence of air photography: elementary comparative studies applied to sites at Mount Down, Hants, and near Malmesbury, Wilts', *Antiq. J.*, 61: 316–21.

Handley, M. (2001) 'The origins of Christian commemoration in Late Antique Britain', *Early Medieval Europe*, 10(2): 177–99.

Harden, D. (ed.) (1956) *Dark Age Britain, Studies Presented to E. T. Leeds*. Methuen, London.

Harding, D. (ed.) (1976) *Hillforts and Later Prehistoric Earthworks in Britain and Ireland*. Academic Press, London.

Harraway, D. (1991) *Simians, Cyborgs and Women*. Routledge, London.

Harries, J. (1992) 'Death and the dead in the late Roman West', in Bassett 1992b, pp. 56–67.

Harris, A. (2003) *Byzantium, Britain and the West*. Tempus, Stroud.

Harris, D. (1980) 'Excavation of a Romano-British round at Shortlanesend, Kenwyn, Truro', *Corn. Arch.*, 19: 63–75.

Harris, D. and Heard, R. (1975) 'Hundred of Stratton 2: parish of Kilkhampton', *Corn. Arch.*, 14: 98–101.

Hartgroves, S. (1996) 'The Sites and Monuments Record', *Archaeology Alive*, 4, Cornwall Archaeology Unit 1995–6, Truro, p. 5.

Harvey, D. (1996) 'Providing a territorial framework for studying medieval settlement patterns, using later material to uncover the nature of early systems of landscape organisation', *Medieval Settlement Research Group Report*, 11: 34–5.

Harvey, D. (1997a) 'The evolution of territoriality and societal transitions in west Cornwall', *Landscape History*, 19: 13–23.

Harvey, D. (1997b) 'The tithing framework of west Cornwall: a proposed pattern and an interpretation of territorial origins', *Cornish Studies*, new series, 5: 30–51.

Haslam, J. (1984) *Anglo-Saxon Towns in Southern England*. Phillimore, Chichester.

Havinden, M. (1987) *The Somerset Landscape*. Hodden and Stoughton, London.

Hawthorne, J. (1997) 'Post processual economics. The role of African red slipware vessel volume in Mediterranean demography', in Meadows *et al.* 1997, pp. 29–37.

Hayes, J. (1972) *Late Roman Pottery*. British School at Rome, London.
Hayward, L. (1972) 'The Roman Villa at Lufton near Yeovil', *PSAHNS*, 116: 59–77.
Head, T. (1990) *Hagiography and the cult of the Saints*. Cambridge University Press, Cambridge.
Henderson, C. (1930) *St Columb Major, Church and Parish*. King's Stone Press, Shipton-on-Stour.
Henderson, C. (1964) *Cornish Church Guide*. Reprinted Bradford Barton, Truro.
Henderson, C. (2001) 'The development of the south gate of Exeter and its role in the city's defences', *PDAS*, 59: 45–124.
Henderson, C. and Bidwell, P. (1982) 'The Saxon minster at Exeter', in Pearce 1982b, pp. 145–77.
Henig, H. and Keen, L. (1984) 'Figures from Duncliffe Hill', *PDNHAS*, 106: 147–8.
Henig, M. (1983) 'A probable chi-rho stamp on a pair of compasses', *PDNHAS*, 105: 159.
Henig, M. (1984) 'James Engleheart's drawing of a mosaic at Frampton, 1794', *PDNHAS*, 106: 143–6.
Henig, M. (1997) 'The Lullingstone mosaic: art, religion and letters in a fourth-century villa', *Mosaic*, 24: 4–7.
Henken, E. (1991) *The Welsh Saints. A Study in Patterned Lives*. D. S. Brewer, Cambridge.
Herren, M. (1990) 'Gildas and early British monasticism', in Bammesberger and Wollmann 1990, pp. 65–78.
Herring, P. (1994) 'The cliff castles and hillforts of West Penwith in the light of recent work at Maen Castle and Tretryn Dinas', *Corn. Arch.*, 33: 40–56.
Herring, P. (1996) 'Transhumance in medieval Cornwall', in Fox 1996b, pp. 35–44.
Herring, P. (1999a) 'Farming and transhumance at the turn of the 2nd Millennium (Part 1)', *Cornwall Association of Local Historians Journal*, Spring: 19–25.
Herring, P. (1999b) 'Farming and transhumance at the turn of the 2nd Millennium (Part 2)', *Cornwall Association of Local Historians Journal*, Autumn: 3–5.
Herring, P. (2000) *St Michael's Mount Archaeological Works, 1995–8*. Cornwall Archaeological Unit/ Cornwall County Council.
Herring, P. and Hooke, D. (1993) 'Interrogating Anglo-Saxons in St Dennis', *Corn. Arch.*, 32: 67–75.
Herval, R. (1966) *Origines chrétiennes de la Lyonnaise gallo-romanie à la Normandie ducale (IVe-VIe siècles)*. Mangard, Rouen.
Higham, M. (1999) 'Names on the edge: hills and boundaries', *Nomina*, 22: 61–74.
Higham, N. (1991) 'Old light on the Dark Age landscape: the description of Britain in the *De Exidio Britanniae of Gildas', J. of Historical Geography*, 127: 363–72.
Higham, N. (1994) *The English Conquest. Gildas and Britain in the Fifth Century*. Manchester University Press, Manchester.
Higham, N. and Hill, D. (eds) (2001) *Edward the Elder 899–924*. Routledge, London.
Hill, D. (1969) 'The Burghal Hidage: the establishment of a text', *Med. Arch.*, 13: 84–92.
Hill, D. (ed.) (1978) *Ethelred the Unready*. BAR British Series 59, Oxford.
Hill, D. (1981) *Atlas of Anglo-Saxon England*. Blackwell, Oxford.
Hill, D. (2000) 'Athelstan's urban reforms', *Anglo-Saxon Studies in Archaeology and History*, 2: 173–85.
Hill, D. and Rumble, A. (eds) (1996) *The Defence of Wessex: The Burghal Hidage and Anglo-Saxon Fortifications*, Manchester University Press, Manchester.
Hill, J. (1914) *The Place-Names of Somerset*. Bristol.
Hill, P. (1952) 'The Cadbury Castle hoard', in Fox 1952, pp. 113–14.
Hinton, D. (1981) 'The topography of Sherborne – early Christian?', *Antiquity*, 55: 222–3.
Hinton, D. (1992) 'The inscribed stones in Lady St Mary Church, Wareham', *PDNHAS*, 114: 260.
Hinton, D. (1994) 'Some Anglo-Saxon charters and estates in south-east Dorset', *PDNHAS*, 116: 11–20.
Hodder, I. (1986) *Reading the Past*. Cambridge University Press, Cambridge.
Hodges, R. and Moreland, J. (1988) 'Power and exchange in middle Saxon England', in Driscoll and Nieke 1988, pp. 79–95.
Hodges, R. and Whitehouse, O. (1983) *Mohammed, Charlemagne and the Origins of Europe*. Cornell University Press, NY.
Holbrook, N. (2001) 'Coastal trade around the south-west peninsula of Britain in the later Roman period: A summary of the evidence', *PDAS*, 59: 149–58.
Holbrook, N. and Bidwell, P. (1991) *Roman Finds from Exeter*. Exeter City Council/University of Exeter, Exeter.
Hollinrake, C. and Hollinrake, N. (1995) 'Carhampton, Eastbury Farm ST0117', *PSANHS*, 138: 177.
Hollinrake, C. and Hollinrake, N. (1997) 'Carhampton, Eastbury Farm ST01127', *PSANHS*, 140: 149–50.
Hollinrake, N. and Hollinrake, C. (1984) 'Glastonbury, Magdelene Street, ST49803870', *PSANHS*, 129: 10–11.
Hollinrake, N. and Hollinrake, C. (1989) 'Bridgwater, Wembdon Hill', *PSANHS*, 133: 171.
Holtorf, C. (1997a) 'Christian landscapes of pagan monuments. A radical constructivist perspective', in Nash 1997, pp. 80–8.
Holtorf, C. (1997b) 'Megaliths, monumentality and memory', *Arch. Review from Cambridge*, 14(2): 45–65.

Hood, A. (1978) *St Patrick: His Writings and Muirchu's Life*. Phillimore, Chichester.
Hooke, D. (1982) 'Pre-Conquest estates in the West Midlands: preliminary thoughts', *J. Historical Geography*, 8(3): 227–44.
Hooke, D. (ed.) (1985) *Medieval Villages: A Review of Current Work*. Oxford University Committee for Archaeology Monograph 5, Oxford.
Hooke, D. (1990) 'Studies on Devon charter boundaries', *TDA*, 122: 193–211.
Hooke, D. (1994) *The Pre-Conquest Charter-bounds of Devon and Cornwall*. Boydell Press, Woodbridge.
Hooke, D. (1998) *The Landscape of Anglo-Saxon England*. Leicester University Press, London.
Hooke, D. (1999) 'Saxon conquest and settlement', in Kain and Ravenhill 1999, pp. 95–104.
Hooke, D. and Burnell, S. (1992) *Landscape and Settlement in Britain AD 400–1066*. University of Exeter Press, Exeter.
Hooke, D. and Burnell, S. (eds) (1995) *Landscape and Settlement in Britain AD 400–1066*. Exeter University Press. Exeter.
Horner, B. (1999) 'Totnes revealed – new evidence of the early town and its defences', *PDAS Newsletter*, 73: 1–3.
Horner, W. (1995) 'A Romano-British enclosure at Butland Farm, Modbury', *PDAS*, 51: 210–15.
Hoskins, G. (1952) 'The making of the agrarian landscape', in Hoskins and Finberg 1952, pp. 289–333.
Hoskins, G. and Finberg, H. (eds) (1952) *Devonshire Studies*. Jonathan Cape, London.
Hoskins, W. (1954) *A New Survey of England: Devon*. Collins, London.
Hoskins, W. (1960) *The Westward Expansion of Wessex*. Dept. of English Local History Occasional Papers 13, Leicester University Press.
Howlett, D. (1994) *Celtic Latin Tradition of Biblical Style*. Four Courts Press, Dublin.
Hudson, H. and Neale, F. (1983) 'The Panborough Saxon Charter, AD 956', *PSANHS*, 127: 55–69.
Hughes, M. (1972) 'A Romano-British sacred well at Norden, Corfe Castle', *PDNHAS*, 94: 76–7.
Humphries, M. (1999) *Communities of the Blessed: Social Environment and Religious Change in Northern Italy, AD 200–400*. Oxford University Press, Oxford.
Hurley, V. (1982) 'The early Church in the south-west of Ireland: settlement and organisation', in Pearce 1982b, pp. 297–332.
Hurst, F. (1936) 'Excavations of Porthmeor, 1933–5', *JRIC*, 24, App 2: 1–81.
Hutchinson, G. (1979) 'The bar-lug pottery of Cornwall', *Corn. Arch.*, 18: 81–103.
Hutchinson, P. (1862) 'On the hill-fortresses, tumuli, and other antiquities of eastern Devon', *J. Brit. Arch. Assoc.*, 18: 53–66.
Hutchinson, V. (1986) *Bacchus in Roman Britain: The Evidence for his Cult*. BAR 151(i) and (ii), Oxford.
Hutton, R. (1997) *The Stations of the Sun*. Oxford University Press, Oxford.
Insley, C. (1998) 'Charters and episcopal scriptoria in the Anglo-Saxon south-west', *Early Medieval Europe*, 7: 173–97.
Isaac, P. (1976) 'Coin hoards and history in the West', in Brannigan and Fowler 1976, pp. 52–64, 214–20.
Isserlin, R. (1997) 'Thinking the unthinkable: human sacrifice in Roman Britain', in Meadows *et al.* 1997, pp. 91–100.
Jackson, J. (1987) 'Selwood Forest', *WAM*, 23: 268–94.
Jackson, K. (1938) 'Nennius and the twenty-eight cities of Britain', *Antiquity*, 12: 44–55.
Jackson, K. (1949–50) 'Brittonica', *J. Celtic Studies*, 1: 69–79.
Jackson, K. (1950) 'Notes on the ogham inscriptions of southern Britain', in Fox and Dickins 1950, pp. 199–213.
Jackson, K. (1953) *Language and History in Early Britain*. Edinburgh University Press, Edinburgh.
Jackson, K. (1959) 'The Arthur of history', in Loomis 1959, pp. 1–11.
Jackson, K. (1982) 'Varia: II. Gildas and the names of the British princes', *Cam. Med. Celtic St.*, 3: 30–40.
Jackson, R. (1990) *Camerton. The Late Iron Age and Early Roman Metalwork*. British Museum Publications, London.
James, H. (1992) 'Early Medieval cemeteries in Wales', in Edwards and Lane 1992: 90–103.
James, H. (1993) 'The cult of St David in the Middle Ages', in Carver 1993, pp. 105–12.
James, M. (1901–2) 'St Urith of Chittlehampton', *Procs. Cambridge Antiquarian Society* X: 230–4.
James, S. (1999a) *The Atlantic Celts*. British Museum Press, London.
James, S. (1999b) 'The community of soldiers: a major identity and centre of power in the Roman Empire', in Baker *et al.* 1999; pp. 14–25.
James, S., Marshall, A. and Millett, M. (1984) 'An early medieval building tradition', *Arch. J.*, 141: 243–51.
Jankulak, K. (2000) *The Medieval Cult of St Petroc*. Boydell, Woodbridge.
Jankulak, K. (2001) 'Fingar/Gwinear/Guigner: an "Irish" saint in medieval Cornwall and Brittany', in Carey *et al.* 2001, pp. 120–39.
Jarvis, K. (1976) 'The M5 motorway and the Peamore–Pocombe link', *PDAS*, 34: 41–72.
Jelley, H. (1998) *Saint Patrick's Somerset Birthplace*. Carey Valley Historical Publication, Somerton.

Jenkins, D. and Owen, M. (eds) (1980) *The Welsh Law of Women*. University of Wales Press, Cardiff.

Jenkins, P. (1988) 'Regions and cantrefs in early medieval Glamorgan', *Cam. Med. Celtic St.*, 15: 31–50.

Jenner, H. (1917) 'The Irish immigration into Cornwall in the late fifth and early sixth centuries', *J. Royal Cornwall Polytechnic Society*, new series 2: 38–85.

Jessup, M. and Hill, D. (eds) (1971) *The Iron Age and its Hill-forts*. Southampton University Press, Southampton.

John, E. (1966) *Orbis Britanniae and Other Studies*. Leicester University Press, Leicester.

Johns, C. (1986) 'Hacked, broken or chipped: a matter of terminology?', *Antiq. J.*, 76: 228–30.

Johns, C. (1992) 'A late Roman silver toothpick with the Christian monogram', *Antiq. J.*, 72: 179–80.

Johns, C. (1995) 'Romano-British precious-metal hoards: some comments on Martin Millett's paper', in Cottam *et al.* 1995: pp. 109–17.

Johns, C. (1996) 'The classification and interpretation of Romano-British treasures', *Britannia*, 27: 1–16.

Johns, C. and Herring, P. (1996) *St Keverne: Historic Landscape Assessment*. Cornwall Archaeological Unit, Cornwall County Council, Truro.

Johns, C. and Potter, T. (1983) *The Thetford Treasure: Roman Jewellery and Silver*. British Museum, London.

Johnson, D. E. (ed.) (1977) *The Saxon Shore*. Council for British Archaeology Research Report 8, London.

Johnson, N. (1980) 'The Bolster Back, St Agnes: a survey', *Corn. Arch.*, 19: 77–88.

Johnson, N. and Rose, P. (1982) 'Defended settlement in Cornwall – an illustrated discussion', in Miles 1982, pp. 151–208.

Johnson, N. and Rose, P. (1984) *Bodmin Moor: An Archaeological Survey Vol 1. Human Landscape to c. 1800*. English Heritage and RCHME, London.

Jones, A. (1966) *The Decline of the Ancient World*. Longman, London.

Jones, A. (1996) 'Liskeard', *Corn. Arch. Soc. Newsletter*, Sept n.p.

Jones, A. (2001) *Bear's Down to Ruthvoes, Cornwall Archaeological Watching Brief*. Cornwall Archaeological Unit, Truro.

Jones, B. and Mattingley, D. (1990) *An Atlas of Roman Britain*. Blackwell, Oxford.

Jones, G. (1953) 'Some medieval rural settlements in north Wales', *Trans. Institute Brit. Geographers*, 9: 51–72.

Jones, G. (1972) 'Post-Roman Wales', in Finberg 1972, pp. 283–382.

Jones, G. (1976) 'Multiple estates and early settlement', in Sawyer 1976b, pp. 15–40.

Jones, G. (1986) 'Holy wells and the cult of St Helen', *Landscape History*, 8: 61–75.

Jones, H. (1992) 'Early medieval cemeteries in Wales', in Edwards and Lane 1992, pp. 90–103.

Juleff, G. (1997) *Earlier Iron-working on Exmoor: Preliminary Survey*. Exmoor National Park Association and National Trust Survey Report.

Juleff, G. (2000) 'New radiocarbon dates for iron-working sites on Exmoor', *Newsletter of the Historical Metallurgical Society*, 44: 3–4.

Kain, R. and Oliver, R. (2001) *Historic Parishes of England and Wales*. History Data Service, Colchester.

Kain, R. and Ravenhill, W. (eds) (1999) *Historical Atlas of South-West England*. University of Exeter Press, Exeter.

Keble, M. (1954) 'A short history of Coffinwell', *TDA*, 87: 165–90.

Keen, L. (1981) 'The topography of Sherborne, Dorset – *Lanprobus*', *PDNHAS*, 103: 132–5.

Keen, L. (ed.) (1997) *'Almost the Richest City': Bristol in the Middle Ages*. British Archaeological Association Conference Transactions 19.

Kelleher, J. (1963) 'Early Irish history and pseudo-history', *Studia Hibernica*, 3: 113–27.

Ker, W. P. (1957) *Epic and Romance. Essays on Medieval Literature*. Dover Publications, New York.

Kerslake, T. (1873) 'The Celt and the Teuton in Exeter', *Arch. J.*, 30: 211–25.

Keynes, S. (1994) 'The West Saxon charters of King Aethelwulf and his sons', *EHR*, 109 (434): 1109–49.

Keynes, S. (1999) 'The cult of King Alfred the Great', *Anglo-Saxon England*, 28: 225–56.

Keynes, S. and Lapidge, M. (eds) (1983) *Alfred the Great: Asser's Life of King Alfred and Other Contemporary Sources*. Penguin Books, Harmondsworth.

Keys, D. (1999) *Catastrophe*. Century Press, London.

Kirby, D. (1974) 'The Old English forest', in Rowley 1974, pp. 120–30.

Kirwan, R. (1871) 'Notes on the prehistoric archaeology of East Devon', *TDA*, 4(2): 641–53.

Knight, J. (1992) 'The early Christian Latin inscriptions of Britain and Gaul: chronology and contexts', in Edwards and Lane 1992, pp. 45–50.

Knight, J. (1993) 'The early Church in Gwent II: the early medieval Church', *Monmouth Antiquary*, 9: 1–17.

Knight, J. (1996a) 'Late Roman and post-Roman Caerwent: some evidence from metalwork', *Arch. Camb.*, 114: 35–66.

Knight, J. (1996b) 'Seasoned with salt: insular-Gallic contacts in the early memorial stones and cross slabs', in Dark 1996, pp. 109–20.

Knight, J. (1996c) *The End of Antiquity*. Tempus, Stroud.
Knight, J. (2001) *Roman France*. Tempus, Stroud.
Knight, J., Thomas, W., Ward, A., Lynch, F. and White, R. (1977) 'New finds of early Christian monuments', *Arch. Camb.*, 126: 60–73.
Kurchin, B. (1995) 'Romans and Britons on the northern frontier: a theoretical evaluation of the archaeology of resistance', in Rush 1995b, pp. 124–31.
Lancley, J. (1992) 'Late Iron Age and Romano-British sites located on the Chalbury to Osmington water main', *PDNHAS*, 114: 254–5.
Lane-Davies, A. (1970) *Holy Wells of Cornwall*. Federation of Old Cornwall Societies, Truro.
Langdon, A. (1896) (facsimile edition 1988) *Old Cornish Crosses*. J. Pollard, Truro.
Langdon, A. (1992) 'Cornish crosses: recent news', *Corn. Arch.*, 31: 154–67.
Langdon, A. (2001) 'A Cornish cross, lot no 473, going, going, gone', *DCNQ*, Spring: 273–7.
Langdon, M. (1986) 'Wembdon, Wembdon Hill', *PSANHS*, 130: 151.
Langdon, M. (1988) 'Bawdrip, Bush Marsh ST32904025', *PSANHS*, 132: 216.
Lapidge, M. (1982) 'The cult of St Indract at Glastonbury', in Whitelock *et al.* 1982, pp. 179–212.
Lapidge, M. and Dumville, D. (1984) *Gildas: New Approaches*. Boydell, Woodbridge.
Lapidge, M. and Herren, M. (1979) *Aldhelm, the Prose Works*. Cambridge University Press, Cambridge.
Last, J. (1998) 'Books of life: biography and memory in a Bronze Age barrow', *Oxford Journal of Archaeology*, 17(1): 43–53.
Leach, P. (1975) *Ilchester By-pass Excavations 1975: Interim Report*. CRAGS.
Leach, P. (1982) *Ilchester Volume 1. Excavations 1974–5*. Wessex Archaeological Trust Excavation Monograph 3, Bristol.
Leach, P. (1990) 'The Roman site at Fosse Lane, Shepton Mallet', *PSANHS*, 134: 47–55.
Leach, P. (1991) 'Shepton Mallet, Mendip Business Park, Fosse Lane, ST632427', *PSANHS*, 135: 148–50.
Leach, P. (ed.) (1994) *Ilchester Volume 2: Archaeology, Excavations and Fieldwork to 1994*. Sheffield Excavation Reports 2, Sheffield.
Leach, P. (1998) 'Ilchester, Almshouses Lane, ST522225', *PSANHS*, 132: 216–17.
Leach, P. and Ellis, P. (1993) 'The medieval precinct of Glastonbury Abbey – some new evidence', in Carver 1993, pp. 119–24.
Leach, P. *et al.* (2001) *Fosse Lane: Excavations of a Romano-British Roadside Settlement at Shepton Mallet, Somerset*. Britannia Monograph Series 18, Society for the Promotion of Roman Studies.
Le Blant, E. (1856) *Inscriptiones Chrétiennes de la Gaul, Vol I Provinces Gallicanes; Vol II Les Septs Provinces*. Paris.
Leech, R. (1975) *Small Medieval Towns in Avon*. CRAGS, Bristol.
Leech, R. (1980) 'Religion and burials in south Somerset and north Dorset', in Rodwell 1980, pp. 329–68.
Leech, R. (1981) 'The excavation of a Romano-British farmstead and cemetery on Bradley Hill, Somerset', *Britannia*, 12: 117–252.
Leech, R. (1982) 'The Roman interlude in the south-west: the dynamics of economic and social change in Romano-British south Somerset and north Dorset', in Miles 1982, pp. 209–68.
Leech, R. (1986) 'The excavation of a Romano-Celtic temple and a later cemetery on Lamyatt Beacon, Somerset', *Britannia*, 17: 259–328.
Leech, R. (1997) 'The medieval defences of Bristol revisited', in Keen 1997, pp. 18–30.
Leeds, E. (1926–7) 'Excavations at Chun Castle in Penwith', *Arch*, 76: 205–40.
Leeds, E. (1931) 'Excavations at Chun Castle in Penwith, Cornwall, second report', *Arch*, 81: 33–42.
Lega-Weekes, E. (1924–5) 'St Sidwell', *DNCQ*, 13: 18–23, 104–7.
Lega-Weekes, E. (1933) 'St Sidwell and her fee', *DCNQ*, 17: 253–6.
Levison, W. (ed.) (1905) *Vitae Sancti Bonifatii, MGH Scriptores Rerum Germanicarum*. Hanover trans. by C. Talbot, *The Anglo-Saxon Missionaries in Germany*, 1954.
Levy, E. (1951) *West Roman Vulgar Law*. University of Baltimore Press, Philadelphia.
Lewis J. and Knight, B. (1973) 'Early Christian burials at Llanvithyn House, Glamorgan', *Arch. Camb.*, 122: 147–53.
Liebermann, F. (1903–6) *Die Gesetze der Angelsachsen*, 3 Vols, University Press, Halle.
Lloyd-Morgan, G. (1991) 'From Ynys Wydrin to Glasynbri: Glastonbury in Welsh vernacular tradition', in Abrams and Carley 1991, pp. 301–16.
Longley, D. (1997) 'The royal courts of the Welsh princes in Gwynedd, AD 400–1283', in Edwards 1997, pp. 55–70.
Loomis, R. (ed.) (1959) *Arthurian Literature in the Middle Ages*. Clarendon Press, Oxford.
Lucas, R. (1991) 'The Halstock mosaic found in 1817', *PDNHAS*, 113: 133–8.
McAvoy, F. (1980) 'The excavations at a multi-period site at Carngoon Bank, Lizard', *Corn. Arch.*, 19: 17–30.
McCrone, P. (1993) 'Carhampton, Eastbury Farm, ST011427', *PSANHS*, 137: 144.
Macdonald, J. (1977) 'Pagan religious and burial practices', in Reece 1977, pp. 35–8.

McGarvie, M. (1978) *The Bounds of Selwood*. Frome, Historical Research Group Occasional Papers 1.

McKee, H. and McKee, J. (2002) 'Counter arguments and numerical patterns in early Celtic inscriptions: a re-examination of *Christian Celts: Messages and Images*', *Med. Arch.* XLVI: 29–40.

McManus, D. (1986) 'Ogham: archaising, orthography and the authenticity of the manuscript key to the alphabet', *Erin*, 37: 1–31.

McManus, D. (1991) *A Guide to Ogham*. Maynooth Monographs 4, Maynooth, An Sagart.

Macquarrie, A. (1992) 'Early Christian religious houses in Scotland: Foundation and Function', in Blair and Sharp 1992: 110–33.

Maddicott, J. (1989) 'Trade, industry and the wealth of King Alfred', *Past and Present*, 123: 3–51.

Maddicott, J. (1992) 'Reply', *Past and Present*, 135: 164–88.

Magilton, J. (1982) *The Church of St Helen-on-the-Walls, Aldwark, York, The Archaeology of York*, 10/1, Council for British Archaeology, London.

Mann, J. C. (1961) 'The administration of Roman Britain', *Antiquity*, 35: 316–20.

Manning, W. (1972) 'Ironwork hoards in Iron Age and Roman Britain', *Britannia*, 3: 224–50.

Manning, W. (1985) *Catalogue of Romano-British Iron Tools, Fittings and Weapons in the British Museum*. British Museum Press, London.

Markham, C. A. (1930) 'The churchyards of Northamptonshire', *Northampton and Oakham Architectural and Archaeological Society*, 39: 132–40.

Mason, J. (1966) 'Keynsham Abbey', in Wedlake 1966, pp. 27–8.

Mathisen, R. (1989) *Ecclesiastical Factionalism and Religious Controversy in Fifth-century Gaul*. Catholic Press of America, Washington.

Mathisen, R. and Sivan, H. (1996) *Shifting Frontiers in Late Antiquity*. Variorum, Aldershot.

Matthews, C. (1981) 'A Romano-British inhumation cemetery at Dunstable', *Bedfordshire Archaeology J.*, 15: 4–137.

Maund, K. (1997) 'Fact and narrative fiction in the Llandaff Charters', *Studia Celtica*, 31: 173–93.

Mawer, C. (1995) *Evidence for Christianity in Roman Britain*. BAR British Series 243, Oxford.

Meade, H. M. (1979) *Archaeological Check-list of Landcross Parish*. Devon Archaeological Society/Devon Committee for Rescue Archaeology 6, Exeter.

Meadows, K., Lemke, C. and Heron, J. (eds) (1997) *Proceedings of the Sixth Annual Theoretical Roman Archaeology Conference, Sheffield, 1996*. Oxbow Books, Oxford.

Meaney, A. (1994) 'Gazetteer of hundred and wapentake meeting-places of the Cambridge region', *Procs. Cambridge Antiquarian Society*, 82: 67–92.

Meates, G. (1979) *The Roman Villa at Lullingstone, Kent Vol. 1: The Site*. Kent Archaeological Society Monograph Series 1, Chichester.

Merriman, N. (1987) 'Value and motivation in pre-history: the evidence for the "Celtic spirit" ', in I. Hodder (ed.), *The Archaeology of Contextual Meanings*. Cambridge University Press, pp. 111–16.

Metcalf, D. (1995) 'Byzantine coins from Exeter', in Efthymiadis 1995, pp. 253–61.

Meyer, K. (1912) *Anedota from Irish Manuscripts IV*. Halle.

Miles, D. (ed.) (1982) *The Romano-British Countryside*. Part I. BAR 103i, Oxford.

Miles, H. (1975) 'Excavations at Woodbury Castle, east Devon, 1971', *PDAS*, 33: 183–208.

Miles, H. and Miles, T. (1973) 'Excavations at Trethurgy, St Austell: interim report', *Corn. Arch.*, 12: 25–30.

Miles, H. and Miles, T. (1975) 'Pilton, north Devon. Excavations within a medieval village', *PDAS*, 33: 267–95.

Miles, H. (1977) 'Excavations at Killibury hill-fort, Egloshayle 1975–6', *Corn. Arch.*, 16: 89–121.

Millett, M. (1990) *The Romanization of Britain*. Cambridge University Press, Cambridge.

Millett, M. (1995) 'Treasure: interpreting Roman hoards', in Cottam *et al.* 1995, pp. 100–5.

Mills, A. (1977) *The Place-names of Dorset*, Part 1. English Place-Name Society, Cambridge.

Mills, A. (1980) *The Place-names of Dorset*, Part 2. English Place-Name Society, Cambridge.

Mills, A. (1998) *A Dictionary of English Place-names*. Oxford University Press, Oxford.

Minter, E. (1972–3) 'Eleven years of archaeological work on Dartmoor', *Trans. Torquay Natural History Soc.*, 16: 112–20.

Molleson, T. (1992) 'Mortality patterns in the Romano-British cemetery at Poundbury Camp, Dorchester', in Bassett 1992b, pp. 43–55.

Moore, S. (1890) *Short History of the Rights of Common upon Dartmoor*. Dartmoor Preservation Society, Plymouth.

Moreland, S. (1984) 'Glaston twelve hides', *PSANHS*, 128: 35–67.

Morris, C. (1998) 'Tintagel', *Current Archaeology*, 159: 84–88.

Morris, C. and Harry, R. (1997) 'Excavations of the Lower Terrace, Site C, Tintagel Island 1990–1994', *Antiq. J.*, 77: 1–143.

Morris, J. (1973) *The Age of Arthur*. Weidenfield and Nicolson, London.

Morris, J. (ed. and trans.) (1980) *Nennius: British History and the Welsh Annals*. Phillimore, Chichester.

Morris, R. (1983) *The Church in British Archaeology*. Council for British Archaeology Research Report 47, London.

Morris, R. (1989) *Churches in the Landscape*. Phoenix, London.

Morris, R. and Roxan, J. (1980) 'Churches on Roman buildings', in Rodwell 1980, pp. 175–209.

Morton, A. (ed.) (1992) *Excavations at Hamwic: Vol. 1*. CBA Research Report 84.

Motteson, T. (1993) 'The human remains', in Farwell and Motteson 1993, pp. 141–234.

Muir, R. (2000) *The New Reading the Landscape*. University of Exeter Press, Exeter.

Murphy, E. (1991) 'Anglo-Saxon Abbey, Shaftesbury – Bectun's base or Alfred's foundation', *PDNHAS*, 113: 23–32.

Mynors, R., Thomson, R. and Winterbottom, M. (ed. and trans.) (1998) *Gesta Regum Anglorum: History of the English Kings Vol. 1*. Oxford University Press, Oxford.

Nash, G. (ed.) (1997) *Semiotics of Landscape: Archaeology of Mind*. BAR International Series 661.

Nash-Williams, V. (1950) *The Early Christian Monuments of Wales*. University of Wales Press, Cardiff.

Nash-Williams, V. (1953) 'Excavations at Caerwent and Caerleon', *Bulletin Board of Celtic Studies*, 15: 165–87.

Nelson, J. (1992) 'Debate: trade, industry and the wealth of King Alfred', *Past and Present*, 135: 151–63.

Newman, C. (1989) 'Fowler's type F3 early medieval penannular brooches', *Med. Arch.*, 33: 7–20.

Newman, C. (1992) 'A late Saxon cemetery at Templecombe', *PSANHS*, 136: 61–71.

Newman, P. (1994) 'Tinners and tenants on south-west Dartmoor: a case study in landscape history, *TDA*, 126: 199–238.

Niblett, R. (1999) *The Excavation of a Ceremonial Site at Folly Lane, Verulamium*. Britannia Monograph Series 14, Society for the Promotion of Roman Studies, London.

Nightingale, J. (1996) 'Oswald, Fleury and continental reform', in Brooks and Cubitt 1996, pp. 23–45.

Nunan, D. (1993) *Introducing Discourse Analysis*. Penguin Books, London.

O'Brien, E. (1992) 'Pagan and Christian burial in Ireland during the first millennium AD – continuity and change', in Edwards and Lane pp. 1992, 130–7.

O'Danachair, C. (1983–4) 'Summer pasture in Ireland', *Folk Life*, 22: 30–44.

O'Donovan, M. (1972) 'An interim revision of the episcopal dates for the province of Canterbury 850–950: Part I', *Anglo-Saxon England*, 1: 23–113.

O'Donovan, M. (1988) *Anglo Saxon Charters III, Charters of Sherborne*. British Academy/Oxford University Press, Oxford.

Okasha, E. (1993) *Corpus of Early Christian Inscribed Stones of South-West Britain*. Leicester University Press, Leicester.

Okasha, E. (1998–9) 'A supplement to *Corpus of Early Christian Inscribed Stones of South-West Britain*', *Corn. Arch.*, 37–8: 137–52.

Okasha, E. and Forsyth, K. (1999) *Irish Early Christian Inscriptions of Munster: A Corpus of the Inscribed Stones (Excluding Ogham)*. Cork University Press, Cork.

O'Kelly, M. (1958) 'Church Island near Valencia, Co. Kerry', *Procs. Royal Irish Acad.*, 59C: 57–136.

Olson, L. (1982) 'Crantock, Cornwall, as an early monastic site', in Pearce 1982b, pp. 177–86.

Olson, L. (1989) *Early Monasteries in Cornwall*. Boydell, Woodbridge.

Olson, L. and Padel, O. (1986) 'A tenth-century list of Cornish parochial saints', *Cam. Med. Celtic Stud.*, 12: 33–71.

Olson, L. and Preston-Jones, A. (1998–9) 'An ancient cathedral of Cornwall? Excavated remains east of St Germans Church', *Corn. Arch.*, 37–8: 153–69.

O'Neil, St. J. (1933) 'A hoard of late Roman coins from Northamptonshire, its parallels and significances', *Arch. J.*, 90: 282–305.

Orme, N. (ed.) (1992) *Nicholas Roscarrock's Lives of the Saints: Cornwall and Devon*, Devon and Cornwall Record Society, New Series Vol 35.

Orme, N. (1995) 'Two unusual Devon saints', *Devon Historian*, 51: 10–13.

Orme, N. (1996) *English Church Dedications*. University of Exeter Press, Exeter.

Orme, N. (2000) *The Saints of Cornwall*. Oxford University Press, Oxford.

Orme, N. (2001) 'English church dedications: supplement No 1', *Devon and Cornwall Notes and Queries* XXXVIII, X: 307–7.

O'Sullivan, D. (1980a) 'Curvilinear churchyards in Cumbria', *Bulletin of the Council for British Archaeology Churches Committee*, 13: 3–5.

O'Sullivan, D. (1980b) 'A reassessment of the early Christian archaeology of Cumbria'. Unpublished M. Phil. thesis, University of Durham.

O'Sullivan, D. and Young, R. (1980) 'Excavations at Gilling West churchyard, North Yorkshire'. University of Durham/University of Newcastle Archaeological Reports 3 for 1979, Durham, pp. 13–14.

Padel, O. (1974a) 'Cornish language notes: 1', *Cornish Studies*, 1: 57–9.

Padel, O. (1974b) 'Cornish language notes: 2', *Cornish Studies*, 2: 75–8.

Padel, O. (1975) 'Cornish language notes: 3', *Cornish Studies*, 3: 19–23.

Padel, O. (1976–7) 'Cornish language notes: 5. Cornish names of parish churches', *Cornish Studies*, 4/5: 15–27.

Padel, O. (1977) 'Kelli Wic in Cornwall', in Miles *et al.* 1977, pp. 115–19.

Padel, O. (1979) 'The text of the Lanlawren Charter', *Cornish Studies*, 7: 43–4.

Padel, O. (1981) 'The Cornish background of the Tristan stories', *Cam. Med. Celtic Stud.*, 5: 53–81.

Padel, O. (1984) 'Geoffrey of Monmouth and Cornwall', *Cam. Med. Celtic Stud.*, 8: 1–28.

Padel, O. (1985) *Cornish Place-name Elements*. English Place-Name Survey Vol. 56/57, Cambridge University Press, Cambridge.

Padel, O. (1987) 'Predannack or Pradnick, in Mullion', *Cornish Studies*, 15: 11–14.

Padel, O. (1988) *A Popular Dictionary of Cornish Place-names*. Alison Hodge, Penzance.

Padel, O. (1991a) 'Glastonbury's Cornish connections', in Abrams and Carley 1991, pp. 245–56.

Padel, O. (1991b) 'Some south-western sites with Arthurian associations', in Bromwich *et al.* 1991, pp. 229–48.

Padel, O. (1994) 'The nature of Arthur', *Cam. Med. Celtic Stud.*, 27: 1–31.

Padel, O. (1999a) 'Cornwall around the year 1000', *Cornwall Association of Local Historians Journal*, 37: 5–6.

Padel, O. (1999b) 'Place-names', in Kain and Ravenhill 1999, pp. 88–94.

Page, J. (1890) *An Exploration of Exmoor*. Seeley and Co., London.

Page, J. (ed.) (1906) *A History of Devonshire: In Five Volumes, Vol. 1*. Victoria History of the Counties of England (VCH), London.

Page, W. (1906) *Victoria County History, Somerset, Vol. 1*. Street, London.

Page, W. (1924) *A History of the County of Cornwall*, Part 5. London.

Painter, K. (1965) 'Excavations of the Roman villa at Hinton St Mary, 1964', *PDNHAS*, 86: 150–4.

Painter, K. (1971) 'Villas and Christianity', in G. Sieveking (ed.), *Prehistoric and Romano-British Studies*. British Museum, London, pp. 156–75.

Painter, K. (1999) 'Natives, Romans and Christians at Uley? Questions of continuity of use at sacred sites', *Journal of Roman Archaeology*, 12: 694–703.

Painter, K. and Künzl, E. (1997) 'Two documented hoards of treasure', *Antiq. J.*, 77: 291–327.

Parry, J. (1867) 'On the remains of ancient fortifications', *TDA*, 2: 99–105.

Parsons, D., Styles, T. and Hough, C. (1997) *The Vocabulary of English Place Names (A–Box)*. Centre for English Place Name Studies, University of Nottingham, Nottingham.

Passmore, M. (2000) 'Castles in the air at Berkeley House', *DAS News*, 77: 4.

Peacock, D. (1969) 'A Romano-British salt working site at Trebarveth, St Keverne', *Corn. Arch.*, 8: 47–65.

Peacock, D. (1974) 'A North African amphora', *TBGAS*, 93, 91.

Peacock, D. (ed.) (1977) *Pottery and Early Commerce: Characterisation and Early Trade in Roman and Later Ceramics*. Academic Press, London.

Peacock, D. (1982) *Pottery in the Roman World*. Longman, London.

Peacock, D. and Thomas, C. (1967) 'Class E imported post-Roman pottery: a suggested origin', *Corn. Arch.*, 6: 35–46.

Peacock, D. and Williams, D. (eds) (1986) *Amphorae and the Roman Economy: An Introductory Guide*. Longman Archaeological Series, London.

Pearce, S. (1970) 'Late Roman coinage in south-west Britain', *TDA*, 102: 19–33.

Pearce, S. (1971) 'The traditions of the royal king-list of Dumnonia', *Trans. Hon. Soc. Cymmrodorion*: 128–39.

Pearce, S. (1973) 'The dating of some Celtic dedications and hagiographical traditions in south-western Britain', *TDA*, 105: 95–120.

Pearce, S. (1978) *The Kingdom of Dumnonia*. Lodenek Press, Padstow.

Pearce, S. (1981) *The Archaeology of South-West Britain*. Collins, London.

Pearce, S. (1982a) 'Church and society in south Devon AD 350–700', *PDAS*, 40: 1–18.

Pearce, S. (1982b) *The Early Church in Western Britain and Ireland*. BAR British Series 102, Oxford.

Pearce, S. (1982c) 'Estates and church sites in Dorset and Gloucestershire: the emergence of a Christian society', in Pearce 1982b, pp. 117–38.

Pearce, S. (1983) *The Bronze Age Metalwork of South-western Britain*, Vols 1 and 2. BAR 120, Oxford.

Pearce, S. (1985) 'The early Church in the landscape: the evidence from north Devon', *Arch. J.*, 142: 255–75.

Pearce, S. (1995) *On Collecting. An Investigation into Collecting in the European Tradition*. Routledge, London.

Pearce, S. (1998) *Collecting in Contemporary Culture*. Sage, London.

Pearce, S. (2000) *Researching Material Culture*. Leicester Archaeology Monographs 8/Material Culture Study Group Occasional Paper 1, Leicester.

Pearce, S. (2003) 'Processes of conversion in north-west Roman Gaul', in Carver 2002, pp. 61–78.

Pearce, S. (forthcoming) 'Enclosed graveyards in south-west Britain.

Pedler, E. (1860) *The Anglo-Saxon Episcopate of Cornwall*. John Petheram, London.

Pelteret, D. (1981) 'Slave raiding and slave trading in early England', *Anglo-Saxon England*, 9: 99–114.

Pelteret, D. (1995) *Slavery in Early Medieval England*. Boydell, Woodbridge.
Penaluna, W. (1957) 'Phillack', *Proceedings of the West Cornish Field Club*, 2 (1): 13.
Penhallurick, R. (1986) *Tin in Antiquity*. Institute of Metals, London.
Penn, K. (1980) *Historic Towns in Dorset*. DNHAS Monograph Series 1, Dorchester.
Percival, J. (1997) 'Villas and monasteries in late Roman Gaul', *J. Ecclesiastical History*, 48(1): 1–21.
Perring, D. (2002a) 'Deconstructing the Frampton pavements: gnostic dialectic in Roman Britain?' in Carr *et al.* 2002, pp. 74–83.
Perring, D. (2002b) *The Roman House in Britain*. Tempus, Stroud.
Petrikovits, H. (1971) 'Fortifications in the north-western Roman Empire from the third to the fifth centuries AD', *JRS*, 61: 178–218.
Petts, D. (1997) 'Elite settlements in the Roman and sub-Roman period', in Meadows *et al.* 1997, pp. 102–12.
Petts, D. (1998) 'Burial and gender in late and sub-Roman Britain', in Forcey *et al.* 1998, pp. 112–24.
Petts, D. (2003) *Christianity in Roman Britain*. Routledge, London.
Phillips, M. E. (1937) 'The ancient stone crosses of Devon', *TDA*, 69: 299–340.
Phillips, M. E. (1938) 'The ancient stone crosses of Devon: Part II', *TDA*, 70: 299–334.
Phillips, M. E. (1939) 'Supplementary notes on the ancient stone crosses of Devon (first paper)', *TDA*, 71: 231–41.
Phillips, M. E. (1940) 'Supplementary notes on the ancient stone crosses of Devon (second paper)', *TDA*, 72: 265–72.
Phillips, M. E. (1943) 'Supplementary notes on the ancient stone crosses of Devon (third paper)', *TDA*, 75: 257–66.
Phillips, M. E. (1954) 'Supplementary notes on the ancient stone crosses of Devon (fourth paper)', *TDA*, 82: 173–194.
Phillips, M. E. (1959) 'Supplementary notes on the ancient stone crosses of Devon (fifth paper)', *TDA*, 87: 83–91.
Phillips, M. E. (1966) 'Excavations at a Romano-British site at Lower Well Farm, Stoke Gabriel', *PDAS*, 23: 3–34.
Phillips, M. E. (1979) 'Supplementary notes on the ancient stone crosses of Devon (sixth paper)', *TDA*, 111: 139–44.
Phillips, M. E. (1987) 'Supplementary notes on the ancient stone crosses of Devon (eighth paper)', *TDA*, 119: 241–50.
Philpott, R. (1991) *Burial Practices in Roman Britain. A Survey of Grave Treatment and Furnishing AD 43–410*. BAR British Series 219, Oxford.
Pickard, J. (1985) 'Structural patterns in early Hiberno-Latin hagiography', *Peritia*, 4: 67–82.
Picken, W. (1960) 'The Landochou Charter', in Hoskins 1960, pp. 36–44.
Picken, W. (1986a) 'Cornish place-names and fiefs in a twelfth-century charter', *Cornish Studies*, 13: 55–61.
Picken, W. (1986b) 'Bishop Wulfsige Comoere: an unrecognised tenth-century gloss in the Bodmin Gospels', *Cornish Studies*, 14: 34–38.
Pickles, C. (1999) *Texts and Monuments: A Study of Ten Anglo-Saxon Churches of the Pre-Viking Period*. BAR British Series 277, Oxford.
Pierce, G. (2000) 'The Welsh *mystwyr*', *Nomina*, 23: 121–40.
Pike, R. and Langdon, M. (1981) 'A Romano-British site at Combwick Passage', *Bridgwater and District Archaeological Society Annual Report*, 4–18.
Pollard, S. (1966) 'Neolithic and Dark Age settlements on High Peak, Sidmouth, Devon', *PDAS*, 23: 23–35.
Pollard, S. (1967) 'Radiocarbon dating, Neolithic and Dark Age settlements on High Peak, Sidmouth, Devon', *PDAS*, 25: 41–2.
Pollard, S. (1974) 'A late Iron Age settlement and Romano-British villa at Holcombe, near Uplyme, Devon', *PDAS*, 32: 59–161.
Pool, P. (1981) 'The tithings of Cornwall', *JRIC*, 8(4): 275–337.
Ponsford, M. (1992) 'Post-Medieval Britain and Ireland in 1991', *Post-Medieval Archaeology* 26: 95–156.
Potter, J. (2001) 'The occurrence of Roman brick and tile in the churches of the London Basin', *Britannia*, 32: 119–42.
Poulton, R. and Scott, E. (1995) 'The hoarding, deposition and use of pewter in Roman Britain', *TRAC*, 2: 115–32.
Pounds, N. (1942) 'Note on transhumance in Cornwall', *Geography*, 27: 34.
Poyntz-Wright, P. and Barlow, M. (1967) 'Padwell Hill, Ashcott', *Arch. Rev.*, 2: 16.
Preston-Jones, A. (1984) 'The excavation of a long-cist cemetery at Carnanton, St Mawgan, 1943', *Corn. Arch.*, 23: 157–79.
Preston-Jones, A. (1992) 'Decoding Cornish churchyards', in Edwards and Lane 1992, pp. 105–24.
Preston-Jones, A. and Langdon, A. (1997) 'St Buryan crosses', *Corn. Arch.*, 36: 107–28.
Preston-Jones, A. and Rose, P. (1986) 'Medieval Cornwall', *Corn. Arch.*, 25: 135–85.

Preston-Jones, A. and Rose, P. (1992) 'Week St Mary, town and castle', *Corn. Arch.*, 31: 143–53.

Price, C. (1987) 'Atlantic Trading Estate, Barry', *Archaeol. Wales*, 27: 60–1.

Price, E. (2000) *Frocester, a Romano-British Settlement, its Antecedents and Successors, Vol. 1: The Sites; Vol. 2: The Finds*. Gloucester and District Archaeological Research Group, Frocester Court, Stonehouse.

Probert, S. and Dunn, C. (1992) 'Denbury Camp, Torbryan Parish: a new survey', *PDAS*, 50: 53–9.

Pryce, H. (1992) 'Pastoral care in early medieval Wales', in Blair and Sharpe 1992, pp. 41–62.

Quensel von Kalben, L. (1999) 'The British Church and the emergence of the Anglo-Saxon kingdoms', *Anglo-Saxon Studies in Archaeology and History*, 10: 89–97.

Quinn, G. (1995) 'A new survey of the prehistoric field system in Kerswell Down and Wilborough Common', *PDAS*, 53: 131–4.

Quinn, P. (1999) *Holy Wells of Bath and Bristol Region*. Logaston Press, Wooton Almeley.

Quinnell, H. (1986) 'Cornwall during the Iron Age and Roman period', *Corn. Arch.*, 25: 111–34.

Quinnell, H. (1987) 'Cornish gabbroic pottery: the development of a hypothesis', *Corn. Arch.*, 26: 7–12.

Quinnell, H. (1992) 'The pottery', in Appleton-Fox 1992, pp. 94–106.

Quinnell, H. (1993) 'A sense of identity: distinctive Cornish stone artefacts in the Roman and post-Roman periods', in Carver 1993, pp. 69–78.

Quinnell, H. (forthcoming) *Excavations at Trethurgy Round, St Austell: Insights into Roman and Post-Roman Cornwall*. Cornwall County Council, Truro.

Quinnell, H. and Harris, D. (1985) 'Castle Dore: the chronology reconsidered', *Corn. Arch.*, 24: 123–32.

Rackham, O. (1987) *The History of the Countryside*. Dent, London.

Radford, C. (1951) 'Report on the excavations at Castle Dore', *JRIC*, 1, Appendix: 1–119.

Radford, C. (1956) 'Imported pottery found at Tintagel, Cornwall', in D. Harden (ed.), *Dark Age Britain*. Methuen and Co. Ltd, London, pp. 59–70.

Radford, C. (1957) 'Sidbury: church of St Giles', *Arch. J.*, 114: 166–7.

Radford, C. (1962) 'The Celtic monastery in Britain', *Arch. Camb.*, 111: 1–24.

Radford, C. (1973) 'Pre-Conquest minsters', *Arch. J.*, 130: 120–40.

Radford, C. (1975) 'The pre-Conquest Church and the old minsters in Devon', *The Devon Historian*, 11: 2–12.

Radford, C. A. R. (1981) 'Glastonbury Abbey before 1184: interim report on the excavations 1908–64', in *Medieval Art and Architecture at Wells and Glastonbury*, British Archaeological Association, pp. 110–34.

Radford, C. and Jackson, K. (1970) 'Early Christian inscriptions', in *An Inventory of Historical Monuments in the County of Dorset, II South-East*, Part 2. Royal Commission on Historic Monuments (England), London, pp. 310–12.

Raftery, B. (1969) 'Freestone Hill, Co Kilkenny: an Iron Age hillfort and Bronze Age cairn', *Proc. Royal Irish Academy*, 68(C): 1–108.

Rahtz, P. (1951) 'The Roman temple at Pagans Hill, Chew Stoke, N. Somerset', *PSANHS*, 96: 112–42.

Rahtz, P. (1963) 'Cannington Hillfort 1963', *PSANHS*, 113: 56–8.

Rahtz, P. (1966) 'Cheddar vicarage', *PSANHS*, 110: 52–84.

Rahtz, P. (1968) 'Sub-Roman cemeteries in Somerset', in Barley and Hanson 1968, pp. 193–5.

Rahtz, P. (1971a) 'Castle Dore – a reappraisal of the post-Roman structures', *Corn. Arch.*, 10: 49–54.

Rahtz, P. (1971b) 'Excavations at Glastonbury Tor', *Arch. J.*, 127: 1–81.

Rahtz, P. (1976a) *Excavations at St Mary's Church Deerhurst 1971–73*. Council for British Archaeology Research Report 15.

Rahtz, P. (1976b) 'Irish settlements in Somerset', *Proc. Royal Irish Academy*, 76(C): 223–30.

Rahtz, P. (1978) 'Grave orientation', *Arch. J.*, 135: 1–14.

Rahtz, P. (1979) *The Saxon and Medieval Palaces at Cheddar. Excavations 1960–1962*. BAR British Series 65, Oxford.

Rahtz, P. (1982) 'The Dark Ages 400–700', in Aston and Burrow 1982, pp. 98–107.

Rahtz, P. (1993) *Glastonbury*. Batsford/English Heritage, London.

Rahtz, P. and Brown, J. (1957) 'Blaise Castle', *Proc. U. Bris. Spel.*, 8(3): 147–71.

Rahtz, P. and Fowler, P. (1972) 'Somerset AD 400–700', in Fowler 1972, pp. 187–217.

Rahtz, P. and Greenfield, E. (1977) *Excavations at Chew Valley Lake*. Dept. of Environment Arch., Report 8, HMSO, London.

Rahtz, P. and Hirst, S. (1974) *Beckery Chapel, Glastonbury 1967–8*. Glastonbury Antiquarian Society, Glastonbury.

Rahtz, P., Wright, S. and Hirst, S. (2000) *Cannington Cemetery*. Britannia Monograph Series 17, Society for the Promotion of Roman Studies, London.

Rahtz, P. and Watts, L. (1979) 'The end of the Roman temples in the west of Britain', in Casey 1979, pp. 183–210.

Rahtz, P. and Watts, L. (1989) 'Pagans Hill revisited', *Arch. J.*, 146: 330–71.

Rahtz, P. and Watts, L. (1997) *St Mary's Church Deerhurst, 1971–1984.* Report of the Society of Antiquaries of London 55, London.

Rahtz, P., Woodward, A., Burrow, I., Everton, A., Watts, L., Leach, P., Hirst, S., Fowler, P. and Gardner, K. (1992) *Cadbury Congresbury 1968–73. A Late/Post-Roman Hilltop Settlement in Somerset.* BAR 223, Oxford.

Rainbird, P. (1998) 'Oldaport and the Anglo-Saxon defence of Devon', *PDAS,* 56: 153–64.

Ramm, H. (1971) 'The end of Roman York', in Butler 1971, pp. 179–99.

Rance, P. (2001) 'Attacotti, Deisi and Magnus Maximus: the case for Irish federates in late Roman Britain', *Britannia,* 32: 243–70.

Rands, S. (2001) 'Ponter's Ball or Porter's', *SDNQ,* 35(354): 55–7.

Randsborg, K. (1991) *The First Millennium in Europe and the Mediterranean.* Cambridge University Press, Cambridge.

Rank, A. and Frend, W. (1992) 'A decorated lead object', *Art. J.,* 72: 168–70.

Ratcliffe, J. (1995) 'Duckpool, Morwenstow: a Romano-British and early medieval industrial site and harbour', *Corn. Arch.,* 34: 81–171.

Rattue, J. (1992) 'An inventory of ancient, holy and healing wells of Dorset', *PDNAHS,* 114: 265–7.

Rattue, J. (1995) *The Living Stream: Holy Wells in Historical Context.* Boydell and Brewer, Woodbridge.

Ravenhill, W. (1970) 'The form and pattern of post-Roman settlement in Devon', *PDAS,* 28: 83–92.

Rawle, E. (1893) *Annals of the Ancient Royal Forest of Exmoor.* Barnicott & Pearce, Taunton.

Rawlings, M. (1992) 'Romano-British sites observed along the Codford–Ilchester pipeline', *PSANHS,* 136: 29–35.

RCAHMW (1997) *An Inventory of the Ancient Monuments in Brecknock (Brycheiniog): The Prehistoric and Roman Monuments. Part I Later Prehistoric Monuments and Unenclosed Settlements to 1000 AD.* Royal Commission on the Ancient and Historical Monuments of Wales, Cardiff.

RCHM (1972) *Dorset, Vol. IV North.* HMSO, London.

RCHMS (1957) *The County of Selkirk.* HMSO, London.

Reade, R. (1885) 'The Roman villa at Great Wemberham in Yatton', *PSANHS,* 31: 643–73.

Reaney, P. (1935) *The Place-names of Essex.* English Place-Names Society, Vol. 12, Cambridge University Press, Cambridge.

Reaney, P. and Smith, A. (1943) *Place-names of Cambridgeshire and the Isle of Ely.* English Place-Names Society, Vol. 19, Cambridge University Press, Cambridge.

Rednap, M. (1994) 'A pre-Norman cross from Caerwent and its context', *Monmouth Antiquary,* 10: 1–6.

Reece, R. (ed.) (1977) *Burial in the Roman World.* Council for British Archaeology Research Report 22, London.

Reece, R. (1988) 'Interpreting Roman hoards', *World Archaeology,* 20(2): 261–9.

Reed, S. (1997) 'First investigation of a Blackdowns iron pit', *DAS News,* May: 1.

Reed, S. and Manning, P. (1994a) 'Archaeological recording at Gittisham', *Exeter Museums Archaeological Field Unit Report* 94: 20.

Reed, S. and Manning, P. (1994b) 'Archaeological recording at Clyst Honiton', *Exeter Museums Archaeological Field Unit Report* 94: 25.

Reyddlet, M. (1994) *Venance Fortunat Poèmes I, Livres I–IV.* Les Belles Lettres, Paris.

Reynolds, A. and Turner, S. (2003) 'Excavations at Holy Trinity, Buckfastleigh, Spring 2002', *DAS Newsletter* 85: 1–2.

Reynolds, P. (1995) *Trade in the Western Mediterranean: AD 400–700. The Ceramic Evidence.* BAR International Series 604, Oxford.

Reynolds, P. (2000) 'The Pimperne House', *Current Archaeology,* 171: 94–7.

Richards, M. (ed. and trans.) (1954) *The Laws of Hywel Dda (The Book of Blegywryd).* Liverpool University Press, Liverpool.

Richards, M. (1960) 'The Irish settlement in south-west Wales: a topographical approach', *J. Royal Society of Antiquities of Ireland,* 90: 133–52.

Richards, M. (1968) 'Ecclesiastical and secular in medieval Welsh settlement', *Studia Celtica,* 3: 10–28.

Richardson, A. (1986) 'Further evidence for centuriation in Cumbria', *Trans. Cumberland and Westmorland Antiquities and Arch. Soc.,* 86: 152–4.

Ridyard, S. (1988) *The Royal Saints of Anglo-Saxon England.* Cambridge University Press, Cambridge.

Rigold, S. E. (1977) 'Litus Romanorum – the shore fronts and missionary stations', in Johnson 1977, pp. 70–5.

Riley, H. and Wilson-North, R. (2001) *The Field Archaeology of Exmoor.* English Heritage, London.

Rippengal, R. (1993) 'A Roman writing tablet from Somerset', *Journal of Roman Studies,* 46: 115–18.

Rippon, S. (1997) *The Severn Estuary Landscape Evolution and Wetland Reclamation.* Leicester University Press, Leicester.

Rivet, A. (ed.) (1969) *The Roman Villa in Britain.* Batsford, London.

Rivet, A. and Smith, C. (1979) *The Place-names of Roman Britain.* Batsford, London.

Roberts, B. (1985) 'Village patterns and forms: some models for discussion' in Hooke 1985, pp. 7–25.

Roberts, T. (1992) 'Welsh ecclesiastical place-names and archaeology', in Edwards and Lane 1992, pp. 41–4.

Robertson, A. (1952) 'The Poundbury hoard of Roman fourth-century copies and their prototypes', *Numismatic Chronicle*, 11: 87–95.

Robertson, A. (2000) *An Inventory of Romano-British Coin Hoards*. Royal Numismatic Society Special Publication 20, London.

Robinson, A. (1921) *Somerset Historical Essays*. London.

Robinson, S. (1992) *Somerset Place-names*. Dovecote Press, Taunton.

Rodwell, W. (1980) *Temples, Churches and Religion in Roman Britain*. BAR British Series 77 i and ii, Oxford.

Rodwell, W. (1982) 'From mausoleum to minster: the early development of Wells Cathedral', in Pearce 1982b, pp. 49–59.

Rodwell, W. (2001) *The Archaeology of Wells Cathedral: Excavations and Structural Studies, 1978–1993*. English Heritage, London.

Rodwell, W. and Rodwell, K. (1977) *Historic Churches: A Wasting Asset*. Council for British Archaeology reports, London.

Rogers, J. (1979) 'Human remains from a sub-Roman cemetery at Station Road, Portishead, Avon', *Rescue Archaeology in the Bristol Area*, 1: 7–14 (ed. N. Thomas).

Rollason, D. (1978) 'Lists of saints' resting-places in Anglo-Saxon England', *Anglo-Saxon England*, 7: 61–93.

Rollason, D. (1986) 'Relic-cults as an instrument of royal policy c. 900–1050', *Anglo-Saxon England*, 15: 91–103.

'Roman Britain in 1939: Cornwall', *Journal of Roman Studies*, 30: 175.

'Roman Britain in 1939: Somerset', *Journal of Roman Studies*, 30: 174–5.

Rose, P. and Preston-Jones, A. (1992) 'Changes in the Cornish countryside AD 400–1100', in Hooke and Burnell 1992, pp. 51–67.

Rose-Troup, F. (1931) 'The ancient monastery of St Mary and St Peter at Exeter', *TDA*, 63: 197–200.

Rose-Troup, F. (1933) 'St Sativola', *DCNQ*, 13: 256–7.

Ross, A. (1968) 'Shafts, pits, wells – sanctuaries of the Belgic Britons?', in Coles and Simpson 1968, pp. 255–85.

Rowlands, M. (1987) 'Introduction', in M. Rowlands (ed.) (1987) *Centre and Periphery*. Cambridge University Press, Cambridge, pp. 1–11.

Rowley, T. (ed.) (1974) *Anglo-Saxon Settlement and Landscape*. BAR 6, Oxford.

Rowley, T. (1981) *Origins of Open-field Agriculture*. Croom Helm, London.

Rumble, A. (2001) 'Edward the Elder and the churches of Winchester and Wessex', in Higham and Hill 2001, pp. 230–47.

Rush, P. (1995a) 'Economy and space in Roman Britain', in Rush 1995b, pp. 141–7,

Rush, P. (1995b) (ed.) *Theoretical Roman Archaeology Conference Proceedings*. Avebury Books, Avebury.

Rushforth, G. (1933) 'The legend of St Sativola', *DCNQ*, 17: 247–53.

Russell, P. (1988) 'The sounds of silence: the growth of Cormac's Glossary', *Camb. Med. Celtic St.*, 15: 1–30.

Russell, V. and Pool, P. (1968) 'The excavations of Chapel Jane, Zennor', *Corn. Arch.*, 7: 43–60.

Russett, V. (1988) 'Cheddar, Milkway, ST454530', *PSANHS*, 132: 216.

Said, E. (1978) *Orientalism*. Penguin, London.

Sauer, E. (1996) *The End of Paganism in the North-western Provinces of the Roman Empire: The Example of the Mithras Cult*. BAR International Series 634, Oxford.

Saunders, A. (1963) 'Excavations at Castle Gotha, St Austell: interim report', *Procs. West Cornwall Field Club*, 2(5): 215–20.

Saunders, A. and Harris, D. (1982) 'Excavations at Castle Gotha, St Austell', *Corn. Arch.*, 21: 109–53.

Saunders, C. (1972) 'The excavations at Grambla, Wendron, 1972: Interim report', *Corn. Arch.*, 11: 50–2.

Savory, H. (1976) 'Welsh hill-forts: a reappraisal of recent research', in Harding 1976, pp. 237–91.

Sawyer, P. (1968) *Anglo-Saxon Charters: An Annotated List and Bibliography*. Royal Historical Society, London.

Sawyer, P. (1976a) 'Introduction: early medieval English settlement', in Sawyer 1976b, pp. 1–7.

Sawyer, P. (ed.) (1976b) *Medieval Settlement: Continuity and Change*. Edward Arnold, London.

Sawyer, P. (1978) *From Roman Britain to Norman England*. Methuen, London.

Sawyer, P. and Wood, I. (eds) (1977) *Early Medieval Kingship*. School of History, University of Leeds, Leeds.

Scarth, R. (1885) 'The Roman villa at Wemberham', *PSANHS*, 31: 1–9.

Schmidt, R. and Voss, B. (eds) (2000) *Archaeologies of Sexuality*. Routledge, London.

Schülke, A. (1999) 'On Christianisation and grave-finds', *European Journal of Archaelogy*, 2 (1): 77–106.

Schweise, J. (1979) 'The Anglo Saxon burials', in G. Wainwright (1979), *Mount Pleasant, Dorset: Excavations 1970–1*. Res. Report Soc. Antiq. London, London, pp. 181–3.

Scott, S. (1992) 'A theoretical framework for the study of Romano-British villa mosaics', *TRAC*, 1: 103–14.

Scott, S. (1995) 'Symbols of power and nature: the Orpheus mosaics of fourth-century Britain and their architectural contexts', *TRAC*, 2: 105–23.

Scott, S. (2000) *Art and Society in Fourth-century Britain: Villa Mosaics in Context.* Institute of Archaeology Monograph 53, Oxford.

Scull, C. (1995) 'Approaches to material culture and social dynamics of the migration period in Eastern England', in Bintliff, L. and Hamerow 1995, pp. 17–24.

'Secrets of the sands' (2001) *DAS News*, 79: 1, 8–9.

Segui, J. (2000) 'Ethnoarchaeology of pastoralism in a Mediterranean mountain area'. Unpublished Ph.D. thesis, School of Archaeological Studies, University of Leicester.

Semple, S. (1998) 'A fear of the past: the place of the prehistoric burial mound in the ideology of middle and later Anglo-Saxon England', *World Archaeology*, 30(1): 109–26.

Sheehan, J. and Monk, M. (1998) *Early Medieval Munster.* Cork University Press, Cork.

Sheppard, P. (1980) *The Historic Towns of Cornwall.* Cornwall Committee for Rescue Archaeology, Truro.

Silvester, R. (1980) 'An excavation at Dunkeswell', *PDAS*, 38: 17–48.

Simpson, S., Griffith, F. and Holbrook, N. (1989) 'The prehistoric, Roman and early post-Roman site at Hayes Farm, Clyst Honiton', *PDAS*, 47: 1–28.

Sims-Williams, P. (1986) 'The visionary Celt: the construction of an ethnic preconception', *Cam. Med. Celtic S.*, 11: 71–96.

Sims-Williams, P. (1990) *Religion and Literature in Western Europe.* Cambridge University Press, Cambridge.

Sims-Williams, P. (2003) *The Celtic Inscriptions of Britain: Phonology and Chronology c. 400–1200.* Blackwell, Oxford.

Slater, T. (1991) 'Controlling the South Hams: the Anglo-Saxon *burh* at Halwell', *TDA*, 123: 57–78.

Slee, A. (1952) 'The open fields of Braunton: Braunton Great Field and Braunton Downs', *TDA*, 84: 142–9.

Smith, A. (1939) *Place-names of the East Riding of Yorkshire and York.* English Place-Name Society, Vol. (14). Cambridge University Press, Cambridge.

Smith, A. H. (1956) *English Place-name Elements.* Cambridge University Press, Cambridge.

Smith, C. (1977) 'Late prehistoric and Romano-British enclosed homesteads in north-west Wales', *Arch. Camb.*, 126: 38–52.

Smith, D. (1969) 'The mosaic pavements', in Rivet 1969, pp. 71–126.

Smith, J. (1978) 'Villas as a key to social structure', in Todd 1978, pp. 149–85.

Smith, J. (1997) *Roman Villas: A Study in Social Structure.* Routledge, London.

Smith, R. Finch (1987) *Roadside Settlements in Lowland Roman Britain.* BAR British Series 179, Oxford.

Smith, V. (1972) *Portrait of Dartmoor.* Robert Hole, London.

Smyth, A. (1998) *The Medieval Life of King Alfred the Great.* Palgrave, London.

Smyth, G. (1973) *Archaeological Supervision of Road Improvements at Phillack.* Information Sheet circulated by Institute of Cornish Studies, Truro.

Somers-Cox, J. (1970) 'Saxon and early medieval times', in Gill 1970, pp. 76–99.

Sørensen, M. (2000) *Gender Archaeology.* Blackwell, Oxford.

Spivak, C. (1993) 'Can the subaltern speak?', in Williams and Chrisman 1993, pp. 66–111.

Snyder, C. (1998) *An Age of Tyrants: Briton and the Britons.* Pennsylvania State University Press, Philadelphia.

Stacey, L. (1988) 'The excavation of burials at 8 Albert Road, Dorchester: interim report', *PDNHAS* 108: 184.

Stafford, P. (1980) 'The "farm of one night" and the organisation of King Edward's estates in Domesday', *Economic History Review*, 33: 491–502.

Stark, R. (1994) *The Rise of Christianity. A Sociologist Reconsiders History.* Princeton University Press, Princeton, NJ.

Stark, R. (1999) 'The community of the soldiers: a major identity and centre of power in the Roman Empire', in Baker *et al.* 1999, pp. 14–25.

Stead, P. and Weddell, P. (1990) *Roadford Reservoir Project. Archaeological Investigations at West Wortha: Summary Report.* Devon County Council.

Stead, P. and Weddell, P. (1991) *Roadford Reservoir Project. Archaeological Investigations at Shop Farm: Summary Report.* Devon County Council.

Stenton, F. (1933) 'Medehamstead and its colonies', in Edwards *et al.* 1933, pp. 313–26.

Stenton, F. (1947) *Anglo-Saxon England.* Oxford University Press, Oxford (2nd edn.).

Stevens, C., Mallalieu, L., Bernier, G. and Radford, C. (1975) 'The Roman pillar in St Lawrence's Church, Jersey: a stocktaking', *Bulletin de la Societé Jersaise*, 21(3): 343–57.

Stevenson, W. (1959) *Asser's Life of King Alfred. Together with the Annals of St Neots Erroneously Ascribed to Asser. New Impression with Article on Recent Work on Asser's Life of Alfred by Dorothy Whitelock*. Clarendon Press, Oxford, repr. 1959.

Stoyle, M. (2003) *Circled with Stone. Exeter's City Walls 1485–1660*. University of Exeter Press, Exeter.

Sunter, N. and Woodward, P. (1987) *Romano-British Industries in Purbeck*. DNHAS, Dorchester.

Swanton, M. and Pearce, S. (1982) 'Lustleigh, South Devon: its inscribed stone, its churchyard and its parish', in Pearce 1982b, pp. 139–43.

Tatlock, J. (1938) 'Caradoc of Llancarfan', *Speculum*, 13: 139–52.

Tatlock, J. (1939) 'The dates of the Arthurian saints' legends', *Speculum*, 14: 345–68.

Tatlock, J. (1950) *The Legendary History of Britain*. University of California Press, Berkeley.

Taylor, C. (1967) 'The later history of the Roman site at Hinton St Mary, Dorset', *British Museum Quarterly*, 5(32): 31–5.

Taylor, C. (1972) *The Making of the English Landscape: Dorset*. Hodder and Stoughton, London.

Taylor, C. (1977) 'Polyfocal settlement and the English village', *Med. Arch.*, 21: 189–93.

Taylor, R. (1993) *Bronze Age Hoards*. BAR 228, Oxford.

Taylor, T. (ed. and trans.) (1925) *The Life of St Samson of Dol*. SPCK, London.

Tew, D. (2000) 'The origins, rise and decline of free mining customs in England and Wales: a legal standpoint'. Unpublished Ph.D. thesis, Department of History, University of Leicester, Leicester.

Thacker, A. (1992) 'Monks, preaching and pastoral care in early Anglo-Saxon England', in Blair and Sharpe 1992, pp. 137–70.

Thomas, C. (1956a) 'Evidence for post-Roman occupation of Chun Castle', *Antiq. J.*, 36: 75.

Thomas, C. (1956b) 'Excavations at Gwithian, Cornwall 1956', Appendix to *Proc. West Cornwall Field Club*, 1.

Thomas, C. (1958) *Gwithian. Ten Year's Work*. West Cornwall Field Club, Gwithian.

Thomas, C. (1959) 'Imported pottery in Dark Age western Britain', *Med. Arch.*, 3: 89–111.

Thomas, C. (1961) *Phillack Church*. British Publishing Co., Gloucester.

Thomas, C. (1963) 'The rediscovery of St Ia's Chapel, Cambourne', *Corn. Arch.*, 2: 77–8.

Thomas, C. (1964a) 'Loban Rath', *Corn. Arch.*, 3: 78.

Thomas, C. (1964b) 'Settlement-history in early Cornwall, I: the antiquity of the hundreds', *Corn. Arch.*, 3: 70–9.

Thomas, C. (1965) 'The hill-fort at St Dennis', *Corn. Arch.*, 4: 31–5.

Thomas, C. (1966) 'A cross-incised slab from Ludgvan churchyard', *Corn. Arch.*, 5: 86–7.

Thomas, C. (1967a) *Christian Antiquities of Camborne*. H. E. Warne Ltd., St Austell.

Thomas, C. (1967b) 'An early Christian cemetery and chapel on Ardwall Island, Kirkcudbright', *Med. Arch.*, 11: 127–88.

Thomas, C. (1968a) 'Grass-marked pottery in Cornwall', in Coles and Simpson 1968, pp. 328–31.

Thomas, C. (1968b) 'Merther Uny, Wendron', *Corn. Arch.*, 7: 81–2.

Thomas, C. (1969) 'Excavations at Crane Godrevy, Gwithian, 1969: interim report', *Corn. Arch.*, 8: 84–8.

Thomas, C. (1971) *The Early Christian Archaeology of North Britain*. Oxford University Press, Oxford.

Thomas, C. (1972) 'The Irish settlements in post-Roman western Britain: a survey of the evidence', *JRIC*, 4: 251–74.

Thomas, C. (1973a) 'Irish colonists in south-west Britain', *World Archaeology*, 5(1): 5–13.

Thomas, C. (1973b) 'Parish churchyard, Phillack', *Corn. Arch.*, 12: 59.

Thomas, C. (1976a) 'Imported late-Roman Mediterranean pottery in Ireland and western Britain: chronologies and implications', *Proc. Royal Irish Academy*, 76(C): 245–55.

Thomas, C. (1976b) 'Towards the definition of the pre-Norman period at Gwithian', *Corn. Arch.*, 1: 61–84.

Thomas, C. (1980) 'Hermits on islands or priests in a landscape?', *Cornish Studies*, 8: 28–44.

Thomas, C. (1981a) *Christianity in Roman Britain to AD 500*. Batsford, London.

Thomas, C. (1981b) *A Provisional List of Imported Pottery in Post-Roman Western Britain and Ireland*. Institute of Cornish Studies Special Report 7, Camborne.

Thomas, C. (1984) 'The occupation of Mary's Hill and its dating – a note', *Cornish Studies*, 11: 78–80.

Thomas, C. (1988a) 'The archaeology of Tintagel parish churchyard', *Cornish Studies*, 16: 79–91.

Thomas, C. (1988b) 'The context of Tintagel: a new model for the diffusion of post-Roman Mediterranean imports', *Corn. Arch.*, 27: 7–26.

Thomas, C. (1988c) 'Tintagel papers: special issue', *Cornish Studies*, 16: 3–96.

Thomas, C. (1989) 'Christians, chapels, churches and charters – or, "proto-parochial provisions for the pious in a peninsula" (Landsend)', *Landscape History*, 11: 19–26.

Thomas, C. (1990) ' "Gallici Nautae de Galliarum Provinciis." A sixth/seventh-century trade with Gaul reconsidered', *Med. Arch.*, 34: 1–26.

Thomas, C. (1993) *Tintagel: Arthur and Archaeology*. Batsford/English Heritage, London.

Thomas, C. (1994) *And Shall These Mute Stones Speak?*. University of Wales Press, Cardiff.
Thomas, C. (1996) 'The Llanddewi-Brefi "*IDNERT*" stone', *Peritia*, 10: 136–83.
Thomas, C. (1997) 'Christian Latin inscriptions from Cornwall in biblical style', *JRIC*, new series 21 (4): 42–66.
Thomas, C. (1998) *Christian Celts: Messages and Images*. Tempus, Stroud.
Thomas, J. (2000) *Understanding the Neolithic*. Routledge, London.
Thomas, N. (1997) 'Four Holes Cross', *Corn. Arch.*, 36: 224.
Thompson, E. (1968) 'Britonia', in Barley and Hanson 1968, pp. 201–5.
Thompson, E. (1984) *St Germanus of Auxerre and the End of Roman Britain*. Oxford University Press, Oxford.
Thorn, C. and Thorn, F. (eds) (1979) *Domesday Book: Cornwall*. Phillimore, Chichester.
Thorn, C. and Thorn, F. (eds) (1980) *Domesday Book: Somerset*. Phillimore, Chichester.
Thorn, C. and Thorn, F. (eds) (1983) *Domesday Book: Dorset*. Phillimore, Chichester.
Thorn, C. and Thorn, F. (eds) (1985) *Domesday Book: Devon*, Parts 1 and 2. Phillimore, Chichester.
Tilley, C. (1994) *A Phenomenology of Landscape. Places, Paths and Monuments*. Berg, Oxford.
Timms, S. (1985) 'The royal town of Lydford', *Devon Arch.*, 3: 19–23.
Todd, M. (ed.) (1978) *Studies in the Romano-British Villa*. Leicester University Press.
Todd, M. (1983) 'A Romano-Celtic silver brooch from Capton, near Dartmouth', *PDAS*, 41: 131–2.
Todd, M. (1987) *The South-West to AD 1000*. Longman, London.
Todd, M. (1988) 'A hill-slope enclosure at Rudge, Morchard Bishop, Devonshire', *Newsletter of the Council for British Archaeology Group 13*, 109: 110.
Todd, M. (1992) *The Early Germans*. Blackwell, Oxford.
Todd, M. (1999) 'Classical sources for Roman place-names', in Kain and Ravenhill 1999, pp. 80–1.
Tomlin, R. (1993) 'An inscription from the lead-lining in Grave 530', in Farwell and Molleson 1993, pp. 132–3.
Tomlin, R. (1988) 'The curse tablets', in Cunliffe 1988, pp. 59–280.
Tongye, M. (1995) 'Lestowder, St Keverne: a previously unidentified stronghold', *Corn. Arch.*, 34: 176–81.
Toynbee, J. (1964a) 'The Christian Roman mosiac, Hinton St Mary, Dorset', *PDNHAS*, 85: 116–21.
Toynbee, J. (1964b) 'A new Roman pavement found in Dorset', *J. Roman Studies*, 54: 1–14.
Toynbee, J. (1968) 'Pagan motifs and practices in Christian art and ritual in Roman Britain', in Barley and Hanson 1968, pp. 177–92.
Transactions of the Devonshire Association (1932) 'Proceedings of the seventy-first annual meeting held at Paignton 20–24 June 1932', *TDA*, 64: 35–63.
Trudgian, P. (1987) 'Excavation of a burial ground at St Endellion, Cornwall', *Corn. Arch.*, 26: 145–52.
Turner, A. (1952) 'Some Somerset place-names containing Celtic elements', *Bulletin Board of Celtic Studies*, 14: 113–19.
Turner, E. (1956) 'A Roman writing tablet from Somerset', *JRS*, 46: 115–18.
Tylecote, R. (1962) *Metalurgy in Archaeology*. Butterworth, London.
Uglow, J. (2000) 'Three Romano–British sites in the Lower Exe Valley', *PDAS*, 58: 227–48.
Uglow, J., Brown, A. and Silvester, R. (1985) 'The investigation of cropmarks in the Lower Exe Valley', *PDAS*, 43: 115–17.
Vachell, E. (1964) 'Milber Down. Excavations encroaching on the site of the Romano-British homestead', *PDAS*, 22: 27–30.
Van Dam, R. (1988a) *Gregory of Tours: The Glory of the Confessors*. Liverpool University Press, Liverpool.
Van Dam, R. (1988b) *Gregory of Tours: The Glory of the Martyrs*. Liverpool University Press, Liverpool.
Varwell, P. (1886) 'The ancient parish of Brixham, and some of its ancient people', *TDA*, 18: 197–215.
Wailes, B. (1964) 'Castle-an-Dinas, St Columb Major', *Corn. Arch.*, 3: 85.
Wakelin, M. (1972) *English Dialects*. Athlone, London.
Wakelin, M. (1976–7) 'Norse influence in Cornwall: a survey of the evidence', *Cornish Studies*, 4/5: 41–9.
Ward, A. (1999) 'Transhumance and place-names: an aspect of early Ordnance Survey mapping, on the Black Mountain commons, Carmarthenshire', *Studia Celtica*, 33: 335–48.
Ward Perkins, J. and Goodchild, R. (1953) 'The Christian antiquaries of Tripolitania', *Arch*, 95: 1–83.
Wareham, A. (1996) 'St Oswald's family and kin', in Brooks and Cubitt 1996, pp. 46–63.
Warner, R. (1965) 'Rediscovery of the chapel at Chapel Porth, St Agnes', *Corn. Arch.*, 4: 41–3.
Watts, D. (1988) 'Circular lead tanks and their significance for Romano-British Christianity', *Antiq. J.*, 68: 210–22.
Watts, D. (1989) 'Infant burials and Romano-British Christianity', *Arch. J.*, 146: 372–83.
Watts, D. (1991) *Christians and Pagans in Roman Britain*. Routledge, London.
Watts, L. and Leach, P. (1996) *Henley Wood, Temples and Cemetery Excavations 1962–69*. Council for British Archaeology Research Report 99, London.

Watts, M. (1993) *Archaeological Assessment of a Proposed Extension to Milber Abattoir, Milber Down, Newton Abbot*. Exeter Museums Archaeological Field Unit Report 93041.

Weatherhill, C. (1982) *The Courtyard Houses of West Penwith: A Survey*. Cornwall Committee for Research Archaeology, Truro.

Weber, W. (1984) *Constantinische Deckengemälde aus dem romischen Palast unter dem Dom*, Bischöfliches Museum, Trier.

Webster, C. (1992) 'Langport, Hanging Chapel ST424267', *PSANHS*, 136: 171.

Webster, C. (1993) 'Blackdown Hills AONB survey', *PSANHS*, 137: 129.

Webster, J. and Cooper, N. (1996) *Roman Imperialism: Post-colonial Perspectives*. Leicester Archaeology Monographs 3, University of Leicester.

Weddell, P. (2000) 'The excavation of a post-Roman cemetery near Kenn', *PDAS*, 58: 93–126.

Weddell, P. and Reed, S. (1997) 'Excavations at Sourton Down, Okehampton, 1986–1991: Roman road, deserted medieval hamlet and other landscape features', *PDAS*, 55: 39–147.

Wedlake, W. (1958) *Excavations at Camerton, Somerset*. Camerton Excavation Club, Camerton.

Wedlake, W. (1966) *A North Somerset Miscellany*. Bath and Camerton Archaeological Society, Bath.

Wedlake, W. (1982) *The Excavation of the Shrine of Apollo at Nettleton, Wilts 1956–1971*. Society of Antiquaries Research Report N40, London.

Wheeler, M. (1943) *Maiden Castle, Dorset*. Report of the Research Committee of the Society of Antiquaries of London 12, Oxford University Press.

Wheeler, M. and Wheeler, T. (1932) *Report on the Excavations of the Prehistoric, Roman and Post-Roman Site in Lydney Park, Gloucestershire*. Report of the Research Committee of the Society of Antiquaries 9, Oxford University Press.

Whightman, E. (1985) *Gallia Belgica*. Oxford University Press, Oxford.

Whimster, R. (1981) *Burial Practices in Iron Age Britain*. BAR British Series 90, Oxford.

White, R. (1988) *Roman and Celtic Objects from Anglo-Saxon Graves*. BAR British Series 191, Oxford.

White, R. and Barker, P. (1998) *Wroxeter: Life and Death of a Roman City*. Tempus, Stroud.

Whitelock, D. (ed.) (1955) *English Historical Documents I 500–1042*. Eyre and Spottiswoode, London.

Whitelock, D., Brett, M. and Brooke, C. (1981) *Councils and Synods with Other Documents relating to the English Church I AD 871–1204*. Oxford University Press, Oxford.

Whitelock, D., McKitterick, R. and Dumville, D. (eds) (1982) *Ireland in Early Medieval Europe*. Cambridge University Press, Cambridge.

Whitelock, D., Douglas, D. and Tucker, S. (eds) (1965) *The Anglo-Saxon Chronicle*. Eyre and Spottiswoode, London.

Whitfield, M. (1981) 'The medieval fields of south-east Somerset', *PSANHS*, 125: 17–29.

Whyman, M. (1993) 'Invisible people? Material culture in "Dark Age" Yorkshire', in Carver 1993, pp. 61–8.

Wicker, N. and Arnold, B. (eds) (1999) *From the Ground Up: Beyond Gender Theory in Archaeology*. Routledge, London.

Wickham, C. (1984) 'The other transition: from the ancient world to feudalism', *Past and Present*, 103: 3–36.

Wilkes, J. (1972) 'A Pannonion refugee', *Phoenix* 26: 377–93.

Wilkinson, F. (1977) 'The Dartmoor husbandman', *Devon Historian*, 14: 5–10.

Williams, D. (2000) 'The Church in medieval Gwent (maps)', *Monmouth Antiquary*, 16: 1–12.

Williams, D. and Carreras, C. (1995) 'North African amphorae in Roman Britain: a reappraisal', *Britannia*, 26: 231–52.

Williams, G. (1988) 'Recent work on rural settlement in later prehistoric and early historic Dyfed', *Antiq. J.*, 68: 30–54.

Williams, G. and Mytum, H. (1998) *Llawhaden, Dyfed: Excavations on a Group of Small Defended Enclosures, 1980–4*. BAR British Series 275, Oxford.

Williams, H. (1998) 'The ancient monument in Romano-British ritual practices', in Forcey *et al.* 1998, pp. 71–86.

Williams, H. (1998) 'Monuments and past in the early Anglo-Saxon England', *World Archaeology*, 30(1): 90–108.

Williams, M. (1970) *The Draining of the Somerset Levels*. Cambridge University Press, Cambridge.

Williams, P. and Chrisman, L. (eds) (1993) *Colonial Discourse and Post-colonial Theory*. Routledge, London.

Williams, S. and Friell, G. (1994) *Theodosius. The Empire at Bay*. Routledge, London.

Wilmot, T. and Wilson, P. (eds) (2000) *The Late Roman Transition in the North*. BAR 293, Oxford.

Wilson, D. and Blunt, C. (1961) 'The Trewiddle hoard', *Arch*, 96: 15–122.

Wilson, P. (1966–7) 'Romano-British and Welsh Christianity: continuity or discontinuity?', *Welsh Historical Review*, Part 1: 1966, 3: 5–19; Part 2: 1967, 4: 103–20.

Wilson-North, W. (1993) 'Stowe: the country house and garden of the Grenville family', *Corn. Arch.*, 32: 112–27.

Winterbottom, M. (ed. and trans.) (1978) *Gildas. The Ruin of Britain and Other Works*. Phillimore, Chichester.

Wood, J. (1997) 'A new perspective on West Cornwall courtyard houses', *Corn. Arch.*, 36: 95–106.

Wood, P. (1963) 'Open field strips, Forrabury Common near Boscastle', *Corn. Arch.*, 2: 29–33.

Wooding, J. (1996) *Communication and commerce along the Western Sealanes AD 400–800*, BAR 5: 654, Oxford.

Woods, H. (1990) 'Bridgwater, Wembdon Hill, ST279278', *PSANHS*, 134: 222.

Woods, H., Kent, D. and Minnitt, S. (1995) 'Excavations at Glastonbury Abbey 1987–1993', *PSANHS*, 138: 7–73.

Woodward, A. (1993) 'The cult of relics in prehistoric Britain', in Carver 1993, pp. 1–7.

Woodward, A. and Leach, P. (1993) *The Uley Shrines. Excavation of a Ritual Complex on West Hill, Uley, Gloucestershire: 1977–9*. English Heritage Archaeological Report 17, London.

Woodward, P., Davies, S. and Graham, A. (1984) 'Excavations on the Greyhound car park, Dorchester, 1984', *PDNHAS*, 106: 99–106.

Worth, R. (1891) 'The thirteenth report of the Barrow Committee', *TDA*, 23: 117–24.

Wrigley, E. (1993) 'Mortality and the European marriage system', in G. Geissler and D. Oddy (eds) (1993) *Food, Diet and Economic Change Past and Present*. Leicester University Press, Leicester, pp. 35–49.

Yorke, B. (1995) *Wessex in the Early Middle Ages*. Leicester University Press, Leicester.

Young, A. (2001) *The National Mapping Programme. Cornwall and the Isles of Scilly Mapping Project: Annual Progress Report 2000/2001*. Cornwall Archaeological Unit, Truro.

Youngs, S. (1998) 'Medieval hanging bowls from Wiltshire', *WAM*, 91: 35–41.

Index